ESSAY ON THE ORIGIN OF LANGUAGES and WRITINGS RELATED TO MUSIC

JEAN-JACQUES ROUSSEAU

ESSAY ON THE ORIGIN OF LANGUAGES and WRITINGS RELATED TO MUSIC

THE COLLECTED WRITINGS OF ROUSSEAU
Vol. 7

TRANSLATED AND EDITED BY JOHN T. SCOTT

ROGER D. MASTERS AND CHRISTOPHER KELLY,
SERIES EDITORS

DARTMOUTH COLLEGE
PUBLISHED BY THE UNIVERSITY PRESS OF NEW ENGLAND
HANOVER AND LONDON

DARTMOUTH COLLEGE
Published by University Press of New England, Hanover, NH 03755
© 1998 by the Trustees of Dartmouth College
All rights reserved
Printed in the United States of America
5 4 3 2 1

This publication has received support from Pro Helvetia
and the Florence Gould Foundation.

Frontispiece: *"Le Devin du village."*
"Album Rousseau," Plate N. *108.*
Courtesy Bibliothèque nationale de France.

Library of Congress Cataloging-in-Publication Data
Rousseau, Jean-Jacques, 1712–1778.
 [Selections. English. 1998]
 Essay on the origin of languages and writings related to music / Jean-Jacques Rousseau.
   p.   cm. — (The collected writings of Rousseau ; vol. 7)
 Includes bibliographical references and index.
 ISBN 0-87451-839-3 (alk. paper)
 1. Music—France—18th century—History and criticism.
 2. Music—18th century—Philosophy and aesthetics. 3. Language and languages—Origin. 4. Music and language. 5. Guerre des Bouffons.
 6. Rameau, Jean Philippe, 1683–1764. I. Title. II. Series:
Rousseau, Jean-Jacques, 1712–1778. Works. English. 1990 ; vol. 7.
 PQ2034.A3   1990 vol. 7
 [ML60]
 780—dc21   98-8043

Contents

Preface   vii

Chronology of Works in Volume 7   ix

Introduction   xiii

Note on the Text   xliii

Plan Regarding New Signs for Music   1

Letter to the *Mercure* on a New System of Musical Notation   21

Dissertation on Modern Music   27

Letter on Italian and French Opera   99

Letter on "Omphale" (Grimm)   106

Remarks on the Subject of the Letter by M. Grimm on "Omphale" (Raynal)   115

Letter to M. Grimm on the Subject of the Remarks Added to His Letter on "Omphale"   121

"Notice" to Rinaldo da Capua's *La Zingara*   133

Letter from a Symphonist of the Royal Academy of Music to His Comrades in the Orchestra   134

Letter on French Music   141

Observations on Our Instinct for Music and on Its Principle (Rameau)   175

Articles from the *Encyclopedia*   198

Errors on Music in the Encyclopedia (Rameau)   222

Continuation of the Errors on Music in the Encyclopedia (Rameau) 251

On the Principle of Melody, or Response to the "Errors on Music" 260

Examination of Two Principles Advanced by M. Rameau in His Brochure Entitled: "Errors on Music in the Encyclopedia" 271

Essay on the Origin of Languages 289

Pronunciation 333

On Theatrical Imitation 337

The Levite of Ephraïm 351

Dictionary of Music 366

Letter to Mr. Burney and Fragments of Observations on Gluck's "Alceste" 486

Extract from a Response by the Underlaborer to His Frontman Concerning a Piece from Gluck's "Orfeo" 506

Appendix: "Enfin, il est en ma puissance," from Lully's *Armide* 511

Notes 515

Index 605

Preface

Although Jean-Jacques Rousseau is a significant figure in the Western tradition, there is no standard edition of his major writings available in English. Unlike those of other thinkers of comparable stature, moreover, many of Rousseau's important works either have never been translated or have become unavailable. The present edition of the *Collected Writings of Rousseau* is intended to remedy this situation.

Our goal is to produce a series that can provide a standard reference for scholarship that is accessible to all those wishing to read broadly in the corpus of Rousseau's works. To this end, the translations seek to combine care and faithfulness to the original French text with readability in English. Although, as every translator knows, there are often passages where it is impossible to meet both of these criteria at the same time, readers of a thinker and writer of Rousseau's stature deserve texts that have not been deformed by the interpretive bias of translators or editors. Wherever possible, existing translations of high quality have been used, although in some cases the editors have felt minor revisions were necessary to maintain the accuracy and consistency of the English versions. Where there was no English translation (or none of sufficient quality), a new translation has been prepared.

Each text is supplemented by editorial notes that clarify references and citations or passages otherwise not intelligible. Although these notes do not provide as much detail as is found in the critical apparatus of the Pléiade edition of the *Oeuvres complètes*, the English-speaking reader should nevertheless have in hand the basis for a more careful and comprehensive understanding of Rousseau than has hitherto been possible.

For Volume 7, we have brought together Rousseau's *Essay on the Origin of Languages* and his writings related to music, along with the works by other authors to whom Rousseau was responding in these writings, principally Jean-Philippe Rameau. Most of Rousseau's musical writings have largely been ignored by scholars of Rousseau's thought, in part because they have been unavailable in a critical edition until the recent appearance of the long-awaited fifth and final volume of the Pléiade edition of Rousseau's works. Even the most important of Rousseau's writings on music and language, the *Essay on the Origin of Languages*, has not in general received a full interpretation because it has not been interpreted in light of his other musical works. Among Rousseau's writings related to music, the *Essay* is the work that most clearly displays the juncture between Rousseau's musical theory and his major philosophical works. Rousseau's linguistic treatise emerged out of both the *Second Discourse* and the contemporaneous polemics of the mid-1750s in which he rethought and developed his musical theory in accordance with his philosophy more generally. Rousseau's writings related to music therefore provide the context in which the *Essay* should be interpreted and also constitute an important part of Rousseau's philosophy often ignored by students of his thought. This volume fills an important gap in Rousseau's writings, and will be of interest to scholars in many fields, including philosophy, political theory, literature, and music.

Several scholars have been particularly helpful in making this volume possible. I would especially like to thank Roger D. Masters and Christopher Kelly, without whose support and criticism this volume would never have appeared, and Cynthia Verba, Matthew Dirst, and James Johnson. I would also like to thank, for their encouragement and advice, Jean Starobinski, Sidney Kleinman, and Philip Gossett. Final preparation of this volume was made possible in part by support from a Limited Grant-in-Aid by the University of Houston and by a faculty research fellowship from the Earhart Foundation.

Chronology of Works in Volume 7

1712
June 28: Jean-Jacques Rousseau born in Geneva.

1728
March 14: Rousseau runs away from Geneva; travels to Italy until Summer 1729.

1729
Summer–Fall: Rousseau studies at the Lazarist Seminary and then begins to study music with M. Le Maître.

1730
Winter: Rousseau teaches music at Neuchâtel.

1731
Rousseau begins copying music as a trade.

1732
June: Rousseau begins to teach music at Chambéry.

1733
July: Rousseau travels to Besançon to study music with the Abbé Blanchard. (Date uncertain.)

1734
Fall: Rousseau acquires and studies Rameau's *Treatise on Harmony*. Directs Mme de Waren's musical evenings at Chambéry.

1737
June: Rousseau's first publication, a song, appears in the *Mercure de France*.

1741
End of December: Rousseau arrives in Paris with his new system for musical notation.

1742
August 22: Rousseau reads his *Plan Concerning New Signs for Music* to the Academy of Sciences.

1743
January: Publication of Rousseau's *Dissertation on Modern Music*.
July 10: Rousseau leaves Paris as secretary to the French Ambassador to Venice. Becomes reacquainted with Italian music.

1744
August 6: Rousseau leaves Venice and returns to Paris.

1745
July: Rousseau completes *Les Muses galantes*.
September: Rousseau's *Les Muse galantes* is presented at the household of La Poplinière, where Rameau accuses Rousseau of plagiarism.
Fall: Rousseau works on *Les Fêtes de Ramire*, with libretto by Voltaire and music by Rameau. The work was presented at Versailles in December without Rousseau being credited.

1749
January–March: Rousseau writes articles on music for the *Encyclopedia*.
October: The "illumination of Vincennes": Rousseau reads the essay topic proposed by the Academy of Dijon.

1750
July: The *First Discourse* is awarded the prize by the Academy of Dijon.

1751
January: Publication of the *First Discourse*.
February: Rousseau leaves his employment with the Dupin family and works as a musical copyist.
July: Publication the first volume of the *Encyclopedia*, containing the first of Rousseau's articles on music.

1752
Winter–Spring: Rousseau writes the *Letter on French Music*.
March: Publication of Grimm's *Letter on "Omphale"* and Raynal's *Remarks on Grimm's Letter on "Omphale."*
April: Anonymous publication of Rousseau's *Letter to Grimm on the Subject of the Remarks Added to His Letter on "Omphale."*
Spring: Rousseau composes *Le Devin du village*.
June: Performance of Rousseau's *Le Devin du village* at Fontainebleau. Rousseau turns down pension offered by Louis XV.
August 1: Eruption in Paris of the "Quarrel of the Bouffons" with the successful performance of Pergolesi's *La Serva padrona* by a traveling Italian troupe.

1753
March 1: Performance of Rousseau's *Le Devin du village* at the Paris Opera.
September: Anonymous publication of Rousseau's *Letter from a Symphonist*.

November: Publication of Rousseau's *Letter on French Music*. Rousseau begins writing the *Second Discourse*.

1754

June 12: Rousseau dates the dedication to the *Second Discourse*.
Anonymous publication of Rameau's *Observations on Our Instinct for Music*.

1755

April 24: Publication of Rousseau's *Second Discourse*.
August: Anonymous publication of Rameau's *Errors on Music in the Encyclopedia*.
Fall: Rousseau writes the first draft of his response to Rameau's *Errors on Music*.

1756

March: Anonymous publication of Rameau's *Continuation of the Errors on Music in the Encyclopedia*.
May: Publication of Vol. VI of the *Encyclopedia*, containing a "Notice" in which Diderot and d'Alembert defend Rousseau against Rameau.

1758

Spring: Composition of Rousseau's *On Theatrical Imitation*, written in preparation for writing the *Letter to d'Alembert*.

1761

September: Rousseau sends the *Essay on the Origin of Languages* to Malesherbes, who advises publication.

1762

June 9: A warrant is issued for Rousseau's arrest after the publication of *Emile*; he flees France for Geneva. Composition of the *Levite of Ephraïm*.

1763

Spring: Rousseau contemplates publishing *On Theatrical Imitation*, the *Essay on the Origin of Languages*, and the *Levite of Ephraïm* together but decides against it.

1764

Winter: Publication of Rousseau's *On Theatrical Imitation*.

1765

Rousseau finalizes the text of his *Examination of Two Errors*, with the intention of using it as a preface to his *Dictionary of Music*. (Date uncertain.)

1768

Publication of Rousseau's *Dictionary of Music*.

1770

May: First performance of Rousseau's *Pygmalion*.
December: Rousseau meets Charles Burney.

1774

February: Rousseau meets Gluck, who publicly places himself under Rousseau's patronage.

August: Gluck's *Orphée* debuts in Paris. Earliest date for drafting of Rousseau's *Extract from a Response by the Underlaborer to His Frontman*

1775

March: Probable date of Rousseau's *Fragments of Observations on Gluck's Italian "Alceste,"* later added to his *Letter to Burney*.

October 20: Performance of Rousseau's *Pygmalion* at the Paris Opéra.

1776

December: Rousseau's *Devin du village* is reprised at the Paris Opera and played along with Gluck's *Orphée*.

1777

October: Probable date of the composition of Rousseau's *Letter to Burney*.

1778

July 2: Rousseau dies at Ermenonville.

Introduction

Rousseau's *Essay on the Origin of Languages*
and Writings Related to Music

Rousseau is best known as the author of philosophic and literary works, but he was a practicing musician and musical theorist for over a decade before he burst onto the European stage with his *Discourse on the Sciences and Arts*. It was with a new system for musical notation that he set off for Paris seeking fame and fortune, and while he earned celebrity as a political theorist he continued to consider music, in one aspect or another, as his primary vocation and avocation throughout his life. The author of one of the most popular operas of his century, main contributor of the articles on music for the *Encyclopedia*, the most controversial and influential polemicist during the "Quarrel of the Bouffons," antagonist of Rameau, inspirer of Gluck: Rousseau made an important contribution to the theory and practice of music of his time and beyond.

The relationship between Rousseau's musical theory and his philosophy as a whole has seldom been extensively analyzed.[1] Rousseau himself explains in his *Dialogues* that his mature musical writings and compositions are animated by the same feelings and ideas as all of his works—that they too are based on the principle of his "system": that "man is good although men are wicked."[2] The discovery of his "system" led Rousseau to rethink and develop his early ideas on music, and his mature musical theory extends his philosophy of human nature and development. Rousseau's musical theory is not an isolated part of his *oeuvre*, but rather an important facet of his philosophy.

This volume brings together Rousseau's major writings on music and language. Because many of these writings are directly or indirectly responses to other writers, principally Rameau, the works to which he was responding are included in this volume so that the reader can better understand Rousseau's writings on music and language and trace their development. This introduction has two aims. First, it will provide the historical context for the writings contained in this volume through an account of Rousseau's career as a musician and musical theorist. Second, it will trace the development of his musical theory and place his writings on music and language in the context of his philosophy as a whole. Rousseau's *Essay on the Origin of Languages* serves as the centerpiece of both this volume and this introduction because it is the work in which the mutual influence of his musical theory and his philosophy is most clearly seen.

Rousseau's Presystematic Musical Training and Writings

"J.J. was born for music," Rousseau writes of himself in the *Dialogues*: "Not to be consumed in its execution, but to speed its progress and make discoveries about it. His ideas on the art and about the art are fertile, inexhaustible."[3] Rousseau's boast was not idle. His musical career spanned several decades during a period that witnessed the culmination of the classical aesthetic and the birth of a new era in music and literature, a birth he played a part in conceptualizing and instigating. During his lifetime, Rousseau's celebrity as a philosophic and literary figure hardly obscured his fame as a composer and musical theorist, or the notoriety of a famous author who continued to earn his living by the lowly trade of copying music. Rousseau's early development as a musician occurred before he became a philosopher, and he learned his trade long before he gained his unfortunate celebrity.

Rousseau speaks in the *Confessions* of "the taste or rather passion for music" that he had experienced almost from birth and that first began to declare itself during his wanderings in Italy after running away from Geneva at age sixteen.[4] Rousseau's mature musical writings might be characterized as his attempt to account for his native love for music and especially his early passionate reaction to the Italian music he would later champion. Rousseau left Italy after about a year and returned to Annecy and his protectress, Madame de Warens. During his stay with his dear "*Maman*," Jean-Jacques pursued his growing passion as a way of avoiding other potential careers, for example applying himself to learning cantatas by heart while at a Lazarist seminary instead of studying for a priesthood for which he felt himself unsuited. Ultimately his penchant for song triumphed. He studied with the music master of the Cathedral at Annecy, M. Le Maître, and these six months in a choir school at about the age of seventeen were almost the only formal musical training he would receive.[5] Despite his limited competence, Rousseau took up the profession of music teacher and even proposed himself as a composer, performing his work with disastrous but comical results later related by him in his *Confessions*.[6] Claims that Rousseau did not know music well enough to be the author of his writings on music and the composer of a celebrated opera would pursue him to the end of his life.[7]

Rousseau began to devote himself exclusively to music during his twenties after unsuccessfully trying trades with more lucrative and permanent prospects. "I surely must have been born for this art, because I began to love it from my childhood, and it is the only one I have loved constantly at all times."[8] He turned again to teaching music and also began more serious practice and study of the art. He directed Mme de Warens's musical gatherings and learned to play the flute, the violin, and keyboard instruments, especially the spinet. And he also tried his hand at composing music, first seeing his name as an author of a song in the June 1737 edition of the *Mercure de France*.[9] His first attempt to write an opera was not so successful, and he later claimed that his lyric-tragedy *Iphis et Anaxarète*, written at Chambéry, was so poor that he had the good sense to throw it into the fire. A similar fate befell his *La Découverte du nouveau monde*, which he wrote around 1740 while serving as a tutor to the Mably family in Lyon, although the libretti to both of his first two operas still exist.[10] As for his musical studies, they were, as was most of his education, autodidactic. He acquired and claimed to have painstakingly mastered Rameau's *Treatise on Harmony*. Rameau's famed obscurity induced Rousseau to write a simpler digest of his master's system to use in his own teaching. He also studied informally at about this time with a young musician who had himself studied under a great Italian organist, and later recalled that he compared his friend's "principles" to those of "my Rameau."[11] At least in retrospect, then, Rousseau remarked the contrast between French and Italian music that would later so involve him and bring him into conflict with Rameau.

During his long stay in Chambéry Rousseau also began to support himself by copying music, a trade to which he would return permanently after abandoning philosophy. "I must admit that later on I chose in this profession the one in the world for which I was least suited."[12] Copying music acquainted him with the difficulty of the ordinary system of musical notation, and he therefore devised a new system. It was with this system of notation and a youthful play, his *Narcisse*, that Rousseau set out for Paris in 1741, with dreams of fame and fortune for himself in the artistic and intellectual capital of Europe.[13]

Rousseau carried to Paris letters of introduction to several important personages and was able to gain an audience for his new system of notation at the Academy of Sciences. He read his "Plan Regarding New Signs for Music" at the Academy on August 22, 1742. He proposed a numerical system that replaced the visual representation of notes, rests, and so on. He maintained that his system was easier to notate and to read than the ordinary system and that it was also better for teaching music, something he claimed to have himself confirmed.[14] His proposal was favorably received, but the report of a select committee concluded that his system was not entirely new and was less practical in most respects than the ordinary system, offering Rousseau encouragement but no official endorsement. The report mentioned that a numerical system of notation had been proposed a half century before by Souhaitti, but Rousseau claimed never to have heard of its proponent. He further argued that his own plan was more general in scope and noted that it employed a mobile system in contrast to the fixed system in use in France and retained in earlier schemes for numerical notation. Disappointed by the Academy's decision, Rousseau showed his plan to Rameau, who raised what he regarded as the only "solid objection" that could be made to his system by pointing out that while his figures clearly determined the value of the notes and their intervals, they did not sufficiently portray for sight the connection of notes in rapid succession, knowledge especially necessary for an accompanist. Rousseau was nonetheless convinced of the utility of his system and decided to present it to the public. After preparing its appearance with a letter to the *Mercure*, he published his proposal as the *Dissertation on Modern Music* (1743), a work that gained little attention and cost Rousseau a part of his small savings to get published.[15] Despite its poor reception, Rousseau continued to champion his notational system, explaining it in the article on notation in his *Dictionary of Music* and perfecting it for his own use. Rousseau's system was finally adopted in the nineteenth century by the influential Galin-Paris-Chevé school and spread by it throughout Europe and then to Japan, China, and other parts of Asia, where a version of it is still used today.[16]

Rousseau came to Paris an adherent of Rameau's musical theory, but several incidents during the next decade before the discovery of his philosophical "system" contributed to his break with the great musician. His early adherence to Rameau's view of musical expression is seen in two writings from this period. First, in a digression in the *Dissertation on Modern Music* Rousseau explains that we are not "touched" by sounds themselves but by the relationships they have among them, and he claims that "it is solely by the choice of these charming relationships that a beautiful composition can move the heart by flattering the ear." He refers his reader to Rameau's writings, where the source of musical expression is "sufficiently explained."[17] In his mature musical writings, Rousseau expounds a theory explicitly opposed to Rameau's theory of the harmonic basis of musical expression. Second, a letter dating from the mid-1740s reveals not only Rousseau's partiality for French music, but also a theory that directly contradicts his analysis a decade later in the *Letter on French Music*. In this early letter, Rousseau compares French and Italian opera and proclaims

French music generally more effective, in part because he does not perceive the close relationship between the Italian language and its "universal music" that he appreciates in French music and language—the close relationship that serves as the basis for his condemnation of French music a decade later.[18] Rousseau's break with Rameau and French music was due both to his reawakened appreciation for Italian music and to his increasingly bitter relationship with the foremost representative of French music.

Several incidents in the decade before the discovery of his "system" and his rethinking of his musical theory seem to have contributed to Rousseau's break with Rameau and French music. First, his year-long stay in Venice from 1743 to 1744 as secretary to the French ambassador reacquainted him with the Italian music he had grown to love years earlier. "From Paris I had brought the prejudice they have in that country against Italian music, but from nature I had also received that sensitivity of discrimination against which prejudices do not prevail. Soon I had for that music the passion which it inspires in anyone made to judge it." He frequented the opera and theaters and visited the famed *scuole*, but he particularly appreciated popular music. "While listening to the bacarolles I found that I had not heard singing until then."[19] Rousseau brought back to Paris a renewed passion for Italian music that would soon play an important role in the development of his musical ideas.

The other two incidents that contributed to Rousseau's break with Rameau involved the great musician himself. Before he had gone to Venice, Rousseau began work on a new opera entitled *Les Muses galantes*, which he completed after returning to Paris. The work is largely in the French style of the time, and perhaps owed its immediate inspiration to Rameau's opera-ballet *Les Indes galantes*, which was reprised in the spring of 1743.[20] Rousseau's work was performed in September 1745 at the household of Alexandre-Jean-Joseph Le Riche de La Poplinière, a wealthy tax farmer, patron of the arts, and, unfortunately for Rousseau, employer of the jealous Rameau. Rameau's reaction to Rousseau's opera was exceedingly galling to his professed "disciple." Rameau accused him of having plagiarized the Italianate portions of the work and having incompetently composed the French ones. Rousseau admitted that his work was uneven, the production of natural genius and too little knowledge of the art, but insisted on his authorship.[21] In a notice to the posthumously published version of the work, he further attributes its shortcomings to his still Gallic tastes: "This work is so mediocre in its genre, and its genre is so bad, that in order to understand how it could have pleased me, one must sense all the force of habit and prejudices. Nourished in my infancy in the taste for French Music and in the type of Poetry that belongs to it, I took noise for harmony, the marvelous for the interesting, and songs for an Opera."[22] A decade later after the opera's performance he would make the same charges against French music. Rousseau reworked his opera after the Duc de Richelieu said he wanted to have it performed at Versailles, and, while it was not put on there, Rousseau did arrange to have it rehearsed at the Paris Opera, but says he withdrew it because he was dissatisfied with it.[23] (Rameau would say that it was rejected.) Finally, a further confrontation with Rameau confirmed Rousseau's growing disenchantment with his former idol. Rousseau was offered the task of adapting a drama by Voltaire to a score by Rameau, but Rameau interfered with his work and then withdrew from the project, and Rousseau was not credited or compensated for his labor on *Les Fêtes de Ramire* (1745).[24] His relations with Rameau were more sour than ever, and his respectful if distant relationship with Voltaire would endure only for a few years. Rousseau's attack on the polite enlightened society of his time in the *First Discourse* surely owed much to his animus against two of its leading exemplars.

While he suffered setbacks in his musical career after his return to Paris, Rousseau soon became intimate with the *philosophes* and was asked by Diderot in late 1748 to write the articles on music for the *Encyclopedia*. His articles were ready after three months of feverish labor during which he completed some two hundred entries.[25] He relates in a letter that he was animated in his labor in part by vengeance: "I am out to get back at people who have done me harm, and bile gives me strength; it even gives me wit and knowledge."[26] He appears to refer to Rameau, and while he had certainly suffered humiliation at his hands, the *Encyclopedia* articles generally follow Rameau's theories and treat him with respect. However, at least the respectful tone of the articles may be due in part to d'Alembert, who appears to have intervened and removed some passages from Rousseau's drafts that betrayed spite.[27] The Encyclopedists were eager to arrogate some of Rameau's prestige to themselves. In the "Preliminary Discourse" to the *Encyclopedia*, d'Alembert celebrates Rameau as an "artist-philosopher" who had made of music a science.[28] Rameau's theory of the fundamental bass, the chord root that remains the cornerstone of modern harmonic theory, was likened in that age to Newton's theory of gravitation.[29] Nonetheless, beneath Rousseau's respectful treatment of Rameau lies pointed criticism. For instance, in the article on accompaniment, Rousseau echoes d'Alembert's praise of Rameau for having made a science of music but then criticizes him for adhering too literally to his "principles," claiming that some chords would be "unbearable" if filled out completely in the manner Rameau contends is required by his theory.[30] Rousseau's criticism of Rameau's overly "harmonic" music anticipates his impending polemic with him over the priority of melody and harmony,[31] but it does not contain any clear signs of the theory of the relationship between language and melody as the direct or imitative expression of the passions, the central idea of his mature musical writings. The *Encyclopedia* articles antedate Rousseau's discovery of his "system" and thus his mature musical theory.

By the time the first volume of the *Encyclopedia* appeared in July 1751, Rousseau was the author of the controversial *Discourse on the Sciences and Arts*, or *First Discourse*. D'Alembert's "Preliminary Discourse" to the *Encyclopedia* therefore not only announces Rousseau as the chief contributor on music, but also discusses his recently published work. D'Alembert suggests in defense of the Enlightenment manifesto that the corruption from the sciences and arts is due only to their abuse by cultivated minds, remarking that in any case Rousseau "seems himself to have given suffrage to our work by the zeal and the success of his collaboration on it."[32] Yet a revolution had occurred in Rousseau's thinking between the completion of the *Encyclopedia* articles and their publication. During the hot summer of 1749 on the road to Vincennes to visit Diderot, who was there in prison, Rousseau read the question for a prize essay competition sponsored by the Academy of Dijon and was transformed: "At the moment of that reading I saw another universe and I became another man."[33] The "illumination of Vincennes" was the revelation of the "system" that Rousseau would explicate in his works, beginning with the *First Discourse*.

Signs of the impact of Rousseau's philosophical vision on his musical theory are evident even in the *First Discourse*, in which he speaks of "the marvels of harmony rejected" in his time as a sign of declining tastes and morals, apparently alluding to the rejection in France of the Italian style that he would soon champion.[34] Numerous replies to Rousseau defended progress and challenged Rousseau's paradoxes. One reader espied a contradiction in Rousseau's participation in the *Encyclopedia* and wondered whether Rousseau would except music from his attack on corrupting effects of the sciences and arts.[35] Rousseau had indeed begun to rethink occupation as a musician and his ideas on the subject within the context of his "system." The simultaneous elaboration of his system in his philosophical works and his continued work on music would be the crucible in which his mature musical theory would develop. That development would occur in two episodes: the "Quarrel of the Bouffons" and his polemical exchange with Rameau.

The "Quarrel of the Bouffons"

Rousseau's participation in the war over the relative merits of French and Italian music known as the "Quarrel of the Bouffons" brought him almost as much celebrity as his *First Discourse*. For the next decade people would associate Jean-Jacques with his broadside against Gallic taste, and the *Letter on French Music*, along with the two *Discourses*, were often paired when their famous author was discussed. Although Rousseau's musical writings are now treated largely as a diversion from his more serious works, the works he produced during the "Quarrel," especially the *Letter on French Music*, exhibit the influence of the "system" he was simultaneously developing in his philosophical works.

Opera had been a serious matter in French literary and artistic circles for nearly a century when the "Quarrel of the Bouffons" erupted on August 1, 1752, upon the successful presentation in Paris of Pergolesi's *La Serva padrona* by an Italian troupe.[36] Bambini's troupe followed up its first success with a run of pieces whose continued success came to be perceived as an affront to the French style and reopened arguments that dated back fifty years and indeed almost to the birth of the French opera. The Italian form was accused of being intricate and frivolous, and its influence on French opera was decried. Similar issues had also arisen in the 1730s with the defense of Lullian lyric-tragedy, now the traditional form, against the novel opera of Rameau. The world of art was divided into two camps, the Lullists and the Ramists. Rameau's complex harmonies reminded his listeners of Italian music and brought down on him the fatal appellation "learned."[37] Nevertheless, by the middle of the century Rameau reigned supreme. Six of his operas were produced at the Paris Opera during the 1748–1749 season, and only the insistence of the King's mistress, Madame de Pompadour, that he be limited to two productions a year slowed the musician's ascent.[38] When French opera came under attack, it was inevitable that Rameau would be implicated even though his music represented something of a middle ground between the Lullist and the Italian sides.

The "Quarrel of the Bouffons" was prepared with a sally precipitated by the 1751 revival of Destouches's *Omphale*, a lyric-tragedy in the style of Lully. Rousseau's new friend Grimm wrote a piece critical of the opera, the *Letter on "Omphale,"* which appeared in February 1752. Grimm compares the Gallic style unfavorably to the Italian, but claims that he does not want to revive these "worn-out parallels" and instead focuses on French music in its own "genre." He laments that Destouches's opera is sadly representative of the operatic form the French so jealously guard and is vastly inferior to Rameau's "sublime" works.[39] Grimm's *Letter* was answered by Raynal's *Remarks on Grimm's Letter on "Omphale."*[40] Raynal also praises Italian music at the expense of French, but he is more generally critical of both, pointing out the common defects of the Italian style and also offering a more critical view of Rameau. Rousseau here entered the fray with his *Letter to Grimm on the Subject of the Remarks Added to His Letter on "Omphale,"* which appeared anonymously in April 1752. Rousseau presses the criticism of French opera begun by Grimm and Raynal even further and elevates Italian music correspondingly. He acknowledges that Rameau has boldly transcended the "trifling Music" of Lully's successors, but his praise is ultimately qualified. While Rameau's great talent must be recognized, his works display "more learning than genius—or at least a genius smothered by too much learning."[41] Rousseau's *Letter* is more satirical than philosophic in character, yet his criticism of Rameau's over-wrought accompaniments and learned harmonies and a brief discussion of the "very wise and very desirable unity" of dramatic and melodic character that should reign in a musical work are the first sketches of what would become the central doctrine of his mature musical theory.

Rousseau's criticism of Rameau redefined the musical debate by putting him on the same side as Lully. The success of the *buffa* style in the musical capital of France split the nation into two camps. In one camp were the admirers of the Italian style, including almost all the Encyclopedists. Bambini's troupe held the stage until the failed performance of Jommelli's *Il Paratojo* in September 1753. This failure elicited Rousseau's *Letter from a Symphonist*, published anonymously shortly afterward. In the letter, Rousseau poses as a player at the Opera conspiring with his fellow symphonists to perform the Italian music badly so they can chase off the Bouffonists and shine anew with their French music.

Rousseau also made a musical contribution to the "Quarrel" with his own triumphant comic opera, *Le Devin du village* (1752). Rousseau's opera was patterned after Pergolesi's *La Serva padrona*, which he was the first to engrave and publish in France. By his own reckoning, Rousseau's own opera remained an essentially French work, so that, paradoxically, as a composer Rousseau weighed into the "Quarrel of the Bouffons" with a piece of French music.[42] His opera was first rehearsed in June 1752 at Fontainebleau and then performed there with great success in October of the same year and then at the Paris Opera in March 1753.[43] *Le Devin du village* would see about four hundred performances in the next fifty years (and was the first work presented at the Paris Opera when it reopened after the fall of the Bastille) until its last, memorable performance in 1829, when Berlioz, it is rumored, threw a powdered wig on stage in disgust.[44] In his *Dialogues*, Rousseau attributed the success of his work to the "perfect accord between the words and the music" and more importantly to its "hidden principle," the unity of melody, and it is in this context that Rousseau claims that his opera exhibits the same ideas and "feelings" as all his works.[45] Rousseau's comic opera represents the first expression of the influence of his philosophy on his musical theory, but the contemporaneously written *Let-*

ter on French Music first elaborates the principle of the unity of melody and is therefore his first fully mature work of musical theory.[46]

The "Quarrel" seemed to be drawing to a close with Bambini's troupe soon to depart, but it took on a new seriousness with the appearance of Rousseau's *Letter on French Music* in November 1753 and then in a second edition a few months later. Rousseau begins the *Letter* by suggesting that one examine not whether French music is excellent, but whether there is even a French music at all. His analysis in the *Letter* concerns the relationship of music to language. "Harmony, having its principle in nature, is the same for all Nations, or if it has some variations they are introduced by those in the melody; thus, it is from melody alone that the particular character of a National Music must be derived; all the more so as, its character being produced principally by the language, song strictly speaking should be affected by its greatest influence."[47] He imagines a language totally unsuited for melodious song, and that language turns out to be French. In order to prove the inaptness of the French language for music, he examines a famed recitative from Lully's *Armide* and finds it wanting. As in so many of his works, Rousseau's conclusion was foreshadowed in the question he posed at the outset: "I believe I have shown that there is neither meter nor melody in French Music, because the language is not susceptible to them; that French song is but a continual barking, unbearable to any ear not prepared for it. . . . From which I conclude that the French do not at all have a Music and cannot have any; or that if ever they have any, it will be so much the worse for them."[48]

Rousseau's almost entirely critical approach in the *Letter on French Music* conceals the constructive theory on which his criticism is based. He elaborates that theory in his later works, but it can be glimpsed within the *Letter* when his argument about the relationship between music and language is brought together with his digression on the "unity of melody." The link is hinted at when Rousseau notes that he could explain the source of an expressive music by inverting his explanation of the inexpressive character of French music. Based on the contrary assumption of a music suited to a language, he would be able to deduce all the qualities of a genuine music, "one made to move, to imitate, to please, and to convey to the heart the sweetest impressions of harmony and of song."[49] The source of musical expression is the imitation of the passions conveyed through the melody. The "unity of melody" is therefore the key to a truly expressive music, and Rousseau considers himself to be the first to articulate that principle.

The reaction to the *Letter on French Music* was immediate and furious. Rousseau was denied entry to the Paris Opera despite the free pass he had earned as a composer whose works had been presented there, and he was burned in effigy by its musicians. His attack on French music began to be read as an attack on France, and it appears that an order for his expulsion from France was drawn up but then suppressed through the influence of his friends.[50] His own later estimation of the effect of his *Letter* is curious: "The Parlement had just been exiled; the fermentation was at its peak; everything threatened an approaching uprising. The Pamphlet appeared; instantly all the other quarrels were forgotten; only the peril of French music was thought of, and there was no longer any uprising except against me.... When you read that this pamphlet perhaps prevented a revolution in the State, you will believe you are dreaming. Nevertheless, it is a very real truth which all of Paris can attest...."[51] As Maurice Cranston remarks, it is ironic that the philosopher so often blamed for provoking the French Revolution would see himself as responsible for averting one. Yet, as Cranston also notes, there is good reason to take Rousseau's claims seriously. The King's attempt in November 1753 to dissolve the Paris Parlement and replace it with a Royal Chamber met with fierce opposition, and the capital seemed to be on the brink of a rebellion. Rousseau's *Letter* created a diversion that occupied the warring spirit of the time.[52]

Rousseau's *Letter on French Music* provoked over thirty mostly angry responses.[53] Among those responses was one by Rameau. Although Rousseau barely mentions Rameau in his examination of French music, his *Letter* had to be considered an attack on France's greatest musician and musical theorist. At least that is how Rameau perceived it.[54] Further, Rameau himself in his earlier works had analyzed Lully's famed recitative as an example of the finest French harmony. Rousseau recalls this examination in his *Letter* when he suggests that Rameau's praise of the piece should be considered "a veritable satire" given Lully's "pedantic regularity" in a scene that called for the liveliest passions.[55] Rousseau's charge of "pedantic regularity" seems directed as much at Rameau's infamously "learned" harmonies as at Lully. Rameau quickly adapted a writing on which he was already at work, the *Observations on Our Instinct for Music and on its Principle*, adding a counter-examination of Lully's recitative.[56] Rameau argues in the *Observations* that our instinct naturally leads us to the harmonic modulations that can be shown to be derived from the resonance of a sounding body, the core of his theory of harmony and, he maintains, the "principle" of all music. Rameau had always contended that melody derived from harmony, but in the *Observations* he takes a more extreme position than previously: "It belongs to Harmony alone to stir the passions; Melody derives its force only from that source, from which it directly emanates."[57] The polemical exchange between Rousseau and Rameau that evolved out of

Rousseau's attack on French music centered on the relative priority of harmony and melody as the source of music's structure and expressive power. However, when he brought out his *Letter on French Music* Rousseau was also beginning his *Second Discourse*, and so the dispute with Rameau evolved into "a serious argument about aesthetics and even metaphysics."[58]

The Polemics with Rameau

The quarrel between Rousseau and Rameau was bitterly personal, but it was also a contest between opposing views about the nature of music as an expressive art.[59] Rameau argued that harmony is the source of music's structure and its expressive power and that the harmonic structure of music is derived from universal, natural principles available to us in inchoate form through our instinct and found out by scientific investigation. Indeed, for Rameau music was the "mother of the sciences," the best subject in which to glimpse the essentially harmonic or proportionate character of nature as a whole. In opposition to Rameau, Rousseau argued, from the *Letter on French Music* onward, that melody is the source of musical expression; music is a semantic system, a language of the passions communicated through the inflections of the melody. Music and language are cultural phenomena, and differences between cultures and the forms of expression that belong to them are based on differences in their characteristic needs and passions. In other words, Rousseau's attack on French music implies the philosophy of human nature and development elaborated just afterward in the *Second Discourse*. For Rousseau, music provides a means for glimpsing the "nature" of a people, and Rameau's purported science of music mistakes the nature of music and its power over the human heart. The debate between Rameau and Rousseau would prove to be one where "two distinct and well-considered philosophies of music confronted one another."[60]

Rousseau articulated his theory of music as the language of the passions in his response to Rameau's continued attacks. Rameau followed up his response to the *Letter on French Music* with a bitter criticism of the articles Rousseau wrote for the *Encyclopedia*. The *Errors on Music in the Encyclopedia*, which appeared anonymously in 1755 but bore the unmistakable stylistic signature of its author, offered a commentary on a number of Rousseau's articles that had appeared to that point, and he continued his attack the next year with the also anonymous *Continuation of the Errors on Music in the Encyclopedia*. Rameau's principal objection to Rousseau is hard to ascertain amidst the line-by-line critique he offers, but his central point is that

Rousseau has failed to understand the harmonic foundation of the structure and expressive power of music. For example, in response to Rousseau's criticism in the article on accompaniment that chords need not always be completely filled out, Rameau argues that the accompaniment represents the harmonic complements produced in the resonance of a sounding body and therefore the harmony "cannot be truncated without violating the laws of Nature itself."[61] The argument between the two musicians is ultimately over the nature of music itself. Rameau therefore reprises his quarrel with Rousseau over the relative priority of harmony and melody, and turns in the midst of his critique of the *Encyclopedia* articles to the *Letter on French Music*.[62] He suggests that Rousseau's "partisanship" for the melody prominent in Italian music betrays an untutored ear. He ridicules Rousseau's doctrine of "the unity of melody" as a "chimera"— "words which strike the ears in discourse, but whose effect has only weak appeal in Music without the aid of harmony." It is in this context that Rameau relates the story of the performance some ten years earlier of Rousseau's *Les Muses galantes*. Although Rousseau would like to present himself as a "Legislator" in music, Rameau argues, his failures as a composer and as a theorist betray a fundamental misunderstanding of music. "As long as Melody alone is considered as the principal moving force of Music's effects there will not be great progress in this Art," he proclaims. "It is therefore only directly from the harmony, mother of this Melody, that the different effects we experience in Music arise."[63] For Rameau, music is explained by the harmonics produced by the resonance of a body in motion. Music is a "physicomathematical science,"[64] a science that investigates a universal nature characterized by harmony and proportion and subject to rational human understanding.

Like Rameau, Rousseau claims "nature" as the source of his own theory of music, but his conception of "nature" is quite different.[65] In Rousseau's eyes, Rameau's musical theory tends toward the reductionist rationalism and materialism he opposes in his philosophical works, and it is in his reaction to Rameau's theory that we can see his musical theory come together with the guiding thread of his philosophy. Rameau's attack stimulated Rousseau to develop the theory of music sketched in the *Letter on French Music* in light of his theory of human nature and development. However, Rousseau's direct response to Rameau's criticism of his *Encyclopedia* articles, the *Examination of Two Principles Advanced by M. Rameau*, remains centered on the dispute over the priority of melody and harmony.[66] Rousseau wrote the *Examination* in 1755, just after the appearance of Rameau's *Errors*, but the final form of the work dates from about ten years later when he considered including it as a theoretical preface to his

Dictionary of Music, although he decided against publishing it in that form and the work was published posthumously.

As its title suggests, Rousseau's *Examination* responds to two principles advanced by Rameau in his critique of the *Encyclopedia* articles. The first principle is Rameau's contention that harmony is the unique foundation of music and its great effects—a principle "which has guided M. Rameau in all his writings and, what is worse, in all his Music." The second principle advanced by Rameau is that the accompaniment represents the sounding body, but since Rameau's argument that the harmony must be completely represented in the accompaniment, the second principle is essentially a corollary to the first. As Rousseau notes, the debate over the source of musical expression is the crux of his disagreement over the "basis for the whole Musical Art."[67] The two thinkers find themselves diametrically opposed on this subject. Whereas Rameau argues that a piece of music with a good harmonic succession "relates directly to the soul" while the pleasure induced by an unadorned melody "does not pass beyond the ear canal,"[68] Rousseau states:

The most beautiful chords, like the most beautiful colors, can convey to the senses a pleasant sensation and nothing more. But the accents of the voice pass all the way to the soul; for they are the natural expression of the passions, and by depicting them they excite them. . . . It is by means of the song, not by means of the chords, that sounds have expression, fire, life; it is the song alone that gives them the moral effects that produce all of Music's energy. In a word, the physical part alone of the art is reduced to very little and harmony does not pass beyond that.[69]

To Rameau's "physical" science of harmony Rousseau opposes a theory of the "moral effects" of the melody as the conduit of the passions. While he admits that simple harmony is natural, Rousseau contends that "the feeling which develops it is acquired and artificial, as are the majority of those attributed to nature," concluding, in the vein of the *Second Discourse*, that "it is an inconvenience inseparable from great cities that nature must be sought far off."[70] Rousseau's remark suggests that he could provide an account of the melodic origin of music and its development—or rather decline—into a science of harmony. In fact, Rousseau originally did just that at this point in the text within a digression that he cut from the final version of the *Examination* but incorporated into his *Essay on the Origin of Languages*.[71] While the philosophical basis of Rousseau's quarrel with Rameau can be glimpsed in his direct reply to his adversary, it is fully evident only in writings that transcend that dispute, in which he could explore the relationship between his musical theory and his philosophy as a whole, especially the *Essay on the Origin of Languages* and his *Dictionary of Music*.

The *Essay on the Origin of Languages*

In the *Essay on the Origin of Languages*, Rousseau brings together his developed ideas concerning music and his philosophy of human nature and development in a way that makes that work the fullest account of his mature musical theory. The full title of the *Essay* indicates its musical content: *Essay on the Origin of Languages, In which melody and musical imitation are treated*. Rousseau himself explains in a draft preface to the *Essay* that it was originally a fragment from the *Second Discourse*, which he omitted as too long and out of place.[72] What portion of the work he could mean is a matter of dispute, but part of the *Essay* can be said with certainty to have originated out of his polemics with Rameau. As noted above, a portion of the *Essay* began as part of the original draft of Rousseau's response to Rameau, which dates from late 1755 and was entitled *On the Principle of Melody or Response to the Errors on Music*.[73] The hypothetical account of the origin and progress of music Rousseau presents in the digression on the origin of melody in that original draft is strikingly similar to the account of human origin and development offered in the *Second Discourse*, which was written at about the same time. As Elisabeth Duchez remarks, the digression marks "the point of juncture of two concurrent preoccupations: the one concerning music and language, the other concerning society and language."[74] Rousseau seems to have reworked the *Essay* several times over the next several years, with the final version dating from about the time of the publication of *Emile* (1762), in which he refers the reader to the work as proof of his contention that "something moral enters into everything connected with imitation."[75] He sent the *Essay* to Malesherbes, then the head of censorship in France, for advice on publication. Although the magistrate reacted favorably, Rousseau decided against publishing it in any form, and the *Essay* appeared only after his death. The origin and form of the *Essay* show that it belongs to the philosophical project of the *Second Discourse* as well as to Rousseau's polemic with Rameau, and thus provides the best view of the links between Rousseau's musical theory and his philosophy as a whole.

The *Essay* has received increasing attention in recent years. Most notably, Jacques Derrida's influential *Of Grammatology* contains an extended analysis of the *Essay* as an exemplar not only of Rousseau's thought but of a decisive "epoch" in Western metaphysics as a whole. Jean Starobinski devotes considerable attention to the *Essay* throughout his monumental interpretation of Rousseau, as does Paul de Man in his important response to Derrida's and other writings.[76] Much earlier scholarship on Rousseau's *Essay* centered on dating the work.[77] The dating of the work is an important issue because of an apparent contradiction between Rousseau's discussions of pity in the *Essay* and in the *Second Discourse*: whereas Rousseau appears to argue in the *Second Discourse* that pity is active in presocial man, in the *Essay* he states that pity fully develops only with the social affections. A genuine contradiction between the two texts would suggest either that the *Essay* is at least in part an early, presystematic writing or that Rousseau's thought changed and developed in important ways between his writing of the *Second Discourse* and his writing of *Emile*, which contains an account of pity similar to that of the *Essay*. However, this apparent contradiction is ultimately a matter of different emphasis, and the *Essay* contains an important elaboration of Rousseau's understanding of pity and the development of the human passions.

In the *Essay*, Rousseau argues that language and music originate as the expression of the human passions as they develop in nascent societies. He depicts a similar origin of speech and song in the *Second Discourse*, but in the *Essay* he explores variations in the development of man's malleable passions and faculties and thus variations in the form of his communication in a way that the unitary plot line of the *Discourse* does not permit. The *Essay* therefore begins with a statement about man's unique capacity for speech and the variation among different languages: "Speech distinguishes man from the animals. Language distinguishes nations from each other; one does not know where a man is from until after he has spoken." Linguistic variations are due to local physical causes such as climate, and at the center of the *Essay* is an extended comparison between northern and southern languages. However, Rousseau's emphasis on physical causes should not obscure his underlying argument about linguistic and cultural variation: physical causes have a variable effect on human beings because of their uniquely malleable passions. Social animals such as beavers and ants have some form of language, Rousseau acknowledges, but he argues their language is natural and invariable. "Conventional language belongs only to man. That is why man makes progress, whether for good or bad, and why the animals do not at all."[78] Both the capacity for speech and the variability of its form are related to what Rousseau identifies in the *Second Discourse* as the distinctively human "faculty of self-perfection," or "perfectibility."[79] In the *Essay*, Rousseau elaborates his theory of the uniquely human capacity for development and explores the closely related capacity for communication within a culturally distinct community.[80]

The origin of languages and music coincides with the origin of human societies, and when Rousseau seeks the passionate origin of human communication he is at the same time challenging prevailing views of the origin and purpose of human society. Language and music do not originate as the expression of our physical needs, as many of his predecessors had claimed, but are originally and essentially the communication of "the moral needs, the passions."[81] The first language, the archetypal form, was animated by the melodic accent of the passions, and as such it would have been sung rather than spoken, poetic and figurative in character. In order to illustrate the figurative character of the first language, Rousseau gives the example of one man encountering another. The first man's fear causes him to see the other as taller and stronger than himself, so he will give such beings the name "giant." Further experience will reveal that these beings are similar to himself and he will give them the name "man."[82] A recognition that the "other" is like one's self is needed before man will try to communicate with his fellows. "As soon as one man was recognized by another as a sentient, thinking Being and similar to himself, the desire or the need to communicate his feelings and thoughts to him made him seek the means for doing so."[83] The origin of communication is tied to the dawning consciousness of fellow humanity that marks man's emergence as a social and moral being. In the *Second Discourse*, just before his consideration of the origin of speech, Rousseau gives a similar description of savage man's view of his "fellows": "The conformities that time could make him perceive among them, his female, and himself led him to judge of those which he could not perceive; and . . . he concluded that their way of thinking and feeling conformed entirely to his own."[84] A consciousness of fellow humanity involves a sympathetic recognition of shared passion. Rousseau's argument about the passionate origin of speech leads him to a consideration of the role of pity as the basis for the recognition of shared passion that leads to our communication with our fellows.

In chapter ix of the *Essay*, Rousseau begins his extended account of the passionate origin of speech in the southern climates with a discussion of the role of active pity in human communication. The early, scattered inhabitants of the earth had no society other than the family and no language beyond gesture and some unarticulated sounds because they lacked the social or moral passions that give rise to society and to true speech. "Social affections develop in us only with our enlightenment. Pity, although natural to the heart of man, would remain eternally inactive without the imagination that puts it into play."[85] Although Rousseau's argument here about the initial inactivity of pity may seem to contradict what he says in the *Second Discourse*, upon careful examination there is no substantial contradiction between the two works.[86] Rousseau's argument in the *Second Discourse* is not precisely that pity is initially active, but rather that it is a "principle" of natural right, which does not assume natural sociability, and his emphasis there is on the presocial foundation of natural right and, in fact, he never argues that pity is fully active by nature: he states that pity is "the *first* relative sentiment which touches the human heart according to the order of nature."[87] Rousseau may overstate the active role of pity in the *Second Discourse* for rhetorical purposes, that is, to shore up his account of the state of nature as a peaceful condition. Indeed, Rousseau's conception of human development, in which pity plays a crucial role, is somewhat difficult to understand from the *Second Discourse* alone, in large measure because of its negative character as an exposition devoted to showing why humans need not have developed. He is not so constrained in the *Essay* and therefore presents an account that reveals that the development of pity is the foundation for the development of the social or moral passions and faculties, including the faculty for communication. In his explanation of pity in the *Essay*, Rousseau describes pity as the sympathetic recognition of commonality. "We suffer only as much as we judge him to suffer; it is not in ourselves, it is in him that we suffer. . . . How could I suffer in seeing another suffer if I do not even know that he suffers, if I do not know what he and I have in common?"[88] Consciousness of what one has in common with another leads to self-consciousness, and the awakening of pity is therefore the catalyst for the development of the passions from the essentially "physical" desires man has by nature into the other-regarding social or "moral" passions he gains in society.

Rousseau's account of the origin of speech and song in the *Essay* centers on the transformation of the sexual passion, as does his parallel account in the *Second Discourse*. After gathering his inhabitants together through natural accidents such as earthquakes or volcanic eruptions, also as in the *Second Discourse*, Rousseau portrays how sustained contact with their fellows develops men's faculties and passions. The arid climate of the south makes common watering places important to its nomadic inhabitants, and it was at these wells that separate families came into contact. "There were formed the first ties between families; here the first meetings between the two sexes took place. . . . There eyes accustomed to the same objects from childhood began to see sweeter ones."[89] The meetings between the sexes of different families offer the conditions for the development of the passions beyond their initially habitual and essentially solipsistic basis:

> Beneath aged oaks, conquerors of years, an ardent youth gradually forgot its ferocity, little by little they tamed one another; through endeavoring to make themselves understood, they learned to explain themselves. There the first festivals took place, feet leaped with joy, eager gesture no longer sufficed, the voice accompanied it with passionate accents; mingled together, pleasure and desire made themselves felt at the same time. There finally was the true cradle of peoples, and from the pure crystal of the fountains came the first fires of love.[90]

Introduction xxxi

Speech and song are born as the melodious accents of the awakened passions. In the parallel account in the *Second Discourse*, Rousseau shows his lovers dancing around a large tree: "song and dance, true children of love and leisure, became the amusement or rather the occupation of idle and assembled men and women. Each one began to look at the others and to want to be looked at himself. . . ."[91] The transformation of the sexual passion from a "physical" desire to a "moral" sentiment coincides with a similar transformation of the passion of self-love, and the development of these passions and the desire to communicate them marks man's transformation into a social or moral being.[92]

The origin of human communication is inextricably tied to the origin of human communities, or what we would call cultures. In the *Essay*, Rousseau describes the fountains around which speech and song originated in the southern climes as "the true cradles of peoples," and in the parallel account in the *Second Discourse* he also suggests the relationship between the origin of language and the birth of what he calls "nations"—communities "unified by morals and character" and among other things by "the common influence of Climate."[93] Rousseau makes linguistic differences resulting from climate a central theme of the *Essay*. He contrasts the amorous origin of language and music in the south to the needy beginnings of speech in the cold regions of the north. Instead of the meridional expression of moral love, "*aimez-moi*," the physically needy peoples of the north have a characteristically harsher demand, "*aidez-moi*." French, a northern language, bears the imprint of its origin; its harsh articulations and muted syllables cannot support a sonorous music; Rousseau thus provides an explanation for his claims in the *Letter on French Music* about the differences between Italian and French music.[94] The linguistic variation Rousseau notes in the *Essay* hints at related social and moral differences, a subject he touches upon in the concluding chapter of the work after preparing it with a discussion of the origin and degeneration of music.

Rousseau's turn from a discussion of the origin and character of the first languages and the contrast between southern and northern languages in the first half of the *Essay* to an analysis of the character and development of music in the remainder of the work may appear abrupt, but his account of the development (that is, degeneration) of music moves from the pole of the passionate melody of the south to that of the harmonic science of the north. The melodic language of the south serves Rousseau as the archetypal origin of language and music, and of their essential nature as the expression of the passions. He describes the first language as "tuneful" in character. The passions are expressed as cadenced melodic accents: "passion makes all the vocal organs speak, and adorns the voice with all their brilliance; thus verses, songs, and speech have a common origin." The first languages were the melodic expression of the passions enunciated by the lovers dancing around the fountains of chapter ix, and "at first there was no music at all other than melody, nor any other melody than the varied sound of speech."[95] The identity or at least cooperation of song and speech are the source of musical expression, and their separation explains their loss of expressive power. The highly articulated languages born of the needy passions of the north represent the separation of speech and song, the fate that looms over the melodic language of the south. As in the *Second Discourse*, man's emergence as a moral and social being carries with it the germ of corruption. The modern languages of Rousseau's Europe, especially French, not only have a northern origin that makes them the unmelodic expressions of selfish need, but they can also be represented as the endpoint of a process of degeneration of music and language that accompanies the degeneration of politics and morals.

The degeneration of music that Rousseau chronicles in the *Essay* culminates in the modern science of harmony. He therefore returns to his polemic with Rameau over the relative priority of melody and harmony, but he recasts it in the historical mode that makes the work so similar to the *Second Discourse*. He further reformulates his dispute with Rameau as part of the quarrel between the ancients and moderns, contrasting the expressive power of the melodic language and music of ancient Greece to the unexpressive modern music dominated by harmony.[96] As in his political thought, where he indicates the superiority of ancient practice while refounding that practice on the basis of modern natural right theory, in his musical theory Rousseau appeals to the powerful influence of music and language experienced among the ancients while seeking to rekindle that influence on the basis of a properly directed modern philosophic approach. His own approach to understanding music's expressive power on the soul takes cognizance of both the natural or physical and the moral or cultural levels in explaining human communication, and thereby tries to avoid the reductionism and materialism toward which he believes modern science tends.

Rousseau's ambition in reconsidering ancient music is clear in the source of his discussion of the development and decline of music in the *Essay*: the digression on the origin of melody he removed from the original draft of his direct reply to Rameau's criticism of his *Encyclopedia* articles. In response to Rameau's questions about the veracity of the reports of the prodigious effects of ancient music and his contention that Greek music was based upon false principles, Rousseau defends his treatment of Greek music by means of an imaginative reconstruction of ancient music and language as forms of social communication. "Never did the vain noise of harmony disturb these divine concerts. Everything was heroic and grand in these antique festivals. Laws and songs bore the same name in those happy times; they maintained unison in all voices, passed with the same pleasure into all hearts, all adored the first images of virtue, and innocence itself gave a sweeter accent to the voice of pleasure."[97] A melodic language binds the community through the unmediated expression of shared passion. The image of the unanimous expression of a common will based upon shared passions recalls the legitimate political community of the *Social Contract* and suggests that Rousseau's "general will" should be conceived less as the combined articulation of rational interests than as a unison of voices, as in the singing of a national anthem, a unison based on the affective cultural foundation of common customs, opinions, and mores.[98] Just as Rousseau anticipates that his modern readers will hardly credit the model of the political community he offers, so he explains Rameau's incredulity about the power of ancient music by saying that we no longer experience these effects ourselves.[99] In addition, he argues that Rameau's attempt to understand ancient music as a defective version of a universal science of harmony is flawed, for that music was based on different "principles" than our own. Rousseau portrays a decline in the expressive power of language and music—and a related decline in politics and mores—that culminates in modern times. Rameau's theory of harmony merely codifies a degenerate music. "Let us therefore not think that the empire Music has over our passions is ever explained by proportions and figures . . . because one cannot discover in them any type of connection between nature and man. The Principle and the rules are only the material of the art; a more subtle Metaphysics is needed in order to explain its great effects."[100] Rousseau supplies this "Metaphysics" in the *Essay*.

A proper explanation of musical and linguistic expression must begin from the nature of man. The theory of musical expression expounded in the *Essay* rests upon Rousseau's analysis of man's uniquely malleable passions. "Man is modified by his senses, no one doubts it; but because we fail to distinguish their modifications, we confound their causes; we attribute both too much and too little dominion to sensations; we do not see that often they affect us not only as sensations but as signs or images, and that their moral effects also have moral causes."[101] Rousseau contrasts the "physical" causes and effects of the sounds of harmony with the "moral" causes and effects of melody as the sign of the passions. His analysis of musical expression rests upon the distinction he makes in the *Second Discourse* between "physical" passions man possesses by nature and the social or "moral" passions that develop as he comes into sustained contact with his fellows and emerges as a "moral" being. This theory of the communication of the passions through the melodic accent of speech or music illuminates his understanding of how the "moral" dimension of human existence develops from an initially purely "physical" basis. As the fullest consideration of the relationship between the "physical" and the "moral," the *Essay* and Rousseau's musical writings more generally offer the best glimpse into Rousseau's metaphysical thought, the "sensitive morality, or the Wise Man's materialism" announced in the *Confessions*.[102]

If music is the expression of the social or moral passions as they develop differently among different peoples as the effect of such causes as climate, then music must be understood as a cultural phenomenon that belongs to man as a moral, social, and cultural being. Music must be understood as a semantic system—indeed cultures in general must be understood in this way. As Rousseau develops his musical theory he continues to contrast it with Rameau's. The effects of harmony are "purely physical" and produce a "pleasant sensation" but nothing more. The full expressive power of song depends upon the melody, but since the melody derives from the particular passions expressed by the people among whom it is used, the full effect of a music is restricted to that musico-linguistic community. "The sounds of a melody do not act on us solely as sounds, but as signs of our affections, of our feelings; it is in this way that they excite in us the emotions which they express, and the image of which we recognize in them."[103] A musical theory that studies only its purely sensual effects will never succeed in understanding musical expression and will produce only a pallid music. As in his philosophy in general, Rousseau fears the reductive materialism represented by Rameau's science of harmony: "in this century, when every effort is made to materialize all the operations of the soul and to deprive human feelings of all morality, I am mistaken if the new philosophy does not become as fatal to good taste as to virtue."[104] Rousseau develops his own "metaphysics" of human nature and communication in order to oppose what he sees as the dominant and inimical philosophy of his time. His mature musical theory is animated by the same spirit and based on the same principles as his "system" as a whole.

In the concluding chapters of the *Essay* Rousseau describes a related decline in music and language on the one hand and in mores and government on the other. He locates the peak of music among the Greeks and then charts its decline. The changes in music are related to a "natural" change in the character of languages. As language was perfected by philosophy, melody assumed a separate existence and music lost its ancient energy. The decay in language and music was accompanied by a political decline: "Greece in chains lost that fire that warms only free souls, and no longer found for the praise of its tyrants the tone with which it had sung of its Heroes." The catastrophic inundation of Europe by the northern barbarians vanquished what remained of freedom and of melodious language.[105] Rousseau concludes the *Essay* with a consideration of the political relevance of language hinted at in his discussion of the history of music's decline. Just as in modern times music becomes a matter of physical forces instead of moral passions, so too does politics. The eloquent persuasion of ancient times has been replaced by force. "Societies have assumed their final form; nothing is changed in them any longer except by arms and cash." There are some languages favorable to liberty, he argues, but the muted and articulated languages of modern Europe are not favorable.[106] The conclusion of the *Essay* is the culmination of an analysis of the origin of language and music that is at the same time a critical study of man's moral and political development. In the *Essay* the two streams of Rousseau's intellectual career are united; his musical theory reaches its fullest development in the work and his theory of human nature and development is in turn enriched by the musical theory it stimulated.

Although he never published the *Essay* during his lifetime, Rousseau considered publishing in two different manners, both of which alternatives are reflected in the organization of the present volume. First, after being encouraged in June 1763 by Malesherbes to publish the work, he thought of issuing it along with the essay *On Theatrical Imitation* and his prose poem *The Levite of Ephraïm*. Rousseau wrote the first work of his proposed volume, *On Theatrical Imitation*, in preparation for his *Letter to d'Alembert on the Theatre* (1758), he describes it as a sort of extract from Plato's treatments of the subject that he has taken out of the dramatic form of the original and put into continuous discourse. The origin of the writing suggests Rousseau's keen interest not only in the moral effect of theater, but also in the "old quarrel between philosophy and poetry," as he says in imitation of Plato. Although the work initially appears to be a simple recapitulation of the Platonic doctrine of imitation, if an artful one, closer examination reveals that Rousseau makes certain changes from the original.[107] The *Levite of Ephraïm*, the third piece in the volume Rousseau proposed to publish, was begun in June 1762 during Rousseau's flight from France after a warrant was issued for his arrest upon the publication of *Emile* and *Social Contract*.[108] Like the essay on theatrical imitation, the *Levite* is an imitation of an ancient original, in this case a story in *Judges*, and also like that work Rousseau generally follows the original but diverges from it in certain important ways, notably by giving it a new ending.[109] Thus placed between an imitation of an ancient philosophical work and an imitation of an ancient scriptural text, Rousseau's *Essay* might be viewed as his attempt to mediate the "quarrel between philosophy and poetry" and the related conflict between philosophy and scripture. This interpretation is suggested by Rousseau's use in the *Essay* of the story of the Levite and of the example of the legislators of the Jews as examples of the lost art of persuasion.[110] Through the combination of an analysis of language and imitation and examples of new imitative forms of literature, Rousseau seeks to reestablish the language of freedom whose loss he laments at the end of the *Essay*. Rousseau's second plan for publishing the *Essay* was to issue it along with his major musical writings, reaffirming the *Essay*'s place among the final statements of his mature musical theory. Rousseau's intentions for the *Essay* have both been honored in the present volume, and it is hoped that by organizing his writings in this manner, his musical theory will be seen in the light of his "system" of the natural goodness of man and as an integral part of it.

The *Dictionary of Music*

Rousseau's other major statement of his mature musical theory is found in the *Dictionary of Music*. Like the *Essay*, the *Dictionary* reached its final form only after a long period of revision and maturation. Indeed, the composition of the *Dictionary* is testimony to the influence on Rousseau's musical theory of his discovery of his philosophical system, since the work had originated in the presystematic articles on music for the *Encyclopedia*. While his musical lexicon was long viewed as a simple reworking and expansion of the *Encyclopedia* articles,[111] subsequent research has shown that "it is more nearly an original work" since over half of the articles in the *Dictionary* were entirely new, including the most important ones, and since the majority of the articles carried over from the *Encyclopedia* were substantially revised.[112] The *Dictionary of Music* is Rousseau's literal revision of his musical theory to make it accord more fully with his philosophy as a whole.

In the Preface to the *Dictionary* Rousseau explains that he has tried to produce a lexicon that is at the same time a coherent treatment with a unified theory, although he adds that he does not believe that he has succeeded. He relates that he was dissatisfied with the quality of the *Encyclopedia* articles he wrote in such haste in early 1749, and therefore began to rework them shortly thereafter. The first independent confirmation we have of Rousseau's labors is the "Notice" to the sixth volume of the *Encyclopedia* (1756), where d'Alembert assures the reader that Rousseau will be able to defend himself against Rameau's criticisms in the dictionary he is preparing.[113] D'Alembert's remark not only helps us date the first drafts of the *Dictionary of Music*, but suggests how that work, like all of his mature musical writings, arose in part out of his polemics with Rameau. This interpretation is confirmed by the fact that, when he first tried to publish the *Dictionary* in about 1765, Rousseau considered using his response to Rameau's criticism of his *Encyclopedia* articles as a theoretical preface to his musical lexicon.[114] Because of interruptions and the exigencies of other work, Rousseau's attention to the *Dictionary* was intermittent. He appears to have done most of the reworking of his original articles in two stages.[115] The first stage took place around 1755 when he did the substantial research at the Royal Library that he mentions in the Preface to the *Dictionary*. This was also the period in which he completed and published the *Second Discourse* and wrote his initial response to Rameau's criticisms of his *Encyclopedia* articles. The second stage was during his stay at the Hermitage at Montmorency (1756–1762), where he says that the "scattered, mutilated, shapeless materials" of his work forced him to begin it anew.[116] Despite his dissatisfaction with the results after a decade and a half of work, Rousseau decided to publish his *Dictionary* in the mid-1760s, largely for much-needed income.[117] It was an immediate success and "soon achieved the status of an indispensable reference work."[118] It was almost immediately translated into several languages, including a full translation into English, and incorporated into numerous lexicons and encyclopedias, including the renowned *Chamber's Encyclopedia*, the inspiration for the very *Encyclopedia* for which Rousseau first wrote his articles. As the "first modern musical lexicon," Rousseau's work also served as the model for others, especially in France and Germany.[119] The musical theory contained in the *Dictionary* was thus disseminated by direct and indirect means throughout Europe and beyond.

The *Dictionary* articles elaborate the musical theory Rousseau develops in the *Essay*, although with a narrower focus on music. The central idea of this theory is that music is an imitative art that realizes its greatest effects as the imitative communication of the human passions. The centrality of imitation in Rousseau's aesthetic theory suggests that he belongs to a long tradition dating back at least to Aristotle, and his understanding of music as the imitation of the passions further shows that his aesthetic theory owes much to the dominant theory of the eighteenth century, represented foremost by Dubos.[120] However, since Rousseau's mature musical theory rests upon a theory of human nature and development that is significantly different from that articulated or assumed by any of his predecessors, his views on musical imitation as the expression of passions and his insistence upon the variability in the forms of their communication ultimately produces a novel aesthetic doctrine.[121]

The theoretical shift represented by Rousseau's philosophy of music can be seen in numerous articles in the *Dictionary*. For example, in the first substantial article of the work, ACCENT [*Accent*], he discusses the natural basis of the melodic accent and its cultural variability: "the universal *Accent* of Nature which draws from every man inarticulate cries is one thing, and the *Accent* of the Language which engenders the Melody peculiar to a Nation is another." While the "same basis of passion" reigns in all souls, there is a prodigious variety of accented expression in different languages and musics.[122] Rousseau takes up the differences among the musics of different peoples in the article MUSIC [*Musique*]. He criticizes the narrowness of the physical approach to music understood as sound and gives an important example to suggest that music must be understood foremost as a moral or cultural phenomenon. He relates that the French have forbidden the playing of the rustic Alpine tune the "Rans-des-vaches" since it would cause their Swiss troops "to melt in tears, desert, or die, so much would it arouse in them the desire to see their country again." He also notes that this effect does not occur in any foreigner. "The music therefore does not precisely act as music, but as a memorative sign."[123] In the same article he provides examples of ancient Greek and Chinese music, as well as others, and argues that they represent unique forms of music that cannot be understood on the basis of the purportedly universal modern European theories of harmony. Rousseau's interest in the variability of music in relation to culture has led Claude Lévi-Strauss to call him an ethnologist and even the founder of the human sciences.[124] For Rousseau, music is a culturally situated form of uniquely human communication.

The theoretical foundation of Rousseau's musical theory leads him to suggest several reforms in the musical practice of his day. The link between theory and practice here is most evident in the article UNITY OF MELODY [*Unité de la mélodie*]. As throughout the *Dictionary*, Rousseau distinguishes the "pleasure of pure sensation" produced by harmony from the "pleasure of interest and of feeling which speaks to the heart" through melody. He therefore argues that a truly effective music must have a unified melodic core.[125] The principle of the unity of melody suggests that the masterpieces of harmony and counterpoint—those elaborate fugues, imitations, duos, and trios upon which French musicians in particular prided themselves—are at best triumphs of ingenuity at the expense of expression, and he provides a persistent critique of such practices in the articles on those subjects.[126] The most important of these articles is the one on opera, where he provides an historical account of the development of opera that owes much to his discussion of the degeneration of music in the *Essay*. The aim of the article on opera is indicated by Rousseau in his article on composition: it is to produce imitative music that moves the listener by "moral effects" that imitate the accents of the human voice, thereby ennobling the art of music and making of it "a language more eloquent than discourse itself."[127] Finally, Rousseau's conception of the composer deserves mention. The great composer has what Rousseau terms "genius," and in the influential article on that subject Rousseau writes: "Seek not, young Artist, what is *Genius*. If you have any, you feel it in yourself. If you do not, you will never know it. The *Genius* of the Musician submits the entire Universe to his Art. He paints every portrait by Sounds; he makes silence itself speak; he renders ideas by feelings, feelings by accents; and the passions he expresses, he arouses them in the bottom of hearts."[128] This statement might be taken as the sum of Rousseau's musical theory. Its influence can be discerned not only in Romantic music and literature, but also in Kant's aesthetic theory and in the Romantic philosophers who followed him.[129]

The Twilight of Rousseau's Musical Career and His Influence

In his last years Rousseau found consolation in the art for which he says he was born. His dotage was actually quite active, producing some of his most innovative ideas on music. Rousseau continued to ply his trade as a musical copyist until almost the last months of his life, and his ledgers show that from September 1770 to February 1777 he copied over 11,200 pages of music.[130] He was also an enthusiastic patron of the opera during this period and thereby kept up with the latest developments in the art, especially the reform opera of Gluck, and was inspired to attempt some innovations of his own.

In his *Dictionary of Music* and other works, Rousseau had discussed the problems of uniting music with drama, and in his *Pygmalion* he attempted a new form of drama that alternated music with pantomime and declamation in a way that sought to overcome the unmelodic character of French recitative. Rousseau's "melodrama" *Pygmalion* was first performed in 1770 in Lyon, where he was staying at the time, and later performed in 1775 at the Paris Opera. His work, called "the first musical melodrama,"[131] had considerable influence on late eighteenth- and nineteenth-century music, especially in Germany. Rousseau also began another opera, *Daphnis et Chloé*, in the last couple of years of his life, but it remained unfinished.

During the last years of his life, Rousseau's musical compositions held the stage and his musical writings gained an ever wider circulation throughout Europe. One of his readers was Gluck, who, having astonished the rest of the continent with the dramatic operas he had fashioned along with Raniero di Calzagibi, his librettist and collaborator in the reform of opera, arrived in Paris in 1774 determined to conquer the cultural capital of Europe and woo its most famous philosopher-musician. Gluck's arrival in Paris was prepared for by his French librettist and unauthorized agent, du Roullet, who proposed a French version of *Iphigénie en Aulide* to the Paris Opera. Du Roullet claimed that, through his study of the language, "Gluck was roused against the bold assertions of those of our famous writers who have dared to calumniate the French tongue, saying that it could not lend itself to great musical creation."[132] Gluck, somewhat embarrassed by du Roullet's efforts, appealed to Rousseau in a conciliatory open letter in which he proposed to consult the famous philosopher and musical theorist, saying "we might have succeeded together, by searching for noble, sensitive, and natural melody and with a careful declamation suited to the prosody of each language and the character of each people, in hitting upon the means I have in view to produce a music fit for all the nations, and in allowing the ridiculous distinctions of national music to disappear."[133] Although initially suspicious of the newcomer, whom he met in February 1774, Rousseau was won over by his music.[134] Gluck's French *Iphigénie* was a triumph, lauded by, among others, Marie Antoinette and Rousseau, both of whom were present at the first performance of the work in April 1774.[135] Gluck continued to court Rousseau, stating in the Dedication to his French *Orphée* (1774): "I have seen with satisfaction that the natural tone is the universal language. . . . M. Rousseau used it successfully in the simple genre. His *Devin du village* is a model which no one has yet imitated."[136] Gluck's *Orphée* debuted in Paris in August 1774, and Rousseau was said not to have missed a single performance of the work.[137] He later saw his own *Devin du village* successfully reprised in a January 1777 production in which it was paired with Gluck's *Orphée*. Rousseau wrote an analysis of the famous passage in Gluck's Italian *Orfeo* where the Furies deny Orpheus entry into the underworld. In the title of his analysis, *Extract from a Response by the Underlaborer to His Frontman Concerning a Piece from Gluck's "Orfeo,"* he playfully alludes to charges that he was merely the "frontman" for the musical writings and compositions he had plagiarized from others, and he presents his analysis as an explanation of the passage from Gluck's opera by the true author, the "underlaborer," to himself, the supposed author. We therefore see in this occasional writing on music, which was not published until after his death, the same literary device Rousseau uses in his *Dialogues*—and also the same anxiety to proclaim himself as the author of his musical works against the charges of plagiarism that had originated with Rameau three decades earlier.

Rousseau's last substantial musical writing was an analysis of another of Gluck's operas. During the winter of 1774–1775 Gluck gave Rousseau a copy of his Italian *Alceste* for his comments before he attempted a French version of the work. Rousseau wrote a series of observations on the opera but was unable to complete them because Gluck took back his score in April 1775 when he left Paris to return to Vienna. Rousseau kept his notes and later sent them to Charles Burney. Rousseau had met the English organist and musicologist in December 1770, when he was touring France and Italy to collect information for his history of music. Burney, a great admirer of Rousseau's musical works, translated his *Devin du village* as *The Cunning Man* (1776) and had it performed by Garrick; and he advertised his own *General History of Music* by saying that Rousseau would be "so to speak, the Hero" of the work.[138] Burney sent Rousseau the first volume of his *History* of ancient music, and around October 1777, Rousseau wrote a long reply in which he expressed his thoughts on Burney's subject; explained his old proposal for musical notation, revealing that he still used the system himself and had improved upon it; and, finally, included his observations on Gluck's *Alceste*. Rousseau's remarks on Gluck's opera —published in 1778 by Grimm, who used them on behalf of the anti-Gluckist cause—embroiled him posthumously in the debate over Gluck's reform opera. He had carefully remained aloof from the dispute between the Gluckists and Puccinists during his lifetime, but his *Letter on French Music*, his *Dictionary*, and his own comments on Gluck's opera were used as ammunition by both sides of the last great operatic battle of the eighteenth century.

Rousseau's influence on Gluck is a disputed matter, as is the question of the impact of his musical work in general. As for his influence on the great operatic reformer, opinions vary from assertions that Gluck's ideas were directly inspired by Rousseau to claims that Gluck sought Rousseau's patronage purely in order to gain access to the Parisian musical world.[139] Gluck himself credits Calzabigi for inspiring his reform of the opera, and while it might be conjectured that the two collaborators were inspired in part by Rousseau's *Letter on French Music*, it can be said with certainty that Rousseau's doctrine of the unity of melody, his insistence on the close connection of music and words, and his more specific suggestions for making opera a unified spectacle appealed to Gluck. Rousseau's appeal extended beyond his musical ideas to his thought as a whole, and the impact of his musical theory must ultimately be seen as one aspect of the influence of the philosophy of which it is an integral part. Gluck and others responded to the ideas and feelings expressed in Rousseau's writings. They responded to the passionate, even melodic style Rousseau used to communicate his thoughts, to create a mood and to provoke a passionate reaction in his listeners and his readers alike. The polemic between Rousseau and Rameau has been characterized as an epochal battle marking the end of the reign of classical aesthetics and the beginning of a new era, the Romantic movement.[140] But that battle was only one front of the war Rousseau was waging as he sought to integrate his early musical interests into his philosophy as a whole and to fill his prose with the unique accent of his voice.

Note on the Text

This translation is an effort to produce an English version that corresponds word for word (as far as possible) with Rousseau's French text. Wherever possible, words have been translated consistently both within and between Rousseau's writings. Although this goal may cause some awkwardness, it has the advantage of permitting readers to come to their own conclusions with the smallest danger that the translation will have imposed a particular interpretation.

In his musical writings, Rousseau uses technical terms current in his time. In keeping with the general policy of the series, Rousseau's technical terms have generally been translated into the equivalent eighteenth-century English terms instead of into contemporary terminology. Terms that are particularly antiquated or difficult to translate into contemporary terms have been explained in the notes. Rousseau's usage of the French terms for notes (*do*, *re*, *mi*, etc.) has been retained instead of using the English equivalents (C, D, E, etc.), in part because of the difficulties in translating his writings on musical notation, in which he retains the French terms but proposes rejecting the French system of fixed notation for a mobile one. Furthermore, despite a certain awkwardness, accidentals for notes have been rendered by combining the French terms for notes with English terms for accidentals (e.g., *mi*-flat instead of *mi-bémol*) because of the potential terminological inconsistency between the terms for notes and the accompanying discussion. Another difficulty in translation has been capitalization. Following the style of this series, original capitalization has been reproduced in translation. Rousseau tends to capitalize technical terms, especially in his *Dictionary of Music*, and with compound terms he generally capitalizes only the first word of the term, but since most terms require inversion in translation, both words are capitalized in the translation (e.g., "*Bass fondamentale*" becomes "Fundamental Bass").

For easy cross-reference, the source text and location within that text for each pair of facing pages is indicated in the right-hand running head. The Pléiade edition of Rousseau's *Oeuvres complètes* has been used where possible as the basic text for the translation of his writings. The original editions of Rousseau's writings were also consulted where available. The basic text used for Rousseau's "Letter to the *Mercure* on a New System of

Musical Notation" was R. A. Leigh's edition of the *Correspondence complète de J.-J. Rousseau* (Geneva: Musée et Institut Voltaire, 1965–). The basic texts used for Grimm's *Letter on "Omphale"* and Raynal's *Remarks on the Subject of the Letter by M. Grimm on "Omphale"* were the facsimiles of the original editions of the works as reproduced in *La querrelle des bouffons*, ed. Denise Launay (3 vols.; Genève: Minkoff Reprint, 1973). The basic text used for Rousseau's articles from the *Encyclopedia* was a facsimile edition of the *Encyclopédie, ou Dictionnaire raisonné des sciences, des arts, et des mètiers* (Stuttgart; Bad-Cannstatt: Friedrich Frommann Verlag, 1966). The basic texts used for Rameau's works were the facsimiles of the original editions of the works as reproduced in *The Complete Theoretical Writings of Jean-Philippe Rameau*, ed. Erwin R. Jacobi (6 vols.; New York: American Institute of Musicology, 1967–1972). For the *Essay on the Origin of Languages*, Rousseau's own manuscript of the work, which was provided thanks to M. René Marti of the Bibliothèque publique et universitaire de la ville de Neuchâtel, was also consulted.

Previous translations and editions of Rousseau's writings on music and language have suggested solutions to numerous problems of translation and sources for Rousseau's references. Chief among these was Victor Gourevitch's excellent translation and edition of the *Essay on the Origin of Languages* (New York: Harper and Row, 1990), which is based on an earlier edition of the work by Charles Porset (Bordeaux: Ducros, 1970), which has also been quite helpful. Also of particular help were two partial translations of Rameau's *Observations on Our Instinct for Music and on Its Principle*, the first by Cynthia Verba in her *Music and the French Enlightenment: Reconstruction of a Dialogue, 1750–1764* (Cambridge: Cambridge University Press, 1993), and the other by Edward A. Lippman in his collection *Musical Aesthetics: A Historical Reader* (New York: Pendragon, 1986).

ESSAY ON THE ORIGIN OF LANGUAGES and WRITINGS RELATED TO MUSIC

Plan Regarding New Signs for Music

Preface

Given the taste today for constantly publishing new methods and new Systems, it is quite advantageous for the public to remain on guard against everything presented to it with a certain air of novelty. Without this precaution, one would soon be inundated with the most extravagant plans, and one would perhaps see the general disruption of arts and letters occur almost without having foreseen it. There is all the more wisdom in a similar mistrust that assumes it is always a very reasonable prejudice to believe what men have long done successfully must be more advantageous than new discoveries that often have no other end than the desire to shine and no other foundation than an overheated imagination.

What I say in general about all the sciences applies to Music as well with much more precision, because all the plans of innovation which people have desired to develop concerning this Art have served only to make the perfect condition in which it seems to be more perceptible through comparisons by which the old method always stands to gain and which never fail to cast new ones into discredit.

All these considerations are present to my mind with all the force they can have in those of the Readers. Despite this, I dare believe that they must fall before the demonstrated truths that I have to establish, if I am judged before the tribunal of experience and of reason; but if I am attacked by prejudices I have nothing to respond, and I know of no arms that are effective against prejudices.

The System I propose turns on two principal objects, the first to notate music and all its complexities in a simpler, more precise manner, and in less volume, and without all that hindrance of lines and staffs, which never fails to be excessively inconvenient. The second, and this is the most important point, to make it easier to learn by diminishing the number of signs and their combinations without however taking from them any of the variety of their expressions. So that, for example, by my method, all things being otherwise equal, a third of the time would be needed to succeed in sight-singing than by following the ordinary system.

My plan is not at all to annihilate the Musical characters in use today. I do not at all dispute whether they are better or worse than mine; it is enough for them to be established to make their destruction impossible, even by the most advantageous substitution.

My aim is solely to establish other signs, more convenient and of lesser quantity, by which, without excluding those which are in use, one may succeed in much less time in singing correctly and at sight all sorts of tunes and songs imaginable. These signs will moreover have the advantage of occupying less space; all sorts of paper will be appropriate for them, and, as the notation will hardly increase the space that the words alone occupy, this system will be equally convenient for tunes one wants to notate on the spot and without lined paper, and for those one might like to send to the provinces without increasing the bulk or the expense of the postage.

I found the utility of my system on its extreme ease. Those who know Music need only cast their eyes over my principles to grasp their whole Theory and, by means of it alone, after very few days its use will be more convenient for them and more familiar to them than that of the ordinary Music. As for those who do not know it at all, aside from the ease they will have in learning it profoundly in very little time by my characters, they will moreover have the advantage that the cares they will have spent on it will not be lost for ordinary music, since, by beginning with mine, still less time will be needed for learning them both one after another than by following the ordinary method for learning solely that which is in use. Although this claim may have a paradoxical air about it, I flatter myself with having proved it by experiment,[1] and the reason for it is that Musical Theory, which is very difficult to sort out by the ordinary System, is developed in mine almost from the first glance, and because this becomes very easy to do by means of this application to other Signs. It should also be noted that a concert would not be in less concord even though some were to play their part by the ordinary music and others by mine. So that, for example, one might notate the instrumental parts in a score by the ordinary music—it is not by necessity that I propose it in this way, for my music suffices for everything, as will be seen in the plan—and the vocal parts by the other, whether because of its lesser volume or because of its extraordinary ease.

It would therefore not be right to treat my method as useless because it does not teach how to play according to the ordinary music. For the Science of the Musician does not consist in knowing whole notes, half notes, rests, or Clefs. Whoever knows the art of expressing all sorts of sounds and of movements[2] with the precision that belongs them, and of reading them when expressed by others, has the right to present himself as a Musician, just as a man doesn't fail to speak French even though he doesn't know how to read or write it by Greek characters, provided that he otherwise knows how to express himself and understands everything others wanted to say to him in French terms by means of these characters.

In the second place, one must not regard as useless a System that abridges the very routes of the ordinary System. The simplest methods are incontestably hardly those which first come to men's minds. Even if mine were regarded as a Theory of sounds from which a greater facility of practice resulted, it would still be advantageous; but if it were added that this supposed Theory is itself a simple and universal practice that sufficed for everything, it should begin to become a more serious object.

In the third place, nothing is easier than to have tunes, Cantatas, selections of Opera, and pieces of Music of every kind printed for singing following the system I propose. It is a task with which I will charge myself and which I shall try to fulfill to the public's liking by the selection and the novelty of the pieces. To the degree that this Music begins to become widespread, there is room to believe that the ease of printing and the convenience of the characters will make its use more general, and, without excluding the ordinary music, if mine is found to be good, I dare say that it will soon suffice by itself and that its extreme ease will at the very least succeed in putting it on the other's level, without saying anything more about it.

But it is superfluous to respond to objections that do not at all attack my System in itself. The extrinsic difficulties do not at all depend upon me. I am responsible for the defects inherent in my method, but not the extraneous inconveniences which might prevent its succeeding, and if for my part I fulfill my promises, it is up to the public to do the rest.

Plan Regarding New Signs for Music

This plan aims at making Music more convenient to notate, easier to learn, and much less diffuse.

That quantity of lines, clefs, transpositions, sharps, flats, naturals, simple and compound meters, whole notes, half notes, quarter notes, eighth notes, sixteenth notes, thirty-second notes, sixty-fourth notes, rests, half rests, quarter rests, eighth rests, sixteenth rests, etc., yields a throng of signs and their combinations, from which result two principal inconveniences: the first, that of occupying too great a volume, and the second, that of overloading the memory of Students in such a way that, the ear being formed and the Organs having acquired all the necessary aptitude long before one is in a position to sight-sing, it follows that the difficulty lies wholly in the observation of the rules, and not in the performance of the song.

The means that will remedy the first of these inconveniences will remedy the second as well; and as soon as equivalent signs are invented, but simpler and fewer in number, they will have greater precision for that very reason, and they will be able to express as many things in less space.

Besides this, it is advantageous for these Signs to be known already, in order that attention be less divided, and to be easy to form, in order to make music more convenient.

Two principal objects must be considered for this result, each separately. The first should be the expression of all possible sounds; and the second, that of all different durations, of sounds as well as of their relative silences, which also includes the difference in movements.

As music is only a linking of sounds heard either together or in succession, it suffices for all these sounds to have relative expressions that assign to each of them the place they should occupy in relation to a certain fundamental sound, provided that this sound be clearly expressed and that the relationship be easily known.

There can be as many of these fundamental sounds as there are different sounds in the chromatic System, that is, twelve. But with regard to singing, their number does not cause any more difficulty than if there were a single one because as soon as one has the key, it is enough to conform one's voice to it without needing to know on which pitch it is taken. With regard to instruments, I shall soon speak of them and it will be seen that they are in just about the same situation.

We shall take *do* for this fundamental sound to which all the others must be related and, expressing it by the numeral 1, following it we have the expression of the seven natural sounds.

1	2	3	4	5	6	7
do	*re*	*mi*	*fa*	*sol*	*la*	*si*

This in such a way that as long as the song moves within the range of seven sounds, it will suffice to notate each of them by its corresponding numeral in order to express everything without equivocation.

But when it is a matter of leaving this range to pass into other Octaves, then this presents a new difficulty.

In order to resolve it, I have made use of the simplest of all Signs, namely the dot. If I leave the octave in which I began in order to produce a note in the range of the octave above and which begins with the *do* above, in that case I put a dot over that note on which I leave my Octave; and, once put in place, this dot is an indication that not only the note over which it is placed, but also all those which follow it without any Sign that cancels it should be taken within the range of that Superior Octave into which I have entered, for example:

$$1 \quad 3 \quad \dot{1} \quad 3 \quad 5$$

The dot you see over the second 1 indicates that you enter there into the Octave above that in which you began, and that, consequently, the 3 and the 5 which follow are also in that Superior Octave and are not at all the same as those which you would have otherwise sounded.

On the contrary, if I want to leave the Octave in which I happen to be in order to pass into that which is below, then I put the dot below the note by which I enter it, for example:

$$5 \quad 3 \quad 1 \quad \underset{.}{5} \quad 3$$

thus, supposing that this first 5 is the same as the last one in the preceding example, by the dot you see here under the second 5 you will ascend in order to reenter into that by which you formerly began. In a word, when the dot is above the note, you pass into the Superior Octave; if it is below, you pass into the Inferior and when you would change Octave on each note, either when you want to ascend or descend two or three Octaves all at once or in a row, the rule is always general and you have only to put as many dots below or above as you have Octaves to descend or to ascend.

This is not to say that on each dot you would ascend or descend an Octave, but that on each dot you enter into an Octave different from the one you are in with respect to the fundamental sound *do* below it, which in this way happens to be in the same Octave when descending diatonically, but not when ascending; about which it must be noted that I make use of the word octave but improperly and in order not to multiply terms uselessly, because properly speaking this range includes only seven notes, the *do* above, which begins another Octave, not being included in it.

Here is a Series of notes which will be easy to *sol-fa* by the rules I have just presented:

$$1 \quad \underset{.}{7} \quad \dot{1} \quad 2 \quad 3 \quad 1 \quad 5 \quad 4 \quad 5 \quad 6 \quad 7 \quad 5 \quad \dot{1} \quad \underset{.}{7} \quad 6 \quad 5 \quad 4 \quad 3 \quad 2 \quad 4 \quad \dot{2} \quad \dot{1} \quad \underset{.}{7} \quad 6 \quad 5 \quad 4 \quad 3 \quad 4 \quad 5 \quad 5 \quad \dot{1}$$

But this *do*, which by transposition should always be the name of the tonic in major keys and that of the mediant in the minor keys, can consequently be taken on each of the twelve pitches of the Chromatic System, and in order to designate it, it will suffice to place in the Margin the numeral—whether natural or altered—which expresses this pitch on the Keyboard in the natural order, that is, if the song is in the key of *do* major or of *la* minor, it will be necessary to write 1 in the margin. If the song is in the key of *re* major or of *si* minor, one must write 2 in the margin. For the key of *mi* major or of *do*-sharp minor, one will write 3 in the margin and so on. By which it is seen that the Numeral in the margin, which can be called the Clef, designates the key of the keyboard that should be called *do*, and that this *do* is always tonic in the major keys and mediant in the minor ones. But, furthermore, the knowledge of this Clef is useful only for instruments, and those who sing do not need to pay attention to it.

One sees by this that the same Clef under the same name of *do* can nevertheless designate two different keys: namely, the major of which it is tonic and the minor of which it is mediant, and in which, consequently, the tonic is a minor third below it. Thus, for the ease of warming up, one will write the Clef quite plain when it is tonic, and when it is mediant one will add a small horizontal line below it in order to designate the major Mode. An Example in *sol* major:

5

1 3 2 1 5 5 7 5 1 3 6 6 2 4 7 5 1 4 5 5 1

An Example in the mode of *mi* minor:

5
—

1 7 6 3 4 6 2 1 7 6 4 7 3 6 2 4 3 2 1 7 6

By this method, the same names are always reserved for the same notes. That is to say that the art of *sol-fa*ing all possible music consists in knowing seven unique and invariable characters that never change as to position, and that are consequently much preferable to that multitude of Clefs and transpositions which, although ingeniously invented, are for that reason no less a torture for beginners.

A third difficulty consists in the range of the keyboard. For it is not enough to know the natural name of the note you should call *do*, nor whether it is tonic or mediant, but one must further know in which of the five octaves this note should be taken. In order to explain this, I am going to represent the entire range of the Keyboard worked out for all twenty-four keys here in a general table*; the fifth column marked by an asterisk represents in it the key of *do* major or of *la* minor, that is, in the Clef of 1 or according to the natural order such as it is established on organs and Harpsichords, and it is this column that should serve as the rule and basis for all the others. As this table has considerable uses and is the principal

* See p. 9.[3]

Clef for my system, I shall treat it in particular detail and I content myself here with developing from it what is absolutely necessary about it for comprehending my method.

Taking the fifth column or the Clef of 1 as an example, the first range from 1 to 7 in ascending will be called Octave A, the second B, the third C, etc., until the last 1, which begins a fifth octave, E, which might be pressed further if one likes. With regard to the portion below that begins on the first 4 and ends on the first 7, as it is incomplete, not beginning with *do*, we shall call it octave X and this letter X shall serve in all sorts of keys to designate the notes which remain on the bass end of the Keyboard below the first tonic.

Let us suppose, then, that I want to notate a tune in the Clef of 1, that is, in the key of *do* major or of *la* minor; I write 1 at the head of the page in the margin and I make it mediant or tonic at my choosing according to whether or not I add the small horizontal line.

Knowing in this way which pitch should carry the key, it is now merely a question of finding which of the five octaves the note that begins my song is in, and this is what is easy to designate by the corresponding letter. Thus, d3 would indicate the *mi* of the fourth Octave, c4 would indicate the *fa* of the third, etc. Now, as soon as one thus has the first note of the song, the dots lead us throughout without equivocation, and it is always easy to know precisely on which portion of the Keyboard one happens to be. Nevertheless, for more clarity one could indicate the letter corresponding to the note that has preceded at the beginning of each line, which is easy to do as a result of my method and from which, moreover, follows still more generally and without exception the means for expressing the relationships and all the intervals, in ascending as well as descending, for reprises and rondos, by writing the letter that indicates the octave in which this note is found after the final note of a tune, of a first part, or of a reprise.

But if I were in another key, the Octaves would no longer be counted as before, but from the notes which take the name of *do*. Thus, in the Clef of 2, the *re* being called *do*, the first octave A would be a tone higher than the first Octave A of the Clef of 1. Octave A of Clef 3 would be two degrees higher than that of the same Clef 1. But octave A of Clef 4, instead of being three degrees higher, on the contrary would be a fifth lower than Octave A of the Clef, because the first *fa*, which would then become *do*, is a fifth below the first *do* natural. With regard to the notes that are found below the lowest tonic in any Clef whatsoever, they will be designated by Octave X, as I have already explained, that is, for example, that there are no notes at all in octave X in Clef 4, that there is one in Clef 5, two in Clef 6, three in Clef 7, four in Clef 1, five in Clef 2, and six in Clef 3.

It must be carefully remembered that one can sight-sing by my method without ever having heard of my table or of this explanation, the reading of which one can even omit by replacing it with what is joined to the table and which will be found more clearly expressed.

The pitch of the key, the mode, and the octave being well designated in this way, instruments as well as the voice will have to make use of transposition, which will present no difficulty to Musicians who are instructed, as they must be, about the keys of the natural intervals in each mode and about the way of finding them on their instruments. On the contrary, this important advantage will result: that it will be no more difficult to transpose all sorts of tunes a semitone or tone higher or lower when needed than to play them in their natural key; or, if some difficulty is found in this, it will lie uniquely with the instrument and never with the notation, which, by the change of a single sign, will represent the same tune in whatever key one might like to propose, so that, finally, an entire Orchestra, on the simple warning of the Conductor, would immediately play in *mi* or in *sol* a piece notated in *fa*, in *la*, or in *si*-flat, or in any other key imaginable—an impossible thing to do in the ordinary Music, and one whose utility is easily enough perceived by those who frequent concerts.

In general, what is called singing and playing naturally is perhaps what is worst devised in Music. For if the names of the notes have any real utility, it can be only to express certain relationships, certain specific affects in the progressions of sounds. Now, as soon as the key changes, since the relationships of the sounds and the progression also change, reason says that the names of the notes must likewise change by relating them analogously to the new key, otherwise, the meaning of the names is overturned and the words are deprived of the sole advantage they can have, which is to arouse other ideas with those of the sounds. The transition from *mi* to *fa*, or from *si* to *do*, naturally raises the idea of the semitone in the musician's mind. Nevertheless, if one is in the key of *si* or on that of *mi*, the interval from *si* to *do*, or from *mi* to *fa*, is always one tone, and never a semitone. Thus, instead of retaining names that deceive the mind and shock the ear habituated to a different practice, it is important to apply ones whose meaning has nothing contradictory about them, but which on the contrary proclaim the intervals they should express. Now, all the relationships of sounds of the diatonic system are expressed in the Major following their natural order, in the octave contained between two *do*s, in ascending as well as in descending, and, in the minor, in the Octave contained between two *la*s, in descending alone. For in ascending, the minor mode is subjected to different affects which present new reflections for theory, but these are not my subject today and do not affect the system I am proposing.

I appeal to experience regarding the trouble students have in intoning, by the natural names, tunes they sing with all the ease in the world by means of transposition, provided always that they have acquired the long and necessary practice of reading the flats and sharps of Clefs, which with their eight positions make up eighty useless combinations, all eliminated by my method.

It follows from this that the principles given for playing instruments are totally worthless, and I am sure there is not a good musician who, after having warmed up in the key in which he must play, does not pay more attention in his playing to the level of the key he finds himself in than to the sharp or flat that affects it. Let Students be taught to know the two modes and the regular arrangement of the sounds appropriate to each thoroughly, let them be trained in warming up in major or in minor on all the sounds of the instrument, a thing they always have to know, whatever method is adopted. Then, let my music be put in their hands: I dare respond that it will not hinder them for a quarter of an hour.

It would be surprising if attention were paid to the quantity of Books and of precepts that have been produced about transposition. Those harmonic scales, those diatonic scales, those imaginary Clefs, make up the most tedious jumble imaginable, and all this for want of having made this very simple reflection, that, since the fundamental pitch of the key is known as the tonic on the natural Keyboard, that is as *do* or *la*, it alone determines the relationship and the key of all the other notes, without regard to the original order.

It is now necessary to speak of changes of key; but as the accidental alterations of the sounds present themselves at every moment, I am going to explain them first.

The sharp is expressed by a small line that intersects the note by rising from left to right. For example, *sol*-sharp is expressed thus: ƒ; *fa*-sharp thus: 4. The flat is likewise expressed by a similar line that intersects the note by descending: ↘, ↘; and these signs, simpler than those in use, further serve to show the eye the sort of alteration they cause.

The natural has become necessary only through a poor choice of sharp and flat, because, being separate from the notes they alter, if several of these notes are found in a row on the same level and under one or the other of these signs, one can never distinguish those which should be affected from those which should not be without making use of the natural. But since in my System the sign of alteration, aside from the simplicity of its shape, is always inherent to the altered note, it is clear that all those on which one does not see it should be played on the natural pitch they should have in the key one is in. I therefore eliminate the natural as useless; and I further eliminate it as equivocal, since it is common to find it used in two entirely opposite senses. For some make use of it to eliminate the alteration caused by the signs of the Clef, and others, on the contrary, for putting the note back onto the pitch it should have in conformity with these same signs.

With regard to changes in key, whether when passing from the major to the minor, or from one tonic to another, it is merely a matter of expressing the first note of this change in a way that represents what it was in the key one is leaving and what it is in that one is entering, which is done by a double note separated by a small horizontal line as in fractions: the numeral above expresses the note in the key from which one is leaving, and that below represents the same note in the key into which one is entering. In a word, the lower numeral indicates the name of the note, and the upper numeral serves to find the key.

An Example of passing to the key of the fourth note:

$$\overset{1}{d} 1\ 2\ 3\ 4\ 2\ 4\ 3\ 4\ 5\ 5\ \dot{1}\ \tfrac{4}{1}\ 2\ 3\ 4\ 2\ 4\ 3\ 4\ 5\ 5\ \dot{1}$$

Another Example for passing from the major to the minor, and vice versa:

$$\overset{5}{c}\ 3\ 4\ 5\ 3\ 6\ 4\ 5\ 4\ 3\ 2\ 1\ 7\ \dot{1}\ \tfrac{3}{1}\ 7\ 6\ \sharp 6\ 7\ \dot{1}\ 2\ 3\ 4\ 3\ 2\ 1$$
$$7\ 6\ \tfrac{\sharp 4}{3}\ 4\ 3\ 1\ 6\ 2\ 5\ 1\ 7\ 6\ 5\ 7\ \dot{1}$$

In the first example, you pass to the key of the fourth note, and you should call *do* the note which was called *fa* in the preceding key.

In the second, the note which should be mi-flat takes the name of *do* because you pass to the minor mode of which it should be mediant, after which, this same *do*-sharp again takes the name of *mi* when you reenter the major mode.

This is how to express all sounds imaginable in whatever key one might be in and whatever progression one might like to consider. It is now necessary to pass on to the second part, which treats the values of notes and their movements.

End of the First Part

EXPLANATION OF THIS TABLE

This table represents the whole range of the Keyboard worked out for the twelve pitches of the Chromatic system. The natural keyboard, in which *do* and all its other notes retain their proper name, is found here on the fifth row, which is marked by an asterisk at each extremity, and it is to this row that all the others should be related.

The interval contained between the first 1 and the second 7 that follows it to the right is called octave A; the interval contained from the second *do* to the next 7 is called octave B; the next, octave C; etc.; until the fifth 1, where Octave E begins, which I have carried out only to *fa*, which is the highest key of Harpsichords, but which might be pressed further if one likes. With regard to the four notes to the left of the first 1, they belong to Octave X, to which I am therefore giving this particular name in order to express the fact that it is not complete, because in order to get to *do* it would be necessary to descend lower than the Keyboard permits.

But if I am in another key, as for example in the key or the Clef of *re*, then this *re* changes name and becomes *do*, which is why octave A, contained from the first tonic to its seventh note, is a tone higher than the octave corresponding to the preceding key, which is easy to see by means of the table, since this *do* on the 3rd row, that is, of the Clef of *re*, corresponds to the 2 of the natural Clef of *do*, on which it falls perpendicularly; and, for the same reason, Octave X here has more notes than the same Octave in the Clef of *do*, because, as they ascend further, the Octaves grow more distant from the lowest note of the Keyboard.

This is why the Octaves proceed by ascending from the Clef of 1 to the Clef of 3, and by descending from the same Clef of *do* to the Clef of 4. For this *fa*, which is the lowest note of the natural Keyboard, then becomes tonic, and consequently begins the first Octave A.

Everything contained between the two first oblique lines to the left is therefore always Octave A, but in different degrees according to the key one is in. For example, the same key of the keyboard will be *do* in the major key of *mi*, *re* in that of *re*, *mi* in that of *do*, *fa* in that of *si*, *sol* in that of *la*, *la* in that of *sol*, *si* in that of *fa*. It is always the same key of the keyboard because it is the same column, and it is the same Octave because this column is contained between the same oblique lines.

Thus, in order to express both the key of the keyboard and the octave in any key whatsoever, the letter of the octave is placed before the numeral of the note and in this way the note is known by the name it bears in the key in which it is found, by its Octave, and by its natural name. For example, in Clef 2, c4 is the *fa* of octave c in the third row, which *fa* is the same thing

Exposition du Clavier général dans tous les tons, suivant le nouveau système.

as the natural *sol* of the fifth row of the same octave on which it falls perpendicularly. In Clef 4, d2 is the same thing as c5 natural, and so on with the others. So as to leave nothing to desire, one could assure oneself by placing at the beginning of each line the letter corresponding to the note that has preceded, and likewise placing after the finales of reprises and of rondos the letter corresponding to these finales.

In order to give a general recapitulation of the use of this table, it must be noted that it contains exactly a range of five octaves, comprising four entire Octaves—A B C D—and three incomplete ones, namely, X, E, F. These Octaves are distinguished by six dark oblique lines, whose darkness makes known how high or low these Octaves are, according to the key one is in. The horizontal lines in pencil separate the various keys practiced on the twelve pitches of the chromatic system. The perpendicular lines serve to show that all the notes traversed by the same line are always merely a single key of the keyboard, whose natural name is found on the fifth row and whose other names are found in the other rows of the same column according to the key one is in. These perpendicular ones are of two sorts. The black ones connect numerals which represent a natural key of the keyboard, and the dashed ones are for the keys of the keyboard altered as a consequence of the key, in such a way that by means of this table one can know on the spot in any key whatsoever which notes must be altered in order to play in that key.

The Clefs you see at the beginning serve to determine which note should bear the name of *do* and to indicate the key, as I have already said. There are five duplicates because in practice the flat of the superior and the sharp of the inferior produce the same effect.

It is also easy by means of this Table to determine precisely the range of each vocal part, and the place it will occupy in these various Octaves according to the key one will be in.

Plan Regarding New Signs for Music

SECOND PART

Musicians recognize at least fourteen different meters used in Music,* meters the distinction of which confuses the minds of Students for an infinite time. Now, I maintain that all the movements of these different meters are reducible to two alone, namely, duple-time and triple-time, and I dare defy the keenest and most astute ear to discover natural ones that can't be expressed with all possible precision by one of these two meters. I will therefore begin by making a clean sweep of all those bizarre numerals, reserving only the 2 and the 3, with which, as will immediately be seen, I will express all possible movements. Now, in order for the numeral that declares the meter not to be confused with those for the notes, I distinguish it by making it larger and by separating it by a double perpendicular line. For example:

I

$$3 \| \ 3 \ 4 \ 5 \ \text{etc.}$$

It is a now matter of expressing the beats and the values of the notes which fill them.

A considerable defect in the ordinary music is that of representing as absolute values notes that have only relative ones, or at least that of giving them poorly applied relationships. For it is certain that the duration of whole notes, Half notes, quarter notes, eighth notes, etc., should be determined not by the quality of the note, but by that of the meter in which it is found. From which it happens that a quarter note in a certain meter will be played much more quickly than an eighth note in another—this eighth note nevertheless being worth only half of that quarter note, and because of this it still happens that Provincial Musicians, deceived by these false relationships, will give tunes wholly different movements than they should have by adhering scrupulously to the absolute value of the notes, whereas a measure in simple triple meter must sometimes be played much more quickly than another in three-eighths, something that depends on the whim of the Composer, and examples of which are offered at the Opera at every moment.

Furthermore, the double subdivision of notes and of their values does not, as it is established, suffice for all the cases, and if, for example, I want

* 2. 3. C. $\frac{2}{2}. \frac{2}{4}. \frac{2}{8}. \frac{3}{2}. \frac{3}{4}. \frac{3}{8}. \frac{6}{4}. \frac{6}{8}. \frac{9}{4}. \frac{9}{8}. \frac{12}{8}.$

to play three equal notes in one beat of a measure in duple-, triple-, or quadruple-time, either the Musician has to divine it or I have to instruct him by an extraneous sign which constitutes an exception to the rule.

Finally, not having the beats separated is yet another inconvenience; it happens from this that, in the midst of a long measure, the student doesn't know where he is, especially when, singing the vocal part, he encounters a number of detached eighth and sixteenth notes, which he himself must allocate.

The separation of each beat by a comma remedies all this with considerable simplicity. Each beat contained between two commas contains one note or several: if it contains only one note, this means that it fills this whole beat, and there is not the least difficulty here. For example:

$$\overset{2}{3}目\, d\, 1, 2, 3 | 7, \dot{1}, 2 | 6, 7, 1 | \overset{*}{5}, \overset{*}{4}, 3 | \dot{1}, 2, 3 | 7, \dot{1}, 2 | 6, 7, \overset{\smile}{5}\, 6\, c$$

Are there several notes contained in each beat? This is no more difficult. Divide this beat into as many equal parts as it contains notes; apply each of these parts to each of these notes, and play them in such a way that all the beats are equal. For example:

$$\overset{1}{2}目\, b\, 1\, 7, \dot{1}\, 2 | 3\, 2, 3\, 1 | 5\, 4, 5\, 6 | 7\, 6, 7\, 5 | \dot{1}\, 4, 5\, 5 | \dot{1}\, b$$

Another example:

$$\overset{4}{3}目\, d\, 3, 4, 5 | 6\, 5, 4\, 3, \overset{\sim}{2}\, 1 | 2, 5, \dot{1} | 1, 6, \dot{2} | 2, 7, \dot{3} | 3, 1, 4 |$$
$$4, 2, 5 | 5, \overset{\smile}{3}, 6 |$$
$$d\, 6\, 2, 3, \overset{\smile}{2} | 1, 5, \dot{1}\, 2 | 7\, \dot{1}, 6, \dot{2}\, 3 | 1\, 2, 7, \dot{3}\, 4 | 2\, 3, 1, 4\, 5 |$$
$$3\, 4, 2, 5\, 6 | 4\, 5, 3, 6 |$$
$$e\, 6\, 2, \overset{\frown}{3, 2} | 1, 5, \dot{1}\, 2\, 1 | 7\, \dot{1}\, 7, 6, \dot{2}\, 3\, 2 | 1\, 2\, 1, 7, \dot{3}\, 4\, 3 |$$
$$2\, 3\, 2, 1\, 2\, 3, 4\, 5\, 4 | 3\, 4\, 3, 2\, 3\, 4, $$
$$e, 5\, 6\, 5 | 4\, 5\, 4, 3\, 4\, 5, 6\, 5\, \dot{1} | 1\, 7\, 6, 5\, 4\, 3, 2\, 1\, 7 | \dot{1}$$

A third example:

$$\overset{1}{2}目, c\, 3\, 6\, \dot{1} | 1\, 7\, 6, 6\, \overset{*}{5}\, 6 | 7\, 3\, \dot{1}, 7\, \dot{1}\, 2 | 1\, 7\, 6, \overset{\frown}{2\, 2}\, \overset{\sim}{1}\, 7, \dot{1}\, 7\, 6 |$$
$$\overset{*}{5}, 3\, 6\, \dot{1} | 1\, 7\, 6, \overset{*}{5}\, 6 | 7\, 3\, \dot{1}, 1$$
$$| c\, \overset{\frown}{2, 2}\, \overset{\sim}{1}\, 7 | \dot{1}\, \overset{\sim}{7}\, 6, 3\, 6\, \overset{*}{5} | 6\, c$$

The comma seen before the first note of this last example designates the end of the first beat and indicates that the song begins on the second.

In *passepied* movements, one sometimes finds certain syncopated meters two times slower than the other meters with which they are intermixed. They will be designated by a double Separation at the beginning of the measure and by double commas or inverted commas between each beat, which will serve to show that the measure and each of its beats should also have twice the duration they would have without this accidental sign. This can also occur in Adagios sometimes found at the end of fast tunes, although to tell the truth, a word placed above it is preferable to this for determining the degree of movement, excepting however the syncopated measures of which I have just spoken. This is what resolves the objection that might be made to me, that fast or slow movements are not at all expressed by my music. For there are good Teachers who, regarding the movement, would like to rely upon the quality of the notes it uses and who do not add words—*gracieusement, lentement, tendrement, vivement, gai*, etc.—to give the precision they are lacking in their expression, and, if it happens that they neglect it, it is because they trust in the character of their music and to the taste of those who will read it, in which their confidence is often found to be misplaced.

Here is an Example of those Syncopated meters of the *passepied*:

$$\begin{array}{l} 4 \\ 3\natural \quad d\ 6,\ 6\ 7,\ \dot{1}|7,\ 3,\ \sharp\|6,,\ 5,,\ 4|3,\ 3\ \sharp,\ 5|\sharp,\ \sharp\ 5,\ 6|\sharp,\ 3,\ 3\| \\ \quad\quad \dot{1},,\ 1\ 7,,\ \overset{\times}{7}|6| \end{array}$$

Notes where two equal ones fill a beat will be called halves; those where three are needed, thirds; those where four are needed, fourths; etc.

But when a beat happens to be divided in such a way that the notes in it are not of an equal value, for example in order to represent a quarter note and two eighth notes in single beat, I consider this beat as divided into two equal parts, of which the quarter note makes up the first one and the two eighth notes together the second; I then tie them by a straight line which I place above or below them, and this tie shows that everything embraced by it represents only a single note, which should be subdivided in two equal parts, or in three, or in four, according to the number of numerals it covers. For example:

$$\begin{array}{l} 4 \\ 2\natural,\ d\ 1\ 7\ 6\ \sharp|6\ 7,\ \dot{1}\ 2\ 1\ 7\ \dot{1}\ 6|7\ 3,\ \underline{1\ 7\ 6\ \dot{\times}\ 2}\ 3\ \underline{2\ 3\ 2},\ \tilde{1}\ 7 \\ \quad 6\ 7|\dot{2}\ 1\ 2\ \underline{1,\ \tilde{7}}\ 6\ \sharp\ 7| \\ \quad d\ \dot{3}\ \overline{2\ 1,}\ \overset{\times}{7}\ |6\ \| \end{array}$$

Another tie below this first one can also be used in order to indicate the different values of the notes it contains, which encompasses all possible cases without there ever being any need to add a third. For example:

$$
\begin{array}{l}
\overset{5}{2\natural}|\mathrm{d}1\,3,\ 5\ \overline{1\ 2\ 1}|7\ \dot{2},\ 5\ \overline{7\ \dot{1}\ 7}|6\ \dot{1},\ 4\ 6\ 7\ \underline{6|5\ 6\ 7\ 5},\ \dot{1}\ 2\ 3\ 1| \\
4\ 6,\ \dot{1}\ \underline{4\ 5\ 4}|3\ 5,\ \dot{1}\ \underline{3\ 4\ 3}|2\ 4, \\
\mathrm{d}\ 7\ 2\ \overline{3\ 2}|1\ 4\ 3\ 4,\ 5\ 5|\dot{1}\|
\end{array}
$$

If there is one note that alone fills an entire measure, it suffices to place it alone between the two lines which enclose the measure; and, by the same rule I have just established, this means that this note should last the entire measure.

With regard to held notes, I also make use of a dot to express them, but in a much more advantageous manner than the one in use; for instead of making it worth precisely half of the note that precedes it, which constitutes only a specific case, I give it, just like the notes, a value that is determined only by the place it occupies, that is, if the dot alone fills a beat or a measure, the sound that preceded it should also be held for this whole beat or this whole measure, and, if the dot is found in a beat with other notes, it makes up part of it just as they do and should be counted as a third or as a fourth, according to the number of notes the beat contains, including the dot.

For example:

$$
\begin{array}{l}
\overset{1}{2\natural},\ \mathrm{C}\ |5\ 4,\ \cdot\ 3|\cdot\ 2,\ 4\ 3|\cdot\ 2,\ \cdot\ 1|5\ \dot{5},\ \cdot\ 4|6\ 4,\ \cdot\ 2| \\
5\ 4\ 3\ 2,\ \cdot\ \dot{1}|7\ 5\ 1|\cdot,\ \overset{\times}{7}\ \dot{1}\ \mathrm{c}|
\end{array}
$$

Furthermore, as is seen by this example, it is not to be feared that these dots will ever be confused with those which serve to change Octaves, their being too easily distinguished by their position to need to be so by their shape. This is why I have not bothered to do so, carefully avoiding making use of special signs which would distract the attention and would express nothing more than the simplicity of my own signs.

Following the principle I have just established above, rests need only a single sign. Zero appears the most suitable, and, since the rules that I have established with regard to notes are completely applicable to their relative rests, it follows that Zero, by its position alone and by the dots which might follow it, which will then express rests, alone suffices to replace all the rests, half rests, quarter rests, and other bizarre and superfluous signs which fill up ordinary music.

Plan Regarding New Signs for Music

An Example drawn from Monteclair:[4]

$$2\text{目},\ \overset{4}{\overset{}{\text{o}}}|\text{d}\ 1|2|3,\ 1|5|3|5\ 6|7\ 5|\overset{}{\overset{\cdot}{1}}|.|\overset{2}{\overset{}{\text{o}}}|.\ ,\ 5|1,\ \text{o}\ 7|6,\ \text{o}\ 5|$$
$$4,\ \text{o}\ 3\ 2\ 1|$$
$$\text{d}\ \overset{\times}{\underset{\cdot}{7}},\ \text{o}\ \overset{\cdot}{1}\ 2\ 3|4\ 3\ \overset{\times}{2}\ .\ 1|1$$

These are, in my system, the general principles from which flow all the rules necessary for practice, without it being possible in this regard for any difficulty to arise that cannot be resolved as a consequence of some one of these principles.

I shall conclude with some observations that arise from the parallel between the two systems.

Are the notes in ordinary music more or less advantageous than the numerals to be substituted for them? This is properly speaking the heart of the issue.

It is clear, on the one hand, that notes have their meaning and their power only with the help of the Clef, and, on the other, that the variations of the Clefs give a great number of entirely different meanings to notes placed in the same manner.

It is no less evident that the relationships of the notes and intervals to one another are expressed in ordinary music by positions that are difficult to remember, and the knowledge of which depends uniquely upon practice and upon a very long practice at that. For what hold does the mind have to grasp with precision, and from the first glance, an interval of a sixth, of a ninth, or a tenth, in ordinary music, unless custom familiarizes the eyes to reading these intervals all at once?

Is it not above all a considerable defect not to preserve anything in the expression of Octaves of the analogy they have between them? When one is on a line the other is in a space, and when, by dint of habit, one soon succeeds in knowing this interval because it is frequently presented, one is no less misled when one encounters leaps of two and three Octaves whose notes are then all on lines or in spaces in the first case, and once again the one in a space and the other on a line in the second? For every hundred Musicians, there are perhaps not ten who are in a position to say right off how it is that a line is found between two notes placed in two Octaves, both of them in each of the two fashions in which they can be, and of responding likewise to all questions of this type. In addition, shouldn't it be admitted in good faith that considerable phlegm and obstinacy are needed to subject oneself to the boredom of these sorts of studies?

Numerals used in the way I propose produce absolutely different results. Their power is in themselves and independent of any other Sign:

their relationships are known by inspection alone, and without training entering into it at all. A lesson of a quarter of an hour can put anyone in a position to name fluently and without hesitation all the notes in any music presented to him, and another quarter of an hour will be enough to teach him likewise to name without hesitation every possible interval, which depends on the clear knowledge of three intervals alone, namely the second, the third, and the fourth, of their inversions, which are the seventh, the sixth, and the fifth, and reciprocally of the inversion of these, which return to the first ones.

The Analogy of Octaves is perfectly preserved by my method, since they are always expressed by the same numeral and since the distinction among them is made by the dots, which do for music just about what Zero does in arithmetic. From this arises this further advantage, that with seven unique characters placed on the same line I nonetheless generally express without equivocation all the sounds of the Keyboard.

What is better about ordinary music is the expression of high or low sounds by notes that are high or low according to their position. It is very useful to know which way one should go, even when one does not know precisely where. It is so to speak to forewarn thought by the eyes, and to dispose the organs almost before the aid of the mind. All those who have proposed new signs have been frustrated above all by the impossibility of preserving this advantage, and it is certain that otherwise ingenious methods will never be able to make up for this loss. It is easily seen that without high or low notes my music does not fail to produce the same result by the different values of the numerals or by the dots placed above or below them, which make you see straightaway whether you ascend or whether you descend with the same obviousness as ordinary music, except that in mine you know the interval with much more precision.

It seems to me that there wouldn't be any more reason in disputing the above argument than if it were claimed that the numerals do not express their different values very well because 6 or 7 are larger than 3 or 4, even though they contain great numbers.[5] In a word, experience proves that it is no less easy to determine the progression of sounds from plain sight by the succession of numerals than by the placement of notes, and that, moreover, the degree of this progression is more clearly expressed by it.

A second Question that is hardly less interesting than the first consists in knowing whether the division of beats I substitute for that of the notes which fill them is a general principle that is simpler and more advantageous than all those different names and shapes one is constrained to apply to the notes in conformity to the duration one wishes to give to them.

A sure means of deciding this would be to examine *a priori* whether the value of the notes is made to regulate the length of the beats or whether, on the contrary, it is not at all by the beats themselves that the duration of the notes should be fixed. In the first Case, the ordinary method would without question be the better, unless one were to regard the elimination of so many shapes as a sufficient compensation for an error in principle from which better results would come. But, in the second case, if I likewise reinstate the cause and the effect, taken until now for one another, and if, by this means, I simplify the rules and if I abridge practice, it must be admitted that reason itself seems to speak in my favor.

Add to this the advantages of detail my method presents in swarms: those hindrances of lines and of staffs entirely eliminated, music made so short to learn, so easy to notate, occupying so little space, requiring less expense to print, and, consequently, costing less to acquire, a more perfect correspondence established between the various parts without one needing all those leaps from one Clef to another, which the most skillful masters still find difficult. Chords and the progression of the harmony presented with an obviousness which the eyes cannot deny. The key clearly specified. The whole succession of the modulation expressed, and the course one has followed, and the point one has reached, and the distance one is from the principal key. But above all the extreme simplicity of the principle joined to the small number and the ease of the rules that follow from it. It is for these considerations that I hope that one will not disapprove of the respectful confidence with which I dare expound my plan to the judgment of the most enlightened body in the world.[6]

Letter to the *Mercure* on a New System of Musical Notation

M. D:[1]

When I devised new characters to maintain our exchanges in Music more conveniently, I hardly thought that the knowledge of this system would go further than between ourselves. Nevertheless, I soon saw myself in the position of expanding its use when, having come to Paris, I was solicited by my friends in the Provinces to send them various pieces of Music; as these commissions came often, I undertook to explain my Method to them, which enabled me to satisfy their curiosity more easily, and without increasing the bulk of my Letters. We found it so suitable that we continue to send to Italy and Paris what is most curious and newest in Music, notated following my Method. Its extreme ease compared to the awkwardness of ordinary Music soon involved me in making a comparison, in which mine seemed to me to win out and merit a more serious examination. The Royal Academy of Sciences wanted to accord me the honor of making this examination. It even prompted a favorable enough judgment there to authorize me to publish my Method; this is what is being done today in a short Work entitled *Dissertation on Modern Music,* which contains, apart from my system as I explain it therein, reflections on the Scale and on ordinary notes in Music that are, I believe, novel enough and interesting enough to merit some attention. I am going to give you a notion of this little Treatise, Sir, expecting that reading it will put you in a position to rely on yourself alone. Moreover, I will not conceal from you that I have the weakness of being among the number of those Authors who imagine that their Works are not capable of being excerpted and that one must read everything in order to judge them well.

As my aim is not to annihilate the Signs of ordinary Music in order to substitute my own for them, I should be excused from responding to the objections usually made, and even reasonably enough, against all the enterprises of this kind; nevertheless, I perceived that these sorts of objections are repeated with such pleasure and with so much confidence that I believed I should show in detail how little applicable they are to my system: my end is only to establish a simpler and more convenient Method that might serve, so to speak, as an aid and supplement to the old one. It is therefore not necessary to wear oneself out with anticipating what will become of the Music already notated if mine does gain a foothold, and one must oppose me still less with the length of time that would necessarily be lost in learning Music twice since, based on the extreme simplicity of my Method, I establish the fact that one would succeed in learning them both by beginning with mine in still less time than is taken to learn only the one in use. This is what I explain in detail in my Preface; I have tried there to exhaust what generally could be said in opposition to my system, and I dare believe that it would be necessary to be in love with quibbling to renew the same objections after having read it.

The Work begins with an examination of the present Signs in Music, such as they were substituted for the numerals of Arithmetic by Jehan des Murs or by Guido of Arezzo, that is, for the letters of the Alphabet of the Greeks.[2] The motives for this substitution having seemed frivolous to me, I explain the basis for my opinion, and after having shown that numerals can preserve all the advantages of Notes, I add that since these numerals are the expression that has been given to numbers, and that since numbers themselves are the exhibitors of the generation of sounds, nothing is so natural as the expression of sounds by the numerals of Arithmetic.

The manner of employing these numerals can be relative only to the relationships of sounds or to their intervals, and it is easy to see that the second meaning is preferable in practice. But it is a matter of finding a fixed and fundamental sound to which one may relate all the others and which serves them as a common term of comparison. There is no such a thing, properly speaking; but there are an infinity of arbitrary ones that can become fundamental, each in its turn; for then none of the other sounds can be employed in the Song except in virtue of certain specific relationships they have with this Tonic sound, and all those that do not have these relationships are for this fact excluded from the modulation.

Now, as only the major mode is indicated to us by Nature, I take it as a model in my new institution, and I establish the numeral 1 for the Bass and the Tonic of all the major Tonics. We have twelve principal sounds on the Keyboard, on each of which a Song can be played; each of these sounds would therefore be capable of being expressed by the numeral 1, and this particular sound will be determined by its natural name, which will be written in the margin. That is, if *do* is written we will be in *do* major, and *do* will be marked by 1; if *sol* is written we will be in *sol* major, and *sol* will be marked 1; etc. Now, as soon as the Key is thus determined, the numeral or the Tonic will always be called *do*, regardless of its natural name; the second Note of the Key will be called *re* and will be marked 2; the third, *mi* and will be marked 3, etc., until the seventh, which will be called *si* and will be marked 7. All those Notes will have to be found between them and with the Tonic in the same relationships as the Notes of the same name in the natural Scale between them and with *C sol do*;[3] in this manner there will always be one Tone between 1 and 2, one Tone between 2 and 3, a semitone between 3 and 4, etc. This wholly eliminates Sharps and Flats from the Clefs, and always expresses the same intervals, major as well as minor ones, with the same characters.

This is pretty nearly reducible to that Method which is called Transposition in vocal Music and which teachers usually regard as a training for ignoramuses, imagining that there is much more science in always singing naturally; it would not be adopted in instrumental music for a much stronger reason, since it further destroys that direct relationship they always assume to be between a certain position of a Note and a certain key on their instrument.

But this relationship is in error at every moment and must serve more to lead one into error than to facilitate playing, which I explain in detail, as well as everything which concerns the idea that should be gotten of the Notes and of the relative sounds in playing, vocal as well as instrumental. If there is anything that is poorly devised in Music it is, without question, the Method of singing and playing naturally; I believe I have demonstrated it; and if there is anything that is ingeniously done in the System I propose that it is the expression of sounds, always relative to the Key in which they are employed. You will judge the solidity of my proofs, Sir, by examining them in the work itself.

Transitions from one Octave to another are made by dots placed above or below the Notes or by their positions on lines, similarly to those in ordinary Music, with this difference, that the distance of one degree makes only an interval of a second by this Music, and nothing else is needed in order to make an Octave by mine, so that a single line and its two contiguous spaces suffice in it to play a part within the range of three Octaves, for which no less than eleven lines would be needed by the ordinary Method.

With regard to the minor mode, as the relationship of sounds that constitute it is found precisely in the Octave contained between two *la*s on the natural Keyboard, this Octave will become the model, and applying the numeral, and the name of *do* to the Mediant of a minor tone, the Tonic will be called *la* and will be marked by the numeral 6; thus, the name written in the margin and which always indicates the Note that should be called *do* is then that of the Mediant and not of the Tonic; this is always known by a Sign added to this word when the Key is minor, and this arrangement has the further advantage of very precisely expressing the analogy found on the one hand between every major Key and the minor mode of its sixth

Note, and on the other hand between every minor Key and the major mode of its Mediant.

The accidental Sharp is indicated by an oblique line that intersects the Note by rising from left to right, and the Flat by another similar line that intersects it by descending in the same way.

This, Sir, is an abridged notion of the Method I use for the expression of all the sounds which make up the Keyboard. The advantages that this Method has over ordinary Notation seem to me considerable; I will speak to you here only of the two most important ones, which are: 1st. The identity of ideas always preserved by the same arrangement of characters; 2nd. The exact knowledge of simple and doubled intervals, as much by the difference in the numerals which express them as by the inversions, the complete knowledge of which depends upon a quarter of an hour of application.

The examination of the manner in which the duration of sounds and the value of Notes has been determined occupies the second part of the Work.

All those different shapes of Notes, relative to the duration of a whole note or to that of a measure in quadruple time, have nothing specific about them relative to duration since nothing is so variable as the term to which they are compared. From thence arise a thousand faults injurious to the precision of movements. Moreover, why this large number of different meters, indicated by as many bizarre figures, while on the other hand the relationships of the Notes have been established only by a subdivided progression which produces only half of the combinations?

I recognize only two different meters, namely in duple- and triple-time, and I likewise recognize two divisions of beats, namely double division and triple division, to which one must necessarily pay attention in the distribution of values, for lack of which attention one falls into the vicious exceptions of which I speak in this Work. As we have no absolute fixed sound that merits serving as fundamental to the others by some specific property, likewise and by the same reason we do not have any absolute duration that should serve as a common measure to the different values of the Notes. But as in each Key I establish the fundamental sound of that Key as the fixed sound, so in each different measure I also take as the term of comparison the duration itself of the measure in question. I divide its beats by commas; each beat is composed of one Note or several; if it is composed of only one, this Note fills that whole beat and should last as long as it. Nothing is so simple: if the beat contains several Notes, you divide its duration into as many equal parts as there are Notes; you apply each of these parts to each of these Notes, and you play them in such a way that all the Beats are equal.

A beat is divided into unequal parts? All possible inequalities are determined with the most exact precision, not by a complexity of bizarre numbers, but by simple horizontal lines added above or below the Notes, to tie all those which are only subdivisions of equal parts, to which it is easy to compare them by this means. These ties produce nearly the same result as eighth notes and sixteenth notes, etc., in ordinary Music, except that they recur much more rarely and can never be more than two in number on the same Note.

I make use of the dot for nearly the same purpose as in ordinary Music, but I give it a much more extensive meaning since it can sustain the Sound of the Note that preceded it not only for half of the duration of this Note, which comprises only a specific case, but for all the different durations of which the measure in which it is employed is susceptible—the dot, just as the Notes, having a specific value only by the place it occupies in the measure or in the beat it is in.

As I have no need to diversify the shape of the Notes in order to represent their different values, and as the same rules are applicable to all their relative rests, it follows that zero alone suffices, along with the dots which might follow it, to replace all those rests, half rests, and other bizarre Signs one is constrained to arrange at every moment in a line for want of having desired to give to the dot a more extensive use.

It is not necessary, Sir, to speak to you further to remind you of an idea of a Method you have cultivated with such pleasure. You have done me the honor of telling me in the past that you would not believe it was possible to devise simpler and more expressive signs than mine. I hope, Sir, that if the Public does not adopt a judgment as wholly favorable, it will at least find them convenient and simple—with which I dare flatter myself to have worked with a success quite different from all those who have until now proposed plans of this sort.

Moreover, it seems to me that many advantages of detail which have long been hoped for will be found in this system. There is perhaps not one enthusiast of Music who has not once in his life sought some more convenient means to notate it in less volume, and without all that difficulty of lines and staves, whether to carry about Collections with them, or to send Music to the Provinces, or, finally, because ruled paper is not found at hand every time there is some tune to be notated.

What is advantageous about my system is that it is enough for those who know Music to read my Work once in order to be able to perform with the same ease by mine as by the other; with regard to those who do not know it at all, if they want to make do with mine, they should know how to sight-sing in at the very least eight months, and if besides this they want to know ordinary Music, they should not have to employ more than double this time for them both, by beginning with mine, for all that difficulty of transpositions, clefs, values, positions, produces a confusion that should be developed in the minds of Students only when they have acquired a training in mensuration and intonation, and when they begin to know something about the theory of keys and modes.

You will find a Tune notated by my characters in the next *Mercure*;[4] I did not want to put it into this one because this Extract does not suffice to explain my System; my Book must be given time to spread into the Provinces so that everyone is in a position to decipher it. I have the honor of being, etc.

Paris, 6 January, 1743.

Dissertation on Modern Music

Immutat animus ad pristina.
Lucr.[1]

Preface

If it is true that circumstances and prejudices often decide the fate of a Work, never has an Author had more to fear than I do. The Public is today so ill-disposed to everything that is called a novelty, so put off by systems and plans, especially with respect to Music, that it is hardly possible any longer to offer it anything of this sort without exposing oneself to the effect of its initial reaction, that is, to see oneself condemned without being heard.

Moreover, it would be necessary to overcome so many obstacles, assembled not by reason but by habit and prejudices much stronger than it, that it does not seem possible to overturn such strong barriers; having only reason on one's side is not to do combat with equal arms, and prejudices are almost always sure of triumphing, and I know that interest alone is able to vanquish them in its turn.

I would be reassured by this last consideration if the Public were always very careful to judge its true interests: but it is ordinarily nonchalant enough to leave them to the direction of people who are totally opposed to them, and it prefers to complain eternally of being badly served rather than to take the trouble to be better served.

This is precisely what happens in Music: the slowness of Teachers and the difficulty of the Art are decried, and those who propose to clarify and abridge it are rebuffed. Everyone agrees that the characters of Music are in a state of imperfection little proportioned to the progress which has been made in the other parts of this Art; nevertheless, every proposal to reform them is guarded against as against a horrible danger. To imagine other signs than those the divine Lully[2] used is not only the most outrageous extravagance of which the human mind is capable, but is also a type of sacrilege. Lully is a God whose finger has forever fixed the state of these sacred characters—good or bad, it doesn't matter; they must be immortalized by his Works. It is no longer permitted to touch them without making a criminal of oneself; and all the young People who henceforth learn Music must, literally, pay the tribute of two or three years of trouble to Lully's honor.

If these are not the precise terms, it is at least the sense of the objections that I have heard made a hundred times against every project that would care to reform this part of Music. What! Must all our Authors be thrown in the fire, everything renovated? Lalande, Bernier, Corelli?[3] All this would be thus lost for us? Where would we get new Orpheuses to compensate ourselves for them? And who are the Musicians that would want to resolve to become Students again?

I do not know very well how those who make these objections understand them, but it seems to me that, by reducing them to maxims and by explaining their consequences somewhat, extremely singular aphorisms would be made of them so as to arrest the progress of Letters and the fine Arts altogether.

Moreover, this reasoning simply leads to falsehoods, and, far from destroying ancient Works, establishing new characters would doubly preserve them by the new Editions which would be made of them, and by the old ones which would still live on. When an Author is translated, I do not see the need to throw the Original into the fire. It is therefore neither the work in itself nor the Copies that would be at risk of perishing, and note above all that, however advantageous a new system might be, it would never destroy the old one quickly enough to abolish its use suddenly; Books would be worn out before being useless, and when they should serve only as a resource for the obstinate, enough of them would always be found to use them.

I know that Musicians are not tractable on this item. Music is for them not the science of sounds, it is that of quarter notes, eighth notes, sixteenth notes, and as soon as these figures cease to affect their eyes, they would never believe that they are really seeing Music. The fear of becoming Students again, and especially the course of that training they take for the science itself, will always make them regard with disdain or with fear all that might be proposed to them of this sort. Their approbation must therefore not be counted upon—all their resistance must even be counted upon—in the establishment of new characters, not as good or as bad in themselves, but simply as new.

I do not know what the particular sentiment of Lully would be on this point, but I am almost sure that he would be too great a man to fall into this pettiness: Lully would have perceived that his science did not at all depend on the characters; that his sounds would never cease to be divine sounds, whatever signs were employed to express them; and, finally, that it would always be an important service to render to his Art and to the advancement of his Works to publish them in a language as energetic but easier to understand, and which by this would become more universal, even though he would have had to give up some old copies, the price of which he assuredly would not have believed compared to the general perfection of the Art.

The misfortune is that it is not with Lullys that we have to deal. It is easier to inherit his science than his genius. I do not know why Music is not enamored of reasoning, but if her Pupils are so scandalized to see a colleague[4] reduce his Art into principles, deepen it, and treat it methodically, all the more reason for them not to allow someone to dare to attack the very parts of this Art.

In order to judge the way in which this would be received, one has only to recall how many years of struggle and obstinacy were needed to substitute the use of *si* for those crude subtleties which are not even yet abolished everywhere. It was quite accepted that the Scale was composed of seven different sounds, but they could not persuade themselves that it would be advantageous to give each of them a specific name, since no one had thought of it until then and since Music hadn't failed to keep going along.[5]

All these difficulties are present to my mind with all the force they can have in those of the Readers. Despite this, I cannot believe that they can withstand the demonstrated truths that I have to establish. That all the systems that have been proposed of this sort have so far failed does not at all astonish me. What's more, in the case of equal advantages and defects the old method should unquestionably prevail, since to destroy an established system, that with which one would like to replace it has to be preferable, not only considering each in itself and what is distinctive about it, but, further, by adding to the first all the considerations of antiquity and all the prejudices which fortify it.

It is in that case of preference that mine seems to me to be, and in that it will indeed be recognized to be if it preserves the advantages of the ordinary method, if it rescues it from its inconveniences, and, finally, if it resolves the superficial objections that are opposed to every novelty of this sort, independently of what it is in itself.

With regard to these first two points, they will be discussed in the body of the Work, and one can know how they stand only after reading it; as for the third, nothing is so simple to decide. For this, it is necessary merely to display the very aim of my plan and the effects that should result from its execution.

The system I propose turns on two principal objects. The first, to notate Music and all its complexities in a simpler, more convenient manner and in less volume.

The second and more considerable one is to make it as easy to learn as it has been discouraging until now, to reduce its signs to a smaller number without taking from them any of their expressiveness, and to abridge its rules so as to make light work of theory and to make practice dependent on only the habituation of the organs, without the difficulty of notation being able to have any part in it

It is easy by experience to justify the fact that Music is learned by my method in half or a third the time of the ordinary method, that Musicians formed by it will be sounder than others given equal knowledge; and, finally, that its ease is such that if one wished to stick to the ordinary Music, it would always be necessary to begin with mine in order to attain it more soundly and in less time. A proposition which, wholly paradoxical as it may seem, does not fail to be strictly true, as much by fact as by demonstration. Now, these facts being supposed true, all the objections fall by themselves and without recourse. In the first place, Music notated according to the old system will not at all be useless, and there will be no need at all to worry about throwing it into the fire, since Pupils of my method will succeed in sight-singing ordinary Music in even less time, including that which they may have given to mine, than is commonly done; as both will therefore be equally well known without having employed more time, already it cannot be said with regard to these things that the old Music is useless.

Let us suppose Students who do not have years to sacrifice, and who would be very willing to be content with knowing how to sight-sing in seven or eight months' time based on my notation. I contend that they will not even be at a loss with ordinary Music. In truth, at the end of this time they will not know how to perform it at sight; perhaps they will not even decipher it without difficulty: but in the end they will decipher it, for, as they will be used to mensuration and intonation anyway, it will be enough to sacrifice five or six lessons in the seventh month to explain the principles to them by means of those already known to them in order to put them in a position to succeed easily by themselves and without the help of any Teacher. And, if they do not want to devote themselves to this effort, they will still be able to translate all sorts of Music on the spot on their own, and consequently be in a position to put it to good use at a point when it is indecipherable for ordinary Students.

Teachers shouldn't fear becoming Students again: my method is so simple that it need only be read, and not studied, and I have grounds for believing that the difficulties that might be found in it would derive more from their frame of mind than the obscurity of the system, since some Ladies, to whom I have had the honor of explaining it, have sung on the spot, and at sight, music notated according to my method, and have themselves notated tunes quite correctly, whereas Musicians of the first order would perhaps have affected to have understood nothing of it.[6]

Musicians—I speak at least of the greater number—hardly pride themselves on judging things without prejudices and without passion, and they commonly consider them much less by what they are in themselves than by the relation they might have to their interest. It is true that, even in this sense, they will have no cause to be opposed to the success of my system, since as soon as it is published they will be its masters as much as I am, and, since the ease it introduces into previous Music naturally gives it a more universal currency, they will only be busier by helping to spread it. It is nevertheless quite probable that they will not be the first to give themselves over to it, and that it is only the settled taste of the Public that could encourage them to cultivate a system whose advantages appear as so many dangerous innovations against the difficulty of their Art.

When I speak of Musicians in general, I do not at all mean to confuse them with the ones among those Gentlemen who are a credit to that Art by their characters and by their enlightenment. It is only too well known that what is called the people always dominate by their number in all societies and all stations; but it is no less well known that there are everywhere honorable exceptions, and all that could be said in particular against the Musical profession is that the people in it are, perhaps, a bit too numerous, and the exceptions more rare.

However this may be, if one wishes to assume and to enlarge all the obstacles that might check the operation of my plan, this fact, clearer than day, cannot be denied, that there are in Paris two or three thousand people who, with much aptitude, will never learn Music for the sole reason of its slowness and its difficulty. If I had worked only for them, this is already one unquestionable utility; and let it not be said that this method will be of no use to them in performing ordinary Music. For, aside from the fact that I have already responded to this objection, it will be even less necessary for them to have recourse to it, as care will be taken to give them Editions of the best pieces of Music of every type and periodic collections of Tunes to sing and of instrumental pieces, while waiting for the system to be widespread enough to make its use universal.

Finally, if mistrust is sufficiently exaggerated so that it is imagined that no one will adopt my system, I contend that even in this case it will still be advantageous for Enthusiasts of the Art to cultivate it for their particular convenience. The Examples notated at the end of this Work will make the advantages of my signs over the ordinary signs sufficiently evident, whether in terms of ease or in terms of precision. There might be a hundred occasions on which there are Tunes to notate without ruled paper; my method gives you a very convenient and very simple means of doing so. Do you want to send some new Tunes, entire scenes of Operas to the Provinces without increasing the bulk of your letters? You can write quite long pieces of Music on the same sheet. In composing do you want to depict the relationship of your parts, the progression of your chords, and the whole ordering of your harmony for the eyes? The practice of my system fulfills all this, and I conclude, finally, that to consider my method only as like that special language of the Egyptian Priests, which served only to treat sublime sciences, it would still be infinitely useful for initiates in Music, with this difference, that instead of being more difficult, it would be easier than the ordinary language, and consequently could not for long remain a mystery to the Public.

My system need not at all be regarded as a project aiming at destroying the old characters. I would like to believe that this enterprise would be chimerical, even with the most advantageous substitution; but I also believe that the convenience of my characters, and especially their extreme ease, makes them worth being cultivated in any case, independently of what might become of the others.

Furthermore, given the state of imperfection in which Musical signs have long been, it is not at all remarkable that several people have tried to recast them or to correct them. It is not even very astonishing that several of them have settled on the most natural and most proper signs for this substitution, such as numerals are. Nevertheless, as the majority of men hardly judge things except on first glance, it might well happen that, by this sole reason of using the same characters, I will be accused of having done nothing but copy and of presenting here a revived system.[7] I admit that it is easy to perceive that it is indeed less the sort of signs than the manner of employing them that constitutes the actual difference among systems: otherwise it would have to be said, for example, that Algebra and the French Language are merely the same thing since they likewise make use of the letters of the Alphabet; but this reflection probably will not be that which will win the day; and it appears such a happy occasion simultaneously to take from me the merit of the invention and to attribute to me the vices of other systems by a single objection that there are people capable of adopting this criticism solely by reason of its convenience.

Although I am not completely indifferent to a reproach of this sort, I would be much less sensitive to it than to those that might fall on my system directly. It is much more important to know whether it is advantageous than to know its Author; and if I were denied the honor of the invention, I would be less affected by this injustice than by the pleasure of seeing it be useful to the Public. The sole favor which I have a right to demand from it, and which few people will grant me, is that it be willing to judge only after having read my Work and those I may be accused of having copied.

I had at first resolved to present here only a very abridged plan, and about as it was contained in a Report I had the honor of reading at the Royal Academy of Sciences, 22 August 1742.[8] I have nevertheless reflected that one must speak to the Public differently than one speaks to an Academy, and that there were numerous objections of all types to anticipate. In order therefore to respond to those I have been able to anticipate, some additions had to be made which have put my Work into the condition it is here. I shall await the approbation of the Public to present it with another one which will contain the absolute principles of my method such as they should be taught to Students.[9] I shall deal in it with a novel means of figuring the accompaniment of the Organ or Harpsichord entirely different from all those of this sort that have appeared until now, and such in way that with four signs alone I figure all sorts of Thoroughbasses in a way that always makes the modulation and the Fundamental Bass perfectly known to the Accompanist, it being otherwise possible for him to be mistaken about it. Following this method, one can, without seeing the Figured Bass, accompany quite correctly by the numerals alone, which, instead of being related to that Figured Bass, are related directly to the Fundamental. But this is not the place to speak further of this matter.

Dissertation on Modern Music

Since Musical signs have for so long remained in the state of imperfection in which we still see them today, it seems astonishing that the difficulty of learning them has not alerted the Public that it was the fault of the characters and not that of the Art, or that, this being perceived, no one has deigned to remedy it. It is true that plans of this sort have often been presented, but of all these plans which, without having the advantages of ordinary Music, have its inconveniences, none, that I know of, has so far attained the objective, whether because too superficial a training has thwarted those who wanted to consider it theoretically, or because the narrow and limited genius of ordinary Musicians has prevented them from embracing a general and reasoned plan and from perceiving the true defects of their Art, the present perfection of which they are usually quite obstinate about.

Music has suffered the fate of the Arts that are perfected only successively. The inventors of its characters considered only the condition in which it was found in their time without foreseeing that to which it might later attain. From this it happened that their system was soon found to be defective, and all the more defective as the Art was perfected. As it advanced, rules were established to remedy present inconveniences and to multiply a too limited expression which could not suffice for the new combinations with which it was burdened every day. In a word, the inventors in this genre, as M. Sauveur says,[10] having had in view only some properties of sounds, and especially the practice of Singing that was in use in their time, contented themselves with making, in relation to that one, systems of Music which others changed little by little as Musical taste changed. Now, it is impossible for one system, be it otherwise the best in the world in its origin, not ultimately to be burdened with inconveniences and difficulties by the changes made to it and by the redundancies added to it, and this could never have produced anything but an extremely muddled and extremely ill-mixed whole.

This is the case for the method we practice today in Music, excluding nevertheless the simplicity of the principle, which is never encountered in it. As its foundation is absolutely bad, it has not exactly been spoiled—it has only been made worse by the additions that had to be made to it.

It is not easy to know precisely what condition Music was in when Guido of Arezzo* took it into his head to do away with all the characters that were used for it in order to substitute for them the notes used today. What is likely is that these first characters were the same ones with which the ancient Greeks expressed that marvelous Music, which, whatever may be said about it, our own will never approach with regard to its effects, and what is certain is that Guido rendered quite a bad service to Music, and that it is pity for us that he did not find in his path Musicians as intractable as those of today.

There is no doubt that the letters of the Greek Alphabet constituted at the same time the characters of their Music and the numerals of their Arithmetic, so that they needed only a single type of signs, in all twenty-four in number, to express all the variations of discourse, all the relations of numbers, and all the combinations of sounds; in which they were much wiser or more fortunate than we are, we who are forced to ply our imaginations to a multitude of uselessly diversified signs.

But, in order to attend only to what relates to my subject, how can it be that this host of difficulties which the use of notes has introduced into Music is not perceived, or that, being perceived, courage is wanting to attempt the remedy, to try to bring it back to its first simplicity, and, in a

---

*Whether Guido of Arezzo or Jehan des Murs, the name of the Author does not matter for the system, and I speak of the former only because he is better known.[11]

word, to do for its perfection what Guido of Arezzo did to spoil it? For, in truth, that's the word, and I say it in spite of myself.

I wanted to discover the reasons that Author must have used so as to have the ancient system abolished in favor of his own, and I haven't ever been able to find any others than the two following ones. 1. The notes are more visible than numerals. 2. And their position better expresses the raising and lowering of sounds to the sight. Here then are the sole principles on which our Aretino built a new system of Music, annihilated all that which had been in use for two thousand years, and taught men to sing with difficulty.

In order to discover whether Guido reasoned justly, even admitting the truth of these two propositions, the question is reduced to knowing whether the eyes must be spared at the expense of the mind, and whether the perfection of a method consists in making signs more perceptible by making them more cumbersome, for this is precisely the case with ours.

But we are spared from entering into the above debate since, these two propositions being equally false and ridiculous, they could never serve as the foundation for any but a very bad system.

In the first place, it is seen right away that since Musical notes fill much more space than the numerals for which they are substituted, one could, by making these numerals much larger, make them at least as visible as notes without occupying more volume. It is moreover seen that notated Music, having dots, sixteenth rests, lines, clefs, Sharps, and other signs as necessary and more minute than numerals, it is by these signs, and not by the size of the notes, that the point of view must be determined.

In the second place, Guido ought not to have so highly stressed the utility of the position of the notes since, without speaking of the throng of inconveniences of which it is the cause, the advantage it procures is already entirely found in natural Music, that is in Music by numerals; it is seen from the first glance, in the one as well as in the other, whether a sound is higher or lower than the one that it precedes or the one that follows it, with this sole difference, that in the numerical method the interval, or the relationship of the two sounds which compose it, is known precisely by inspection alone, whereas in ordinary Music you know by looking that it is necessary to ascend or descend, and you know nothing more.

It cannot be believed what application, what perseverance, what deft machinations are necessary to acquire passably the science of intervals and relationships in the established system: it is the tedious work of a training that is always too long and never extensive enough, since after fifteen and twenty years of practice the Musician still encounters leaps that confound him, not only as regards intonation, but even as regards knowing the interval, especially when it is a question of jumping from one clef to another. This matter merits being gone into more deeply, and I shall speak of it at length.

Guido's system is altogether comparable, as regards its idea, to that of a man who, having reflected that numerals have nothing in their shape that answers to their different values, should propose to establish among them a certain relative size, and one proportional to the numbers they express. Two, for example, would be double the size of the unit one, three half again the size of two, and so on. This system's defenders would not fail to prove to you that it is quite advantageous in Arithmetic to have uniform characters before the eyes which, without any difference in shape, have it only in their size, and which would after a fashion depict for the eyes the relations of which they would be the expression.

Furthermore, this ocular knowledge of highs, lows, and intervals is so necessary in Music that there is no one who does not perceive the ridiculousness of certain plans which have sometimes been proposed for notating it on a single line by characters that are the most bizarre characters, the worst devised, and the least analogous to their meaning; tails turned to the right, to the left, up, down, and at an angle, in all ways, in order to represent *Dos*, *Res*, *Mis*, etc.[12] Heads and tails differently placed in order to answer to the denominations *Pa*, *ra*, *ga*, *so*, *bo*, *lo*, *do*, or other signs altogether as singularly applied.[13] It is perceived right away that all this says nothing to the eyes and has no relation to what it should signify, and I dare say that men will never find characters as convenient or natural as numerals alone to express sounds and all their relationships. The reasons for this will be made known a thousand times in the course of this reading: while waiting, it suffices to remark that, numerals being the expression that has been given to numbers and the numbers themselves being the exponents of the generation of sounds, nothing is so natural as the expression of the various signs by the numerals of Arithmetic.

It should therefore not be surprising that the attempt has sometimes been made to restore Music to this natural expression. As little as one may reflect on this Art, not as a Musician but as a Philosopher, its defects are soon perceived: one further perceives that these defects are inherent in the very basis of the system and depend uniquely on the poor choice, and not the poor use, of its characters; for, moreover, it cannot be denied that a long practice, supplementing reason in this regard, has not taught us to combine them in the most advantageous manner possible.

Finally, reasoning leads us as far as knowing palpably that Music, depending on numbers, ought to have the same expression as they do: a necessity which arises not only from a certain general suitability, but from the very basis of the physical principles of this Art.

When one has once reached this point by a chain of well-founded and consistent reasonings, it is then that one has to leave Philosophy and become a Musician again, and it is precisely this that none of those who have proposed systems in this genre have, until now, done. Some, sometimes starting off with a very fine theory, have never been able to follow it through to the point of reducing it to use; and others, really embracing only the mechanics of their Art, have not been able to go back to the great principles they do not know, and from which one must nevertheless necessarily begin in order to encompass a coherent system. The lack of training among the first, the lack of theory among the others—and perhaps, it has to be said, the lack of genius in all of them—has made it so that until now none of the plans that have been published has remedied the inconveniences in ordinary Music while preserving its advantages.

It is not that any great difficulty is found in the expression of sounds by numerals, since they could always be represented numerically, or by the degrees of their intervals, or by the relationships of their vibrations; but the predicament of employing a certain number of numerals without bringing back in the inconveniences of ordinary Music, and the need to determine the kind and progression of sounds in relation to all the different modes, requires more consideration than at first appears; for the question is properly speaking one of finding a general method in order to represent all the sounds of Music considered in each of twenty-four modes with a very small number of characters.

But the great difficulty on which all the inventors of systems have foundered is that of the expression of the different duration of rests and sounds. Deceived by the false rules of ordinary Music, they have never been able to raise themselves above the idea of whole notes, quarter notes, and eighth notes; they have made themselves the slaves of this mechanics, they have adopted the bad relations that it establishes. Thus, in order to give specific values to the notes, it was necessary to invent new signs, to introduce into each note a complexity of shapes with respect to the duration and with respect to the sound; from which ensue inconveniences which ordinary Music does not have, so that it is with reason that all these methods have fallen into discredit. But, ultimately, the defects of this Art remain no less for having been compared with greater defects, and, if a thousand more worse methods were published, one would always be at the same point in the matter, and all this would not make the one we practice today any more perfect.

No one, excepting Artists, stops complaining of the extreme length that the study of Music demands before possessing it passably: but, as Music is one of the sciences which has been least reflected upon, whether because the pleasure one takes from it injures the sang-froid needed to meditate or because those who practice it are not too commonly people given to reflection, it has hardly been thought of until now to seek the genuine causes of its difficulty, and the Art itself has been unjustly taxed with the defects that the Artist has introduced into it.

It is easily perceived that, in truth, that quantity of lines, clefs, transpositions, sharps, flats, naturals, simple and compound meters, whole notes, half notes, quarter notes, eighth notes, sixteenth notes, thirty-second notes, whole rests, half rests, quarter rests, eighth rests, sixteenth rests, etc., yields a throng of signs and their combinations, from which result considerable difficulty and considerable inconvenience. But what precisely are these inconveniences? Do they arise directly from Music itself, or from the poor manner of expressing it? Are they susceptible of correction, and what are the appropriate remedies that might be provided for them? It is rare for the examination to be pressed this far, and, after having had the patience during entire years to fill one's head with sounds and one's memory with verbiage, it often happens that one is wholly astonished to have understood nothing for all that, so that one acquires a distaste for Music and the Musician and then leaves them both more convinced of the tiresome difficulty of that Art than its much-vaunted charms.

I am undertaking to justify Music from the wrongs of which it is accused, and to show that one can, by shorter and easier routes, succeed in possessing it more perfectly and with more intelligence than by the ordinary method, so that, if the public persists in wanting to hold on to it, it will have only itself to blame for the difficulties it encounters.

Without wanting to enter here into the details of all the defects of the established system, I shall nevertheless take this occasion to speak of the most considerable ones, and it will be proper to remark that, since these inconveniences are the necessary result of the very basis of the method, it is absolutely impossible to correct them otherwise than by a general recasting such as I propose. It remains to examine whether my system actually remedies all these defects without introducing equivalent ones, and it is to this examination that this small work is dedicated.

In general, all the vices of ordinary Music can be reduced to three principal classes. The first is the multitude of signs and their combinations which uselessly overloads the minds and memories of Beginners, so that, the ear being formed, and the organs having acquired all the necessary aptitude long before one is in a position to sight-sing, it follows that the difficulty is wholly in the observation of the rules, and not at all in the performance of the song. The second is the lack of conspicuousness in the kind of intervals expressed on the same or on different Clefs—a lack of such a great extent that not only is it the principal cause of the slowness of the progress of Students, but further there is no fully formed Musician who is not sometimes inconvenienced by it when performing. The third, finally, is the extreme diffuseness of the characters and the too great a volume they occupy, which, joined to those lines and those staffs, so tiresome to draw, becomes a source of inconvenience of more than one type. Perhaps the point will appear to many readers to be of scant consideration; but if they reflect on what constitutes the perfection of signs of every kind and especially in Music, they will perceive that it consists essentially in expressing a great deal in a small amount of space, and that, finally, the least benefit is never a small defect.

At first it seems difficult enough to find a method which might simultaneously remedy all these inconveniences. How to make our signs more conspicuous without increasing their number? And how to increase their number without making them on the one hand more lengthy to learn, more difficult to retain, and on the other hand more extensive in their volume?

Nevertheless, considering the thing closely, it is soon perceived that all these defects come from the same source: namely, from the poor institution of signs and from the quantity of them that had to be established in order to supplement the limited and poorly understood expression they were given in the first place. And it is manifest that as soon as equivalent signs are invented, but simpler and fewer in quantity, they will at the same time have more precision and be able to express as many things in less space.

It would be advantageous, besides this, for these signs to be known already, in order that attention might be less divided, and easy to form, in order to make Music more convenient.

Here are the aims I have set for myself in meditating on the system I am presenting to the public. As I am dedicating another work to the details of my method, such as it should be taught to Students,[14] one will find here only a general plan which will suffice to give a perfect understanding of it to persons who cultivate Music at present, and in which I hope that, in spite of its brevity, the simplicity of my principles will give rise neither to obscurity nor to equivocation.

Two principal objects must first be considered in Music, each separately: the first should be the expression of all possible sounds, and the second, that of all different durations, of sounds as well as of their relative rests, which also includes the difference in movements.

As Music is only a linking of sounds that are heard either together or in succession, it suffices for all these sounds to have relative expressions that assign to each of them the place they must occupy in relation to a certain natural or arbitrary fundamental sound, provided that this sound be clearly expressed, and that the relationship be easily known. These are advantages not at all possessed by ordinary Music, in which the fundamental sound has no particular prominence, and in which all the relationships of notes need to be studied for a long time.

But how should one proceed in order to determine this fundamental sound in the most advantageous manner possible? This is a question that well merits being examined first. It is already seen that there is no sound in nature that contains any specific and known property by which it can be distinguished every time it is heard. You cannot decide by a unique sound that it is a *do* rather than a *la* or a *re*. and as long as you hear it alone you cannot perceive anything about it that should commit you to attribute to it one name rather than another. This has already been noted by M. de Mairan.[15] There is in nature, he says, no *do* nor *sol* that are a fifth or a fourth in themselves, because *do*, *sol*, or *re* exist only hypothetically according to the fundamental sound that has been adopted. The sensation of each of the tones has nothing in itself that properly belongs to the place it occupies in the range of the keyboard, nothing that distinguishes it from the others taken separately. The *Re* of the Opera may be the *Do* of the Chapel, or the contrary:[16] the same rate, the same frequency of vibrations that constitutes the one could serve, if one liked, to constitute the other; they differ in feeling only by the quality of higher or lower, as eight vibrations differs, for example, from nine, and not by a specific difference in sensation.

Here, then, all imaginable sounds are reduced to the sole faculty of exciting sensations by the vibrations which produce them, and the specific property of each of them is reduced to the particular number of these vibrations during a specific time. Now, as it is impossible to count these vibrations, at least in a direct manner, it is still demonstrated that no specific property can be found in the sounds by which they may be recognized separately, and all the more reason in that there is not one that merits, by preference, being distinguished from all the others and serving as fundamental for the relationships they have among themselves.

It is true that M. Sauveur has proposed a means for determining a fixed sound that might serve as the basis for all the sounds of the general scale: but his reasonings themselves prove that there is no such sound in nature at all; and the very ingenious and very impractical artifice he has imagined for finding an arbitrary one further proves how far from Hypotheses or even, if one likes, from truths of speculation it is to the simple rules of practice.[17]

Let us nevertheless see whether, by spying upon nature more closely, we cannot dispense with resorting to Art in order to establish one or several fundamental sounds that can serve us as a principle of comparison to which all the others may be related.

To begin with, since we are working only for the sake of practice, we shall speak in our research into sounds only of those that make up the tempered system such as it is universally adopted, counting as nothing those that do not at all enter into the practice of our Music, and considering as just without exception all the chords that result from temperament. It will be soon seen that this supposition, which is the same one that is admitted in ordinary Music, will take away nothing of the variety that the tempered system introduces into the effect of the different modulations.

By thus adopting the series of all the sounds of the keyboard, such as it is practiced on Organs and Harpsichords, experience teaches me that a certain sound to which the name *do* is given, made by an open pipe six feet in length, makes heard fairly distinctly, aside from the principal sound, two other weaker sounds, one on the major third, and the other on the fifth,* to which the names *mi* and *sol* are given. I write these three names separately, and looking for a pipe on the fifth of the first that produces the same sound, which I am going to call *sol* or its octave, I find one of ten feet eight inches in length, which, aside from the principal sound *sol*, also produces two others, but more weakly; I call them *si* and *re*, and I find that they are in precisely the same relationship with *sol* as *sol* and *mi* are with *do*; I write them after the others, omitting writing *sol* a second time as useless. Looking for a third pipe in unison with the fifth *re*, I find that it further produces two other sounds aside from the principal sound *re*, and always in the same proportion as the preceding ones; I call them *fa* and *la*,† and I write them after the preceding ones as well. By continuing likewise on *la*, I should further find two other sounds: but as I perceived that the fifth is the same *mi* that the third of the first sound *do* produced, I stop there, so as not to redouble my experiments uselessly, and I have the following seven names, answering to the first sound *do* and to the six others that I have found by twos:

Do, mi, sol, si, re, fa, la

*That is to say to the twelfth, which is the replica of the fifth, and to the seventeenth, which is the duplicate of the major third. The octave, and even several octaves, are also heard distinctly enough, and would be heard even better if the ear did not sometimes confound them with the principal sound.

†The *fa* that makes the third major of *re* is consequently found to be sharp in this progression, and it is must be admitted that it is not easy to develop the origin of *fa*-natural considered as the fourth note of the key: but observations would have to be made above that would take us far off and would not be appropriate for this work. Furthermore, we must stop even less so for this slight exception, which could show that *fa*-natural could be treated in the key of *do* only as a dissonance or a preparation for a dissonance.

Then bringing together all these sounds by octaves in the smallest intervals in which I can place them, I find them arranged in this fashion:

Do, re, mi, fa, sol, la, si

And these seven notes arranged in this way indicate precisely the diatonic progression assigned to the major mode by nature itself. Now, as the first sound *do* has served as principle and fundamental for all the others, we shall take it for that fundamental sound for which we had been looking, since it is in reality the source and origin from which all those that succeed it have emanated. To go through all the sounds of this scale in this way by beginning and ending with the fundamental sound, and by always preferring the one engendered first to those later, is what is called modulating on the tone of *do*-major, and it is properly speaking there that the fundamental scale, which it has been agreed to call natural in preference to the others, and which serves as the rule of comparison to which the fundamental sounds of all the practicable keys conform. Furthermore, it is quite evident that, taking the sound produced by every other pipe for the fundamental sound *do*, we would arrive by different sounds at a wholly similar progression, and that, consequently, this choice is only a pure convention and as wholly arbitrary as that of this or that meridian for determining the degrees of longitude.

It follows from this that what we have done in taking *do* for the basis of our operation we can likewise do by beginning with one of the six sounds that follow it, at our choice, and, that calling this new fundamental sound *do*, we shall arrive at the same progression as beforehand, and we shall find entirely anew:

Do, re, mi, fa, sol, la, si

With this sole difference, that these latter sounds being placed with respect to their fundamental sound in the same manner as the preceding ones were with respect to theirs, and these two fundamental sounds being taken on different pipes, it follows that their corresponding sounds are also produced by different pipes, and that, for example, since the first *do* is not the same as the second one, the first *re* is not the same as the second one either.

At present, the first of these two keys being taken for the natural one, if you want to know what the different sounds of the second are with respect to the first one, you have only to look for which natural sound of the first key is related to the fundamental of the second one, and the same relationship will always persist between the sounds of the same denomination of both keys in the corresponding octaves. Supposing, for example, that the *do* of the second key is a *sol* in the natural one, that is, the fifth of the natural *do*, the *re* of the second key will surely be a natural *la*, that is, the fifth of the natural *re*; the *mi* will be a *si*, the *fa* a *do*, etc., and then it will be said that it is in the major key of *sol*, that is, that the natural *sol* has been taken in order to produce the fundamental sound of another major key.

But if, instead of stopping at *la* in the experiment of the three sounds produced by each pipe, I had continued my progression by fifths until I found myself again at the first *do* from which I first began, or at one of its octaves, then I would have passed through five new sounds altered from the first ones, which along with them make up the sum of twelve different sounds contained in the range of the octave, and together making up what is called the twelve pitches of the chromatic system.

These twelve sounds, replicated on different octaves, make up the entire range of the general scale without any other ever being able to be introduced, at least in the tempered system, since after having gone through all the sounds that the pipes make heard by fifths, I have arrived at the replica of the first by which I began, and since, consequently, by carrying on the same operation, I would always have only replicas, that is, the octaves of the preceding sounds.

The method that nature has indicated to me and that I have followed in order to find all the sounds practiced in Music thus teaches me in the first place not to find a fundamental sound properly speaking, which does not at all exist, but to derive from a sound established by convention all the same advantages as would be possible if it were really fundamental, that is, by truly producing from it the origin and the generator of all the other sounds which are in use and which can in consequence only exist by certain specific relationships they have with it, like the keys of the keyboard with regard to *C sol do*.[18]

In the second place, it teaches me that after having determined the relationship of each of these sounds with the fundamental, each of them in its turn can itself be considered as fundamental, since the pipe that produces it makes its major third and its fifth heard just as the fundamental does; by beginning with this sound as generator, one finds a scale that differs in no regard as to its progression from the scale established in the first place. That is, in a word, that each key of the keyboard can be and even should be considered in two entirely different senses: according to the first, this key represents a sound relative to *C sol do*, and which in this capacity is called *re*, or *mi*, or *sol*, etc., according to whether it is the second, the third, or the fifth degree of the octave contained between two natural *do*s. According to the second sense, it is the fundamental of a major key, and then it should continually bear the name of *do*, and all the other keys of the keyboard coming to be considered only by the relationships they have with the fundamental, it is this relationship that then determines the name they should bear, according to the degree they occupy; as the octave contains twelve sounds, it must indicate the one that is chosen, and then it is a natural *la* or a *re*, etc., which specifies the sound; but when one must make it fundamental and thereby establish the key, then it is constantly a *do*, and this determines the progression.

It results from this explanation that each of the twelve sounds of the octave can be considered fundamental or relative according to the manner in which it is employed, with this distinction, that the placement of the natural *do* in the scale of the notes makes it naturally fundamental, but that it can always become relative to every other sound one might like to choose as fundamental, whereas those other sounds, naturally relative to that of *do*, become fundamental only by a particular specification. Moreover, it is evident that it is nature itself that leads us to this distinction of a fundamental and of relationships among the sounds: each sound can be naturally fundamental since it makes its harmonics heard, that is, its major third and its fifth, which are the essential pitches of the key of which it is the root,[19] and each sound can still be naturally relative since there is not one of them that is not one of the harmonics or one of the essential pitches of another fundamental sound, and which may not be engendered in this capacity. Why I am insisting on these observations will be seen in the following.

We therefore have twelve sounds which serve as roots or as tonics for the twelve major keys practiced in Music, and which, in this capacity, are perfectly alike as to the modifications which result from each of them treated as fundamental. With regard to the minor mode, it is not at all indicated to us by nature, and as we do not find any sound that makes its harmonics heard, we can see that it has no absolute fundamental sound at all, and that it can exist only by virtue of the relationship it has with the major mode from which it is engendered, as it is easy to make seen.*

The first object we should therefore propose for ourselves in the institution of our new signs is that of coming up with one sign that clearly designates on all occasions the fundamental pitch one means to establish and the relationship it has with the fundamental by comparison, that is, with the natural *do*.

Let us assume that this sign is already chosen. The fundamental being

---

*See M. Rameau, *New Sys.*, p. 21; and *Tr. on Harm.*, pp. 12 and 13.[20]

specified, it will be a matter of expressing all the other sounds by the relationship they have with it, for it is it alone that determines their progression and alterations. This is not, it is true, what is practiced in ordinary Music, in which the sounds are constantly expressed by certain specific names which have a direct relationship to the keys of instruments and to the natural scale without regard to the key one is in or to the fundamental which determines it; but as it is a question here of what is most suitable to do, and not of what is done at present, is there any less right in rejecting a bad practice, if I make it clear that the one which I substitute for it is preferable, than there would be in quitting a bad guide for another who showed you a more convenient and shorter path? And wouldn't the first not make a laughing-stock of himself if he wanted to compel you always to follow him, for this sole reason, that he's been leading you astray for a long time?

These considerations lead us directly to the choice of numerals to express the sounds of music, since numerals indicate only relationships and since the expression of sounds is also only that of the relationships they have among themselves. In addition, we have already noted that the Greeks made use of the letters of their Alphabet for this purpose only because those letters were at the same time the numerals of their arithmetic, whereas the characters of our Alphabet, not usually carrying with them the ideas of number or of relationships, would not be anywhere near as appropriate for expressing them.

It should not be surprising after this that substituting numerals for Musical notes has been attempted so many times; it would assuredly have been the most important service that could have been rendered to this Art if those who had undertaken it had had the patience or the necessary knowledge to embrace a general system in its whole extent. The great number of tentative ones that were produced on this score makes it clear that the defects of the established characters had long been perceived. But it must be further seen that it is much easier to perceive them than to correct them. Must it be concluded from this that the thing is impossible?

We have therefore already decided here on the choice of the characters. It is now a question of reflecting on the best way of applying them. It is certain that this requires some care, for if it were only a question of expressing all the sounds by as many different numerals, then there wouldn't be any great difficulty; but there also wouldn't be any great merit in doing so either, and this would be to bring back into Music a confusion still worse than that which arises from the position of the notes.

In order to move away from the spirit of the ordinary method as little as possible, I shall first attend to the natural keyboard, that is, to the black keys of the Organ and of the Harpsichord,[21] retaining signs of alternation which are similar to those commonly used for the others. Or, rather, in order to fix on a more universal notion, I shall consider solely the progression and the relationship of sounds affected in the major mode, abstracting from modulation and changes of key, quite certain that, through the regular application of my characters, the fertility of my principle will suffice for everything.

Furthermore, as the entire range of the keyboard is only a succession of several redoubled octaves, I shall content myself with considering one octave in particular, and shall then seek a means of successively applying to all of them the same characters I will have appointed to the sounds of this one. By doing so, I shall conform simultaneously to usage, which gives the same names to the corresponding notes of different octaves; to my ear, which takes pleasure in confounding these sounds; to reason, which makes me see the same relationships multiplied among the numbers which express them; and, finally, I shall correct one of the great defects of ordinary Music, which is to destroy the analogy and the resemblance which should always be found among different octaves by means of a faulty position.

There are two manners of considering sounds and the relationships they have among them: the first, by their generation, that is, by the different lengths of the strings or the pipes that make them heard; and the second, by the intervals that separate them from low to high.

With regard to the first, it could not be of any consequence in the establishment of our signs, whether because it would require numbers too large to express them, or, finally, because such numbers have no advantage as to the ease of intonation, which should be our main object here.

On the contrary, the second manner of considering sounds by their intervals encompasses an infinite number of utilities: it is on it that the system for position was founded such as it is practiced at present. It is true that, following this system, since the notes having nothing in themselves nor in the space which separates them that clearly indicates to you the kind of their interval, an infinite amount of time must be spent fumbling about before having acquired all the training necessary to recognize it at first glance. But as this defect comes solely from the bad choice of signs, nothing can be concluded against the principle on which they are based, and it will soon be seen how, to the contrary, all the advantages which can make intonation easy to learn and to practice are drawn from this principle.

Taking *do* for this fundamental sound to which all the others should be related, and expressing it by the numeral 1, we will have following it the seven natural sounds *do, re, mi, fa, sol, la, si* expressed by the seven numerals 1, 2, 3, 4, 5, 6, 7; so that, when the song moves within the range of these seven sounds, it will suffice to notate each by its corresponding numeral in order to express everything without equivocation.

It is obvious that this manner of notating fully preserves the much-vaunted advantage of their position; for you know at a glance, as clearly as is possible, whether one sound is higher or lower than another; you see perfectly that one must ascend to go from 1 to 5, and that one must descend to go from 4 to 2; this does not permit of the slightest objection.

But I shall not enlarge here upon this point, and I shall content myself with touching upon the principal reflections which arise from the comparison of the two methods at the end of this work; if my plan is followed with some attention, they will present themselves of their own accord at every instant, and, by leaving to my readers the pleasure of anticipating me, I hope to procure for myself the glory of having thought as they do.

Aside from the degree of their intervals, the first seven numerals arranged in this way will indicate the degree each sound occupies with regard to the fundamental sound *do*, in such a way that there is no interval whose expression by numerals does not present you with a double relationship: the first, between the two sounds which make it up, and the second, between each of them and the fundamental sound.

Let it be thus established that the numeral 1 will always be called *do*, 2 will always be called *re*, 3 always *mi*, etc., in conformity with the following order:

1,	2,	3,	4,	5,	6,	7
Do,	*re,*	*mi,*	*fa,*	*sol,*	*la,*	*si*

But when it is a matter of leaving this range to pass into other octaves, then this presents a new difficulty. For one must necessarily multiply the numerals or provide for this by some new sign which determines the octave in which one is to sing, otherwise, since the *do* above is written as 1 just like the *do* below, the Musician would not be able to avoid confusing them and the equivocation would necessarily stand.

This is the case in which position can be admitted with all the advantages it has in ordinary Music without retaining either its obstacles or its difficulty. Let us establish a horizontal line on which we shall place all the notes contained within the same octave, that is, from the *do* below and including it to the one above, exclusively. Is it necessary to pass into the octave which begins with the *do* above? We shall place our numerals above the line. Do we on the contrary want to pass into the inferior octave which begins in descending with the *si* which follows the *do* placed on the line? Then we shall place them below the same line. This is to say that the position one is constrained to change at each degree in ordinary music will change in mine only at each octave and, consequently, will have six times fewer combinations. (See the plate [p. 98], Example 1.)[22]

After this first *do*, I descend to *sol* of the inferior octave; I return to my *do*, and, after having played the *mi* and the *sol* of the same octave, I pass to the *do* above, that is, to the *do* which begins the superior octave; I then descend again all the way to the *sol* below by which I return to conclude on my first *do*.

You can see in these examples (See the plate [p. 98], Examples 1 and 2) how the progression of the voice is always announced to the eyes, either by the different values of the numerals if they are of the same octave, or by their different positions if their octaves are different.

This mechanics is so simple that it is understood on first inspection, and its practice is the easiest thing in the world. With a single line you modulate within the range of three octaves; and if you happen to want to pass still further beyond than this, which hardly occurs in proper Music, you always have the freedom to add accidental lines above and below, as in ordinary Music, with the difference that in the latter eleven lines are needed for three octaves whereas only one is needed in mine, and that I can express the range of five, six, and nearly seven octaves, that is, much more than the range of the large keyboard, with only three lines.

Position, such as my method adopts it, must not be confused with that practiced in ordinary Music: its principles are entirely different. Ordinary Music has it in view only to indicate the intervals to you and to dispose your organs in a certain way by the appearance of a greater or lesser distance between notes, without troubling to distinguish the kind of these intervals or the degree of this distance, so as to make knowing this independent of training. On the contrary, the knowledge of intervals, which properly speaking constitutes the basis of the Musician's science, seemed to me such an important point that I believed I should make it the essential object of my method. The following explanation shows how one can succeed by my characters in determining all the possible intervals by their kinds and by their names, without any effort other than that of reading these remarks a single time.

We first divide intervals into direct and inverted, and both of these further into simple and doubled.

I am going to define each of these intervals as it is considered in my system.

The direct interval is that which is contained between two sounds whose numerals are in accord with the progression, that is, the higher sound should also have the larger numeral, and the lower sound the smaller numeral. (See the plate [p. 98], Example 3.)

The inverted interval is that whose progression is contradicted by the numerals, that is, if the interval ascends, the second numeral is the smaller, and if the interval descends, the second numeral is the larger. (See the plate, Example 4.)

The simple interval is that which does not pass beyond the range of an octave. (See the plate, Example 5.)

The doubled interval is that which passes beyond the range of an octave. It is always the replica of a simple interval. (See Example 6.)

When you enter from one octave into the next one, that is, you pass from the line above or below it, or vice versa, the interval is simple if it is inverted, but if it is direct it will always be doubled.

This short explanation suffices to know in all profundity the kind of every possible interval. It is now necessary to learn to find its name on the spot.

All intervals can be considered as formed of three primary simple intervals, which are the second, the third, and the fourth, whose complements at the octave are the seventh, the sixth, and the fifth; to which, if you add this octave itself, you will have all the simple intervals without exception.

In order to find the name of every simple direct interval, then, one need only add one unit to the difference of the two numerals which express it. For example, let this interval be 1, 5: the difference of the two numerals is 4, to which adding one unit gives you 5, that is, the fifth for the name of this interval; it would be the same if you had had 2, 6, or 7, 3, etc. Let this other interval be 4, 5: the difference is 1, to which adding one unit gives you 2, that is, a second for the name of this interval. The rule is general.

If the direct interval is doubled, after having proceeded as before, 7 must be added for each octave, and you will again have very precisely the name of your interval. For example, you already see that $1\frac{3}{-}$ is a doubled third; you therefore add 7 to 3 and you will have 10, that is, a tenth for the name of your interval.

If the interval is inverted, you take the complement of the direct one: this is the name of your interval; thus, since the sixth is the complement of the third, and since this interval $-1\frac{}{3}-$ is an inverted third, I find that this is a sixth; if, moreover, it is doubled, you add 7 to it as many times as there are octaves. With these few rules, in whatever situation you are, you can name whatever interval you are presented with on the spot and without the least difficulty.

You see, then, by what I have just explained, what point we have reached in the art of *sol-fa*ing by the method I am proposing.

To begin with, all the notes are known without exception; not much effort was needed to retain the names of the seven unique characters, which are the sole ones for the expression of the sounds with which the memory had to be burdened; let one learn to sing them justly by ascending and descending, diatonically and by intervals, and we are all of a sudden relieved of the difficulties of their position.

To grasp this correctly, the knowledge of the intervals with respect to their naming is not an absolute necessity, provided that one correctly know the key from which one is leaving and that one know how to find that into which one is going. One can sing *do* and *fa* exactly without knowing that one is producing a fourth; and surely this would always be much less necessary by my method than by the common one, in which the clear and precise knowledge of the notes cannot make up for that of the intervals, whereas in mine, if the interval were unknown, the two notes which make it up would always be evident, without one ever being able to be mistaken about it in whatever Key and on whatever Clef one might be. Nevertheless, all the advantages are here found brought together in such a way that, by means of three or four very simple observations, my Student is in a position boldly to name every possible interval, whether on the same part or in jumping from one to another, and knowing more in this regard after an hour of application than Musicians with ten or twelve years of practice: for it must be noted that the operations of which I have just spoken are done all at once by the mind and with a speed very far from the long gradations indispensable in ordinary Music in order to arrive at the knowledge of intervals, and that, finally, rules would always be preferable to training, whether for their certainty or for their brevity, even when they only produce the same effect.

But it is nothing to have reached this point; there are other objects to consider and other difficulties to overcome.

When I assigned the name *do* to the fundamental sound of the natural scale above, I merely conformed to the spirit of the first institution of the name of notes and to the general custom of Musicians, and when I said that the fundamental of each key had the same right to bear the name *do* as this first sound, to which it is not assigned by any specific property, I was further authorized by the universal practice of that method called *transposition* in vocal Music.

In order to eliminate every scruple that might be thought of on this matter, my thinking must be explained at a bit more length. Should the name *do* necessarily and always be that of a fixed key of the keyboard or, on the contrary, should it preferably be applied to the fundamental of each key? This is the question that must be discussed.

To hear it enunciated in this way, it might perhaps be imagined that this is merely a question of words. Nevertheless, it influences practice too much to be disregarded; it is less a matter of the names in themselves than of determining the ideas that should be attached to them and on which there has not been too much agreement up until now.

Ask someone who sings what a *do* is, and he will tell you that it is the first tone of the scale; ask the same thing of an instrumentalist, he will respond to you that it is a certain fingerboard on his violin or key of his harpsichord.[23] They are both right; they are in accord only in one sense, and they would be in complete accord if the first did not represent this scale as mobile and the second this *do* as invariable.

Since it was agreed that a certain more or less determined sound would regulate the range of voices and the diapason of instruments by being so determined, this sound necessarily had to have a name, and a determinate name like the sound it expresses; let's give it the name *do*, I agree to this. Let's then regulate all those of the different sounds of the general scale by this name, so that we might indicate the relationship they have with it and with the different fingerboards or keys of the instruments; I further agree to this, and up to this point the instrumental player is right.

But these sounds to which we have just given names, and those keys which make them heard, are arranged in such a way that they have certain relationships among themselves and with the key of the keyboard called *do* that properly speaking constitute what is called a key, and this key, of which *do* is the fundamental, is the one that the black keys of the organ and of the harpsichord make heard when they are played in a certain order— otherwise it would be impossible to employ all the same keys on the keyboard for any other key of which *do* was not fundamental, nor in that of *do* to employ any of the black keys of the keyboard, which do not even have any specific names, and by taking different ones are sometimes called sharps and sometimes flats, according to the keys in which they are employed.

Now, when one wants to establish another fundamental, one must necessarily make such a choice of the sounds one wants to employ that they have precisely the same relationships with it as *re, mi, sol*, and all the other sounds of the natural scale have with *do*. This is the case in which the Singer is right to say to the Instrumental player: Why do you not make use of the same names to express the same relationships? Furthermore, I believe it is hardly necessary to remark that one must always determine the fundamental by its natural name, and that it is only after this determination that it takes the name *do*.

It is true that, by always assigning the same names to the same keys of the instrument and to the same notes of the Music, it seems at first that a more direct relationship is established between this note and this key of the keyboard, and that the one more easily raises the idea of the other than would be the case in always seeking an equality of relationships between the numerals of the notes and the fundamental numeral on the one hand, and on the other between the fundamental sound and the keys of the instrument.

It can be seen that I am not trying to weaken the force of the objection: shall I for my part dare flatter myself that prejudices will take nothing away from that of my answers?

I shall first remark that the relationship determined by the same names existing between the keys of the instrument and the notes of the Music has many exceptions and difficulties to which sufficient attention is not always paid.

We have three Clefs in Music, and these three Clefs have eight positions; thus, in accordance with these different positions, there are eight different keys of the keyboard for the same position, and eight positions for the same key of the keyboard and for each key of the instrument. It is certain that this multiplication of ideas impairs their clarity; there are even many Instrumental players who never grasp them all in a certain aspect, even though all eight of these Clefs are used on a number of instruments.

But let us limit ourselves in this examination to what happens on a single Clef. It is imagined that the same note should always express the idea of the same key, and this is nonetheless quite false: for by very common accidentals, caused by the sharps and the flats, it happens at every moment not only that the note *si* becomes the key of the keyboard called *do*, that the note *mi* becomes the key called *fa*, and reciprocally, but also that a note made sharp on the clef, and sharp by an accidental, ascends an entire tone; that a *fa* becomes a *sol*, a *do* a *re*, etc.; and that, on the contrary, by a double flat, a *mi* will become a *re*, a *si* a *la*, and so with the others. Where in this, then, is the precision of our ideas? What! I see a *sol* and I must play a *la*! Is this that relationship, so exact, so vaunted, to which one wants to sacrifice that of the modulation?

I nonetheless do not deny that there is something very ingenious about the invention of the accidentals added to the Clef in order to indicate, not the different keys, for they are not always known by this, but the different alterations they cause. They do not explain the theory of progressions so poorly; it is a pity that they make us pay so dearly for this advantage by the difficulty they cause in the practice of singing and of playing instruments. What does it matter to me to know that a certain semitone has changed place, and that it has thereby been transported to that place so as to produce a leading tone, a fourth or a sixth note, if I cannot succeed in playing it without tormenting myself anyway, and if I need to remember exactly those five sharps or those five flats in order to apply them to all the notes I may find on the same positions or at their octaves, and this precisely at the point when playing becomes most difficult by the specific difficulty of the instrument? But let us not imagine that Musicians devote themselves to this effort in practice; they follow a much more convenient route, and there is not a skillful man among them who, after having warmed up in the key in which he must play, pays more attention to the degree of the key in which he finds himself and whose progression he knows than to the sharp or to the flat that affects it.

In general, what is called singing and playing naturally is perhaps what is worst devised in Music: for if the names of the notes have any real utility, it can be only to express certain relationships, certain specific affects in the progressions of sounds. Now, since the relationships of the sounds and the progression also change as soon as the key changes, reason says that the names of the notes must likewise change by relating them analogously to the new key; otherwise, the meaning of the names is overturned and the words are deprived of the sole advantage they can have, which is to arouse other ideas with those of the sounds. The transition from *mi* to *fa*, or from *si* to *do*, naturally raises the idea of the semitone in the Musician's mind. Nevertheless, if one is on the key of *si* or on that of *mi*, the interval from *si* to *do* or from *mi* to *fa* is always one tone, and never a semitone. Thus, instead of retaining names that deceive the mind and shock an ear habituated to a different practice, it is important to apply others whose recognized meaning is not contradictory and proclaims the intervals they should express. Now, all the relationships of sounds of the diatonic system are expressed in the major, whether in ascending or descending, in the octave contained between two *do*s following the natural order, and in the minor in the octave contained between two *la*s following the same order in descending alone, for in ascending the minor mode is subjected to different affects which present new reflections for theory, which are not my subject today and which in no way affect the system I am proposing.

I do not deny that, with regard to instruments, my method does not deviate very much from the spirit of the ordinary method; but as I do not believe the ordinary method to be extremely sound, and as I even believe that I am demonstrating its defects, before condemning me for this reason it would always be necessary to put oneself in a position to convince me not of the difference, but of the disadvantage of my own.

Let us continue by explaining the mechanics. I recognize in Music twelve original sounds or pitches, the first of which is C *sol do*, which serves as root for the natural scale: to take one of the other sounds as fundamental is to attribute to it all the properties of *do*; this is properly speaking to transpose the natural scale higher or lower by as many degrees. In order to determine this fundamental sound, I make use of the corresponding word, that is, of *sol*, *re*, *la*, etc., and I write it in the margin above the tune I want to notate; then this *sol* or this *re*, which can be called the Clef, becomes *do* and, thus serving as root for a new key and for a new scale, all the notes of the Keyboard become relative to it, and then it is only in virtue of the relationship they have with this fundamental sound that they can be employed.

Whatever may be said about it, this is the true principal to which one must adhere in composing, in warming up, and in Singing; and if you would have the notes retain their natural names, you would necessarily have to consider them simultaneously under a double relationship, namely, in relation to C *sol do* and to the natural scale, and in relation to the particular fundamental sound according to which you are constrained to regulate the progression and its alterations. It is only an ignoramus who plays the sharps and flats without thinking of the key he is in, and then God knows what precision there can be in his playing!

In order then to form a Pupil by following my method, I speak of instruments—for, as for Singing, the thing is so easy that it would be superfluous to pause over it—it is first necessary to teach him to know and to play all the keys of his instrument by their natural name, that is on the Clef of *do*. These first names should serve him as a rule for then finding other fundamentals and all the possible modulations in the major keys, to which alone it suffices to pay attention, as I shall soon explain.

I then come to the Clef *sol*, and, after having him play the *sol*, I inform him that this *sol*, becoming the fundamental of the key, should then be called *do*, and I have him go through the whole natural scale on this *do*, above or below, according to the range of his instrument; as there will be some difference in the key of the keyboard or in the placement of the fingers due to the transposed semitone, I will have him note it. After having practiced in these two keys for some time, I will lead him to the Clef *re*; and having him call *do* the natural *re*, I have him recommence a new scale on this *do*, and thus running through all the fundamentals by fifths, he will finally find himself in a position of having warmed up in major mode on the twelve pitches of the chromatic system, and of knowing perfectly the relationship and the different affects of all the keys of his instrument in each of these twelve different keys.

Then I put easy Music in his hands. The Clef shows him which key of the keyboard should take the name *do*, and as he has learned to find *mi* and *sol*, etc., that is, the major third and the fifth, etc., on this fundamental, a 3 and a 5 are soon familiar signs for him, and if the movements are familiar to him and the instrument does not have its particular difficulties, he would then be in a position to play at sight every sort of Music in all the keys and on all the Clefs. But before speaking any further about this point, the explanation of the part that pertains to the expression of sounds must be completed.

With regard to the minor mode, I have already remarked that nature does not at all teach it to us directly. Perhaps it arises from a succession of the progression of which I spoke in the experiment of the pipes, in which it is found that at the fourth fifth, this *do* that had served as the basis of the operation, makes a minor third with *la*, which is then the fundamental sound. Perhaps it is also from thence that that great correspondence arises between the major mode *do* and the minor mode of the sixth note, and reciprocally between the minor mode *la* and the major mode of its mediant.

Furthermore, the progression of the sounds affected by the minor mode is precisely the same one found in the octave contained between two *la*s, since, according to M. Rameau, it is essential for the minor mode to have its minor third and sixth, and for there to be only that octave in which, all the other sounds being ordered as they should be, the third and the sixth naturally happen to be minor.

Taking *la* for the name of the tonic of minor keys, then, and expressing it by the numeral 6, I always leave to its mediant *do* the privilege of being not tonic, but characteristic fundamental; in this I will be conforming to nature, which does not at all make a fundamental properly speaking known to us in minor keys, and at the same time I will be maintaining uniformity in the notes and in the numerals which express them and the analogy found between the major and the minor modes taken on the two pitches *do* and *la*.

But this *do*, which, by transposition, should always be the name of the tonic in the major keys and that of the mediant in the minor keys, can consequently be taken on each of the twelve pitches of the chromatic system; and, in order to designate it, it will suffice to place the name of that pitch taken on the keyboard in the natural order in the margin. It is seen by this that if the song is in the key of *do* major or of *la* minor, one will have to write *do* in the margin; if the song is in the key of *re* major or of *si* minor, one must write *re* in the margin; for the key of *mi* major or of *do*-sharp minor, one will write *mi* in the margin, and so on. That is, that the note written in the margin, or the Clef, precisely designates the key of the keyboard that should be called *do* and as a consequence should be tonic in the major key, mediant in the minor one, and fundamental in them both—about which it will be noted that I have always called this *do* fundamental, and not tonic, since it is only such in the major keys, but that it serves as fundamental to the relationship and to the name of the notes and even to the different octaves in both modes alike. But, to grasp this properly, the knowledge of this Clef is of use only for instruments, and those who sing never need to pay attention to it.

It follows from this that the same Clef under the same name of *do* nevertheless designates two different keys, namely, the major of which it is tonic and the minor of which it is mediant, and consequently that the tonic is a third below it. It further follows that the same names of the notes and the notes affected in the same way, at least in descending, serve for both modes alike, so that, not only is there no need to make a special study of the minor modes, but that one might quite possibly even be excused from knowing them, since the relationships expressed by the same numerals are not at all different when the fundamental is tonic than when it is mediant; nevertheless, for the sake of the conspicuousness of the key of the keyboard and for ease in warming up, the Clef will be written entirely simply when it is tonic, and when it is mediant a small horizontal line will be added below it. (See the plate [p. 98], Examples 7 and 8.)

Changes of key must now be spoken of; but as the accidental alterations of the sounds often present themselves, and as they always occur in the minor mode in ascending from the dominant to the tonic, I should first explain the signs.

The sharp is expressed by a small slanted line that intersects the note by rising from left to right; for example, *sol*-sharp is expressed thus: ⸌; *fa*-sharp thus: 4. The flat is also expressed by a similar line that intersects the note by descending: ⸍, ⸍; and these signs, simpler than those in use, further serve to show the eye the sort of alteration they cause.

As for the natural, it has become necessary only through the poor choice of sharp and flat, because, being separate characters from the notes they alter, if several are found in a row under one or the other of these signs, one can never distinguish those which should be affected from those which should not be without making use of the natural. But since in my system the sign of alteration, aside from the simplicity of its shape, further has the advantage of always being inherent in the altered note, it is clear that all those on which one does not see any should be played at the natural tone they should have on the fundamental one is in. I therefore eliminate the natural as useless, and I further eliminate it as equivocal, since it is common to find it employed in two entirely opposite senses: for some make use of it to eliminate the alteration caused by the signs of the Clef, and others, on the contrary, to put the note back onto the tone it should have in conformity to these same signs.

With regard to changes in key, whether when passing from the major to the minor or from one tonic to another, it might suffice to change the Clef; but as it is extremely advantageous to make knowing their Clef unnecessary for those who sing, and as, moreover, it would require a sure training to find the relationship of one Clef to the other easily, this is the precaution that must be added. It is merely a matter of expressing the first note of this change in such a way that represents what it was in the key from which one is leaving and what it is in that into which one is entering. For this, I first write this first note between two double perpendicular lines by the numeral which represents it in the preceding key, adding above it the Clef or the name of the fundamental of the key into which one is going to enter; I then write this same note by the numeral which expresses it in the key it begins. So that, with regard to the course of the Song, the first numeral indicates the key of the note and the second serves to find its name.

You see (plate [p. 98], Example 9) not only that from the key of *sol* you pass into that of *do*, but that the note *fa* of the preceding key is the same as the note *do* which happens to be the first in the one you are entering.

In the other example (see [p. 98] Example 10), the first note *do* of the first change would be the *mi*-flat of the preceding mode, and the first note *mi* of the second change would be the *do*-sharp of the preceding mode—a very convenient comparison for voices and even for instruments, which moreover have the advantage of the change of Clef. It can also be noted that the fundamental always changes in changes of mode, even though the tonic remains the same, which depends on the rules I have explained above.

There remains a difficulty concerning the range of the keyboard of which it is time to speak. It is not enough to know the progression assigned to each mode, the fundamental that belongs to it, whether this fundamental is tonic or mediant, nor, finally, to know how to relate it to the place that suits it within the range of the natural scale, but it must further be known to which octave and, in a word, to which precise key of the keyboard it should pertain.

The ordinary large keyboard is five octaves in extent, and I shall restrict myself to it for this explanation, while remarking solely that one is always free to extend it on one end or the other as far as one likes without making notation more diffuse or more inconvenient.

Let us therefore suppose that I am in the Clef of *do*, that is, on the sound of *do* major or of *la* minor, which constitutes the natural keyboard. The keyboard is then found to be arranged in such a way that from the first *do* below it to the last *do* above I find four complete octaves, aside from the two portions which remain above and below, between the *do* and the *fa* that end the keyboard on the one end and the other.

I call A the first octave contained between the *do* below and the following one toward the right, that is, everything contained between 1 and 7, inclusively. I call B the octave that begins on the second *do*, counting likewise toward the right; C, the third; D, the fourth; etc.; until E, where a fifth octave begins that might be pressed further if one likes. With regard to the portion below, which begins on the first *fa* and ends on the first *si*, as it is incomplete, not beginning with the fundamental, we shall call it Octave X; and this letter X will serve in every sort of key to designate the notes that remain at the low end of the keyboard below the first tonic.

Let us suppose that I want to notate a tune in the Clef of *do*, that is, in the key of *do* major or of *la* minor. I write *do* at the top of the page in the margin, and I make it mediant or tonic, according to whether or not I add a small horizontal line.

Knowing in this way which pitch should be the fundamental of the key, it is now merely a question of finding in which of the five octaves the Song I have to express is best played, and of writing the letter at the beginning of the line on which I place my notes. The two spaces above and below will represent the adjoining stages and will serve for notes which might exceed above or below the octave represented by the letter I have put at the beginning of the line. I have already noted that if the Song happens to be bizarre enough to pass beyond this range, one is always free to add a line above or below, which can sometimes occur with instruments.

But as Octaves are always counted from one fundamental to another, and as these fundamentals are different, according to the different keys one is in, the octaves are also taken on different degrees and are sometimes higher or lower accordingly as their fundamental is distant from *C sol do* natural.

In order to represent this operation clearly, I have added here (see the plate [p. 98]) a general table of all the sounds of the keyboard, arranged in relation to the twelve pitches of the chromatic system taken successively as fundamental.

In it the progression of the different sounds in relation to the key one is in is seen in a simple and perceptible manner. One will also see, from the following explanation, how it facilitates the playing of instruments to the point of making a game of it, not only in relation to instruments with separate key pads, such as the Bassoon, the Oboe, the Flute, the Bass Viol, and the Harpsichord, but also with regard to the Violin, Cello, and every other type without exception.

This table represents the whole range of the keyboard, combined on twelve pitches: the natural keyboard in which *do* retains its proper name is found here at the sixth rank, marked by an asterisk at each extremity, and it is to this rank that all the others should be related as to the common term of comparison. One sees that it extends from the *fa* below to that above for a distance of five octaves, which is what makes up the larger keyboard.

I have already said that the interval contained from the first 1 to the first 7 that follows it toward the right is called A; that the interval contained from the second 1 to the next 7 is called octave B; the next, octave C; etc.; until the fifth 1, on which the octave E begins, which I have carried here only to *fa*. With regard to the four notes which are to the left of the first *do*, I have also already said that they belong to octave X, to which I thus give a letter out of order in order to express the fact that this octave is not complete, since it would be necessary to descend lower than the keyboard allows in order to reach *do*.

But if I am in another key, as for example in the Clef of *re*, then this *re* changes name and becomes *do*; this is why octave A, contained from the first tonic to its seventh note, is one degree higher than the corresponding octave of the preceding key—which is easy to see by means of the table, since this *do* of the third rank, that is, of the Clef of *re*, corresponds to the *re* of the natural Clef of *do*, on which it falls perpendicularly, and, by the same reason, octave X has more notes than the same octave of the Clef of *do*, since in rising the octaves grow more distant from the lowest note of the keyboard.

This is why the octaves ascend from the Clef of *do* to the Clef of *mi*, and descend from the same Clef of *do* to that of *fa*: for this *fa*, which is the lowest note of the keyboard, then becomes fundamental and consequently begins the first octave A.

Everything contained between the two first oblique lines toward the left always belong to octave A, therefore, but at different degrees according to what key one is in. For example, the same key of the keyboard will be *do* in the major key of *mi*, *re* in that of *re*, *mi* in that of *do*, *fa* in that of *si*, *sol* in that of *la*, *la* in that of *sol*, *si* in that of *fa*. It is always the same key of the keyboard since it is the same column, and it is the same octave since this column is encompassed between the same oblique lines. Let us give an example so as to express the Key, the octave, and the key of the keyboard without any equivocation. (See the plate [p. 98], Example 11.)

This example is in the Clef of *re*; it must therefore be related to the fourth rank answering to the same Clef, octave B, marked on the line, showing that the superior interval, in which the song begins, answers to the superior octave C; thus, the note 5, marked by an *a* in the table, is precisely that which answers to the first of this example. This is enough to make understood that in each part one should place the letter corresponding to the octave in which this part is played most at the beginning of the line, and that the spaces which are above and below will be for the superior and inferior octaves.

The horizontal lines serve to separate, from semitone to semitone, the different fundamentals whose names are written to the right of the table.

The perpendicular lines show that all the notes traversed by the same line are always merely the same key of the keyboard, whose natural name, if it has one, is found on the sixth rank, and the other names in the other ranks of the same column according to the key one is in. These perpendicular lines are of two sorts: the black ones, which serve to show that the numerals they join represent this natural key of the keyboard, and the dotted ones, which are for the white or altered keys of the keyboard, in such a way that by means of this table one can know on the spot in any key whatsoever which notes must be altered in order to play in that key.

The Clefs you see at the beginning serve to determine which note should bear the name of *do*, and to indicate the key, as I have already said; there are five of them that can be duplicates since the flat of the highest one—marked *b*—and the sharp of the lowest one—marked *d*—produce the same effect.* It will nonetheless not be a bad idea to retain the denominations I have chosen and which, abstracting from every other reason, are preferable at least because they are the most commonly used.

It is also easy by means of this table precisely to indicate the range of each part, vocal as well as instrumental, and the place it will occupy in these various octaves according to the key one will be in.

I am convinced that, by following exactly the principles I have just explained, there is no Song that one will not be in a position to *sol-fa* in very little time and play on any instrument whatsoever with all possible ease. Let us recall in some detail what I have said on this point.

Instead of first beginning by having this Student perform Tunes mechanically, instead of having him play, sometimes sharps, sometimes flats, without his being able to conceive why he is doing so, let the Teacher's first care be to make him understand profoundly all the sounds of his instrument in relation to the different keys in which they can be played.

For this, after having taught him the natural names of all the keys of his instrument, they must be presented to him with another point of view and related back to a general principle. He already knows all the sounds of the octave according to the natural scale; it is now a question of his making an analysis of them. Let us assume him before a Harpsichord. The Keyboard is divided into sixty-one keys. One explains to him that these keys, taken in

---

*It is only by virtue of temperament that the same key of the keyboard can serve as the flat of the one and the sharp of the other, since, moreover, no one is ignorant of the fact that two major semitones can make up a whole tone.

succession and without distinguishing whites or blacks, express sounds which go from left to right by ascending by semitones. Taking the key *do* for the basis of our operation, we will find the others of the natural scale arranged with regard to it in the following manner.

The second note, *re*, at an interval of one tone to the right; that is, an intermediary key must be left between the *do* and the *re* for the division of the two semitones.

The third, *mi*, at an interval of another tone from *re* and two tones from the *do*, in such a way that between the *re* and the *mi* an intermediary key must also be left.

The fourth, *fa*, at a semitone from the *mi* and at two and one-half tones from the *do*; consequently, the *fa* is the key which immediately follows the *mi*, without leaving any between them.

The fifth, *sol*, at a tone from the *fa* and at three and one-half tones from the *do*; an intermediary key must be left.

The sixth, *la*, at a tone from the *sol* and at four and one-half tones from the *do*; another intermediary key.

The seventh, *si*, at a tone from the *la* and at five and one-half tones from the *do*; another intermediary key.

The eighth, *do* above, at a semitone from the *si* and at six tones from the first *do* of which it is the octave; consequently, the *si* is contiguous to the *do* which follows it, without an intermediary key.

By continuing thus the whole length of the keyboard, only the replicas of the same intervals will be found, and the Student will easily be made familiar with them as with the numerals which express them and which indicate their distance from the fundamental *do*. He will be made to note that there is an intermediary key of the keyboard between each degree of the octave, except between the *mi* and the *fa* and between the *si* and the *do* above, where two intervals of a semitone each are found which have their fixed position on the scale.

It will also be observed that in the Clef of *do* all the black keys are precisely those which he must take and that all the whites ones are the intermediary ones which he must leave alone. One will not at all seek to have him discover the mystery of this distribution, and he will only be told that, as the keyboard would be too extended or the keys too small if they were all uniform, and that as, moreover, the Clef of *do* is the one most used in Music, for more convenience the white keys, which are only little used, have been expelled from the class of intervals. One will also be very careful to affect a knowing air in speaking to him of major and minor tones and semitones, of commas, and of temperament; all this is absolutely useless for practice, at least at this time. In a word, as little intelligence as a Teacher may have and as poorly as he may possess his Art, he has so many occasions to shine while instructing that it is inexcusable when his vanity is a total loss for the Disciple.

When it is found that the Student has a good enough grasp of his natural keyboard, then one will begin to have him transpose in other Clefs by first choosing those in which the natural sounds are least altered. Let us take, for example, the Clef of *sol*.

This word *sol*, you will say to the Student, written thus in the margin, means that one must transfer the name and all the properties of the *do* and of the natural scale to *sol* and to its octave. Then, after having exhorted him to recall the arrangement of the tones of that scale, you will invite him to apply this in the same order to *sol* considered as fundamental, that is, as a *do*. At first, it will be a question of finding *re*; if the Student is well directed, he will find it himself and will play the *la* natural, which is precisely in relation to *sol* in the same situation as *re* is in relation to *do*; and to find *mi*, he will play *si*; to find *la*, he will play *do*; and you will have him note that in actuality these two latter keys of the keyboard leave a semitone as an intermediary interval, just like the *mi* and the *fa* in the natural scale. Continuing on in this way, he will play *re* for *sol*, and *mi* for *la*. Until now he will have encountered only natural keys of the keyboard to express the scale of the Octave *do* in the Octave *sol*; so that, if you continue and were to ask him for *si* without adding anything, it is almost inevitable that he will play *fa* natural; then you will stop there and will ask him if he doesn't recall whether between natural *la* and *si* he didn't find an interval of one tone and an intermediary key of the keyboard; at the same time you will show him this interval on the Clef of *do*, and, returning to that of *sol*, you will place his finger on *mi*-natural, which you will name *la* while asking where *si* is; then he will surely correct himself and play *fa*-sharp; he will perhaps play *sol*, but instead of growing impatient, one must seize this occasion to explain to him quite clearly the ordering of tones and semitones in relation to the octave *do*, and without distinguishing the black and white keys, about which he is no longer in a position of being capable of being mistaken.

Then one must have him go through the keyboard from high to low and from low to high, while having him name the keys of the keyboard in keeping with this new key; you will also have him observe that the white key employed in it becomes necessary in order to make up the semitone which should be between *la* and *si*, which is against the order of the scale. You will take care, above all, to make him understand that in this Clef *sol*-natural is really a *do*, *la* a *re*, *si* a *mi*, etc. So that these names and the position of their relative keys of the keyboard become as familiar to him as in the Clef of *do*, and that, as long as he is in the Clef of *sol*, he envisions the keyboard only through this second explanation.

When he is found to be sufficiently trained, he is to be put in the Clef of *re* with the same precautions, and he will easily be led to find the *mi* and the *si* on two white keys by himself; this third Clef will succeed in enlightening him about the location of all the tones of the scale relative to any fundamental whatsoever, and in all probability no explanation will be needed to find the order of the tones on all the other fundamentals.

It will then be merely a question of training, and it will depend more on the Teacher to contribute to forming him if he applies himself to making it easy for the Student to practice all the intervals by remarks about the positioning of the fingers, which soon makes the mechanics familiar.

After this, from short explanations of the minor mode, of the alterations that belong to it, and of those which arise from the modulation in the course of a single piece, a Student who is well directed by this method should profoundly understand his keyboard on all the keys in less than three months; let's give him six months for this, at the end of which we will leave off this to put him to playing, and I maintain that, if he also has some knowledge of movements, he will then play at sight tunes notated by my characters, at least those that do not require a great deal of training in fingering. Let him take six more months to perfect his hand and his ear, whether for harmony or for rhythm, and in the space of one year you have a Musician of the first rank, practicing all Clefs alike, knowing the modes and all the keys, all the pitches that belong to them, the whole succession of modulation, and transposing every piece of Music into all sorts of keys with the most perfect ease.

This is what seems to me evidently to follow from the practice of my system and which I am ready to confirm not only by proofs from reasoning, but by experience, to the eyes of whoever wants to see the result.

Furthermore, what I have said of the Harpsichord applies likewise to every other instrument, with some slight differences with regard to stringed instruments, which give rise to different alterations that belong to each key. As I am writing here only for Teachers to whom this is known, I shall say about it only what is absolutely necessary in order to bring an objection to light that might be opposed to me and in order to provide its solution.

It is a fact of experience that the different keys in Music have every one of them a certain character that belongs to them and which distinguishes each in particular. *A mi la* major, for example, is brilliant; *F do fa* is majestic; *si*-flat major is tragic; *fa* minor is sad; *do* minor is tender; and all the other keys likewise have, by some privilege, I don't know what ability to arouse this or that feeling, which skillful masters well know how to make prevail.[24] Now, since modulation is the same in all the major keys, why should one major key arouse a certain passion rather than another major key? Why does the same transition from *re* to *fa* produce different effects when it is taken on different fundamentals, since the relationship remains the same? Why does this tune played in *A mi la* no longer produce that expression it had in *G re sol*?[25] It is not possible to attribute this difference to the change in the fundamental, since, as I have said, each of these fundamentals taken separately has nothing in itself which can arouse any feeling other than that which its higher or lower octave makes heard. It is not at all properly by sounds that we are touched; it is by the relationships they have among themselves, and it is solely by the choice of these charming relationships that a beautiful composition can move the heart by flattering the ear. Now, if the relationship of a *do* to a *sol* or of a *re* to a *la* is the same in each of the keys, why does it produce different effects?

Perhaps Musicians might be found who are at a loss to provide an explanation; and it would in fact be quite inexplicable if this identity of relationships were rigorously admitted between the sounds expressed by the same names and represented by the same intervals in all the keys.

But these relationships have slight differences between them, according to the pitches on which they are taken, and it is these differences, so small in appearance, that cause that variety of expression in Music, perceptible to every refined ear and perceptible to such a degree that he is hardly a Musician who, hearing a concert, does not recognize in what key it is being played at that time.

Let us compare, for example, *C sol do* minor and *D la re*.[26] These are two minor modes all of whose sounds are expressed by the same intervals and by the same names, each relative to its tonic; nevertheless, the affect produced is not at all the same, and it is incontestable that *C sol do* is more touching than *D la re*. In order to discover the reason for this, it is necessary to enter into a fairly long investigation whose result is more or less the following. The interval found between the tonic of *re* and its second note is a little bit smaller than that which is found between the tonic of *C sol do* and its second note; on the contrary, the semitone found between the second note and the mediant of *D la re* is a little bit larger than that which is between the second note and the mediant of *C sol do*, so that, the minor third remaining about equal in both cases, in *C sol do* it is divided into two intervals slightly unequal to those in *D la re*. This makes the interval of the semitone smaller than the quantity of which that of the tone is larger.

One also finds that the semitone contained between *sol* natural and *la*-flat is, by the usual tuning of the Harpsichord, a little bit smaller than that which is between *la* and *si*-flat. Now, the more the two sounds which form a semitone approach one another, the more tender and touching is the transition; it is experience which teaches us this, and this is, I believe, the genuine reason why the minor mode of *C sol do* moves us more than that of *D la re*. If however the diminution goes to the point of causing an alteration in the harmony, and throwing harshness into the Song, then the feeling changes into sadness, and this is the effect we experience in *F do fa* minor.²⁷

By continuing our investigations into this matter of taste, we might perhaps nearly succeed in finding the reasons for the different feelings aroused by the various keys of Music by these slight differences that remain in the relationships of sounds and of intervals. But if one also wanted to find the cause of these differences, it would be necessary for this to enter into a detail of which my subject excuses me, and which one will find sufficiently explained in the works of M. Rameau. I shall content myself with saying here in general that, as it was necessary to make use of the same notes for several uses so as to avoid multiplying sounds, they have only been able to have been altered a little, which makes it so that they lose something of the precision they should have with regard to their different relationships. For example, *mi* considered as the minor third of *do*, is not at all strictly speaking the same *mi* which should make up the fifth of *la*; the difference is small, true, but after all it exists, and to make it vanish this fifth had to be tempered slightly; by this means the same sound has been employed for these two uses, but from this it also arises that the tone from *re* to *mi* is not the same type as that from *do* to *re*, and so with the others.

I might then be reproached with having eliminated the differences with my new signs, and with thereby having destroyed that variety of expression so advantageous in Music. I have many things to respond to all this.

In the first place, temperament is a true defect; it is an alteration which art has made to harmony for want of being able to do better. The harmonics of a pitch do not at all give us the tempered fifth, and the mechanic of temperament introduces tones so harsh into modulation, for example *re*- and *sol*-sharp, that they are not bearable to the ear. It would not be an error, therefore, to avoid this defect, and especially in Musical characters, which, not participating in the vice of the instrument, should preserve all the purity of the harmony at least by their meaning.

Furthermore, the alterations caused by the different keys are not at all practiced by voices; for example, one does not intone the interval 4 5 differently than one would intone this one, 5 6, although this interval is not entirely the same, and one modulates it in singing with the same precision in all keys, in spite of the particular alterations that the imperfection of the instruments introduces into these different keys, and to which the voice never conforms itself, at least if it is not constrained to do so by its unison with the instruments.

Nature teaches us to modulate in all keys precisely in all the justness of the intervals; voices guided by it do exactly this. Must we move away from what it prescribes in order to subject ourselves to a defective practice, and must we sacrifice the natural expression of the most perfect of all not only to the benefit, but to the vice of the Instruments? It is here that one should recall everything I said above about the generation of sounds, and it is by this that one will be convinced that the use of my signs is simply a very faithful and very exact expression of the operations of nature.

In the second place, in the most important instruments, as the Organ, the Harpsichord, and the Viol, the keys of the keyboard or the keypads are fixed, the various alterations of each key depend uniquely upon tuning, and they are practiced in the same way by those who play them, although they do not at all think so. It is the same with Flutes, Oboes, Bassoons, and other wind Instruments; the placement of the fingers is fixed for each sound, and the same will be the case for the characters, without Students practicing temperament any less in order to understand its expression.

Furthermore, no difficulty could be raised against me regarding the above discussion that did not at the same time attack ordinary Music, in which, very far from the small differences of intervals of the same type being indicated by any mark, even the specific differences are not so indicated, since major and minor thirds or sixths are expressed by the same intervals and the same positions, whereas in my system the different numerals employed in intervals of the same denomination at least make it known whether they are major or minor.

Finally, in order to remove this difficulty all at once, it is for the Teacher and for the ear to guide the Student in the practice of the different keys and the alterations that belong to them; ordinary Music does not at all give rules for this practice which I may not apply to mine with even more advantage, and the Student's fingers will be much more happily guided by having him practice the intervals on his Violin with the alterations that belong to them in each key by moving his finger back and forth a little, than by that throng of sharps and flats which, producing small intervals between them and not contributing to form the ear, trouble the Student with differences which are imperceptible to him for a long time.

If the perfection of a system of Music consisted in being able to express a great quantity of sounds, it would be easy by adopting that of M. Sauveur to divide the whole extent of a single octave into 3010 decameridians or equal intervals, whose sounds would be represented by differently shaped notes.[28] But what use would all these characters serve, since the diversity of sounds which they would express would neither be within the range of ears nor within that of our vocal organs? It is therefore no less useless to learn to distinguish *do*-double-sharp from *re*-natural, as soon as we are constrained to practice it on this same *re*, and since we will never find ourselves in the position to have to express in notation the difference which should be found in it because these two sounds cannot be relative to the same modulation.

Let us hold as a certain maxim that all the sounds of a mode should always be considered by the relationship they have with the fundamental of that mode; that, therefore, the corresponding intervals should be perfectly equal in all the keys of the same type; also, let them be considered as such in composition, and if they are not rigorously so in practice, Keyboard Makers at any rate lavish all their skill in tuning so as to make the difference imperceptible.

But this is not the place to go on any further about this point. If in the view of the most Learned Academy of Europe my system has marked advantages over and above the ordinary method for vocal Music, it seems to me that these advantages are much more considerable in the instrumental part[29] — at least I shall expound the reasons I have for believing this is so: it is for experience to confirm their solidity. Musicians will not fail to cry out with indignation, and to say that they play with the greatest ease by the ordinary method and that they do with their instruments all that can be done with them by any method whatsoever. I agree; I admire them in this regard, and in fact it does not seem that performance may be pushed to a higher degree of perfection than it has been today; but in the end, when they are made to see that this point of perfection can be reached more certainly in less time and with less trouble, perhaps they will be constrained to admit that the marvels they accomplish are not so inseparable from bar lines, quarter notes and eighth notes that they may not be attained by other routes. Specifically, I am undertaking to prove to them that they have even more merit than they think, since they make up for the defects of the method of which they make use by dint of their talent.

If the part of my system that I have just explained is clearly understood, it will be perceived that it presents a general method for expressing all the sounds used in Music without exception, not, in truth, in an absolute manner, but relative to a specified fundamental sound, which produces a considerable advantage by always keeping the key of the piece and the succession of the modulation before you. It now remains for me to present another still easier method to enable one to notate all these same sounds in the same manner on a horizontal line without ever needing lines or intervals to express the different octaves.

In order to furnish this, then, I make use of the simplest of all signs, namely the dot; and here is how I have used it. If I leave the octave in which I began in order to produce a note in the range of the superior octave and which begins with the *do* above, then I put a dot over that note on which I leave my octave, and, once put in place, this dot is an indication that not only the note over which it is placed, but also all those which follow it without any sign that cancels it should be taken within the range of that superior Octave into which I have entered. For example:

$$\text{Do}$$
$$c\ 1\ 3\ 5\ \dot{1}\ 3\ 5$$

The dot you see over the second *do* indicates that you enter there into the octave above that in which you began, and that, consequently, the 3 and the 5 which follow are also in that same superior octave and are not at all the same as those you would have otherwise intoned.

On the contrary, if I want to leave the octave in which I happen to be in order to pass into that which is below, then I put the dot below the note by which I enter it:

$$\text{Do}$$
$$d\ 5\ 3\ 1\ \underset{.}{5}\ 3\ 1$$

Thus, this first 5 being the same as the last one in the preceding example, by the dot you see here under the second 5 you are informed that you leave the octave into which you ascended and reenter that by which you formerly began.

In a word: when the dot is above the note you pass into the superior octave, if it is below, you pass into the inferior, and, if you would change octave on each note, or when you might desire to ascend or descend two or three octaves all at once or in a row, the rule is always general, and you have only to put as many dots below or above as you have octaves to descend or ascend.

This is not to say that on each dot you would ascend or descend an octave, but that on each dot you will enter into a different octave, into another level, whether by ascending by descending, in relation to the fundamental sound *do*, which is indeed therefore found in the same octave when descending diatonically, but not when ascending. By this fashion of notating, the dot is equal to two lines and to two intervals by the preceding fashion; everything that is in the same position pertains to the same dot, and you need another dot only when you pass into another position, that is, into another octave. About which it must be noted that I make use of this word octave but improperly and in order not to multiply terms uselessly, because properly speaking the range I designate by this word is filled only by a tier of seven notes, the *do* above not being included in it.

Here is a series of notes which will be easy to *sol-fa* by the rules I have just established.

Sol
    d 1 7 1̇ 2 3 1 5 4 5 6 7 5 1̇ 7 6 5 4 3 2 4 2̇ 1 7 6 5 3 4
    d 5 5̣ 1̣.

And here (see the plate [p. 98], Example 12) the same example notated according to the first method.

Although the dots always lead you quite precisely in a long succession of Song, they nonetheless do not make known to you which octave you find yourself in relative to that which has preceded; this is why, in order to know precisely the place you are on the keyboard, it would be necessary to go by reascending to the letter at the beginning of the tune—an exact process, true, but in other respects a bit too lengthy. In order to avoid this, I put the letter of the octave in which one finds oneself at the beginning of each line, not the first note of this line, but the last of the preceding line, and this so that there is no exception to the ordering of the dots.

Example

Fa
    d 1 7 1̇ 2 3 4 5 6 7 5 1̇ 5̣ 2̇ 5̣ 3 1 4 3 2 1 7 6 5 5̣ 5 4 6 4
    e 4 2 7 5 6 4 5 1̣.

The *e* I have put at the beginning of the second line indicates that the *fa* which ends the first one is in the fifth octave, from which I leave in order to reenter the fourth one *d* by the dot you see below the *si* of this second line.

Nothing is easier than finding this letter corresponding to the last note of a line, and here is the method for doing so.

Count all the dots that are above the notes of this line; also count those that are below: if they are equal in number with the first ones, this is a proof that the last note of the line is in the same octave as the first, and such is the case with the first example on the preceding page, where, after having found three dots above and as many below, you conclude that they cancel each other out, and consequently that the last note *fa* of the line is in the same octave *d* as the first note *do* of the same line—which is always true, whatever way the dots may be arranged, provided that there be as many above as below.

If they are not equal in number, take their difference: count from the letter at the beginning of the line and move back as many letters toward *a* if the excess is below, or, if it is above, on the contrary advance as many letters in the Alphabet as this difference contains units, and you will have exactly the letter corresponding to the last note.

Example

Do
    c 6 3 6 7 i̇ 2 1 7 6 i̇ 5 i̇ 2 3 4 3 2 1 3 6 8̇ 6 7 3 i̇
    c 2 7 i̇ 6 7 8̇ 6 i̇ 4 3 2 1 8̇ 6 2 1 7 6 3 3 4 4̇ 5 8̇ 6 7 i̇
    d 2 7 8̇ 6.

In the first line of this example, which begins at the level *c*, you have two dots below and four above, and consequently two in excess for which as many letters must be added to the letter *c* following the order of the Alphabet, and you will have the letter *e* corresponding to the last note of the same line.

On the contrary, in the second line you have a dot in excess below, that is, you must move back one letter from the letter *e* at the beginning of the line toward *a*, that is, to *d*, for the letter corresponding to the last note of the second line.

One must likewise be sure to put the letter of the octave after every first and every last note of reprises and rondos, so that in leaving from them one always knows with certainty whether one should ascend or descend when taking a reprise or recommencing. All this will be better clarified by the following example, in which this mark 𝄋 is a sign for a reprise.

Mi
    c 3 4 5 7 i̇ 2 3 4 3 2 1 4 3 2 1 7 6 2 5 b 𝄋 5 c 5 5
    b⸕ 6 4̇ 4 6 2̇ 7 5 i̇ 2 5 7 i̇ c.

The letter *b* you see after the last note of the first part tells you that you must ascend a sixth to return to the *mi* at the beginning, since it is in the superior octave *c*, and the letter *c* which you likewise see after the first and the last note of the second part tells you that they are both in the same octave, and consequently that it is necessary to ascend a fifth to return from the finale to the reprise.

These observations are very simple and very easy to remember. It must nevertheless be admitted that the method of dots has some lesser advantages than that of the positioning by levels which I first presented and which never has need of all these differences in letters; however, both of them have their convenience, and, as they are learned by the same rules and as they can both be learned together with the same ease as they can be learned separately, each will be used in the situations for which they seem most suitable. For example, nothing will be more convenient than the method of dots for adding a tune to words that are already written, for notating short tunes, detached pieces, and those one wants to send to the Provinces and in general, for vocal Music. On the other hand, the method of positions will serve for scores and large pieces of Music, for instrumental Music, and especially for starting off Students, since its working is even more obvious than the other manner, and since the latter is understood from the first instant when moving from this former one after it is already familiar. Composers will also prefer to make use of it because of its visual distinction of the different octaves. By utilizing it, they will perceive the extent of its advantages, which I dare say are such for the conspicuousness of the harmony that, even should my method gain no currency, there is no composer who ought not employ it for his own use and for the instruction of his pupils.

This is what I have to say about the first part of my system, which regards the expression of sounds. Let us pass to the second, which treats their durations.

The topic I have just spoken about is not nearly so difficult as this one, at least in practice, since in the former only a certain number of sounds are admitted, all of whose relationships are fixed, and nearly the same ones in all the keys, whereas the differences which can be introduced into their durations can vary almost infinitely.

It is quite likely that the establishment of quantity in Music was at first relative to that of the language, that is, that it was necessary to play sounds by which short syllables were expressed more quickly and to draw out somewhat those to which long ones were adapted. Things were soon pressed further, and, in imitation of Poetry, a certain regularity in the duration of sounds was established by which they were subjected to uniform recurrences, which they took it into their heads to measure by equal movements of the hand or foot and which for this reason took the name of measures. The analogy between Music and Poetry is evident in this regard. Verses are relative to measures, feet to beats, and syllables to notes. Surely, to discover relationships as natural is not to leave oneself open to absurdities, provided that one not go on, like Father Souhaitti, to apply to the one the signs of the other and to conflate their differences on account of their similarities.[30]

This is not the place to examine as a Physicist from whence arises that wondrous equality that we experience in our movements when we beat time; not one beat that surpasses another, not the least difference in their successive duration without our having any other rule than our ear to determine it: there is room to conjecture that a such a singular effect comes from the same principle that makes us naturally intone every consonance. However this may be, it is clear that we have a sure feeling for judging the relationship of movements, as entirely as for that of sounds, and organs always ready to express them both in accordance with the same relationships, and, considering what I have to say, it is enough for me to note the fact without seeking the cause.

Musicians draw huge distinctions among these movements, not only regarding the various degrees of speed they can have, but also regarding the very type of meter, and all this is merely a result of the poor principle by which they have fixed the different durations of sounds; for in order to find the relationships of some to others, it was necessary to establish a term of comparison, and it pleased them to choose for this term a certain quantity of duration which they have specified by a round figure;[31] they then thought of notes of several other shapes, whose value is fixed in relation to this round figure, by diminishing proportion. This division would be bearable enough, although it would still require a great deal to have the necessary universality, if the term of comparison, that is, if the duration of the whole note, were a little less vague; but the whole note is sometimes played more quickly, sometimes more slowly according to the movement of the meter in which it is employed, and one must not flatter oneself with producing anything more precise by saying that a round figure is always the expression of the duration of a measure in quadruple-time, since, aside from the fact that the very duration of this measure has nothing determinate about it, measures in quadruple and duple-time are commonly seen in Italy that contain two and sometimes four whole notes.

This is nonetheless what is assumed about the numerals in duple-time meters: the lower numeral indicates the number of notes of a certain value contained in a measure in quadruple-time, and the upper numeral indicates how many of these same notes are needed to fill a measure in the tune one is going to notate. But why this relationship of so many different meters to that in quadruple-time, which is so little similar to them? Or why this relationship of so many different notes to a whole note whose duration is so unspecific?

It might be said that the inventors of Music set themselves the task of doing exactly the contrary of what they ought to have done; on the one hand, they disregarded the specification of the fundamental sound indicated by nature and so necessary to serve as a common term in relation to all the others, and, on the other hand, they wanted to establish an absolute and fundamental duration without being able to determine its value.

Must one be surprised if the error in the principle caused so many defects in its consequences? Defects essential to practice, and all suited to long retard the progress of students?

Musicians recognize at least fourteen different meters, whose signs are:

2, 3, C, 3/2, 2/4, 3/4, 6/4, 9/4, 12/4, 3/8, 6/8, 9/8, 12/8, 3/16, 6/16

Now, if these signs are instituted to specify how many different types of movements there are, there are many more of them, and if, besides this, they are to express the different degrees of quickness of these movements, they are not sufficient for this. Furthermore, why torment oneself so much in order to establish signs which are not useful for anything, since, independently of the kind of meter, one is almost always constrained to add a word at the beginning of the tune which specifies the type and the degree of the movement?

Nevertheless, one cannot deny that the diversity of these meters confounds beginners for an infinite time, and that all this arises from the extravagant thought that one need only be willing to relate them to quadruple-time, or to be willing to relate the notes to the value of the whole note.

To give relationships to the movements and to the notes that are entirely foreign to the meter in which they are employed is actually to give them absolute values while preserving the obstacle of the relationships. In addition, one sees that terrible equivocations thereby follow which are so many traps for the Music's precision and for the Musician's style. In fact, is it not obvious that by determining the duration of whole notes, half notes, quarter notes, eighth notes, etc., not by the quality of the meter in which they are encountered, but by that of the note itself, at every moment you find the relationship in opposition with the proper meaning? From this it happens, for example, that a half note in a certain meter is played much more quickly than a quarter note in another, in which the quarter note is nevertheless worth half of that half note, and from this it still happens that Provincial Musicians, deceived by these false relationships, often give tunes wholly different movements than they should have by adhering scrupulously to this false relationship, whereas a measure in simple triple meter must sometimes be played much more quickly than another in three-eighths, something that depends on the whim of Composers, and examples of which are offered at the Opera at every moment.

There might be other remarks to make at this point over which I shall not pause. For example, when the double subdivision of notes such as it is established was devised every case was apparently not foreseen, or, rather, they could not all be embraced by a general rule; thus, when it is a question of dividing one note or one beat into three equal parts in a meter in duple-, triple-, or quadruple-time, the Musician has to divine it, or rather one must warn him of it by means of an extraneous sign which constitutes an exception to the rule.

It is by examining the progress in Music that we are able to discover the remedy for these defects. Two centuries ago this art was still extremely unrefined. Whole notes and half notes were almost the only notes that were used, and an eighth note was looked upon only with fright. A Music so simple did not lead to great difficulties in practice, and that made it so that great care was not taken to give the signs precision, the separation of measures was neglected, and they contented themselves with expressing them by the shape of the notes. In proportion as the Art was perfected and as the difficulties increased, they perceived the obstacles they had in distinguishing the measures with such a great diversity of notes, and they began to separate them by perpendicular lines; they further set about tying eighth notes together so as to make the beats easier, and they found this so good that, ever since then, Musical characters have remained in about the same state.

A portion of the inconveniences nevertheless still remains, the distinction of the beats is not always very well observed in instrumental Music, and has no place at all in the vocal sort; it happens from this that, in the midst of a long measure, the Student doesn't know where he is, especially when he encounters a number of detached eighth and sixteenth notes, which he himself must allocate.

A very simple reflection on the use of perpendicular lines for the separation of measures will furnish us with a sure means for eliminating these inconveniences. All the notes contained between two of those lines of which I have just spoken make up precisely the value of one measure. Let them be of a great or small number—this does not at all affect the duration of this measure, which is always the same; simply divide it into equal or unequal parts, according to the value and the number of the notes it contains; but, finally, without knowing precisely the number of these notes, nor the value of each of them, one knows with certainty that all together they make up a duration equal to that of the measure in which they are found.

Let us separate the beats by commas just as we separate measures by lines, and let us reason about each of these beats in the same way we reason about each measure. We shall have a universal principle for the duration and the quantity of notes that will let us dispense with inventing new signs to determine it, and which will put us in a position to diminish greatly the number of different meters used in Music without taking away anything from the variety of movements.

When one note alone is contained between the two lines of a measure, it is a sign that this note fills all the beats of this measure and should last as long as it; in this case, the separation of the beats would be pointless: one has only to sustain the same sound through the whole measure. When the measure is divided into as many equal notes as it contains beats, one might also dispense with separating them: each note marks a beat, and each beat is filled by one note. But in the case where the measure is laden with notes of unequal values, then the separation of beats by commas must necessarily be practiced; and we shall practice it even in the preceding case in order to preserve the most perfect uniformity in our signs.

Each beat contained between two commas, or between a comma and a perpendicular line, contains one note or several. If it contains only one note, it is understood that it fills this whole beat; nothing is so simple; if it contains several, the thing is no more difficult: divide this beat into as many equal parts as it contains notes, apply each of these parts to each of these notes, and play them in such a way that all the beats are equal.

Example of the First Case

Re

3‖ d, 1, 2, 3|7, 1̇, 2|6, 7, 1|5̆, 4̆, 3|1̇, 2, 3|
d 7, 1̇, 2|6, 7, 5̆|6 c.

Example of the Second Case

Do

2‖ c 1 7, 1̇ 2|3 2, 3 1|5 4, 5 6|7 6, 7 5|1̇ 4, 5 5|1̇ c.

Example of Them Both

Fa

3‖ d 3, 4, 5|6 5, 4 3, 2̆ 1|2, 5, 1̇|1, 6, 2̇|2, 7, 3|3,
d 1, 4|4, 3 2, 3 4|2̆|3, 4, 5|6 5, 4 3, 2̆ 1|2, 5, 1̇ 2|
d 7 1̇, 6, 2̇ 3|1 2, 7, 3 4|2 3, 1, 4 5|3 4, 2 5 6|4 5,
d 3, 6|6 2, 3,̆ 2̇|1, 5 6 7, 1̇ 2 1|7 1̇ 7, 6 7 1̇, 2 3 2|
d 1 2ʳ, 7 1̇ 2, 3 4 3|2 3 2, 1 2 3, 4 5 4|3 4 3, 2 3 4,
d 5 6 5|4 5 4, 3 2, 3 4|2̆, 5 5 6 7, 1̇|1 2 1 7, 6 6 7 1̇,
d 2̇|2 3 2 1, 7 7 1̇ 2, 3|3 4 3 2, 1 1 2 3, 4|4 5 4 3,
d 2 2 3 4, 5|5 6 5 4, 3 3 4 5, 6 6 7 1̇|1 2, 3,̆ 2 1 d.

One sees in the preceding examples that I preserve trills and liaisons as in ordinary Music, and that in order to distinguish the numeral that marks the measure from those for the notes, I have taken care to make it larger and to separate it from them by a double perpendicular line.

Before entering into greater detail concerning this method, let us first note how much it simplifies the use of the meter by eliminating double meters altogether; for, as the division of the notes is taken uniquely by the value of the beats and of the measure in which they are found, it is obvious that these notes no longer need to be compared to any exterior value in order to fix theirs; thus, the meter being determined uniquely by the number of these beats, it can very nicely be reduced to two types: namely, duple-time and triple-time. With regard to the meter in quadruple-time, everyone agrees that it is merely the assemblage of two meters in duple-time: it is treated as such in composition, and one can count upon those who might claim to find in it any specific property to rely much more on their eyes than on their ears.

That the number of beats of a natural, perceptible meter agreeable to the ear is limited to three is a fact of experience that all the speculations in the world do not destroy; one might very well seek subtle analogies between the beats of the measure and the harmonics of a sound, one might discover a sixth consonance in the harmony as soon as a movement in quintuple-time in the meter, and, whatever may be the reason, it is incontestable that the pleasure of the ear and likewise its sensitivity to the meter extends no further.

Let us therefore keep to these two kinds of meters, in duple- and triple-time; each of these times can both be divided into two or three equal parts, and sometimes in four, six, eight, etc., by subdivisions of these, but never by other numbers which are not multiples of two or of three.

Now, whether a meter is in duple- or triple-time, and whether the division of each of these beats is in two or three equal parts, my method is always general, and expresses everything with the same ease. This was already able to be seen by the last preceding example, and it will further be seen by this one, in which each beat of a measure in duple-time, divided into three equal parts, expresses movement in six-eighths in ordinary Music.

Example

Do

2‖ d, 3 6 i|1 7 6, 6 *8* 6|7 3 i, 7 i 2|1 7 6, 2̂|2̇ î 7,
d i 7 6|*8*, 3 6 i|1 7 6, 6|*8* 6|7 3 i, 1 4 7|2̂, 2 1 7|
c i 7 6, 3 6 *8*|6.

Notes where two equal ones fill a beat will be called halves; those where three are needed, thirds; those where four are needed, fourths; etc.

But when a beat happens to be divided in such a way that all the notes in it are not of an equal value, in order to represent, for example, a quarter note and two eighth notes in a single beat, I consider this beat as divided into two equal parts of which the quarter note fills the first and the two eighth notes the second; I then tie them by a straight line which I place above and below them, and this tie shows that everything embraced by it represents only a single note that must then be subdivided in two equal parts, or in three, or in four, according to the number of numerals it covers.

EXAMPLE

Fa

2|| d, 1 7 6|8̆|6 7, 1̄ 2 1 7 1̄ 6|7 3, 1̄ 7 6 x̆ 2|3 2̄ 3̄ 2̄,
d 1̆ 7 6 7|2̇ 1̄ 2̄ 1, 7 6 8̆ 7|3 |2̄ 1, 7̇|6 .

The comma found before the first note in the two preceding examples designates the end of the first beat and indicates that the Song begins on the second.

When unequal subdivisions are found in a single beat, one can then make use of a second tie; for example, in order to express a beat made up of a quarter note, an eighth note, and two sixteenth notes, one goes about it in this way:

Sol

2|| d 1 3, 5 1̄ 2̄ 1̄|7 2̇, 5 7̄ 1̄ 7|6 1̇, 4 6̄ 7̄ 6̄|5 6 7 5,
c 1̇ 2 3 1|4 6, 1̇ 4 5̄ 4̄|3 5, 1̇ 3̄ 4̄ 3̄|2 4, 7 2̄ 3̄ 2̄|
d 1 4 3 4, 5 5|1̇ d .

You see here that the second beat of the first measure contains two equal parts, equivalent to two quarter notes, namely, the 5 for the first, and for the other the sum of three notes—1, 2, 1—which are under the long tie; these three notes are subdivided into two other equal parts, equivalent to two quarter notes of which the first is the first 1 and the other the two notes 2 and 1 joined by the second tie, which are thus each a quarter of the value contained under the long tie and an eighth of the entire beat.

In general, in order to express the value of notes with regularity, the division of each beat by equal parts must be followed closely, which is always done by the method I have just presented by adding to its use that of the dot of which I shall soon speak, without its being possible to be checked by any exception. It will not even ever be necessary, however bizarre a piece of Music may be, to place more than two ties over any of these notes or for any of them to be accompanied by more than two dots, unless one wanted to imagine great inequalities in values of quintuple and sextuple eighth notes whose comparative quickness is not at all within the capacity of the voice or of instruments, and examples of which would hardly ever be encountered in the most teeming of our composers' brains.

With regard to held notes and syncopations, I can express them as in ordinary Music with notes tied together by a curved line which we shall call a hold tie or crescent, in order to distinguish it from the value tie of which I have just spoken and which is marked by a straight line. I can also employ the dot for the same use by giving it a more universal and more convenient meaning than in ordinary Music. For, instead of making it always worth half of the note that precedes it, which constitutes only a specific case, I give it, just like the notes, a value that is determined only by the place it occupies, that is, if the dot alone fills a beat or a measure, the sound that preceded it should also be held for this whole beat or this whole measure, and if the dot is found in a beat with other notes, it makes up part of it just as they do and should be counted as a third or as a fourth, according to the number of notes the beat contains, including the dot. In a word, the dot is worth as much, or more, or less, as the note that precedes it and whose continuation it indicates, according to the place it occupies in the beat in which it is used.

Example

Do
2|| C, 1|5 4, ·3|·2, 4 3|·2, ·1|5 5̇ , · 4 |
C 6 4, · 2|5 4 3 2, · 1|7 5, i|· , 7̊|1 ·

Furthermore, as we see from this example, it is not to be feared that these dots will ever be confused with those which serve to change octaves; they are too easily distinguished by their position to need to be so by their shape. This is why I have not bothered to do so, carefully avoiding making use of special signs which would distract the attention without expressing anything more than the simplicity of my own.

With regard to the degree of movement, if it is not determined by the characters of my method, it is easy to supply it by a word placed at the beginning of the tune, and this provides no argument against my system since even ordinary Music has need of the same assistance. For example, in the space of three simple beats you have five or six movements that are very different from one another, all expressed by a half note on each beat; it is not, therefore, the quality of the notes employed that serves to determine the movement, and if there happen to be negligent Teachers who, on this point, rely upon the character of their Music and upon the taste of those who should read it, their confidence is very often found to be misplaced when wrong movements are given to their tunes, which should make them perceive how necessary it is to have, in this respect, more precise indications than the quality of the notes.

The gross imperfection of Music regarding the point about which we are speaking would be perceptible to anyone who had eyes; but Musicians do not see it at all, and I dare boldly predict that they will never see anything of what might tend to correct the defects of their Art either. It has not escaped M. Sauveur, and it is not necessary to meditate upon Music as much as he has in order to perceive how important it would be not to leave such a vague expression to the movements of the various meters, and not to abandon its determination to those whose taste is often so poor.

The singular system he proposed, and in general all he has done in Acoustics, although chimerical enough according to its aims, did not fail to contain excellent things which might well have been put to profitable use in any other Art. For example, nothing would be more advantageous than the use of his general Echometer to determine precisely the duration of measures and of beats, and that by the easiest method in the world: it would only be a question of determining the length of a simple pendulum by a measure of a known duration, which would give a certain exact number of vibrations during a beat or a measure of a certain type.[32] A single numeral, put at the beginning of a tune, would express all that and, by this means, one would be able to specify the movement with as much precision as the Author himself. The pendulum would be necessary only in order to once grasp the idea of each movement, after which—this idea being awakened in other tunes by the same numerals, which would cause it to arise, and by the tunes themselves that one had already sung in accordance with it—an assured habit, acquired by a practice that is as precise, would soon take the place of the rule and render the pendulum useless.

But these very advantages—which would become true inconveniences by the ease they would give beginners in being able to do without Teachers and in forming their taste on their own—have, perhaps, been the reason why the plan has not at all been admitted into practice; it seems that if one proposed to make the Art more difficult, this would sooner be a reason to be listened to.

However this may be, while awaiting the approbation of the Public to give me the right to elaborate further on the means that might be taken to make the knowledge of movements easier, and likewise with that of many other parts of music about which I have remarks to propose, I can limit myself here to the expressions of the ordinary method, which indicate the movement well enough by means of the words that are put at the beginning of each tune. These words, when well chosen, should, I believe, compensate and more for those double figures and all those different meters which, despite their number, leave the movement indeterminate and teach nothing to students; thus, by adopting only 2 and 3 as signs for the meter, I take away the confusion of the characters without altering the variety of the expression.

Let us return to our plan. It is known how many strange figures are used in Music in order to express rests; there are as many of them as there are different values and, consequently, as many as there are different shapes of their relative notes; one is even constrained to use a proportionately greater number of them since it did not please their inventors to admit the dot after rests in the same manner and for the same use as after the notes, and they preferred to multiply quarter rests, eighth rests, and sixteenth rests one after another rather than to establish such a natural analogy among the relative signs.

But as it is not at all necessary in my method to give specific shapes to the notes in order to determine their value, one is also excused from the same precaution for rests, and a single sign suffices to express them all without confusion and without equivocation. The choice of whatever character one might like to employ for this use appears indifferent enough given this unity of shape. Nevertheless, zero has something about it that is so convenient for this effect, as much by the idea of privation it usually carries with it as by its quality as a numeral, and especially by the simplicity of its shape, that I believed I should prefer it. I shall therefore employ it in the same way and in the same meaning with regard to the value as the ordinary notes, that is, as the numerals 1, 2, 3, etc., and since the rules I have established with regard to the notes are wholly applicable to their relative rests, it follows that zero by its position alone and by the dots which might follow it, which then will express rests, alone suffices to replace all the rests, quarter rests, eighth rests, and other bizarre and superfluous signs which fill up ordinary Music.

Example Drawn from the Lessons of M. Montéclair[33]

Fa

$2\|\ \overset{4}{0}\ |d\ \ 1|2|\ 3,\ \ 1|5|3|5,\ \ 6|7,\ \ 5|\dot{1}|\overset{2}{0}|\cdot,\ \ 5|\dot{1},\ \ 0\ \ 7|$

$d\ \ 6,\ \ 0\ \ 5|4,\ \ 0\ \ 3\ \ 2\ \ 1|\overset{x}{7},\ \ 0\ \ \dot{1}\ \ 2\ \ 3|4\ \ 3,\ \ \dot{2}\ \ \overline{\cdot1}|1\ .$

The numerals 4 and 2 placed here above the zero indicate the number of measures that should be passed by in silence.

Such are the general principles from which flow the rules for every sort of imaginable expression without its being possible in this regard for these to be any difficulty that has not been foreseen, and that is not resolved in consequence of certain of these principles.

I shall conclude with some observations that arise from the parallel between the two systems.

Are the notes in ordinary Music more or less advantageous than the numerals to be substituted for them? This is properly speaking the heart of the issue.

It is clear, first of all, that the notes vary more by their position alone than my numerals do by their shape and by their position combined; that, besides this, there are seven different shapes in it, as many numerals as I allow to express them; that the notes have their meaning and their power only with the help of the Clef and that the variations of the Clefs give a great number of entirely different meanings to notes placed in the same manner.

It is no less evident that the relationships of the notes and intervals to one another have nothing in their expression by ordinary Music to indicate their kind, and that they are expressed by positions that are difficult to remember and the knowledge of which depends uniquely upon practice and a very long practice at that: for what hold does the mind have to grasp exactly and from the first glance an interval of a sixth, of a ninth, or a tenth, in ordinary Music, unless custom familiarizes the eyes in reading these intervals all at once?

Is it not a terrible defect in Music not to be able to preserve anything in the expression of octaves of the analogy they have between them? Octaves are merely the replicas of the same sounds; nevertheless, these replicas are presented under expressions absolutely different from those of their first term. Everything in the position is muddled at the distance of a single octave; the replica of a note which was on a line is found in a space between two lines, that which was in the space has its replica on a line. Are you ascending or descending two octaves? Another difference entirely contrary to the first: then the replicas are placed on lines or in spaces, like their first terms; thus, the difficulty increases by changing object, and one is never assured of knowing exactly the type of an interval traversed by such a great number of lines, so that, from octave to octave, one needs to make use of specific rules which never end, and which make of the study of intervals the fearsome and very rarely attained culmination of the Musician's science.

From this comes that other defect, almost as harmful, of not being able to distinguish the simple interval within the doubled interval. You see a note placed between the first and the second line, and another note placed on the seventh line: in order to know their interval, you count back from the one to the other, and after a long and tiresome process, you find a twelfth; now, as it is easily seen that it surpasses an octave, one must start anew with a second search to assure oneself ultimately that it is a doubled fifth, further, to determine the type of this fifth, great attention must be paid to the signs of the Clef, which might make it a true or diminished fifth according to their number and their position.

I know that Musicians usually make use of more abridged rules so as to make training and the knowledge of intervals easier; but these very rules prove the defect of the signs in that one must always count the lines by one's eyes and in that one is constrained to fix one's imagination from octave to octave in order to leap from there to the following interval, which is called making up with genius for the vice of expression.

Furthermore, when, by dint of practice, one reaches the point of easily reading every kind of interval, of what use will this knowledge be inasmuch as you will have no sure rule for distinguishing their type? Major and minor thirds and sixths, diminished and augmented fifths and fourths, and in general all intervals with the same name, true or altered, are expressed by the same position independently of their quality, which makes it so that, according to the different locations of the semitones in the octave, which change place on each key and on each Clef, the intervals also change quality without changing name or position—from whence the uncertainty about their intonation and the uselessness of training in the cases when it would be most necessary.

The method that has been adopted for instruments is manifestly dependent upon these defects, and the direct relationship which had to be established between the keys of the instrument and the position of the notes is only a pathetic last resort for making up for the science of intervals and of *tonic relations*, without which one would forever know how to be only a poor Musician.

What should the great care of the Musician be while performing? Doubtless to enter into the mind of the Composer and to appropriate his ideas in order to render them with all the fidelity which the taste of the Piece requires. Now, the idea of the Composer in the choice of sounds is always relative to the tonic, and, for example, he will never use *fa*-sharp as a certain key of the keyboard, but as a certain chord or a certain interval with its fundamental. I therefore say that, if the Musician considers sounds by these same relations, he will play his intervals more exactly and will perform with more precision than by solely producing sounds one after another, without connection and without dependence other than that of the position of the notes before his eyes, and of the throng of sharps and flats which he must continually have in mind. Of course he will always observe the modifications specific to each key, which are, as I have said, the result of temperament, and whose practical knowledge, independent of any system, can be acquired only by the ear and by training.

If a bad principle is once adopted, one slides from inconvenience to inconvenience, and one often sees the very advantages that were proposed vanish. This is what happens in the practice of instrumental Music; the difficulties it presents come in droves. The number of different positions, of sharps, of flats, of changes of Clef, are eternal obstacles to the progress of Musicians; and, after all this, half the time one must also lose that much-vaunted advantage of the direct relationship of the key of the keyboard to the note, since it happens a hundred times by force of signs of alteration or doubling that the same notes become relative to different keys from those they represent, as was noted above.

Do you want to transpose the piece a semitone or a tone higher or lower for the convenience of the voices? Do you want to present Music to the Instrumental player notated on a Clef foreign to his instrument? Behold him hampered and, often, totally checked, if the Music is somewhat intricate. I believe, in truth, that great musicians will not be in this position; but I also believe that great Musicians do not become such without labor, and that it is this labor that it is a matter of abridging. Because it is not totally impossible to attain perfection by the ordinary route, does it follow that there is not an easier one?

Let us suppose that I want to transpose and play in *B fa si* a Piece notated in *C sol do* on the clef of *sol* on the first line.[34] Here is all I have to do: I put aside the idea of the Clef of *sol*, and I substitute for it that of the Clef of *do* on the third line; then I add to this the ideas of the five sharps, the first placed on *fa*, the second on *do*, the third on *sol*, the fourth on *re*, and the fifth on *la*; finally, to all this I add the idea of an octave above this Clef of *do*, and I must continually retain this whole complexity of ideas in order to apply it to each note, otherwise behold me off key at every moment. Let the ease of all this be judged.

Numerals used in the way I propose produce absolutely different results. Their power is in themselves and independent of any other sign. Their relationships are known by inspection alone, and without training at all entering into it; the simple interval is always evident within the doubled interval: a lesson of a quarter of an hour should put anyone in a position to *sol-fa*, or at least to name the notes in any Music presented to him; another quarter of an hour suffices to teach him likewise to name, and without hesitation, every possible interval, which depends, as I have already said, on the clear knowledge of the intervals, their inversions, and reciprocally of the inversion of these, which return to the first ones. Now, it seems to me that habit should form much more easily when the mind has done half the work, and when it itself no longer has anything to do.

Not only are the intervals known by their kind in my system, but they are further known by their type. Thirds and sixths are major or minor: you make the distinction without being capable of being mistaken. Nothing is as easy as knowing at once that the interval 2 4 is a minor third; the interval 2 4 a major sixth; the interval 3 1 a minor sixth; the interval 3 1 a major third; etc. Fourths and thirds, seconds, fifths and sevenths, true, diminished, or augmented, cost no more to know; accidental signs hinder one still less, and the natural interval being known, it is so easy to determine this same interval, altered by a sharp or by a flat, by both of them at the same time, or by two of the same type, that to enter into this detail would be to prolong this discourse uselessly.

Apply my method to instruments: its advantages will be striking. It is a question merely of learning to form the seven sounds of the natural scale and their various octaves on a fundamental *do* taken successively on the twelve pitches* of the scale; or, rather, it is a question merely of knowing how to find a fifth, a fourth, a major third, etc., and all their octaves, on a given sound, that is, of possessing the knowledge that should be the least unknown by Musicians in any system whatsoever. After these preliminaries, so easy to acquire and so appropriate for forming the ear, a few months given to the use of meters put the student in a position all at once to play at sight—but with a playing incomparably more intelligent and more certain than that of our ordinary Instrumental players. All the Clefs will be equally familiar to him; all the keys will have the same ease for him, and, if he finds any difference in them it will always depend only on the particular difficulty of the instrument and not on a confusion of sharps, of flats, and of different positions, which are so awkward for beginners.

Add to this a perfect knowledge of keys and of the whole modulation, a necessary result of my method; and especially the universality of the signs, which produces with the same notes the same tunes in all the keys by the change of a single character; from which results an ease of transposing a tune into every other key equal to that of playing it in that in which it is notated: this is what will be known by an Instrumental player formed by my method in very little time. Every young person, with talent and ordinary preparation and who might not know a single note of Music, should,

---

*I say the twelve pitches so as not to omit any of the possible difficulties, since one might content oneself with the seven natural pitches, and since it is rare for the fundamental of a key to be established on one of the seven altered sounds, except, perhaps, *si*-flat. It is true that these are attained often enough by the succession of the modulation; but then, although one may have to change key, the same fundamental always persists, and the change is brought about by particular alterations.

led by my method, be in a position at the end of eight months to accompany with the Harpsichord, at sight, any Music which does not surpass in difficulty that of our Operas, and, at the end of ten, that of our Cantatas.

Now, if one can teach at the same time enough Music and accompaniment to play at sight in such a short time, so much the stronger reason for a Flute or Violin Teacher, who has only the notation to add to the playing of the instrument, to be able to form a Pupil in the same amount of time by the same principles.

I say nothing about Singing in particular because it seems to me to be impossible to dispute the superiority of my system in this regard, and because I have stronger and more convincing examples to present on this point than all these reasonings.[35]

After all of the advantages of which I have spoken, it is permissible to count as something the little volume which my characters occupy compared to the diffuseness of the other Music, and the ease of notating without all that hindrance of lined paper, on which, five lines per staff almost never being enough, it is necessary at every moment to add others which sometimes run into neighboring staffs or get mixed up with the words and cause a confusion to which my Music will never be exposed. Without wanting to establish the value of this advantage, it nevertheless does not fail to have an influence that merits attention. How much more convenient it will be to keep up a correspondence in Music without increasing the bulk of letters! What difficulties of turning the page at every moment will be avoided in Instrumental Parts and in scores! And what a resource of entertainment there will be for being able to carry books and collections of Music, as one carries literature, without being burdened by a cumbersome weight or bulk, and, for example, of having an extract of the Music added to that of the words at the Opera, almost without increasing the price or the size of the book! These considerations are not, I admit, of great importance—also, I present them merely as accessories; furthermore, it is but a canvas of similar trifles that adds charm to human life, and nothing would be as miserable as it if attention were never paid to small objects.

I shall conclude my remarks on this point by concluding that, having removed the different position that Clefs and accidentals produce in ordinary Music in a single sweep by means of my characters; having established an invariable and constant sign for each sound of the octave in all keys; having likewise established a very simple position for the different octaves, having fixed all the expression of sounds by intervals that belong to the key one is in; having preserved for the eyes the ease of discovering at first glance whether the sounds ascend or descend; having fixed the degree of this progression with a manifestness that ordinary Music does not at all have; and, finally, having abridged by more than three quarters the time needed to learn to *sol-fa*, and the volume of the notes, it stands demonstrated that my characters are preferable to those of ordinary Music.

A second question that is hardly less interesting than the first is to know whether the division of beats I substitute for that of the notes which fill them is a general principle that is simpler and more advantageous than all those different names and shapes one is constrained to apply to the notes in conformity to the duration one wishes to give them.

A sure means of deciding this would be to examine *a priori* whether the value of the notes is made to regulate the length of the beats or whether, on the contrary, it is not at all by the beats themselves that the duration of the notes should be fixed. In the first case, the ordinary method would without question be the better, unless one were to regard the elimination of so many shapes as a sufficient compensation for an error in principle from which better results would come. But, in the second case, if I reinstate the cause and the effect, taken until now for one another, and if, by this means, I simplify the rules and abridge practice, I have room to hope that this part of my system—which, moreover, no one will accuse me of having copied from anyone—will not appear less advantageous than the preceding.

I postpone many details which I cannot place in this one to the work of which I have spoken.[36] Aside from the new method of accompaniment of which I spoke in the Preface, in it will be found a means of recognizing long cascades of notes when ascending or descending at first glance, in such a way that one will have to pay attention only to the first and the last; the expression of various syncopated meters which are sometimes found in lively movements in triple-time; a table of all the words proper for expressing the different degrees of movement; the means of finding first the highest and the lowest note of a tune and, consequently, of warming up; finally, other specific rules which are all yet simply developments of the principles I have proposed here; and, above all, a system of conduct for Teachers who teach singing or playing instruments very different in method, and I hope in progress, from that used today.

If, therefore, to the general advantages of my system, if to all those eliminations of signs and of combinations, if to the precise development of theory, one adds the utilities my method presents for practice—those hindrances of lines and of staffs entirely eliminated, Music rendered so short to learn, so easy to notate, occupying so little volume, requiring less expense to print, and, consequently, costing less to acquire—a more perfect correspondence established between the different parts without jumps from one Clef to another being more difficult than the same intervals taken on the same Clef, chords and the progression of the harmony presented with an obviousness to which the eyes cannot refuse themselves, the key clearly specified, the whole succession of the modulation expressed, as well as the course one has followed, and the point one has reached, and the distance one is from the principal key, but above all the extreme simplicity of the principles joined to the ease of the rules that follow from them: perhaps one will discover in all this what justifies the confidence with which I dare present this plan to the Public.

Notice

Since the characters that were to be engraved were not yet ready, I preferred to present the following examples notated solely by the method of dots rather than to delay this edition. It will be a long time before this Music will be seen printed in the other manner,[37] it is only then that its advantages will be able to be judged properly. Furthermore, having found it more convenient to place the notation below the words, I did not believe I should have qualms about doing so after having lifted the yoke of habit regarding more important points.

What a poor impression I have gained of Musicians in the Provinces in which I have lived will be seen by reading this Work. My stay in Paris has taught me to render them more justice, and I know that there are several of them who are not only enlightened enough to make the most judicious judgments, but also obliging enough to communicate their knowledge to me. This is what I ask of everyone in general, while assuring them of my thanks and of my docility in profiting from them. I am sorry that I do not have the time to correct the pages of my Work; I at least hope that the Public will recognize by the very fashion in which these Gentlemen receive it how far they are above the unjust opinion I had conceived of them.

Minuet from *Dardanus*[38]

Re   Volez, plaifirs, volez, Amour prête leur tes char-
3||d 3,4   3,2   3|4,·,3| 2 , 3 2,1   2˙|3,·,
mes , répare les allarmes qui nous ont troublez.
d 2 | 1,2 1,7 6|5,4, 3 | 6, 5 ; 1 |⁷₇ c⁀
Que ton empire eſt doux, vien, vien, nous voulons
c 5c,4   3,4   5 | 6 | 4˙ | 5˙ | 1 , 3 2,
tous ſentir tes coups, enchaîne nous; mais ne te fers
d 1 | 1,3 2, 1 | 1,3 2, 1 | 6 |4 5,6
que de ces chaînes dont les peines font des bienfaits.
c 7,i̇ 2 | 3 4, 5   6;7 1 |4˙, 5, 7| id.

Milanais Carillon in Trio[39]

Do
1er Dessus.

Campana che sona da lu to è da fes- - - -
c,, 3 | 6,7, 1 | 7,6,5 | 6,7,1 |·,2,7 | 1,2,3 |

2d Dessus. 3

Campana che
c,, o | · | · | · |·,·,3 | 6,7,1 |

Basse.

b,, o | · | · | · | · | · |

- - - - - - - - - - - - ta   Fa
d 2,1,7 | 1,2,3 |·,2,1 |·,7, o | · | 4 |

sona da lu to è da festa   Fa
d 7,6,5 | 6,7,1 |·,7,6 | 6,5, o | · | 2 |

                    Fa romper la tes - - -
b o | · | · |·,·,3 | 6,7,1 | 2,3,4 |

romper la tes - - - - - - - - - -ta , Din di ra din di
d 4, 3, 2 | 3 |·4,5,3 |·, 2 , 5 | 5,4,3 | 2,

romper la tes - - - - - - - - -ta , Din di ra din di
d 2, 1, 7 | 1 |·2,3,1 |·, 7, 3 | 3,2, 1 | 7,

- - - - - - - - - - - - - - - ta   don
b 5, 6, 7 | 1,2,3 |·, 2,1 | 5,5, o | · | 5,

ra din di ra din don don don , dan di ra din
d 3, 4 | 5, 4, 3 | 2 | 3 | 4,·, 3 | 4, 3, 2 |

ra din di ra din don don don , dan di ra din
c 1, 2 | 3, 2, 1 | 7 | 1 | 2,·, 1 | 2, 1, 7 |

    don   don don don dan di ra din
b ·, · | 5 | 5 | 1 | 6,·, 1 | 4, 2, 5 |

```
        don         don      don.
‖d       3    |      3     | 3,·,d.𝄇
         don         don      don.
‖d       1    |      1     | 1,·,d.𝄇
     don don don don don don don.
‖b   1 , 3 , 5 | 1 , 5 , 3 | 1,·,b.𝄇
```

```
    Campa na che fo na da lu - - - - to è da fef-
‖d   5 |5,3 2,34|5,3 2,34| 5  |·, 4 , 3 | 4 ,
    Campa na che fo na da lu - - - - to è da fef-
‖d   3·|3,1 7,1 2|3,1 7,1 2| 3 |·, 2 , 𝟙 | 2 ,
                              Fa romper la tef-
‖b   o |    ·   |    ·    |·,·, 6| 6, 6, 6| 2 ,
```

```
    - - - - - - - - - - - - - - - - - - - ta, din di
‖d   2 1,2 3|4,2 1,2 3| 4 |·, 3 , 2|3, 3, 3 |3,
    - - - - - - - - - - - - - - - - - - - ta, din di
‖d   7 6,7 1|2,7 6,7 1| 2 |·, 1 , 7|1, 1, 1 |1,
     ta                    Fa romper la testa
‖c   2 , 0 |    ·    |·,·, 5| 5 , 5, 5| 1, 1, 0 |·,
```

```
     ra din di ra din di ra din don, Fa romper la tef-
‖d   2, 1 |7, 1, 2 | 3, 2, 1 | 7,·, 3| 3 , 2, 3| 4 ,
     ra din di ra din di ra din don, Fa romper la tef-
‖d   7, 6 |5, 6, 7 | 1, 7, 6 | 5,·, 1| 1 , 7, 1| 2 ,
        don      don    don, Fa romper la tef-
‖b   o,· |  3  |   3   | 3,·, 3| 6, 7, 1| 2 ,
```

$$
\begin{array}{l}
\|d\cdot,\cdot|\cdot 5,43,42|\ 3\ |\cdot 4,32,31|\ 2\ \downarrow\\
\|d\cdot,\cdot|\cdot 3,21,27|\ \dot{1}\ |\cdot 2,17,\dot{1}6|\ 7\ |\\
\|b\ 3,4|\ 5,6,7\ |1,2,3|\ 4,5,6\ |7,\dot{1},2|
\end{array}
$$

```
                                 - ta din di ra din di ra din di ra din
‖d · 3,21,27| i,1,3 |3,2, 1,|7,i, 2 |3,2, 1|
                                 - ta din di ra din di ra din di ra din
‖c · i,76,75|6,6, i |1,7, 6 |5,6, 7 | i,7, 6|
            -- ta            don      don
‖b 3 , 4, 5 |6,6, 0|  ·      |  3     |  3  |
```

```
       don don don dan di ra din      don
‖d      7  |  i  | 2,·,1 |2,1,7 |      i       |
       don don don dan di ra din      don
‖c      5  |  6  | 7,·,6 |7,6,5 |      6       |
       don don don dan di ra din don don don
‖b      3  |  6  | 4,·,1 |4,2,3 | 6 , i , 3|
```

```
        don    don.
‖d       1   | 1,·, d‖
        don    don.
‖c       6   | 6,·, c‖
       don don don don.
‖b      6, 3, 1 | 6,·, a‖
```

92   *Dissertation on Modern Music*

Ariette from *Les Talens Lyriques*[40]

Vivement.

Mi
Symphonie.
Basse-continue.

```
  ‖c o ⁻5̣,5 ·1̇|1 7̄6̣,5645|3̇ ⁻2̇,1234.|
2 ‖
  ‖b o 1,3 1| 5 5, 7 5 |1̇ 1̣, 1 1 |
```

```
‖c 5̄1 5,·645|6 5 6,·7 1̇ 6|2 5̇ 2,·7|3 3̄ 2̇,1 7 6 5|
‖b 7̣ 7, 7 7| 6 6, 6 6 | 5 5,75| 1̇ 1, 3 1 |
```

```
‖c 4̲6̲2̲,0 2̇ 6 1̇|7 2̇ 5 7, 6 1̣4̣6̣|7 2̇ 5 6,6·5̲6̲|
‖b 2 2, 4̲ 2 | 5 , 4̲ 2 | 5 5, 4̲ 2 |
```

```
‖c 7 2̇ 5 6, 6·5̲6̲|7 2̇ 5 6,6·5̲6̲|5 7̲5̲·2 5 7 2̇|
‖a  5 ,4̲ 2 | 5 7̇1̇,2 2 | 5 7̲5̲,2 5 7 2̇|
```

```
‖c 5̇ ,0 5̲3̲|6̲4̲1 1,·4̲6̲|5̲1 1̇,·5̲3̲|6̲4̲1 1,·4̲6̲|
‖b 5̣ 5̲4̲,3 1 | 4 4 ,44 |3 3 ,33 | 4 4 , 44 |
```

```
‖c 5 1 1̇,·5̲3̲|6 6,·7 1̇ | 2 1,·7̄6̣|7̄6̣, 5 5 2 4|
‖a 1  , 0 3 |4 4̲, 4 4 |4 4̲, 4 4̲|5 5, 7 5 |
```

```
‖d 3 5 1 3, 2 5 7 2̇|3 5 1 2,2·1 2|3 5 1 2,2·1 2|
‖b 1̣ 1̣, 7 5 | 1̇ , 7̣ 5 | 1̇ 1, 7 5 |
```

L'objet qui

```
‖d 3 5 1 2, 2·1̲2̲|1 3̲1̲,5 1̇ 3 5| 1̇ ‖b, o 5| 5,·1̇|
‖b 1̣ ,4̲ 5 |1 3̲1̲,5 1̇ 3 5| 1̇   , o |o 1̇,3 1|
```

```
          ré - - - - - - - - - - - - - - - - - - - - gne dans mon
c 1 7̇6,5 645 | 3·2, 1 2 3 4 | 5,·645 | 6·7, i̇ · 6 |
b 5 5,  7 5 | i̇ i, i i    | 77,77   | 6 6, 6 6   |


         ame des mortels & des Dieux doit être le vain-
b 2̇,2  1  7̇ | i̇,  1·2 | 3,  · 1 | 6,6 6   7 |
a 5,·     4 | 3,  · 2 | 1,  · 3 | 2̇,      2 |


c o,  ·   5̄ 3 | 6̄ 4 1 1,·4̄ 6 | 5̄ 1 i̇,· 5̄ 3 |
  queur,                           chaque inſ-
b 5,  o       |   ·           | ·  ,5  5      |
a 5 5̲ 4,  3 1 | 4 4,   4 4    | 3 3,  3  3    |


c 6̄ 4 1 1,·4̄ 6 | 5̄ 1 i̇,·5̄ 3 | 6̄ 6̇ 4,7̄ 7 5 | 1̇ 3̇ 1,5̇ 1̇ 3 5 |
  tant il m'en flam - - - - - - - - - - - me
b  6, 7 i̇   |  5 ,·6̲5̲ | 5 ,·4̲3̲ |   3̇       |
a 4 4, 4 4  | 3 3, 3 3 | 2 2,  5 5 |   1,  o   |


c  i̇,  o   | 0 4̄ 3,2 4 6̇ | 7̄ 2 5,o | · | ·2̇ 5̇ 7̈, 
  d'une nouvel - le ar  deur,  il m'enflam- - -
b 6,6  5 | 5 , 4̲.  3 | 2     | 2̇,2 |    2
a 4,·  5 | 6,   ·  4 | 5     | o   | ·5̇,


c,6̇ 1̇ 4̇ 6 | 7̇ 2̇ 5 6̇,6̈ ·5̄ 6̈ | 7̇ 2̇ 5 6̇,6̈ ·5̄ 6̈ | 7 2̇ 7,
  - - - - - - - me         il       m'en       flam-
c, ·       | ·   ,2 o         | 2  ,  2          | 5,
b, 4̇ 2     | 5 5, 4̇ 2         | 5 5, 4̇ 2         | 7,
```

94 — Dissertation on Modern Music

```
||c, 5725| 3 ·4̄, 4̈·34|5̄2 2, 0 | 0 2̇,
||b, ·645|6545,6756|7ṡ7,6146|7ṡ6,
||a,  ·  |  ı̇ , 2  | ,5̇5̇ , 42 | 5 5̇,

||d, 2̇ |  0   | 0̄3̇2,17̄65|1̄17̄,
||b, 6·56|717̇ı̇,2312|   3   | · ,
||a, 4̈2 |  5 , 7̣ |  ı̇ , 17̣  | 6 ,

||c, 6543|4,2 ·5̄|5̂,4̈·5|5,·27̄|331̄,4̄4̄2|
         me   d'u ne nouvelle ardeur
||c, 3 0 |6,7·ı̇ |7,6·5̣| 5 | 0 |
                    ẍ
||a, 0 6 |2̇,5·ı̇|2,2̣|5,·7| ı̇ , 2 |

||d 54̄3̄,2312|7̄65̄,24̈| 5 |0̄17̄,6543|
   ẍ                      l'objet qui
||b   0 |  ·  |  ·,0·5̣|5̣,·ı̇ |
||b 3 ,4̈·34̄|51,22|55̣4̣,3432|1 1,3 1 |
        ẍ

*||c 2̈ , 0·5̄|53̄ı̇, 1 3̄ı̇|5̄75, 2̇ |·1̄6̣,
   ré - - - - - - - - - - - - - - - -gne
 ||c 176̄,5645|3·ẍ2,1234| 5 ,·645|6·7̣,
*||b 5̇ ,·5̣ |ı̇ ı̇, 1 1 |77̣, 7 7|66,

||c, 4̈ 1 6̄|55̄2̄,527 2̇| 5̈ |51̄3̄, 5 |
    dans mon   ame des mortels & des Dieux doit
||b, 1 ·6̣| 2̇,2 17̣ |ı̇,1·2̣| 3,· 1 |
||a, 6 6̣ | 5, · 4 |3,·2| 1,· 6̣ |
```

Pl., V, 240–242

être le vainqueur. Chaque inftant il m'en-

flam — — — — — — — — — — — — — — — — —

— — — me d'une nouvelle ar deur il m'en-

flam me il m'en-

flam — — — — — — — — — — — — — — — —

— — — — — — — — — — — me il m'en-

H ij

```
‖d o 6̄5̄,4 3 2 1 |7̇2̇ 1,7 1̄ 7 6| 5    | 2̇,3 ·4̇|
  flam - - - - - - - - - - - - - me d'une nou-
 c    4     |    ·    |   ·, 4 o |7, 5 · 1̇|
 b    2     |    5    |  |o 5̲ 6,7 1̇ 2 3|4,3 ·1̲|

‖d 3̂,2̄·1̇| 1 ,0 5̲3 |6̄4 1 1 ,·4̲ 6| 5̄ 1 1̊,·5̲ 3 |
  vel - le ardeur
 c 1,7 ·1̲|  ʻ1     |  o       |   ·      |
 b 5̣, 5̣  |1 1̇,1 1| 4̲ 4 ,4̲ 4 | 3̲ 3 ,3̲ 3 |

‖c 6̄4 1 1,·4̲ 6|5̄ 1 1̊,·5̲ 3|6̇6̇,·7̲ 1̇|2 1̇,·7̲ 6̲|
 a 4̲ 4 ,4̲ 4 | 1 , o  |4̲4̇, 4̲4̇|4̲4̇, 4̲4̇|

‖c 7 6̊,5̣ 5̣ 2 4| 3 5̣ 1 3, 2 5̣ 7̇ 2̇ | 3 5̣ 1 2,2̈ ·1̄2̄|
 a 5̣, o | o ï , 7 5̣ | 1̇ 1̇ , 7 5̣ |

‖d 3 5 1 2,2̊·1̄2̄|3 5 1 2,2̊·1̄2̄|1 3̇1̇,5̣1̇ 3 5|1̊ Fin.
 a 1 1̇ , 7 5̣ | 1̇ , 4 5 |1 3̄1̇,5̣1̇ 3 5|1̊ Fin.

‖   Je m'abandonne à mon amour extrême, & je
 c o·3̲, 3  6|5̌ |6 , 7·1̇| 2 ,·7̲ | 1̇ 6̇,1·2̲|
 a 6 , 1̇ 6̇|3̇,2|1 , 2·1̇| 7 , 3̇ |6̇| o , 6̇|

‖c  o  |·3 6̇1̇,7 3̧ 8̣ 7|1̇ 3̇ 6̇7,7̊·6̄7̄|1̇ 3̇ 6̇ 7,
  fixe à ja mais - - - - - - - - -
 c 7̲,7 ·6̲| 3 | · | · ,
 b 5̣,4 | 3̲ 6,5̲ 3 |6̇ 6̇,5̲ 3 | 6̇ ,
```

```
|c, 7·67|1 3 1, 6 1♯6|3, 2·3| 3 | 5 5 , 5 5 |
   mes plai firs         en  ces lieux : C'eſt où l'on
|c, 7 ·1 | 7 , ·6 5 | 5 , 4·3| 3 |  1 ,  1·5 |
|a,  5  |    6    | 7 , 7 | 3 | 3 3 , 3  3 |


|c 5 5 , 4 3| 2 , 0 |  ·  | 7 7 , 7 7|  3 |6 ,
   aime que font les Cieux : c'eſt où l'on aime que
|b 6 , 6 0| 2 , ·1 2|  7  | 3 , ·3 7 |1 , 1 0|2 ,
|b 4 , 0 |4 4 , 4 4| 5 , 0|5 5 , 5 5 |6 , 5 |4 ,


|c, ·6 7| 5 |0·5 , 5·1|1 7 6 , 5 6 4 5|3 1 7 , 6 5 4 3|✢
   font les Cieux.                    L'ob jet  qui
|c, ·1 2| 3 |  0  | · , · 5| 5 , ·1 |
|b,  :  | 3 |  0  |0 5 , 7 5|1 1 , 3 1|✢
```

END

GENERAL TABLE
Of All the Keys of All the Clefs

Clef							X							A							B							C							D							
Clef of Fa	1	2	3	4	5	6	7	1	2	3	4	5	6	7	1	2	3	4	5	6	7	1	2	3	4	5	6	7	1	2	3	4	5	6	7	1	2	3	4	5	6	7
of Mi	2	3	4	5	6	7	1	2	3	4	5	6	7	1	2	3	4	5	6	7	1	2	3	4	5	6	7	1	2	3	4	5	6	7	1	2	3	4	5	6	7	1
of Mi-Flat																																										
of Re	3	4	5	6	7	1	2	3	4	5	6	7	1	2	3	4	5	6	7	1	2	3	4	5	6	7	1	2	3	4	5	6	7	1	2	3	4	5	6	7	1	2
of Do-Sharp																																										
of Do	4	5	6	7	1	2	3	4	5	6	7	1	2	3	4	5	6	7	1	2	3	4	5	6	7	1	2	3	4	5	6	7	1	2	3	4	5	6	7	1	2	3
of Si	5	6	7	1	2	3	4	5	6	7	1	2	3	4	5	6	7	1	2	3	4	5	6	7	1	2	3	4	5	6	7	1	2	3	4	5	6	7	1	2	3	4
of Si-Flat																																										
of La	6	7	1	2	3	4	5	6	7	1	2	3	4	5	6	7	1	2	3	4	5	6	7	1	2	3	4	5	6	7	1	2	3	4	5	6	7	1	2	3	4	5
of La-Flat																																										
of Sol	7	1	2	3	4	5	6	7	1	2	3	4	5	6	7	1	2	3	4	5	6	7	1	2	3	4	5	6	7	1	2	3	4	5	6	7	1	2	3	4	5	6
of Fa-Sharp	1	2	3	4	5	6	7	1	2	3	4	5	6	7	1	2	3	4	5	6	7	1	2	3	4	5	6	7	1	2	3	4	5	6	7	1	2	3	4	5	6	7

1. Example Page 48. . . . .
2. Ex. Page 48 . . . .
3. Ex. of Direct Intervals Page 48 . . . .
4. Ex. of Inverted Interv. Page 49 . . . .
5. Ex. of Simple Interv. Page 49. . . . .
6. Ex. of Doubled Int. Page 49 . . . .
7. Ex. for the Major Mode of Sol Page 56 . . . .
8. Ex. for the Minor Mode of Sol Page 56 . . . .
9. Ex. of the transition from one Key to another Page 57 . . . .
10. Ex. of the transition from the Major to the Minor, and vice versa P. 57
11. Ex. P. 59 . . . .
12. Ex. transcribed by the 1st method P. 69 . . . .

Letter on Italian and French Opera

Finally, Sir,[1] obedience prevails over vanity. If you complain about my bad taste you will at least praise my kindness and I am sure that you will agree that faced with the alternative the heart does itself honor at the expense of the mind. At least this is the way I should act following the laws of prudence, so as to gamble only on the side on which there is less to lose. I am therefore going to speak to you about the spectacles of Italy, to you who has already judged those of France so well.[2] I would have only too much to be glad about if my letter could furnish you with some materials to judge the former as well.

It is a misfortune for opera that neither Aristotle nor Horace gave us rules for it. I imagine that our modern Greeks and Latins would not have spoken about it with so much scorn. Boileau would have removed it from his satires in order to place it in a position of honor in his *Poetic Art*.[3] La Bruyère would have grown bored with it only with knowledge, and Dacier, turning his criticisms into Praises, would have spared many of the rather dull ironies against the enthusiasts of that charming spectacle.[4] What is singular about this is that they were disposed to scorn opera precisely in Lully's and Quinault's time and that ever since the miserable Rhapsodies with which we are inundated, it began to be judged more favorably: apparently only the useless efforts that were seen to be made by those modern Amphions made the difficulty of the enterprise understood, and it was judged that a genre in scattered pieces in which it is difficult to succeed has more rigorous laws than was at first imagined;[5] whatever these laws may be, it is certain that aside from the general rules of the Theater they should encompass others that belong to the genre of the spectacle alone; for since the music gives it a singular and extraordinary character, the genre of the Poem should lend itself to it and correspond to it. Tragedy and comedy, aside from rules that are common to them both, each have their specific ones which make for two types of the same genre; opera is a third which is distinguished no less from the others and it is certainly a mistake to confound them and not to follow in each of these Poems its specific genius. Concerning this Principle it must be admitted that the Words of Italian Opera are not as good as ours even when they are better and more reasonable. It has already been noted that Tragedy is nothing less than the representation of a human action—men and above all Heroes do not speak in verse, they do not justify themselves for the idiocies love makes them do by grand words, their discourse is not a canvas of gigantic thoughts, of mixed expressions; they do not make those ridiculous cries nor those wild gestures which fill our theater. Nevertheless, when the Poet is wise and the actor skillful, it must be admitted that they can create an illusion; a well-directed and well-recited scene has nothing about it that is shocking, so if I can take Grandval for Cinna, I might sometimes take Sarrazin for Augustus.[6] At the opera it is not the same thing: it is not possible to imagine that two persons naturally converse by singing, and in this manner have a conversation that is often very serious; the more serious the subject the more the extravagance increases, so that it would be the height of ridiculousness to make a King converse with his Minister or his General about affairs of state or those of war and to hold counsel in music. This is precisely the vice of Italian Operas: their subjects are good and well chosen, but they are no good for the Opera, because instead of being selected from what is most wondrous in fable, they are drawn from what is most illustrious in History. Instead of *Isis*, *Phaeton*, *Persée*, *Iphegénie*, it is Antiochus, Caesar, Cato, Themistocles, and even Tamerlane who come by long and clear peals grossly to shock taste and decency, by representing to us those ancient and respectable Heroes in the guise of vile weaklings who torture their gullets to make us admire their quavering.[7] What, I ask, would the Shades of those great men say if, as spectators in a corner of the Theater, they were to see themselves so unworthily represented and what effect could Cato's and Themistocles' bizarre and humming song produce on our minds other than making us suppose that Themistocles and Cato had gone mad? The direction of the Piece answers to the choice of subject, love never departs from the majesty of the buskin; always heroic, rarely gallant, it knows how to count flowerets only by getting lost in figures of speech and comparisons. In this way, the sad and serious speeches of the actor make a shocking contrast with the liveliness of the tune to which they are put. This is one of the reasons why Italian operas, although interesting on Reading, are always glacially cold in the Theater; they are genuine Tragedies made to be declaimed, and which are in fact declaimed in Theaters by omitting some tunes the author had added on account of the music and which are usually saddled for any horse and have only a distant general relationship to the subject for which they are employed precisely like the detached tunes of festivals in our Operas.[8] These Operas represented in this way without music have much more effect than at the opera itself, where they are supremely boring, which does not happen in ours, which, although charming when performed at the Opera, are unbearable to read. I doubt that Italy has cause to make a merit of this difference; a work can be good only relative to the object the author proposed to himself, operas must be sung and it is for the author who has taste and discernment to apply to this genre what is proper to it, it being certain that a work can be absolutely good only when it is so with respect to its goal. It is in this that Quinault seems to me to be admirable and much superior to Metastasio, whose pieces are nonetheless more regular and more noble than his.[9] Quinault consulted nature and, as creator in the genre he undertook, he gave to his pieces precisely the genius they ought to have had with regard to their use; he wrote a poetry specifically for them from which one can draw from his operas the best rules they may be given. Metastasio wrote Tragedies as a thousand people had done before him. Quinault wrote neither Tragedies nor Comedies, he invented a third genre of spectacle, he wrote distinct Operas. He perceived that there had to be a single means to disguise from the spectators the ridiculousness that there was in carrying on conversation in music; he had to take them away from themselves, transport them to an enchanted world, into an abode of fairies; to stun them by dint of the surprising and marvelous, so that in the midst of so many extraordinary things they were less surprised to see speaking by means of singing and walking by means of dancing there. To this precaution he added another which succeeded in making the opera entirely suitable: it was to put in it only subjects which naturally entailed singing. Sacrifices, evocations, public rejoicings, gallant festivals, cries of War, songs of victory: all this is made for music and the imagination does not have to force itself to suppose it there. Furthermore, those choruses and the Pomp of those festivals contribute to the spectator's enthusiasm. A brilliant spectacle accompanied by a harmonious Music seduces the senses and prevents the mind from reflecting on the implausibility of the things it sees. In addition, one must not think of following in the opera the system of the Tragic scene and of seducing the spectator by degrees. One would never succeed in this manner: it is necessary to take him away, charm him all at once; and opera would only improve its effect if it always began with grand choruses and with the most imposing splendor of the spectacle. Moreover, I do not claim to say that our *merveilleux*[10] is exempt from inconveniences; first of all, it has that of touching much less than what is natural: one is only moderately interested in the misfortunes of people who have so many resources to save themselves—a God has only to arrive in a machine, or a Devil, a fury leaves from hell: behold all dangers dissipated without much fatigue and as one is warned in advance of the ease of all these things, one relies a great deal upon the opera's machinist for the salvation of the Heroes who are in peril there. It is for this reason that one fears little for a Dardanus and for a Perseus, one trusts too much to the power of the Father to be in pain for the son, but one can say that the coldness of those Pieces in this genre comes much more often from the bad choice of subject than from the *merveilleux* that enter into them.[11] Thus, *Thésée, Atys, Thétis et Pélée*[12] are Pieces to which the *merveilleux* adds much interest, by increasing the dangers for the Heroes by the inevitable power of their adversaries; and then one can establish conflicts of interest and jurisdiction among the Gods themselves, which leaves the same hold over the art and over situations as in an ordinary Tragedy in the direction of the Piece and gives rise to more hold over the whole spectacle than opera demands. On the contrary, the historical and natural turn of Italian Operas is the source of an infinite number of unbearable defects in that genre of spectacle, a tiresome monotony in scenes spun out without vigor and with as little wit, eternal recitatives intermixed at formalized distances with arias all cast in the same mold without variety and without contrast; scenes which one would say were always the same, so much do they resemble one another. In a word, a tissue of wholly trivial conversations of fourteen- to fifteen-hundred verses divided into three acts and sung for four deathly hours. So much for the taste of Italian operas in relation to the poem.

As for the Music, this is the main point. But that famous Italian music has already been spoken of so much, so many comparisons have already been made of it with ours that it appears impossible to say anything more about it without falling into tiresome repetitions.[13] Nevertheless, privately and for you alone, this is the opinion I have conceived on this point.

The Italians have brought Music to the ultimate point of perfection with respect to the end they proposed for themselves, which is that of arranging and combining sounds with taste to make voices and instruments shine. In this sense one can say that they have exhausted the beauties of the art; the ear is equally charmed by the variety, by the elegance of their passages and by the agility of the organs which make them heard. As for me, I devour them every day with new eagerness and I do not believe that there is a man on earth so little sensitive to beautiful sounds as to be able to hear without pleasure those who make this admirable music heard. All the Nations of Europe join in praise in its favor in this regard and the eagerness with which they have adopted it sufficiently indicates the esteem they have for it; while adopting it like the others, our suffrage should have more merit, since it is by taste and not by necessity that we make use of it. What would the Germans, the Spanish, and the English do without Italian music? A miserable racket in the fashion of their nations would be their entire resource; but whatever may be said, beautiful French music is quite capable of pleasing, even Foreigners. We therefore savor Italian music and we cultivate it because we are capable of recognizing and of loving beauty without regard to the climate which produces it. From this the Italians derive a reasoning that according to them unquestionably shows the excellence of their music. You hear them say: every Nation without excepting our own admires and practices our music; it is Music *par excellence*; all voices join in its favor, yet you alone through bad taste and through stubbornness for the productions of your own country claim to place your French music on a parallel with our own, but you are partial, and all the other judges, who are not so, unanimously condemn you: therefore you are mistaken. To this the French content themselves with responding that Italian Music has its particular genius, and French its own, and as the difference found between them does not admit of comparison, they should pass as equally good each in its own genre. It seems to me that Foreigners are hardly mistaken not to make a great deal of that reasoning. For, aside from the fact that they are right to reject the Hypothesis on which it is based, even if they were to admit it they would be quite justified in denying the consequence. First, the Music of the Italians is not at all so peculiar to the language and the genius of their nation that it still does not suit all the others; thus, German words go quite well with Italian Tunes, and even French words would not be ridiculous if the tune were written expressly for them or at least if they were adjusted to them with a little taste. Italian Music is incontestably a universal music and if it belongs particularly to the Italians, it is not that its own character is peculiar to their language and to their nation exclusively of the others, but that they happened to have enough genius and fire to give the former that brilliant character. In this regard who could deny that this music has the advantage over our own, which simply suits only the particular turn and genius of the French language, from which it follows that if one were to acknowledge that particular character in Italian music it would always be preferable to our own as being more universally pleasing.

From whence there thus arises that obstinacy of the French in cultivating and cherishing their music, whatever pleasure they may take from the Italian, however sensitive they may be to its beauties; it is known with what intensity all people with good taste are opposed to the introduction of the Italian genius into our own song and, despite the natural predilection of the French in favor of everything the French do not produce, the mixture of those foreign accents with the sweetness of our own has never been able to be admitted. The true reason for this is that the beauties of Italian Music are not of the same genre as those of our own and do not produce the same effects. Italian music supremely pleases me, but it does not at all touch me, the French pleases me only because it touches me. The trills, flowing movements, virtuoso passages, ornamented melodies of the first make the [vocal] organ shine and charm the ear, but the seducing sounds of the second go straight to the heart. If music is made solely to please, let us give the palm to Italy, but if it should also be moving, let us keep it for ourselves, and above all when it is a question of opera, where it is proposed to arouse the passions and to touch the spectator. How many times have our tears and our tender feelings honored the art of the musician and the talent of the actor at the Theater in Paris![14] Never has all the divine Italian music in those grand and majestic Theaters been able to boast, I do not say of drawing a tear, but of causing the least emotion in the most touching scenes—there one is always in a tranquil chill, one analyzes the sounds one hears, one admires the throat that forms them, but one never takes it into one's head to be touched, because instead of a passionate woman who expresses the raptures of her soul with feeling, for example, one always sees only a singer who grimaces and tortures her glottis to make us admire the agility of her voice. How many pretty eyes will weep at the beautiful scene of Atys and Sangride, at the third act of Pyramus and Thisbe, at Iphegenia's recognition scene, at Dardanus's monologue, and at a thousand other passages in which the most insensitive spectator feels himself stirred and softened despite himself![15] Mistaking their two roles, the actor acts badly and the musician composes in Italian, that is, coldly. The rage for ornamented melodies, trills, exquisitely flowing passages sweeps along their genius, nothing remaining of it for the natural character to which even they are not sensitive; they load their music with notes for the same reason they load their writings with flourishes, their houses with columns and reliefs, and their gardens with statues: to make up with their art for nature's avarice in not having made them sensitive to her beauties.

One of the great vices of Italian Music is also its monotony and lack of contrast. Their Opera, as I have told you, is composed of a long recitative, and then an aria, another long recitative, and yet another aria, and thus always alternately, but these arias which follow one another at formalized distances are all cast from the same mold, and divided into two parts, the first subdivided into two others, of which the first is further subdivided into two, namely the ritornello and the cadenza in the dominant, and the other contains the final cadenza, after which comes the second part of the aria, always modulated on the fourth note of the key, a modulation which, parenthetically, is neither as natural nor as agreeable as the note on the Dominant or on the sixth note. This whole series of arias, so similar with regard to their distribution, is still more so with regard to their style and movement, and it is hardly otherwise possible considering the quantity in which they are put into it, for an opera is usually composed of thirty grand arias all of about the same length and all distributed in the same way, without any admixture of those rhythmic recitatives, or of those little tunes, or of those light dialogues that serve among us to vary the style of the singing and the music and to contrast the various parts.

A further monotony in the Orchestra and the accompaniments; instead of taking advantage of the various instruments of which the orchestra is composed, it is always the violins that truly play with an admirable exactness and precision, but which always make the same passages heard perpetually accompanied by four large hunting horns which, whatever good effect they may produce when properly placed, make my head burst horribly by their continual racket in tunes for which they are least suited. As for accompaniment by flutes, oboes, cellos and Bassoons, violins of a low register and of other sorts which our musicians employ so happily, the former simply don't know what they are. Given this, their bass parts are in the worst taste in the world, bass parts without singing, without effort, and without grace; scraped glumly by a half dozen double basses which certainly serve more to keep the beat than to flatter the ear. In addition, the beautiful song and melody they put into the principal parts are the sole value of their compositions, for, as for the harmony, there is more of it in my view in the *Indes galantes* alone than in all the Italian operas put together.[16] I do not speak at all of fugal imitations, of ground Basses, and other torments they have with great reason banished from their music, at least from opera, so as not to place any obstacles before good taste and beautiful singing, which should alone be consulted in this genre of music.

But I should not finish this point without also reproaching them for the omission of Choruses, which produce such a beautiful effect in opera, whether by themselves or by the decoration that the girls and men who sing them add to the theater. We have such beautiful ones that one need only hear them in order to judge that they are a very advantageous and very suitable ornament for opera in more than one respect. Twenty times I have seen the spectator, seized with admiration and respect, transported as outside of himself by the famous chorus in *Jephté*; earth, hell, heaven itself all tremble before the lord; the chorus of the shining sun and that of the sailors who perish in the *Indes galantes*, the hymn of Ceres in *Pyrame et Thisbé*, the chorus of hurled thunderbolts in *Hippolyte et Aricie* are pieces which are not heard calmly.[17] Italy has nothing to my taste that makes up for this beauty in the least. For the few choruses there are in its opera, sung solely by the principal actors, are not worthy of bearing that name.

It must be admitted that if the defects of which I have spoken could be redeemed, they would be so by the beauties they accompany. The most beautiful singing of . . .[18]

Letter on "Omphale"
A Lyric Tragedy, reprised by the Royal Academy of Music, 14 January 1752[1]

(Grimm)

*Ingenium cui sit, cui mens divinior, atque os
Magna sonaturum, des nominis hujus honorem.*[2]

I dared to condemn *Omphale*, Madame,[3] before knowing that you protect it. You order me to justify my judgment publicly, and you are doubtless right: I need a justification for having judged French Music, and still more so for not having been of your opinion.

I do not at all wish to repeat here the worn-out parallels between European Music and French Music, for, as all the judges belong to one side, it is a trial that will never end. I shall speak of it, as much as is necessary, only in order to authorize the liberty I am taking of examining the latter; otherwise, instead of weighing my reasons, I would perhaps be asked by what right I meddle in speaking of it.

I am not unaware that every time it is a question of their Music the French flatly deny competence to all other peoples, and they have their reasons for this. Nevertheless, when these same French assure us that Chinese Music is detestable, I do not believe they have taken the trouble to take into account the view of the Chinese when pronouncing this judgment. Why should they deprive us with regard to them, at least concerning Music, a right they employ quite freely, and on more than one point, with regard to other Nations?

Italian Music promises and gives pleasure to every man who has ears—no more preparation is needed than that. If all the peoples of Europe have adopted it, despite the differences in languages, it is because they have preferred their pleasure to their pretensions.

I therefore believe I can say that, since the aim of Music is to arouse pleasant sensations by harmonious and rhythmic sounds, every man who is not deaf has a right to decide whether it has fulfilled its object. I admit that to judge a national Music well, the character of the Language in relation to song must also be known, and this is also a study I have tried to make: whether I may flatter myself with some success is what I will learn from you, Madame, after you have read this Letter.

Let us therefore begin by conceding the genre; this I do quite sincerely, and I find great beauties in it, although always inferior to those of Italian Music. French Music is very well adapted to the genius of the Language; and French Opera also makes up a genre apart, of which the Nation has reason to be jealous, for everything that is a genuine genre cannot be preserved with too much care.

You see, Madame, that I am equitable. Not only have I judged French Music in itself—a law always neglected in the mania for comparisons, but I have had no trouble in accustoming myself to its genius and to feeling its beauties. Luck, it is true, has been for me. I arrived in Paris as predisposed against your Opera as all Foreigners are; I rushed to it, quite sure to find it even worse than I had imagined. To my great astonishment I found two things I was far from looking for in it: Music and a voice that sang. It was *Platée*, a sublime Work in a genre M. Rameau created in France, which some people of taste appreciated and which the multitude has judged.[4] It was Mademoiselle Fel,[5] who, with the most felicitous vocal organ in the world, with a voice always even, always fresh, brilliant, and light, still knew the art we call in sacred language *singing*—a term shamefully profaned in France and applied to a way of pushing sounds out of one's gullet with effort and of crashing them against the teeth by a movement of a convulsive chin; this is what is called among us *shouting*, and which is never heard in our Theaters, it is true, but as much as one likes in public Marches. My surprise, I admit, was odd, and this experience cured me forever, so I hope, of the desire to judge precipitously based on a vague and uncertain rumor. Nevertheless, I had only to arrive two days earlier, when *Medée et Jason* was produced, and I would have been reaffirmed in all my ideas.[6]

After the confession I have just made, I will be allowed, I hope, to obey your orders and to hazard some remarks on *Omphale*'s Music, with all the frankness natural to me. The interest of the arts, of taste, and above all of the Nation demand that one always be able to speak the truth, and it is a glory that France alone has among all the Peoples of Europe that every Foreigner can speak freely in its bosom, even in order to call attention to the defects he finds there. That noble confidence of this People, the object of our admiration and sometimes of our jealousy, says more about it than we know how to, and it is our Critics themselves who give it its finest praise.

You will allow me, Madame, to not speak at all of the Poem; the respect I have for the Creator* of the Ballet, for the Author of *L'Europe Galante*, of

---

*M. De La Motte.[7] I name him in addition to the other men celebrated for their merit and for their talent, so that no one might misunderstand me here. It is in order to prevent any misunderstanding on the part of certain of my compatriots into whose hands this Letter might fall, and who, due to being in the heart of Saxony or of Bavaria, are no less worthy of honoring true merit.

Issé, and of so many other beautiful Works, would put me in the position of proving that *Omphale* is not worthy of him. I prefer to limit myself to the Music, whose Author* can merit consideration which is less well known to me.

I foresee that *Omphale*'s partisans will relinquish many parts of this Opera to me, and especially that called Music *par excellence*. They will admit that one must seek in it neither treasures nor harmony. They will speak to me of the taste, of the naturalness, and of the expression in the singing of this Opera, and it is precisely concerning these things that I wish to attack it. In my opinion, this singing is in bad taste from one end of it to the other, and filled with contradictions, sad, expressionless, and always beneath its subject, which is the worst of all vices—not to mention the thoroughbass, always wandering haphazardly, following the keyboard uncertainly, without knowing where to stop, not meeting up with the dominant in the end, in order to conclude, almost always in the wrong way, on a perfect cadence.

In order to prove all these things, one must follow this Music line by line; but I do not claim to write a Book, and when clarification is desired in good faith, a few well-chosen examples, and a few well-meditated reflections suffice to judge many things.

M. Rameau is reproached with not at all understanding Recitative; it even seems to me that some of his friends, not daring at the outset to justify him on this count, have preferred to claim that anyone can compose a Recitative rather than to uphold the goodness of his. It is, however, well attested that nothing in the world is so difficult as composing Recitative,†

---

* M. Destouches.[8]

† The character of Italian Recitative is so sublime that by itself it assures this Music a superiority to which no other approaches. I conceive of nothing beyond its truthfulness. Equally capable of every expression and every character, it declaims and proceeds with pomp and majesty in Tragedy; it speaks the language of all the passions with fire and speed; and it makes joy, gaiety, sentimentality, playfulness, pleasantry, buffoonery speak with the same felicity. French Recitative, in contrast, is by its genre sad, slow, monotonous, yet susceptible nonetheless of great beauties. The praise I have just given to Italian Recitative will appear strange only to those who, without having a principle and without reflection, are accustomed to repeat what they have heard others say. They will tell me that Recitative is often not listened to in Italy, and that they have ears there only for Ariettas. But there are people in Italy who prefer Ariosto to Tasso, and there are those there whom I would like to forbid from listening to *Pergolesi*, *Buranello*, and *Adolfati* altogether as much as I would like to stop certain people in Paris from going to hear *Pygmalion*.[9] I beg those who will not want to rely on me concerning this inferiority of the French Recitative to look for the word *Recitative* in the future Volumes of the *Encyclopedia*, and other articles related to it. I believe I can rely on the sentiment and the reasons of the Author of that portion (M. Rousseau, Author of the Discourse of Dijon), for although he proudly affects to be ignorant about so many things, one cannot do him the honor of believing that he is ignorant of the beauties of French Recitative after having seen that of *Les Muses galantes*.[10]

for it is the work of a most pure genius. But it is precisely on this point that I find M. Rameau very often great, and always original.*

I respect the Creator of French Recitative. In order to dare judge it, it does not suffice to see it on paper and to read the Score; one must have seen the scene staged. I very much long to admire *Armide*, that masterpiece by Quinault, that Opera the Nation never wearies of seeing. People whose judgment is as a demonstration for me have assured me that Lully's talent in Recitative is as great as his fame. I believe it, but I would not believe that ears accustomed to the truthfulness and to the beauty of the singing in *Armide*, *Atys*, *Thésée*, etc.,[12] could ever have listened to *Omphale*, and especially to its Recitative, if I did not know that immediately after the Century of Racine and during that of M. de Voltaire Tragedies were played with great success in which there were not three French verses in succession.[13]

* * *

It is in appearance an inexplicable problem how the same Spectators who applauded that masterpiece of the art, that divine *Pygmalion*, in the evening dared show the least pleasure in *Omphale* the next day. But it is not difficult to make sense of these contradictions. It is to Philosophers and men of Letters that the Nation owes, even without its suspecting it, its taste for good Music, as well as for all the fine arts, having become general of late. It is to their praise that M. Rameau principally owes the justice and the honors the whole Nation today renders him. But in Italy and elsewhere nature and instinct make more proselytes of good taste in a single day than Philosophers make here in several years by their dissertations. This taste, although general in France, is still vague; it is often counterbalanced by old prejudices which seem respectable by their very weakness, as sometimes age has no other title to consideration than its decrepitude. It remains for the Philosophers and for time to fix this taste, and to make it secure in the Nation. Ten years from now the repertoire of the Opera will be rid of many pretended treasures, and will not be the poorer for it.

---

*It is a very curious anecdote in the History of French Music that in 1735 M. Rameau dared not print the Recitative of the *Indes galantes* because all Paris found it detestable. And what is even more singular is that in his Preface the Author asks pardon of the Public, who, without saying it, today finds it very beautiful. Let us listen to one of those barbarous scenes from the *Indes galantes*, that, for example, between Huascar and Phani, in the act of the Incas. With what dignity, with what majesty the Musician makes the Inca speak! Follow the progression of that Bass, always simple and natural. Note that ease and that variety in the modulations, those bold passages, when nature and the declamation require them. I know only of the bad taste of the Poet for having made a traitor of a man who speaks with such majesty of his Gods, and who makes such a sublime cult of the Sun.[11]

Atys, *Armide*, *Hippolyte et Aricie* will be at the head of Tragedy; *L'Europe galante*, *Les Fêtes d l'Hymen et de l'Amour* at the head of Ballet; *Issé* will be the model for pastorals, and I greatly fear that *Platée* will remain without rival as it was without a model.[14]

The authority and the credit of Literary People will doubtless hasten this very glorious period for France. It is for them, as Professors of that Nation and of the Universe, to enlighten the multitude by their enlightenment and to guide it by their precepts. In the matter of taste, the Court gives fashions to the Nation and Philosophers give Laws. They require merely the courage they do not always have to go against the most generally received and often the most absurd opinions, to attack them with all the force of reason, and to exterminate them everywhere they are found. The Philosopher* who has written the preliminary discourse to the *Encyclopedia* has given them the signal. He has dared to admire his Contemporaries and his Compatriots. He has dared, with a boldness worthy of him and of every man who thinks, to speak of those superior geniuses whose labor and glory he shares, whose merit the ungrateful Nation—sometimes more through lack of enlightenment than through envy and jealousy—has often misunderstood, and tarnished the brightness that only redounded to it. The time is not far off, I hope, when the Public will learn the art of listening, and when it will decide about things of taste and the agreeable Arts with the same finesse and with the same delicacy that the people of Athens once did. It is then that it will no longer name in an Actor "expressiveness of singing" what is merely overdone playing, an effort of the lungs, sometimes a gesture of the arm, or a movement of a stick. It is then that it will no longer call "singing" what is only a series of shouts, often off-key, always disagreeable. It is then that great talents will be genuinely flattered by the applause they receive, which they will regard as their most precious privilege, whereas today they often blush at the homage lavished on them by the same hands that prostitute themselves a moment later with the same passion by applauding what they should boo or at least what they should only tolerate with an indulgent silence in order to make easier the passage from nothingness to mediocrity.

I require the hope of all these revolutions in order to calm the sadness that the striking success of *Pygmalion* causes me. I notice every day with regret that only what is pretty in it is perceived and that what is beautiful is forgotten. This is a result of that taste for little things, of that malady of the shrinking of the mind that seems to have infected our century, and this is the reason in another sense why everyone is occupied with the ornamen-

---

*M. D'Alembert.[15]

tation of his fireplace and the tops of his doors and that no one dreams of the portal of his house.

It is the Ariette* *Regne Amour, etc.*, that produces the great success of this act; the beauty of the two monologues is lost on the multitude. They are found to be well written, it is said coldly, but there is always enthusiasm for the Ariette. Nevertheless, this Ariette, the happiest canvas of the world, which has M. Jelyotte[16] display all the charms and riches of his enchanting talent, is merely the production of a man of taste, whereas the Author of the monologues must have been warmed by that divine fire we call genius. It is the same workman, I know, who wrote both portions, but men should be affected wholly differently by what is beautiful than by what is merely pleasing.

I admit that I find new objects for admiration in these monologues at each performance. What regularity in the design, what harmony in the instrumental part, what simplicity, what learning in the thoroughbass, what nobility in its progression, what expression in the song, how touching and true it always is, as all this comes together to seize me, to transport me outside of myself! With what art he always takes up these words again:

> Fatal love, cruel victor,
> What features have you chosen to pierce my heart!
> [*Fatal amour, cruel vainqueur,*
> *Quels traits as-tu choisi pour me percer le coeur!*]

How he renders them by more touching gradations at each reprise, especially by the bass that leads them! How he expresses the words to me through flutes and violins on the same plan:

> Unfeeling witness of the turmoil that overwhelms me;
> [*Insensible témoin du trouble qui m'accable*;]

when he says to me:

> Its enchanting grace
> Draws from me, despite myself, cries and sighs.
> Gods! What confusion! What vain tenderness!

---

*I cannot keep myself from noting here another great advantage of Italian Music over French. Their Aria, precisely like their Recitative, is capable of every expression and of every form. You see before you two equally beautiful and agreeable figures: the one in noble and simple dress, the other covered with all the richness of a refined luxuriousness. You see the reason why this last one dazzles the multitude, and the ease that it has in hiding its defects under the splendor of its finery. The Ariette, on the contrary, will never make up a very brilliant part of the French Opera: it is not the daughter of genius; no, in France it does not claim such a sublime origin. It permits only the pleasant painting of certain words. The Musician is reduced to frolic eternally around a word such as *"lance," "vole," "chaîne," "ramage,"* etc.[17] Grand portraits, the language of feeling and of the passions are relegated to the monologues, which are but an embroidered, ornate, and sometimes overburdened Recitative. . . .[18]

> [*Sa grace enchanteresse*
> *M'arrache, malgré moi, des pleurs & des soupirs!*
> *Dieux! Quel égarement! Quelle vaine tendresse!*]

In vain I command my tears, in vain I try to stop them. This belongs only to him who makes them flow. He seizes me all of a sudden by a stroke of genius: two chords which precede Pygmalion's prayer to Venus, and which are all the more sublime, which he makes with extreme simplicity and a straight change from the minor to the major mode. With what felicity he expresses these words by the song, and by the bass, and by the instrumental part:

> Could you condemn the source of my tears?
> [*Pourrois-tu condamner la source de mes larmes?*]

In a word, if the Statue did not come alive, and if I were not seized at the moment of the miracle by that bold and felicitous change of key from *G re sol* to *E si mi* major,[19] what happens to its Lover would happen to me when he says to it in a modulation which tears at my soul:

> If Heaven were not to make you live,
> It would condemn me to death!
> It would condemn me to death!
> [*Si le Ciel ne vous eut fait vivre,*
> *Il me condamnoit à mourir!*
> *Il me condamnoit à mourir!*]

You see, Madame, that the enthusiasm these pieces inspire prevents me from speaking to you of that brilliant overture, of that admirable saraband danced by the Statue,* of that majestic Chorus, *l'amour triomphe*, of that original character of the innocent Pantomime, finally, of each piece which makes up part of this immortal work. But my astonishment is at its height when I think that the Author of *Pygmalion* is that of the fourth act of *Zoroastre*, that the Author of *Zoroastre* is that of *Platée*, and that the Author of *Platée* has written the divertimento of the Rose in the act of the flowers.[20] What a Proteus, always novel, always original, always grasping the true and the sublime of each character, and of whom one can say precisely what the Philosopher I have already cited says of M. de Voltaire: that he is never either above or below his subject.[21]

I admit, Madame, that I regard the admiration and the respect I have for all that is true talent, in whatever genre, as my greatest good after the love of virtue. Heaven, by favoring these men with its blessings, distinguishes them from the crowd of ordinary mortals. High rank, birth, riches,

---

* Mademoiselle Puvignée.[22]

frivolous distinctions, chimerical honors: you all disappear in my eyes. The preference for a man of talent over one who does not have them is alone just and founded. It is nature which has imprinted this sacred mark on them in order to attract for them the worship and the homage of humanity.

I erect in my heart a Temple to those privileged mortals, and I allow all those who are fortunate enough to perceive what is beautiful to assist in the worship I render them. I do not at all fear being outshone in zeal. Sublime devotion does not at all fear rivals.

I believe, Madame, that I perceive you among the small number of those fortunate spirits who hasten to honor this Temple. Who could be more worthy than you to discern and to admire talents! You find in this Temple the images of the illustrious dead; Altars and Incense for the living. They are delighted with what you accord them. You are not surprised to find the altar of the God of Dance* nearby that of the immortal Maurice.[23] You are not at all so to find the Conqueror of Silesia, sometimes before the altar consecrated to the man who does not wound, to the Bard of Henri IV, to the Historian of Charles XII, who alone merits being his;[24] sometimes before that other altar consecrated to the Orpheus of France next to that of the divine Pergolesi,[25] dividing his devotion between the Sublime—*Venite exultemus*†—and the Pathetic—*Salve Regina*;‡ here stopped short by the grace and suppleness of that unique voice§ which by her talent has taught her nation that one could sing in French, and who has dared to give an original expression to Italian Music with the same boldness; there listening with admiration to Astroa and Salimbeni**; seduced by the expression, the soulfulness, and the ease, that infallible mark of the great talent of the singer†† of the French Nation; sometimes busied in the workshops of the Praxiteles‡‡ of the century; or quite astonished by the proudness of Carle's§§ brush, by the boldness of his emulator,*** by the truthfulness and the force of expression in those lively Pastels†††; quivering, trembling at the features of the sublime Merope‡‡‡; seized with Orosmane's§§§ acting; touched by the truthfulness of that ven-

---

* M. Dupré.[26]
† Motet by M. Mondonville, who has written so many masterpieces in this genre.[27]
‡ Short Motet by Pergolesi.[28]
§ Mademoiselle Fel.[29]
** The first is from Berlin, M. Salimbeni is from Dresden. Their equal talent is famous.[30]
†† M. Jelyotte.[31]
‡‡ M. de Bouchardon, M. Pigale.[32]
§§ M. Vanloo.[33]
*** M. Pierre.[34]
††† By M. De la Tour.[35]
‡‡‡ Mademoiselle Dumesnil.[36]
§§§ M. Lekain.[37]

erable Luzignan* or by that quick-tempered Old Man†; sometimes charmed by Zeneide's‡ grace and unique talent; sometimes enchanted by the art and finesse of the acting of that original and charming couple§; sometimes attracted by those two other inimitable subjects, the Momus** and the Thalie of the century; sometimes admiring the wisdom of the vast and profound views of the Philosopher,†† Legislator of Nations, and sometimes distracted by the pathetic playing of that inimitable Violin.‡‡

This extraordinary man, who alone has time for everything, finds his altar raised in the middle of this temple. You see him there with the governance of his states in one hand, and his flute in the other; dictating on one side the System of Laws to his Chancellor, and on the other the plans for a Symphony to his Musician. And Heaven, in order to compensate him for the misfortune he has of ruling, accords him the precious privilege, of which he is worthy, of spreading his blessings over the talents he has the happiness of admiring.

THE END

* M. Sarrazin.[38]
† In *Andrienne*.[39]
‡ Mademoiselle Gaussin.[40]
§ M. Grandval, Mademoiselle Grandval.[41]
** M. Armand, Mademoiselle Dangeville.[42]
†† The Author of *The Spirit of the Laws*, and other works consecrated to immortality.[43]
‡‡ M. Pagin.[44]

Remarks on the Subject of the Letter by M. Grimm on "Omphale"

(Raynal)

What pleasure you have given the Public, Sir, by showing it the weakness of its ideas on Music! You approach the most astute and boldest truths, but ones which still leave a cloud behind them. I would not have noticed it at all if I had not followed the advice of the Author in the *Mercure* this month, who *exhorts those who have not read you to read you, and those who have read you to reread you.*[1]

I do not at all wish to renew the issue of *Omphale* here. I would be obliged to follow you line by line, and I would not have the time to say to you one word about what you call *Music par excellence*.[2]

You pour forth many charming things in the various praises you give M. Rameau; they are so ingeniously placed that the Public would regard the pompous titles with which you decorate him as insipidness and a marked affectation from every other quarter. Like you, I admire this great Artist; but I am no longer of your view when you direct your efforts to persuade us that he is a creator, when he is only an imitator, and when he is truly a creator, not to have demonstrated it is to force him to complain about you, despite that beautiful zeal you inspire.

He who speaks of a creator of a sublime genre in France,* does not suppose that in other countries just about the same things have been done. The genre of the Music in *Platée* is not at all new; all the Opera buffa in Italy belong very much to this genre. If it is due to the croaking of frogs that you call him original, those others make horses whinny, and cats meow, and by a more marked singularity, put a Medical prescription into Music.† The character of the Music in *Platée* is a buffa character, and *not sublime*[3] (two things surely quite incompatible). This is what designates it —we knew this before *Platée*. You see, Sir, that he is not at all a creator, but an imitator.

M. Rameau is the first who devised the system of the Fundamental

---

* *Platée.*[4]
† *Recipe triginta viginta quinquaginta sexaginta lumacas amaras & ravana rara misce con borgogna.*[5]

Bass. He has in addition enriched us by his own taste: behold him a creator twice over—this is perhaps what you meant to say.

I read with pleasure the praise you gave Italian Recitative; but it does not suffice to say that it *is sublime, nothing is beyond its truthfulness, that it proceeds with pomp and majesty in Tragedy.*[6] It should instead have been defined rather than dressed so magnificently. Acclaim is not at all taken account of in a country where it is so very fashionable.

Italian Recitative, steady in its pace, gives each feeling enough time for the Orchestra to facilitate its changes in key, and by this means avoids final cadences, and often knows rest only at the end of the Recital. The Orchestra does not at all obscure the declamation of the Actor by a heap of chords; but to each different expression it confirms the same feeling by a new way of expressing it. This is what makes it susceptible of variety.

French Recitative, you say, Sir, *is by its genre sad, slow, monotonous.*[7] Criticism is no better received than praise when nothing is proved.

French Recitative is *slow* because it has the misfortune to be sung with trills, and because more portamenti are put into it than into true declamation, which causes the Listener to flag by the slowness of its expression. It is *monotonous* because it is the melody that decorates it, and this melody often calls for final cadences, which can only be the same for the ear, and which by this means have a uniformity of tone that makes the whole monotonous.

The Recitative or Melopoeia of the Ancients might have been another type of simple and natural declamation which had no melodic character, but which borrowed from the melody what could be used to make it progress in succession by the various analogous keys to the true key of the declamation.

You fear that someone might object to you, Sir, that Recitative is not at all listened to in Italy. Do not give as reasons (p. 10) *that there are people there whom you would like to prevent listening to the Music of Pergolesi, of Buranello, and of Adolfati;*[8] that is, that there are numbed organs in that country as there are in this one. One might perhaps give a reason more natural and more in favor of Recitative.

It is almost always the same people who go to the Opera, the Recitative is always listened to for the first five or six performances; the repetition of things which have a serious character cannot be focused upon for much longer. The Opera lasts only during Carnival; it is a time consecrated to dissipation and to liberty. In Italy as in France fanatic cabalists or pitiless gossips are not wanting, but with this sole difference, that custom does not at all permit the military guard to repress their self-conceit.[9] Recitative finds itself the victim of abuse and of circumstances; but one should not conclude against it from this that it is not listened to.

I take the liberty to tell you that Adolfati is misplaced in your citation of Pergolesi and Buranello.[10] It is as if Lully and Rameau were cited along with a mediocre Composer; to confound them so lightly is to little respect their fame. Hasse, called the Saxon,* would have figured better in his place.

You celebrate a *Philosopher who has dared, with a boldness (p. 37) worthy of him, to admire his contemporaries and his compatriots*, etc.[13] — such sentiments make up the praise of your Philosopher. But, Sir, do you not do precisely the contrary? Hasse, called the Saxon, is surely your contemporary and your compatriot; and you admire Adolfati. I am quite persuaded that it is not at all from *want of enlightenment* that you have forgotten him in the general list, which is at the end of your Letter.[14] But there will be surprise at seeing you spread such beautiful maxims without making use of them.

Handel is also Saxon, and I sought handsome long for his number and did not find it: these two great Masters have a right to cite you to the tribunal of your Philosopher.[15]

(P. 40). The Ariette is so beautiful that it pleases all Europe in general. It is not at all reduced to frolic eternally, like the French Ariette, around a word such as "*lance*," "*vole*," "*chaîne*," "*ramage*," etc.[16] What is the cause of this fecundity? This is what I wish you had defined, rather than your saying that it is *covered with all the richness of a refined luxuriousness, and that it hides its defects under the splendor of its finery*.[17] If the richness of your style gave us the slightest idea of the Ariette, I would be the first to applaud the fecundity of your images; but in a work in which the Public, eager for reasons, might wish for some details, this does not suffice.

The Italian Arietta had its defects of old. A single word varied several times comprised its whole merit. The mind, by the skillfulness and vivacity of its execution, alone found what suited it; feeling was not at all its object. But the famous Bernacchi imagined that rules were needed for this brilliant part of music. He first dared attempt this plan at Bologna: he succeeded.[18] Likewise, Mainard first perceived that the third verse should have a final meaning, or pause in the stanza: good minds will follow this model. Maigret was the first who, by imitating Trissino's *Sofonsibe*, introduced the rule of the three unities into Tragedy: people of good taste sense

---

*Hasse, Composer of Opera to the King of Poland, Elector of Saxony, is recognized by all Italy as the most fecund and most felicitous genius that ever existed, especially in Music for the Theater. At forty-eight he had put fifty-four Operas to Music. He is the sole foreigner whose Music the Italians grant the glory of performing. He is so very cherished in Italy, that cradle of the Arts, that impresarios have done the impossible by establishing him there. But he is attached to the service of a Prince who will never regard it as a *misfortune to rule*,† because he is just, and creates the happiness of his Subjects.[11]

†Page 52, in speaking of the King of Prussia: And heaven for compensating him *for the misfortune he has of ruling*.[12]

the necessity of it; these are things enclosed, so to speak, within a frame well-decorated by its form.[19] So the famous Bernacchi* behaved: he put the minor between two majors,† and had the first and principal motif of the song repeated by the different transitions in key, so that the ear would better grasp, by this repetition, the character of the thoughts of the music. (The celebrated Abbé Metastasio was obliged to conform to these laws.)[20] The Italian Musicians place all the happy productions of their genius in this frame; often inspired by the features of love, of hate, of fury, of despair: all the passions can enter into it. This, without doubt, is what assures the Italian Arietta its superiority over the French Ariette.

(P. 35) *It is to Philosophers and to men of Letters that the Nation owes, even without its suspecting it, its taste for good Music, as well as for the fine arts, having become general of late.* (p. 36) *In the matter of taste, the Court gives fashions to the Nation and Philosophers give Laws.*[22]

Has this taste for the arts become general of late by the aid of your Philosophers, who today cause the Magots of China, vases of fragile porcelain, to be preferred to the antique bronzes that used majestically to decorate our apartments? Are these the same laws that today cause India paper, illuminated prints to be preferred to the paintings of the greatest painters? Music, it is true, seems in our time to have received some increase in France, but this is not at all on the side of taste: do not confuse taste with the dryness of calculation. The principles are better known and better demonstrated, but taste is in the genius of the Musician and all the Philosophers in the world cannot make one compose good music if he has not received a special gift from nature. M. de Voltaire has quite ingeniously said "that almost all the arts have been overwhelmed with a prodigious number of rules, the majority of which are useless or false. We find lessons everywhere; but very few examples. For nothing is so easy to do than to speak in the tone of a master of things one cannot execute."[23] Italy owes its progress in all the arts and above all in music to emulation and to the great number of models that are before their eyes. The Philosophers are not owed much credit for the arts in that country. Music seems to have established its abode in Naples, where a thousand young people, brought together in several Academies, cultivate the happy gifts of Nature. It is

---

 * Bernacchi was not at all a Composer, but he was a celebrated Singer; he conceived of this plan and it was put into practice by Porpora, Bononcini, etc.,[21] by which we see that great Composers could not wholly glimpse it and how attentive they should be to the good advice given to them.
 † What I have called minor is often only the correlate key. It is for the skill of the Composer to seek the correlate which is relative to the subject, and which best enters into the major. The minor or correlate always changes the movement: that is, if the major is C the minor will be slow, and retakes the major C. This is what produces the shading of the picture.

there that from infancy they vie with one another in the art of immortalizing their name: it is from there that all the famous Musicians have come, such as Leo, Vinci, Taradellas, Pulli, Hasse, Jomelli, and a hundred others.[24] Practice, natural taste, and emulation have formed these great masters. This is precisely what we lack: where there is no emulation, there is no talent. Louis XIV desired painters and sculptors; he established an Academy that still exists,* and which counts among its members subjects who honor him.[25] When true music is desired in France, one will be obliged to create the same establishments.

(P. 37) *The time is not at all far off,* you say, *when the public in France will learn the art of listening.*[27] What do you mean by *the art of listening*? There is no other theater in Europe where more decency reigns than at the Opera, and no nation more attentive, whether for music or for Poetry, than the French nation. This great *art* of *listening* is so very much neglected in Italy that people of good taste openly complain of it. I would complain that the *art* of understanding is neglected by many people, since they regard declamation as a thing of little importance in our lyric- tragedies.

(P. 38) *It is then that the Public will no longer name in an Actor "expressiveness of singing" what is merely overdone playing, an effort of the lungs, a gesture of the arm or a movement of a stick.*[28] It is seen by this proposition that you want to spread a ridiculous veneer over the Actors whom the nation cherishes the most by the truth of their talents. The Poems put to Music by M. de Lully could not be performed without these talents you claim to despise. We know their price, and we see with regret festivals, ballets perpetually occupying our Theater; it is, as you say quite well (p. 39), *occupied with the ornamentation of his fireplace without being occupied with the portal of his house.*[29]

Mademoiselle Fel, who with the same boldness dared to give an original expression to Italian Music, etc.[30] One could not be at all timid to have formulated this plan; and if it were formulated, the Italians will likely profit from this discovery.

(P. 49, 50, 51, 52).[31] The number of people you cite and whom you group in singular fashion breathes all the license of that beautiful poetic fire that enraptures you. He has *seduced you by expression*; he *makes you tremble and shake*; the other *seizes you and touches you*. Finally, he *charms* you, *has enchanted you*: this presupposes a temperament susceptible to many im-

―――――――
* Monsieur de Tournehem has revived the ancient rights and privileges of the Academy of painting.[26] He has assigned pensions to the young pupils, who, gathered under a famed Professor, have the advantage of being animated by emulation. The honors and pensions they have been obtained by the most skillful Masters are living proof of his love for the Arts, of which he is the protector. M. de Tournehem has done more in a day than all our Philosophers have done in ten years.

pressions. But since you are so well organized, why does that *inimitable violin only cause you to become distracted by its pathetic playing*, above all you, Sir, who have (p. 49) *erected in your heart a temple to those privileged mortals?*[32] I would have taken great pleasure in reading in your letter to what point the nation ungrateful to such a sublime talent dared publicly humiliate him.[33] Here is where it was necessary to take the tone of your Philosophers and to say that the love of his talent made him cross the Alps to seek a teacher worthy of him. It is the Music of that Teacher who inspires noble sensations. Original in everything, he received as laws only those from his genius. The sublimity of his Works causes him to be esteemed by every man capable of perceiving the truth. He knew how to banish cosmetics from Music so as to serve nature. He is known throughout Europe, but cherished by few people, as very few people have the happiness of distinguishing noise from feelings and expression. Such is the teacher M. Pagin has faithfully followed in his studies. He wanted to enrich us with a new genre, and the nation disdained what it will doubtless admire in another time. Foreigners accustomed to enriching themselves by our losses would like to attract him to their homes; but a PRINCE[34] who has protected Science from his youth, who has known how to win in war, and whom in the heart of peace we enjoy, compensates talented men, has called him to his Court, where true merit finds a refuge from cabal.

I do not believe, Sir, that you could be ungrateful to me for having hazarded some Remarks on your Work. I have abandoned *Omphale* to you; I have *declaimed* like you on the French and Italian Recitative. I have said what you might have said if you had wished to do so. I have praised M. Rameau, who is surely above praise; I have avoided citing him too often, for fear of appearing *partial*. I have not said a word about *Pygmalion*, since unless its score is presented, it is impossible to embellish your praise.

I have only spoken of Handel, of Hasse, and of Tartini, because they came up on their own, and I am quite persuaded that they are well worth the trouble. You have your *Gods* and I *mine*. I have the honor of being, Sir, with all the esteem owed to your merit,

Your very humble and very obedient Servant,
D.***

Letter to M. Grimm on the Subject of the Remarks Added to His Letter on "Omphale"

Picas quis docuit verba nostra, conari?[1]

I congratulate you, Sir, on your new fame. You are now in possession of an honor which Homer and Plato had only long after their deaths, and which Boileau alone enjoyed among us during his lifetime: You have a Commentator.[2] The remarks on your letter do not, it is true, bear the title of Commentaries; but you know that Commentators suppress the essential things and expand on those which have no need of it, that they have passion for interpreting everything that is clear, that their explanations are always more obscure than the text, and there is nothing they fail to perceive in their Author, except for grace and finesse.

Now, the remarks do not say a word about *Omphale*, which is the subject of your letter. On the other hand, they expand at great length on your somewhat overlong digressions. You have spoken of Recitative, and the remarks make a sermon about it of which your words are the text. French Recitative is slow; *first point*. French Recitative is monotonous; *second point*. Care is taken to supplement the definition they claim you should have given of Italian Recitative. After this the *Recitative or the Melopee* of the ancients is defined.[3] Soon the Arietta will be defined; and what is not defined?

A grand Commentary on the fact that you would like to forbid certain people from listening to the Music of Pergolesi, Buranello, Adolfati; a Commentary which proves very methodically that you are right to say that nothing should be concluded against Italian Recitative from the fact that it is not listened to at the Opera.[4]

Another grand Commentary on the Arietta, invented in Bologna by the famous Bernacchi, but put into practice by others, given that the famous Bernacchi was not a Composer at all, but a famous Singer.[5]

A second Commentary on the art of listening, which the Commentator takes for the art of opening one's ears. About which he complains very wittily about the art of understanding being neglected.[6]

A Commentary on what you have said about the abuse of gestures: but here the Commentator takes the liberty of not being of your opinion, because gesture is essential to Lully's Music.[7]

Item, a grand Commentary on your sensitivity for the fine arts and for talents in every genre. You have raised a Temple to the God of Taste and of talent. One ought to believe the Commentator on this matter when he declares to us that your Gods are not at all his. In saying this he has proved it, and he can be quite sure that he will never be suspected of that idolatry.

Let us pass to the clarity of interpretations. The Commentator, who has the charity to supply the definitions which he maintains you are wrong for having omitted, dictates to you this one for Italian Recitative. *Italian Recitative, steady in its pace, gives each feeling enough time for the Orchestra to facilitate its changes in key, and by this means avoids final cadences, and often knows rest only at the end of the Recital. The Orchestra does not at all obscure the declamation of the Actor by a heap of chords; but to each different expression it confirms the same feeling by a new way of expressing it. This is what makes it susceptible of variety.*[8] To tell you my view of such a clear definition frankly, I think that the Author must have heard some Italian Recitative by chance, shorn of ritornelli and of the features of instrumental playing, and he must simply have taken this for the general character of the Recitative. What is quite certain in all this is that the Author of this definition, whoever it may be, has never known Music.

But another definition which must be heard out of curiosity is that of the Arietta. I am going to transcribe it very exactly. *The famous Bernacchi put the minor between two majors, and had the first and principal motif of the song repeated by the different transitions in key, so that the ear would better grasp by this repetition the character of the thoughts of the Music.* You laugh: patience, you are not at the end; you must still suffer through the footnote, if you please. *What I have called minor is often only the correlate key. It is for the skill of the Composer to seek the correlate relative to the subject, and which best enters into the major. The minor or correlate always changes the movement: that is, if the major is C the minor will be in 3/4, slow, and retakes the major C. This is what produces the shading of the picture.*[9] Let us not wrong the Author by believing that he has taken all this gibberish out of his head. I think I glimpse the truth here yet. These passages must have been transcribed from some old Italian book and translated somehow or other by someone who understood nothing at all about Music, and not much about Italian.

I agree to spare you the continuation on the condition that you acknowledge that the remarks are true Commentaries. Never have the Lexicographers and all the learned in *usage* had a more clearly marked character. Thus I suppose the proof made.

I am utterly unaware of who the Commentator is, but I do not at all believe him to be on bad terms with you: for, in my opinion, it is not in his own way without some finesse that he pretends to set aright so many pretty passages in your letter. It is a sort of a Crony who repeats Punch's maxims, and who pretends to mock them only in order to make them more understandable to the Spectators. I well know that you do not have Punch's manner; but as for the Crony, I tell you again, I suspect him of being one of your friends.

Allow me therefore to address myself to you in order to submit some advice to him which I imagine he ought to take before inserting his Commentary into your letter. As I might well, from contagion, grow a bit dull over the remarks, in order to avoid at least monotony I shall give different names to their Author. When he takes the trouble to explain at length why he does you the honor of being of your opinion, I shall name him *The Commentator*. When he pretends to refute you, he will be *The Crony*, and he will be *The Critic* every time he is right—but I shall be constrained to be somewhat sparing in using this last name.

Should a Commentator be obscure, diffuse, dull, it is the right of the trade; but there is nonetheless a certain point he should not exceed. With regard to the Arietta, Matanasius himself cannot be permitted to cite either Mainard, who first perceived that the third verse should have a final sense or rest in the stanza, or Trissino's *Sofonisba*, a model of the three unities, or Mairet, who was the first to introduce this rule of the three unities to Tragedy, and who consequently instructed Sophocles, Euripides, and Seneca in this matter, or the famous Bernacchi, of whom neither you, nor I, nor many others have ever heard—which should not, however, surprise you: there are likewise many of those famous people whom no one knows, and who pass their lives celebrating one another without getting themselves known any better![10] Be that as it may, here are the clear reasons why the Italian Arietta is not at all reduced to frolicking eternally like the French one around a word such as "*lance*," "*vole*," "*chaîne*," "*ramage*," etc.[11] —reasons with which the Crony reproaches you for not having stated, and which he has the goodness to state in your place.[12]

The Crony claims that, since the buffa genre is known in Italy, it is not true that M. Rameau was its creator in France. This is extremely amusing. For if the buffa genre had never existed in Italy, it would have been quite ridiculous to say that M. Rameau had created one *in France*. I do not inquire whether the buffa genre really exists in French Music. What I do know quite well is that it must necessarily be different from the buffa genre of Italian Music; a fat goose does not fly at all like a swallow.[13] With regard to the Music of *Platée*, which the Critic reproaches you for having treated as sublime, call it divine, if he so prefers, but never repent having considered it as M. Rameau's masterpiece and as the most excellent piece of

Music that has ever been heard in our Theater.[14] You will, I admit, have to do without the approbation of all those who have no other means for assessing a work than that of counting the voices that have applauded it. But you aren't going to take your stand on that.

I would like to ask this great man, who takes the trouble to assign the limits of the sublime, what epithet he would give to the first scene of *Tartuffe*, especially to the last two verses, "Go, slut, be off,"[15] and to these other verses in the same piece:

That's it, I renounce all godly men!, etc.[16]

Beseech him to try to decide whether this is sublime or not. One might ask him as much about the music of the *Serva padrona*, but perhaps he's never heard of it.[17]

The Crony, who takes the liberty of telling you that Adolfati is poorly placed in your citation of Pergolesi and of Buranello,[18] will find it good that we take the liberty of asking of him—he who wishes to allow others only demonstrated propositions—for his reasons, or at least reasonings. He can have no knowledge of the masterpieces of this Author: but ignorance does not at all excuse a man for having misspoken, it only obliges him to remain quiet, especially when it is a question of publicly condemning a living Author whose career has only begun. It is true that this Adolfati, who does not have the honor of pleasing the Crony, very cordially despises French Musicians, but he must be pardoned a bit for this: the poor devil has passed through the goose's beak.[19]

It would be absolutely necessary to substitute Hasse[20] in the place of Adolfati, and this for four irrefutable reasons. The first, that Hasse is your compatriot; the other, that at the age of forty-eight he had composed fifty-four Operas; the third, that he is the sole foreigner whose Music the Italians perform.

Oh! the wicked Boileau for not having heaped praise on Monsieur de Scudéry, Monsieur le Gouverneur de Notre-Dame de la Garde, who was his Compatriot and his Contemporary, who wrote so many books, and who enchanted so many decent Readers![21] And this culpable Philosopher, who has dared to admire his Compatriots, might he not have unfortunately forgotten the Crony? Also, did he not have the honor of being, not his Philosopher, but yours; and I would have indeed doubted that you two would have the same Philosophers any more than the same Gods. Hasse is the sole Foreigner whose Music the Italians have adopted? Has the Crony, by citing Terradeglias, thus forgotten that he is Spanish?[22] Hasse is admired by the Italians? The Italians greatly admire Ariosto.*[23]

---

* I do not at all claim to speak badly here of Hasse, who really has a great deal of merit, talent, and a prodigious fecundity, although in my opinion he is very far from being Pergolesi's

And the fourth reason? the Crony will ask. He will be quite cross for having forgotten it. It is that your name beginning with a "G" and those of Hasse and Handel with an "H," the proximity of the initial letters was for you a new obligation to name these two Authors. I ask your forgiveness for having furnished this weapon against you, but, in imitation of the Commentator, I too reserve myself the right of sometimes being a Crony.

The Commentator enlarges on the praise for Pagin and for his illustrious Teacher,[24] and we applaud him, you and I, quite wholeheartedly. He would have liked you to have said to what extent the Nation, ungrateful toward a talent so sublime, has dared to humiliate him publicly. He should have said, *humiliated itself publicly*. Midas did not at all humiliate Apollo, and a Swan is perhaps hooted by Geese without being humiliated.

I want to be equitable, Sir, and I am no less ready to grant to the Author of the remarks the praise due to him than to submit my doubts to him. For example, you have said that the taste for the Arts was general in France, and it is assuredly much too much so. The imbecilic multitude of so-called connoisseurs without enlightenment engenders a greedy and deplorable multitude of Artists without talent, and genius remains stifled amidst the crowd of fools. You have also said that, as regards taste, the Court gives fashions to the Nation and Philosophers laws. The Crony answers you with the Magots of China, vases of *fragile porcelain*, India papers, illuminated engravings. These are, in his opinion, the laws given by Philosophers; as for the fashions we derive from the Court, he does not speak of them at all. You say that the Philosophers imperceptibly give taste to the People, that is, discernment for great talents and admiration for those who possess them. The Crony answers you that Philosophy does not inspire talents, and gravely warns you not to confound taste with the dryness of calculation.[25] Well! I say very wholeheartedly, the Crony seems to me an admirable man.

Let the Crony speak; do not doubt that we are indeed indebted to Philosophers for that pleasant enlightenment that begins to enlighten us, and believe that if Philosophy does not produce great Artists, money produces them still less. Happy is Italy, where the Inhabitants have received from nature that exquisite taste which makes them sensitive to the charms of the fine Arts! Happier is France for acquiring this same taste by means of study and knowledge, and for owing to the art of thinking the more precious art of feeling! Philosophy, I know, does not at all engender genius,

---

equal. I only examine the reasons for which the Crony pokes his nose into prescribing for M. Grimm the Authors he should name, and those he should reject. Which of the two is the more reprehensible: the one who says nothing of Hasse or the one who speaks badly of Adolfati?

but if it teaches nations to recognize it and to love it, this gives to it a new being no less rare and no less useful than the one it derives from nature.

He warrants that there is in Europe no nation more attentive to the Theater than the French, and he agrees that Paris is the sole city where Guards must be stationed in the Theaters to contain the squawking of the judges of Corneille, Racine, and Quinault.[26] He says in one place, *that in our time Music has not at all received any increase in France on the side of taste*, and in another, *that M. Rameau has enriched us by his own taste*.[27] These are the refinements of the art, Sir, these contradictions: it is a sure means of not lacking truth concerning the things about which one wants to reason without understanding anything about them.

You have ended your letter with a stroke of the greatest beauty, and you ought not doubt that the one whom it regards has felt the force and the truth of it; it belongs to such men there, if they are men, to appreciate the sublime. Do not forget, I beg you, some little thanks to the Crony concerning this subject: for he has surpassed himself in this passage.

It is again by a stroke of skill that merits some sort of compliment, that the Commentator does not say a word on the subject matter of your letter. These mysteries are closed subjects for him; believe that he had very good reasons for not speaking of them at all. You have taught us, everyone like us, to analyze a piece of Music; you have found the art of expressing the ideas, the faults, the contradictions of the Musician by parodying the Poet's words. You have made an exquisite selection of pieces for comparison; you have spoken of Duos, of the Arietta, of Recitative as a man of taste who understands Music and who knows how to reflect. And fleeing alike the stupidly self-important air and the treacherous and malignant hypocrisy of fashionable writings, you have had the difficult modesty to judge only by reasons, and the courage to pronounce with firmness. I content myself with exhibiting these things; perhaps they will not be praised by anyone, but many people will definitely profit from them.

As for me, who tells you freely what I think in charge and debit, and to whom your writings give the right to be difficult with you, I would first of all have liked you to have chosen a text other than *Omphale*; that miserable rhapsody was not worthy of occupying you. I would also have liked you to have made clearer the difference that characterizes the two Recitatives and the decisive reason that assures the superiority of the Italian Recitative: namely, the greater relationship of the latter to Italian declamation than of French Recitative to French declamation. The French do not, strictly speaking, have a Recitative at all; what they call such is merely a kind of song mixed with shouts—all this gets mixed up, one does not know what all this is. I believe I could defy any man to assign some precise difference in French Music that distinguishes what they call Recitative from what they call an aria. For I do not think that anyone dares allege the meter; the proof that there is none at all in French Music is that someone is always needed to keep the beat. How many Foreigners has this cursed baton caused to desert our Opera?

While quite nicely showing the great superiority of the Italian Arietta, by the power and the variety of passions and of portrayals, you perhaps ought to have set aright a ridiculous misinterpretation that is often found in it and that is the sole thing French Musicians have faithfully copied from it. It is that, since the words ordinarily turn on a comparison, since the first part of the Arietta constitutes the first term and the second one the second, when the Musician takes up the rondo in order to conclude on the first part, he presents us with a meaning just like that of an exactly punctuated discourse that were to end with a comma.

But let us return to the poor crony who is perhaps fretting over listening and not at all over understanding.

The Critic has given you a warning from which I advise you to profit: it is to be sober in your praises in a country where they are so very fashionable.[28] Tear to pieces or praise to the skies: this is the lot of base souls. You are always ready with pleasure to render justice to merit, this is enough for you, and would be a great deal too much for an ordinary man. I won't tell you never to flatter anyone, if I believed you capable of it I wouldn't say anything to you. But I shall tell you wholeheartedly: you despise praise too much to be allowed to disturb the people worthy of your esteem with it. As for the Critic, one might believe in reading his remarks that his pretended indifference to praise could very well be a deft maneuver in order to attempt to give some value to his, that is, to the praise he gives, and it is at any rate very clearly seen from this that he is not a man to deprive himself of any when needed.

The crony does not seem to me extremely content with your Temple,[29] and as he can see it only from without, there is no great evil in that; but the Critic reproaches you for singular Groupings, and I confess to you that I am of his opinion. I well know that this singularity, which he must take for a blunder, is a very methodical arrangement and the effect of a reasoned system; but it is the system itself that I condemn. You admire all talents, and it is so much the better for them and for you, but you admire them all equally, and here is what I cannot allow you. You claim that they all have the same origin, and that the genius that engenders them ennobles them equally. But the geniuses themselves, will you say that they are all equal? It is not time to enter here into a long dissertation on this subject. I would at least want to make you admit that there are many differences in the requisite elements, in the difficulties to surmount, and that the narrow genius who composes a very beautiful *adagio* is very far from the powerful genius who dares to explain the universe.[30]

I love Music perhaps as much as you do, but I no less love the saying of Philip, who shamed his son for singing so well: he did not shame him for being as wise as his teacher.[31] You will perhaps cite me a King who plays the flute, and I shall respond to you that it is not without effort that he has acquired the right of playing it.[32]

Only give me taste and organs and I will dance like Dupré or sing like Jelyotte.[33] Join to taste knowledge and imagination, and I will compose an opera like Rameau. In order to compose a passable Novel, great knowledge of the human heart and of the extravagances of love is further needed. Dialectic, and it is a talent like the others, is needed along with all this in order to compose a good Tragedy in dialogue: this will still not be enough to write a book of Philosophy, if you do not have an exact, elevated, penetrating mind practiced in meditation. A good General should be robust, courageous, prudent, firm, eloquent, foresighted, and rich in resourcefulness. Finally, all these qualities, I say all without exception, and beyond all these yet, a great and sublime soul, mastery of one's passions, and an unheard of excellence in virtue: these are the talents that he who governs a People is obliged to have. Talents are thus not equal by their nature. They are even much less so by their object. All the others are good for amusing, spoiling, or grieving men. This last one is alone made for making them happy. This decides the question, so it seems to me.

The critic also warns you no longer to show yourself partial, and he tells you this with regard to M. Rameau. This is another very wise opinion for which I thank him on your behalf. This will also be the subject of the last point of my letter, for I take a true pleasure in commenting on your Commentator.

I first want to try to fix on approximately the idea a reasonable and impartial man should have of M. Rameau's works; for I count as nothing the babbling of cabals for and against.[34] As for me, I might be capable of judging this poorly for want of enlightenment, but if reason is not found in what I shall say about it, impartiality will certainly be found in it, and this will always have been the most difficult thing.

M. Rameau's theoretical works have this very singular thing about them, that they have become quite popular without having been read, and they will be much less so henceforth now that a Philosopher has taken the trouble to write a summary of this Author's doctrine.[35] It is quite certain that this abridgment will wipe out the originals, and with such compensation that there will be no reason for missing them. These various works contain nothing new or useful other than the principle of the Fundamental Bass*: but it is no small thing to have given a principle, even be it arbitrary, to an art that seemed to have none at all, and to have made its rules so much easier that the study of composition, which beforehand was a matter of twenty years, is at present one of a few months. Musicians have eagerly seized on M. Rameau's discovery while pretending to disdain it. Pupils have multiplied with an astonishing speed; everywhere one turns nothing is seen but little composers of two days' training, the majority without talent, who create scholars at the expense of their master; and the very real, very great, and very solid services that M. Rameau has rendered to Music have at the same time led to this inconvenience, that France finds itself inundated with bad Music and bad Musicians, since, each believing he knows all the fine points of the art as soon as he has learned the elements, all have meddled in composing harmony before their ear and experience have taught them to discern good harmony.

With regard to M. Rameau's Operas, to begin with we are obliged to them for their having been the first to raise the Opera Theater above the level the Traveling Troupes of the Pont-Neuf.[37] He has boldly gone beyond the small circle of trifling Music around which our little Musicians ceaselessly revolved ever since the death of the great Lully. So that if one were unjust enough to refuse M. Rameau his superior talents, one would at least not be able deny that he had in some fashion opened up a career for them, and that he put the Musicians who should come after him in the position of deploying theirs with impunity, which assuredly was not an easy enterprise. He felt the thorns, his successors will cut the roses.

He is too readily accused, it seems to me, of having worked with only poor words; moreover, in order for this reproach to be reasonable, it would have to be shown that he was in a position to choose good ones. Would we like it better if he had done nothing at all? A more just reproach is that of not having always understood those with which he was burdened, of having often poorly grasped the ideas of the Poet, or of not having substituted more suitable ones for them, and of having made many misinterpretations. It is not his fault if he worked with poor words, but it might be doubted whether he would have turned better ones to account. He is certainly far below Lully in point of mind and intelligence, although he may always be superior in point of expression. M. Rameau would no more have composed Roland's monologue† than Lully that of Dardanus.[38]

One must recognize in M. Rameau a very great talent, a great deal of

---

* It is not at all because of an oversight that I say nothing here of the pretended physical principle of harmony.[36]

† Act 4, Scene 2.

ardor, a quite sonorous faculty, a great knowledge of harmonic inversions and all the things of effect, a great deal of art in appropriating, denaturing, ornamenting, embellishing someone else's ideas, and of overturning his own, rather little facility in inventing new ones, more skill than fecundity, more learning than genius—or at least a genius smothered by too much learning, but always force and elegance, and very often beautiful song.

His recitative is less natural, but much more varied than Lully's; admirable in a small number of scenes, poor nearly everywhere else, which is perhaps as much the fault of the genre as his own, for it is often for having desired too much to subject himself to the declamation that he has made his song baroque and his transitions harsh. If he had possessed the power of devising true recitative, and of getting it accepted among that sheep-like troupe, I believe that he might have excelled in it.

He is the first who composed intricate instrumental pieces and accompaniments, and he has misused them. Before him, the Orchestra of the Opera resembled a troupe of Blind Men[39] attacked by paralysis. He has warmed them up a bit. They assure us that they can now perform, but I myself say that these people will never have either taste or soulfulness. There is still nothing of being together, of playing loud or soft, and of following the Actor carefully. Strengthen, weaken, accentuate, conceal the sounds, as good taste or expression demand, take up the spirit of an accompaniment, highlight and sustain the voices: this is the art of all Orchestras except our Opera's.

I say that M. Rameau has misused this Orchestra such as it is. He has made his accompaniments so confused, so overcharged, so frequent, that the head has difficulty in following the continual racket of the various instruments during the performance of those Operas, which would be quite pleasant to hear if they deafened the ears a little less. This makes it so that the Orchestra, because it is ceaselessly playing, never grabs, never strikes one, and almost always fails in its effect. After a recitative scene an unexpected blow of the baton is needed to awaken the most distracted spectator, and to force him to be attentive to the images that the Author is going to present to him, or to lend himself for the feelings that he wants to arouse in him. This is what an Orchestra will not at all do when it does not cease scraping.

Another still stronger reason against overly-wrought accompaniments is that they do completely the opposite of what they should do. Instead of fastening the attention of the spectator more agreeably, they destroy it by dividing it. Before I am persuaded that it is a fine thing for three or four designs to be piled one atop the other by three or four types of instruments, it must be proven to me that three or four actions are needed in a

Comedy.⁴⁰ All those beautiful delicacies of the art, those imitations, those double motives, those thoroughbasses, those counterfugues, are only deformed monsters, monuments of bad taste that should be relegated to the Cloisters as though to their last exile.⁴¹

To return to M. Rameau and complete this digression, I think that no one has grasped the spirit of details better than he, no one has better understood the art of contrasts; but at the same time no one has known less how to give his Operas that very wise and very desirable unity, and he is perhaps the only one in the world who could not in the end produce a good work from several beautiful, very well arranged pieces.

> Et ungues
> Exprimet, et molles imitabitur aere capillos.
> Infelix operis summa, quia ponere totum
> Nesciet.⁴²

Here, Sir, is what I think of the works of the celebrated M. Rameau, to whom the Nation would have to give many honors to accord him what it owes to him. I know very well that this judgment will satisfy neither his partisans nor his enemies; also, I wish only to give it equitably, and I propose it to you not as a rule for you but as an example of the sincerity that suits an honest man speaking of great talents he admires and does not believe to be flawless.⁴³

I approve your taste for all that bears the imprint of genius; but if you believe the opinion of a sincere man who has some experience, for the sake of the honor of the arts and the purity of your pleasures, retain it for admiring the works and never desire to know their Authors. You will live in societies in which you will find only cabals and enthusiasts and all of whose members already know very decidedly whether they will find works that are yet to be composed good or bad. Protect yourself from all that vile fanaticism as from a vice fatal to judgment and even capable at length of staining the heart. May your mind always remain as free as your soul; recall Plato's just raillery against that Actor, that the verses of a single Poet took him outside of himself and who was merely cold while reading all the others.⁴⁴ And know that there is no man in the world at all, whatever genius he may have, who has the right to subject your reason; not even M. de Voltaire, of all living men the master in the art of writing. In a word, I want to see you going through the *Henriade*, when your heart beats and you feel yourself touched, enraptured in admiration, daring to exclaim while shedding tears: No, great man, you are not yet Homer's rival.⁴⁵

Pardon me, Sir, for a zeal perhaps indiscreet, but dictated by the esteem that those of your writings I have seen have inspired in me for you. The

Public has judged and applauded them, and has recognized in them with pleasure the man of intelligence and of taste; as for me, I believed with still more pleasure to recognize in them the true Philosopher and friend of men. Continue, therefore, to love and to cultivate the talents that are dear to you and of which you have made good use. But nevertheless do not forget to cast the glance of the wise man over all this from time to time, and to laugh sometimes at all these children's games.

I am, etc.

THE END

"Notice" to Rinaldo da Capua's *La Zingara*[1]

We offer to the public an Intermezzo by the famous Rinaldo to which many great changes had to be made in order for it to conform as well as possible to the nation's taste. It would be impossible to say that the subject is drawn from an incident that happened in an Italian city, for we are not ignorant of the fact that the truth demanded at the theater is not a truth of morals and of characters. It would be no less possible to want to excuse the scene with the bears if the public disapproves of it. One would point out to it in vain that it refuses to tolerate in a buffa work a spectacle less shocking than the monstrosities it passively endures in numerous serious operas, and that the costume of a man as a bear before the eyes of the spectators, and, so to speak, in concert with them, is a thing less puerile than seeking to terrify them with truly ferocious beasts poorly represented. These reasons, which every reasonable and impartial spectator will very well be able to state for himself, will not at all gain the good graces of those for whom our very efforts to please serve us as obstacles to succeeding, of those who make it a crime for us to have dishonored by the mere name of an apothecary that same theater that was not so by Pourceaugnac's syringes,[2] as if the glory of a theater could depend upon the rank of the characters presented there, and as if more talent were needed to play the role of a prince than that of a bourgeois or of an artisan. It is only bad Music that may dishonor an Academy of music,[3] and we do not fear that we will be reproached with debasing in this regard the theater in which we have the honor of performing. It is for us to endure with respect the severity it pleases the public to exercise toward us, by making all our efforts in order to have need only of justice. We feel with sadness how far we are from meriting its suffrage, but if our greatest crime is to have sought to please it, we shall spare nothing to make ourselves still more culpable.

Letter from a Symphonist of the Royal Academy of Music to His Comrades in the Orchestra[1]

Finally, my dear Comrades, we are triumphant: the bouffonists have been sent away.[2] We are going to shine anew with M. de Lully's instrumental parts, we will no longer be so heated in the Opera nor so fatigued in the Orchestra. Admit, Sirs, that it was a hard job playing that bitch of a Music in which the Meter went on mercilessly and never waited so that we could follow it. As for me, when I felt myself being observed by one of those cursed inhabitants of the Queen's corner,[3] and some remnant of shame obliged me to play approximately what was on my part, I found myself the most perplexed person in the world, and at the end of a line or two, no longer knowing where I was, I pretended to count the rests or quite got myself out of the predicament by leaving to take a piss.

You wouldn't believe what harm we have done to that Music that moves so quickly, nor how far the reputation for ignorance some supposed Connoisseurs dared give us already extends. For his forty sous, the least rascal believed himself to have a right to grumble when we played falsely, which quite frequently disturbed the Spectators' attention. There were even certain people who are called, I believe, Philosophers, who, without the slightest respect for a Royal Academy, had the insolence brazenly to criticize persons of our sort.[4] Finally, I forsee the time when, shamelessly infringing our ancient and respectable privileges, the King's Officers are going to be obliged to know Music and to play quite well the instrument for which they are paid.[5]

Alas! What has become of the happy times of our glory? What has become of those happy days when, with a unanimous voice, we passed among the Ancients of the Chambre des Comptes and the best bourgeois of the rue Saint Denis for the foremost Orchestra in Europe,[6] when they swooned over that celebrated overture to *Isis*, over that beautiful storm in *Alcyone*, over that brilliant Logistille in *Roland*,[7] and when the sound of our first stroke of the Bow raised the cheers of the Parterre to the heavens. Now each impudently meddles in inspecting our performance, and since we do not play too correctly and we hardly ever play together, we are treated without further ado as gut sawers, and would readily be chased from the theater if the guards, who like us are in the service of the King, and consequently honest people and of the good camp, did not maintain a little insubordination. But, my dear comrades, what need have I to arouse your just anger, to recall for you our ancient splendor and the affronts which have cast us from it? They are all present in our memory, these cruel affronts, and you have demonstrated by your ardor for extinguishing their odious cause how little disposed you are to endure them. Yes, Sirs, it is that dangerous foreign Music, which, without any help other than its own charms, in a country where everything was against it: it almost destroyed our own, which is played so comfortably. It costs us our honor, and it is against it that we all have to remain united until the last breath.

I recall that, warned of the danger by the first successes of the *Serva Padrona*,[8] and we being secretly assembled in order to find the means of mangling that enchanting Music as much as possible, one of us, whom I have since recognized as a false brother,* took it into his head to say in a half-mocking tone that we need not deliberate so and that we must boldly play everything as best we can. Judge what would have happened if we had had the bumbling modesty to follow that advice, since all our cares, joined to our great talents for leaving to the Works we play all the credit for the pleasure they can give, have hardly stopped the Public from perceiving the beauties of the Italian Music handed over to our bows. We have thus flayed both this Music and the ears of the Spectators with a fearlessness unparalleled and capable of rebuffing the most determined bouffonists. It is true that the enterprise was hazardous, and that everywhere else half of our band would have gotten themselves thrown into the dungeon twenty times over; but we know our rights and we make use of them. It is the Public, if it complains, who will be thrown into the dungeon.

Not content with this, we have joined intrigue to ignorance and ill will. We did not forget to speak as badly of the Actors as we have done of their Music, and the rumor of the treatment they have received from us has produced a very good effect by making all the good subjects whom Bambini[11] tried to attract disgusted with coming to Paris so as to be insulted there. United by a powerful common interest and by the desire of avenging the

---

* A few days ago, ambling along with him to the Opera, as we were accustomed to do, I discovered in his pocket a paper that contained that scandalous Epigram,

O, inimitable Pergolesi,
When our merciless Orchestra
Made you scream under its ponderous violin,
I believe that, contrary to the Fable,
Marsyas flays Apollo.[9]

There are two or three in the Orchestra like that who take it into their heads to blame our cabals, who dare to approve Italian Music in public, and who, without regard for the corps, want to meddle in doing their duty and being honest people.[10] But we count on them being soon sent packing by dint of snubs, and we wish to put up only with those Comrades who make common cause with us.

glory of our bow, it was not difficult for us to crush the poor Foreigners, who, being ignorant of the mysteries of the shop, had no protectors other than their talents, no partisans other than sensitive and equitable ears, nor any scheme other than the pleasure they tried hard to produce for the spectators. They did not know, the good People, that this pleasure itself aggravated their crime and speeded their punishment. They are finally ready to receive it without their even suspecting it, for, in order for them to feel it even more, we shall have the satisfaction of seeing them abruptly dismissed, without being forewarned or paid, and without their having had the time to seek some exile where they might be permitted to please the public with impunity.

We also hope for the consolation of true Citizens and especially of people of taste who frequent our Theater, that the French Comedians,[12] abandoned by everyone and overwhelmed with insults, will be soon obliged to close their own, which will give us all the more pleasure as the queen's box is composed of their most ardent partisans, worthy admirers of the farces of Corneille, Racine, and Voltaire, as well as those of the Intermezzi. It is thus that the Foreigners, who have all the uncouthness of seeking French Comedy and Italian Opera, no longer finding in Paris anything but Italian Comedy and French Opera, precious monuments to the Nation's taste, will cease rushing there with such eagerness—which will be a great advantage for the Kingdom, seeing that better living will be had there and that rents there will not be so expensive.

All that we have done is something, but it is still not enough. I have discovered a fact, about which it is good for you all to be forewarned in order to coordinate the conduct that must be maintained on this occasion: this is that the said Bambini, encouraged by the success of the *Bohémienne*, is preparing a new Intermezzo which may well even appear before his departure.[13] I cannot understand where in the Devil he gets so many Intermezzi, for we assured everyone that there were only three or four in all of Italy. I believe, for my part, that these cursed Intermezzi fell from Heaven ready made by the Angels expressly to have us damned.

It is therefore a matter, Sirs, of uniting at this moment in order to prevent this one from being put on in the Theater, or at least to make it fail there resoundingly, especially if it is good, so that the bouffonists may be loaded down with public hatred and so that all Paris may learn by this example to fear our authority and to respect our decisions. With this plan in mind, I have skillfully wormed my way in with the said Bambini under the pretext of friendship, and as the good man distrusts nothing, for not only does he not have the mind for perceiving the tricks we are playing on him, he has even shown me his Intermezzo without making any mystery about it. The title of it is the *Oiseleuse Angloise*, and the Author of the Music is a certain *Jommelli*.[14] Now you know that this *Jommelli* is one of those ignorant Italians who knows nothing, and who composes, I don't know how, the ravishing Music that we sometimes have so much trouble disfiguring. In order to meditate the means at my leisure, I examined the score with as much care as was possible; unfortunately, I am not, any more than the others, very skilled at sight-reading, but I saw enough of it to know that this instrumental part appears composed expressly to favor our plans: it has short phrases, quite varied, full of precious moments, of short responses of various instruments that enter one after another: in a word, it requires a singular precision for its performance. Judge the ease with which we will muddle all this without affectation and with a completely natural manner. If only we wish to cooperate, we will make a Devilish din: this will be delightful. Here, then, is a set of rules we have meditated upon with our illustrious Leaders, and among others with M. the Abbé and M. Caraffe,[15] who on all occasions have deserved so much from the good camp and done so many bad things to good Music.

1

The usual method, followed with success in the other Intermezzi, will not at all be followed on this occasion. But, before speaking badly of this one, we will wait until we become acquainted with it through rehearsing it. If its Music is mediocre we shall speak of it with admiration, we shall all unanimously feign to praise it to the skies in order that marvels will be expected from it and so that it will be found far wide of the mark at the first performance. If, unfortunately, the Music is found to be good, as there is only too much ground to fear, we shall speak of it with disdain, with outrageous contempt, as the most miserable thing ever composed; our judgment will seduce the fools who never make a retraction except when they are right, and the majority will be for us.

2

We will have to play at our best in the rehearsals in order to exculpate the Leaders, who, without this, would be reproached for not having repeated the rehearsals until the whole thing went well. These rehearsals will not for that be a total loss, for it is there that we will reach accord among ourselves on the means of being as discordant as possible in the performances.

3

The pitch shall be taken, in accordance to the rule, on the notice of the first Violin, seeing that he is deaf.

4

The Violins will distribute themselves into three bands of which the first will play a quarter tone too high, the second a quarter tone too low, and the third will play as justly as possible. This cacophony will be done easily by subtly raising or lowering the pitch of the Instrument during the performance. As for the oboes, there is nothing to say to them and they will proceed by themselves as one would wish.

5

The meter will be treated just about the same as the pitch: a third will follow it, a third anticipate it, and another third will go after the others. In all their entrances the Violins will above all guard against being together, but starting successively one after another they will produce all manner of little fugues or imitations, which will produce a most grand effect. As for the Cellos, they are exhorted to imitate the edifying example of the one among them who piques himself with a just pride on never having accompanied an Italian Intermezzo in key and on always playing major when the mode is minor and minor when it is major.

6

Great care will be taken to soften the *fortes* and strengthen the *dolces*, principally under the singing. It will be necessary above all to saw away with full arm's strength when Tonelli[16] sings, for it is above all of great importance to keep her from being heard.

7

Another precaution that must not be forgotten is that of overdoing the second parts as much as possible, and of weakening the first ones in order that only the melody of the second part above be heard everywhere. It will also be necessary to urge Durant not to take the trouble to copy the parts of the fifths every time they are on the octave of the Bass in order that this lack of connection between the lower and the higher parts make the harmony drier.[17]

8

It is recommended that the young Gut-Sawers not fail to take the octave, to caterwaul on the bridge, and to double and disfigure their part, especially when they can't play the simple one, in order to allay suspicions of their blundering, to scrawl over the whole Music, and to show that they are above the laws of all the Orchestras of the world.[18]

9

As the public might in the end lose patience with all this hullabaloo, if we perceive that it is observing us too closely, the method must be changed in order to avoid gossip. Then, while three or four Violins are playing as best they know how, all the others will set about getting into harmony during the arias, and will take care to saw with all their power, and to make a Devil of a racket with unfingered strings precisely in the softest spots. By this means we shall ruin the most beautiful music without anyone saying anything to us, for it is after all quite necessary to be in accord. And should we be caught in this, we would have the finest pretext in the world for playing as falsely as we please. Thus whether we are allowed to put ourselves in accord or whether we are prevented from being so, we shall always find the means of never being in accord.

10

We shall all continue to cry out in indignation and desecration: we shall complain loudly that the abode of the Gods is dishonored by Jesters; we shall try to prove that our Actors are not Jesters like the others, seeing that at the very most they sing and gesture, but do not at all play their parts, that the little Tonelli makes use of her arms to play her role with an ignominious intelligence and gentility, whereas the illustrious Mlle Chevalier[19] makes use of hers only to aid the effort of her lungs, which is much more decent; that, what is more, it is only talent that demeans and our Actors have never demeaned themselves. We shall also make it seen that Italian Music dishonors our Theater, by the reason that a Royal Academy of Music should sustain itself with the pomp of its title and its privilege alone, and that it is not in keeping with its dignity to need good Music for this.

11

The most essential precaution we have to take on this occasion is to keep our deliberations secret. Such great interests should not be exposed to the eyes of a stupid vulgarian who foolishly imagines that we are paid to serve him. The spectators are so arrogant that if this Letter happens to be divulged by the indiscretion of one of you, they will believe they have the right to observe our conduct more closely, which would not fail to have its inconvenience. For, finally, as superior as one may be to the Public, it is not at all pleasant to endure its Gossiping.

Here, Sirs, are some preliminary Articles on which it seems fitting for us to reach accord in advance. With regard to the specific discussions we ought to hold when the work in question is in progress, as they should be modified by the manner in which they are received, it is proper to reserve them for that time to agree upon them. Each of us, almost to a man, has until now behaved so much in agreement with the common interest that it does not appear that anyone will fail in this at the moment of crowning the work. And we hope that if we are reproached with lacking talent, it will at least not be with that of plotting well.

It is thus that, after having ignominiously expelled all that Italian elegance, we will establish a redoubtable tribunal; soon the success, or at least the failure, of pieces will depend on us alone. Authors, seized with just fear, will come trembling to pay homage to the bow that can flay them, and from the band of miserable sawers for which we are now taken, we shall one day become the supreme judges of the French Opera, and the sovereign arbiters of the chaconne and the rigadoon.[20]

I have the honor of being with very profound respect, my dear Comrades, etc.

Letter on French Music

by J. J. Rousseau

Sunt verba et voces, praetereaque, nihil.[1]

Notice

As the quarrel that arose last year at the Opera resulted only in abuse, delivered on the one side with much wit and on the other with much animosity, I did not want to take any part in it, for this type of war did not in any sense suit me and I was well aware that it was not the time to give only reasons. Now that the Bouffonists have been dismissed, or nearly so,[2] and there is no longer a question of Cabals, I believe I can hazard my sentiment, and I shall state it with my ordinary frankness, without fearing that I will offend anyone by doing so. It even seems to me that on such a subject any precaution would be insulting to the Readers; for I admit that I would have quite a bad opinion of a People* who attached a ridiculous importance to Songs, who made more of their Musicians than of their Philosophers, and among whom it was necessary to speak of Music with more circumspection than of the gravest questions of morality.[3]

It is for the reason I have just put forward that, although some accuse me, it is said, of having lacked respect for French Music in my first edition, the much greater respect and esteem which I owe to the Nation prevent me from changing anything, in this respect, in this one.

An almost unbelievable thing, if it regarded anyone else but me, is that I should dare to be accused of having spoken of the language with scorn in a Work in which it could be an issue only in relation to Music. I have not changed a single word herein on that point in this edition, so, by going through it with a cool head, the Reader will be able to see if this accusation is just. It is true that, although we have had excellent Poets and even some Musicians who have not been without genius, I believe our language to be little suited to Poetry, and not at all so to Music. I do not fear relying on

---

* For fear lest my readers take the last lines of this paragraph for a satire added after the fact, I should warn them that they are taken exactly from the first edition of this Letter; all that follows was added in the second.[4]

the Poets themselves on this point; for, as for Musicians, everyone knows that one can dispense with consulting them on any matter of reasoning. On the other hand, the French language seems to me that of Philosophers and the Wise*: it seems made for being the organ of truth and reason. Woe to whoever offends either of them in Writings that dishonor it! As for me, the most worthy homage I believe I can render to that beautiful and wise language of which I have the good fortune of using, is to endeavor not to debase it.

Although I do not wish and ought not at all to change tone with the Public, as I do not expect anything from it, and as I trouble myself quite as little about its satires as its praises, I believe I respect it much more than that crowd of mercenary and dangerous Writers who flatter it for their interest. This respect, it is true, does not consist in the empty posturing which indicates the opinion one has of the dimness of his Readers, but in paying homage to their judgment by supporting the sentiment one offers to them with solid reasonings, and it is this that I have always tried to do. Thus, in whatever sense one wishes to envision things, in assessing equitably all the clamors this Letter has excited, I greatly fear that in the end my greatest wrong will be to have been right; for I know only too well that I shall never be pardoned for that.

Letter on French Music

Do you remember, Sir, the story of that child from Silesia about whom M. de Fontenelle speaks, who was born with a gold tooth?[6] At first all the Learned of Germany wore themselves out with learned dissertations in order to explain how someone could be born with a gold tooth: the last thing they thought of doing was to verify the fact, and it was found that the tooth was not made of gold. In order to avoid a similar drawback, before speaking of the excellence of our Music, it would perhaps be good to be assured of its existence, and to examine first not whether it is golden but whether we have one.

The Germans, the Spanish, and the English have long claimed to possess a Music suited to their language; in fact, they have National Operas they admire in very good faith, and they were quite persuaded that their glory would be at stake in allowing these masterpieces, unbearable to all ears except their own, to be abolished. In the end, pleasure won out among them over vanity, or at least they have gotten a better understand-

---

*This is the sentiment of the author of the *Letter on the Deaf and the Dumb*, a sentiment that is very well upheld in the addition to that Work, and which he proves still better by all his Writings.[5]

ing of sacrificing to taste and reason prejudices that often make Nations ridiculous by the very honor they attach to them.

We still have in France, with regard to our music, the sentiments they then had about their own. But who will assure us that, for having been more obstinate, our stubbornness is better founded? Should we ignore how much the practice of the worst things can bewitch our senses in their favor,* and how much reason and reflection are needed in order to rectify, in all the fine arts, the badly understood approbation the people often give to productions in the worst taste, and to destroy the false pleasure they take from them?[7] Would it not therefore be appropriate, in order to judge French Music well, independently of what the populace of all stations thinks, to attempt for once to submit it to reason's cupel, and to see whether it will withstand the test? *Concedo ipse hoc multis*, said Plato, *voluptate musicam judicandam; sed illam fermè musicam esse dico pulcherrimam, quae optimos satisque eruditos delectet.*†[8]

It is not my intention to delve into this examination here: this is not the business of a letter, nor perhaps is it mine. I would like only to try to

---

* The curious will perhaps be pleased to find here the following passage, taken from an ancient partisan of the Queen's Corner,[9] and which I abstain from translating for very good reasons:

"*Et reversus est rex piissimus Carolus, et celebravit Romae pascha cum domno apostolico. Ecce orta est contentio per dies festos Paschae inter cantores Romanorum et Gallorum: dicebant se Galli meliùs cantare et pulchriùs quam Romani: dicebant se Romani doctissimè cantilenas ecclesiasticas proferre, sicut docti fuerant à sancto Gregorio papâ; Gallos corruptè cantare, et cantilenam sanam destruendo dilacerare. Quae contentio ante domnum regem Carolum pervenit. Galli verò, propter securitatem domni rgis Caroli, valdè exprobrabant cantoribus romanis. Romani verò, propter auctoritatem magnae doctrinae, eos stultos, rusticos et indoctos, velut bruta animalia, affirmabant, et doctrinam sancti Gregorii praeferebant rusticitati eorum. Et cùm altercatio de neutrâ parte finiret, ait domnus piissimus rex Carolus ad suos cantores: Dicite palàm, quis purior est, et quis melior, aut fons vivus, aut rivuli ejus longè decurrentes? Responderunt omnes unâ voce, fontem, velut caput et originem, puriorem esse; rivulos autem ejus quantò longiùs à fonte recesserint, tantò turbulentos et sordibus ac immuniditiis corruptos. Et ait domnus rex Carolus: Revertimini vos ad fontem sancti Gregorii, quia manifestè corrupistis cantilenam ecclesiasticam. Mox petiit domnus rex Carolus ab Adriano papâ cantores qui Franciam corrigerent de cantu. At ille dedit ei Theodorum et Benedictum, doctissimos cantores, qui à sancto Gregorio eruditi fuerant, tribuitque Antiphonarios sancti Gregorii, quos ipse notaverat notâ romanâ. Domnus verò rex Carolus, revertens in Franciam misit unam cantorem in Metis civitate, alterum in Suessonis civitate, praecipiens de omnibus civitatibus Franciae magistros scholae Antiphonarios eis ad corrigendum tradere, et ab eis discere cantare. Correcti sunt ergò Antiphonarii Francorum, quos unusquisque pro suo arbitrio vitiaverat, addens vel minuens; et omnes Franciae cantores didicerunt notam romanam, quam nunc vocant notam francicam: excepto quòd tremulas et vinnulas, sive collisibiles vel secabiles voces in cantu non poterant perfectè exprimere Franci, naturali voce barbaricâ frangentes in gutture voces, quàm potiùs exprimentes. Majus autem magiterium cantandi in Metis remansit; quantùmque magisterium romanem superat metense in arte cantandi, tantò superat metensis cantilena caeteras scholas Gallorum. Similiter erudierunt romani cantores supradictos cantores Francorum in arte organandi. Et domnus rex Carolus iterùm à Româ artis grammaticae et computatoriae magistros secum adduxit in Franciam, et ubique studium litterarum expandere jussit. Aute ipsum enim domnum regum Carolum, in Galliâ nullum studium fuerat liberalium artium.*"[10]

† De Leg. bk. II.

establish some principles by which, while waiting for better ones to be found, the Masters of the Art, or rather the Philosophers, may direct their researches. For, a Wise Man once said, it is for the Poet to write Poetry, and the Musician to compose Music: but it belongs only to the Philosopher to speak finely of them both.[11]

All Music can be comprised of only three things: melody or song, harmony or accompaniment, movement[12] or meter.*

Although song derives its principal character from the meter, as it arises immediately from harmony and always subjects the accompaniment to its march, I shall unite these two parts in the same consideration, then I shall speak of the meter separately.

Harmony, having its principle in nature, is the same for all Nations, or if it has some variations they are introduced by those in the melody; thus, it is from melody alone that the particular character of a National Music must be derived; all the more so as, its character being produced principally by the language, song strictly speaking should be affected by its greatest influence.

One can conceive of some languages as being more appropriate to Music than others; one can conceive that some would not at all be so. Such might be one that was composed of only mixed sounds, of mute, indistinct, or nasal syllables, few sonorous vowels, many consonants and articulations, and that further lacked other essential conditions of which I shall speak under the subject of meter. Out of curiosity, let us try to find what would result from a Music applied to such a language.

First, the want of vividness in the sound of the vowels would require giving a great deal to that of the notes, and because the language would be indistinct, the Music would be piercing. In the second place, the harshness and the frequency of the consonants would force one to exclude many words, to proceed on others only by elementary intonations, and the Music would be insipid and monotonous, its progress would also be slow and tiresome for the same reason, and if one wanted to press the movement a little, its haste would resemble that of a heavy and angular body rolling along on cobblestones.

As such a Music would be devoid of all pleasant melody, one would attempt to make up for it with sham and quite unnatural beauties; it would be loaded down with frequent and regular modulations, but cold, graceless, expressionless ones; trills, cadenzas, portamenti and other fake pleasures would be invented which would be lavished on the song and which

---

*Although by "meter" is understood the determination of the number and the relation of beats, and by "movement" that of the degree of speed, I believed I could here mingle these two things under the general idea of modifications of duration or of time.

would only make it more ridiculous without making it less dull. The Music, with all this gloomy finery, would remain tiresome and expressionless, and its images, devoid of power and of energy, would portray few objects in many notes, like that gothic writing in which the lines, filled with strokes and figurative letters, contain only two or three words, and which contain very little meaning in a great deal of space.

The impossibility of inventing pleasant songs would oblige Composers to turn all their attention to the side of harmony, and, lacking real beauties, they would introduce conventional beauties, which would have almost no merit but the difficulty overcome.[13] Instead of a good Music, they would devise a learned Music; to substitute for song they would multiply accompaniments; it would cost them less to place many bad parts one on top of another than to make one that was good. In order to take away insipidness, they would augment the confusion; they would believe they were making Music, and they would be making only noise.

Another effect which would result from the lack of melody would be that Musicians, having only a false idea of it, would everywhere find a melody in their style: not having any genuine song, the parts of the song would cost them nothing to multiply—since they would boldly give that name to what would not be such, even to the Thoroughbass, to the unison of which they would without scruple make Countertenors do the recitative—except to cover the whole with a kind of accompaniment in which the pretended melody would have no relation to that of the vocal part. Wherever they saw notes they would find song, seeing that in effect their song would be only notes. *Voces, praetereàque nihil*.[14]

Let us proceed now to meter, in the perceptibleness of which the beauty and expression of song in great part consists. Meter is approximately to melody as Syntax is to discourse: it is what constitutes the link among the words, what distinguishes phrases, and what gives a meaning, a connection to the whole. All Music in which the meter is not perceptible resembles, if the fault comes from the one who performs it, a writing in ciphers for which the key must be found in order to disentangle the meaning; but if this Music in fact has no perceptible meter, it is then only a confused collection of words chosen at random and writing without coherence in which the Reader finds no meaning because the Author has not put any into it.

I have said that every National Music derives its principal character from the language to which it belongs, and I should add that it is principally the prosody of the language that constitutes this character. As vocal Music long preceded instrumental, the latter has always received from the former its melodic character and its meter, and the different meters in vocal Music could have arisen only from the different manners in which discourse can be scanned and the shorts and longs can be placed with regard to one another; this is quite evident in Greek Music, in which all the meters are only formulas for so many rhythms furnished by all the arrangements of long or short syllables, and of the feet of which the language and the Poetry were susceptible. So that, although one might very well distinguish the measure of the prosody, the meter of the verse, and the meter of the song in the musical rhythm, it must not be doubted that the most pleasant Music, or at least the most rhythmic, would be that in which these three meters concurred as perfectly as possible.

After these clarifications, I return to my hypothesis, and I suppose that the same language of which I was just speaking would have a poor prosody, indefinite, without exactitude and without precision; that in terms of duration or in number the longs and the shorts would not have simple relations among themselves and ones fit for making the rhythm pleasant, exact, and regular; that it would have some longs more or less long than others, shorts more or less short than others, syllables neither short nor long, and that the differences between them both would be indeterminate and almost incommensurable. It is clear that the National Music, being constrained to take the irregularities of the prosody into its meter, would have but an extremely vague, unequal, and hardly perceptible meter; that the recitative would especially feel this irregularity; that one would hardly know how to make the values of the notes and those of the syllables coincide; that one would be constrained to change its meter at every moment, and that one could never render the verses in an exact and cadenced rhythm; that, even in tunes in meter, all the movements would be hardly natural and without precision; that, as little slowness as may be added to this defect, the idea of the equality of the beats would be entirely lost in the mind of the Singer and of the Listener, and that, finally, the meter no longer being perceptible nor its recurrences equal, it would be subject to the caprice of the Musician alone, who could, at each moment, hurry or retard it at his whim so that it would not be possible in a concert to do without someone to mark it for everyone, according to the fancy or the convenience of one person alone.

It is thus that Actors would so contract the habit of subjecting the meter that they are even heard ruining it on purpose in pieces in which the Composer has succeeded in making it perceptible. To mark the meter would be a wrong against the composition, and to follow it would be one against the taste of the song: defects would pass for beauties, and beauties for defects; vices would be established as rules, and, to compose Music to the Nation's taste one would have only carefully to follow what displeased every other one.

Furthermore, with whatever artfulness one sought to cover up the defects of such a Music, it would be impossible for it ever to please ears other than those of the natives of the country in which it was in use: by dint of enduring reproaches about their bad taste, by dint of hearing genuine Music in a more favorable language, they would seek to draw their own closer to it and would only deprive it of its character and of the affinity it had with the language for which it had been made. If they wished to denature their song, they would make it harsh, baroque, and almost unsingable; if they contented themselves with ornamenting it with accompaniments other than the ones suited to it, they would only make its flatness more marked by an inevitable contrast; they would deprive their Music of the sole beauty of which it was susceptible by depriving all its parts of the uniformity of character that made it a one, and by accustoming their ears to despise song in order to listen only to instrumental music, they would finally come to the point of making use of voices only as an accompaniment to the accompaniment.

We see by what means the Music of such a Nation would be divided into vocal Music and instrumental Music; how by giving different characters to these two types a monstrous whole would be created. The instrumental would want to proceed in time and, since the song could not bear any constraint, the Actors and the Orchestra would often be heard contradicting each other and proving an obstacle to one another in the same pieces. This uncertainty and the mixture of the two characters would introduce a coldness and feebleness into the manner of accompaniment that would turn into such a habit that the Instrumental players could not, even when performing good Music, leave it any power and energy. By playing it like their own, they would entirely enervate it; they would make the *dolces* loud, the *fortes* soft,[15] and would not know any of the nuances of these two terms. Those other terms, *rinforzando*, *dolce*,* *risoluto*, *con gusto*, *spiritoso*, *sostenuto*, *con brio*, would not even have synonyms in their language, and that of *expression* would have no meaning at all; they would substitute I do not know how many cold and gloomy little ornaments for the vigor of the stroke of the bow. However numerous the orchestra might be, it would produce no effect at all, or it would produce only a very disagreeable one. As the performance would always be careless and as the Instrumental players would prefer to play finely than to play in time, they would never be together: in the end they would not be able to emit a precise and exact sound or to perform anything according to its character;

---

*There are perhaps not four French Instrumental players who know the difference between *piano* and *dolce*;[16] and it is quite useless for them to know it, for who among them would be in a position to produce it?

and Foreigners would all be surprised that, with a few exceptions, an orchestra praised as the first in the world would hardly be worthy of a dance hall stage.* It would naturally have to come to pass that such Musicians should acquire a hatred for the Music that made their shame manifest, and soon, joining ill will to bad taste, they would also put premeditation into a ridiculous performance in which they could very well have relied on their lack of skill.

Based on another assumption contrary to the one I just made, I would easily be able to deduce all the qualities of a genuine Music, one made to move, to imitate, to please, and to convey to the heart the sweetest impressions of harmony and of song; but, as this would draw us too far away from our subject and especially from ideas very familiar to us, I prefer to limit myself to some observations on Italian Music which may help us to judge our own better.

If it were asked which of all the languages ought to have the best Grammar, I would reply that it is that of the People who reason best; and, if it were asked which of all the Peoples ought to have the best Music, I would say that it is the one whose language is most suited to it. This is what I have already established above and what I shall have occasion to confirm in the remainder of this Letter. Now, if there is in Europe a language suited to Music it is certainly Italian; for that language is sweet, sonorous, harmonious, and accented more than any other, and these four qualities are precisely those most fitting for song.

It is sweet because its articulations are not very compounded, because in it the grouping of consonants is rare and without roughness, and, since a great number of syllables are formed of vowels alone, the frequent elisions make its pronunciation more flowing. It is sonorous because the majority of its vowels are bright, and because it has no compounded diphthongs, because it has few or no nasal vowels, and because its rare and smooth articulations better distinguish the sound of the syllables, which become clearer and fuller because of it. With regard to the harmony, which depends on number and prosody as much as on sounds, the advantage of the Italian language is manifest on this point; for it must be remarked that what makes a language harmonious and genuinely picturesque depends less on the real force of its components than on the distance there is from soft to loud among the sounds it employs and on the choice that can be made for the portraits to be painted. This supposed, let those who think

---

*As I have been assured that there were among the Instrumental players of the Opera not only some very good violinists (which I confess they almost all are taken individually), but also some genuinely honest people that do not fall in with the cabals of their fellows in order to serve the public badly, I hasten to add this distinction here in order to make amends, as much as is in my power, being in the wrong with respect to those who deserve such a name.[17]

that Italian is the language only of softness and of tenderness take the trouble to compare these two stanzas from Tasso with one another:

> Teneri sdegni e placide e tranquille
> Repulse e cari vezzi e liete paci,
> Sorrisi, parolette, e dolci stille
> Di pianto e sospir, tronchi e molli bacci:
> Fuse tai cose tutte, e poscia unille,
> Et al foco temprò di lente faci;
> E ne formò quel sì mirabil cinto
> Di ch' ella aveva il bel fianco succinto.[18]

> Chiama gl'abitator de l'ombre eterne
> Il rauco suon della tartarea tromba;
> Treman le spaziose atre caverne,
> E l'aer cieco a quel romor rimbomba;
> Ne sì stridendo mai dalle superne
> Regioni del Cielo il folgor piomba,
> Ne sì scossa giammai trema la terra
> Quando i vapori in sen gravida serra.[19]

And if they despair of rendering into French the sweet harmony of the first, let them try to express the hoarse harshness of the second.[20] It is not necessary, in order to judge of this, to understand the language: only ears and good faith are needed. Furthermore, you will observe that the harshness of the latter stanza is not at all indistinct, but quite sonorous, and that it is only so for the ear and not for pronunciation; for the language no less easily articulates the multiple *r*'s that make for the severity of this stanza than the *l*'s that make the first one so flowing. On the contrary, every time we want to give harshness to the harmony of our language we are forced to heap up consonants of every type, which forms difficult and crude articulations, which slows the progress of the song and always constrains the Music to go more slowly precisely when the meaning of the words requires greater speed.

If I wanted to expand upon this point, I could perhaps also make it clear to you that the inversions of the Italian language are much more favorable to good melody than the didactic order of ours, and that a Musical Phrase is developed in a more pleasant and more interesting manner when the meaning of the discourse, long suspended, is resolved on the verb with the cadence rather than when it is developed in proportion, and is thus allowed to weaken or to satisfy the desire and the mind by degrees while that of the ear is increased in the inverse ratio until the end of the phrase. I would prove to you as well that the art of suspensions and of parentheses, which the happy constitution of the language makes so familiar to Italian Music, is entirely unknown in ours, and that we have no other means of making up for it than with silences which are incompatible with the singing and which, on these occasions, display rather the poverty of the Music than the resources of the Musician.

It would remain for me to speak of accent, but this important point requires such a profound discussion that it would be better to reserve it for an abler hand. I am therefore going to move on to things more essential to my aim and to try to examine our Music in itself.

The Italians claim that our melody is flat and without any tuneful character, and all neutral Nations* unanimously confirm their judgment on this point; for our part, we accuse theirs of being bizarre and baroque.† I prefer to believe that both are mistaken than to be reduced to saying that in the countries where the Sciences and all the Arts have attained such a high degree Music alone is yet to be born.

The least prejudicial among us‡ content themselves with saying that Italian and French Music are both of them good, each in its kind, each for the language which belongs to it; but, aside from the fact that other Nations do not accept this parity, it would still remain to know which of the two languages can accommodate the best type of Music in itself: a question much debated in France, but which will never be elsewhere; a question which can be decided only by a perfectly neutral ear, and which, consequently, becomes every day more difficult to resolve in the sole country in which it is problematic. Here are some experiments on this subject which everyone is capable of verifying and which seem to me capable of being used in answering it, at least as far as melody is concerned, to which alone almost the entire dispute is reducible.

I have taken arias from the two Musics, each of which is equally esteemed in its genre, and, stripping from the first their portamenti and their perpetual trills, from the others the implied notes which the Composer does not take the trouble to notate and which he leaves to the understanding of the Singer,§ I *sol-fa*ed them exactly in accordance with the notation,

---

*There was a time, says Milord Shaftesbury, when the custom of speaking French made French Music fashionable among us. But soon Italian Music showing us Nature more closely, made us disgusted with the other and we were made to perceive it as being as heavy, as flat, and as gloomy as it is in actuality.[21]

†It seems to me that one no longer dares make this reproach to Italian melody since it has been heard among us; it is thus that this admirable Music has only to show itself such as it is in order to justify itself against all the wrongs of which it has been accused.[22]

‡Some condemn the complete exception Devotees of Music grant without hesitation to French Music; these conciliatory moderates would not want there to be exclusive tastes, as if the love of good things must cause bad ones to be liked.

§Going about it in this way gives every advantage to the French Music, for these implied notes in the Italian are no less of the essence of the melody than those which are written out. It is less a question of what is written than of what should be sung, and this manner of notating ought simply to pass for a sort of abbreviation, whereas the trills and the portamenti of

without any ornamentation, and without myself furnishing anything to the sense or to the connection of the phrase. I will not tell you what effect the result of this comparison had on my mind, because I have the right to propose to you my reasons and not my authority. I am merely giving you an account of the means I adopted to make a decision so that if you find them good you may employ them in your turn. I should warn you only that this experiment requires many more precautions than it may appear. The first and the most difficult of all is to be of good faith and to make oneself equally equitable in the choice and in the judgment. The second is that, in order to attempt this examination, one must necessary be equally versed in the two styles; otherwise the one that was more familiar would at every instant present itself to the mind to the prejudice of the other; and this second condition is hardly easier than the first, for of all those who are well acquainted with both Musics, no one hesitates in the choice, as one can see by the laughable scribbling of those who have gotten involved in attacking the Italian what knowledge they have of it and of the Art in general.

I should add that it is essential to proceed exactly in tempo, but I foresee that this warning, superfluous in every other country, will be quite useless in this one, and this sole omission necessarily carries with it an incompetence of judgment.

With all these precautions, the character of each genre is not slow in declaring itself, and then it is quite difficult not to endow the phrases with the ideas which are suited to them and not to add, at least mentally, the turns and ornaments which one has the power to refuse them by the song simply. Nor must one confine oneself to a single trial either, for one aria may please more than another without this determining which genre has the preference, and it is only after a great number of attempts that a reasonable judgment can be established. Furthermore, by taking away the knowledge of the words, that of the most important part of the melody is taken away, which is the expression; and all that can be decided by this route is whether the modulation is good and whether the song possesses naturalness and beauty. All this shows us how hard it is to take enough precautions against prejudices, and how necessary reason is for us to put ourselves in a position to make sound judgments in matters of taste.

I made another trial which demands fewer precautions and which will perhaps seem more decisive to you. I gave Lully's most beautiful arias to some Italians to sing and some of Leo's and Pergolesi's arias to some French

---

French song are, if you will, demanded by taste, but do not at all constitute the melody and are not of its essence; they are for it a sort of rouge that covers its ugliness without destroying it and that only makes it more ridiculous to perceptive ears.

Musicians, and I observed that, although the latter were very far from grasping the true taste of these pieces, they nevertheless perceived their melody and drew from them, after their manner, tuneful, pleasant, and well-cadenced phrases of Music. But the Italians, *sol-fa*ing our most pathetic arias quite exactly, were never able to recognize in them either the phrasing or the melody; for them it was not Music that had any meaning, but only series of notes set down indiscriminately and as if at random; they sang them precisely as you would read Arabic words written in French characters.*

A third experiment. In Venice I saw an Armenian, a man of intelligence, who had never heard any Music and before whom in the same concert were performed a French monologue which begins with this verse:

Temple sacré, séjour tranquille

and an aria by Galuppi which begins with this one:

Voi che languite senza speranza.[23]

Both were sung, the French one indifferently and the Italian one badly, by a man accustomed only to French Music and at that time quite enthusiastic about that of M. Rameau. I observed more surprise than pleasure in the Armenian during the entire French song, but everyone observed from the first bars of the Italian aria that his face and eyes grew soft; he was enchanted, he gave his soul over to the impressions of the Music, and although he understood little of the language, the mere sounds perceptibly enraptured him. From that moment he could no longer be made to listen to any French aria.

But without seeking examples elsewhere, do we not have among us several people who, knowing only our Opera, believed in good faith that they had no taste for singing, and have been disabused only by Italian intermezzi? It is precisely because they liked only genuine Music that they believed they did not like Music.

I admit that so many facts made me doubt the existence of our melody and made me suspect that it may be only a sort of modulated plain-song which possesses nothing pleasant in itself, which is pleasing only with the aid of some arbitrary ornaments, and only to those who have agreed to find them beautiful. Furthermore, our music is hardly bearable to our own ears when it is performed by mediocre voices which lack the art to bring it

---

* Our musicians claim to derive a great advantage from this difference: *We perform Italian Music*, they say with their accustomed haughtiness, *and the Italians cannot perform ours; therefore our music is better than theirs.* They do not see that they ought to draw a completely opposite conclusion and say, *therefore the Italians have a melody and we have none.*

out. It takes a Fel and a Jelyotte[24] to sing French music, but any voice is good for Italian music, because the beauties of Italian song are in the Music itself, whereas those of French song, if it has any, are only in the art of the Singer.*

Three things seem to me to cooperate toward the perfection of Italian melody. The first is the sweetness of the language, which, making all the inflections easy, leaves to the Musician's taste the freedom of making a more exquisite choice, of varying the combinations more, and of giving to each Actor a particular melodic contour, so that each man has the mannerism and the tone that belong to him and that distinguish him from another man.

The second is the boldness of the modulations, which, though less servilely prepared than our own, make them more pleasant by making them more perceptible, and, without giving any harshness to the song, add a lively energy to the expression. It is by this means that the Musician, passing abruptly from one key or mode to another, and suppressing when necessary the intermediary and pedantic transitions, can express the reticences, the interruptions, the faltering speeches which are the language of impetuous passions, which the seething Metastasio has so often employed, which a Porpora, a Galuppi, a Cocci, a Jomelli, a Perez, a Terradeglias have known how to render with success, and of which our lyric Poets know as little as do our Musicians.[25]

The third advantage and that which lends melody its greatest power, is the extreme precision of the meter, which makes itself felt in the slowest movements as well as in the gayest: a precision which makes the singing animated and interesting, the accompaniments lively and rhythmic, which in reality multiplies the songs by making out of the same combination of sounds as many different melodies as there are ways of scanning them; which conveys every feeling to the heart, and every portrait to the mind; which gives the Musician the means of putting into an aria all the characters of words imaginable, about many of which we do not have even an ideal†; and which renders all the movements proper for expressing all

---

*Furthermore, it is a mistake to believe that Italian Singers generally possess weaker voices than the French. On the contrary, they must have a stronger and more harmonious timbre to be able to make themselves heard in the immense theaters of Italy without ceasing to keep the sounds under control, as Italian Music demands. French singing requires the utmost effort of the lungs, the whole extent of the voice. Louder, our Teachers tell us; make the sounds swell, open your mouth, give it your whole voice. Softer, Italian Teachers say; do not force it at all—sing without effort; make your sounds soft, flexible, and flowing; save the outbursts for those rare and passing moments when you have to surprise and rend. Now, it seems to me that, it being necessary to make oneself heard, the one who can do so without shouting must have the stronger voice.

†In order not to depart from the comic genre, the only one known to Paris, consider these arias: *Quando sciolto avrò il contratto*, etc.; *Io ò un vespajo*, etc.; *O questo o quello t'ai a risol*

characters,* or a single movement proper for contrasting and changing the character at the whim of the Composer.

Here, it seems to me, are the sources from which the Italian song derives its charms and its power; to which can be added a novel and very strong proof of the advantage of its melody, in that it does not require, as much as ours, those frequent inversions of harmony which give to the Thoroughbass the melody that is genuinely that of the treble. Those who find such great beauties in French melody ought indeed tell us to which of these things it is indebted or show us the advantages it has to substitute for it.

When one begins to become acquainted with Italian melody, one at first finds in it only graces and believes it suited only for expressing pleasant feelings, but after studying its pathetic and tragic character a bit, one is soon surprised by the power the art of the Composers imparts to it in the greatest pieces of Music. It is by the aid of those learned modulations, of that simple and pure harmony, of those lively and brilliant accompaniments that these divine songs rend or enrapture the soul, putting the Spectator outside of himself and extracting from him, in his rapture, the cries with which our placid Operas have never been honored.

How does the Musician manage to produce these grand results? Is it as a result of contrasting the movements, of multiplying the chords, the notes, the parts? Is it as a result of heaping up design upon design,[28] instrument upon instrument? All this jumble, which is only a poor substitute where genius is lacking, would stifle the song, far from animating it, and would destroy the interest by dividing the attention. Whatever harmony several parts, each quite tuneful, may be capable of producing together, the effect of these beautiful songs vanishes as soon as they are heard all at the same time, and there remains only that of a series of chords which, whatever may be said, is always cold when not animated by the melody; so that the more the songs are heaped up inappropriately, the less the Music is pleasant and tuneful, because it is impossible for the ear to lend itself to several melodies at the same time, and because—since the one effaces the impression of the other—the result of all this is merely confusion and noise. For a Music to become attractive, for it to convey to the soul the feelings it is intended to excite, all the parts must concur to fortify the im-

---

vere, etc.; *A un gusto da stordire*, etc.; *Stizzoso mio, stizzoso*, etc.; *Io sono una Donzella*, etc.; *Quanti maestri, quanti dottori*, etc.; *I Sbirri già lo aspettano*, etc.; *Ma dunque il testamento*, etc.; *Senti me, se brami stare, O che risa! che piacere!* etc.; all characters of Arias of which French Music does not have the first elements and of which it is not in a position to express a single word.[26]

*I shall content myself with citing a single example, but a very striking one: it is the aria *Se pur d'un infelice*, etc., from *The Intriguing Chambermaid*, a very pathetic Aria on a very gay movement, which wants only a voice to sing it, an orchestra to accompany it, ears to hear it, and the second part, which must not be suppressed.[27]

pression of the subject: the harmony must serve only to make it more energetic; the accompaniment must embellish it without covering or disfiguring it; the Bass must, by a uniform and simple progression, somehow guide the person who sings and the one who listens, without either of them perceiving it; in a word, the whole ensemble must convey only one melody to the ear and only one idea to the mind.

    This unity of melody seems to me an indispensable rule and no less important in Music than the unity of action in a Tragedy, for it is founded on the same principle and directed toward the same object.[29] In addition, all good Italian Composers conform to it with a care that sometimes degenerates into affectation, and, however little one may reflect upon it, one soon perceives that it is from this that their Music derives its principal effect. It is in this great rule that one must seek the cause of the frequent accompaniments in unison seen in Italian Music, and which, fortifying the idea of the song, at the same time make the sounds mellower, softer, less tiring for the voice. These unisons are not at all practicable in our music, unless it be in some sorts of arias chosen and adapted expressly for that purpose; a pathetic French aria would never be tolerable accompanied in this manner, because, since vocal and instrumental Music have different characters among us, one could not apply to the one the same devices which suited the other without sinning against the melody and taste—not to mention that, since the meter is always vague and indeterminate, especially in slow arias, the instruments and the voice would never be able to be in agreement or would not keep step together well enough to produce a pleasant effect. One beauty that further results from these unisons is that of giving a more perceptible expression to the melody, sometimes by suddenly reinforcing the instruments in a passage, sometimes by softening them, sometimes by giving them an energetic and leaping melodic feature which the voice would not be able to produce and which the adroitly deceived Listener does not fail to attribute to it when the orchestra knows how to deliver it at the right time. From this also arises that perfect correspondence between the instrumental part and the song which makes it so that all the features admired in the one are only developments of the other, so that it is in the vocal part that one must always seek the source of all the beauties of the accompaniment. This accompaniment goes so well with the song and is so exactly proportioned to the words that it often seems to determine the action and to dictate to the Actor the gesture he should make,* and someone who would not play the role from the words alone

---

    * Frequent examples are found in the Intermezzi which have been performed for us this year, among others in the aria *a un gusto da stordire*, from *The Music Teacher*; in *son Padrone*, from *The Proud Woman*; in *vi sto ben*, from *Tracollo*; in *tu non pensi no signora*, from *The Gypsy Girl*; and in almost all those which require acting.[30]

will play it quite correctly from the Music, because it performs its function of interpreter so well.

Furthermore, it is very important that Italian accompaniments always be in unison with the voice. There are two rather frequent cases where the Musician separates them. The first, when the voice, running lightly over the pitches of the harmony, so holds the attention that the accompaniment cannot share it; yet even then this accompaniment is endowed with such simplicity that the ear, affected only by pleasant chords, does not perceive in it any song which might distract it. The other case demands a bit more attention to make it understood.

When the Musician knows his art, says the Author of the *Letter on the Deaf and the Dumb*, *the parts of the accompaniment will concur either to fortify the expression of the vocal part or to add new ideas which the subject requires and which the vocal part will not be able to express.*[31] This passage seems to me to contain a very useful precept, and this is how I think it must be understood.

If the song is of such a nature as to require some additions, or, as our old Musicians said, some *diminutions** which add to its expression or pleasantness without thereby destroying the unity of melody with the result that the ear, which might perhaps blame these additions if made by the voice, approves of them in the accompaniment and lets itself be gently affected without thereby ceasing to be attentive to the song, then the skillful Musician, handling them appropriately and employing them tastefully, will embellish his subject and make it more expressive without making it less of a unity; and although the accompaniment might not be exactly like the vocal part, they will both nevertheless produce only one song and only one melody. If the meaning of the words includes an accessory idea which the song is not able to render, the Musician will insert it into the rests or into the held notes in such a way that he may present it to the Listener without distracting him from that of the song. The advantage would be even greater if this accessory idea could be rendered by a restrained and continuous accompaniment, which produced rather a light murmur than a genuine song, as if it were the sound of a river or the chirping of birds, for then the Composer would be able completely to separate the song from the accompaniment, and, devoting the latter uniquely to rendering the accessory idea, he will arrange his song in such a manner as to give frequent openings to the orchestra by taking care that the instrumental part is always dominated by the vocal part, which depends even more on the art of the Composer than on the performance of the Instruments; but this requires a consummate experience in order to avoid a doubling of the melody.

This is all that the rule of unity can concede to the taste of the Musician

---

* The word *diminution* will be found in the fourth volume of the *Encyclopedia*.[32]

in order to adorn the song or make it more expressive, whether by embellishing the principal subject or by adding another to it that remains subordinate to it. But to make the Violins play by themselves on one side, the Flutes on the other, the Bassoons on another, each with a particular design and almost without any relationship among them and to call all this chaos Music is to insult equally the ear and the judgment of the Listeners.

Another thing which is no less contrary to the rule I have just established than the multiplication of parts is the abuse or rather the use of fugues, imitations, double designs, and other arbitrary and purely conventional beauties which have almost no merit other than that of the difficulty overcome and which were all invented in the infancy of the Art in order to make learning shine while awaiting for genius to enter the picture.[33] I do not say that it is altogether impossible to preserve the unity of melody in a fugue by skillfully leading the attention of the listener from one part to another as the subject goes by, but this labor is so difficult that almost no one succeeds in it, and so thankless that success can hardly compensate for the strain of such a work. Since all this only ends up making noise, like the majority of our much-admired choruses* it is equally unworthy of busying the pen of a man of genius and the attention of a man of taste. With regard to counter-fugues, double fugues, inverted fugues, thoroughbasses, and other difficult foolishness which the ear cannot bear and which reason cannot justify, they are evidently the remnants of barbarism and of bad taste which subsist, like the portals of our gothic Churches, only to the shame of those who had the patience to make them.

There was a time when Italy was barbarous, and, even after the renaissance of the other Arts, all of which Europe owes to it, Music, more tardy, did not easily assume that purity of taste with which it is seen to shine today, and a worse idea of what it was then can hardly be given than by observing that for a long time there was only one Music in France and in Italy,† and that the Musicians of the two countries communicated familiarly with one another, not without one nonetheless already being able to

---

* The Italians have not themselves altogether shaken off this barbarous prejudice. They still pique themselves on having noisy Music in their Churches; they often have Masses and Motets with four Choirs, each on a different design: but the great Masters only laugh at all this jumble. I remember that Terradeglias, telling me about several Motets of his composition in which he put Choruses worked with great care, was ashamed of having composed such fine ones and excused himself on account of his youth. Previously, he told me, I used to love to make noise; now I try to compose Music.[34]

† The Abbé Du Bos took a world of pains in order to do honor to the Low Countries for their revival of Music, and this might be allowed if the name Music were given to a continual filling in of chords; but if harmony is only the common basis and melody alone constitutes the character, not only was modern Music born in Italy, but there is some ground for thinking that in all our living languages, Italian Music is the only one that may in reality exist. In Roland's and Goudimel's time they produced harmony and sounds; Lully added a little rhythm; Corelli, Buononcini, Vinci, and Pergolesi were the first who composed Music.[37]

notice in our own the seed of that jealousy which is inseparable from conscious inferiority. Lully himself, alarmed at Corelli's arrival, hastened to have him driven away from France—which was all the easier to do as Corelli was the greater man, and consequently less of a courtier.[35] In those times when Music had barely been born, it had in Italy that ridiculous emphasis of harmonic science, those pedantic pretensions of doctrine which it has lovingly preserved among us and by which one distinguishes that methodical, stiff Music, but without genius, without invention, and without taste, which is in Paris called *written Music par excellence* and which is in fact, at the very most, good only for writing and never for performing.[36]

Even though the Italians made harmony purer, simpler, and gave all their attention to the perfection of melody, I do not deny that there still remains among them some slight traces of fugues and gothic designs, and sometimes of double and triple melodies. I might cite several examples of this among the Intermezzi with which we are acquainted, and among others the shoddy quatuor at the end of *The Proud Woman*.[38] But aside from the fact that these things overstep the bounds of the established character, aside from the fact that nothing similar is ever found in Tragedies, and since it is no more just to judge Italian Opera by its farces than to judge our French Theater by *L'Impromptu de Campagne* or *Le Baron de la Crasse*,[39] justice must also be rendered to the artfulness with which composers have often avoided, in these Intermezzi, the traps that were set for them by the Poets, and have turned to the benefit of the rule situations which would seem to force them to break it.

Of all the parts of Music the most difficult to treat without departing from the unity of melody is the Duo; and this point merits our pausing for a moment. The Author of the *Letter on "Omphale"* has already observed that Duos are beyond Nature; for nothing is less natural than to see two persons speaking together all at once for some time, either to say the same thing or to contradict one another, without ever listening or responding to one another.[40] And although this supposition might be admitted in certain cases, it is quite certain than it never would be so in Tragedy, in which this impropriety is suited neither to the dignity of the personages that are made to speak nor to the education they are supposed to have. Now, the best way of avoiding this absurdity is to handle the Duo as much as is possible in Dialogue, and this first concern regards the Poet; what regards the Musician is to find a song suited to the subject and distributed in such a fashion that, each of the Interlocutors speaking alternately, the whole series of the Dialogue forms only one melody, which, without changing subject or at least without spoiling the movement, passes in its course from one part to another without ceasing to be a unity and without going out of its path. When these two parts are joined together, which should rarely take place and should last for a short time, a song must be found which is susceptible to a progression in thirds, or sixths, in which the second part produces its effect without distracting the ear from the first. The harshness of dissonances, piercing and reinforced sounds, the Orchestra's *fortissimo*, must be saved for the moments of disorder and of rapture in which the Actors, seeming to forget themselves, convey their distraction to the soul of every sensitive Spectator and make him experience the power of a soberly handled harmony. But these moments should be rare and induced with artfulness. It is necessary, by a sweet and affecting Music, to have already disposed the ear and the heart to the emotion in order for them both to lend themselves to these violent disturbances, and they must pass with the quickness that suits our weakness; for, when the agitation is too strong it cannot last, and all that is beyond Nature no longer touches.

In saying what Duos should be, I have said precisely what they are in Italian Operas. If anyone has been able to hear a tragic Duo sung in an Italian Theater by two good Actors and accompanied by a genuine Orchestra without being affected, if a dry eye has been able to witness the Farewells of Mandane and Arbace, I hold him worthy of weeping at those of Lybia and Epaphus.[41]

But, without insisting on tragic Duos, a genre of Music of which they don't even have a notion in Paris, I could cite for you a comic Duo known to everyone, and I shall boldly cite it as a model of song, of unity, of melody, of dialogue, and of taste, to which, in my opinion, nothing will be lacking when it is well performed other than Listeners who know how to hear it: it is that of the first act of *La Serva Padrona*, *Lo consoco a quegl' occhietti*, etc.[42] I admit that few French Musicians are in a position to feel its beauties, and I would readily say of Pergolesi, as Cicero said of Homer, that it is already to have made much progress in the Art to be pleased in reading him.[43]

I hope, Sir, that you will pardon me for the length of this point on account of its novelty and the importance of its object. I believed I should elaborate a bit on a rule as essential as that of the unity of melody; a rule of which no Theorist, that I know of, has spoken to this day, which the Italian Composers alone have felt and practiced, without perhaps suspecting its existence, and on which depend the sweetness of the song, the force of its expression, and almost all the charm of good Music. Before leaving this subject, it remains for me to show you that new advantages result from it for harmony itself, at whose expense I seemed to give all the advantage to melody, and that the expression of the song gives rise to that of the chords by forcing the Composer to handle them sparingly.

Do you recall, Sir, having sometimes heard, in the Intermezzi which have been played for us this year, the son of the Italian Impresario, a young boy at most ten years old, sometimes play the accompaniment at the Opera?[44] We were struck from the first day by the effect produced by the accompaniment of the Harpsichord under his little hands; and the whole theater perceived from his precise and brilliant playing that he was not the usual Accompanist. I immediately sought the reasons for this difference, for I did not doubt that Signor Noblet[45] was a good harmonist nor that he did not accompany very exactly; but what was my surprise, when observing the little gentleman's hands, to see that he almost never filled out the chords, that he omitted many notes and very often employed only two fingers, one of which almost always sounded the octave of the Bass! What! I said to myself, complete harmony produces less of an effect than mutilated harmony, and by filling out all the chords our Accompanists produce only a confused noise, while this one, with fewer notes, makes its accompaniment more perceptible and more pleasant! This was a disturbing problem for me, and I understood its whole importance still better when, after other observations, I saw that the Italians all accompanied in the same manner as the little lad, and that, consequently, this spareness in their accompaniment must depend on the same principle as that which they apply to their scores.

I understood very well that the Bass, being the foundation of the whole harmony, should always dominate over the rest, and that when the other parts stifle it or cover it up, a confusion results which can make the harmony less distinct; and I thus saw why the Italians, so economical with the right hand in the accompaniment, usually redouble the octave of the Bass with the left, why they put so many Double-basses in their orchestras, and why they so often make their cellos*[46] proceed with the Bass, instead of giving them another part, as the French never fail to do. But this, which might reasonably account for the clarity of the chords, does not account for their power, and I soon saw that there had to be some more hidden and subtler principle for the expression which I noticed in the simplicity of Italian harmony while I found ours so complicated, so cold, and so slack.

I then recalled having read in some work of M. Rameau's that each consonance has its particular character, that is, a manner of affecting the soul proper to it; that the effect of the third is not at all the same as that of the fifth, nor the effect of the fourth same as that of the sixth. Likewise, the

---

* One can observe in the orchestra of our Opera that in Italian Music the cellos almost never play their part when it is on the octave of the Bass: perhaps in such a case they do not deign to copy it. Could those who lead the orchestra be unaware that this lack of connection between the Bass and the treble makes the harmony too dry?

minor thirds and the sixths ought to produce affects different from those which the major thirds and sixths produce; and these facts once granted, it follows evidently enough that the dissonances and all the intervals possible will also be in the same situation. An experience which reason confirms, since every time the relations are different the impression cannot be the same.

Now, I said to myself while reasoning from this supposition, I see clearly that two consonances joined to each other inappropriately, although in accordance with the rules for the chords, may, even while augmenting the harmony, weaken, fight against, or divide one another's effect. If I require the whole effect of a fifth for the expression I need, I may risk weakening this expression by a third sound which, dividing this fifth into two other intervals, will necessarily modify its effect by that of the two thirds into which I resolve it; and these same thirds, even though the whole ensemble makes a very good harmony, being of different types, may still both damage one another's impression. Likewise, if I required the simultaneous impression of the fifth and the two thirds, I would inappropriately weaken and spoil this impression by omitting one of the three sounds which form the chord. This reasoning becomes even more perceptible when applied to the dissonance. Let us suppose that I require all the harshness of the tritone, or all the insipidness of the diminished fifth—an opposition, by the way, which proves how much the various inversions of chords can change their effect; if, in such a circumstance, instead of conveying to the ear the two unique sounds which form the dissonance, I take it into my head to fill out the chord with all those that belong to it, then I add to the tritone the second and the sixth and to the diminished fifth the sixth and the third, that is, by introducing into each of these chords a new dissonance, at the same time I introduce into it three consonances which must necessarily temper and weaken their effect by making one of these chords less bland and the other less harsh. It is therefore a certain principle and one founded in nature that every Music in which the harmony is scrupulously filled out, every accompaniment in which all the chords are complete, must produce a great deal of noise, but have very little expressiveness: which is precisely the character of French Music. It is true that the selection becomes difficult when handling the chords and the parts and requires much experience and taste so as always to make it properly; but if there is one rule to assist the Composer in acquitting himself well on such an occasion, it is certainly that of the unity of melody which I have tried to establish, which conforms to the character of Italian Music and accounts for the sweetness of its song along with the power of expression which reigns in it.

It follows from all this that after having studied well the elementary rules of harmony, the Musician should not at all hasten to lavish it indiscriminately, nor believe himself to be in a position to compose because he knows how to fill out chords, but that before putting his hand to the work he should apply himself to the much longer and more difficult study of the various impressions which the consonances, the dissonances, and all the chords make on perceptive ears, and to say to himself often that the great art of the Composer consists no less in knowing how to discern at the time the notes he should omit than those he should use. It is by continually studying and leafing through the masterpieces of Italy that he will learn to make this exquisite choice, if nature has given him enough genius and taste to feel its necessity; for the difficulties of the art let themselves be perceived only by those who are made to vanquish them, and these individuals will not take it into their heads to look with disdain upon the vacant spaces of a score, but seeing the ease a Novice would have in filling them out, they will suspect and seek the reasons for this deceptive simplicity, the more admirable as it conceals prodigies beneath a feigned negligence, and as *l'arte che tutto fà, nulla si scuopre*.[47]

Here, so it seems to me, is the cause of the surprising effects produced by the harmony of Italian Music, although much less encumbered than our own, which produces so few. This does not mean that the harmony must never be filled out, but that it must be filled out only with selection and discernment; nor is this to say that for this selection the Musician would be obliged to go through all this reasoning, but that he must be sensitive to their result. It is for him to have the genius and the taste to discover the things of effect; it is for the Theorist to seek their causes and to say why these things are effective.

If you cast your eyes over our modern compositions, above all if you listen to them, you will soon recognize that our Musicians have so very badly understood all this that, while trying to arrive at the same goal, they have followed exactly the opposite route; and, if I am permitted frankly to state my thinking to you, I find that the further our Music is perfected in appearance, the more it is ruined in actuality.[48] It was perhaps necessary for it to come to the point where it is for our ears to be accustomed imperceptibly to reject the prejudices of habit and to enjoy tunes other than those with which our Nurses put us to sleep; but I foresee that in order to bring it to the very mediocre degree of goodness of which it is susceptible, sooner or later it will be necessary to begin by redescending—or reascending—to the point where Lully left it. Let us admit that the harmony of this celebrated Musician is purer and less convoluted, that his Bass parts are more natural and proceed more briskly, that his song is more consistent, that his accompaniments, less burdened, spring better from the subject and depart from it less, that his recitative is much less mannered, and consequently much better than our own. This is confirmed by the style of the performance, for the old recitative was rendered by the Actors of that time altogether differently than we do it today; it was livelier and less drawling; it was sung less and declaimed more.* Trills, portamenti have been multiplied in ours; it has become still more languid and there is hardly anything found in it any longer that distinguishes it from what we are pleased to call an *air*.[49]

Since airs and recitatives are in question, you will permit me, Sir, to end this Letter with some observations on them both which will perhaps turn out to be useful insights into the solution of the problem in question.

The idea our Musicians have of the constitution of an Opera can be judged by the singularity of their nomenclature. Those great pieces of Italian Music which enrapture, those masterpieces of genius which draw tears, which offer the most striking portraits, which portray the liveliest situations and convey to the soul all the passions they express, the French call *ariettes*. They give the name *airs* to those insipid ditties which they interpolate into the scenes of their Operas, and reserve that of "monologues" *par excellence* for those drawn-out and tiresome lamentations which need only be sung justly and without shouting in order to numb everyone.

In Italian Operas all the arias are properly situated and make up part of the scenes. Sometimes it is a despairing father who believes he sees the shadow of a son whom he unjustly killed reproach him for his cruelty; sometimes it is an easygoing prince who, forced to give an example of severity, asks the Gods to take the empire away from him or to give him a less sensitive heart. Here it is a tender mother who sheds tears on regaining her son, whom she believed dead. There it is the language of love, not filled with that vapid and puerile rigmarole of *flammes* and *chaînes*, but tragic, lively, ardent, faltering, and such as befits the impetuous passions.[50] Upon such words it is well to lavish all the riches of a Music full of power and expression and to add to the power of the Poetry by that of the harmony and the song. On the contrary, the words of our ariettes, always detached from the subject, are but a miserable honeyed jargon which one is only too happy to not understand; it is a haphazard collection of the very small number of sonorous words that our language can furnish, turned and returned in every manner except the one that would give them meaning. It is upon these ridiculous bits of nonsense that our Musicians waste their taste and their knowledge and our Actors their gestures and their lungs; it is over these extravagant pieces that our women swoon in admi-

---

* This is proved by the duration of Lully's Operas, much longer today than in his time according to the unanimous report of all those who saw them long ago. Thus, whenever these Operas are put on again, one is obliged to make considerable omissions from them.

ration; and the most striking proof that French Music knows neither how to depict nor how to speak is that it can develop the few beauties of which it is susceptible only on words that have no meaning. Nevertheless, to hear the French speak of Music, one would believe that it is in *their* Operas that music portrays great pictures and great passions, and that mere ariettes are found in Italian Operas, in which the very name of "ariette" and the ridiculous thing that it expresses are equally unknown. One must not be surprised at the crudeness of these prejudices: Italian Music has no enemies, even among us, except those who know nothing about it; and all the Frenchmen who have tried to study it with the sole design of criticizing it with knowledge have soon become its most zealous admirers.*

After the ariettes, which constitute the triumph of modern taste in Paris, come the famed monologues which are admired in our old Operas. About which it should be noted that our most beautiful airs are always in the monologues and never in the scenes, because, since our Actors possess no skill in pantomime and since the Music indicates no gesture and depicts no situation, the one who remains silent does not know what to do with himself while the other sings.

The drawling character of the language, the little flexibility of our voices, and the doleful tone which perpetually reigns in our Opera place almost all French monologues on a slow movement; and as the beat does not make itself felt either in the song, or in the Bass, or in the accompaniment, nothing is so drawling, so slack, so languid as those beautiful monologues, which everyone admires while yawning; they would like to be sad and are only boring; they would like to touch the heart and only afflict the ears.

The Italians are more skillful in their Adagios; for when the song is so slow that there is any danger of allowing the idea of the meter to be weakened, they make the bass proceed by equal notes which indicate the movement, and the accompaniment indicates it as well by the subdivisions of the beats, which, keeping the voice and the ear in time, only make the song more pleasant and especially more energetic by this precision. But the nature of French song forbids our Composers this resource; for as soon as the Actor is forced to stay in time, he can no longer deploy his voice or his acting, dwell on his song, swell and prolong his sounds, or shout at the top of his lungs, and, consequently, can no longer be applauded.

But what prevents monotony and boredom in Italian Tragedies still more efficaciously is the advantage of being able to express all the feelings and portray every character with whatever meter and whatever movement

---

* It is a prejudice that is hardly favorable to French Music that those who despise it most are precisely those who know it best; for it is as ridiculous when one examines it as it is unbearable when one listens to it.

the Composer pleases. Our melody, which says nothing by itself, derives all its expressiveness from the movement it is given; it is inevitably sad on a slow meter, furious or gay on a lively movement, grave on a moderate movement: the song counts almost for nothing in it, the meter alone, or, to speak more exactly, the degree of quickness alone, determines the character. But Italian melody finds in every movement expressions for every character, portraits for every object. It is, if it so pleases the Musician, sad on a lively movement, gay on a slow movement, and, as I have already said, it changes character on the same movement at the whim of the Composer, which gives it the ease of contrasts without depending for this on the Poet and without exposing itself to inconsistencies.

This is the source of that prodigious variety which the great Masters of Italy know how to diffuse into their Operas without ever departing from nature: a variety that prevents monotony, dullness, and boredom, and that French Musicians cannot imitate because their movements are imposed by the meaning of the words, and because they are forced to adhere to them if they do not want to fall into ridiculous inconsistencies.

With regard to recitative, of which it remains for me to speak, it seems to me that in order to judge it well it would be necessary to know precisely what it is for once; for up until now I do not know whether any of all those who have disputed about it has thought of defining it. I do not know, Sir, what idea you may have of this word; as for me, I call recitative a harmonious declamation, that is, a declamation in which all the inflections are produced by harmonious intervals. It follows from this that as each language has a declamation that belongs to it, each language must also have its particular recitative; which does not prevent one from being very well able to compare one recitative with another to find out which of the two is the better, or which relates to its aim better.

Recitative is necessary in lyric dramas: 1. To link the action and make the spectacle a unity. 2. To set off the arias, whose continuous succession would become unbearable. 3. To express a number of things which cannot or should not at all be expressed by tuneful and rhythmic Music. Simple declamation would not be suited to all that in a lyric work, because the transition from speech to song, and especially from song to speech, has a harshness to which the ear lends itself with difficulty, and constitutes a shocking contrast which destroys the whole illusion, and consequently the interest; for there is a sort of verisimilitude which must be preserved, even at the Opera, by making the discourse so uniform that the whole may at least be taken for a hypothetical language. Add to this that the help of the chords increases the power of harmonious declamation and compensates advantageously for what is less natural about the intonations.

It is evident, according to these ideas, that the best recitative, in whatever Language one may take, if it otherwise meets the necessary conditions, is that which most approaches speech; if there were one that so approached it by preserving the harmony which suits it that the ear or the mind might be deceived by it, one would boldly pronounce that it had attained all the perfection of which any recitative may be susceptible.

Let us now examine in accordance with this standard what is called recitative in France; and tell me, I ask you, what relation you can find between that recitative and our declamation? How could you ever conceive that the French Language, whose accent is so uniform, so simple, so modest, so untuneful, would be well rendered by the noisy and shrill intonations of that recitative, and that there was any relation between the soft inflections of speech and those sustained and swollen sounds, or rather those eternal shouts which make up the fabric of that part of our Music even more than the airs? For example, have someone who knows how to read recite the first four verses of the famous recognition scene in *Iphigénie*.[51] You will hardly recognize some slight irregularities, some weak vocal inflections in a tranquil recital that has nothing lively or passionate about it, nothing that must compel the person doing it to raise or lower the voice. Then have these same verses recited by one of our Actresses according to the Musician's notation, and try, if you can, to endure that extravagant squawking which passes at each instance from low to high and from high to low, covers the entire range of the voice without a subject and inappropriately interrupts the recital in order *to string together some beautiful sounds* on meaningless syllables, and which makes for no pause in the meaning.

Add to this the *frédons*, the trills, and the portimenti which recur at every moment, and tell me what analogy there can be between speech and all this glum drapery, between declamation and this so-called recitative. At least show me, on what ground might one reasonably praise this marvelous French recitative whose invention constitutes Lully's glory.

It is rather amusing to hear the Partisans of French Music take refuge in the character of the Language, and to shift onto it the defects of which they dare not accuse their idol, whereas it is quite obvious that the best recitative that could suit the French Language must be almost entirely opposite to the one that is in use: that it must range within very small intervals, neither much raising nor lowering the voice, few sustained sounds, never outbursts, still fewer shouts, above all nothing which resembles singing, little inequality in the duration or value of the notes, nor in their degrees either. In a word, true recitative in French, if it can have one, will be found only by a route directly opposed to that taken by Lully and his successors, by some new route that assuredly French Composers, so proud of their false knowledge and consequently so far from feeling and loving the genuine thing, will not soon take it into their heads to seek, and which they will probably never find.

Here would be the place to show you, by the example of the Italian recitative, that all the conditions I have supposed in a good recitative can actually be found in it; that it can have at the same time all the vivacity of declamation and all the power of harmony; that it can proceed as rapidly as speech and be as melodious as a genuine song; that it can indicate all the inflections with which the most vehement passions animate discourse without straining the voice of the singer or deafening the ears of those who listen. I could show you how, with the aid of a particular fundamental progression, the modulations of the recitative can be multiplied in a manner that suits it and that contributes to distinguishing it from the arias, where, in order to preserve the graces of the melody, the key must be changed less frequently; how, above all, when one wishes to give passion the time to display all its movements, one can, with the aid of a skillfully handled instrumental part, make the Orchestra express through pathetic and varied songs what the actor must only recite: a masterpiece of the Musician's art, by which, in an accompanied recitative,* he joins the most touching melody to all the vehemence of declamation without ever confusing the one with the other. I could display for you the innumerable beauties of that admirable recitative of which so many accounts are given in France which are as absurd as the judgments which people presume to pass on them—as if someone could deliver a verdict on a recitative without knowing profoundly the language to which it belongs. But to enter into these details it would, so to speak, be necessary to create a new Dictionary, to invent terms at each instant in order to offer to French readers ideas unknown to them and address discourses to them which would seem to be gibberish to them. In a word, in order to be understood it would be necessary to speak to them in a language they understood, and consequently of science and of arts of every genre, except Music alone. I will therefore not go into an affected detail in this matter which would do nothing for the instruction of Readers and concerning which they might presume that I owe the apparent force of my proofs only to their ignorance in this area.

*I had hoped that Signor Caffarelli would give us some piece of grand recitative and of pathetic song at the Concert Spirituel in order to enable the so-called Connoisseurs to hear for once what they have been judging for such a long time; but, based on his reasons for not doing anything of the kind, I have found that he knew the capacity of his Listeners even better than I.[52]

Nor for the same reason will I try to draw the parallel which was proposed this Winter in a Writing addressed to the Little Prophet and his adversaries between two pieces of Music, one Italian and the other French, which were specified there.[53] Since the Italian scene, mingled with a thousand other equal or superior masterpieces in Italy, is hardly known in Paris, few people would be able to follow the comparison, and it would turn out that I would have spoken only for the small number of those who already know what I had to tell them. But, as for the French scene, I shall gladly sketch an analysis of it, with all the more pleasure since, as it is the piece sanctioned by the most unanimous suffrage in the Nation, I shall not fear that I will be charged with partiality in the selection nor of having wanted to shield my judgment from the Readers' by the selection of a little-known subject.

Furthermore, as I cannot examine this piece without embracing its genre, at least hypothetically, this is to give French Music all the advantage which reason has forced me to take from it in the course of this Letter; this is to judge it by its own rules, so that if this scene were as perfect as is claimed, nothing else could be concluded but that it is well-written French Music, which would not, its genre being demonstrated to be bad, exclude it from being absolutely bad Music. It is therefore here a matter only of seeing whether it can be admitted as good, at least in its genre.

To do this I am going to try to analyze in a few words that celebrated monologue by Armide, *enfin il est en ma puissance*, which passes for a masterpiece of declamation and which the Masters themselves present as the most perfect model of true French recitative.[54]

I observe first that M. Rameau has cited it with reason as an example of an exact and very well-connected modulation;[55] but this praise, applied to the piece in question, becomes a veritable satire, and M. Rameau would himself be wary of deserving similar praise in a like case; for what can be more badly conceived than that pedantic regularity in a scene in which rage, tenderness, and the contrast of opposed passions put the Actress and the Spectators into the liveliest agitation? Furious Armide comes to stab her enemy. At the sight of him, she hesitates, she relents, the dagger drops from her hands; she forgets all her plans of vengeance, and does not forget her modulation for a single instant. The reticences, the interruptions, the intellectual transitions which the Poet offered the Musician have not once been grasped by him. The Heroine ends by adoring the person she wanted to slaughter in the beginning; the Musician ends with *E si mi*,[56] as he began, without ever having for an instant left the pitches most analogous to the principal key, without having a single time put into the Actress's declamation the slightest exceptional inflection which might give credit to the agitation of her soul, without having given the slightest expressiveness to the harmony. And I defy anyone who would assign to the Music alone, whether in the key, the melody, the declamation, or the accompaniment, any perceptible difference between the beginning and the end of this scene by which the Spectator might judge the prodigious change that has taken place in Armide's heart.

Look at this Thoroughbass. How many eighth notes! How many little fleeting notes to run after the harmonic succession! Is this then how the Bass of a good recitative progresses, in which only the long notes should be heard, here and there, as seldom as possible and only so as to prevent the voice of the reciter and the ear of the Spectator from wandering?

But let us see how the beautiful verses of this monologue, which can actually pass for a masterpiece of Poetry, are rendered:

> *Enfin il est en ma puissance.*
> [At last, he is in my power.]

Here is a trill,* and, what is worse, a perfect close on the first verse, while the sense is completed only in the second. I admit that the Poet might perhaps have done better to omit this second verse and to leave to the Spectators the pleasure of reading its meaning in the Actress's soul; but since he has employed it, it was for the Musician to render it.

> *Ce fatal ennemi, ce superbe vainqueur.*
> [This mortal enemy, this haughty conqueror.]

I would perhaps pardon the Musician for having put this second verse into another key than the first if he allowed himself to change it more often on the necessary occasions.

> *Le charme du sommeil le livre à ma vengeance.*
> [Sleep's charm delivers him to my vengeance.]

The words *charme* and *sommeil* were an inevitable snare for the Musician; he has forgotten Armide's fury, in order to take a little nap here from which he wakes up on the word *percer*. If you believe that it is by chance that he has employed soft sounds for the first hemistich, you have

---

* I am constrained to frenchify this word in order to express the fluttering of the throat which the Italians give this name because, finding myself at every instant having to make use of the word *cadence* in another sense, it was not otherwise possible for me to avoid continual equivocations.[57]

only to listen to the Bass: Lully was not a man to employ those sharps for nothing.

> *Je vais percer son invincible coeur.*
> [I will pierce his invincible heart.]

How ridiculous this final cadence is in such an impetuous movement! How cold and graceless this trill is! How badly placed it is on a short syllable in a recitative that should fly and in the midst of a violent outburst!

> *Par lui tous mes Captifs sont sortis d'esclavage;*
>   *Qu'il éprouve toute ma rage!*
> [Through him all my Captives have left their servitude
>   Let him feel all my fury!]

One sees here is an adroit reticence of the Poet. Armide, after having said that she is going to pierce Renaud's invincible heart, feels in her own the first movements of pity, or rather of love; she seeks reasons to harden herself, and this intellectual transition directs these two verses quite nicely, which without this would be poorly connected with the preceding and would become altogether superfluous for what is not unknown either to the Actress or to the Spectators.

Let us now see how the Musician has expressed this secret progress of Armide's heart. He has indeed seen that he had to put an interval between these two verses and the preceding, and he has produced a rest which he has not filled with anything at a moment when Armide has so many things to feel and, consequently, the orchestra to express. After this pause, he begins again in exactly the same key, on the same chord, on the same note on which he just finished, passes successively through all the sounds of the chord through an entire measure, and finally with difficulty leaves the key which he has just gone round so inappropriately at a moment when it is no longer necessary.

> *Quel trouble me saisit? Qui me fait hésiter?*
> [What tumult seizes me? What makes me hesitate?]

Another rest, and then that's all. This verse is in the same key, almost on the same chord as the preceding. No alternation that might indicate the prodigious change taking place in Armide's soul and in her speech.[58] The tonic, it is true, becomes dominant by a movement of the Bass. But Heavens! Is it indeed a question of tonic and dominant at a time when all harmonic connection should be interrupted, when everything should portray disorder and agitation! Furthermore, a slight alteration which takes place in the Bass alone can give more energy to the voice's inflections but never take their place. In this verse, Armide's heart, eyes, expression, gestures, everything is changed—save her voice: she speaks lower, but keeps the same tone.

> *Qu'est-ce qu'en sa faveur la pitié me veut dire?*
> *Frappons.*
> [What does pity wish to say to me in his behalf?
> Strike.]

As this verse can be taken in two different senses, I do not wish to quibble with Lully for not having preferred the one I would have chosen. Nonetheless, it is incomparably more lively, more animated, and turns what follows to better account. Armide, as Lully has her speak, continues to soften while asking herself the reason:

> *Qu'est-ce qu'en sa faveur la pitié me veut dire?*
> [What does pity wish to say to me in his behalf?]

Then all at once she regains her fury with a single word:

> *Frappons.*
> [Strike.]

Armide, indignant, as I understand her, after having hesitated, precipitously rejects her vain pity, and pronounces sharply and all in one breath while raising the dagger:

> *Qu'est-ce qu'en sa faveur la pitié me veut dire?*
> *Frappons.*
> [What does pity wish to say to me in his behalf?
> Strike.]

Perhaps Lully himself has understood this verse this way, although he rendered it differently. For his notation fixes the declamation so little that it can be given the meaning one prefers without risk.

> *. . . . Ciel! qui peut m'arrêter?*
> *Achevons . . . Je frémis. Vengeons-nous . . . Je soupire.*
> [. . . Heavens! What can be stopping me?
> End it . . . I tremble. Avenge myself . . . I sigh.]

Certainly here is the most violent moment in the whole scene. It is here that the greatest struggle is taking place in Armide's heart. Who would believe that the Musician has left all this agitation in the same key, without the slightest intellectual transition, without the slightest harmonic distinction, in a manner so insipid, with a melody so little distinguished and so inconceivably clumsy, that instead of the last verse spoken by the Poet,

> *Achevons; Je frémis. Vengeons–nous; Je soupire*
> [End it; I tremble. Avenge myself; I sigh]

the Musician says precisely this:

> *Achevons, achevons. Vengeons-nous, vengeons-nous.*
> [End it; end it. Avenge myself; avenge myself.]

The *trills* have an especially fine effect on such words, and it is quite fortunate to have the perfect cadence on the word *soupire*!

> *Est-ce ainsi que je dois me venger aujourd'hui?*
> *Ma colère s'éteint quand j'approche de lui.*
> [Is this how I must avenge myself today?
> My anger abates when I draw near him.]

These two verses would be well declaimed if there were a greater interval between them and if the second did not end with a perfect cadence. These perfect cadences are always the death of expression, especially in French recitative, where they fall so heavily.

> *Plus je le vois, plus ma vengeance est vaine.*
> [The more I behold him, the more my vengeance is vain.]

Everyone who has a feeling for the genuine declamation of this verse will judge that the second hemistich is a misinterpretation; the voice should be raised on *ma vengeance*, and fall again softly on *vaine*.

> *Mon bras tremblant se refuse à ma haine.*
> [My trembling arm refuses my hatred.]

A poor perfect cadence! So much more so because it is accompanied by a trill.

> *Ah! quelle cruauté de lui ravir le jour!*
> [Ah! what cruelty to rob him of life.]

Have Mlle Dumesnil[59] declaim this verse and you will find that the word *cruauté* will be the highest and that the voice will always lower toward the end of the verse. But the manner of not emphasizing *le jour*! Here I recognize the Musician.

For brevity's sake, I pass over the rest of this scene, which has nothing more of interest or remarkable about it other than the ordinary misinterpretations and the continual trills, and I end with the verse with which it concludes,

> *Que, s'il se peut, je le haïsse.*
> [Let me, if it is possible, hate him.]

This parenthesis, *s'il se peut*, seems to me a sufficient proof of the Musician's talent; as this is found in the same key, on the same notes as *je le haïsse*, it is quite difficult to fail to perceive how little Lully was capable of putting Music to the words of the great man he kept in his hire.

With regard to the little dance-hall tune at the end of this monologue, I quite prefer to consent to say nothing about it, and if there are some devotees of French Music who know the Italian scene which was put into parallel with this one,[60] and especially the impetuous, pathetic, and tragic aria with which it concludes, they will doubtless be pleased with this silence.

To sum up my sentiment about the celebrated monologue in a few words, I say that if one looks upon it as singing, neither meter, nor character, nor melody is found in it; if one wishes to see it as recitative, neither naturalness nor expressiveness is found in it; whatever name one wanted to give it, it is found full of spun-out sounds, of trills and other ornaments of song even more ridiculous in such a situation than they usually are in French Music. Its modulation is regular, but puerile for the same reason, pedantic, without power, without perceptible feeling. Its accompaniment is limited to the Thoroughbass in a situation where all the powers of Music should be deployed; and this Bass is rather one that would be written by a Pupil for his Music lesson than the accompaniment of a lively Opera scene, in which the harmony should be chosen and applied with an exquisite discernment in order to make the declamation more perceptible and the expression more lively. In a word, if one took it into one's head to perform the Music of this scene without joining the words to it, without shouting or gesticulating, it would not be possible to sort out anything in it analogous to the situation it wants to depict and the feeling it wants to express, and all this would seem only a tiresome series of sounds, modulated by chance and only in order to make it last.

Yet this monologue has always effectively produced in the theater, and I don't doubt that it will still be so, because its verses are admirable and the situation lively and interesting. But without the arms and the acting of the Actress, I am persuaded that no one could endure the recitative, and that such a Music has great need of the help of the eyes in order to be bearable to the ears.

I believe I have shown that there is neither meter nor melody in French Music, because the language is not susceptible to them; that French song is but a continual barking, unbearable to any ear not prepared for it; that its harmony is crude, expressionless, and uniquely feels its Schoolboy padding; that French arias are not at all arias; that the French recitative is not at all recitative. From which I conclude that the French do not at all have a Music and cannot have any*; or that if ever they have any, it will be so much the worse for them.

I am, etc.

---

* I do not call not having a Music to borrow that of another language in order to try to apply it to one's own, and I would prefer that we keep our glum and ridiculous song than combine, still more ridiculously, Italian melody with the French language. This disgusting combination, which will perhaps henceforth constitute the study of our Musicians, is too monstrous to be allowed, and the character of our language will never lend itself to it. At the very most some comic pieces may be able to pass due to their instrumental part; but I boldly predict that the tragic genre will not even be attempted. At the comic Opera this summer the work of a man of talent was applauded,[61] someone who seems to have listened to good Music with good ears, and who translated the genre into French as closely as was possible; his accompaniments were well imitated without being copies, and if he did not produce song at all, it is because it was not possible to produce it. Young Musicians who sense talent in yourselves: continue to despise Italian Music in public—I am well aware that your present interest requires it; but hasten to study that language and that Music in private if you want to be able one day to turn against your Comrades the disdain which you today affect for your Masters.

Observations on Our Instinct for Music and on Its Principle

In Which the Means for Recognizing the One by the Other Leads to Being Able to Account with Certainty for the Different Effects of that Art

by Monsieur Rameau

Preface

In order to enjoy the effect of Music fully, one must be in a state of pure self-abandonment, and in order to judge it, it is to the Principle by which one is affected that one must resort. This principle is Nature itself; it is from it that we derive that feeling which moves us in all our musical Operations, it has given us a gift which may be called *Instinct*. Let us therefore consult it in our judgments, let us see how it develops its mysteries in us before we make pronouncements. And if men are still found so full of themselves as to dare decide upon it on their own authority, there is room to hope that there will no longer be any so weak as to listen to them.

A mind preoccupied while listening to Music is never in a free enough position to judge it. If in its opinion, for example, it attributes the essential beauty of that Art to transitions from low to high, from soft to loud, from fast to slow, means which are used to vary sounds, it will judge everything in accordance with this prejudice without reflecting on the feebleness of these means, on the little merit there is in employing them, and without perceiving that they are foreign to Harmony, which is the unique basis of Music and the principle of its greatest effects.

A truly sensitive soul judges quite otherwise! If it is not penetrated by the power of the expression, by those vivid portraits of which Harmony alone is capable, it is not at all fully satisfied: not that it does not know how to lend itself to everything that can amuse it, but at least it values things in proportion to the effects it experiences from them.

It belongs to Harmony alone to stir the passions; Melody derives its force only from that source, from which it directly emanates;[1] and as for the differences from low to high, etc., which are only the superficial modifications of the Melody, they add almost nothing to it, as is demonstrated by striking examples in the course of the Work, wherein the principle is verified by our Instinct and this Instinct by its principle, that is, wherein the cause is verified by the effect one experiences and this effect by its cause.

If the imitation of noises and of motions is not as frequently employed in our Music as in Italian, it is because the dominant object of ours is feeling, which does not at all have determinate motions and which, consequently, cannot be everywhere subjected to a regular meter without losing that truth which constitutes its charm. The expression of the Physical is in the meter and the movement,[2] that of the Pathetic, in contrast, is in the Harmony and the inflections: which must be weighed carefully before determining what should prevail.

Since the Comic genre almost never has feeling for its object, it is consequently the sole one which is constantly susceptible of those rhythmic movements for which Italian Music is honored, without its nevertheless having been perceived that our Musicians have employed them happily enough in the small number of Attempts which the delicacy of the French taste has permitted them to venture: Attempts in which we have proven, by child's play, how easy it was for us to excel in this genre.*

This small Work may be regarded as the result of all the others I have presented on the same subject, and I hope that, given this, I will be pardoned some repetitions necessary for the comprehension of what happens to be connected to what is new in it. If I have elaborated a bit on certain points which will perhaps not be equally interesting to all Readers, some Authors, at least, will be able to recognize through this wherein they may have been mistaken.

While I was laboring on this Work, in which at first I had in view our Instinct for Music and its Principle, there appeared several Writings on the Theory of the Art,† to which I believed I could not better respond than by profiting from my first ideas in order to put everyone in a position not only to judge for himself, but to be able to account for the different effects of Harmony, without overly taxing the mind or the memory.

To attain knowledge of what has until now appeared as almost impenetrable, it is in actuality a matter simply of attending to the products of the Sounding Body,[4] products which can be distinguished into two kinds, kinds which are recognized by the position these same products occupy in the order of their generation, a position which, for its part, is recognized by two terms of the Art that are, moreover, very significant, namely, the *Dominant*, the *Fifth* above, and the *Subdominant*, the *Fifth* below: the first indicating only that the Voice should be raised, the other that it

---

* *Les Troqueurs* presented at the last Fairs of St. Laurent and St. Germain, and *La Coquette Trompée* presented at Fontainebleau in 1753.[3]

† Perhaps the Authors of these Writings will be grateful for not being named.

should be lowered; the first always being seconded by a new *Sharp* or *Natural*, the other by a new *Flat*; the first generally having for its part vigor, joy, the other feebleness, gentleness, tenderness, sadness. Both of them, finally, serve us most often as interpreters for our expressions, for example, when we cite the *Sharp* or the *Natural* as a sign of vigor and we raise our Voice in such a case, and when we lower it and cite the *Flat* as a sign of softness, of weakness — so much so that, considered with a little reflection, the whole is reduced to the greatest simplicity.

The Examples contained in my Observations confirm the truth of the precepts I give to attain the knowledge of the causes, and go so far as to justify the taste of the Nation concerning the Works of Music to which they have given their suffrage.

In order to give these precepts all the necessary force, I had to prove the Instinct by its Principle and this Principle by the same Instinct. They are, both of them, the work of Nature. Let us therefore no longer abandon her, this mother of the Sciences and the Arts. Let us examine her well and henceforth no longer try to be led by anything but her.

The Principle in question is not only that of all the Arts of taste, as is already confirmed by a *Treatise on the Beauty Essential in the Arts, Applied Principally to Architecture*,* it is also that of all the Sciences subject to calculation. This cannot be denied without at the same time denying that these Sciences are founded on the proportions and progressions, which Nature lets us know about through the Phenomenon of the Sounding Body in such marked circumstances that it is impossible to dismiss the evidence. And how deny it! No proportions, no Geometry.

Every Hypothesis, every arbitrary System must vanish in the face of such a Principle; one should not even hope ever to discover one as enlightening: if the seed of all the Elements of Geometry, of all the rules of Music and of Architecture has already been found in it, what may one not expect by grounding it even more scrupulously than has so far been done?

Observations on Our Instinct for Music and on Its Principle

Music is natural to us; we owe to pure Instinct alone the pleasant feeling it makes us experience. This same instinct sometimes acts on us through several other objects which may well have some relation to Music, which is why people who cultivate the sciences and arts should not be indifferent to knowing the principle of such an Instinct.

* By M. Briseux.[5]

This principle is now known: it exists, as one cannot be unaware, in the Harmony that results from the Resonance of every Sounding Body, such as from the sound of our voice, of a string, of a pipe, of a bell, etc., and in order to be further convinced, one need only examine oneself in all the steps one takes in Music.

For example, the man without experience in Music, just like the most trained, ordinarily takes the first Note he intones in the middle of his vocal range when he sings at fancy, and always then ascends, even though his vocal range is about equal below as well as above this first Note. This is entirely conformable to the resonance of the Sounding Body, all the Sounds that emanate from which being above that of its totality, which one believes to be the sole one that one hears.

In another respect, as little experience as one has, one hardly fails, when one wants to warm up by oneself, to intone in succession, always by ascending, the perfect chord made up of the harmony of the Sounding Body, whose genre, which is *Major*, is always preferred to the *Minor*, unless this latter is suggested by certain recollections.

If one ordinarily intones the *Third* first in the perfect chord, in ascending, even though the Sounding Body produces it only on the double *Octave*, which is the seventeenth, and thus above the *Octave* of the *Fifth*, which is its twelfth, this is because we naturally reduce all the intervals to their smallest degrees since the ear perceives them more promptly and since the voice arrives at them more easily. But it will not be the same for a man without experience, someone who has never heard Music, or who has not at all listened to it: for there is a difference between hearing and listening. If this man intones a note a little too low, quite clearly and quite distinctly, and then promptly allows his voice to go, without being preoccupied by any object, not even with the interval he wants to cover, since the succeeding operation is purely mechanical, he will certainly intone the *Fifth* first in preference to any other interval, according to the experiment we have made more than once.

It is quite well known that the *Fifth* is the most perfect of all the consonances: the remainder of these Observations will serve only to confirm it.

The smallest natural degrees, called *Diatonics*, those, in a word, of the scale *do re mi fa*, etc., are suggested only thanks to the consonances to which they conform and which they form in succeeding one another, so that these consonances always present themselves first to any person without experience. Furthermore, as soon as one wants to follow the order of these smallest degrees without the help of some recollection, one always ascends one *tone*, and descends a *semitone*, especially when one wants to go back immediately afterward to the first Note from which one began. For example, if this first Note, which represents a Sounding Body, is called *do*, its *Fifth*, *sol*, which resonates with it, will immediately seize the ear, and, wanting to go from *do* to its nearest degree, this *sol* will then present itself as a new Sounding Body with all its harmony, which consists of its *Major Third*, *si*, and its *Fifth*, *re*, so that one will thereby be forced to ascend one *tone* from *do* to *re*, and to descend one *semitone* from *do* to *si*.

On the other hand, after the *tone* in ascending, one will naturally be led to intone another: the *semitone* will present itself only through recollection, because two *tones* form the *Major Third* that resonates in the Sounding Body, whereas the *tone* and the semitone form only a *Minor Third*, which does not at all resonate in it; but also, after these two *tones*, one will feel oneself forced to intone a half one in order to pass to the *Fourth*, the third whole *tone* being rejected at that point since it produces a dissonance. And it is for this reason that it has always been said, because it has been felt, that three whole *tones* in succession are not natural. After this last *semitone* more, never does another one present itself; the *tone* will prevail in every ear in order to arrive at the consonance of the *Fifth*.

Such is the empire of the consonances over the ear, which is then preoccupied only with the degrees that form them, or that lead to them, these consonances being moreover merely the product of the resonance of the Sounding Body: which must be well noted, since nothing else can be inserted into it, so that the principle demonstrated is the instrument of all those faculties that have just been recognized as natural to us.

There is more; and however little experience one may have, one discovers by oneself the Fundamental Bass of every cadence in a song, according to the explanation given in our *New System*, etc., p. 54.[6] This proves even better the empire of the principle over all its products, since in this case the progression of these products recalls to the ear that of the principle which has determined it, and consequently which suggested it to the Composer.

This last experience, in which Instinct alone acts, just as in the preceding ones, proves quite well that melody has no other principle than the harmony produced by the Sounding Body: a principle with which the ear is so preoccupied, without one thinking of it, that it alone suffices to make us immediately discover the harmonic basis on which that melody depends. This happens not only to the Author who imagined it, but also to every person of a middling experience; one thus finds a number of Musicians capable of accompanying a song they hear for the first time by ear.

What, moreover, is the driving force behind those beautiful preludes, those happy caprices performed as soon as they are imagined, principally on the Organ? The fingers, in a position to obey instantaneously the imagination guided by the ear, would move in vain through every possible song if their guide were not of the simplest sort.

That guide for the ear is in fact none other than the harmony of a primary Sounding Body, by which it is no sooner struck than it drives forward everything that can follow this harmony, and lead back to it: and this all consists simply in the *Fifth* for the less experienced, and in the *Third* as well when experience has made greater progress.

But let us not go so far, and let us always note that, however little experience one may have, one never fails initially to follow the order of the *Mode* announced by the first harmony, and that the first new *mode* into which one then passes is generally that of that same *Fifth* from which we receive the feeling of the *tone* in ascending and that of the *semitone* in descending, in accordance with what has already been said about this: a *Fifth* on which is founded all the melody that can be drawn with justness from natural Instruments, such as the Trumpet and the Hunting Horn, and which is given to Kettledrums to serve as the Bass of this melody. And what other Bass, then? The *Fundamental Bass*, even without one having had it in mind, since it has been recognized only in our time.

These natural Instruments are themselves sounding Bodies, which have in their whole range only just what belongs to their harmony and to that of their *Fifth*, so that, by confirming the Instinct which generally leads us in the direction of this *Fifth* or of its harmony, this Instinct confirms, in its turn, the principle which guides it.

Such a behavior on our part, a purely mechanical behavior, should indeed open our eyes to the principle which is its sole and unique driving force. And people who cultivate the other Sciences should also closely examine the behavior they follow: they will doubtless recognize in it this same principle, at least in the proportions on which they base almost all their operations. Who would prefer to owe these to chance, these proportions, rather than to a phenomenon in which Nature has embraced them all, under circumstances which may well extend to objects other than Music?

Instead of consulting Nature about Music, the Philosophic mind has from the earliest times turned to it from the direction of Geometry, in order therein to follow Pythagoras without first examining whether that Author was well- or ill-founded. He is made to speak, made to act as one believes he may have done. Hypotheses are imagined with him, or after his fashion, to make the ratios he gave to the Sounds square with the different orders that experience suggests. Each says what he thinks about it, and all are equally mistaken.

Who is the Philosopher, who is the man, who with a little common sense will not recognize that he owes that pleasant feeling he experiences in hearing certain relationships between Sounds to nature, to his pure Instinct? And who is it that will not therefore profit from the means he can discover in this Mother of the Sciences and the Arts to act consistently? But not at all; it is wished that Pythagoras, after having recognized the *Octave* was composed of two unequal intervals, which are the *Fifth* and the Fourth, of which the major *tone* constitutes the difference, had of his own authority added that *tone* to itself, to form the *Major Third*. Is this consistent, and can such an error be supposed of so great a Man? What! He finds in Nature an interval made up of two unequal ones, and it is wished that he himself had made another one of two equal ones? One is surely deceived on his account, in this case and every time. It is much more probable that this Author, fertile in progressions, as can be judged by what remains to us of him, having recognized the ratio of the *Fifth* or double *Fifth*, called the twelfth, between 1 and 3, would have formed a triple progression of this first ratio, and would have carried it all the way to the twelfth power, as all the intervals presented as belonging to his system confirm, and in particular his *comma* formed of the comparison of the unit with this twelfth power: the *comma* whose source has been unknown in all times, even by Pythagoras' sectarians, since it has never been spoken of except under the heading of *Pythagoras' Comma*, without any other explanation.

As soon as one no longer consults the ear, one will always be seduced by the product of a triple progression, in which all the intervals necessary for Music are found, with the exception of the *Enharmonic*, whose usage has been known only in our times, although the Ancients spoke about it, but very confusedly; now, there is room to believe that Pythagoras no more consulted his ear concerning the intervals produced by his progression than all the Authors who have adopted his system, since there is nothing just in this progression except the *Major Tone* and the *Fifths*, from which *Fourths* are formed by inversion, all the rest in it being false, without *Minor Tones* being found in it; and from which it happens that its *Major Third* is made up of two *Major Tones*.*

In Music, the ear obeys only Nature; it takes no heed of either moderation or accuracy; Instinct alone guides it. Our Moderns were therefore mistaken to conclude, from the falsity of Pythagoras' system, that the Ancients did not practice harmony. We have, ourselves, contributed to this error by too much confidence in those who have anticipated us in this matter; and without the fanciful ideas uttered every day on Music, a reflection so just and so simple would perhaps still have escaped us. In Music,

---

* One ought to judge from this account that the authority of Pythagoras, any more than that of all the Ancients, can hardly carry any weight in Music.

the ear obeys only Nature, we repeat it again, and all the false systems recanted up until now, the false relationships that are found, even in the perfect system, have not prevented our Musicians from singing justly and from carrying their Art to a very high degree of perfection.[7]

* * *

If one first looks into the resonance of sounding Bodies, from which the natural feeling for Harmony comes to us, one will likewise see in the Sounds common to the Harmony the various fundamental Sounds which immediately succeed one another, from which there comes to us that of its succession, called *Melody* in each part in particular. And here is the explanation.

When *do* resonates, its *Fifth*, *sol*, resonates with it; thus, this *sol* is present for us in hearing *do*, and the moment the ear fixes on it, its harmony naturally turns out to be implied in it, so that everything then induces us to pass from *do* to *sol*, or to one of its harmonic Sounds. The return from this *sol* to *do* is quite simple. Thus, we have a presentiment of the *fifth* below as well as that above; from which it follows that in hearing *do* we can likewise have a presentiment of the *fa*, of which it is the *Fifth*. There is a common Sound on each side, which is the *Fifth* above or below. And is by such springs that the ear is guided from one Sound to another.

Since the presentiment of one fundamental Sound entails that of its Harmony, there naturally follows for us the freedom of choice among all the harmonic Sounds that then follow it; and it is from this choice, dictated by good taste, that the most pleasant Melody is formed.[8]

* * *

As soon as one wants to experience the effect of a Song, it is always necessary to support it with all the Harmony from which it derives; it is in that Harmony itself that the cause of the effect resides, not at all in the Melody, which is only its product—a truth that will be recognized in a moment on the subject of the *Chromatic*. It is moreover necessary to sing what precedes this Song, because it is the impression received from the *Mode* in which one begins that gives rise to the feeling one experiences in the *Mode* which follows it.[9]

* * *

Often what is due only to the Words is believed to pertain to the Music, or, one tries to submit them to the expression one wants to give them by forced inflections, and this is not the means for being able to judge them. One must, on the contrary, let oneself be drawn along by the feeling it inspires, this Music, without thinking about it, without thinking at all, and then this feeling will become the instrument of our judgment. As for the reason, it is now in everyone's hands; we have just drawn it from the very bosom of Nature; we have even proved that Instinct reminds us of it at every moment, both in our actions and in our discourses. Now, as soon as reason and feeling are in accord, there is no further appeal.

The Modulation, at first fixed in the two *Fifths** of the generator, is not limited to them, and in order to extend the limits, this generator has further reserved its two *Major Thirds*, of which it forms, with itself, a quintuple progression, in this order taken by whole numbers: 1, 5, 25, where 5 represents it at the center, a place it occupies in every context; so that from the products of its Harmony and of that of one of the extremes—it does not matter which, 1 or 25—there arises the *minor semitone*, called the *Chromatic*; and from the products of the Harmony of these two extremes, 1 and 25, arises a *quarter-tone*, called *Enharmonic*, which is absolutely indiscernible. This confirms quite well the superiority of the *Fifth*, in accordance with our opening remarks, since it is the unique source of the true naturalness, the true beauty of what alone can furnish us with a sufficiently pleasant Music. As proof, we appeal to Lully's Operas and even to the Italian Music of his time, which was hardly more varied than his own. And in order to judge this equitably, it is necessary to transport oneself to those times. Furthermore, as one can never interrupt the Diatonic order except by a single *Chromatic* or *Enharmonic interval*, which then serves for the transition from one *Mode* to another, whose relation is more or less remote, and as this transition is in general practicable thanks to the Diatonic, excepting that which depends on the Enharmonic, which has not yet been used in French Operas, except in a Monologue in *Dardanus*,[10] it must necessarily be concluded from this that whatever advantage one might derive from these latter intervals, all Music is able to please without their aid; and this reflection should always be kept in mind so as not to let it be imposed upon by big words that signify nothing.

Is it not said every day, by some to find fault, by others to praise: that is *Chromatic* Music. Oftentimes, though, it is not a question of it at all. On the other hand, this *Chromatic* is not suspected in a Music in which it abounds, since it is again represented only in the interval, when this interval is only the accidental caused by the products of a fundamental succession, from which arises the feeling one experiences from it. Examine, for

---

* There is a *Fifth* and a *Third* below as well as above.

this effect, the Rondo from the Monologue *Tristes apprêts*, etc., in the Opera *Castor et Pollux*.¹¹ The feeling of doleful sorrow and gloom which reigns in it belongs wholly to the *Chromatic* furnished by the fundamental succession, while not a single interval of this genre is found in any of its parts*—a feeling which is not the same in the previous Chorus, in which the *Chromatic* intervals, which abound in descending, there depict the sobs and the groans caused by intense regrets.

We cite this *Chromaticism* principally in order to make it known that, if the feeling one experiences from it is always confined to sadness, sometimes to softness, to tenderness, its source, as that of the *Enharmonic*, lies in the *Minor Mode*, the sphere of the multiples, as we have already stated: a new set of additional proofs in support of the resonance of the totality of the Bodies, from which there arises the Arithmetical proportion on which this *Mode* is founded and from which there also arises the *Minor Third*, the *Subdominant*, and the *Flat Keys*, something that cannot be too often repeated. But perhaps we shall gain more through examples than through reasons—and this will properly furnish us with the occasion to render to Lully the justice owed to him, and of which he would have been robbed through a Criticism which is all the more ill-founded as it is in general contradictory to the Principles which the Author has himself laid down in the *Encyclopedia*.¹² Let us therefore see what it's all about.

> *Enfin il est en ma puissance.*
> [At last, he is in my power.]†

Here is a Trill and, what is worse, a perfect close on the first Verse.

The Trill‡ produces beauty in our Music, especially in the present case, where it adds force to the word *puissance*, on which the entire meaning of the Verse rests; and if some abuse it, it is wrong to blame the thing itself.

Armide congratulates herself here on having Renaud in her power, and to express her triumph in this, nothing is better imagined than the *Trill* she uses: a *Trill* exactly like that of Trumpets in Victory Songs. Example B.¹⁵

As to what a *perfect cadence* is, there is no hint of it in the Music even according to the principles the Author has given for it.§

M. Rousseau cannot be unaware that as long as a Song moves along on

---

*The feeling one experiences of Chromaticism, which strictly speaking does not exist at all in this Monologue, proves the necessity there is of joining to the Melody all the Harmonic bases on which it depends [...] in order to be able to judge its full effect.

† Page 81 of the *Letter on French Music* by M. Rousseau.¹³

‡ *Trill*: this term is more suitable than that of *Cadenza*, which we make use of inappropriately in such a case.¹⁴

§ In the *Encyclopedia* at the word *Cadence*, one finds nearly everywhere the word *Close* for that of *cadence*, and notably in the penultimate paragraph of page 514, which has: *To establish* the same Harmony, the variety of Sounds employed in it serves only to form the embellishment of the Melody, and that, at bottom, this variety never represents anything but a single Sound, as one sees in the Bass of Example B.[19] Now, how could he have imagined that there was a close, or more, a *perfect close* on *puissance*, when not only does the same *Tonic*, its same Harmony, persist throughout the entire Verse, but even up to the hemistich of the second? What becomes of the principles laid down on this subject in the *Encyclopedia*?

A forced close in order to regain breath, actually forced in order to detach the first *ce* with which *puissance* ends from the *ce* that begins the following Verse, as every Performer will likewise be forced to do: can a close of this nature, I say, be taxed with that name—and *what is worse* that of a *perfect close*—in Music? Does the *Trill* have this character in itself when, on the contrary, it is generally employed only in order to announce the close? Is such a contradiction with the precepts given pardonable?

> *Ce fatal Ennemi, ce superbe Vainqueur.*
> [This mortal enemy, this haughty Conqueror.]

An Author who has done me the favor of adopting my principles is doubtless not unaware of the intimate relation already cited between the *Major Mode* and the *Minor*, nor is he any more unaware that the latter owes its origin to the former, that it depends upon it, and that if it partakes of softness, the other is on the contrary virile, vigorous.* If this is so, why reproach Lully by saying: *I would gladly pardon*, etc.,[20] for what is most admirable in the treatment of the first two Verses? To avoid any close from the opening to the end of the second verse in order to make the connection of the meaning perceptible, since the same *Tonic* persists until the hemistich of the second, where it passes to another *Tonic*: this is already quite a lot. But to employ first the *Minor Mode*, so that its softness, opposed to the vigor of the *Major*, adds to it a new spur and, so to speak, re-

---

a perfect close, etc.[16] Now, a perfect close, an absolute close, a perfect cadence, a final conclusion after which one no longer desires anything, all these are synonymous.

Then in the second paragraph one reads: *What is called an Act of cadence always results from two fundamental Sounds of which the first announces the cadence and the other terminates it.*[17]

In the third paragraph: *The chord formed on the first Sound of a cadence*, precisely that which announces it, *should therefore always be dissonant*. There is thus an error at the end of the first paragraph, where it is said precisely: *It follows that all Harmony is properly only a series of cadences*, since the Tonic, never carrying dissonances, can consequently never announce *cadences*.[18] Also, there are never any in the transition from a Tonic to any note whatsoever, unless from the *Tonic* that it was it becomes *Dominant* or *Subdominant*; which must be carefully noted before making a determination, and this reflection will not be useless in what follows.

* One can see on pages 54 and 55 of the *Letter*, etc.,[21] that the Author does recognize these sorts of differences and should as a consequence judge what use can be made of them for contrast.

doubles it at the moment this *Major* is going to terminate a perfect close on these words, *ce superbe Vainqueur*: this is the great stroke of the Master. For, in short, it is only on these last words that all Armide's spite rests, it is not at all *ce fatal Ennemi* that occupies her, any more than her liberated captives, as she says afterward to rouse herself to an action her heart belies: it is only Renaud's contempt for her charms that wounds her pride.

Let one reflect on this, after having really gotten down to the basis of the Art, and one will see what Instinct is capable of all by itself; for Lully, led by feeling, and by taste, did not have any knowledge of this basis, unknown in his time.

In seeing what Instinct can do by itself, one sees at the same time the simplicity of the principle that guides it. Two *Tonics* of which the first is subject to the laws imposed on it by the other: this is all that is employed to render an expression with the greatest perfection that could be desired.

Furthermore, one should always mistrust one's judgment, when, not knowing the Principles, one wants to detach it from the impressions one has received or is receiving. Let us abandon ourselves over to pure feeling, let us listen without thinking about it, and we shall see that the *Trill* in question is struck only as a simple deceptive close, on which the triumph Armide claims to enjoy is expressed; we shall likewise feel the forcefulness of expression that falls on these words, *ce superbe Vainqueur*, without knowing that it arises from the Artfulness with which the modulation is observed here; but what does it matter: if we are genuinely sensitive, and if we judge only according to feeling, we shall always judge well.

> *Le charme du sommeil le livre à ma vengeance.*
> [Sleep's charm delivers him to my vengeance.]

Could a man of taste and of feeling be mistaken when reason enlightens him about the great artfulness there is in softening a first expression in order to direct all the force to the principal one by the opposition of the contrast?* *Le charme du sommeil* does not yet conclude anything, and it is to *le livre à ma vengeance* that everything should be directed. See Example C.[22]

Lully thinks in Grand terms, and he has certainly not nodded on this last Verse. He begins, in the first place, in the Mode of the *Subdominant* announced by the *Sharp* cited by the Author of the Criticism,[23] then, stepping over the *Tonic*, he passes to its *Dominant*, where the force is redoubled† in order to express *le livre à ma vengeance*, he carries the voice in the

---

* See the preceding note.

† Let us recall that the sphere of the *Dominant*, that of the *Fifth* in ascending, is precisely the sphere of forcefulness; so that the more *Fifths* there are in ascending, the more the force is redoubled; the same reasoning applies in inverted fashion for softness, the sphere of the *Subdominant*.

bass in order then, by ascending rapidly, to make felt all the furor to which Armide strives to abandon herself in saying *je vais percer*, etc. There is more, which is that the *Dominant*, chosen for the close which precedes this last Verse, makes a new close desired on the *Tonic* which is to follow it, so that one thereby senses that Armide still has something to say while the meaning that concludes with the Verse nonetheless gives no hint of it. Shall the skill of the Musician be counted as nothing in this case? And can this be passed over in silence in order to attack it as inappropriately as has been done?

A contrast on the one hand between the *Subdominant* and the *Dominant* and on the other between the bass and the treble, the whole mindful of the regularity which the expression demands.

One might have dispensed with citing, as proof of what is advanced, a *Sharp* that has no virtue other than from its Fundamental Bass.[24] This could easily be judged by substituting this Bass for it: the effect of the Melody will not be changed by this. There is more, and this same *Sharp* can take a Song which will not have the appearance of a *Sum*.[25] Example D.[26]

What precedes a Melody whose effect one wants to experience must always be sung, as has already been remarked; moreover, if Lully had followed another route in his Melody other than that found here under its same *Sharp*, and which could not fail to present itself to his ear, for it presents itself wholly naturally with this *Sharp*, which is what is seen at D, this would destroy the whole contrast, otherwise it is easily perceived that he could not give to the two expressions that come afterward all the power they demand, and that by degrees.

> *Je vais percer son invincible coeur.*
> [I will pierce his invincible heart.]

If all *the impetuosity of the movement* falls on *Je vais percer son invincible*, can it be better rendered than by ascending by degrees and rapidly until the moment when Armide must have spent all her fire in order to end it with a *Trill* which, it is true, displeases our Author? Let us pass over this weakness without, however, passing over what this *Trill* does *on a short syllable*.[27]*

---

*It is to be quite ignorant of and little sensitive to our Prosody to tax as *short* the last masculine syllable of a word, whereas there is not one in it that is not *long*. After this, one must not be astonished by the conclusions that are drawn from this about our Recitative. Sometimes one has one's reasons: taste, feeling, and the ear do not do too much to make them succeed, and one is not always equally favored with these gifts. It is true that they are almost useless in the Italian Recitative, in which Art plays a much greater role than Nature. The more one strikes the ear disagreeably with the Chromatic and the Enharmonic, the better one believes one has succeeded, such is the mania of the Italian School: it is not at all made for the ear. Also, the Italians themselves are not seen to take much pleasure in hearing it.

Let us moreover note that Lully has done more here than in a simple declamation, in which the voice would naturally be decreased on the word *Son*, whereas in the Music it ascends to *invin* . . . , being forced by the style of the Song, which should finish on the Tonic, to then descend on the *Trill*.

> *Par lui mes Captifs sont sortis d'esclavage:*
> *Qu'il éprouve toute ma rage.*
> [Through him all my Captives have left their servitude
> Let him feel all my fury.]

To require accompaniments from the Orchestra when one can do without them, is this not an uncalled-for quibble? Does the Player need his interior feelings to be depicted, and does the Singer need anything other than silence in this case? It is not at all a matter here of what could be done better, provided that what is found here is done well.

If the first paragraph of p. 84 of the *Letter* in question is read,[28] one will recognize in it the ascendancy of passion over reason, since the whole Criticism there is contradictory to the very principles the Author himself has laid down.

In the second paragraph of the word *Cadence*, already cited in a Note,[29] one reads: *What is called an act of Cadence results from two fundamental Sounds of which the first announces the Cadence and the other terminates it*; then in the third paragraph: *The chord formed on the first Sound of a Cadence should always be dissonant.*[30] This first Sound of the *Cadence* is that which announces it, it therefore cannot be a *Tonic*, since it never carries a Dissonance. Now, even though the note which concluded the preceding Verse might be the same as that which begins the following, as is said, the ear and the judgment decide this very differently than the eyes, since, from the *Tonic* that it was it becomes *Dominant* for the close, or of the Cadence, that terminates at the end of the Verse.

Par lui mes Captifs sont sortis d'esclavage. This close should be announced—it can be so only by the note that precedes the one that concludes it; this note that announces should carry a Dissonance according to the Author himself; it is therefore not the previous Tonic. It is true that its Bass is not figured.* But are the eyes enough in Music? Ears are needed, and above all an impartial judgment in which reason does not allow itself to be blinded. Soon this *Tonic* will be seen to become *Dominant*, as soon as it is believed it can be allowed to do so.

To take advantage of the notes that are cited as being of the same Chord, because they are effectively the same notes, while its Chord changes;

---

* See the third paragraph of *Cadence* in the *Encyclopedia* on the expressed or implied Dissonance.[31]

to remain silent about those which are actually of the same Chord at the Verse, *Enfin il est dans ma puissance*, so as to deduce from this a *perfect close* on *puissance*—against the Principles that were presented on this subject; to applaud himself for his very error with regard to this *close*; and to pass over in silence the one that is so perceptible at the word *esclavage*, since the Song concludes on a *note* called *leading*, in the terms of the Art—a silence apparently feigned so as to be able to say that the chord of the former *Tonic* is the same as that of the *Dominant* into which it is transformed from one verse to the other; even to fasten on a naught, that is a short vowel, which should not be a factor in the present case, gives him the weight to authorize what is advanced against all truth. What can be thought of such a Critic?

As soon as a Chord takes on some new Sounds, expressed or implied,* its effect totally changes; but care is taken not to talk about this with regard to the second Verse: *Qu'il éprouve*, etc. There was no intention to praise, and he would have had to recall the *Dominant* of the *Dominant-Tonic*, which so happily makes one desire a conclusion which could not be expected since the meaning is ended on the first Verse, *Par lui*, etc., on this *Dominant-Tonic*. The Critic would have been foiled by that.

> *Quel trouble me saisit? qui me fait hésiter?*
> [What tumult seizes me? What makes me hesitate?]

To conceal here the nature of closes, of their different *Modes*, in order boldly to say that everything is in *the same key, almost in the same chord as the preceding*[32]—this can hardly be excused in a Musician, still less a Theorist, who works for the *Encyclopedia*. The *Mode* changes on each phrase, and the word *almost*, which leaves an equivocation, which does not proclaim good faith and which may seduce everyone poorly versed in the Art, has no value in this case here: everything or nothing. *The Tonic, it is true, becomes Dominant*, etc.; it is as if one were to say, day, it is true, becomes night; for the *Mode* is actually changed into another on the side of the *Subdominant*, exactly that which requires reflection. But to whom is he speaking? Doubtless he counts upon the Reader not having very much knowledge. The *key* changes, then, at this point. Example F.[33] From *re* it passes to *sol* for the first hemistich, then to *do* for the second—as is proved by the Note *la* that follows it and in whose *key* the first hemistich of the next Verse concludes, *Qu'est-ce qu'en sa faveur*, etc. This Note immediately afterward becomes the Subdominant of *mi*, which in its turn concludes the same Verse—so very nicely that the *Minor mode* of *mi*, the one that reigns in the whole

---

* See the preceding Note on the expressed or implied Dissonance.

Monologue, that alone predominates in it and that was just made to be desired more strongly than ever by all the different *Keys* or *Modes* which have been used since the fourth verse, namely those of *re*, *sol*, *do*, and *la*—so very nicely, I say, that this same so much desired *Mode* of *mi* announces itself, returns, and will all suddenly strike on the *Tonic* by ascending a *Fourth*, precisely in order to express the decisive word, *Frappons*.

The Tonic, it is true, becomes Dominant. Well! Is that all? Must what has just been observed regarding the same subject be recalled? Are there other fundamental Sounds in the Harmony than *Tonics*, *Dominants*, and *Subdominants*? *Well, Heavens!*, it is said, *is it indeed a question of the Tonic*, etc.—and of what, then, if that is all? Is it not said, at the word *Cadence*, although mistakenly: *It follows that every Harmony is properly only a series of Cadences.*[34] Let us now see in the same paragraph what Cadences are made up of and judge. We do not believe that one may, by a similar judgment, blind oneself as much as the one who says to us: *This Verse is in the same key, almost in the same chord as the preceding*. Can one come down against all truth with such boldness?

The Tonic, it is true, becomes Dominant. We repeat it again. Well! Why not make the same observation concerning the Verse, *par lui tous mes captifs*, etc., and the one that precedes it. Would it actually be the figuration found there, would it be the *leading note*, which has no place on the other side, would it have been done on purpose? Think about it what one wants, but an enlightened man does not need such signs to decide.

> *Qu'est-ce qu'en sa faveur la pitié me veut dire?*
> *Frappons.*
> [What does pity wish to say to me in his behalf?
> Strike.]

The deceptive close on the first Verse in the middle of the vocal range leaves it enough space to ascend a *Fourth* on *Frappons*, then yet a third further on the exclamation, *Ciel!*: the first presenting the *Tonic* as a decided thing—*Frappons*; the other ascending to the *Third* of this *Tonic* in order to mark the surprise she has in seeing herself suddenly checked. Here the change of *Mode* is not at all suitable because the surprise is so subtle that the first sound that presents itself when elevating the voice is the genuine and most suitable sound for the exclamation and this first Sound is precisely the *Third*—according to the order of the principle and of instinct, and, consequently, to the range that remains to the voice. Thus this verdict of the critical Author, *for his notation fixes the declamation so little*,[35] seems to have been pronounced quite without reflection.

If the nature of the *Modes* used in the preceding Verses were also observed in order always to hold the listener in suspense until the moment when the great blow should be felt, and if it were considered, along with this, how the treble and the bass parts are handled, it would be admired instead of blamed.

> *Ciel! qui peut m'arrêter!*
> *Achevons . . . je frémis! vengeons-nous . . . je soupire!*
> [Heavens! What can be stopping me?
> End it . . . I tremble. Avenge myself . . . I sigh.]

Who would believe, says M. Rousseau, *that the Musician left all this agitation in the same key*, etc.[36] Who would believe that one could have been mistaken after such an absolute affirmation? Not only is all this agitation not in the same *Key*, but it changes by the implied Chromatic every half hemistich.

After the *Key* of *mi*—*qui peut m'arrêter*—passes to the Dominant-Tonic of *sol*, where this Dominant ascends on the word *achevons*, this *sol* afterward becomes Dominant-Tonic of its Subdominant *do*, to which it passes in order to express by descending, *je frémis*; and from there comes the Dominant-Tonic of *re*, on which *re* the Song ascends to express *Achevons*; then, this *re*, becoming in its turn Dominant-Tonic of *sol*, will finally expire by descending on the *Third* of this *sol* to put an end to all the whole agitation with *Je soupire*, in the same *Key* on which it began.

So many Dominant-Tonics, so many new Sharps or Flats, which produce a Chromatic distributed as perfectly as is possible in the basis of the Harmony, as can be verified by examination; but it will perhaps be said that none of these Sharps or Flats is seen in the Song, not in the Bass any more than in the Figuration. Again, more than the eyes are needed to judge in such a case. See Example G.[37]

The Harmony is here made to be intoned before the Melody that is its product, in order that it inspire the Singer with the feeling with which he should be affected independently of the words: a feeling that will strike every unbiased man who wants to abandon himself to the pure effects of Nature; from which one is forced to conclude that Harmony is the principal mover of this feeling, and that if the Melody alone can inspire it, it is because it implies, without one thinking of it, the basis of the Harmony on which it depends.

This can be settled only on the basis of the Music; the Figuration of the Bass—at every moment full of errors, by an error of copying, of printing, or of the Author himself, who will have passed lightly over this point—should not have any weight. Nevertheless, to judge only by Lully's Figuration, one sees various types of deceptive closes at every half hemistich;

they occur on different fundamental Sounds, and this alone is enough to be able to conclude that the same line of reasoning suits each of these half hemistiches, especially after having said some pages previously, *Every time the relations are different, the impression cannot be the same*.[38] But there is more. The words are not at all enough for the Singer to put himself in a state to express well the feeling they depict; it is necessary, at the same time, for the Music to answer to it. For proof of this, let one present at *je frémis* the Melody of *Vengeons-nous*, right after *Achevons*, as the Modulation allows: the sudden agitation, the turmoil the Author wants to depict will seem gauche, forced: he himself will need all his presence of mind to produce as best he can what the Melody, and especially the whole basis of the Harmony, does not inspire in him, and despite all his artfulness a discrepancy will always be felt between his acting and the Music. This must be carefully noted so as not to fall into the error of believing that the Actor's acting may compel in such a case: one would have to be quite limited in his knowledge and quite insensitive to think in such a way.

It is principally from the basis of the Harmony, from which the Melody applied to the words is drawn, that the Singer receives the impression of the feeling he should depict. These words serve him, so to speak, only as an indication; the proof of this has just been given, as it has already been given, but in still more particular cases—whether at the *Parenthesis* on page 57, or at the words *Le charme du sommeil*, page 81.[39] Further, when the Singer recognizes by the words that he should indicate the turmoil at *je frémis*, his voice expresses it as though on its own and without thinking of the cause that makes him act, without even suspecting it he finds himself led to this expression by the basis of the Harmony that inspires it in him. The Listener, for his part, finds himself moved: let him not seek the reason for this, then, since he can be mistaken about it, or at least let him recognize it in the expressed or implied *Flat* that conveys the basis of the Harmony by a species of Chromatic in descending, let him likewise recognize that the feeling of fury he experiences when hearing *Vengeons-nous* comes from the two new *Sharps*, the first of which forms the Chromatic in ascending with the Subdominant *do* that immediately precedes it, this same *Sharp* afterward descending to its *Flat* to express *je soupire*.

There is an interplay of Chromatics here that which does not actually appear at all in Lully's Figuration, but which appears to be the foundation of the different expressions, so very much so that it is enough to accompany them with a Harpsichord to be absolutely convinced of it. Whatever the Figuration may be, one should judge, by the different feelings which the Actor and the Listener experience here, that the Author could only have been guided by the Harmonic basis which we prescribe to it.

Is it not a merit to know so well how to conceal Art through Art itself? Let us assume that this is only the work of feeling, as it is in all appearance: its merit is perhaps even greater for having known so well how to render the impetuosity of so many different emotions with a Harmonic basis as simple as the one that is employed there. Let no one be mistaken about this, however; the required *harmonic departures* found in this simplicity are not, in truth, those which one perhaps thought, those whose harshness always makes itself felt and which are the usual resource of limited geniuses who can only take fire by forcing Nature, but those gentle *departures* in which the *connection*, although pleasant, does not fail to make felt the various emotions they depict. The effect of this Music has already been experienced quite often; it will always be experienced as before, as long as one allows oneself to be guided by feeling alone, without any extraneous concern.

It is good to remind people that there is in all Music only the Diatonic, the Chromatic, and the Enharmonic; that this last genre was not at all in use in Lully's time, that it can hardly be employed, that a certain harshness results from it and that it has been used only a single time in our Theatrical Music, so that there remains the Chromatic for all *departures*. Now, if this was not perceived in the present case, who is at fault? This is not the sole piece of Music in which the Harmonic basis involves the Chromatic, without the slightest appearance of it in any of the parts and where the feeling one experiences from it arises directly from this same Harmonic basis.

More than eyes are needed, I have already said, in order to judge an Art in which the cause resides as much in what is implied as in what is expressed, as he allows one to glimpse at the word *Cadence* in the *Encyclopedia*.

Trills have an especially fine effect, etc.[40] Something said ironically, but without refinement, characterizes its Author more and more; for a short and quickly struck Trill at the end of *vengeons-nous*, and suspended by a single soft fluttering on *je soupire*, adds to the expression. Why further involve the *perfect Cadence* in this irony? Isn't the meaning complete at *je soupire*? Is it then on the *Third*, whose effect is less absolute than that of its *Tonic*?

Every person who wants to judge the Music of the last Verse,

> *Achevons . . . je frémis! vengeons-nous. . . je soupire!*
> [End it . . . I tremble! Avenge myself . . . I sigh.]

by the aid of the eyes alone, will certainly not judge it like our Critic, since he will at least see the high and low in it; if he adds his ear to this, this difference will strike him as belonging to closes of a different nature on different fundamental Sounds, and if he also adds to this some knowledge of the Art, he will recognize in it the cause of this feeling, such as we have just depicted it. But some Readers decide without going deeply into anything and let themselves be seduced by the style. The thing is well written, true or false, it doesn't matter, one trusts it. Well! What should be sought in works, if it is not imagination, genius, discernment, judgment, taste, feeling, an ear, finally, if it is a matter of Music. One could also well amuse oneself with the character of the Author, for he gladly portrays himself in his writings; but one should follow only the truth. The wise man fears and avoids the flowers whose perfume is often poisoned.

> *Est-ce ainsi que je dois me venger aujourd'hui?*
> *Ma colere s'éteint quand j'approche de lui.*
> [Is this how I must avenge myself today?
> My anger abates when I draw near him.]

To approve of the declamation* of these two Verses is to criticize his own criticism since this declamation is founded on the same principles as everything that has preceded. The greater interval to be hoped for between the two Verses depends upon the Actor, and this is apparently said without reflection, as is the greatest part of the whole Work. As for the *Perfect Cadence* that is reproached, it is the Author's tic; no other is known for concluding a completed sense.

> *Plus je le vois, plus ma vengeance est vaine.*
> [The more I behold him, the more my vengeance is vain.]

The difference of high and low, of loud and soft, is therefore recognized here since he would like the voice to ascend on *vengeance* and fall again softly on *vaine*, but it will soon be forgotten anew, as it has been forgotten before,† so as to give himself the pleasure of saying something clever.

A poor Perfect Cadence, he says; but it is up to those who have an ear to decide: *so much more so because it is accompanied by a Trill*—a good reason.[41]

> *Ah! quelle cruauté de lui ravir le jour?*
> *A ce jeune Héros tout cede sur la terre.*
> [Ah! what cruelty to rob him of life.
> To this young Hero everything on the earth accedes.]

Have the second Verse declaimed after the first and you will see (we speak to the Author himself who cites Mlle Dumesnil here)[42] that one will lower the voice after *jour* in order to pass to the second Verse, that, therefore, the Musician could not have done better than to raise it on *jour* in order to soften it again when descending on *ce jeune Héros*, etc., and further in such a manner when passing to the *Major Mode* relative to that of

---

*The musical declamation of these two Verses is approved of in effect.
† This reflection would made the criticism of the Verse *Vengeons-nous*, etc., collapse if the time were taken. When one does not judge by Principles, one at least needs a memory.

the *Subdominant* of the *Mode* that it left on *jour*, and where one actually experiences a very perceptible resoftening. But care is taken not to cite this second Verse—it would have gotten in the way of the pleasantry. It is here that one can say with reason what this Author says on the occasion of the Verse: *The more I look at it*, etc., *the voice should ascend on "jour" and fall again softly on "à ce jeune Héros"*, etc.[43]

The Criticism now turns on only a Parenthesis which isn't worth the trouble of pausing over: what we have cited sufficiently proves what Lully was capable of in this regard. M. Rousseau's triumph on this matter will not shelter him from his contradictions, from his false statements, any more than from his silence on the very accidentals he proclaims and which he suppresses when it seems good to him, in accordance with the advantages he claims to derive from them. And in order to inform the Reader all at once, here is a brief recapitulation along with some new remarks, which will perhaps not be useless.

An error, and at the same time a contradiction with himself, on the occasion of the *Trill*, where he says there is a *perfect close*.

Another contradiction when he says, page 85 of the *Letter*; *But Heavens! Is it indeed a question of the Tonic*, etc.,[44] after having proclaimed in the *Encyclopedia* at the word *Cadence* that the Harmonic basis consists only in this, so that all the different features the Melody might possibly be given can arise only from this same basis.

Still another contradiction, but a tacit one, when, after having reprimanded Lully for what he should have done in ascending and descending, p. 88,[45] and when, after having agreed that *every time the relations are different the impression cannot be the same*, he wants the same meaning to be rendered by the Melody of each half hemistiche, p. 87,[46] whereas the relations between the closes are different, some of which are used in the treble, the others in the bass, on different fundamental Sounds, in such a way that the two means of variety, which he honors himself for knowing, happen to be employed properly and at the same time.

By this manner of acting, the road to perfection is hidden from the Reader in order to show him only imaginary defects, as can now be perceived.

If it is said, p. 82, *I would perhaps pardon the Musician for having put this second Verse into another key*, etc., this is precisely at the point where the new key brings the expression to the climax: and if it is added, *if he had allowed himself to change it more often on the necessary occasions*:[47] this sufficiently proves the little knowledge he has of the basis of the Art, since the *keys* in the entire Monologue are varied as much and as appropriately as possible. A blind man would not pronounce so boldly on what he does not see; he at least knows that others see.

To conceal on the one hand what is cited on the other, to carry abuse to the point of sharp raillery, where he is himself mistaken: this is incomprehensible.

For example, by concealing the Perfect Avoided Cadences on the *Dominant-Tonics* at the end of the third and of the fifth Verses—Cadences mentioned in the *Encyclopedia*—he conceals from the Reader who has little instruction the merit of the Harmony, which makes one desire what is not at all proclaimed by the words, since the meaning is complete on each of these two Verses when it is not, however, in Armide's mind; it is after this that it concludes. Also hidden is the merit of the Melody, in which the cadences are handled in a manner so that enough of the vocal range is left for it to ascend quickly up to the word that should make all the force of the expression felt.

Why say at the seventh Verse, *The Tonic, it is true, becomes Dominant*, etc., and conceal it at the fifth verse when they are wholly similar, except that the one becomes *Dominant-Tonic* and the other simply *Dominant*? Why say at the fifth Verse, page 84, *He begins again exactly in the same key, on the same chord*, and at the seventh, almost on the same chord, when the thing is the same in both parts?[48] The *almost* has no value at all, it is even excessive and against good faith; but if this is the same chord, it is not the same fundamental note—*the Tonic, it is true, becomes Dominant*, he agrees to this with regard to the seventh Verse, and that in order to disguise the error into which he wants to make one fall by saying, *this verse is in the same key*, when nevertheless it is wholly the contrary, for the *key* actually changes.

These are unpardonable errors; but still more, to cite a *Sharp*, when railling, p. 83, as a cause of an effect in which it has a share only as a harmonic sound of the fundamental; a *Sharp* upon which, I say, a Song could be formed which will not have in any respect the appearance of a *little Sum*.[49] What does this mean?

When it is said, p. 87, *These two Verses would be well declaimed if there were a greater interval between them*,[50] this greater interval depends not only on the Actor, but it is even forced by the close that terminates the first Verse. Thus, these two Verses are very well declaimed according to M. Rousseau himself, thus his Criticism collapses by this acquiescence, since the same Principles reign in the whole course of the Scene.

If this Author's *Letter* swarms with an infinity of Sophisms which we are forced to pass over in silence because we can better employ our time, we nevertheless cannot be silent about a contradiction with himself which should equally surprise everyone: it concerns Musical Choruses.

In the *Encyclopedia* at the word *Chorus* one reads: *A Chorus in Music is a piece of complete Harmony, etc. One looks for an pleasant and harmonious sound in a Chorus that charms and occupies the ear. A beautiful Chorus is the Masterpiece of a skillful Composer. The French are taken as succeeding better in this Part than any other Nation of Europe.*[51]

In the *Letter*, p. 43, after having employed a vain Rhetoric against Fugues, Imitations, and Motives, which nonetheless comprise the most beautiful ornaments for Choruses, he believes that in order to disgust people with them it suffices to say, *almost no one succeeds in it, success can hardly compensate for the strain of such a Work*. What a reason! *All this only ends up making noise, like the majority of our much-admired Choruses*. Then in the Note he relies on a certain *Terradeglias*, who is made to say, *I used to love to make noise, now I try to compose Music*.[52]

First of all, there is here a transposition of the order, and of the form, and of the basis, which should be surprising: it was hardly a year ago that the Letter C was presented in the *Encyclopedia*, and it was ten years ago or so that the conversation with *Terradeglias* must be supposed to have occurred.[53] It was therefore only a year ago that the *sound* of Choruses was for M. Rousseau *pleasant and harmonious*, capable of *charming and of occupying the ear*, and if it was ten years ago that he had heard the contrary, he now takes it into his head to remember it: a fortunate memory!

THE END

Articles from the *Encyclopedia*

ACCOMPANIMENT [*Accompagnement*] is the execution of a complete and regular harmony[1] on some instrument, such as the organ, the harpsichord, the theorbo, the guitar, etc. We shall here take the Harpsichord as an example.

One of the parts of the Music is taken as a guide, which is ordinarily the Bass. This bass is played with the left hand, and the harmony is indicated with the right by the progression of the bass, by the singing of the other Parts which are heard at the same time, by the score one has before one's eyes, or by the figures which are commonly found added to the bass. The Italians scorn figures; the score itself is hardly necessary for them; the quickness and finesse of their ear substitute for it, and they accompany very well without all this apparatus; but it is to their natural disposition alone that they owe this facility, and other peoples, who are not like them born for Music, find infinite difficulties in the practice of *accompaniment*; they need ten to twelve years to manage it passably. What, then, are the causes that retard the progress of students and hamper teachers for such a long time? The difficulty of the art does not alone produce this.

There are two principal ones: the first in the manner of figuring Basses; the second in the methods for *accompaniment*.

The signs which are used to figure basses are far too numerous. There are so few fundamental chords! Why are so many figures needed to express them? The same signs are equivocal, obscure, and insufficient. For example, they almost never determine the nature of the intervals they express, or, what is worse, they indicate opposed ones. Some are barred to take the place of a sharp, others are barred to take the place of a flat; the major intervals and augmented ones, even the diminished ones, are often expressed in the same manner. When the figures are doubled they are too complicated; when they are simple they almost never offer anything but the idea of a single interval, so that there are always several of them to infer and determine.

How to remedy these inconveniences? Must the signs be multiplied to express everything? But it is complained that there are already too many. Must they be reduced? More things will be left to be divined by the accompanist, who is already only too occupied. What to do, then? New signs would have to be invented, fingering perfected, and two combined means would have to be produced from the signs and the fingering which mutually concur to relieve the accompanist. This is what M. Rameau has endeavored to do with great sagacity in his Dissertation on the different methods of *accompaniment*.[2] We shall expound upon the means he proposes at the words FIGURING [*Chiffrer*] and FINGERING [*Doigter*]. Let us pass on to the methods.

As ancient Music was not so complex as ours either as to the song or as to the harmony, and as it had hardly any other bass than the fundamental, the whole *accompaniment* consisted merely in a series of perfect chords, wherein the accompanist substituted from time to time a sixth for the fifth, as his ear led him. They didn't know more about it than this. Nowadays, as the modulations have been varied, overloaded, and perhaps have ruined the harmony by crowds of dissonances, one is constrained to follow other rules. M. Campion devised what is called the *rule of the octave*, and it is by this method that the majority of teachers teach *accompaniment* today.[3]

The chords are determined by the rule of the octave relative to the rank held by the notes of the bass in a given key. Thus, the key being known, the note of the thoroughbass is also known. The rank of this note in the key, the rank of the note that immediately precedes it, the rank of the note that follows it: one will not often be mistaken when accompanying by the rule of the octave, if the composer has followed the simplest and most natural Harmony. But this is what must hardly be expected in today's Music. Besides, by what means will one have all these things present? And, while the accompanist is instructing himself about it, what becomes of the fingers? Hardly has a chord been attained when another is presented; the moment of reflection is precisely that of the execution. There is only one consummate practice in Music, a well-considered experience, the facility of reading a line of Music at a single glance which may help; still, the most skillful make a mistake with this aid.

Can one expect, even to accompany, that the ear be formed, that one know how to read all music easily and rapidly, that one be able to disentangle a score on reading at sight? But, even if one were, one would still need a practice in fingering founded on principles of *accompaniment* other than those given out before M. Rameau.

Zealous teachers have clearly perceived the inadequacy of their principles. In order to remedy them they have had recourse to the enumeration and knowledge of the Consonances from which dissonances are prepared and are resolved. A prodigious detail which the multitude of dissonances sufficiently evinces.

There are those who counsel learning composition before passing on to *accompaniment*: as if *accompaniment* were not composition itself, except for talent, which must be added to the first in order to make use of the second. How many people, on the contrary, want one to begin with *accompaniment* in order to learn Composition?

The progression of the Bass, the rule of the octave, the manner of preparing and of resolving dissonances, composition in general work only toward showing the succession of a single Chord by another; so that there is at each Chord a new object, a new subject for reflection. What continual labor for the mind! When will the mind be sufficiently instructed and the ear be sufficiently trained so that the fingers might no longer be checked?

It is M. Rameau who, by the invention of new signs and the perfection of the fingering, has sufficiently indicated to us the means of making *accompaniment* easier; it is to him, I say, that we owe a new method which prevents the inconveniences of all those which have been followed until now. It is he who first made the Fundamental Bass known and who thereby revealed for us the true foundations of an art in which everything appeared arbitrary.

Here, in a few words, are the principles on which his method is founded:

In harmony there are only consonances and dissonances; there are therefore only consonant and dissonant chords.

Each of these chords is fundamentally divided by thirds. (This is M. Rameau's system.) The consonant chord is composed of three notes, such as *do*, *mi*, *sol*, the dissonant of four, such as *sol*, *si*, *re*, *fa*.

Whatever distinction or distribution one may make of the consonant chord, there will always be three notes, such as *do*, *mi*, *sol*. Whatever distribution one may make of the dissonant chord, one will always find in it four notes, such as *sol*, *si*, *re*, *fa*, putting aside supposition and suspension, which introduce others into the harmony as through license. Either consonant chords succeed one another, or dissonant chords are followed by other dissonant chords, or consonant and dissonant ones are interlaced.

Since the perfect consonant chord suits only the tonic, the succession of consonant chords furnishes so many tonics, and consequently so many changes of key.

Dissonant chords ordinarily follow one another in the same key. The dissonance ties together the harmonic sense. One chord makes one wish for another and at the same time makes one feel that the phrase is not complete. If the key changes in this succession, this change is always announced by a sharp or by a flat. As for the third succession, namely the interlacing of consonant and dissonant chords, M. Rameau reduces this succession to two cases alone, and he declares that in general a consonant chord cannot be preceded by any dissonant other than that of the dominant seventh or by that of the subdominant six-five chord, except in the deceptive cadence and in suspensions; he further claims that there is no exception as regards the basis. It seems to us that the perfect chord could still be preceded by the diminished seventh chord, and even by that of the augmented sixth: two original chords, the latter of which is not at all inverted.

Here, then, are the three different textures of harmonic phrases: tonics that succeed one another and that cause the key to be changed; consonances that ordinarily succeed one another in the same key; and consonances and dissonances that are interlaced and in which, according to M. Rameau, the consonance is necessarily preceded by the dominant seventh or by the subdominant six-five chord. What, then, remains to be done for the facility of the *accompaniment* other than to indicate to the accompanist which of these textures reigns in what he accompanies? Now, this is what M. Rameau expects to be done with the characters.

A single sign could easily indicate the key, the tonic, and its chord.

From that is derived the knowledge of the sharps and flats which must enter into the course of chords from one tonic to another.

The fundamental succession by thirds, or by fifths, in ascending as well as in descending, gives the first texture of harmonic phrases, composed wholly of consonant chords.

The fundamental succession by fifths, or by thirds, in descending gives the second texture, composed of dissonant chords, namely the chords of the seventh; and this succession gives the descending harmony.

The ascending harmony is furnished by a succession of fifths in ascending or of fourths in descending, accompanied by the dissonance that belongs to this succession, which is the added sixth; and this is the third texture of harmonic phrases, which has not until now been observed by anyone, although M. Rameau may have discovered its principle and origin in the irregular cadence. Thus, by the ordinary rules, the harmony that arises from a series of dissonances always descends, although, according to the true principles and according to reason, it must have a progression entirely as regular in ascending as in descending. *See* CADENCE [*Cadence*].

The fundamental cadences produce the fourth texture of harmonic phrases, in which consonances and dissonances are interlaced.

All these textures can be designated by characters that are simple, clear, and few in number which, when necessary, will at the same time indicate the dissonance which is generally required, for its type is always determined by the texture itself. *See* FIGURING [*Chiffrer*]. One begins by practicing each of these textures taken separately, then one has them succeed each other successively on each key and on each mode.

With these precautions, M. Rameau claims that more *Accompaniment* is learned in six months than was formerly learned in six years, and he has experience on his side. (*See* MUSIC [*Musique*], HARMONY [*Harmonie*], FUNDAMENTAL BASS [*Bass fondamentale*], THOROUGHBASS [*Bass continue*], PARTITION [*Partition*], FIGURING [*Chiffrer*], FINGERING [*Doigter*], CONSONANCE [*Consonnance*], DISSONANCE [*Dissonnance*], RULE OF THE OCTAVE [*Règle de l'octave*], COMPOSITION [*Composition*], SUPPOSITION [*Supposition*], SUSPENSION [*Suspension*], KEY [*Ton*], CADENCE [*Cadence*], MODULATION [*Modulation*], etc.

With regard to the manner of accompanying with intelligence, it depends more on practice and on taste than on any rules that can be given for it. Here, nonetheless, are some general observations on what should always be done in accompanying.

1st. Although following M. Rameau's principles it is necessary to strike all the notes of each chord, this rule must not always be taken literally. There are chords which would be unbearable with all this filling out. In the majority of dissonant chords, above all in chords by supposition, some note has to be omitted in order to diminish their harshness. This note is often the seventh, sometimes the fifth, sometimes both. The fifth or the octave of the bass is also fairly often omitted in dissonant chords in order to avoid consecutive octaves or fifths, which often produce a bad effect, especially in the treble; and for the same reason, when the leading tone is in the bass, it is not put into the *accompaniment*; instead of this, the third or the sixth is doubled by the right hand. Intervals of the second, and keeping two fingers together, must also be avoided, for this produces too harsh a dissonance, which must be saved for those occasions when the expression demands it. In general, one should think in accompanying that, when M. Rameau wants all the chords to be filled out, he has given more consideration to the facility of the fingering and to his particular system of *accompaniment* than to the purity of the harmony.[4]

2nd. It is always necessary to proportion the sound to the character of the music and to that of the instruments or the voices one must accompany; thus, in a chorus one strikes full chords in the right hand, and one doubles the octave or the fifth, and sometimes the whole chord, in the left hand. On the contrary, in a slow and soft solo, when there is only a flute or a weak voice to accompany, one omits notes, one softly arpeggiates, one takes the secondary manual; in a word, attention is always paid that the *accompaniment*, which is made only to sustain and embellish the song, does not spoil it and does not cover it up.

3rd. When one has to strike the same keys on a sustained note or on a held note, let it be rather at the beginning of the measure or on a strong beat than at another point; in a word, one should restrike it only while clearly marking the beat.⁵

4th. Nothing is so disagreeable as those virtuoso passages, roulades, embroideries which some accompanists substitute for the *accompaniment*. They cover up the voice, spoil the harmony, confuse the subject, and often it is only through ignorance that clever ones are produced, inappropriately for not knowing how to discover the harmony suited to a passage. The genuine accompanist always goes to the heart of the matter and accompanies simply. It is not that one may not place some pretty virtuoso passages into certain empty places due to the lack of instruments, but this must be done very aptly and always in the character of the subject. The Italians sometimes play the whole song instead of the *accompaniment*, and this is done well enough in their genre of music. But whatever they may say about it, there is often more ignorance than taste in this manner of accompanying.⁶

5th. One should not accompany Italian music like French. In the latter, one must sustain the sounds, arpeggiating them gracefully and continually from low to high, stick to filling out the harmony as much as possible, play the bass properly—for French composers today give it all the small ornaments and grace notes of the treble. On the contrary, when accompanying the Italian, one must strike the notes from the bass simply, produce neither trills⁷ nor embroidery, reserve for it the grave and steady progression which suits it; the *accompaniment* should be dry, and without arpeggios. One may suppress notes without scruple, but those that are to be made heard must be well chosen. The Italians attach little importance to noise; a third, a well-adapted sixth, even a simple unison when good taste demands it, is more pleasing to them than all our din of parts and of *accompaniment*; in a word, they want nothing to be heard in the *accompaniment* or in the bass that might distract the ear from the principal subject, and they are of the opinion that attention vanishes for having been divided.

6th. Although *accompaniment* by the organ might be the same as that by the harpsichord, the style is different. Since the sounds of the organ are sustained, their progression should be sweeter and less uneven. One must lift the entire hand as little as possible, glide the fingers from one key to another without removing those which, in the place where they are, can be used in the chord into which one is passing. Nothing is so disagreeable as hearing that type of dry and detached *accompaniment* that one is forced to practice on the harpsichord. *See the word* FINGERING [*Doigter*].

One also calls *accompaniment* every part of bass or other instrument which is composed on the principal song in order to produce its harmony. Thus, a violin *solo* is accompanied by the cello or by the harpsichord, and an *accompaniment* by the flute is joined quite nicely to the voice; this harmony adds charm to the song. With regard to voices, there is even a specific reason for having them always accompanied by certain instruments, for although some claim that in singing one naturally modifies one's voice according to the laws of temperament, experience nevertheless shows us that the more precise and best trained voices have much difficulty in maintaining the same key for a long time when nothing sustains them in it. By dint of singing, one imperceptibly ascends or descends, and in finishing one rarely finds oneself quite justly in the same key from which one began. It is in view of preventing these variations that the harmony of an instrument is employed to maintain the voice always in the same *diapason*, or in order promptly to call it back when it strays from it. *See* THOROUGH-BASS [*Basse continue*]. (S)

CHORD [*Accord*], *in Music*, is the union of two or more sounds heard at the same time together forming a regular harmony.

The natural harmony produced by the resonance of a sounding body is composed of three different sounds, without counting their octaves, which together form the most pleasant and the most perfect *chord* that may be heard, from whence it is called a *perfect chord par excellence*. Thus, in order to make the harmony complete, each *chord* must be composed of three sounds. In addition, Musicians find harmonic perfection in the *trio*, whether because in it they employ *chords* in their entirety or because, on the occasions when they do not employ them in their entirety, they at least possess the artfulness to make the ear believe the contrary by presenting it with the principal sounds of the *chord*: as in consonances, the third with the octave implying the fifth, the sixth with the octave implying the third, *etc.*, and in dissonances, the seventh with the third implying the fifth, likewise the ninth, *etc.*, in the large sixth, the sixth with the fifth implying the third, the fourth with the second implying the sixth, *etc.* Nevertheless, since the octave of the principal sound produces new relations and new consonances by the complements of the intervals (*see* COMPLEMENT [*Complément*]), this octave is ordinarily added in order to keep the ensemble of all the consonances within the same *chord*. Moreover, since the addition of the dissonance (*see* DISSONANCE [*Dissonnance*]) produces a fourth sound added to the perfect *chord*, it is a necessity, if one wants to fill out the chord, to have a fourth part in order to express this dissonance. Thus, when one wants to hear the complete harmony, it can only be done by the means of the four parts connected together.

Chords are divided into perfect and imperfect. The perfect *chord*, the one we have just been speaking about, is composed of its fundamental sound in the bass, of its third, of its fifth, and of its octave; and, in general, one sometimes calls *perfect* every *chord*, even dissonant ones, whose fundamental is in the bass. *Imperfect chords* are those in which the sixth reigns instead of the fifth, and in general all those in which the low sound is not the fundamental. These denominations, which were given before the Fundamental Bass was known, are very badly applied. Those of direct or inverted chords are much more suitable for the same meaning. *See* INVERSION [*Renversement*].

Chords are further distinguished as consonant and dissonant. Consonant *chords* are the perfect *chord* and its derivatives; every other *chord* is dissonant.

Table of All the Chords Accepted in Harmony

FUNDAMENTAL CHORDS

Perfect Chord and Its Derivatives

The fundamental sound in the bass	Its third in the bass	Its fifth in the bass

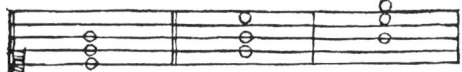

Perfect chord	Sixth chord	Six-four chord

This chord constitutes the key, and takes place only on the tonic. Its third can be major or minor, and this is what constitutes the mode.

Leading or Dominant Chord, and Its Derivatives

The fundamental sound in the bass	Its third in the bass	Its fifth in the bass	Its seventh in the bass

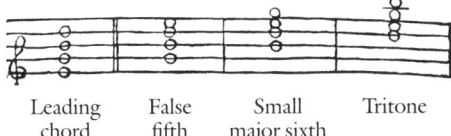

Leading chord	False fifth	Small major sixth	Tritone

None of these chords can be altered.

Added Sixth Chord with the Minor Third, and Its Derivatives

The fundamental sound in the bass	Its third in the bass	Its fifth in the bass	Its sixth in the bass

Added sixth chord	Small added sixth	Augmented second	Augmented seventh

Diminished Seventh Chord

The fundamental sound in the bass	Its third in the bass	Its fifth in the bass	Its sixth in the bass
Diminished seventh chord	False fifth and major sixth	Minor third and tritone	Augmented second

None of the sounds of this chord can be altered.

Added Sixth Chord with Its Minor Third, and Its Derivatives

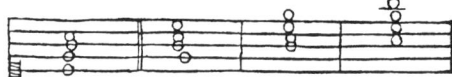

The fundamental sound in the bass	Its third in the bass	Its fifth in the bass	Its sixth in the bass
Added sixth chord	Small added sixth	Augmented second	Augmented seventh

I add here the word *added* in order to distinguish this chord and its inversions from the similar productions of the seventh chord.

Augmented Sixth Chord

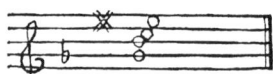

Augmented sixth chord

This chord has no inversion, and none of its sounds can be altered. It is properly speaking only a small major sixth chord, made sharp by an accidental.

CHORDS BY SUPPOSITION
(See SUPPOSITION [*Supposition*].)

Ninth Chord, and Its Derivatives

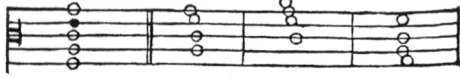

The supposed sound in the bass	The fundamental sound in the bass	Its third in the bass	Its seventh in the bass
Ninth chord	Seventh and sixth	Six-five and fourth	Seventh and second

This is a seventh chord, to which is added a fifth sound from a third beneath the fundamental.

One usually omits the seventh, that is the fifth, of the fundamental sound, which is here the note *mi*; and in this case the ninth chord can be inverted, by further omitting from the accompaniment the octave of the note that is borne in the bass.

Augmented Fifth Chord

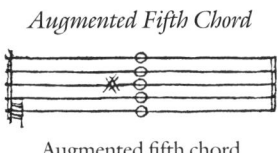

Augmented fifth chord

This is the dominant chord of a minor key, beneath which the mediant is made to be heard; thus, this is a genuine ninth chord, but it has no inversions, due to the diminished fourth which with the leading tone would give the supposed sound borne in the treble, which fourth is an interval banished from harmony.

Eleventh or Fourth Chord

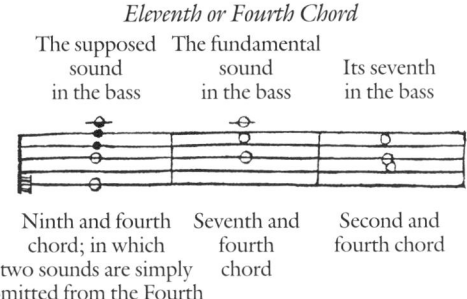

This is a seventh chord, beneath which one adds a fifth sound to the fifth of the fundamental. This chord is hardly ever struck fully due to its harshness, and in order to invert it the ninth and the seventh are omitted from it.

Augmented Seventh Chord

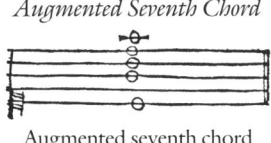

Augmented seventh chord

This is the dominant chord under which the bass makes the tonic.

Augmented Seventh, and Minor Sixth, Chord

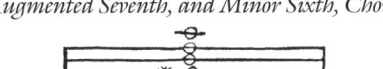

This is the diminished seventh chord, under which the bass makes the tonic.

These last two chords have no inversions, because the leading tone and the tonic would be heard together in the upper parts, which cannot be tolerated.

We shall discuss the manner of employing all these *chords* in order to form a regular harmony from them at the words HARMONY [*Harmonie*], FUNDAMENTAL BASS [*Bass fondamentale*], MODULATION [*Modulation*], COMPOSITION [*Composition*], DISSONANCE [*Dissonnance*]. We shall add here only the following observations.

1. It is a great error to think that the choice of the various inversions of a single chord is indifferent for harmony or for expression; there is not one of these inversions that does not have its own proper character. Everyone senses the opposition found between the sweetness of the diminished fifth and the sharpness of the tritone, and, nevertheless, one of these intervals is the inversion of the other; it is the same for the diminished seventh and the augmented second, for the ordinary second and the seventh. Who does not know how much more sonorous the fifth is than the fourth? The great sixth *chord* and the minor sixth are two faces of the same chord, but how much more harmonious is the one than the other! The major small sixth chord, on the contrary, is it not more brilliant than that of the diminished fifth? And, to speak of only the simplest of all the *chords*, consider the majesty of the perfect chord, the sweetness of the sixth *chord*, and the insipidness of the six-four chord, all of them being composed of the same sounds. In general, augmented intervals, sharps in the treble are appropriate by their harshness to express rage and anger; on the contrary, flats and diminished intervals form a plaintive harmony that melts the heart. There are a multitude of similar observations, when one knows how to take advantage of them, which make an intelligent Musician the master of the dispositions of those who listen to him.

2. The choice of intervals is hardly less important than that of *chords* when it comes to the place one wants to use them. For example, it is in the bass that fifths and octaves must be placed, thirds and sixths in the treble. Transpose this order and you will spoil the harmony while leaving the same *chords*.

3. Finally, *chords* are made more harmonious by bringing them together in small intervals, which are more suitable to the capacity of the ear; this is what is called *tightening the harmony*, and is what so few Musicians know how to practice in the composition of their choruses, in which one often hears parts so removed from one another that they no longer seem to have any relation to one another. (S)

CADENCE [*Cadence*], *in Music*, is the termination of a harmonic phrase on a close or on a perfect chord, or, to speak more generally, it is every transition from a dissonant chord to any chord whatsoever, for a dissonant chord can never be left except by a *cadence*. Now, as every harmonic phrase is necessarily linked by expressed or implied dissonances, it follows that every harmony is properly speaking only a series of *cadences*.

What is called an *act of cadence* always results from two fundamental sounds, of which one announces the *cadence* and the other terminates it.

As there is no dissonance without a *cadence*, there is no *cadence* without a dissonance either, expressed or implied; for, in order to make the close agreeably felt, it must be preceded by something that causes it to be desired, and this thing can be only the dissonance, otherwise, the two chords being equally perfect, one might remain on the first: the second one would not be announced and would not be necessary; the chord formed on the first sound of a *cadence* should therefore always be dissonant. With regard to the second one, it can be consonant or dissonant according to whether one wants to establish or avoid the close. If it is consonant, the *cadence* is regular; if it is dissonant, the *cadence* is deceptive.

Four types of *cadences* are usually reckoned, namely: *perfect cadence*, *interrupted cadence*, *deceptive cadence*, and *irregular cadence*. These are the names M. Rameau has given them.

1. Every time the Fundamental Bass descends a fifth to a perfect chord after the seventh chord it is a *perfect cadence*, which always proceeds from a dominant to a tonic; but if the *cadence* is avoided by a dissonance added to the second note, it can be begun anew on this second note, and be continued as long as one likes by ascending a fourth or descending a fifth on all the pitches of the key, and this forms a series of *perfect deceptive cadences*. In this series, which is the most perfect of all, two sounds, namely the seventh and the fifth, descend on the third and on the octave of the following chord, while the two other sounds, namely the third and the octave, remain to make the seventh and the fifth and then descend alternately with the two others. Thus such a series produces a descending harmony; it must never stop except on a dominant in order to then fall by the *regular cadence* to the tonic.

2. If the Fundamental Bass descends only a third, instead of descending a fifth, after a seventh chord, the *cadence* is called *interrupted*: this one can never be regular, but the second note of this *cadence* must necessarily contain another seventh chord. One can likewise continue to descend by thirds or ascend by sixths from seventh chord to seventh chord, which produces a second succession of *deceptive cadences*, but much less perfect than the preceding one, for the seventh, which is resolved on the third in the *perfect cadence*, is resolved here on the octave, which makes it less of a harmony and even causes two octaves to be implied, so that in order to avoid them one omits the dissonance or inverts the harmony.

Since the *interrupted cadence* can never be regular, it follows that a phrase cannot terminate with it, but recourse must be had to the *perfect cadence* to make the dominant chord heard.

The *interrupted cadence* also forms, by its succession, a descending harmony, but there is only a single sound which descends; the three others remain in place in order to descend successively each in its turn. Some people mistake for an *interrupted cadence* an inversion of the *perfect cadence*, in which the bass, after a seventh chord, descends by a third while carrying along a sixth chord, but it is evident that such a progression, not being at all fundamental, cannot constitute a specific *cadence*.

3. A *deceptive cadence* is one in which the Fundamental Bass, instead of ascending a fourth after a seventh chord, as in the *perfect cadence*, ascends only one degree. This *cadence* is avoided most often by a seventh on the second note. It is certain that it can be made regular only by license, for in that case there is necessarily a lack of connection.

A series of *deceptive cadences* is also descending. Three sounds in it descend and the octave alone remains to prepare the dissonance; but such a succession is harsh and is very rarely used.

4. When the bass descends a fifth from the tonic to the dominant, this is, as I have said, an act of *perfect cadence*; if, on the contrary, the bass ascends a fifth from the tonic to the dominant, this is an act of *irregular cadence*, according to M. Rameau, or of *imperfect cadence*, according to the common denomination. In order to announce it, a major sixth is added to the chord of the tonic, from whence this Chord takes the name of an *added sixth*. See CHORD [*Accord*]. This sixth, which produces a dissonance on the fifth, is also treated as a dissonance on the Fundamental Bass, and, as such, must be resolved by ascending diatonically on the third of the following chord.

It must be noted that the *imperfect cadence* constitutes an almost completely opposed cadence with respect to the *perfect cadence*. In the first chord of them both, the fourth which is found between the fifth and the octave is divided by a dissonance which produces a new third, and this dissonance should be resolved on the third of the following chord by a fundamental progression of the fifth. This is everything that these two *cadences* have in common; here is what they have in opposition.

In the *perfect cadence*, the added sound sets out from the treble of the interval of a fourth, next to the octave, forming a third with the fifth, and produces a minor dissonance which is resolved by descending while the Fundamental Bass ascends a fourth or descends a fifth from the dominant to the tonic in order to establish a perfect close. In the *imperfect cadence*, the sound added starts out from the bass of the interval of the fourth, next to the fifth, and, forming a third with the octave, it produces a major dissonance which is resolved by ascending while the Fundamental Bass descends a fourth or ascends a fifth from the tonic to the dominant in order to establish an imperfect close.

M. Rameau, who first spoke of this *cadence*, and who has allowed several inversions of it, prohibits us, in his *Treatise on Harmony, p. 117*,[8] from allowing that one in which the added sound is in the bass and contains a seventh chord. He has taken this seventh chord as fundamental, so that he has a seventh resolved by another seventh, a dissonance by another dissonance, by a similar movement on the Fundamental Bass. But the harmony under which this author has put such a Fundamental Bass is manifestly inverted from an *irregular cadence* avoided by an augmented seventh on the second note. And this is so true that the thoroughbass which strikes the dissonance is necessarily obliged to ascend diatonically in order to resolve it, otherwise the transition would be of no avail. Besides, in the same work, *p. 272*, M. Rameau gives an example of a similar transition with the true Fundamental Bass; it can be further remarked that in a later work (*Harm. Gener. p. 186*),[9] the same author seems to recognize the true foundation of this transition thanks to what he calls *double employment*. See DOUBLE EMPLOYMENT [*Double Emploi*].[10] (S)

[M. Rameau gives the following reasons for the denominations which have been given to the different types of *cadence*.

[The *perfect cadence* consists in a progression of a fifth in descending and, on the contrary, the *imperfect* consists of a progression of a fifth in ascending. Here is the reason: when I say *do, sol, sol* is already contained in *do* since the very sound of *do* carries with it its twelfth, of which *sol* is the octave. Thus, when one goes from *do* to *sol*, it is the generator sound that passes to its product, in such a way, nonetheless, that the ear always desires to return to this first generator; on the contrary, when one says *sol, do*, it is the product that returns to the generator, the ear is satisfied and no longer desires anything. Moreover, in this progression *sol, do*, the *sol* is also heard in the *do*, thus the ear hears the generator and its product at the same time, whereas in the progression *do, sol*, the ear, which in the first sound has heard *do* and *sol*, no longer hears in the second but *sol* without *do*. Thus, the *close*, or *cadence*, from *sol* to *do* is more perfect than the *close*, or *cadence*, from *do* to *sol*.

[It seems that one can further explain the effect of the *deceptive cadence* and of the *interrupted cadence* by M. Rameau's principles. Let us imagine for this that after a seventh chord, *sol si re fa*, one ascends diatonically by a *deceptive cadence* to the chord *la do mi sol;* it is obvious that this chord is the inversion of the chord of the subdominant *do mi sol la;* thus, the progression of the *deceptive cadence* is equivalent to this one: *sol si re fa, do mi sol la* —which is nothing else but a *perfect cadence* in which *do*, instead of being treated as tonic, is made subdominant by changing mode. See DOMINANT [*Dominante*], SUB-DOMINANT [*Sous-Dominante*], FUNDAMENTAL BASS [*Bass Fondamentale*], etc.

[With regard to the *interrupted cadence*—which consists in descending from one dominant to another by the interval of the third in descending, in this way: *sol, si, do, fa, mi sol si re*—it seems that it can also be explained. In actuality, the second chord *mi sol si re* is the inversion of the chord of the subdominant *sol si re mi*; thus, the *interrupted cadence* is equivalent to this succession: *sol si re fa, sol si re mi*—in which the note *sol*, after having been treated as dominant, is made subdominant by changing mode, which is permitted and depends on the composer. See MODE [*Mode*], etc. (O)][11]

The *irregular cadence* also starts out from the subdominant to the tonic; in this manner one can give it a succession of several notes whose chords will form a harmony in which the sixth and the octave ascend on the third and the fifth of the chord while the fifth and the third remain in order to produce the octave and to prepare the sixth, *etc.*

No author has spoken of this harmonic ascent until now, and it is true that a long series of such *cadences* cannot be practiced because of the major sixths which would take the modulation too far afield, and would not, without precaution, even fill out the whole harmony. But, finally, if the best works of Music, those, for example, by M. Rameau, are full of such transitions, if these transitions are established on good principles, and if they please the ear, why have they not been spoken of? (S)[12]

[One could moreover observe, it seems to me, that M. Rameau has at least spoken indirectly of this sort of *cadence* when he says in his *Harmonic Generation* that every subdominant should ascend by a fifth on the tonic and that every tonic can be made a subdominant to one's liking.[13] For it follows from this that one can have in a Fundamental Bass a succession of subdominants which go along by ascending by fifths or by descending by fourths, which is the same thing. (O)]

There is also another type of Cadence that Musicians do not at all regard as such and that, according to the definition, is nevertheless a genuine one: this is the transition from the Diminished Seventh Chord on the Leading Tone to the Chord of the Tonic. In this transition no *harmonic connection* is found, and it is the second example of this defect in what is called Cadence. Enharmonic transitions might be regarded as ways of avoiding this same Cadence, as the *Perfect Cadence* is avoided from a Dominant to its Tonic by a chromatic transition, but we limit ourselves to explaining what is established.

CADENCE, *as a term of singing*, is called that beating of the voice which the Italians call *trillo*, which we otherwise call *tremblement* and which is ordinarily done on the penultimate note of a musical phrase, from which it doubtless takes the name of *cadenza*.[14] Although this word is here very ill-adapted, and although it has been condemned by the majority of those who have written on this matter, it has nevertheless completely prevailed; it is the sole one of which use is made today in Paris in this sense and it is useless to dispute against usage.

CADENCE, *in our modern dances*, means the uniformity of the dancer's steps with the beat marked by the instrument, but it must be noted that the *cadence* is not always marked as the beat is struck. Thus, the Music teacher marks the movement of a minuet by striking at the beginning of each beat, whereas the dance teacher beats only every two beats because as many are needed in order to form the four steps of the minuet. (S)

CHORUS [*Choeur*] is, *in Music*, a piece of complete harmony, in four parts or more, simultaneously sung by all the voices and played by the whole orchestra. In *choruses* one seeks a pleasant and harmonious sound that charms and fills ears; a beautiful *chorus* is the masterpiece of a skillful composer. The French pass for succeeding better in this part than any other nation in Europe.

The *chorus* is sometimes called a *large-chorus* in opposition to the *small-chorus*, which is composed of solely three parts, namely, two sopranos and the countertenor, who serves as the bass. This small *chorus*, whose sweetness contrasts agreeably with the noisy harmony of the larger one, is heard from time to time. (S)

[The large *chorus* is composed of eight basses, which are placed above the two sides of the orchestra. The double bass belongs to the large *chorus*, as do violins, oboes, flutes, and bassoons. It is the entire orchestra that forms it. See ORCHESTRA [*Orchestra*]. (B)]

One also calls a *small chorus* a small number of the better instruments of each sort in the orchestra of the opera that forms, like a separate orchestra, around the harpsichord and the person who strikes the beat. This small *chorus* is destined for accompaniments which require the greatest delicacy and precision.

There are pieces of music with two or more *choruses* which answer one another and sometimes sing all together; one can see an example of this in the opera *Jephté*.[15] But this plurality of *choruses*, which is fairly often practiced in Italy, is hardly used in France; it is found that it does not produce a very grand effect, that its composition is not very easy, and that too great a number of musicians is needed to perform it. (S)

[There are beautiful *choruses* in *Tancrède*; that of *Phaéton*, *Allez répondre la lumière*, etc., has a very great reputation, although it is inferior to the chorus, *O l'Heureux tems*, etc., from the prologue to the same opera.[16] But the most beautiful that is now known of at this theater is the chorus, *Brillant soleil*, etc., from the second entry in *Indes galantes*.[17] M. Rameau has pressed this part as far as it seems it may be pressed; almost all his *choruses* are beautiful, and many of them are sublime. (B)]

CHROMATIC [*Chromatique*], adj. (*Music*.) a genre of Music that proceeds by several consecutive semitones. This word comes from the Greek χρωμα, which means *color*, whether because the Greeks marked this genre with red or variously colored characters; or, as others say, because the *chromatic* genre is the mean between the two others, as color is the mean between white and black; or, according to others, because the chromatic genre varies and embellishes the diatonic genre by its semitones, which produces the same effect in Music as the variety of colors produces in painting.

Boethius attributes the invention of the *chromatic* genre to Timotheus of Meletus, but Athenaeus gives it to Epigones.[18]

Aristoxenus divides this genre into three types, which he calls *molle*, *hemiolion*, and *tonicum*.[19] Ptolomy divides it into only two, *molle* or *anticum*, which progresses by the smallest intervals, and *intensum*, in which the intervals are larger.[20] We shall explain the *chromatic* of the Greeks at the word GENRE [*Genre*]; as for the modifications which this same genre received in its types, this is a detail which must be sought in the authors themselves.

Today the *chromatic* genre consists in giving such a progression to the Fundamental Bass that the various parts of the harmony may progress by semitones, in ascending as well as in descending, which practically suits only the minor mode on account of the alterations to which the sixth and the seventh notes are subject by the very nature of the mode.[21]

The most common route for the Fundamental Bass in engendering the ascending *chromatic* is alternately to descend a third and ascend a fourth, the minor third being borne throughout. If the same Fundamental Bass progresses from dominant-tonic to dominant-tonic by perfect avoided cadences, it will engender the descending *chromatic*.

As one changes key on every note, it is necessary to limit these successions for fear of going astray. For this, it should be recalled that the most suitable time for *chromatic* movements is between the dominant and the tonic when ascending and the tonic and the dominant when descending. In the major mode one can also descend *chromatically* from the dominant on the second note. This transition is quite common in Italy, and, in spite of its beauty, is beginning to be a little too much so among us.

The *chromatic* genre is admirable for expressing suffering and affliction; it is still more energetic when descending: then one believes one hears true moaning. Full of its harmony, this genre becomes appropriate for everything; but like those delicate dishes whose abundance soon satisfies, as much as it enchants, when soberly handled, so it becomes repulsive in the hands of Musicians who use it prodigally at every opportunity. (S)

DISSONANCE [*Dissonance*], n. fem.[22] *in Music*, is every chord disagreeable to the ear, every interval that is not consonant; and as there are no other consonances than those which form among themselves the sounds of the perfect chord (See CONSONANCE [*Consonnance*]), it follows that every other interval is a genuine *dissonance*. The ancients even added to this number *thirds* and *sixths*, which they did not accept as consonant chords.

There are therefore an infinity of possible *dissonances*; but in Music, as all the intervals that the received system does not furnish must be excluded, they are reduced to a relatively small number; further, for practice one should choose among these only those which suit the genre and the mode, and, finally, even exclude from these latter ones those that cannot be employed according to the prescribed rules.

The physical principle of harmony is found in the production of the perfect chord by any sound whatsoever. All the consonances arise from it, and it is nature itself that furnishes them. There is thus no *dissonance* in it. We do indeed find, if you like, its generation in the differences among the consonances, but we do not at all perceive the physical reason that authorizes us to introduce it into the very body of the harmony. Father Mersenne contents himself with showing the generation and the various ratios of the *dissonances*, those that are rejected as well as those that are accepted, but he does not say anything about the right to employ them.[23] M. Rameau specifically says that the *dissonance* is not natural to harmony, and that it can be used only by the assistance of art. Nonetheless, in another Work he tries to find its principle in the ratios of numbers and of harmonic and arithmetic proportions.[24] But after having quite exhausted the analogies, after many metamorphoses of those various proportions, the ones in the others, after many operations, he ends by establishing, by means of weak conformities, the *dissonances* he has worn himself out to find. Thus, because the arithmetic proportion in the order of the harmonic sounds gives, as he claims, a minor third in the bass, he adds a new minor third to the bass of the subdominant; the harmonic proportion gives him a minor third on the treble, and he adds a new minor third to the treble. These added thirds do not, it is true, form any proportion with the preceding ratios; the ratios they themselves should have are found to be altered. But M. Rameau believes he can reconcile everything: the proportion allows him to introduce the *dissonance*, and the lack of proportion allows him to make it felt.

No one therefore having until now discovered the physical principle of the *dissonance* employed in harmony, we shall content ourselves with explaining its generation mechanically and shall dispense with the calculations.

I assume the necessity of the *dissonance* to be recognized. (*See* HARMONY [*Harmonie*] and CADENCE [*Cadence*].) It is a matter of seeing where one should place this *dissonance* and how it must be employed.

If all the sounds of the diatonic scale are successively compared with the fundamental sound in each of the two modes, one will find for every *dissonance* only the second and the seventh, which is merely an inverted second and which actually makes a second with the octave. Certain other altered intervals can become *dissonances*, but if the second is not found expressed or implied, these are only accidents of modulation which harmony does not take into consideration, and these *dissonances* are not then at all treated as such. Thus, it is certain that where there is no second there are no *dissonances* either, and the second is properly speaking the only *dissonance* that may be employed.

To reduce all the consonances to their least range, let us not leave the limits of the octave. Let us take the perfect chord, *sol si re sol*, and see where in this chord we might place a *dissonance*, that is a second, in order to make it as little shocking to the ear as possible. On the *la* between the *sol* and the *si* it would make a second with them both and, consequently, it would be doubly *dissonant*. It would be the same between the *si* and the *re*, as between every interval of a third; there remains the interval of the fourth between the *re* and the *sol*. Here a sound could be introduced in two ways. 1st. One could add the note *fa*, which would make a second with the *sol* and a third with the *re*. 2nd. Or the note *mi*, which would make a second with the *re* and a third with the *sol*. It is evident that the least harsh *dissonance* one could find will be had in each of these two ways, for it will *be dissonant* with a single sound, and it will engender a new third, which, as with the two preceding ones, will contribute to sweetness of the total chord. On the one hand we will have the seventh chord, and on the other the added sixth chord, as M. Rameau calls it.

It is not enough to make the *dissonance* heard; it must be resolved. You initially shock the ear only then to flatter it more agreeably. Here are two adjoining sounds: on the one side the fifth and the sixth and on the other the seventh and the octave; as long as they thus produce the second they will remain *dissonant*, but let them move away from one another by a degree, let the one ascend or the other descend diatonically, and your second, on one side and the other, will become a third, that is, one of the most pleasant consonances. Thus after *sol fa* you will have *sol mi* or *fa la*; and after *re mi*, *mi do* or *re fa*: this is what is called *resolving the dissonance*.

It remains to determine which of the two adjoining sounds should ascend or descend and which should remain in place: but the grounds for determining it leap to the eyes. Let the fifth or the octave remain as principal pitches, let the sixth ascend and the seventh descend, as accessory sounds, as *dissonances*. Furthermore, if, of the two adjoining sounds, it is for the one that has less distance to cover to do so, the *fa* will further descend on the *mi*, after the seventh, and the *mi* of the added sixth chord will ascend on the *fa*, by opposition.

Let us now see what progression the fundamental sound should possess relative to the movement assigned to the *dissonance*. Since one of the two adjoining sounds remains in place, a connection should be made with the following chord. The interval that the Fundamental Bass should form in leaving the chord should therefore be determined in accordance with these two conditions. 1st. In such a way that the octave of its preceding fundamental sound may remain in place after the seventh chord, the fifth after the added sixth chord. 2nd. In such a way that the sound on which the *dissonance* is resolved be one of the harmonics of the one to which the Fundamental Bass passes. Now, the best movement of the bass being by intervals of a fifth, if it descends a fifth in the first case, or ascends a fifth in the second, all the conditions will be perfectly fulfilled, as is evident solely by inspection of the example:

Perfect Chord   Seventh   Added Sixth

From thence is derived a means of knowing which pitch of the key each of these two chords best suits. What are the two most essential pitches in each key? They are the tonic and the dominant. How can the bass progress when descending a fifth on the two essential pitches of the key? It is by passing from the dominant to the tonic. Thus, the dominant is the pitch that the seventh chord best suits. How can the bass progress when ascending a fifth on the two essential pitches of the key? It is by passing from the tonic to the dominant. Thus, the tonic is the pitch that the added sixth chord best suits. The bass can have other progressions, but these are the most perfect, and the two principal cadences. (*See* CADENCE [*Cadence*].)

If these two *dissonances* are compared with the fundamental sound, one finds that the one that descends is a minor seventh, and the one that ascends a major sixth, from whence is derived this new rule, that major *dissonances* should ascend and minor ones descend, for, in general, a major interval has less distance to travel.

When the seventh chord contains a major third, this third makes another *dissonance* with the seventh, which is the diminished fifth, and by inversion the tritone. This third vis-à-vis the seventh is also called a major *dissonance*, and it is prescribed that it will ascend, but this is in its quality as leading tone, and without the second this pretended *dissonance* would not exist at all or would not at all be treated as such.

I have made it clear at the word CADENCE [*Cadence*] how the introduction of these two principal *dissonances*, the seventh and the added sixth, gives the means for connecting a succession of harmony by making it ascend or descend as one chooses.

I am not speaking here at all of the preparation of the *dissonance* because it has too many exceptions to make a general rule of it. (*See* PRÉPARE [*Préparer*].) With regard to *dissonances* by *supposition* or *suspension*, see *these two words*. Nor, finally, do I say anything about the diminished seventh, which is a very singular chord, but I will touch on it somewhat at the *word* ENHARMONIC [*Enharmonique*]. *See also the word* CHORD [*Accord*]. (S)

[It seems to me that, without having any recourse to progressions and even without departing from the basis of M. Rameau's principles, the *dissonance* can be accounted for in this way. *Do* being supposed tonic, *sol* and *fa* are the dominant and the subdominant. If I can only carry the perfect chord on *sol*, I can no longer do so if I am in *do* or in *sol*, but if I join to this chord the subdominant *fa* in this way, *sol si re fa*, then this union of the dominant and of the subdominant of *do* in a single chord serves to indicate to me that I am in the mode of *do*. Likewise, in the chord *fa la do* of the subdominant, I should join the sound *sol*; but as that would produce two fecund *dissonances*—*fa sol, sol la*, I can take instead of *sol re*, which is its fifth, and I have *fa la do re* for the chord of the subdominant and the *dissonance* is *re*. Moreover, all this is not at all a physical explanation of the addition of the *dissonance* to harmony; an addition which, according to M. Rameau, is the work of art and not of nature.

[After the example of the *dissonance* or seventh *fa* added to the chord of the subdominant, several chords have been formed from *dissonant* sevenths, such as *re fa la do, si re fa la* (See DOUBLE EMPLOYMENT [*Double emploi*], *do mi sol si*, etc., in which the *dissonance* is a major or minor seventh. See my "Elements of Music," part I, chaps. xi, xiv, xv, xvi.[25] (O)]

ENHARMONIC [*Enharmonique*], adj. taken subst.[26] (*Music*.) One of the three genres of the music of the Greeks, also very frequently called *harmony* by Aristoxenus and his sectarians.[27]

It resulted from a particular division of tetrachords according to which the interval which is found between the *lichanos*, or the third Pitch, and since the *mese*, or the fourth, was one ditonon, or one major third, there remained only a semitone to divide into two intervals in order to complete the tetrachord on the lower end, namely, from the hypate to the parhypate, and from the parhypate to the lichanos. We shall explain *at the word* GENRE [*Genre*] how this division was made.

The *enharmonic* Genre was the sweetest of the three, according to Aristide Quintilianus' report;[28] it passed as very ancient, and the majority of authors attributed its invention to Olympus. But his tetrachord, or rather his diatessaron of this genre, was made up of only three pitches, and it was only after him that they thought of inserting a fourth one between the first two in order to make the division of which I was just speaking.

This Genre, so marvelous, so praised by the ancient authors, did not long retain its vigor. Its extreme difficulty soon caused it to be abandoned by musicians, and Plutarch testifies that it was entirely out of use in his time.[29]

Today we have a type of *enharmonic* genre entirely different from that of the Greeks. It consists like the other two in one particular harmonic progression that engenders *enharmonic* intervals in the progression by simultaneously employing between two notes that are one tone apart the sharp from the inferior and the flat from the superior. But, although according to the strictness of the ratios this sharp and this flat should form an interval between them, this interval happens to be null by means of temperament, which in the established system makes the same sound serve two uses, which does not prevent such a transition from producing, by the force of the modulation and of the harmony, part of the effect that is sought in *enharmonic* transitions.

As this genre is rather poorly known, and as our authors have contented themselves with giving too general notions of it, we believe we should explain it here a little more clearly.

It is necessary to note first that the diminished seventh chord is the only one on which *enharmonic* transitions may be practiced, and that in virtue of that singular property it has of dividing the entire octave into exactly four equal intervals. Take from among the four sounds which make up this chord that which one wants as fundamental; one will always likewise find that the three other sounds form a diminished seventh chord on this sound. Now, the fundamental sound of the diminished seventh chord is always a leading tone, so that, without changing anything in this chord, one could make it serve successively on four different fundamentals, that is, on four different leading tones.

Let us suppose the chord on *do*-sharp in the natural key of *re*, for this chord can take place only in the minor mode; let us suppose, I say, the diminished seventh chord on a *do*-sharp leading tone. If I take the third *mi* as fundamental, it will become leading tone in its turn, and will consequently introduce the minor mode of *fa*; now, this *do*-sharp remains in the chord taken in this manner, but it is in its capacity as *re*-flat, that is, of the sixth note of the key, and of the diminished seventh of the leading tone; thus, this *do*-sharp, which as leading tone was obliged to ascend in the key of *re*, having become *re*-flat in the key of *fa*, is obliged to descend as a diminished seventh: this is an *enharmonic* transition. If instead of the third one takes the augmented fifth *sol*, in the same chord, as a new leading tone, the *do*-sharp will again become *re*-flat in its capacity as the fourth note: another *enharmonic* transition. Finally, if one takes as leading tone the diminished seventh itself, instead of *si*-flat it must necessarily be considered as *la*-sharp, which constitutes a third *enharmonic* transition on the same chord.

Thanks, then, to these two different manners of successively considering the same chord, one passes from one key to another one which seems quite remote; one gives to the parts progressions different from the one that they ought to have had in the first place, and these transitions, when properly handled, are capable not only of surprising but of delighting the listener when they are well done. The misfortune is that one must change so brusquely the ideas on the same notes and apply them to such different modulations, to such distant relations, that this genre seems absolutely impracticable for voices such as they are trained by today's music. This is at least what was seen a number of years ago in a memorable example at the Paris Opera.[30] (S)

[*Enharmonic quarter-tone*. One calls thus the difference of the major semitone 15/16 to the minor semitone 24/25, or, to speak more exactly, although not in the manner of ordinary musicians, it is the ratio of 15/16 to 24/25, that is, of 125 to 128. This is how this quarter-tone is formed. Given the Fundamental Bass by major thirds, *do*, *mi*, *sol*♯, and above that this song, *do*, *mi*, *si*♯, one will find that this *si*♯ differs from the *do* by an *enharmonic* quarter-tone. See my "Elements of Music," p. 87.[31]

[M. Rameau observes, 1st, that the diatonic genre, which is the simplest and easiest of all, comes from the progression by fifths of the Fundamental Bass, a progression which is in effect the simplest and most immediately indicated by nature.[32] See SCALE [*Échelle*], DIATONIC [*Diatonique*], SCALE [*Gamme*].

[2nd. That the chromatic genre or the minor semitone, which is the simplest after the preceding one, comes from the progression by major thirds of the Fundamental Bass, a progression also indicated by nature, but nevertheless less natural than the progression by fifths. *See* HARMONY [*Harmonie*]. In fact, if one forms this Fundamental Bass, *do mi*, one will be able to place above this song *sol sol*♯, one will be able to form a minor semitone. 3rd, finally, the *enharmonic* genre, the least natural of the three, has its origin in a bass *do mi sol*♯, of which the two extremes, *do*, *sol*♯, which produce the *enharmonic* quarter-tone, form a progression which is not natural. (O)

[*Enharmonic diatonic*. One calls thus a song that proceeds by a series of semitones, all major, which immediately succeed one another; this song is diatonic because each semitone in it is major (*See* DIATONIC [*Diatonique*] and CHROMATIC [*Chromatique*]); and it is *enharmonic* because two consecutive major semitones form too large a tone of *enharmonic* quarter-tone. In order to form this type of song, one must compose a Fundamental Bass which ascends alternately by a fifth and by a third, such as *fa do mi si*, and this bass will produce the song *fa mi mi re*♯, in which all the semitones are major. A part of the *Trio of the Furies* in the opera *Hippolyte* is in this genre, but it has never been possible to perform it at the Opera; it was performed elsewhere by very able and good-willed musicians, and M. Rameau assures us that its effect was surprising.[33] (O)

[*Enharmonic chromatic*. One calls thus a song that proceeds by a series of minor semitones, which immediately succeed one another. This song is chromatic because each semitone in it is minor (*See* CHROMATIC [*Chromatique*]); it is *enharmonic* because two consecutive minor semitones form too small of a tone of *enharmonic* quarter-tone. In order to form this type of song, one must have a Fundamental Bass composed of minor and major thirds in this way, *do do la do*♯ *do*♯, and to place above this song *mi*♭ *mi mi mi mi mi*♯; one will find by calculation that *mi*♭, *mi*, *mi*, *mi*, *mi*♯ form minor semitones. M. Rameau teaches us that he has composed in this genre of music an earthquake in the second act of the *Indes galantes* in 1735, but that he was so badly served that he was obliged to change it into ordinary music.[34] *See my "Elements of Music," pp. 91, 92, and 116.*[35] (O)]

Errors on Music in the Encyclopedia

(Rameau)

Numerals such as 1, 2, 3, 4, etc., will indicate the Paragraph of the Article which is in question.[1]

ACCOMPANIMENT [*Accompagnement*], p. 75.

1. *Is the execution of a complete and regular harmony,* etc.,[2] to which I would add, *representing the sounding body* in order to avoid any equivocation, any dispute in the following.

It seems, in fact, that the Musician may have been thinking of the Accompaniment of the Organ or of the Harpsichord, in order continually to present to the ear that fundamental *complete and regular harmony*, which Nature offers us in every Sounding Body.

2. *One takes as a guide, etc. The Italians scorn figures; the score itself is hardly necessary for them; the quickness and finesse of their ear substitute for it, and they accompany very well*—for those who do not know it (it must be added) *without all this apparatus*.[3]

It is precisely because the Italians have only their ear for a guide in Composition, as well as in Accompaniment, that Figuration is not a great help to them, for lack of Method; and this is also the reason why they err at every moment in this Accompaniment regarding the fullness of the harmony and regarding its natural succession, as is going to be confirmed.

In order to pass judgment in an Art, especially as a Legislator, one must not only know it, one must also be endowed with all the expected requisite talents in order to be able to account for the effects experienced from it.

It is said that the Italians accompany very well without Figures, even without a Score: a frivolous remark, to which I shall respond in the same spirit that the French do more, since they accompany by ear with their eyes closed. Thus, among them the quickness and finesse of the ear prevail over the former.

---

*A definition which must be kept in mind in all the following.

The least experienced accompany Rondos without figures and with a score, since they almost always turn on only two or three related keys; but when it is a matter of those transitions which the ear cannot anticipate and of which I shall soon speak, it is then that the greatest talents fail for lack of Method.

The greatest proof that can be given that one lacks an ear for Music is to desire to have it believed that one nation can be more favored in this respect than another.

Experience forms the Ear. There are heads equally well constituted in all Nations in which Music reigns, but someone who has passed his first years in a place where Music is rarely heard cannot at all be counted among their number.[4]

Pg. 76, ¶6, 8th line, *M. Rameau reduces this succession to two cases and he declares generally that a consonant Chord can be preceded only by that of the dominant seventh or by that of the subdominant six-five chord, except in deceptive cadences and in suspensions; he further claims that there is no exception as regards the basis. It seems to us that the perfect Chord could also be preceded by the Diminished Seventh Chord, and even by that of an augmented sixth.*[5]

This citation from M. Rameau is taken from his *Plan for Accompaniment*, p. 22,* where he presents *cadences* as a principle (which must be said) and to which he opposes exceptions only relative to his method and to his fingering (which must also be said), otherwise he would not have added immediately afterward, *where* (this word refers to cadences) *I shall prove nevertheless that there is no exception as regards the basis*; since, actually, the consonant Chord which terminates the deceptive cadence is preceded in the same way as the one that terminates the perfect one, and since the suspension only suspends the route of one or two notes of any Chord for an instant.

As for the objection, *He seems to us, etc.*, it is a lack of knowledge and of an ear not to recognize the leading-tone Chord, the sole one annexed to any Dominant that precedes a consonant Chord, in the diminished seventh and the Augmented Sixth Chords, which always announces, just like the leading-tone chord, a more or less Absolute Perfect Cadence, wherein the whole distinction lies. If a difference in fact exists between the major and the Minor Modes, this is not the time to mention it since here it is solely a matter of Cadences practiced likewise in both Modes by all these same chords—it being noteworthy that M. Rameau gave the name of *leading-tone* Chord to the one of the Dominant seventh that precedes the Consonant, a Dominant that he later calls *Dominant-Tonic*, so that this same chord

---

* *Dissertation on the different methods of Accompaniment.*[6]

may always be recognized in all its different combinations or imitations, as long as it is the leading-tone chord, and that relative to the tonic, with which alone one should be principally occupied in the Accompaniment.

Into what a labyrinth a Curious Devotee is thrown by all those differences which can be gathered under a single item! The detail of the rules of Music is immense; it is impossible to be able to communicate them by this detail, whereas their principle is simple, precise, and easy to understand.

It was in a Work such as the *Encyclopedic Dictionary* that it was necessary solely to follow the principle without entering into details which, even when they are correct, cause confusion and are ultimately discouraging.

After the principle is posed, the detail which depends upon it can ultimately be presented, but with a recommendation that they be followed more or less closely as necessity may require, as I shall say at the proper time and place.

Pg. 76, 2nd column, 1st ¶. *Although following the principles, etc., there are chords that would be unbearable with all that filling-out. . . .*[7] A chord is only such with all its filling-out, by definition it must be complete. If it is unbearable, why employ it? But in this case it is no longer a Chord, and if it is a Chord it is therefore bearable.

The lack of an ear is a great obstacle to whoever claims to present himself as a Legislator in Music.

Ibid. *In the majority of dissonant Chords . . . some note has to be suppressed. . . . This note is . . . sometimes the Fifth.* Can one present oneself as a Musician and speak against the Fifth, which is the mainstay of harmony and which should consequently be preferred everywhere it can be employed? Has it been forgotten that the *Accompaniment is the execution of a complete and regular harmony*? Completion is already here decided against, but how will regularity be found in a Chord from which some sounds are omitted? The regularity of harmony consists as much in its succession as in its fullness. A sound should be preceded and succeeded by such and such another, and if you omit it, what becomes for the ear of the sound that precedes it, and how will the one that ought to follow it be recognized when the ear is not at all predisposed in its favor? For delicate ears, this lack of succession is like a man who loses his voice in the middle of a sentence.

Let us compare the definition of Accompaniment with the omissions proposed: we shall see that it is not at all in agreement with itself. Let us now see to what point the Author is going to carry his indiscretion: we shall soon recognize either that he has allowed himself to be imposed upon by it or that he himself wants to impose on us.

P. 77, 5th ¶, 14th line. *The Italians attach little importance to noise. . . . A third, a well-adapted sixth, even a simple unison,* that is, nothing *is more pleas-*

ing to them, when need demands it, in preference to our din, etc. In a word, they want nothing to be heard in the Accompaniment, in the Bass, which might distract the ear from the principal object, and they are of the opinion that attention vanishes for having been divided.[8] The French go still one step further in this opinion, for they claim that one should not perceive the Accompaniment in a Concert, that one should only perceive that it is not there when it is lacking.

M. *Rousseau* goes further in his *Letter on French Music*, p. 51 through 56, where he claims to offer us as a refinement of taste a harmony stripped of its fullness: a sheer result of the ignorance common to all those who have only their ear for a guide in the Accompaniment.[9]

That which can present itself to the ear by dint of trial and error does not present itself in the same way to the judgment, nor to the fingers in the haste of performance, where there is no time to reflect. And it is then that, being unable to perform a certain harmonic foundation right away, one grasps at a few notes of the Score, or rather confines oneself to the Octave of the Bass. Such is that pretended refinement, that choice, so happily practiced and so happily conceived, common to nearly all Accompanists lacking Method.

If the choice of intervals and of the place they should be put, if, further, the resonance of some ought to prevail over others, this can be with regard only to the principal object of the Concert, which should alone occupy the Listener; but in an Accompaniment which is not supposed to distract from this principal object and which is permitted only in order to represent the Sounding Body, this choice becomes not only useless, but pernicious, as soon as it is made to the prejudice of the full completion of the harmony ordained by Nature itself and confirmed by the given definition; otherwise, lacking the full completion, the succession is interrupted by the omitted parts, so much so that it is precisely in this case that the Accompaniment will err, since the ear will no longer find that nourishment of harmony which is offered by the resonating sounding body.

If we reflect on this a little, we shall see how necessary the fullness of harmony in the Accompaniment is for the Players, whether when the eye or the ear itself is misled, or by an error in copying, or especially when they want to add some ornaments to their taste to the Song. They see in their part only a single note of a harmony which can itself contain up to five different ones; now, however well constituted they may be, they will often fall into error by anticipating a wholly natural modulation from which the Composer has expressly departed in order to surprise, if the Accompanist is not careful at that point to make his harmony complete, given the uncertainty in which he must be, concerning the interval capable of guiding the ear in such a case.

The greatest Musicians, that is to say only those who have the most talent in their Art, are sometimes predisposed against certain intervals for lack of reflection. The Italians, for example, have for a long time affected not to employ the augmented fifth in their harmony, even though this be the *leading-tone Note* itself, and consequently the most capable of putting the ear onto the path of the modulation. I do not know whether this is the case at present. And it is apparently on account of similar prejudices that the so-called omission and the imaginary choice absolutely contrary to the definition are founded.

The Italians attach little importance to noise. I recall this statement in order to make it noticed that the word *noise*, all too familiar to the Author, as regards the harmony, can scarcely be pronounced except against a bad harmony, rather it is the ear of he who so taxes it that must be blamed.

When it is a matter of resolving a question in Music, it is nature which must be consulted and not one's opinion.

If the harmony of the accompaniment should be produced with a certain discretion, our unique model in this case is the sounding body which it represents. The fundamental sound of this sounding body so dominates over its harmonics that they can scarcely be distinguished from it. Thus, one cannot overly multiply the Bass Notes nor diminish the strength of those of its harmony; this is why not only is the Bass doubled with its Octaves, but why still other instruments also perform it along with the Harpsichord. And as for the Chords, if their effect dominates too much, it is the loudness of the instrument which must be diminished, and not that which is wrongly supposed to be in the harmony, which cannot be truncated without violating the laws of Nature itself, as much in the fullness of the harmony which it prescribes to us as in the most perfect succession which it indicates to us by the fundamental routes which are received from it.

Amour-propre is a great seducer, especially when it favors our passions, we cannot then imagine that there are limits beyond our own point of view.

If Rhythm[10] is natural to all the Animals, it is also the first effect which strikes us in Music. We become sensitive to the relations of sounds only after having heard this Music for some time; our sensitivity on this point at first has only Melody for its object, and it is only after a certain number of years, according to whether one is more or less well constituted, to whether one listens to Music more or less frequently, and to whether one pays more or less attention to it, that finally the harmony begins to prevail. Now, it is sufficiently perceived from all the Author's reasonings that he is still sensitive to Rhythm alone, since he has subscribed to an omission of the parts in the Chords, which interrupts the succession of these parts and consequently the Melody which should arise from them, especially when a dissonance is found before or after the omitted part. It is true that this defect readily escapes notice in the Accompaniment, but nothing should escape notice in an Art which one wants to account for, in which each part of a successive harmony has its natural melody—something which should even be made law before everything else. In addition, it is the most generally followed in the most pleasant Songs.*

It is therefore, all in all, solely Rhythm that has seduced M. Rousseau here, seeing that it holds one of the first ranks in Italian arias; in addition, he goes on at length about this Point in the *Letter* I have already cited, to the point of reproaching our Music for not being susceptible to it, when it has so erred only in Recitative, including as well that of the Italians; furthermore, the Rhythm of the Verses makes up for it. This was, on the contrary, the occasion for praising it, since the sentiments of the heart, the passions, can be well rendered only by altering the Rhythm.

A Person who needs to be aroused, to be animated by the movement,[11] because he is still sensitive only to the difference of high and low, of soft and loud, is forgivable; but a Musician, at least someone presenting himself as one, who wishes to dogmatize. . . .

One therefore sees clearly enough that, uniquely occupied by the Rhythm, everything else has eluded him. Lacking an ear, he saw the Italian employ sometimes more, sometimes fewer fingers in the Chords, from which he concluded that they did not always complete those Chords. Predisposed in favor of such an Accompaniment, he saw so much good coming from it that he wanted to offer it to us in his *Letter* as a model, and to better convince us on this subject he has applied it to what is of no importance and what M. Rameau claimed applied only to the predominant parts of the Concert. These are the very words of the *Letter*†: *I recalled then having read in some Work of M. Rameau's that each consonance has its particular character, that is, a manner of affecting the soul proper to it: that the effect of the third is not the same as that of the fifth, etc.* Further on, p. 57. *It is therefore a certain principle and one founded in Nature, that every Music in which the harmony is scrupulously filled out, every Accompaniment in which all the Chords are complete, must produce a great deal of noise, but have very little expressiveness, etc.*

All the consequences drawn from these principles can be only highly praised, except that they do not at all belong to the accompaniment of

---

* It is the order of the smallest natural degrees of the voice, called *Diatonic*.
† *Letter on French Music*, pp. 54 to 58.
See also in the *Dictionary*, Article I, p. 79.[12]

the Harpsichord, for which they are invoked: since this Accompaniment everywhere represents the sounding body, whose harmony is always complete—I repeat this again—aside from the other reasons I have mentioned in favor of this completion.

Lack of knowledge and of an ear has therefore caused him to apply such pretty principles inappropriately to an object which is not all susceptible to them, so that by this means he believed he had the right to be able to cite as a perfection what was a genuine mark of ignorance, without having either seen or felt that it arose from an essential error, against melody itself, in whose favor so many pretty arguments have been imagined.

Let us recall those words cited only a moment ago: *they*, that is the Italians, *they want nothing to be heard in the Accompaniment, in the Bass, which might distract the ear from the principal object, and they are of the opinion that attention vanishes for having been divided*. If this is so, then what purpose does this selection, so happily conceived, serve, since attention must not be drawn to it?

To surprise a Legislator in Music in a case of insensitivity to melody, that is to say here, in the natural and indispensable progression which the parts of several successive chords must have amongst themselves, is already a lot; but what is to be concluded from that surprising contradiction which is found between the whole article and its definition? Is not judgment just as necessary as the ear?

For a Partisan of Melody it really shows spite to set his name down against the fullness of the harmony in general.

Although the effect of the third may be different from that of the fifth, this does not mean that a consonance must be omitted in favor of that whose effect should dominate. It is most often in the lack of proportion between the voices, between the instruments, that the part which should predominate happens to be extinguished by that which should barely be heard, just as with the harmonic sounds of the sounding body. Let us recall the effect produced upon every sensitive soul by *L'Amour triomphe*, in a Chorus from *Pygmalion*,[13] where the Actor alone repeats, with the Chorus, those same words on the seventeenth, double octave of the third, while its fundamental sound is extremely multiplied by unisons and octaves, and while the twelfth, the octave of the fifth of this same fundamental sound, is also multiplied, but less so. It is here that harmony *triumphs*, without the aid of a melody that has an affect on its own, nor with any of the accessories which this melody needs in order to make itself pleasant—namely, rhythm, the difference of high and low, of soft and of loud, the sound of the voice or of the instrument, the situation and the Actor—to which often belong what is attributed to the melody alone—leaving aside the harmony, which prescribes the modulation and the intervals proper to the effect and whose absolute empire everywhere reigns like a mother over her children.

This single example should destroy all that beautiful reasoning employed in the *Letter* to establish a chimera: *the unity of melody*—words which strike the ears in discourse, but whose effect has only weak appeal in Music without the aid of harmony—aside from the fact that this word *unity* does not prevent each part of a *duo*, of a *trio*, of a *quartet* from having its particular melody. What then does it mean? One must discern from this, if I am not mistaken, that M. Rousseau counted on the little knowledge of the Readers and on ears still less versed in the Art. Who, however, would believe that he himself overturns his entire edifice after having raised it to the heavens, by saying, pp. 48 and 49 of the *Letter*: *one must save the harshness of dissonances, piercing and reinforced sounds, the Orchestra's* fortissimo, *for the moments of disorder and of rapture in which the Actors, seeming to forget themselves, convey their distraction to the soul of every sensitive Spectator and make him experience the power of well-handled harmony*.[14] What power! The truth here slips out despite himself. What a confession for an excessive Partisan of melody! What remains to him, then, of this melody? The use the Italians make of it will soon tell us.

Aside from the above-mentioned example, how many other Choruses by M. Rameau are there, without speaking of that of the Opera *Jephté*,[15] that have equally penetrated to the soul? It is true that the majority are supported in this by an interesting situation.

Furthermore, the situations conveyed by the Monologues of *Thésée* in the Fourth Act of *Hippolyte et Aricie*, of *Télaire* in the Second Act of *Castor et Pollux*, or *Tirtée* in the Second Act of *Les Talens Lyriques*, and of *Dardanus* in the Fourth Act of the Opera by that name,[16] would be almost imperceptible with the voice alone, unless the Actor were capable of seducing us by his playing and by his acting; whereas, make him immobile, and the harmony will certainly make up for his lacking by maintaining complete balance between the voice and the instruments—a balance whose absence is almost never suspected by those who have it in mind to criticize, even though their criticism be in bad faith.

If it is claimed that the unity of melody is founded on unisons wherein the violins augment the *noise* of the vocal part, I no longer have anything to say. I make use here of the word *noise*, so familiar to the Author, when it is in actuality harmony. Would it not better suit the melody?

Let a Song be performed stripped of all these accessories, especially of rhythm, and where it does not appear that words may be added: one will be much less affected by this than by a drum beaten rhythmically. Let one do as much with *L'Amour triomphe*, which I have cited: its effect will not change at all, its harmony will always triumph.

Moreover, these sorts of unisons suit only lively and gay airs exempt from action, from interest, from feelings, from passions, such as are almost all the Rondos in Italian arias, in which this gaiety is even abused in situations that are the opposite. Italian Musicians seek in general merely to amuse the ear by movements which cheer it, excite it, animate it by roulades in which the Singer makes himself admired, and by softs, louds, highs, lows in the range of every Musician, so that to imitate them properly depends on nothing more than our Poets.

No reflection at all is needed in order to judge whether Music pleases or not; this is what makes People of taste not want to look into it, and the more penetrating they are, the more they yield to a discourse, although mistaken, which accords with their taste, which is moreover limited by their little experience. They do not limit themselves to this; they present themselves as Composers, they believe they are able with impunity to represent to them Music in entirely opposite genres as coming from the same source, imagining, doubtless through lack of feeling and of knowledge, that no one will be able to notice such a disparity. Here is an event I recall to memory, of which there are numerous witnesses and which I believe I can cite so as to make known how easy it is to impose on someone who does not examine anything closely.

Ten or twelve years ago, a Person performed a Ballet of his composition at M. ***'s house which was later presented to the Opera and refused.[17] I was struck to find in it some very beautiful Violin tunes in a decidedly Italian style, and, at the same time to find that everything in it in bad taste was in French Music, vocal as well as instrumental, including even some Ariettes of the most unremarkable vocal quality supported by the prettiest Italian accompaniments. This contrast surprised me and I asked the Author some questions, to which he responded so badly that I clearly saw, as I had already suspected, that he had composed only the French Music and had plagiarized the Italian.

I have now derived a conclusion from this event which seems to me just, namely, that if the Ballet had been presented at the Opera and the Public had been able to judge it as I did, M. Rousseau would not have failed to derive from this an advantage in favor of all the paradoxes he has advanced in his *Letter, etc.* Nevertheless, he would have been quite wrong, since this Ballet would have proved merely that good Italian Music is preferable to unremarkable French Music, that, in the work of a bad Author, what he has plagiarized is preferable to what he has composed himself, that, finally, it is not possible for this Author to plagiarize very good things since, without any genius, destitute of an ear, of feeling, of experience, and of knowledge, he cannot be absolutely lacking in a certain taste, but the degree of taste is so common that it does not merit any praise, not even the name of taste, which is reserved for a finer feeling—aside from the fact that this may perhaps still be doing him a favor, since he may well have made the choice based only on the testimony of a third person or based on its general celebrity.

As long as Melody alone is considered as the principal moving force of Music's effects there will not be great progress in this Art, since even [Melody] has less empire in it than rhythm, according to what I have already touched upon and what can moreover be easily tested by performing a tune slowly that delights by its gaiety. Furthermore, it is neither from the highs nor the lows that expression arises, and it is uniquely from the relationship of modes linked to one another by a kind of transition—unless one wants to play with words, where it is a matter of imitating some Meteors.[18]

Let one pass, for example, from the mode of *do* to that of *sol* by the interval of *do* to *fa*-sharp, and let this *fa*-sharp be produced above or below the *do*: as long as the inflection is directed by the same feeling, the effect will be absolutely the same—an alternative which is observed every day relative to the range of voices and which can be noted in many other cases.

It is therefore only directly from the harmony, mother of this Melody, that the different effects we experience in Music arise; not that its accessories, namely Melody, rhythm, etc., do not contribute to them, but that without it these same accessories are totally wasted—a reflection which should not be insignificant.

It is quite necessary that the harmony be at the height of its perfection; I have cited only weak sketches of it in comparison to what it can produce when Nature is imitated in all its aspects.

If the Reverend Father Castel had confined himself to harmony in order to confirm his analogy with colors, I believe that he would have had as many Partisans as Readers.[19] In actuality, harmony, just like colors, requires a certain duration for its relations to be able to penetrate to the soul, and just as a rapid series of colors forms only a confusion which can at most amuse the eyes, so likewise a rapid series of sounds, which is usual for melody, especially in lively movements, merely amuses the ear.

A like analogy considerably resolves the issue in favor of harmony, whose necessary duration, for producing its effect on the soul, was recognized by our first Moderns: see Zarlino, Kircher, and others;[20] they say precisely that the Bass should progress at a slow pace while the other parts can double, triple the pace, and more, implying harmony in the word

"Bass" since every harmony of any Music whatsoever may be supported by the Bass. But in this case do we need any authority other than our own experience?

Every Musical Chorus which is slow and whose harmonic succession is good always pleases without the aid of any Design, or of a Melody which might affect on its own; and this pleasure is entirely different from that which is usually experienced from a pleasant Song or a simply lively and gay one; the former relates directly to the soul, the latter does not pass beyond the ear canal. I again recur to *L'Amour triomphe*, already cited more than once: let the pleasure experienced from it be compared to that which a tune, whether vocal or instrumental, will produce: the difference will soon be felt.

Let us go further and remark that, when it is a matter of depicting a situation in a Melody whose vivacity must correspond to a lively, gay, fiery, unrestrained character, if its movement is not slowed, or at least if one does not give to the Note on which the expression must make itself felt a value that is double, triple, quadruple, or even more than the one which the playing of the song requires, the effect is unsuccessful. This will be recognized in every piece of Music in which some perceptible features of a marked expression are found.

Does one believe that the effect experienced arises from the Melody? One is mistaken: this forced rest, of which I have just spoken, merely serves to make the soul feel the relationship of the two harmonies which succeed one another, the latter acquiring all its strength from the former by the greater or lesser relationship they have between them.

Everyone, without excepting the Musician, has believed until now that the cause of the effect resided in the Note of the Song by which it is experienced, or at least in the interval by which one fulfills it—an error, an error, a hundred times an error, from which one ought to have recovered since M. Rameau's *New System*,* in which he proves the contrary very clearly.

It is known that our senses are deceivers; nevertheless, one swears only by them, examines nothing, and always decides provisionally. The product is taken for the generator, the effect for the cause, finally everything is turned upside down. Will one never open one's eyes, will I be able to disabuse them? Let's try; what do I risk? I hope for everything from the following example, in which I return to the same interval from *do* to *fa*-sharp which has already been at issue.

When an interval exists in a single Chord, or in two Chords in the same

---

* *New System of Theoretical Music*, Chapter VIII.[21]

mode, its effect has nothing specific about it unless it is with the help of the Actor. The interval from *do* to *fa*-sharp, for example, can be used for apostrophes, interrogations, exclamations, affirmations, negations, but when the mode changes from one sound to another it is then that one feels, in the same interval formed by these two sounds, almost as many different expressions as there are different relations between the two modes which follow one another, these expressions having something of tenderness, of sadness, of gloominess, of fearfulness, of pleasantry, of joy, of menace, of rage, of horror, depending on whether the transition is made to the fifth above or below, and whether the modes are major or minor, while supporting them with a movement suited to the situation.

Example

The name of the Notes identifies the Bass, and the figures above are the figures used in the Accompaniment, so that, however little someone may possess this Art, he will able to instruct himself, by his own feeling, concerning the different effects produced by the difference in the relationship of the modes by singing *do* above the first note and *fa*-sharp above the second one, and then again above or below the *do*.

$\overset{7}{\underset{\times}{}}$
re, *re** or $\overset{7}{} \overset{7}{\underset{\times}{}}$ *la*, *re*, in the major or minor mode of *sol*.

$\overset{7}{\underset{\times}{}} \overset{7}{\underset{\times}{}}$
re si: an interrupted cadence while passing from the major mode of *sol* to the minor of *mi*.

$\overset{\times 6}{}$
do la: a transition from the major or minor mode of *do* to the major or minor of *sol*.

$\overset{\times 4}{}$
do la: a transition from the major mode of *do* to the minor of *mi*.

$\flat \quad \flat 7$
do la: a transition from the minor mode of *do* to the minor of *si*-flat.

$\flat 7$
la × *re*: a transition from the minor of *la* to the minor of *mi*, or to the minor of *sol*, by giving to *re*-sharp the name of *mi*-flat without anything otherwise changing in its chord.

$\overset{7}{\underset{\times}{}}$
la re: a transition from the minor mode of *la* to the major or minor of *sol*.

* The small × takes the place of a Sharp and the ♭ of a Flat.

fa re: a transition from the major of *fa* to the major or minor of *sol*.

fa la: a transition from the major or minor of *fa* to the minor of *si*-flat, by giving to *fa*-sharp the name *sol*-flat, which is effectively the diminished seventh, ♭7, of *la*.

Everywhere a Diminished Seventh Chord is found, figured ♭7, the enharmonic can take place, by taking as the leading tone there whichever of the four notes that make up this Chord one wishes, all of them being formed of Minor Thirds. In this way, since the Tonic announced by this arbitrary leading tone is also capable of being considered dominant-tonic of a major or a minor mode, one can pass into twelve different modes thanks to this same Chord, which one must know how to recognize in its different combinations. But in this case, a third note in the Bass should follow in order to establish the mode implied by the specific leading tone chosen; and it is principally from this that those strongly defined images I have just enumerated arise, at least in part.

Further, everywhere a sharp is found, figured X, below or beside a figure in a minor mode, the same diminished seventh chord can take place, and consequently the enharmonic, by raising the dominant-tonic a semitone higher, without the modulation or the harmony suffering for it.

To feel the effect of each of these transitions well, they must be directed by different modulations made up of a certain number of harmonic phrases. See how the Chorus of *L'Amour triomphe* is directed in its Act in *Pygmalion*.[22] After having, so to speak, caused the principal and dominant mode to be overshadowed by the other modes, it returns precisely when it is least expected so as to make one experience, by its return, one of harmony's most pleasant effects.* On the subject of enharmonics see also the Monologue in *Dardanus*[23] with which the fourth Act commences: the harshness of the harmony makes the effect of the situation strongly felt. I can also refer to the *Trio of the Furies* in *Hippolyte et Aricie*,[24] in which all the horror they proclaim is found painted in a *diatonic enharmonic genre*; but not only are three great Musicians needed to sing it, but there is moreover a way of handling it of which one might be unaware, or to which one also may not have the patience to apply oneself.

---

* As for the effect at the moment when Pygmalion joins the Chorus to sing *L'Amour triomphe*, if the Bass had begun and concluded it in the Mode of *fa*, thus *fa do fa*, instead of beginning it by the mode of *si*-flat, this same *si*-flat then becoming subdominant of the *fa* into which it passes, one would have been much less agreeably affected by it, so true is it that the harmony alone gives to the melody its distinctive character.

To cite a single instance for different proofs is to save Devotees the trouble, time, and effort of leafing through Books to satisfy their curiosity.

I now ask whether the effect of this single interval from *do* to *fa-sharp* could ever produce the different expressions to which the different modulations lead for the eyes, or for the ear.

An even simpler example, and consequently one more within everyone's reach, is that which is found in the *Demonstration of the Principle of Harmony*, p. 40, on the subject of an absolute close after which nothing else is desired, namely, a *Perfect Cadence*.[25] In fact, let any of the three parts that form this close be sung—*si do, re do, fa or sol mi*; let them be sung together if one likes: the harmony of their Fundamental Bass *sol do* will make this close perceptibly felt, whereas if one gives them as Bass *sol la*, where one then passes from the mode of *do* to that of *la*, a continuation is desired.

He who seeks the harmony with which he can accompany a song he has imagined seeks precisely the principle which has suggested it to him, a principle whose seed is in himself and all of whose dependent ones are developed by it to the extent that experience may favor him.

Successive harmony engenders melody, that is, all possible songs, whose basis lies uniquely in a well directed accompaniment such as M. Rameau prescribes it in his *Plan*,[26] wherein the succession of consonances, *and* of dissonances—whether *preparing* them or *resolving* them—is much more regularly observed than it has ever been by means of the rules which had been given until then. All the variety that can be introduced into this melody consists merely in the different combinations of this basis and in ornaments of taste, derived, however, from this same basis, whether by forming a song from the different notes of the same chord, or by passing from one of these notes to another by the smallest natural degrees, or by passing from one harmony to another by these same degrees,* such as is practiced naturally by the mechanics of the fingers alone in that *Plan* by M. Rameau. How, then, could a Partisan of melody have been able to think that some sounds, some notes of a chord must be omitted? Should he not have seen that the order of this melody is thereby destroyed and that he has suppressed precisely that sound which is perhaps the most favorable to the happiest combination?

Thus, all Music being included in the harmony, it must be concluded from this that it is only to this harmony alone that any science whatever must be compared.

Let us take up the continuation of our Article; the Author is therein always the same.

At the end of the Article, ¶10, p. 76, 2nd column, one reads: *When*

---

*The sevenths are merely inverted seconds, and the ninths, tenths, elevenths, twelfths, etc., are merely octaves of the second, third, fourth, and fifth.

M. Rameau wants all the Chords to be filled out, he has given more consideration to the facility of the fingering and to his particular system . . . than to the purity of the harmony.[27]

In what does *the purity of the harmony* consist if it is not in its *full completion* and in its *regularity*? Such is the definition given at the head of this Article. Now, if M. Rameau's system and his fingering address both of these, as it is acknowledged on the whole of page 76 and at the word FIGURING [*Chiffrer*],[28] it is therefore to this *purity of harmony* alone that he principally attends. Every truncated harmony is not pure, either in itself or in its succession.

When examining M. Rameau's *Plan of Accompaniment*, it should have been recognized that it was principally devised in order to form the ear. It would suffice, in order to convince oneself of this, to practice the mechanics of the fingering he prescribes there for a few months and then, far from glossing over the signs which serve to guide this mechanics, as is done at the end of the word FIGURING [*Chiffrer*], p. 337, it would be seen, on the contrary, that these signs, since they are not varied, release one from all reflection; that the fingers then proceed mechanically without being capable of being mistaken; that, since the eye indicates where the sign changes, the fingers, accustomed to all the different routes indicated by this change of signs, immediately lend themselves to this change; that the ear, likewise formed by these same routes, indicates the order and finds itself instantaneously obeyed; finally, that the knowledge of the different cadences which this same change of signs indicates, in accord with the Ear, soon enough warns the fingers so that they not do fall into error.

After having made the most perfect execution of the Accompaniment depend solely on the ear, how did he not sense that this ear, once formed and supported by knowledge as well as by a mechanics of fingering, must be much more promptly obeyed in this performance?

At the beginning of the last Paragraph of this same word FIGURING [*Chiffrer*], still p. 337, it is said that the Method *does not at all express . . . the genuine fundamental harmony*. He should have said merely that it is not at all expressed by its fundamental sounds, since everything relates to the Tonic, which should be essentially a presence for the Accompanist; and he should, on the contrary, have concluded in favor of this discovery, since for the Composer it is a matter merely of knowing, for example, that the leading-tone Chord indicated by an X is the fundamental harmony of a Dominant-Tonic, as this is definitely explained in the *Plan*, if I am not mistaken.

In the Paragraph that precedes the one that has just been cited, we have: *it is clearly perceived that it is necessary to suppose here that every dissonance is re-*

solved by descending, for if there were some that should be resolved by ascending, M. Rameau's points would be insufficient.[29]

This is pronounced in a manner that leaves ambiguity, for by saying, *if there were dissonances which should be resolved by ascending*, it is left in doubt whether there are any or not. There are actually two: the leading tone in its chord and the added sixth. Now, the method makes the succession of these two dissonances so familiar to the fingers by the mechanics that they can always alert the judgment and the ear to them, all the more so as they are always followed by a Perfect Chord indicated by the sign. What is more, these dissonances alone always ascend—which will be verified at the word *Cadence*.[30]

Furthermore, M. Rameau should be quite satisfied with the justice rendered to his *Plan* in this Dictionary. And if he had wanted faithfully to follow all his principles without adding anything of his own, the Reader would be better instructed, since the majority of the exceptions, of the objections, even of the applications that are added are false.

Already nearly everything explained in the Article on Accompaniment is contradictory to his definition. This is carried to the extreme of wanting to make pass for a perfection one of the greatest proofs of ignorance. The exceptions and the objections have been set aright. As for the applications, M. Rameau has already condemned one of them in his observations, to which I shall soon refer; those which relate to the Italians are no less erroneous, but he will find others even much more reprehensible.

CHORD [*Accord*], p. 78.

I did not expect to find here those *unbearable Chords* about which he apparently wanted to speak in the 1st Paragraph of p. 76.[31]

Despite the voice of nature, despite the ear, its faithful interpreter in Music, despite what M. *Rameau* has been able to draw from them both to confirm the chord by *supposition*, despite the simplest means which ought to have come forward to M. *Rousseau* to pass his errors on this subject before his eyes, which I say, despite his very verdict upon the generation of dissonance—a judgment wholly the opposite of what one will read—he attributes to this chord by *supposition* a right of inversion that can belong only to the fundamental harmony.

In his verdict upon dissonance, p. 1049, he rejects the *la* placed between *sol* and *si*, which makes *sol la si*, and *would be doubly dissonant*.[32] Now, *sol la si*, or *fa sol la*, which is found in the penultimate Chord of the last example of p. 78,[33] and which is likewise implied in the two others called *derived* chords, are the same thing entirely. How then did he not perceive that he condemned as a *dissonance* what he wants to be approved as a *Chord*?

Every Chord derived or inverted from another should contain the same number of sounds; nevertheless, the Ninth Chord contains five different ones and those which are then called its *derivatives* contain only four.

The same harmony that precedes and follows a fundamental Chord should likewise precede and follow its derivatives. The intervals which form these latter ones with the fundamental sound should never vary. Furthermore, they should be able to be members of the same modes, assuming that they may belong to several. Finally, since they all make up merely one chord differently combined, they should consequently all be susceptible of having the same accidentals; nevertheless, none of all this happens to the pretended derivatives, as I am going to explain in a moment. All of this has escaped the eyes, the ear, the judgment. How many means there nonetheless are for preventing oneself from going astray in such a case, and how simple they are for an intelligent man, at least for an ear that is just a little sensitive!

There is not a Musician a bit versed in the art who does not in fact know of these peculiarities by his experience alone, and however little sensitive as he may be to harmony, he will perceive the enormous discord found in the Chords claimed to be *derived*, the Chord by supposition being bearable even only in successions in which it then forms a type of suspension. But all this is nothing next to what nature prescribes in such a case, this is at least what should not have escaped the notice of someone who wishes to dictate its laws to us.

The sounding body causes its harmony to resonate, whereas it simply causes its twelfth and its seventeenth below to vibrate by taking from them the right to produce any Sound other than its unison by the division it simultaneously forces upon them, so that, indeed, by assuming each part of the divided body to be susceptible of harmony, it would render precisely the same harmony as that of the body which puts it into motion, since each of these parts gives the unison of this latter body; therefore, since this twelfth and this seventeenth below, which contain the octaves of the fifth and the third below the fundamental, those alone employed in the chord by supposition, are no longer capable of being felt as harmonious in their totality, they consequently cannot be represented by their octaves in a harmony they would then infect, since they are entirely foreign to it and consequently should be allowed only in the place where nature has put them; otherwise, these octaves, always implied everywhere they can be inserted, would produce a triple dissonance in the ninth chord among these four sounds, *mi fa sol la*, which would then be encountered there. This proves very well that the ear is in no way struck by them. What a cacophony a triple dissonance would produce when the double one, like *fa sol la*, is already unbearable! I do not know whether I have made myself very well understood, but one can contest the truths I have just deduced only in order to provide me with the means for shedding greater light on them. It is here that this passage from the Psalmist would be quite appropriate: *Oculos habent & non vident, aures habent & non audiunt*.[34]

From this error he passes on to another. Would one actually believe that the fundamental sound of the ninth, for which the Author preserves the same quality when he has it contain, on the second chord in the example, that of a *seventh* and a *sixth*, would one believe, I say, that this fundamental sound is then no longer such? This is no longer anything but a mediant or a super-dominant, depending on whether the close is going to terminate afterward on a tonic or on its dominant. What Musician will not perceive this by his experience alone? He will see that, while a single harmony exists, there occurs in the Bass a note of taste, which the fundamental harmony with its seventh then receives as a *seventh* and *sixth*, and, that immediately afterward the same harmony, regaining all its rights, progresses in the legitimate order, wherein the first dissonance, this seventh of the fundamental sound which alone occupies the ear from the moment it has been heard, is resolved in accordance with our liking. One could likewise have several other notes of taste put into the Bass on which the harmony, which is already given and which is afterward still preserved, would form Chords as wholly unbearable as the three derived from the example. But mention is never made of these sorts of notes anywhere where it is a question of the basis of the harmony. The ear does not take account of them and the choice is always abandoned to the discretion of the great Masters.

If this Bass of the second Chord [of the example] is no longer the fundamental sound, then those which are afterward called its third and its seventh are no longer so except relative to an arbitrary and absolutely indifferent note.

P. 79 contains no fewer errors.[35] If, for example, there are two Seventh Chords where the presence of the leading tone differentiates between them, they each consequently have their particular supposition, as can be noted between the preceding Ninth Chord and that of the *augmented fifth*, in which the sharp, which is not at all in the first, marks this leading tone.[36] Why, then, has the same distinction not been made between the *Eleventh, or Fourth* Chord, and that of the *augmented seventh*, which is presented with the same notes? A flat should have been added to the quarter note *si* in order in effect to designate the first Chord and in order to distinguish it from the other, which alone contains the leading tone.

It cannot be known what this difference of names for the same Chord means. The two notes are blackened so as to indicate that they may be omitted, for that changes nothing in it; furthermore, the Fourth Chord, putting aside the name of the eleventh, is generally formed on a supertonic and it is only so on a tonic, or on a dominant from which one ordinarily omits the two blackened notes; on the other hand, the Augmented Seventh Chord annexed solely to the tonic is always completed. It is well known that if there are fewer parts in a Music than there are notes in a Chord that it is necessary to omit these notes proportionally, the choice of which depends on taste. This is why it would be necessary to add the octave of the note by supposition in the given Chord with the omission of the two blackened notes in order to indicate the fourth part that is always joined to it when one composes in four parts; but this would not square with the imagined derivations which are proposed.

The three Chords of the example of the fourth, where the latter two are given as derivations of the first, are on the contrary three original ones of the same type in which the same supposition takes place.

1st. Since the fourth is recognized in every dissonant Chord as principal dissonance, since it is always the seventh of the fundamental sound, not at all being given by the same note in the first two Chords, this proves that both are first of their type, the seventh having been inserted in the second only so as to make it square with the first.

2nd. The fourth, unreasonably omitted from the last Chord, further proves that it is also first of its type, and the augmented seventh *mi*, which should be found in it, is likewise omitted from it only because the lowest bass note *fa* suspends this same *mi* in the Bass. This is a fact of practice for which all good Composers can account.

3rd. Every dissonant Chord should contain at least four different sounds. Why, then, are only three presented here?

4th. Every Chord should contain the same sounds in the same number as that from which it is derived. Why, then, further present here only three in the derivatives when the original contains five? What! Since different Chords will have several common notes, will I choose at my pleasure those which please me in order to square those Chords with one another? I had only to say, then, that every consonant Chord derives from that of the seventh, *do mi sol si*, since by omitting *si* I have the perfect major chord and its derivatives, *do mi sol*, and since, on the contrary, by omitting *do*, I have the Perfect Minor Chord and its derivatives, *mi sol si*. In a Music in two or three parts the choice is necessary, as I have already made understood. But is this the place to speak of it, or at least ought not one be warned about it?

5th. If one had been given the 4th and the 5th as possible sounds for the two last Chords, however little of an ear one might have, one would have sensed that the fifth remains while the fourth descends diatonically, which, I say, is so even without the aid of the fifth; the progression of this fourth is perceptible, aside from the fact that it is specifically specified as a dissonance at the word DISSONANCE [*Dissonnance*], p. 1050, at the end of ¶1, where it is said, *thus after sol fa you will have sol mi*.[37] *Sol* in the present case being the fifth which remains and *fa* the fourth which descends diatonically on *mi*.

It must be recalled that the seventh of a note by supposition is not at all still the principal dissonance, for it is the fifth or the third of the fundamental sound; it is solely the seventh of the latter, which makes a ninth or a fourth of the note by supposition, with which the ear is uniquely occupied until it is resolved.

I clearly perceive that this is not within everyone's reach and that in order to pass judgment about it one must be somewhat initiated into the practice of Composition, or at least into its Theory. It is, nevertheless, only by such means that one can attain the knowledge necessary to account for Music's effects. What! Would one rather be seduced than instructed by truths which appear arbitrary only because one doesn't want to take the trouble to delve into them? Let people who want to decide at least rely on an Accompanist who is a good harmonist: he will make them hear and see the order and the succession of Chords in which they would like to be instructed, and, however little a head they may have for sonority, they will judge by the effects they experience from them. Still, if those who were not at all knowledgeable, would they remain silent? But no. The Author of so many errors has recently been praised excessively in the *Journal des Sçavants*,* in which the articles CONSONANCE [*Consonnance*] and DISSONANCE [*Dissonnance*] are cited as proof. As there is no means of being mistaken about consonances, the Panegyrist then goes almost as far as his Hero, but as to what a dissonance is he does not say a word. Why then cite it? And what does such a silence augur? A novelty of his competence could nevertheless have been noted, namely, that when it is a matter of telling how to prepare a dissonance, he refers to PREPARE [*Préparer*], p. 1050, ¶3, 2nd column. The reasons given there are not admissible; rather, he would have the right to do as much with all the articles by means of well-coordinated excuses, which in the end is merely to abbreviate one article in order to elongate another. It would therefore be better to leave things in place: this is custom, this is reason. Besides, I more than anyone desire that the curious not have the time to grow impatient.

* 2nd. From the month of June, 1755.

CADENCE [*Cadence*], p. 513.

At the end of the 1st paragraph. *Now, as every harmonic phrase is necessarily linked by expressed or implied dissonances, it follows that every harmony is properly speaking only a series of cadences.*[38]

It is this last conclusion, *it follows, etc.*, that M. Rameau has set aright in his *Observations*,[39] but he would not have relied upon it if he had examined the article on Accompaniment, p. 76, ¶5, where it is said, *since the perfect consonant chord suits only the tonic, the succession of consonant chords furnishes so many tonics, and consequently so many changes of key*, since he would have recognized a manifest contradiction between these two articles, which he would not have failed to mention. In fact, as soon as it is agreed that two consonant Chords can succeed one another, this is to agree that there are no Cadences there either, consequently to agree to this statement ¶3: *As there is no dissonance without a cadence, there is no a cadence without dissonance either, etc.*[40]

Page 514, last paragraph. *No Author until now has spoken of this ascent, etc.*[41] M. d'Alembert first caused the little weight of this reflection to be noticed, but if one examines: 1. the 2nd column of p. 76, letter A, one will read there, *the ascending harmony is furnished by a succession of fifths in ascending . . . accompanied by . . . the added sixth, etc.*, which is precisely the statement of the rule given by M. Rameau in his *Plan*.[42] He has therefore spoken of this ascension; it is agreed to here while it is denied further on—another contradiction. This is not all. The Author who believes he has found a fortunate distinction between the progression of *sevenths* and that of *added sixths* characterizes the first as *Descending* and the other as *Ascending*. Yet if he had taken as proof the Fundamental Bass, which descends a fifth in the first case and ascends likewise in the other, he would have had some reasons. But none of this: it is of the progression of the harmony itself that he wants to speak, not of the fundamental, nor that of the dissonance in particular either, consequently what follows in the paragraph I have just cited at A: *thus, by the ordinary rules, the harmony that arises from a series of dissonances always descends, although, according to the true principles and according to reason, it must have in ascending a progression entirely as regular as in descending*. See CADENCE [*Cadence*].[43]

There is nothing in the article on *Cadence* that justifies the preceding. If the dissonance ascends in the irregular cadence, this does not at all prove that the entire harmony ascends on it, just as it always descends in a series of dominants, in which the leading tone has no place. On the contrary, while the added sixth ascends, the octave and the third always descend on the third and the fifth of the fundamental sound. Moreover, for someone who sees only one part of the object, this ascending harmony cannot be continued with added sixths without being interrupted from one to the other by the perfect chord, to which the sixth can actually be added immediately afterward; the cadence cannot be simulated in it as in a series of dominants, in which the leading tone, which always ascends, alone determines the perfect cadence; without this leading tone the cadence is simply imitated in the fundamental progression, whereas when the added sixth, which is a major dissonance, is the leading tone, the irregular cadence is necessarily announced and should produce its full effect before passing to another. Such is the character of the major dissonance: by determining the cadence, it alone is forced to ascend and the consonances it accompanies have full liberty to ascend or descend as the style of the song and the relation of the parts among themselves may require, excepting, however, the consonance against which the dissonance strikes as second or seventh and which remains on the same level or takes an opposite route.

This shock of the dissonance is explained in a rather interesting manner in the supplement to the *Treatise on Harmony*, p. 6.[44]

Chorus [*Choeur*], p. 362.

I shall not refer to the contradiction found here with what the same Author says of Choruses in his letter on Music; what this regards can be seen at the end of M. Rameau's *Observations*.[45]

Chromatic [*Chromatique*], p. 387.

1. *A genre of Music that proceeds by several consecutive semitones.*[46]

It ought to have been explained in the Article that there are never two chromatic semitones in succession; instead, it is even left in doubt whether the diatonic semitone is not also chromatic; it should have also been declared that the chromatic semitone always announces a new *key* or *mode*.

Dissonance [*Dissonnance*], p. 1049.

¶1, 2nd Column. After having given a general, but in no way solid idea of dissonances, after having said that Father Mersenne *contents himself with showing the generation*, a generation which, however, is founded only on calculations dictated by simple experimentation, he falls upon M. Rameau with rather pronounced irony: this Author, it is said, *after having specifically said that the dissonance is not natural to harmony . . . tries to find the principle in the ratios, analogies, conformities, metamorphoses, etc.*[47]

If dissonance were natural to harmony, it would suffice to explain the fact; and it is precisely because it is not so, although the ear adopts it, that in order to satisfy reason on this point as much as possible, one cannot overly exhaust *the ratios, the analogies, the conformities, even the metamorphoses*, if there are any. The instinct which has suggested this dissonance to us should doubtless make us seek in its principle what authorizes it. See Chap. IX of the *Harmonic Generation*, p. 107;[48] you will find there not only all the means on which it is thought the criticism in question can be established, you will also find there the reasons M. d'Alembert makes use of, at the end of the Article (O) in order to destroy this criticism and in order to conclude from it that, *without departing from M. Rameau's principles*, the addition of dissonance to harmony *is the work of Art and not of Nature*.[49]

Why has not this Chapter IX been cited anywhere? He would have made it understood, on the one hand, that he was not at all exploiting it, and, on the other, he would have openly rendered justice to its Author, whereas it seems that he desired to do him a favor by saying, *without departing from the basis of M. Rameau's principles*, when it ought simply to have been said, *according to M. Rameau's principles*.

Furthermore, although this addition of the dissonance seems to be due only to Art, the reasons derived from the chapter in question—those, indeed, which M. d'Alembert cites—prove clearly enough that Nature has a large part in it, if not directly at least indirectly, by the need one has to employ it so as to distinguish, in the mode, the tonic from its dominant and from its subdominant. Is not the instinct which suggests it to us the work of Nature? When, for example, one descends from the octave of the dominant to the third of its tonic and when one ascends from the fifth of the subdominant to this same third of the tonic, the less experience one has the more one is naturally led to progress by the smallest diatonic degrees and, consequently, to pass from one side to the other by the dissonance which leads to these thirds, while the same harmony always persists, whose Fundamental Bass also becomes that of these two dissonances, which are the only ones that can be employed in the fundamental harmony: the *leading tone*, known under the name of *tritone*, of *augmented fifth*, etc., not being at all a dissonance by itself, since it is, in its origin, the major third of a dominant-tonic, as this is proved in M. Rameau's Works.

In order to give more weight to the criticism, the two following remarks are principally relied upon.

Because the Arithmetic proportion gives him, as he claims—note, *as he* claims—*the minor third in the bass, etc.*⁵⁰ The claim is certainly well-founded, since the effect of this proportion can be judged only after having arranged it in the order of its principle, which requires one to invert the one in which it was first presented and in which one then finds: 1/10, 1/12, 1/15, namely *La, Do, Mi.*

Reducing the proportion given by the multiples to its least terms or degrees, from which every harmony is banned according to the explanation on pages 76 and 77,⁵¹ is to follow the law that Nature dictates, both in the harmonic proportion susceptible to the same reduction and in the functioning of the ear, which naturally makes us reduce all the intervals to their least degrees*: the difference that is then found between this last proportion and that of the Arithmetic one now in question, consisting only in the transposition of the order between the two thirds on each side of the fifth that make it up.

If he here follows the laws of Nature, he on the contrary contradicts them by supposing the totality of these multiples susceptible of its harmony, as is done with regard to supposition, pp. 76 and 77.⁵³

By always following these same laws, one should note that in each proportion the principle engenders, in Geometry itself, from which the *Mode* is formed,† the fifth or twelfth is the middle term and, consequently, the numerator of each of these proportions! It is, then, for it to order the *Mode*, and as soon as its fifth below is no longer derived from the Multiples it is found to be naturally harmonious.

From this remark there follows this other one, namely, that the principle, by ceding to the fifth the right of ordering the *Major Mode* also cedes to its third, or seventeenth, that of ordering the *Minor*. If, though, by supposing that this principle is called *fa*, its fifth, *do*, orders on the one hand and its third, *la*, on the other; from thence comes the intimate relation between these two Modes.

*M. Rameau believes he can reconcile everything: the proportion serves him to introduce the dissonance, and the lack of proportion serves him to make it felt.*⁵⁵ The play on words seems to have been employed merely to cast more ridicule.

The dissonance added to the perfect Chord is in no way proportionate to it; thus, it is not in this case *the proportion which serves to introduce the dissonance*. On the other hand, the alteration of the third added so as to form a dissonance shows a lack of relation between two sounds and not of proportion where at least three [sounds] are needed; it is therefore not in this case either *that the lack of proportion serves to make it felt.*

---

* See M. Rameau's *Response to M. Euler on the Identity of Octaves*, p. 5 and following.⁵²
† *Demonstration of the Principle of Harmony*, p. 19 to 32, then again p. 62 to 70.⁵⁴

What fruit is to be derived from such a criticism, in which he only jokes and in which, far from sustaining it with good reasons, he is mistaken about all the points by which he establishes it? Did he have it in mind to exploit a means he later proposes (¶3) *in order to know where one should place it*, this dissonance, *and how it must be employed?*[56]

This means, which consists of the *second*, has already been exhausted by M. Rameau in pages 3, 4, 5, 6, 7 of the supplement to his *Treatise on Harmony* and in chaps. XI, XII, XIII, XIV of his *New System*.[57] He even adds a remark there utterly forgotten in the article in question and without which, however, one can easily fall into error, namely, that this *second* is received into the harmony only as an inversion of the *seventh*, the sole and unique dissonance that may contain the Fundamental Bass; and if one can oppose to it the *sixth* added to the chord of a subdominant, the same Author proves that, since this chord can be reduced to that of the seventh thanks to a *double employment* with which he has enriched his Art, every dissonance can very well be conceived under the idea of the seventh alone.

¶ 5. In order to authorize this *second*, it is said, *on the La, between the Sol and the Si, it would make a second with them both and, consequently, it would be doubly dissonant*—a doubleness which, nevertheless, was not at all considered at the word CHORD [*Accord*], if he indeed wanted it to be recalled.[58]

If the fundamental Chord, *Sol Si, Re, Sol*, is proposed, to which is sometimes added *Fa*, sometimes *Mi*, in order to have *on the one hand*, p. 1050, *the Seventh Chord, and on the other the Added Sixth Chord*, what does this amount to when it is not said immediately that these Chords are the sole fundamentals by which one must be guided?[59]

If the Fundamental Bass is still recalled when teaching the progression of the two dissonances found by means of the *second*, it is made to depend on that of this bass when it is on the contrary by the fundamental progression that all the others are directed. The effect is here given for the cause, and the cause for the effect.

Instead of always leading the Reader along the paths of the principle, he is drawn away from it at every instant. If one undertakes to teach how the dissonance is *prepared* and is *resolved*, aside from the fact that it is made the arbiter of its progression whereas it depends on its Fundamental Bass alone, as I have just remarked, one is obliged to refer to the word PREPARE [*Préparer*] for what pertains to its *preparation*.

Can it be, in a Work such as the *Encyclopedic Dictionary*, which should be a compendium of truths for posterity as for the present, that what is done from an Art, from a Science whose principle, given by nature, should indubitably influence the other Arts and Sciences and should foster a connection worthy of finding its place in such a Work is so poorly treated?

This principle consists in the resonance of a sounding body, from which three different sounds result,* which, when perfectly united, are always believed to be heard as merely a single one, except when a well-constituted mind gives it express attention: which confirms more than ever the infallibility of the ear's judgment, since it is the unique judge of this and since it is extremely shocked by the slightest alteration among the consonances formed from these same three sounds.

Nothing further is needed to compose good Music and to enjoy its effects, as is proved by the past, when experience alone led the Musician.

Why, then, did anyone want to know what the relationships of the harmonic intervals consisted in, by measuring for this effect the bodies which made them heard, in a word, by submitting Music to Geometry?

Doubtless recognizing the infallibility of the ear's judgment, not being able to count on that of any other Sense, not even being able to be assured of a relationship of equality perceived by the eye, and finding in Music alone the means of making these two principal senses—hearing and sight—mutually concur, they counted wholly on the help of the ear in the part peculiar to it concerning the certainty of the relationships among the different objects which strike our senses; but deaf to the voice of nature, insensitive to the harmony of the sounding body, the Geometers were foiled in all their research on this subject and the sole fruit they were able to derive from it was to recognize that like intervals had like numerical ratios, applicable to size, without the Art being more advanced for that.

They were not at all deceived: the mind required certainty concerning the relationships[60] which the different objects that strike our senses have among them; of all these senses, the ear alone has this right of certainty in Music alone. And in what circumstance, then? Precisely in that which concerns all these Mathematical truths and the first principles of this Science.

Like a root, which from the first moment it sprouts, produces trunks, branches, and fruits, the sounding body, from the moment it resonates, engenders proportions, progressions, and ratios.† It first makes heard in its aliquots the most perfect of all the progressions, namely the harmonic, in the ratio of 1 1/3 1/5, or of 15 : 5 : 3, when the difference in the sizes of bodies is taken account of. It further makes seen another, less perfect proportion in its aliquots, namely the Arithmetic, in the ratio of 1 : 3 : 5, and the route it prescribes on from one side and the other, finally makes it engender all the geometric proportions, the three first of which—where

---

*This is a generally recognized fact of experience.

†*Demonstration of the Principle of Harmony*, pages 19, 20, 21, 22, 25, 30, 31, 32, and 90. See also the Table of progressions, A, at the end of the Book, a Table still more detailed in the *New System of Music*, p. 24.[61]

the same terms of the Harmonic, as well as that of the Arithmetic, become the denominators—constitute all Music, the octave of the principal one 2, or 1/2, being contained in it, whether in order to combine the fundamental harmony to our liking or in order to reduce the ratios to their smallest terms.

From the two first proportions arise the most simple progressions and from these latter arise new progressions, called, consequently, Geometric, in accordance with the Tables to which I have already referred, which contain all the progressions.

From these proportions and progressions arise all the possible ratios. How, then, would Music not have an intimate connection, to say no more, as had already been guessed, with all the other Sciences, inasmuch as they are founded solely on the same laws which its principle prescribes?

If every Physicist, every Geometer wanted to take the trouble to verify the relationship Music has with the Art, or the Science, he practices, he would perhaps discover merely what was still only glimpsed in all the comparisons with which writings, ancient as well as modern, are filled.

It is well known that every Art, every Science has its particular properties. But could they not all depend upon a single principle? Are there two principles in Nature? Could we discover it by means of a medium other than by that of our senses? And can they offer us one which would be as palpable to them as the resonance of the sounding body and from which the certainty of the relationships may arise as it arises here from the effect the ear experiences?

For lack of the ear's help, for lack of the certainties which might be drawn from it, in the Sciences they were forced to follow an order diametrically opposed to the one which the resonance of the sounding body prescribes. They clung to the first branch from which they believed they could derive fruit in order, from there, to go back to its root, to its principle; and in this inverted order they were likewise forced to substitute the Arithmetic proportion for the harmonic, and the latter for the former, perhaps without even thinking of it. Why, in effect, was the least perfect preferred to the most perfect unless it was that they were constrained to do so by the inversion in question?

Despite all the beautiful discoveries of which we are now in possession, they were still not able to go back to their principle. They contented themselves with having arrived at the proportions it gave. But did they correctly understand the original order? This at least does not appear in the rules of Geometry: there it confounds their first order with their different combinations, that is I say, with simple imitations. This principal order— which is 15 : 5 : 2 for the harmonic proportion and 1 : 3 : 5 for that of the Arithmetic is almost never indicated as the model: on the one side they give 6 : 4 : 3, where the seventeenth and the sixth are lacking, or even 5 : 12 : 10, which is only one combination; on the other they give 1 2 3, 2 3 4, 3 4 5, 4 5 6, when only imitations are everywhere found, in which some consonances are lacking, except in 4, 5, 6, which is only one combination.

The octave is everywhere found substituted for the consonances which should make the proportion complete and regular according to its first order, which adds still more to Music's rights.

I do not know whether these last remarks have some weight in Geometry. Might it nevertheless have happened that, not having been scrupulous enough about the greatest perfection of one proportion, truths even more luminous than those which have been drawn from it were allowed to escape? Everything has not been discovered and if something remains to be learned after having scrutinized Nature in everything that can be glimpsed in it, we have resources other than the conclusions which can be drawn from the principle that today presents itself for the first time, and doubtless for the last, since in everything that strikes our senses the certainty of the relations can be given only by the ear, which has rights only in Music.

How does it happen that in Music one proportion observed in its great regularity enchants,* whereas one gets only mediocre pleasure from one of its combinations, with which almost all of Music's beats are filled? Geometry depends in this on Physics, since the difference of the effects are occasioned only by that of the relations.

It matters little to me to know that what pleases me in an Art arises from such a disposition between its parts: feeling suffices for me both to put it to work and to judge it. Why, then, does my mind find itself enlightened by the numerical relationships analogous to the greater or lesser pleasure I experience from them? What need do I have to know, for example, that such an interval that is as 4 to 5, is for me a *Third from do to mi*? And this suffices for me. Also, the Musician, who has only his ear for a guide, can he understand anything in a calculation which seems, on the contrary, to offer him only contradictions?

A third is as 4 to 5, or as 5 to 6. An Octave is as 1 to 2. So swears whoever is led only by feeling.

Nevertheless, Nature is not explained in vain! Would it be a sheer waste for it to favor us with an Art in which the infallibility of the ear's judgment makes us feel both the exactitude and the perfection of relationships and the greater or lesser degree of perfection among them, while every re-

---

* Pages 33 and 49.[62]

flection must be banished from it if one wants fully to enjoy its effect? Whereas in all the objects which strike our other senses, reflection is necessary in order to make up for their lack concerning the certainty of these relations and concerning the greater or lesser degree of perfection among them.

On the one hand, Sense is our unique arbiter; on the other hand, it can do nothing without the help of the mind's operations. But on what do we base these operations if sense does not at all alert one to the greater or lesser perfection among the relationships it perceives? How many researches has man made use of in order to attain this knowledge? If by his great perspicacity he has finally cleared the hurdle which opposed his passage, the glory which comes to him should not thereby prevent him from admiring the Author who has warned him by presenting him with an Art whose pleasantness might engage him to take his amusement from it to the point of probing it sufficiently in order to discover in it the principle that could guide him with certainty in his researches, by making him pass thus from the pleasant to the useful.

I have gone on at length in digressions about an Art from which one can still derive enlightenment merely in order to put the Editors of the *Encyclopedic Dictionary* onto the path of the truths which they are ignorant of, neglect, or dissimulate, in order to substitute for them errors, criticisms without solution, even opinions: as if authority, still less than opinion, had some rights in the Sciences, especially in Music, where it is a matter merely of being the Interpreter of Nature, as I have tried to be throughout. There is room to hope that they will pay more attention to it in the future.[63]

Continuation of the Errors on Music in the Encyclopedia

Rameau

ENHARMONIC [*Enharmonique*], p. 688.

Here shine M. Rousseau's erudition and the understanding he has derived from it so as to enlighten us concerning the *Enharmonic Genre*. Some Greek words on the subject of this genre are offered up to his eyes as so many torches with which he has allowed himself to be dazzled and with which he apparently believed he might likewise dazzle us.

If the marvelous effects of the Music of the Greeks have been able to impose upon us, their theory has wrongly been included among them since it sins equally both against the ear and against reason. The proof of this is in the false ratios they gave throughout for *Thirds* and *Sixths*, which they consequently treated as dissonances for nearly a century.

Could it possibly be that, during the time when those marvelous effects recounted by the Greeks were experienced, they were insensitive to the consonance of the *Thirds* and *Sixths* contained in the harmony, which is alone capable of producing those effects, since it alone is capable of penetrating to the soul?

Even if those effects had been due only to the melody, which is hardly probable,* could a song exist without *Thirds* or *Sixths*, would it not be unbearable however little these consonances might be corrupted? Did the Greeks not hear these very consonances in all their exactitude between the *do*, the *mi*, and the *sol* of the Trumpet, consonances on which every tune belonging to this instrument alone turn? Did they consult the ear, or not, in order to tune their Lyres, wherein, according to the order of their Tetrachords, a *Minor Third* was found from *si* to *re*, a *Major* one from *do* to *mi*, and *Sixths* of the same genre thanks to their octaves? A corrupted consonance is imperceptible to the ear, so that, even when sounding it without thinking of it, one can only sound it justly. Nature guides the ear, the ear guides the voice, thus no ratio given to an interval will ever bring the ear to lend itself to it if it is not natural.

---

*This question is treated in the preceding *Errors on Music*, issued in 1755, p. 44 and following.[1]

How many reasons there are against Ancients' procedure in their system of Music! How is it that none of these reasons have presented themselves to the minds of their admirers, and especially of our Moderns, to whom the invalidity of these systems has been sufficiently known since Zarlino?[2]

It is not understood how the Greeks could have dispensed with consulting the ear in their systems of Music, while it is by its canal alone that the effects of this Art could have been judged. From whence, for example, did the idea of harmony, which derives from ἁρμος, that is, *a proportion of things that is maintained between them*, come to them if not, doubtless, from *the octave* divided by the *Fifth* and the *Fourth*, from which this proportion is formed: 2, 3, 4? And how is it that they were not curious to experience the same proportion between 3, 4, 5, and 4, 5, 6, whereby they would have then experienced the consonance of *Thirds*? Everything speaks against them, whatever reason may be brought forward to palliate their error.

As for the fable which would have had Pythagoras by his own authority determine the ratio of the *Ditonon*, namely, the *major Third*, I do not believe that it has been found in his writings; apparently, not having been able to discover the source of his system, this fable has been ascribed to him, while at the same time supposing an error of judgment in him, as M. Rameau has already noted.*

Are the relations of any objects whatsoever ever known to us before having been able to make a judgment concerning their relation to our senses? Can I claim that two sizes are alike without having seen, touched, or measured them? How did Pythagoras make a judgment concerning the ratios of the *Octave*, of the *Fifth*, and of the *Fourth*, on which his system is founded, if not by hearing these consonances and by then attributing the ratios to the bodies which made him hear them? Why, then, would he not have done as much with the *Ditonon*, if he had not been seduced, doubtless, by the progressions which these first ratios suggested to him?† Progressions in which are found the ratios, good or bad, of every interval belonging to Music, and concerning which his prejudice in favor of his discovery apparently made him ignore every other proof. But this Philosopher's Sectarians, in a word all the Greeks: ought they have held on to this? What happened to their ear in adopting his system?

Nothing is more conclusive concerning the ignorance of the Ancients in Music than the various *Diatonic Systems* which they passed on to us, when there is only one in Nature that is alone suggested to us. What is

---

* *Observations on Our Instinct for Music*, p. 16 and following.[3]
† Ibidem.

more, what do these *Chromatic* and *Enharmonic Systems* which they propose mean when there is only a single interval in each of these genres and when the Diatonic, which presides everywhere, can never be interrupted except by one of these intervals? What am I saying? The Enharmonic cannot even exist by the interval which constitutes it, as I am going to explain.

As regards the *Diatonic-Enharmonic* and *Chromatic-Enharmonic* genres, they constitute exceptions which belong to no system and concerning which it is enough to explain the order, which consists on the one hand in two consecutive *major semitones* and on the other in two *minor* ones.

The *quarter-tone*, of which the Enharmonic genre is formed, can never have a place in harmony, nor in melody either, because it is inappreciable to the ear. And if by *miolant*, by sliding the finger over a string one can pass over it, one can never fix on it, as one can on the *tone* and on the *semitone*, neither can one make out which of the two *semitones* is sounded, the *major* or the *minor*, as long as no feeling of modulation participates in it, since their difference, which is that of this *quarter-tone*, cannot be appreciated.

In addition, it is neither on the quarter-tone of the Greeks nor on that which produces the difference between the two semitones that the Enharmonic genre should be founded, but rather on the two sounds differing by a quarter-tone, namely, for example, *do* and *si-sharp*, which can form only one of them in execution, considering the inappreciability of their difference. Now, as many differences are found between these two sounds as there are columns in the [table of] progressions.* In the first column *si*-sharp exceeds *do* by a *maximum comma*, called *Pythagoras'*; in the second, it does not surpass it by any more than the excess of this *comma* beyond the *major*; in the third, *do* in its turn exceeds *si*-sharp by a *minor comma*; and in the fourth, finally, it exceeds it by the true quarter-tone, formed from the *major* and from the *minor comma*.† Is it then to be believed that the same interval will be the difference between these two sounds everywhere they might immediately succeed one another? Should the twelve *Modes*‡ into which one can pass thanks to the *diminished seventh* chord, the sole chord proper to the genre in question, all be taken from the same column, given

---

* *New System of Music*, etc.; *Harmonic Generation*; and *Demonstration of the Principle of Harmony*.[4]

† Maximum Comma		Major Comma	
18th octave of *do*	*si*-sharp	4th octave of *mi*	*mi* of the first column
524288	531441	80	81
Minor Comma		Quarter-tone	
si-sharp of the 5th column	11th octave of *do*	*si-sharp* of the 4th column	7th octave of *do*
2025	2048	125	128

‡ P. 56 of the preceding *Errors*.[5]

the extreme difference which must be found between their different ratios? A proof can be produced for it, and it will be perceived from it that every difference similar to that from *do* to *si*-sharp will be differently perceived, and that it will even cost the Singer more or less effort according to the greater or lesser relationship between the two *Modes* which succeed them.

If it could be gathered from the *Modes* given by the Greeks that they above all knew about the *Minor Mode*, in which the *Enharmonic* is alone practicable, likewise the *Chromatic*, more or less so; if one could gather, moreover, that they practiced transpositions of *Modes,* and that by this means they possessed the art of passing from one *Mode* to another, one would then still have reason to doubt the regularity of their practice, given the proofs they give elsewhere of their ignorance concerning harmony; but all their different *Modes* produce only the same *Major Mode* derived from their conjoint or disjoint diatonic Tetrachord, and in which the order of sounds is varied simply by having the one begin with *do*, the other with *re*, etc.

The semitone from *si* to *do* by which the Tetrachord I have just cited begins in ascending and without which any absolute close, called in the terms of the art a *perfect cadence*, cannot terminate harmonically on the *Tonic*, namely, on the note by which the Mode begins and concludes and on which it moves. This same semitone, I say, rightly has a place only in the Mode subordinate to this Tetrachord; so that all the other ancient Modes have only apparent conclusions in ascending to this tonic and no real ones, as is sufficiently perceived in the majority of Church Songs.

Everywhere this semitone is lacking in ascending to the Tonic, the feeling of the Mode it constitutes cannot be communicated to the ear, and further, everywhere it is lacking, the Enharmonic cannot be practiced. If, then, the Greeks have given to this last genre the title of *soft*, apparently because they made its softness consist in the meowing, the sole means by which they could have experienced it. And this bad taste: didn't it not long endure among them and was it not soon entirely banished?

How can the partisans of the ancient Modes not have known that different Peoples attributed different expressions to the same Mode? Some would have it that the Phrygian Mode was menacing, furious since lively Tunes were performed in it whose movement could alone arouse courage, anger on loud and noisy instruments. On the contrary, others would have it that this same Mode was sad, lugubrious since they listened to it during Burials on sweet instruments, with slow tunes.* In this way, they both therefore attributed to the same Mode what occurred only by way of the

---

* Chap. V of the IVth Part of *Harmonic Institutions* by Zarlino. What sanctions this citation is also found in Ptolemy.[7]

sound of the instrument and the character of the tunes. The same contrariety of feelings, with regard to some other Modes, can be noted among different Greek Authors, but it was necessary either to pass over similar anecdotes in silence or to remain silent about the explanation of an antiquity which he wished to advocate at any cost whatsoever. M. Rousseau seems to want to follow the same course of action regarding the present question, and if he does not carry it all the way through to the end, it is apparently in order to take the opportunity to prescribe laws for us, according to what will soon appear, or at least in order to suspend judgment until the word GENRE [*Genre*], to which he refers one—which is rather customary for him, having likewise referred to GENRE [*Genre*] on the subject of *Chromatic*,* to PREPARE [*Préparer*] for the preparation of the dissonance,† and to CADENCE [*Cadence*] in order to sanction a false conclusion of his imagination, where he says quite perceptibly *the true principles, reason*.[6] Has he never gone astray? It will be seen, at least here, what should be thought of this. Moreover, if he has already forgotten to recall this last reference, is there not room to fear that he has done as much with the others?

These sorts of references are adroit enough means to elude difficult and sometimes impossible solutions, or at least to leave them in suspense with chimerical ideas, with poor criticisms. That relating to *Cadence*, for example, whose contents here are precisely instances of both types: *thus, by the ordinary rules, the harmony that arises from a series of dissonances always descends, although, according to his true principles and according to reason, it must have in ascending a progression entirely as regular as in descending.* See CADENCE [*Cadence*].‡ An opinion completely demolished in the preceding *Errors*, page 96 and following,[10] but nevertheless capable of seducing the Reader to the point of believing the thing possible, or of holding it in doubt until its verification is found in the article CADENCE [*Cadence*], where he will not refer to it at all, except insofar as he might like to make it correspond to the following rule, which is full of errors§: *the Sixth and the octave ascend on the third and the fifth of the following chord while the fifth and the third remain in order to produce the octave and to prepare the Sixth*—a rule which nevertheless is not at all proclaimed as proof of the article from which one has been referred.

In order to feel all the incongruity of such a rule, it is enough to go about acquainting oneself with the first laws of Nature regarding successions, fundamental as well as harmonic.

---

* *Encyclopedic Dictionary*, letter C, p. 387, 1st column, ¶1.[8]
† Ibid. letter D, p. 1050, 2nd column, ¶3.[9]
‡ Ibid. p. 76, Letter A, 2nd column, ¶1.[11]
§ Ibid. p. 514, Letter C, second column, penultimate paragraph.[12]

One sees in every succession given by the ratios drawn from the principle that the numbers are never exceeded except by one unit, a means which Zarlino himself made use of, as of a fortunate discovery, everywhere it presented itself to him, in order to demonstrate the truth of a succession. On the other hand, the regularity of the accompaniment, the fullness of the harmony, the ear, the style, everything subscribes to it.

Here is an example of the *Irregular Cadence* in question, where the added *Sixth* is then added to the first of the two perfect chords that form this *Cadence*.

$$\left\{\begin{array}{ll} 5\text{th} & 8\text{th} \\ sol & sol \\ 12 & 11 \end{array}\right.$$
$$\left\{\begin{array}{ll} 5\text{th} & 3\text{rd} \\ mi & re \\ 10 & 9 \end{array}\right\}$$
$$\left\{\begin{array}{ll} 8\text{th} & 3\text{rd} \\ do & si \\ 16 & 15 \end{array}\right.$$
$$\left\{\begin{array}{ll} do & sol \\ 2\text{nd} & 3\text{rd} \\ \text{Fundamental Bass} & \end{array}\right.$$

Here the *fifth* remains in order to make the octave, as is said: 12.12, 6.6, or 3.3 — it is all the same, the doubled numbers never representing anything but octaves. But the *third* 10 descends on the *fifth* 9 and the *octave* 16 on the *third* 15. Such is the primitive order from which one cannot deviate without destroying all the pleasantness of a harmonic basis, except as the style of the song engages one to vary the legitimate succession of the consonances, as can be done by giving to the one what falls by right to the other.

When the *Sixth* is added to the perfect chord of *do* in order to form the *Irregular Cadence*, it is an addition of taste which is not at all absolute and which serves merely to inform the ear more decisively about a cadence otherwise effected by the sole fundamental harmony of *do* to *sol*.

It is true that since the *Added Sixth* forms a major dissonance which absolutely should ascend on the *third*, it would be preferable in this case to have the *octave* ascend on the *fifth* rather than to have it descend on the *third*, because, according to the laws of the basis, the *fifth* happens to be doubled before the *third*. But this preference is not absolutely right: 1st. the style of the song can be opposed to it; 2nd. one can do without the *Added Sixth*, and then that *octave* regains all its rights.

As for the *third*, it should necessarily descend on the *fifth* without ever being able to *prepare the Sixth*, as he says.¹³ The *Added Sixth* added to the first chord announces a *Cadence*, or close, which should always terminate on the second chord before the latter can receive the *Added Sixth* anew, according to the pronouncement in the preceding *Errors* after p. 96, to which I have just referred.¹⁴ What is worse, the *Sixth* that is claimed to have been *prepared* by this *third* is a major dissonance which should never be prepared. I would be no more astonished if he had referred to PREPARE [*Préparer*] on the subject of the preparation of the dissonance, since he here proves, without knowing it, the state of ignorance he is in concerning this point.

In order to arouse a further mystery concerning the Enharmonic, M. Rousseau says: *As this genre is rather poorly known, and as our Authors have contented themselves with giving some notions of it, we believe we should explain it here a little more clearly.*¹⁵

As this genre is but little known: did the Greeks themselves know it? Is this authority enough and a sufficient interval of time to conclude that? Ah! How conclude this on the basis of the authority and of the interval of time if they must have appeared diametrically opposed? Shouldn't this opposition be treated before everything? Does it not fall within the competence of Dictionaries first to give the etymology of complex words, above all when they are scientific terms whose parts ordinarily aim at giving the most distinct idea of the thing they express?*

If in this case we find in all the Greek roots that ἐν means *in* and never *out*, how do we make this word *Enharmonic*, which then means *in harmony*, accord with the quarter-tone, which is in fact out of harmony?

It is sufficiently seen by this sole opposition of the authority and of the interval that all the Admirers of ancient Music have applauded it only because they have not understood anything about it. Moreover, what could they have understood by systems always filled with false ratios and by Modes founded on these systems? If ἐν means *out* among the Greeks on this occasion, this is something which no one has yet explained, and even if this meaning had currency among those Greeks, all their reasonings on this subject would not be any less exempt from errors.

---

*Why neglect this etymology after having given that of *Diatonic* and of *Chromatic*? Why refer to GENRE [*Genre*] on the subject of *Enharmonic* and of *Chromatic* without having done as much on that of *Diatonic*? Are they not three different genera? And when the word carries with it a particular genre, is this not the first thing of which we ought to have been informed? Would not an entire volume be needed to explain the different genera of things susceptible to it if one were referred to GENRE [*Genre*] at every word that expresses them? Is it not to abuse the confidence of the Curious, who count on finding at a word what they do not at all find? They must then wait. Well! Patience! At least the word GENRE [*Genre*] will come sooner than that of PREPARE [*Préparer*], to which one has also been referred for what concerns the *Preparation of Dissonances*.

As this genre is rather poorly known, and as our Authors have contented themselves with giving some notions of it. Ah! What notion can one have given of an incomprehensible thing, of what is impracticable in the manner in which it is explained? M. Rameau, for example, does not seem to have claimed to speak of the Enharmonic of the Greeks when he gave laws for it in his *Harmonic Generation*, p. 149, article II.[16] He only employed the term in use, and I do not at all doubt that, like myself, not having consulted the Greek roots, he has always believed that εν means *out*.

We believe, continues the Author, *we should explain it here a little more clearly*. What is this explanation? It is precisely the one that M. Rameau gives, word for word, in the article of his *Harmonic Generation* to which I have just referred and where it is in actuality only a question of the four Modes cited in the explanation—but it should be recalled that I have shown twelve in the preceding *Errors*, p. 56.[17]

How to make these two phrases accord—*and as our Authors have contented themselves with giving some notions of it, we believe we should explain it*, etc.—when the explanation is drawn word for word from an Author who, consequently, has given more than *some notions* of the thing?

Moreover, the notion that Zarlino gives of the Enharmonic of the Greeks is of the clearest nature,* and I believe one can number him among our Authors. One finds there, among other places, a remark which proves very well the state of ignorance in which these Greeks were regarding the origin of Pythagoras' system. The Ancients wanted, he says, the *Diesis*, that is to say here the *quarter-tone*, to be half of the minor semitone.

Aside from the fact that Nature teaches us that it is always from the division of the larger of two intervals that compose another one that the one that belongs to the harmony, and consequently the melody, should be formed, so that the quarter-tone must then have been derived from the division of the major semitone, if it can be derived from it, it is the case that in triple progression, the semitone from *si* to *do*, the sole natural one, which should be major, that very one which Pythagoras named *Leimma*, so as to pass from the major Third to the Fourth, is found to be less than the minor one from *do* to *do*-sharp, by precisely the false ratios that this progression, joined to the double, assigns to them. It is true, as I have already said, that the difference of these two semitones is inappreciable when they are isolated, that is when one wants to sound the one or the other alone, without the help of some feeling of modulation, whereas by sounding them consecutively, the major, the *Leimma*, flows from the source by always presenting itself first, and the minor which comes afterward does not

---

*End of Chap. 16 of the second Part of the *Institutions*, where one finds the *Tetracordo Enharmonico antico* explained.[18]

at all express itself without it costing in one way or another. This proves very well that the Greek Dogmatists in Music have scarcely consulted their ears, since they have been insensitive to the astonishing contrast between their semitones and those which are derived from the resonance of the sounding body and which alone are suggested to us, the major as natural and the minor as being much less so.

Doubtless infatuated by their hypothesis, they held fast to the calculations that follow from them: calculations whose falsity derives from the false idea they have of Thirds and of Sixths. An Idea whose falsity derives from having been related solely to the octave divided by the Fifth and the Fourth. A Fifth whose division they have all rejected, gives, for its part, two equally consonant Thirds. Doesn't one still see Ptolemy applauded, not for having found the minor tone, and consequently the true relations of Thirds and of Sixths, but rather for having found it all with the aid of the same hypothesis?

These are the guarantors with which M. Rousseau authorizes himself today; he prefers shadows to the light which is offered him on every side, and he sends us very far back at the risk of forgetting the references he has already made. Could I have in view anyone else but him when I said, at the end of the preceding *Errors, I have not gone on at length*, etc., *merely in order to put the Editors onto the path*, etc., since he alone is reprehensible?[19]

Moreover, these words, *the Editors*, are not by my own initiative, and I certainly wouldn't have adopted them if I had been able to suppose that those who have no part at all in the *Errors* would have believed themselves included. What is more, M. Rameau, to whom I have communicated these *Errors* and who has even aided me by his counsel, has always recommended to me that I have the greatest regard for the principal Editors of the *Dictionary*. It is the Philosophers, he has told me, whom I esteem infinitely, and whom I dare regard as my friends, having taught one of them during several months everything that he desired to know about Theoretical Music, having furnished him with very numerous Manuscripts on the Theory and the Practice of this Art and having even offered to him to examine those which might be furnished to him by others.[20]

On the Principle of Melody, or Response to the "Errors on Music"
[The Origin of Melody]¹

It seems to me, then, that Melody or song, a pure work of nature, does not owe, either among the learned or among the ignorant, its origin to harmony, a work and production of art, which serves as the evidence for a beautiful song and not its source and whose most noble function is that of setting it off to advantage.

But let us search, if there is a means, for the genuine origin of melody, and let us see whether the idea as M. Rameau has conceived of it accords with the one which the exact observation of the facts furnishes us. As it is necessary for this to go back to the sources, after having warned readers who might want to follow me to arm themselves with patience, I am going to be as prolix as I shall please without scruple.

We are so perfectly ignorant of the natural state of man that we do not even know if he had a sort of cry that belonged to him;² but, on the other hand, we know him as an imitative animal who is not slow to appropriate all the faculties he can derive from the example of the other animals. He will therefore at first imitate the cries of those who surround him, and depending on the various species that inhabit each country, before having languages men might have had different cries from one land to another. Aside from this, their organs were more or less nimble and flexible in accordance with the temperature of climates, and here we already have the origin of national accent even before the formation of the language.

I shall not examine along with Lucretius whether the invention of song is due to the imitation of that of birds, or according to Diodorus to the blowing of the wind in the reeds of the Nile, nor whether the echo itself after having long frightened men might ultimately have contributed to amusing them and instructing them.³ These uncertain conjectures cannot contribute to the perfection of the art and I like only those researches into antiquity from which moderns can derive some fruit. Moreover, it is quite useless to appeal to foreign causes for effects which can be deduced from the nature of the things themselves, and such is that modification of the voice called song, a modification which must naturally arise and be formed with language: for it is quite clear that every language must at its birth make up for less numerous articulations by more modified sounds, at first putting inflections and accents in the place of words and syllables and singing all the more as it spoke less. Let us clarify this with more care.

It is a very judicious observation by M. Rameau that sound differs from noise in that the first is appreciable and the second is not.[4] This does not at all prevent noise from being merely modified sound, as one can convince oneself with a little reflection. It suffices for me to remark here that the sound of the singing voice is the same sound as the speaking voice, but permanent and sustained, whereas in speech it is in a state of continual flux and is never sustained.[5] In fact, nothing is seen in the formation of the glottis that could lead to the idea of two sorts of voices. As soon as someone who is speaking stops on a sustained syllable and prolongs the sound of his voice to the same extent, the speaking voice instantly changes into the singing voice and the sound becomes appreciable. Furthermore, like musical sound, the speaking voice causes sounding bodies to resonate and vibrate and if it causes several strings to resonate at the same time it is because the inflections of the speaking voice make it pass through, almost at the same instant, a great number of continuous sounds to which the various harmonics simultaneously respond. Finally, let one glide one's finger by small intervals along the strings of an Instrument, the bow will draw sounds from it which lack nothing to resemble speech except the articulations of words and the Timbre of the human voice. In this way, with the aid of some pistons similar to those flutes with which children imitate birds, I would not regard it as an impossible undertaking to make the playing of reeds speak if I saw a means of giving them articulations. But let us return to the origin of melody.

If the speaking voice and the singing voice are absolutely of the same nature, the transition from the one to the other, even in speaking, becomes the most conceivable thing in the world and communication will be all the easier as the language is the more accentuated. In this way, since Greek, of all known languages, was without any question that which had the greatest amount of resonance and of accent, it follows that it is also of all of them that in which discourse must be the most similar to song.

From this moment on we are now out of the land of conjectures and we can proceed with a surer step in the search for the truth.

As melody arises with language, it is enriched, so to speak, by the latter's poverty. When one has only a few words to render many ideas, one must necessarily give various meanings to these words, combine them in various manners, give them various acceptations that tone alone distinguishes, employ figurative turns, and as the difficulty of making oneself understood permits saying only interesting things, one says them with fire by the very fact that they are said with difficulty; fervor, accent, gesture, everything animates discourses one must make felt rather than understood. It is thus that eloquence preceded reasoning and that men were Orators and Poets long before being Philosophers.

There was a time, and all the records of antiquity attest it for us, when souls warmed by admiration for the first bits of knowledge and for the men who spread them were, so to speak, fermented with the leaven of the truth. The first moments when the human species opened its eyes to itself were moments of rapture and of enthusiasm which all the discoveries of philosophy have since done no more than use up and absorb. As soon as great men began to obtain that ascendancy that true genius always acquires over the vulgar in the Centuries of Barbarism, their teachings, passing from mouth to mouth, naturally took the turn most favorable to the fire which inspired them, to the memory that caused them to be retained, and were soon in number and in cadence. The natural feeling that dictated number was not slow to metamorphose it into rhythm by the equal recurrences of the beats and the measures; the taste for onomatopoeia and for imitation added to the unequal force that more or less muted vowels and various articulations gave to the sounds of words submitted the grammatical accent to consistent rules; the pathetic accent animated everything since, saying only important and necessary things, nothing was said but with interest and warmth, and finally, from the effort of retaining along with the verses the tone in which they were pronounced, there then emerged the first seed of genuine Music, which is not so much the simple accent of speech as this same accent imitated.

Hardly had the first sparks of this celestial genius set hearts ablaze than assembled peoples saw themselves singing in a sublime tone of the Gods engendered by their heated imagination, of heroes whose loss they deplored, and of the virtues that their nascent vices made necessary. All their feelings were Raptures, the rustic sounds of a flute with three openings sufficed to put them outside of themselves; this boiling ardor being transmitted to the whole person animated their first steps, the gesture of those present responded to the discourse of the Chorus Leader and registered universal applause. Never did the vain noise of harmony disturb those divine concerts. Everything was heroic and grand in those antique festivals. Laws and songs bore the same name in those happy times;[6] they maintained unison in all voices, passed with the same pleasure into all hearts, all adored the first images of virtue and innocence itself gave a sweeter accent to the voice of pleasure. Reader, pardon me this lapse: who could calmly ponder the time of the innocence and happiness of men?

It is in this way that everything which the art of communicating one's thoughts could possess that is most pathetic and most touching developed from the time of the birth of this great art, animated the first accents and gave energy and grace to discourse, even before it had exactness and clarity.

It is at the same time in this way that language became melodious and tuneful, that, instead of being a particular art, music was one of the parts of grammar, and that, finally, whoever did not know its rules was considered as not knowing the language. As a matter of fact, Pythagoras and Philolaus calculated the ratios of consonances and of all the intervals, and this knowledge was necessary for the construction and the use of the instruments that could be accurately tuned only by consonances; but the constitution of the various systems of the Greeks obviously proves that their authors were not guided by any true feeling for harmony, and whoever should dare to sustain the contrary would soon be overwhelmed with proofs and reduced to silence and to disavowal. If the harmonic science of the Greeks was debated about for so long it is because these disputes took place among Literary Men hardly versed in the art who imagined that slight notions of our music ought to suffice to judge that of the Greeks, whereas with a little more knowledge they would have seen that the two arts do not and cannot have any common parts by which they may be exactly compared.

[The Greeks recognized as consonances only those we call perfect consonances; they excluded thirds and sixths from that class.[7] Why so? It is because, since the interval of the minor tone was unknown to them or at least proscribed from practice, and since their consonances were not tempered at all, all their major thirds were too strong by a comma and their minor thirds too weak by as much and, consequently, their major and minor sixths were reciprocally impaired in the same way. Consider now what notions of harmony one could have and what harmonic modes one could establish after banishing thirds and sixths from the class of consonances. If even the consonances which they did accept had been known to them by a true feeling for harmony, they would have likewise felt them in the melody; they would have, so to speak, under-stood them underneath their songs; the tacit consonance of fundamental progressions would have made them give this name to the diatonic progressions they engendered; far from having had fewer consonances than we do, they would have had more of them, and preoccupied by the example of the bass *do sol*, they would have given the name of consonance to the interval from *do* to *re*.]

I ask readers not go grow impatient if I take such a long detour; it is not that I am losing the end in sight, but that I do not see any shorter road to reach it.

The melody which resulted from the progress of which I have just spoken was composed of beats and of tones, that is, of accent, properly speaking, and of rhythm; the accent was the rule for the raising and lowering of the voice, rhythm was that for the meter and the feet. The whole had for its principle both the ease of intonation and the appropriateness of the language and the pleasure of the ear, but above all that other, more lively pleasure which goes all the way to the heart and to which that of the ear serves only as the vehicle.

As the feet and the verses naturally take a certain meter, so tones and intervals naturally take one in the same way; this meter ended up being fixed by Pythagoras' calculations, and from the most common order of these intervals resulted the genre called diatonic. This genre was subdivided into various species none of which could have a harmonic foundation, and if it is found that the tones which resulted from it had ratios approaching those of our own, it is an effect of the nature of Greek prosody and of the ease they must have had in sounding those intervals rather than others. [For between the overly strong modification which must be given to the glottis in order to intone large intervals of consonances continually and the difficulty of distinguishing the intonation in very complicated ratios, the organ took the middle course and naturally hit on a diatonic progression that fatigued the glottis less than the intonation of the consonances and was more easily distinguished than smaller intervals, which did not prevent the smaller intervals from also having their use in the more pathetic genres.[8]]

That rhythm or meter was one of the constituent parts of melody is what is deduced from the notion of this melody alone, which was merely the strong, sustained, distinguished expression of the grammatical and oratorical accent; for this accent consisted no less in the relative duration of sounds than in their degrees, and number was no less essential to it than intonation. If the ancient authors sometimes distinguish melody from rhythm in their writings, which is rare, it is a purely metaphysical distinction as of two qualities of the same subject and not as two really different parts; in addition, Aristotle expressly declares that he understands the melos and the harmony, that is, the intonation and the number, at the same time under the name of melody.[9]

[What, then, is M. Rameau thinking of in giving us the meter, the difference of high and low, of soft and loud as accessories of the melody, whereas all these things are merely the melody itself, and if they were separated from it it would no longer be anything.[10] High or low sounds represent the like accents in discourse, the shorts and the longs the like quantities in the prosody, equal and constant meter the rhythm and feet of verses, the softs and the louds the slack or vehement voice of the orator. Is there a man in the world sufficiently deprived of feelings to say passionate things without ever softening or strengthening his voice?

[It seems that as speech is the art of transmitting ideas, melody would be that of transmitting feelings, and, nevertheless, M. Rameau wants to strip it of everything that serves it for language and that he cannot give to the harmony.

[Let us return for a moment to the meter. What is a series of notes indeterminate as regards their duration? Sounds isolated and deprived of every common effect that one hears separately, the ones apart from the others, and that, although engendered by a harmonic succession, do not offer any ensemble to the ear and await the connection which the meter gives them in order to form a phrase and say something. Let the Musician be presented with a series of notes of indeterminate value, he will make fifty entirely different melodies from them solely by the various ways of scanning them, of combining and varying their movements—an invincible proof that it belongs to the meter to determine every melody. If the diversity of harmony that can be given to them also varies their effects, it is because it actually makes of them yet as many different melodies by giving to the same intervals various locations on in the scale of the mode, which entirely changes the relations of the sounds and the meaning of the Phrases.] But let us return to the historical account.

[Nevertheless, language was perfected; melody, by imposing on it—by imposing on itself—new rules, imperceptibly lost its ancient energy, and the calculation of intervals was ultimately substituted for the subtlety of intonations.[11] It is in this way, for example, that the practice of the enharmonic genre was gradually eliminated; once Theaters had assumed a regular form, one no longer sang in them except in the prescribed modes, and imitative language grew weaker in proportion as the rules of imitation were perfected.

[But this progress was slow in the beginning, and several particular causes which afterward accelerated it finally destroyed all the enchantment of the melody, for nothing has as much accent as the natural language that is merely the animal cry. The developments of reason rendered the artificial language colder and less accented: logic by degrees succeeded eloquence, tranquil reasoning the fire of enthusiasm, and by dint of learning to think one learned not to feel any longer.

[The study of philosophy and the progress of reason, which gave more perfection and a different turn to language, in this way took away from it that lively and passionate tone which had at first made it so tuneful; and it is then that melody, beginning no longer to be so attached to the language in the declamation, imperceptibly assumed a separate existence, and that music became more independent of the words.[12] It is also then that those wonders it had produced when it was only the lively and passionate accent of poetry and that gave it that dominion over the passions which human discourse has since exercised only over reason gradually ceased. Also, ever since Greece was filled with Sects and Philosophers neither famous poets nor musicians were seen there any longer.[13] By cultivating the art of convincing, that of moving was lost. Plato himself in the bosom of wisdom, jealous of Homer and of Euripides, decried the one and was unable to imitate the other.[14]

[Soon servitude added its influence to that of philosophy.[15] Greece in chains lost that celestial fire that warms only free souls and no longer found for the praise of Tyrants that sublime tone with which it had sung of its Heroes. The intermixture of the Romans further weakened what harmony and accent the language retained. Latin, a more muted and less musical language, wronged music in adopting it. The singing employed in the capital imperceptibly corrupted that of the provinces; the Theaters of Rome harmed those of Athens; when Nero was carrying off prizes, Greece had ceased to merit them, and the same melody shared by two languages no longer suited either of them.

[Ultimately the catastrophe occurred that was to destroy all the progress of the human mind.[16] Europe, inundated with Barbarians and enslaved by the unlearned, lost at the same time its sciences, its arts, and the universal instrument of them both, namely, perfected harmonious language. These crude men whom the north had engendered imperceptibly accustomed all ears to the coarseness of their organ. According to Julian's report[17] they croaked, so to speak, instead of speaking, and their harsh voices stripped of accent were noisy without being harmonious. Since all their articulations were otherwise harsh and muted and their vowels hardly sonorous, they could give only a sort of mildness to their singing, which was to stress the sound of the vowels in order to cover up the abundance and harshness of the consonants.

[This noisy singing, joined to the inflexibility of their organs, obliged these newcomers and the subjugated peoples who imitated them to slow down all their sounds in order to make them more striking; tedious articulation and stressed sounds likewise contributed to drive away from melody every feeling for meter and rhythm; as what was always difficult was the transition from one sound to another, there was nothing better to do than to pause at each one as long as possible; song was thus nothing more than a tiresome and slow series of sounds drawn out and shouted at the top of one's lungs, without sweetness, without meter, and without any graces; and if some scholars have from time to time observed that the long and short syllables in Latin song had to be observed, it is at least certain that it was almost no longer a question of feet and of rhythm, nor of any species of measured song.[18]

[Song thus stripped of all melody and consisting uniquely in the strength and duration of sounds must finally have suggested ways of making it still more sonorous with the aid of consonances.[19] For several voices endlessly drawing out in unison sounds of an indefinite duration, chance naturally led them to hit upon certain chords whose diversified vibrations strengthened the noise, while the same vibrations when brought together made it pleasant, and it is in this way that the first practice of Discant and of Counterpoint began.

[It cannot be said how many centuries Musicians twiddled about frivolous questions where the known effect of an unknown cause made them debate for such a long time.[20] The most tireless reader cannot endure the verbiage of eight or ten large chapters in Jehan des Murs in order to learn whether in the interval of the octave divided into two consonances it is the fifth or fourth that must be the lower one; and four hundred years later, one still finds in Bontempi no less tiresome enumerations of all the basses that must carry the sixth instead of the fifth.[21] Nevertheless, harmony imperceptibly took the routes that nature prescribed to it until the invention of the minor mode and of dissonances, in a word, of all the arbitrariness of which it is full and which prejudice alone prevents us from perceiving.

[It is in this way that, melody being nothing and the attention of the musician having been turned entirely toward harmony, everything was directed toward this new object; the Genres, the modes, the scale, everything imperceptibly took on a new appearance; it was harmonic successions that regulated the progression of the parts, this progression having taken the name of melody, it was indeed impossible to mistake its mother's features in this so-called melody; and as our musical system thus became purely harmonic, it is not surprising that melody suffered for it and that music lost for us a great part of the energy that it once had.[22]

[This is how song gradually became an art entirely separated from the language from which it takes its origin, how the feeling for sound and for its harmonics have made it lose that for the oral accent, for numerical quantity, and consequently for meter and rhythm, and how, finally, limited to the purely physical effect of the combination of vibrations, music found itself completely deprived of the moral effects that it used to produce when it was doubly the voice of nature.[23]]

But, when introducing Music into our theaters, it was desired to restore it to its ancient rights and to make an imitative and passionate language of it; it was then that it had to be brought closer to the grammatical language from which it derives its primary being and that, regulating the modulations of the singing voice by the various inflections that the passions give to the speaking voice, melody found, so to speak, a new existence and new powers in its conformities with the oratorical and passionate accent. Then, already subject to the harmonic progressions from which it ought not to have been separated nor from which was it desired to separate it, song, rigorously subjected by the language and doubly hampered by the harmonic system and by the declamation, taking in each country the character of the language from which it derived its form, became as melodious and varied insofar in proportion as that language had more rhythm and accent, and as to those which, having but little of either of them, were, so to speak, only the organ of reason, this same song remained languishing and cold, as is the tone of people who do nothing but reason. In those regions made for wisdom where judgment has more empire than lively passions, melody, having acquired little ascendancy, harmony preserved all its own; and it is there that, physical pleasure supplanting moral pleasure, chords were preferred to song and the noisy sounds of a strong voice or a large chorus to the touching sounds of a tender and passionate voice.

    This entire historical account rests upon facts and furnishes, as one sees, conclusions directly contrary to M. Rameau's System. Let us now endeavor to get back to the essence of things, and in order to avoid every sophism regarding their qualities let us consider them as much as is possible by their nature. Let us give the most pleasant Effect to whatever sound and to the combination of its harmonics; let us imagine a succession of the simplest and most harmonious chords, or the harshest and least natural as possible. What can result from all this but a purely physical sensation, and the flattering or displeasing impression which the combination or the discord of the vibrations of the sounding body will make on the organ? What connection can reason perceive between those more or less concordant vibrations and those emotions of the soul which cast it by turns at the Composer's pleasure into the raptures of the most opposed passions? Beyond the cases which immediately touch upon our preservation, they are never purely physical causes which can move us to this point. You may have beautifully nuanced and combined colors: never will the most learned painter arrange them in a manner to arouse either pity or anger; if he wants to awaken our passions, let him make use of these same colors to represent to us moral effects by the design. Let him paint for us the wily Ulysses carrying off the prize for bravery over the intrepid Ajax;

let him prostrate the unfortunate Priam at the feet of his son's murderer; let him display for us Andromacha's and Hector's farewells, and this Hero's tender caresses for the little Astianax, and the child's fright at seeing the terrible plume flutter upon Hector's head, and the smiles mixed with tears that the present object and the presentiment of the future draw from the most chaste of wives and the most unfortunate of mothers.[24] These are the touching objects with whose help the Painter will arouse in us interest, pity, terror, and all the movements of which the soul is susceptible. Without this the most learned Physicist may well write learned dissertations on the power of the colors, on the modifications of the retina and the disturbances of the optic nerve; he may well convey, by dint of angles and of refractions, his visual rays to the brain: never will he be able to convey the impression all the way to the heart. This is the point where the physicist stops; it is for the painter to do the rest and for the philosopher to explain it.

One is likewise mistaken in Music as soon as one takes for the first cause harmony and sounds, which are actually only the instruments of the melody. Not that the melody in its turn has this cause in itself, but it derives it from the moral effects of which it is the image: namely, the cry of nature, accent, number, measure, and the pathetic and passionate tone which the agitation of the soul gives to the human voice.[25]

This analogy, so clear and so simple, obviously shows that the principle of imitation and of feeling is wholly in the melody; harmony can only concur with it by making the sensations more flattering and consequently more interesting, either by more or less noise or by strengthening the expressiveness of the song, and it is above all in this that the utility of harmony in imitative music consists; for it would be a great error to think that, although it is not the source [of imitative music], it might nonetheless be displaced by it. Far from it: it serves to sustain melody, to determine the modulation with the most exact precision, to render the feeling always present in it, to strengthen or conceal sounds by more or less perceptible intervals, to mark the measure and the rhythm clearly, finally, to make more perceptible that *piano-forte*[26] which is the soul of melody as well as of the discourse it imitates; and it is in this manner that harmony renders in part to music what it takes from its energy by the exclusion of a multitude of irregular intervals. But if the Musician thinks only of his harmony, if he neglects the essential part, which is the song, in order to chase after chords and filling it out, he will produce a great deal of noise and little effect, and his deafening Music will give much more pain to the head than emotion to the heart.

Let us therefore not think that the empire Music has over our passions is ever explained by proportions and numbers. All these explanations are only nonsense and will never produce anything but disbelievers because experience constantly belies them and because one cannot discover in them any type of connection with the nature of man. The Principle and the rules are only the material of the art; a more subtle metaphysics is needed in order to explain its great effects.

Examination of Two Principles Advanced by M. Rameau in His Brochure Entitled: "Errors on Music in the Encyclopedia"

I dashed this Writing onto paper in 1755 when M. Rameau's Brochure appeared, and after having publicly declared that I would no longer respond to my adversaries concerning the great dispute I had to sustain.¹ Content merely with having noted down my observations on M. Rameau's Writing, I did not publish them; and now I assemble them here only because they serve to clarify some Articles in my *Dictionary*, where the form of the Work did not permit me to enter into long discussions.²

Examination of Two Principles Advanced by M. Rameau in His Brochure Entitled: "Errors on Music in the Encyclopedia"

It is always with pleasure that I see new Writings by M. Rameau appear: in whatever way they may be greeted by the public, they are precious for enthusiasts of the Art, and I do myself the honor of being among those who try to profit from them. When this illustrious Artist sets aright my faults he instructs me, he honors me, I owe him thanks; and, as in renouncing quarrels that might trouble my tranquillity I do not at all refrain from those for sheer amusement, I shall on occasion discuss certain points he determines, quite sure of always having done a useful thing if for his part new clarifications can result from them. This is even to share the views of this great Musician, who says that one cannot contest the propositions he advances without providing him with the means for shedding greater light on them,³ from which I conclude that it is good to contest them.

I am, moreover, very far from wanting to defend my Articles in the *Encyclopedia*; nobody, in truth, should be more content with them than M. Rameau, who attacks them, but nobody in the world is more discontented with them than I am. Nevertheless, when one is informed of the time during which they were written, of the amount of time in which I had to do them, and of the incapacity I have always had for taking up again a work once finished, when one learns, moreover, that I did not have the presumption to propose myself for that work, but that it was, so to speak, a task imposed by friendship, one will perhaps read with some indulgence Articles which I hardly had the time to write in the interval that was given me to meditate upon them and which I would not at all have undertaken if I had only consulted my time and my powers.[4]

But this is a justification before the Public, and for another place. Let us return to M. Rameau, whom I have greatly praised and who makes it a crime for me not to have praised him even more. If Readers wish to cast their eyes over the articles he attacks, such as FIGURE [*Chiffrer*], CHORD [*Accord*], ACCOMPANIMENT [*Accompaniment*], etc., if they distinguish the true praise that equity assesses to talents from the vile flattery that adulation lavishes on everyone, finally, if they are informed of the weight that M. Rameau's proceedings with respect to me add to the justice I would like to render him, I hope that, while blaming the faults I might have made in explaining his principles, they will be content, at least, with the homage I have rendered to the Author.[5]

I shall not feign to acknowledge that the writing entitled *Errors on Music* seems to me in fact to swarm with errors and that I see nothing more just about it than the title. But these errors are not at all in M. Rameau's mind, they have their source only in his heart, and when passion no longer blinds him, he will judge better than anyone concerning the proper rules of his Art. I shall therefore not at all limit myself to setting aright a number of small faults which will disappear with his hatred; still less shall I defend those of which he accuses me and several of which cannot in fact be denied. For example, he makes it a crime for me to write so as to be understood; it is a defect which he ascribes to my ignorance and which I am scarcely tempted to justify. I admit with pleasure that for lack of learned things I was reduced to saying only reasonable ones, and I do not envy anyone the profound knowledge that engenders only unintelligible writings.

Once again, it is not at all for my justification that I write, it is for the good of the thing. Let us leave alone all those personal disputes which do nothing for the progress of the Art, or for the instruction of the Public. Those little squabbles must be left to Beginners who want to make a name for themselves at the expense of names already known, and who, for every error they correct, do not fear committing a hundred of them. But what cannot be examined with too much care are the principles of the Art itself, in which the slightest error is a source of aberrations and in which the Artist cannot be mistaken in anything lest all the efforts he takes to perfect the Art put its perfection further off.

I note two of these important principles in the *Errors on Music*. The first, which has guided M. Rameau in all his Writings, and, what is worse, in all his Music, is that Harmony is the unique foundation of the Art, that Melody derives from it, and that all of Music's great effects derive from Harmony alone.

The other principle, newly advanced by M. Rameau and which he reproaches me for not having added to my definition of Accompaniment, is that this *accompaniment represents the sounding body*.[6] I shall examine these two principles separately. Let us begin with the first and more important one, whose demonstrated truth or falsity should serve in some manner as the basis for the whole musical Art.

It must first of all be noted that M. Rameau has all harmony derived from the resonance of the sounding body. And he is certain that every sound is accompanied by three other concomitant or accessory harmonic sounds, which with it form a perfect Major Third Chord. In this sense, Harmony is natural and inseparable from Melody and from Song, whatever sort it may be, since every sound carries with it its Perfect Chord. But, apart from these three harmonic sounds, each principal sound produces many others which are not at all harmonics and do not at all enter into the Perfect Chord. Such are all the aliquots not reducible by their Octaves to some one of these first three. Now, there are an infinity of those aliquots that can elude our senses, but whose resonance is demonstrated by induction and is not impossible to confirm by experiment. The Art has rejected them from Harmony, and it is here that he began to substitute his rules for those of Nature.

Does one want to present the three sounds that make up the perfect chord a peculiar prerogative, since they form among themselves a sort of proportion which it pleased the Ancients to call harmonic, even though it has only a property of calculation? I say that this property is found in the ratios of sounds which are not at all harmonics. If the three sounds represented by the numbers 1 1/3 1/5, which are in harmonic proportion, form a consonant Chord, the three sounds represented by these other numbers, 1/5 1/6 1/7, are likewise in harmonic proportion and form only a discordant Chord. You can divide harmonically a Major Third, a Minor Third, a major tone, a minor tone, etc.; and the sounds given by these divisions will never produce consonant chords. It is, therefore, neither because the sounds that make up the perfect chord resonate with the fundamental sound, nor because they correspond to the aliquots of the entire String, nor because they are in harmonic proportion that they have been exclusively chosen to make up the perfect chord, but only because they offer the simplest ratios in the order of the Intervals. Now, this simplicity of ratios is a rule common to Harmony and to Melody, a rule from which the latter nevertheless departs in certain cases to the point of rendering every harmony impracticable—which proves that Melody has not at all received its Law from it, and is not at all naturally subordinate to it.

I have spoken only of the Major Perfect Chord. What shall be done when one must show the generation of the Minor Mode, of the dissonance, and the rules of Modulation? I instantly lose sight of nature, arbitrariness riddles every part, the pleasure of the ear itself is the work of habit; and by what right does harmony, which cannot give itself a natural foundation, want to be that of the melody, which produced prodigies two thousand years before it was a question of harmony and chords?

That a consonant and regular progression of the Fundamental Bass engenders harmonics that proceed diatonically and that form among themselves a sort of song is known and can be accepted. One could even invert this generation, and as, according to M. Rameau, each sound has not only the power of setting in motion its aliquots above, but also its multiples below, simple song would be able to engender a sort of bass, as the bass engenders a sort of song, and this generation would be as natural as that of the minor mode; but I would like to ask M. Rameau two things: first, if these sounds engendered in this way are what he calls melody; and second, if it is in this way that he finds his own, or if he even thinks that anyone might ever have found it in this way? May we protect our ears from every music in which the Author begins by establishing a beautiful Fundamental Bass, and, in order to lead us learnedly from dissonance to dissonance, changes key or mode on each note, constantly heaps up chords upon chords without dreaming of the accents of a simple, natural, and passionate melody, which does not derive its expressiveness from the progressions of the bass, but from the inflections that feeling gives to the voice!

No, it is doubtless not this that M. Rameau wants to be done, still less what he does himself. He means simply that harmony guides the artist, without him thinking of it in the invention of his melody, and that every time he composes a beautiful song he follows one regular harmony—which must be true, by the connection the art has established between these two parts, in every country in which harmony has directed the progression of sounds, the rules of Song, and musical accent; for what is called song then takes on a beauty of convention which is not at all absolute, but relative to the harmonic system, and what is more highly esteemed than the song in this system.[7]

But if the lengthy routine of our harmonic successions guides the trained man and the professional Composer, what was the guide of those ignorant people who have never heard harmony in those songs which nature dictated long before the invention of the art? Did they therefore have a feeling for harmony anterior to experience, and if someone made them hear the Fundamental Bass of the tune they had composed, is it to be thought that any of them would recognize his guide there, and that he would find the slightest relation between that bass and that tune?

I shall say more. Judging the melody of the Greeks by the three or four tunes which are left to us, just as it is impossible to adapt a good Fundamental Bass beneath these tunes, so too is it impossible that the feeling for this Bass, all the more regular as it is more natural, suggested these same tunes to them. Nevertheless, that melody which carried them away was excellent to their ears, and it cannot be doubted that ours would have seemed an unbearable barbarism to theirs. Thus, they judged it based on another principle than ours.

The Greeks recognized as consonances only those that we call perfect consonances; they rejected from among that class thirds and sixths. Why so? It is because, since the interval of the minor tone was unknown to them or at least proscribed from practice, and since their consonances were not tempered at all, all their major thirds were too strong by a comma and their minor thirds too weak by as much, and consequently their major and minor sixths were impaired in the same way. Consider now what notions of harmony one could have and what harmonic modes one could establish by banishing thirds and sixths from among the class of consonances! If even the consonances which they did accept were known to them by a true feeling for harmony, they must have likewise felt them in the melody, they would have, so to speak, understood them underneath their songs; the tacit consonance of fundamental progressions made them give this name to the diatonic progressions they engendered; far from having had fewer consonances than we do, they would have had more of them, and preoccupied, for example, by the tacit bass *do sol*, they would have given the name of consonance to the melodious interval from *do* to *re*.

"Although the author of a song," says M. Rameau, "may not know the fundamental sounds from which this song derives, it is no less taken from this unique source of all our productions in Music."[8] This doctrine is doubtless extremely learned, for it is impossible for me to understand it. Let us try, if it is possible, to explain this.

The majority of men who do not know Music and who have not learned how fine it is to produce great noise, take all their songs in the *Middle* of their vocal range, and its Diapason does not ordinarily extend to being able to intone the Fundamental Bass, even if they knew it. Thus, not only does this ignorant person who composes a tune have no notion of the Fundamental Bass of this tune, he is even equally far from being able either to perform this Fundamental Bass himself or to recognize it when someone else performs it. But this Fundamental Bass which has suggested his song to him, and which is neither in his understanding, nor in his organ, nor in his memory: where is it then?

M. Rameau claims that an ignorant person will naturally intone the most perceptible fundamental sounds, as, for example, in the key of *do* a *sol* under a *re* and a *do* under a *mi*. Since he says he has done the experiment, I do not want to reject his authority in this matter.[9] But what subjects has he taken for this test? People who, without knowing music, have heard Harmony and Chords a hundred times, so that the impression of the harmonic intervals and the progression corresponding to the Parts in the most frequent passages had stayed in their ears, and were transmitted to their voices without their even suspecting it. The playing of the gutscrapers in Guinguettes[10] alone suffices to train the people in the environs of Paris in the intonation of thirds and of fifths. I have done the same experiments on more rustic men whose ear was accurate; they have never produced anything similar for me. They heard the Bass only when I whistled it for them; often they still could not grasp it. They never perceived the slightest relationship between two different sounds heard at the same time: this ensemble even always displeased them, however exact the interval may have been; their ear was disturbed by a third as ours is by a dissonance, and I can affirm that there was not one of them for whom the deceptive cadence couldn't terminate a tune entirely as well as the perfect cadence, if unison was likewise found in it.

Although the principle of harmony might be natural, since it offers itself to the sense only under the appearance of unison, the feeling that develops it is acquired and artificial, as are the majority of those attributed to nature, and it is especially in this part of music that there is, as M. d'Alembert says quite nicely, an art of listening as there is an art of performing.[11] I admit that these observations, although just, make the experiments difficult in Paris, for ears are hardly less prejudiced than minds there: but it is an inconvenience inseparable from great cities that nature must be sought far off.[12]

Another example from which M. Rameau *expects everything*, and which seems to me to prove nothing, is the interval of the two notes *do fa*-sharp, under which, by applying different basses that show different harmonic transitions, he claims to demonstrate by the various affections which arise from them that the strength of these affections depends on the harmony and not on the song.[13] How has M. Rameau allowed himself to be misled by his eyes, by his prejudices, to the point of taking all these various transitions for the same song, since it is the same apparent interval, without considering that an interval must not be supposed to be the same, and especially in melody, except to the extent it has the same relation to the mode—which does not occur in any of the transitions he cites? They are the same keys on the keyboard, surely, and this is what has deceived M. Rameau, but they are in reality so many different melodies, for not only do they all present themselves to the ear under various ideas, but even their precise intervals almost all differ from one another. Who is the Musician who will say that a tritone and a false fifth, a diminished seventh and a major sixth, a minor third and a augmented second form the same melody because the intervals which they produce are done in the same way on the keyboard? As if the ear did not always perceive the intervals according to their justness in the mode, and did not correct the errors of temperament regarding the relations of the modulation! Although the Bass sometimes determines the change of key with greater promptitude and energy, these changes would nevertheless not fail to be made without it, and I have never claimed that accompaniment was useless to melody, but only that it should be subordinated to it. Even were all these transitions from *do* to *fa*-sharp exactly the same interval, they would not any the less be so many different song employed in their different places, being taken or supposed on different pitches of the mode, and made up of greater or lesser degrees. Their variety therefore does not come from the harmony, but only from the modulation, which incontestably belongs to the melody.

We are speaking here only of two notes of an indeterminate duration; but two notes of an indeterminate duration are not enough to make up a song, since they indicate neither the mode nor the phrasing, neither the beginning nor the end. Who can imagine a song deprived of all that? What is M. Rameau thinking of by giving us the meter, the difference of high and low, of soft and loud, of fast and slow as accessories of the melody,[14] whereas all these things are merely the melody itself; and if they were separated from it, it would no longer exist. Melody is a language like speech; every song which says nothing is nothing, and this alone can depend on the harmony. High or low sounds represent the like accents in discourse, the shorts and the longs the like quantities in the prosody; equal and constant meter the rhythm and the feet of verses; the softs and the louds the slack[15] or vehement voice of the orator. Is there a man in the world sufficiently cold, sufficiently deprived of feeling to say or read passionate things without ever softening or reinforcing his voice?[16] In order to compare melody to harmony M. Rameau begins by stripping the first of everything that, belonging to it, cannot be suited to the other. He does not consider melody as a song, but as a filling out; he says that this filling out arises from harmony, and he is right.

What is a series of sounds that are indeterminate as regards their duration? Sounds isolated and deprived of every shared effect, which one hears, which one grasps separately, the ones apart from the others, and which, although engendered by a harmonic succession, do not offer any ensemble to the ear and await the connection which meter gives them in order to form a phrase and say something. Let the musician be presented with a series of notes of indeterminate value, he will make fifty entirely different melodies from them solely by the various ways of scanning them, of combining and varying their movements—an invincible proof that it belongs to the meter to determine every melody. If the diversity of harmony that can be given to these series also varies their effects, it is because it actually makes of it yet as many different melodies by giving differing locations in the scale of the mode to the same intervals, which, as I have already said, entirely changes the relations of the sounds, and the meaning of the phrases.

The reason why the ancients had no purely instrumental Music at all was that they did not have the idea of a song without meter, nor of any meter other than that of Poetry. And the reason why Verses were always sung and never prose was that prose possessed only the part of song that depends on intonation, whereas verses also possessed the other constituent part of melody, namely rhythm.

No one, not even M. Rameau, has ever divided Music into melody, harmony, and meter, but rather into harmony and melody, after which they are both considered in terms of sounds and of beats.

M. Rameau claims that all the charm, all the energy of music is in the harmony, that melody is only a subordinate part and gives to the ear only a slight and sterile pleasure. He himself must be heard reasoning. His proofs would lose too much by being rendered by someone other than himself.

Every musical Chorus, he says, *which is slow and whose harmonic succession is good always pleases without the aid of any design, or of a melody which might affect on its own, and this pleasure is entirely different from that which is usually experienced from a pleasant Song or a simply lively and gay one.* (This parallel of a slow song and a lively and gay tune seems to me quite singular.) *The former relates directly to the soul* (note carefully that it is the large Chorus in four parts), *the latter does not pass beyond the ear canal.* (This is the song, according to M. Rameau.) *I again recur to "L'Amour triomphe," already cited more than once:* (This is true.) *Let the pleasure experienced from it be compared to that which a tune, whether vocal or instrumental, will produce.*[17] I grant this. Let me be left the choice of the voice and the tune, without restricting myself to a lively and gay movement, for this is not just, and let M. Rameau for his part come with his chorus *L'Amour triomphe* and all that terrible apparatus of instruments and voices; he may well choose judges who are affected only as a result of noise and who are more touched by a drum than by a nightingale, in the end they will be men. I desire no more in order to make them feel that the sounds most capable of affecting the soul are not at all those of a musical chorus.

Harmony is a purely physical cause; the impression it produces remains of the same order; chords can only impart to the nerves a passing and sterile disturbance; they would produce vapors rather than passions.[18] The pleasure one takes in hearing a slow Chorus deprived of melody is one purely of sensation and would soon turn to boredom if care were not taken to make this chorus quite short, especially when the voices are always placed in their *Middle* range. But if the voices are slack and low, they can affect a soul without the help of the harmony, for a slack and slow voice is a natural expression of sadness; a chorus in unison could produce the same effect.

The most beautiful chords, like the most beautiful colors, can convey to the senses a pleasant sensation and nothing more. But the accents of the voice pass all the way to the soul; for they are the natural expression of the passions, and by depicting them they arouse them. It is by means of them that music becomes oratorical, eloquent, imitative, they form its language; it is by means of them that it depicts objects to the imagination, that it conveys feelings to the heart. Melody is in music what design is in Painting, harmony produces merely the effect of colors. It is by means of the song, not by means of the chords, that sounds have expression, fire, life; it is the song alone that gives them the moral effects that produce all of Music's energy. In a word, the physical part alone of the art is reduced to very little and harmony does not pass beyond that.

If there are some movements of the soul which seem to be aroused by harmony alone, as the ardor of soldiers by military instruments, it is because every great noise, every striking noise can be good for that, since it is a merely question of a certain agitation that is transmitted from the ear to the brain, and since the imagination, thus disturbed, does the rest. Still, this effect depends less on the harmony than on the Rhythm or on the meter, which is one of the constituent parts of melody, as I have already shown above.

I shall not at all follow M. Rameau into the examples he draws from his works to illustrate his principle. I admit that it is not difficult for him to show by this means the inferiority of melody; but I have been speaking about Music and not about his Music. Without desiring to contradict the praise he gives himself, I cannot be of his opinion on this or that piece, and all these particular judgments, for or against, are of no great advantage for the progress of the art.

After having established, as has been seen, the fact that harmony engenders melody, which is true in relation to us but very false generally speaking, M. Rameau concludes his dissertation in these terms: *Thus, all Music being included in the harmony, it must be concluded from this that it is only to this harmony alone that any science whatever must be compared*, p. 64.[19] I admit that I do not see anything to respond to this marvelous conclusion.

The second principle advanced by M. Rameau, and of which it remains for me to speak, is that *harmony represents the sounding body*. He reproaches me for not having added this idea in the definition of accompaniment. It has to be believed that if I had added it he would have reproached me even more, or at least with more reason. It is not without repugnance that I enter into the examination of this addition which he demands, for, although the principle I just examined is in itself no more true than this one, it ought very much to be distinguished from it, in that, if it is an error, it is at least the error of a great Musician who goes astray due to science. But here I see only words devoid of meaning, and I cannot even suppose good faith in the author who dares to present them to the public as a principle of the art he professes.

Harmony represents the sounding body! This word *sounding body* has a certain scientific splendor, it proclaims a Physicist in the person who employs it; but what does it mean in music? The musician does not consider the sounding body in itself, he considers it only in action. Now, what is the sounding body in action? It is sound; harmony thus represents sound. But harmony accompanies sound. The sound does not therefore need to be represented, since it is there. If this gibberish seems laughable it is surely not my fault.

But it is perhaps not the melodious sound that harmony represents, it is the collection of harmonic sounds which accompany it; but these sounds are merely the harmony itself. The harmony therefore represents the harmony, and the accompaniment the accompaniment.

If the harmony represents neither the melodious sound nor its harmonics, what then does it represent? The fundamental sound and its harmonics, in which the melodious sound is contained. The fundamental sound and its harmonics are, then, what M. Rameau calls the sounding body. Perhaps. But let us see.

If the harmony should represent the sounding body, the Bass should always contain only the fundamental sounds, for, on each inversion, the sounding body does not at all produce the inverted harmony of the fundamental sound on the Bass, but the direct harmony of the inverted sound which is in the Bass and which, in the sounding body, thus becomes fundamental. Let M. Rameau take the trouble to respond to this objection alone, but let him respond clearly, and I grant him the victory in the contest.

Never does the fundamental sound or its harmonics, taken for the sounding body, produce the Minor Chord. Never do they produce the dissonance. I am speaking according to M. Rameau's system. The harmony and the accompaniment are full of all this, principally in practice; thus, the harmony and the accompaniment cannot represent the sounding body.

There must be an inconceivable difference between this Author's manner of reasoning and my own; for here is what the first consequences that his principle, admitted for the sake of argument, suggest to me.

If the accompaniment represents the sounding body, it should produce only the sounds produced by the sounding body. Now, these sounds form only perfect chords. Why, then, sprinkle the accompaniment with dissonances?

According to M. Rameau, the concomitant sounds produced by the sounding body are limited to two: namely, the major third and the fifth. If the accompaniment represents the sounding body, it must then be simplified.

The instrument with which one accompanies is itself a sounding body whose every sound is always accompanied by its natural harmonics. If, then, the accompaniment represents the sounding body, only unisons should be struck, for the harmonics of harmonics are not at all found in the sounding body.[20] In truth, if this principle which I contest had occurred to me, and if I had found it to be solid, I would have used it against M. Rameau's system and I would have believed it overturned.

But let us, if possible, give precision to his ideas. We shall better be able to sense their correctness or falseness.

In order to understand his principle, it must be understood that the sounding body is represented by the bass and its accompaniment in such a way that the Fundamental Bass represents the generator sound and the accompaniment its harmonic products. Now, as the harmonic sounds are produced by the Fundamental Bass, the Fundamental Bass in its turn is produced with the assistance of its harmonic sounds; this is not a principle of a system, it is a fact of experience, known in Italy for a long time.[21]

It is therefore now only a matter of seeing what conditions are required in the accompaniment to represent exactly the harmonic products of the sounding body and to furnish with their assistance the Fundamental Bass that suits it.

It is evident that the first and the most essential of these conditions is to produce a unique fundamental sound on each chord; for, if you produce two fundamental sounds, you represent two sounding bodies instead of one, and you have a doubled harmony, as has already been observed by M. Serre.[22]

Now, the perfect major third chord is the sole one that gives only one fundamental sound; every other chord multiplies it. This requires no demonstration for any theorist, and I shall content myself with one very simple example which, without figuration or notation, may be understood by those readers least versed in music, provided they are familiar with the terms.

In the experiment of which I have just spoken, one finds that the major third produces the Octave of the lower sound for its fundamental, and that the minor third produces the major tenth, that is, that this Major Third *do mi* will give you the octave of *do* for its fundamental sound and that this minor third *mi sol* will also give you the same *do* for its fundamental sound. Thus, this entire chord *do mi sol* gives you only one fundamental sound; for the fifth *do sol* which gives the unison of its lower note can be supposed to give the octave, or rather in lowering this *sol* to its Octave, the chord is a unity with the utmost rigor; for the fundamental sound of the major sixth *sol mi* is on the fifth of the lower one and the fundamental sound of the fourth *sol do* is also on the fifth of the lower one. In this manner, the harmony is well-ordered and exactly represents the sounding body; but instead of harmonically dividing the fifth by placing the major third in the bass and the minor in the treble, let us transpose this order by dividing it arithmetically; we shall have this perfect minor third chord, *do mi*-flat *sol*, and taking other notes for more convenience, this chord is similar to *la do mi*.

Then one discovers the tenth *fa* as fundamental sound of the minor-third *la do*, and the octave *do* for fundamental sound of the Major Third *do mi*. One could not, then, strike this complete chord without producing two fundamental sounds at the same time. Still worse, as neither of these two fundamental sounds is the true basis of the chord and of the mode, we need a third bass *la* which produces this basis. Then it is manifest that the accompaniment cannot represent the sounding body except by taking the notes two by two, in which case one will have *la* as an engendered Bass under the fifth *la mi*, *fa* under the minor third *la do*, and *do* under the major third *do mi*. As soon as you add a third sound, therefore, you make a perfect major chord or you have two fundamental sounds, and consequently the representation of the sounding body will disappear.

What I say here of the perfect minor chord should for all the more reason be understood of every complete dissonant chord, in which the fundamental sounds are multiplied by the complexity of the chord, and it should not be forgotten that all this is deduced simply from M. Rameau's very principle, adopted for the sake of argument. If the accompaniment ought to represent the sounding body, how circumspect must one therefore be in the choice of the sounds and of the dissonances, although regular and well resolved! This is the first conclusion that must be drawn form this supposedly true principle. Reason, the ear, experience, the practice of all peoples who have the greatest precision and sensitivity in their organ would all suggest this conclusion to M. Rameau. He nevertheless draws an entirely opposed one; and, in order to establish it, he lays claim to the rights of nature, words which as an artist he ought never pronounce.

He makes it a great crime for me to have said that one should sometimes omit sounds in the accompaniment, and a still greater one to have counted the fifth among these sounds which must be omitted upon occasion. *The fifth*, he says, *which is the mainstay of harmony and which should consequently be preferred everywhere it can be employed.*[23] Quite so, let it be preferred when it should be employed; but this does not prove that it should always be so. On the contrary, it is precisely because it is too harmonious and sonorous that it must often be omitted, especially in chords too remote from the principal pitches, for fear lest the idea of the key go astray and be extinguished, for fear lest the uncertain ear divide its attention between the two notes that form the fifth, or lest it give it precisely to that which is foreign to the melody and to which one ought to listen to least. The Ellipsis has no less use in harmony than in grammar; it is not always a matter of saying everything, but of making oneself sufficiently understood. He who wanted to play the fifth in every chord into which it entered in a written accompaniment would produce an unbearable harmony, and M. Rameau himself is quite wary of using it in this way.

To return to the Harpsichord, I call out to every man for whom a deep-rooted habit has not corrupted his organs: let him listen, if he can, to the strange and barbarous accompaniment prescribed by M. Rameau, let him compare it to the simple and harmonious accompaniment of the Italians, and if he refuses to judge by reason, let him at least judge between theirs and his by feeling. How could a man of taste ever imagine that he must fill out every chord in order to represent the sounding body, that he must employ every dissonance that can be employed? How was he able to make it a crime for Corelli not to have figured all those that might be able to enter into his accompaniment?[24] How is it that the pen did not fall from his hands at every mistake he blamed this great harmonist for having made? How is it that he did not sense that confusion never produces any pleasing product, that an overly burdened harmony is the death of all expression, and that it is for this reason that all the music which has issued from his school is merely noise without effect? How is it that he does not reproach himself for having sprinkled French basses with those forests of figures which hurt the eyes simply by looking at them? How is it that the power of the beautiful Songs that are sometimes found in his Music has not disarmed his paternal hand when he ruins them on his Harpsichord?

His system seems to me hardly better founded in the theoretical principles than in the practical ones. His whole harmonic generation is limited to progressions of perfect major chords; nothing more is comprehended in it as soon as it is a question of the minor mode and of dissonance, and the virtues of Pythagoras' numbers are no less murky than the physical properties he claims to give to simple relationships.

M. Rameau says that the resonance of a sounding string puts into motion another sounding string triple or quadruple the length of the first, and makes it vibrate perceptibly in its totality even though it does not at all resonate. Here is the fact upon which he establishes the calculations he uses for the production of the dissonance and of the minor mode. Let us examine it.

That a vibrating string, divided into its aliquots, causes each of them to vibrate and resonate in such a way that the strongest vibrations of the string produce weaker ones in its parts, this phenomenon is known and has nothing contradictory about it. But that an aliquot might move its entirety by producing in it slower, and consequently larger, vibrations*; that any force whatsoever produces another triple and another quintuple itself is what observation belies and what reason cannot admit. If M. Rameau's experiment is true, M. Sauveur's must necessarily be false. For, if a resonating string causes its triple and its quintuple to vibrate, if follows that M. Sauveur's knots could not exist, that by the resonance of a part the entire string could not vibrate, that the white and red papers should likewise fall, and that the testimony of the whole academy must be rejected concerning this fact.[25]

Let M. Rameau take the trouble to explain to us what a sounding string is that vibrates and does not resonate. This is certainly a new physics. It is therefore no longer the vibrations of sounding bodies that produces sound, and we simply have to seek another cause.

Moreover, I do not at all accuse M. Rameau here of bad faith; I even conjecture how he may have deceived himself. First, in a fine and delicate experiment, a man of systems often sees what he has a great desire to see. Furthermore, since the large string was divided into parts equal to one another and to the small one, he saw all its parts vibrate at the same time, and

---

* What makes the vibrations slower is either more material to move in the string or its greater movement away from the line of rest.

he took this for the vibrating of the entire string. He did not hear a sound either; this is still quite natural. Instead of the sound of the entire string he expected, he had only the unison of the smallest part and he did not discern it. The important fact about which he had to assure himself, and on which all the rest depended, was that immobile knots did not at all exist, and so while he heard only the sound of a part he saw the string vibrate in its totality—which is false.

Even if this experiment were true, the origins M. Rameau deduces for it would be no more real; for harmony does not consist in the relationships of vibrations, but in the concourse of the sounds that result from them. And if these sounds are nothing, how would all the proportions in the world give them an existence they do not have?

It is time for me to stop. This is the point up to which the examination of M. Rameau's *Errors* can matter to the harmonic science. The remainder interests neither readers nor myself. Armed with the right of a just defense, I have contested two principles of this Author, of which the first produces all the bad music with which his school has inundated the public for a number of years; the other the bad accompaniment which is learned by his method. I have shown that his harmonic system is insufficient, badly proved, founded on a false experiment. I believed these researches interesting; I have given my reasons, M. Rameau has given or will give his; the Public will judge us. If I end this writing so soon, it is not that I lack material; but I have said enough for the utility of the art and for the honor of the truth, I do not believe I have to defend my own against M. Rameau's insults. As long as he attacks me as an artist, I will make it a duty for myself to respond to him and willingly discuss with him the contested points. As soon as the man shows himself and attacks me personally, I no longer have anything to say to him and I see in him merely the musician.

Detached Fragments

I

In renouncing quarrels that might trouble my tranquillity, I do not at all wish to refrain from those for sheer amusement, such as the discussions I can have with M. Rameau about his art. As long as it is only a question of Music and of songs, I believe I can sufficiently count on myself not to refrain from disputes where I shall not be more proud to be right than ashamed to be wrong. I owe to the reputation of this musician the honor of a response.

2

What, then, are M. Rameau's strange pretensions, and what honors can satisfy him, if he is not content with those which have been given him, as though out of envy, in the *Encyclopedia*? Is he unaware that his art holds but one of the lowest ranks, and that he himself holds the first in his art only by the suspicion which his proceedings with respect to me have aroused in me contrary to my own opinion, by M. d'Alembert's extreme deference and my own for the Nation's taste, finally, because the *Encyclopedia* is produced in France.[26] Let M. Rameau know that everywhere else his very name would be forgotten, and that the work would not be any less for it.

3

I have used M. Rameau's system throughout, I have named him with praise throughout. I have made objections, doubtless; the good of the art required it. Does M. Rameau wish to be thought infallible? Must he be adopted wholesale, including his errors? If I raised them, it was with all the consideration one could have for the greater man, and about which M. Rameau has rendered me more justice than to himself, if he expects them from my part.

4

But if he does not do honor to my talent, on the other hand he has done so to my knowledge more than I merit by supposing that I am in a position to insert French vocals into an Italian instrumental part.[27] This alliance requires more practice in harmony than I had, and I am far from being as skillful in this regard as M. Rameau.

5

If so as to give a learned air to his work it is enough to write unintelligible things, M. Rameau is doubtless right, and nothing is more learned than his writings. But it always seems funny to hear it said to the public: You understand everything this man says to you because he is merely an ignoramus, but I who am truly learned, and who teach you [. . .]

6

It hardly seems that song is natural to man. Savage man never sings; mutes do not sing, they form unarticulated and hideous sounds, and which need wrests from them. Children scream, cry, and do not at all sing. The first expressions of nature in them are only those of pain, and they learn to sing as they learn to speak: after our example. Melodious and appreciable song is only a possible and artificial imitation of the accents of the speaking voice; one cries out or one complains without singing, but one sings by imitating cries and complaints. And as of all imitations the most interesting is that of the human passions, of all the ways of imitating the most pleasant is singing.[28]

7

It is as far from counterpoint to composition as it is from grammar to eloquence.[29]

8

But on whom does it depend but M. Rameau to end this dispute once and for all before the eyes of all Paris, let him climb before a tribunal, put his learned hands to a keyboard, lavish all the secrets of his art in a full playing, make the most divine harmony triumph, but let him omit the meter from it, and let us see what raptures he will arouse among the spectators, to what martial ardor he will lead them, what tenderness those admirable enharmonic transitions and those learned modulations to which he attributes so much power are going to cause! I do not at all doubt that he would make himself admired by the people of the art and my applause, so vile to his eyes to be counted, will not be given to him less good-heartedly. But what I ask of him, these are not marvels of harmony, I expect them from him: I ask him to move his audience, and allow him to choose it. The organ is certainly an admirable instrument, he will have it tuned it to his liking, he will be the master of drawing his playing from it, the musicians will be his fingers, and he will have nothing at all to complain about in the performance. What, then, will be lacking to make it perfect? Perhaps the lack of meter will spoil it? Well, I grant it to him as well, but no melody, and always full playing, that is, at least four parts. Here, I believe, are all the conditions that M. Rameau can ask for to prove authentically the power of harmony, and in spite of all the reasons that favor me, I will not hesitate, after this experiment, to acknowledge my fault publicly.

9

It is useful and appropriate for M. d'Alembert, the editor, to write after my articles, but since it is neither appropriate nor possible for me to write after him, is it less appropriate for M. Rameau to draw an advantage from this situation?[30] But I don't know what name to give to the freedom he takes of censuring M. d'Alembert himself, to whom he assuredly owes everything.

10

If great principles escape M. Rameau, I admit that he attentively and skillfully sets aright small faults, and I shall take care to profit from his corrections.

11

No one is more circumspect about the imputation of ignorance than he who by dint of instructing himself has learned how much all human knowledge can still harbor errors. Thus, when a learned man such as M. Rameau wants to persuade the public that another man is an ignoramus, it is appropriate for him rather to show it than to tell it. The author who is most capable of success may very well hope to produce a good Dictionary, but cannot hope not to make of it a poor article.

12

Of all artists Musicians are those who have the least time for reading, and that appears only too clearly in the manner in which several artists speak of their art.

13

If there is a natural melody derived from harmony, it should be one for all men, since harmony, having its source in nature, is the same in all the countries of the world. But the songs and tunes of each nation have a character that belongs to them, because they all have an imitative melody derived from the accents of the language.

14

He works for his interest, it is quite necessary for him to endeavor to be right.

Essay on the Origin of Languages
In Which Melody and Musical Imitation are Treated

By J. J. Rousseau[1]

[Draft Preface]

The second piece[2] was also at first merely a fragment of the discourse on inequality which I omitted from it as too long and out of place.[3] I took it up again on the occasion of the Errors by M. Rameau on music, a title which—after the two words I've omitted—is perfectly fulfilled by the work that bears it.[4] In the mean time, held back by the absurdity of discoursing upon languages while hardly knowing one of them and, in addition, dissatisfied with this piece, I had resolved to suppress it as unworthy of the public's attention. But an illustrious magistrate[5] who cultivates and protects letters thought more favorably of it than I did. Thus, I am subordinating my judgment to his with pleasure, as can well be believed, and I am attempting to make this one, which I might perhaps not have risked alone, accepted under the aegis of the other two writings.

Essay on the Origin of Languages

CHAPTER I

ON THE VARIOUS MEANS OF COMMUNICATING OUR THOUGHTS[6]

Speech distinguishes man from the animals. Language distinguishes nations from each other; one does not know where a man is from until after he has spoken. Usage and need make each learn the language of his country; but what causes this language to be that of his country and not of another? In order to tell, one has to go back to some reason that pertains to locality, and precedes even morals:[7] speech, being the first social institution, owes its form only to natural causes.

As soon as one man was recognized by another as a sentient, thinking Being and similar to himself,[8] the desire or the need to communicate his feelings and thoughts to him made him seek the means for doing so. These means can be derived only from the senses, the only instruments by which one man may act upon another. Hence the institution of perceptible signs to express thought. The inventors of language did not go through this reasoning, but instinct suggested the conclusion to them.

The general means by which we can act upon the senses of others are limited to two: namely, movement and the voice. Movement is immediate through touch or is mediate through gesture; the first, having an arm's length for its limit, cannot be transmitted at a distance, but the other reaches as far as the line of sight. That leaves only sight and hearing as passive organs of language among dispersed men.

Although the language of gesture and that of the voice are equally natural, nonetheless the first is easier and depends less on conventions: for more objects strike our eyes than our ears and shapes are more varied than sounds; they are also more expressive and say more in less time. Love, it is said, was the inventor of drawing. It might also have invented speech, though less happily. Little contented with speech, love disdains it: it has livelier ways of expressing itself. What things she who traced the shadow of her lover with so much pleasure told him! What sounds could she have used to convey this movement of a stick?[9]

Our gestures signify nothing but our natural uneasiness; it is not about these that I want to speak. Only Europeans gesticulate while speaking. One would think that all the force of their speech was in their arms. They further add to this the force of their lungs, and all this is hardly of any use to them. When a Frenchman has quite strained himself, quite tormented his body to say a lot of words, a Turk removes his pipe from his mouth for a moment, softly speaks two words, and crushes him with one aphorism.

Ever since we learned to gesticulate we have forgotten the art of pantomime, for the same reason that with so many fine grammars we no longer understand the symbols of the Egyptians. What the ancients said most vividly they expressed not by words, but by signs; they did not say it, they showed it.[10]

Open ancient history; you will find it full of those ways of presenting arguments to the eyes, and never did they fail to produce a more assured effect than all the discourses that could have been put in their place. The object, presented before speaking, stirs the imagination, arouses curiosity, holds the mind in suspense and anticipation of what is going to be said. I have noticed that the Italians and Provençals, among whom gesture usually precedes discourse, in this way find the means of making themselves better heeded and even with greater pleasure. But the most energetic language is the one in which the sign has said everything before one speaks.

Tarquin, Thrasybulus lopping off the heads of poppies, Alexander applying his seal to the lips of his favorite, Diogenes walking in front of Zeno: did they not speak better than with words? What circumlocution would have expressed the same ideas as well? Darius, engaged in Scythia with his army, receives a frog, a bird, a mouse, and five arrows from the King of the Scythians; the Herald delivers his gift in silence and departs. This terrible harangue was understood, and Darius was in a hurry to do nothing but to get back to his country as best he could. Substitute a letter for these signs: the more menacing it is the less it frightens; it will be no more than bluster, at which Darius would only have laughed.[11]

When the Levite of Ephraïm wanted to avenge the death of his wife, he did not write to the Tribes of Israel; he divided the body into twelve pieces and he sent them to them. At this horrible sight they ran to arms, crying with one voice: *No, never has anything like this happened in Israel, from the day our fathers left Egypt to this day*! And the tribe of Benjamin was exterminated.[12]* In our day, the affair would have dragged along, been turned over to legal pleadings, to deliberations, perhaps to jests, and the most horrible of crimes would have gone unpunished in the end. King Saul, returning from his plowing, likewise dismembered his plow oxen and used a similar sign to make Israel march to the aid of the town of Jabes.[13] The Prophets of the Jews, the Legislators of the Greeks, by often presenting perceptible objects to the people, spoke to them more effectively through these objects than they could have done through long discourses, and the way in which, according to Athenaeus, the orator Hyperides got the courtesan Phryne acquitted without adducing a single word in her defense, is yet another mute eloquence the effect of which is not rare in all times.[14]

Thus one speaks to the eyes much more effectively than to the ears: no one fails to perceive the truth of Horace's judgment in this regard.[15] The most eloquent discourses are even seen to be those embedded with the most images, and sounds never have more energy than when they produce the effect of colors.

But when it is a question of moving the heart and enflaming the passions, it is an altogether different matter. The successive impression of discourse, striking with repeated blows, gives you a very different emotion from the presence of the object itself, which you have seen completely with a single glance. Assume that someone is in a painful situation which you know perfectly well: you will not easily be moved to cry in seeing the afflicted person, but give him time to tell you everything he feels, and soon you will burst into tears. Only in this way do the scenes of a tragedy have

---

* Only six hundred men were left of it, without any women and children.

their effect.* Pantomime alone, without discourse, will leave you almost unperturbed; discourse without gesture will wrest tears from you. The passions have their gestures, but they also have their accents, and these accents, which make us tremble, these accents, from which we cannot shield our organ, penetrate by it to the bottom of the heart, and in spite of us carry to it the movements that wrest them, and make us feel what we hear. Let us conclude that visible signs convey a more precise imitation, but that interest is aroused more effectively by sounds.

This makes me think that if we had never had anything but physical needs, we might very well never have spoken and would have understood one another perfectly by the language of gesture alone. We might have established societies little different from what they are today, or ones which might even have proceeded to their end better. We might have instituted laws, chosen leaders, invented arts, established commerce, and, in a word, done almost as many things as we do with the aid of speech. The epistolary language of salaams† transmits the secrets of oriental gallantry across the best guarded Harems without fear of the jealous. The Grand Vizier's mutes make themselves understood among one another and understand everything that is said to them by signs quite as well as could be done by discourse. Master Pereyre and those who like him teach mutes not only how to speak but to know what they are saying, are first compelled to teach them another language, no less complicated, with whose aid they help them understand spoken language.[17]

Chardin says that in the Indies traders, by taking one another by the hand and modifying their grip in a way no one can perceive, in this way transact all their business in public yet secretly, without having said a single word to each other.[18] Assume that these traders are blind, deaf, and mute: they will make themselves understood among themselves no less well. This shows that of the two senses by which we are active, a single one would suffice to form a language for ourselves.

It would further seem from the same observations that the invention of the art of communicating our ideas depends less on the organs we use for that communication than on a faculty that belongs to man, which makes him employ his organs for that use, and which, if he lacked them, would make him employ others to that same end. Give man a physical organization as entirely crude as you please: doubtless he will acquire fewer ideas,

---

*I have said elsewhere why feigned miseries touch us much more than genuine ones.[16] He sobs at a Tragedy who in all his days has not pitied one wretched person. The invention of the theater is admirable for flattering our amour-propre with all the virtues we lack.

† Salaams are a number of the most common things, like an orange, a ribbon, a piece of coal, etc., the sending of which constitutes a meaning known to all the lovers in the countries in which this language is in use.

but provided only that there be some means of communication between him and his fellows by which one might act and the other feel, they will succeed at length in communicating altogether as many ideas as they have to one another.

Animals have a physical organization more than sufficient for such communication, and none of them has ever made this use of it. Here, it seems to me, is a most characteristic difference. Those who, among them, work and live in common, such as Beavers, ants, and bees, have some natural language in order to communicate amongst themselves—I raise no doubt about it. There is even reason to believe that the language of Beavers and that of ants are in gesture and speak only to the eyes. Be that as it may, precisely because all such languages are natural, they are not acquired; the animals that speak them do so from birth, they all possess them, and everywhere the same one; they do not change them, nor do they make the slightest progress in them. Conventional language belongs only to man. That is why man makes progress, whether for good or bad, and why the animals do not at all.[19] This single distinction seems to lead a long way. It is said that it is explained by the difference in organs.[20] I would be curious to see that explanation.

CHAPTER II

THAT THE FIRST INVENTION OF SPEECH DERIVES NOT FROM NEEDS BUT FROM THE PASSIONS

It is therefore to be supposed that needs dictated the first gestures and that the passions wrested the first voices.[21] By following the path of the facts with these distinctions in mind, it might perhaps be necessary to reason about the origin of languages altogether differently than has been done until now. The genius of the oriental languages, the most ancient known to us, absolutely contradicts the didactic course that is imagined in their formation. These languages have nothing methodical and reasoned about them; they are lively and figurative. The language of the first men is put before us as though it were the languages of Geometers, while we see that they were the languages of Poets.[22]

This must have been so. We did not begin by reasoning but by feeling.[23] It is claimed that men invented speech in order to express their needs;[24] this opinion seems untenable to me. The natural effect of the first needs was to separate men and not to bring them together. This had to have been so for the species to spread and the earth to be populated promptly, otherwise mankind would have been crammed into one corner of the world while the rest of it remained deserted.

From this alone it evidently follows that the origin of languages is not at all due to men's first needs; it would be absurd for the cause that separates them to come to be the means that unites them. From where, then, could this origin derive? From the moral needs, the passions. The passions all bring men together, but the necessity of seeking their livelihood makes them flee one another.[25] Neither hunger nor thirst, but love, hatred, pity, anger wrested the first voices from them. Fruit does not elude our grasp, one can feed on it without speaking, one stalks in silence the prey one wishes to devour; but in order to move a young heart, to repulse an unjust aggressor, nature dictates accents, cries, complaints. The most ancient words are invented in this way, and this is why the first languages were tuneful and passionate before being simple and methodical. All this is not true without qualification, but I shall come back to it below.[26]

CHAPTER III

THAT THE FIRST LANGUAGES MUST HAVE BEEN FIGURATIVE

As the first motives that made man speak were the passions, his first expressions were Tropes. Figurative language was the first to arise, proper meaning was found last. Things were not called by their true name until they were seen in their genuine form.[27] At first, only poetry was spoken. Only long afterwards did anyone take it into his head to reason.

Now, I am well aware that the reader will stop me here, and will ask me how an expression could be figurative before having a proper meaning, since it is only in the translation of the meaning that the figurativeness consists. I admit this; but in order to understand me it is necessary to substitute the idea that the passion presents to us for the word that we transpose; for words are transposed only because ideas are also transposed, otherwise figurative language would signify nothing. I therefore respond with an example.

Upon encountering others, a savage man will at first be afraid. His fright will make him see those men as taller and stronger than himself. He will give them the name *Giants*.[28] After many experiences he will recognize that as these supposed Giants are neither taller nor stronger than himself, their stature does not agree with the idea that he had first attached to the word Giant. He will therefore invent another name common to them and to him, such as the name *man* for example, and will leave that of *Giant* for the false object that had stuck him during his illusion. That is how the figurative word arises before the proper word, when passion fascinates our eyes and the first idea it offers us is not the true one. What I have said about words and names is applied without any difficulty to turns of phrase. The illusory image offered by the passions being presented first, the language which corresponded to it was likewise the first to be invented. It then became metaphorical when the enlightened mind, recognizing its first error, employed the expressions only with the same passions that had produced it.

CHAPTER IV

ON THE DISTINCTIVE CHARACTERISTICS OF THE FIRST LANGUAGE AND THE CHANGES IT MUST HAVE UNDERGONE

Simple sounds issue naturally from the throat, the mouth is naturally more or less open; but the modifications of the tongue and palate that produce articulation require attention, practice; one does not make them unless one wants to make them, all children need to learn them and some do not easily succeed in doing so. In all languages the most lively exclamations are unarticulated; cries and groans are simple voices. Mutes, that is the deaf, utter only unarticulated sounds. Father Lamy cannot even conceive how men could ever have invented others unless God had not expressly taught them to speak.[29] Articulations are few in number, sounds are infinite in number, and the accents which mark them can be multiplied in the same way. All musical notes are so many accents; we have, it is true, only three or four in speech, but the Chinese have many more of them; on the other hand, they have fewer consonants. To this source of combinations add that of tense or quantity, and you will have not only a greater variety of words, but of syllables, than the richest language needs.

I do not at all doubt that, independent of vocabulary and of syntax, if the first language still existed it would have retained the original characteristics that would distinguish it from all the others. Not only would all the turns of phrase in this language have to be in images, in feelings, and in figures of speech; but in its mechanical aspect it would have to answer to its first object, and to present to the sense as well as to the understanding the almost inevitable impressions of the passion that is sought to be communicated.

As natural voices are unarticulated, words would have few articulations;

a few interposed consonants eliminating the hiatus between the vowels would suffice to make them flowing and easy to pronounce. In contrast, its sounds would be quite varied, and the diversity of accents would multiply these same voices. Quantity and rhythm would provide further sources of combinations; in this way—since voices, sounds, accent, and number, which are from nature, would leave little to be done by articulations, which are conventional—one would sing it rather than speak it. Most of its root words would be imitative sounds, either of the accent of the passions, or of the effect of perceptible objects. Onomatopoeia would constantly make itself felt.

This language would have many synonyms to express the same being in its different relations*; it would have few adverbs and abstract words to express these same relations. It would have many augmentatives, diminutives, compound words, and expletive particles to give cadence to periods and roundness to phrases. It would have many irregularities and anomalies, it would neglect grammatical analogy to stick to the euphony, number, harmony, and beauty of sounds. Instead of arguments it would have aphorisms; it would persuade without convincing, and depict without reasoning.[30] It would resemble Chinese in certain respects, Greek in others, and Arabic in others. Develop these ideas in all their ramifications, and you will find Plato's *Cratylus* is not as ridiculous as it seems to be.[31]

CHAPTER V

ON WRITING[33]

Whoever studies the history and progress of languages will see that the more voices become monotone, the more consonants multiply, and that as accents are eliminated and quantities are equalized, they are replaced by grammatical combinations and new articulations; but it is only by dint of time that these changes are brought about. In proportion as needs increase, as affairs become entangled, as enlightenment extends, language changes character; it becomes more precise and less passionate; it substitutes ideas for feelings, it no longer speaks to the heart but to reason. As a result, accent is extinguished, articulation extends, language becomes more exact and clearer, but more drawn out, more muted, and colder. This progress appears completely natural to me.

*Arabic is said to have more than a thousand different words to say *camel*, more than a hundred to say *sword*. Etc.[32]

Another means of comparing languages and judging their antiquity is drawn from writing, and this being in inverse ratio to the perfection of this art. The cruder the writing, the more ancient the language is. The first manner of writing is not to depict sounds but the objects themselves, whether directly as the Mexicans did, or by allegorical figures as the Egyptians did of old. This state corresponds to passionate language, and already presupposes some degree of society and some needs to which the passions have given rise.

The second manner is to represent words and propositions by conventional characters, which can be done only when the language is completely formed and when an entire people is united by common Laws; for there is already here a double convention.[34] Such is the writing of the Chinese: this is truly to depict sounds and to speak to the eyes.

The third is to break down the speaking voice into a certain number of elementary parts, whether vowels or articulations, with which one could form all imaginable words and syllables. This manner of writing, which is our own, must have been devised by commercial peoples who, traveling in several countries and having to speak several languages, were forced to invent characters that could be common to all of them. This is not precisely to depict speech, it is to analyze it.

These three manners of writing correspond fairly accurately to the three different states in terms of which one can consider men assembled into nations. The depiction of objects suits savage peoples; signs of words and propositions barbarous peoples; and the alphabet civilized peoples.[35]

This last invention must not therefore be thought to be a proof of the great antiquity of the people who invented it. On the contrary, it is probable that the people who discovered it had in view an easier communication with other peoples speaking other languages, those who were at least their contemporaries and may have been more ancient than them. The same thing cannot be said about the two other methods. I admit, nevertheless, that if one confines oneself to history and known facts, Alphabetical writing seems to go back as far as any other. But it is not surprising that we lack the records of times when people did not write.

It is hardly likely that those who first took it into their heads to resolve speech into elementary signs would have made exact divisions at first. When they afterwards perceived the inadequacy of their analysis, some, like the Greeks, multiplied the characters of their alphabet, others contented themselves with varying their sense or sound by different positions or combinations. The inscriptions on the ruins of Tchelminar, whose Ectypes Chardin has traced for us,[36] would appear to have been written in that way. Only two figures or characters are distinguishable in them,* but of various sizes and placed in different positions. This unknown language of an almost awesome antiquity must nonetheless have been well developed by that time, to judge from the perfection of the arts which the beauty of the characters proclaim† and by the admirable monuments on which these inscriptions are found. I do not know why there is so little discussion of these astonishing ruins; when I read the description in Chardin I feel myself transported to another world. All of this seems to me intensely thought-provoking.

The art of writing does not at all depend upon that of speaking. It depends upon needs of another nature which arise earlier or later according to circumstances completely independent of the time span of peoples, and which might never have arisen in very ancient Nations. It is not known for how many centuries the art of hieroglyphics was perhaps the Egyptians' only writing, and that such a system of writing can suffice for a civilized people is proved by the example of the Mexicans, who had an even less convenient one.

In comparing the Coptic Alphabet to the Syriac or Phoenician alphabet, it is readily judged that the one is derived from the other, and it would not be surprising if this latter one were the original or if the more modern people had taught the more ancient in this respect. It is also clear that the Greek Alphabet is derived from the Phoenician alphabet; one even sees that it must derive from it. Whether Cadmus or someone else brought it from Phoenicia,[39] it appears certain anyhow that the Greeks did not go in search of it and that the Phoenicians brought it themselves: for of the Peoples of Asia and Africa, they were the first and almost the only ones‡ that

---

* *People are astonished*, says Chardin,[37] *that two figures could make so many letters, but as for myself, I do not see what is so astonishing about that, since the letters of our Alphabet, which are twenty-three in number, are nonetheless composed of only two lines, the straight and the curved, that is, only a "C" and an "I" are used to make up our words.*

† *This character is quite beautiful in appearance and has nothing confused or barbarous about it. [. . .] One would say that the letters had been gilded, for there are several of them, and especially the capitals, on which the gold still shows, and it is surely something admirable and inconceivable that the air has not been able to eat away at this gilding over so many centuries. [. . .] Moreover, it is no wonder that not one of the world's scholars has ever understood anything of this writing, since it does not come close in any way to any writing with which we have become acquainted, whereas all the systems of writing known today, except the Chinese, have much affinity with one another, and seem to come from the same source. What is most wondrous about this is that the Parsis, who are what is left of the ancient Persians and who preserve and perpetuate their Religion, are not only no better acquainted with these characters as we are, but that their own characters no more resemble them than do ours. [. . .] From which it follows either that it is a cabalistic character, which is not likely since this character is the common and natural one all throughout the edifice, and there is none other by the same chisel, or that it is of such great antiquity that we should hardly dare state it.*[38] Indeed, Chardin would make one surmise, from this passage, that from the time of Cyrus and of the Magis this character had already been forgotten and was as little known as it is today.

‡ I count the Carthaginians as Phoenicians, since they were a colony of Tyre.

had commerce⁴⁰ in Europe and they came among the Greeks much earlier than the Greeks went among them. This in no way proves that the Greek People is not as ancient as the People of Phoenicia.

At first the Greeks adopted not only the Phoenicians' characters but even the direction of their lines from right to left. Later they took it into their heads to write in furrows, that is, by turning round from left to right then from right to left alternately.* Eventually they wrote as we do today, beginning every line anew from left to right. This progress is only natural. Writing in furrows is undeniably the most convenient to read. I am even surprised that it was not established along with printing; but being difficult to write by hand, it must have been abolished when manuscripts multiplied.

But even though the Greek alphabet derives from the Phoenician alphabet, it does not at all follow that the Greek language derives from the Phoenician. The first of these propositions does not entail the other, and it appears that the Greek language was already very ancient, that the art of writing was still recent and even inadequate among the Greeks. Until the siege of Troy they had only sixteen letters, if they even had that many. It is said that Palamedes added four and Simonides the other four.⁴² All this is rather farfetched. On the other hand, Latin, a more modern language, had a complete alphabet almost from its birth, of which the first Romans nevertheless hardly made use, since they began to write down their history so late and since the lustra were only marked off with nailheads.⁴³

Moreover, there is no absolutely determinate quantity of letters or elements of speech; some have more of them, others fewer, according to the languages and the various modifications that are given to the vowels⁴⁴ and the consonants. Those who count only five vowels are quite mistaken: the Greeks had seven written ones, the first Romans six,† and the Gentlemen of Port Royal count six,⁴⁵ M. Duclos seventeen,⁴⁶ and I do not doubt that many more would have been found if habit had rendered the ear more sensitive and the mouth more practiced in the various modifications of which they are susceptible. In proportion to the refinement of the organ, more or fewer of these modifications will be found: between the acute *a* and the grave *o*, between *i* and open *e*, etc. This is something that anyone can test by passing from one vowel to another by a continuous and finely shaded voice, for these shades can be more or less fixed and marked by particular characters, to the extent that one has made oneself more or less sen-

---

* See Pausanias, *Arcad*. In the beginning the Latins wrote in the same way, and from that, according to Marius Victorinus, came the word *versus*.⁴¹

† *Vocales quas Graeci septem, Romulus sex, usus posterior quinque commemorat, y velut graeca rejecta*. Mart. Capel. Bk. III.⁴⁷

sitive to them by dint of habit, and this habit depends on the sorts of voices used in the language to which the organ is imperceptibly formed. Nearly the same thing can be said about articulated letters or consonants. But most nations did not do it in this way. They took the alphabet from one another, and represented very different voices and articulations by the same characters. That makes it so that however exact orthography may be, one always sounds ridiculous reading a language other than one's own, unless one is exceedingly well practiced in it.

Writing, which seems as if it should fix language, is precisely what alters it; it changes not its words but its genius; it substitutes precision for expressiveness. Feelings are conveyed when one speaks and ideas when one writes. In writing, one is forced to take all the words according to common acceptation; but he who speaks varies the meanings by the tone of his voice, he determines them as he pleases; less constrained to be clear, he grants more to forcefulness, and it is not possible for a language one writes to keep for long the liveliness of one that is only spoken. Words[48] are written and not sounds: now, in an accented language it is the sounds, the accents, the inflections of every sort that constitute the greatest energy of the language; and that make a turn of phrase, even a common one, belong only in the place it is found. The means taken up to compensate for this quality diffuse, elongate written language and, passing from books into discourse, enervate speech itself.* To say everything as one would write it is to do no more than read while speaking.

CHAPTER VI

WHETHER IT IS PROBABLE THAT HOMER KNEW HOW TO WRITE

Whatever we may be told about the invention of the Greek alphabet, I believe it to be much more modern than it is made out to be, and I base this opinion principally on the character of the language.[50] It has quite often occurred to me to doubt not only that Homer knew how to write,

---

*The best of these means, and one that would not have this defect, would be punctuation, if it had been left less imperfect. Why, for example, do we not have a vocative mark? The question mark we do have was much less necessary, for one sees by construction alone whether or not a question is being asked, at least in our language. *Are you coming* and *you are coming* are not the same thing.[49] But how does one distinguish in writing a man who is being mentioned from one being addressed? Here is a real equivocation, which the vocative point would have removed. The same equivocation occurs in irony, when accent does not make it felt.

but even that anyone wrote in his time. I very much regret that this doubt is so categorically contradicted by the Story of Bellerophon in the *Iliad*; as I have the misfortune, as much as Father Hardouin does, to be a bit obstinate in my paradoxes, if I were less unlearned I would be quite tempted to extend my doubts to this Story itself, and to charge it with having been uncritically interpolated by Homer's compilers.[51] Not only are few traces of this art seen in the rest of the *Iliad*, but I dare suggest that the whole *Odyssey* is but a tissue of stupidities and ineptitude which a letter or two would have reduced to thin air, whereas this Poem is made reasonable and even quite well executed by supposing that its Heroes did not know how to write. If the *Iliad* had been written, it would have been sung much less, the Rhapsodies would have been in less demand and would not have become so numerous. No other Poet has been sung in this way unless it is Tasso in Venice, even so it is only by the Gondoliers, who are not great readers.[52] The variety of dialects used by Homer constitutes yet another very strong presumption. Dialects distinguished by speech come together by means of writing and are confounded by it, everything imperceptibly conforming to a common model. The more a nation reads and teaches itself, the more its dialects are effaced, and finally they no longer remain except as a form of slang among the people, which reads little and do not write at all.

Now, since these two Poems are posterior to the siege of Troy, it is hardly obvious that the Greeks who conducted this siege knew about writing, and that the Poet who sang of it did not. These Poems remained for a long time written only in men's memories; they were assembled in writing quite late and with considerable difficulty. It was when Greece began to abound in books and written poetry that all the charm of that of Homer came to be felt by comparison.[53] The other Poets wrote, Homer alone had sung, and these divine songs ceased to be listened to with rapture only when Europe was covered with barbarians who meddled in judging what they were incapable of feeling.

CHAPTER VII

ON MODERN PROSODY[54]

We have no idea of a sonorous and harmonious language that speaks as much by its sounds as by its words.[55] It is a mistake to believe that accent can be made up for by accent marks.[56] Accent marks are invented only when accent is already lost.* What is more, we believe that we have accents in our language, but we do not have them at all. Our supposed accents are only vowels or signs of quantity; they do not indicate any variation in sound. The proof of this is that these accents are all conveyed either by unequal duration or by modifications of the lips, the tongue, or the palate, which produce the diversity of voices, none by the modifications of the glottis, which produce the diversity of sounds. Thus when our circumflex is not a simple vowel, it is a long vowel or it is nothing. Let us now see what it was for the Greeks.

Dionysius of Halicarnassus says that the raising of tone on the acute accent and the lowering on the grave was a fifth; thus the prosodic accent was also musical, above all the circumflex, on which, after having risen by a fifth, the voice drops by another fifth on the same Syllable.† It is clear enough from this passage and the one to which it refers that M. Duclos does not recognize a musical accent in our language, but only the prosodic and the vocal accents. In addition to these there is an orthographic accent which in no way modifies the voice, or the sound, or the quantity, but which sometimes indicates an omitted letter, like the circumflex, and sometimes de-

---

* Some scholars claim,[57] against common opinion and against the evidence drawn from all the ancient manuscripts, that the Greeks knew about the signs called "accents" and used them in writing, and they base this opinion on two passages, both of which I am going to transcribe so that the reader can judge their true meaning.

Here is the first, taken from Cicero out of his treatise *On the Orator*, Bk. III, sect. 44:

Hanc diligentiam subsequitur modus etiam et forma verborum, quod iam vereor ne huic Catulo videatur esse puerile. Versus enim illi in hac soluta oratione propemodum, hoc est numeros quosdam nobis esse adhibendos putaverunt; interspirationis enim, non defatigationis nostrae neque librariorum notis, sed verborum et sententiarum modo interpunctas clausulas in orationibus esse voluerunt; idque princeps Isocrates instituisse fertur, ut inconditam antiquorum dicendi consuetudinem delectationis atque aurium causa, quem ad modum scribit discipulus eius Naucrates, numeris adstringeret.

Namque haec duo musici, qui erant quondam idam poëtae, machinati ad voluptatem sunt, versum atque cantum, ut et verborum numero et vocum modo delectatione vincerent aurium satietatem. Haec igitur duo, vocis dico moderationem et verborum conclusionem, quoad orationis severitas pati posset, a poëtica ad eloquentiam traducenda duxerunt.[58]

Here is the second, taken from Isidore out of his *Origins*, bk. I, chap. xx:

Praeterea quaedam sententiarum notae apud celeberrimos auctores fuerunt, quasque antiqui ad distinctionem scripturarum carminibus et historiis apposuerunt. Nota est figura propria in litterae modum posita ad demonstrandam unamquamque verbi sententiarumque ac versuum rationem. Notae autem versibus apponuntur numero XXVI quae sunt nominibus infra scriptis, etc.[59]

For my part, I see here that good copyists in Cicero's time made a practice of separating words and using certain signs equivalent to our punctuation. I further see in this that the invention of meter and of prose declamation is attributed to Isocrates. I see nothing at all in this of the written signs of accents,[60] and even if I did, only one thing could be concluded from it, one which I do not dispute and which completely conforms with my principles: namely, that when the Romans began to study Greek, the Copyists invented accent marks, aspirations, and prosody in order to indicate their punctuation; but it does not in the least follow that these signs were in use among the Greeks, who had no need of them.

† M. Duclos, *Rem. on the Gener. and Reasoned Gram.*, p. 30.[62]

termines the equivocal meaning of a monosyllable, such as the so-called grave accent that distinguishes the adverb *où* from the disjunctive particle *ou*, and *à* used as an article from the same *a* used as a verb.[61] This accent distinguishes these monosyllables for the eyes alone, nothing distinguishes them in pronunciation.* Thus the definition of the accent that the French have generally adopted does not suit any of the accents of their language.

I fully expect that some of their grammarians, having been told that accents mark a raising or lowering of the voice, will again exclaim a paradox here, and, for want of paying sufficient attention to experience, will believe that they are making the very accents by the modifications of the glottis which are made uniquely by varying the opening of the mouth or the position of the tongue. But here is what I have to tell them in order to verify experience and make my proof irrefutable.[64]

Attune your voice perfectly to some musical instrument, and on this unison pronounce in succession all the most variously accented French words you can muster; since there is no question here of an oratorical accent but only of grammatical accent, these various words need not even comprise a coherent meaning. As you are speaking in this way, observe whether you do not express all the accents as plainly, as clearly on the same tone as you would if you pronounced them unhampered, varying your tone of voice. Now, this being assumed, and it is incontestable, I say that because all your accents are expressed on the same pitch, they therefore do not indicate different sounds. I cannot imagine what might be said in response to this.

Any language in which the same words can be set to several musical tunes has no determinate musical accent. If the accent were determinate, the tune would be as well. As soon as the tune is arbitrary, the accent counts for nothing.

The modern languages of Europe are all more or less in the same situation. I do not except even Italian. The Italian language by itself is no more a musical language than is French. The difference is merely that the one lends itself to music and the other does not.

All this leads to the confirmation of this principle: that by a natural progression all lettered languages must change character and lose force as they gain clarity, that the more one aims at perfecting grammar and logic the more one accelerates this progress, and that in order to make a language

---

* It might be believed that it is by this same accent that the Italians distinguish, for example, the verb *è* from the conjunction *e*; but the first is distinguished by the ear by a stronger and more emphatic sound, which makes the accent with which it is marked a vocal accent, an observation which Buonmattei erred in not making.[63]

cold and monotonous in no time, one has only to establish academies among the people that speaks it.[65]

Derivative languages are known by the discrepancy between spelling and pronunciation. The more ancient and original languages are, the less arbitrariness there is in the way they are pronounced, consequently the less complicated are the characters for determining that pronunciation. *All the ancients' prosodic signs*, says Mr. Duclos, *even assuming that their usage had been well established, were still not worth as much as their use.*[66] I will go further: they were substituted for it. The ancient Hebrews had neither points nor accents; they did not even have vowels.[67] When the other Nations wanted to meddle in speaking Hebrew and the Jews spoke other languages, their own lost its accent; points, signs were needed to regulate it, and this restored the meaning of the words much more than it did the pronunciation of the language. The Jews of our day, speaking Hebrew, would no longer be understood by their ancestors.

In order to know English it must be learned two times: once to read it and another time to speak it. If an Englishman reads out loud and a foreigner glances at the book, the foreigner will not perceive any relationship between what he sees and what he hears. Why is that? Because while England has been successively conquered by various peoples, and while the words have always been written the same, the manner of pronouncing them has often changed. There is a great difference between the signs that determine the meaning of the writing and those that regulate pronunciation. It would be easy to construct with consonants alone a language that was extremely clear in writing, but which could not be spoken. Algebra has something like such a language about it. When a language is clearer by its spelling than by its pronunciation, it is a sign that it is written more than it is spoken. Such may have been the scholarly language of the Egyptians; such are the dead languages for us. In those languages burdened with useless consonants, writing even seems to have preceded speech, and who would not believe that such is the case with Polish? If this were so, Polish would have to be the coldest of all languages.

CHAPTER VIII

GENERAL AND LOCAL DIFFERENCE IN THE ORIGIN OF LANGUAGES

Everything that I have said so far suits primitive languages in general and the progress that results from their duration, but explains neither their origin nor their differences. The principal cause that distinguishes them is local, deriving from the climates in which they are born and the manner in which they are formed; it is to this cause to which one has to go back in order to understand the general and characteristic difference that is noted between the languages of the South and those of the North.[68] The great flaw of the Europeans is always to philosophize about the origin of things according to what happens around them.[69] They do not fail to show us the first men inhabiting a barren and harsh earth, dying of cold and hunger, anxious to get shelter and clothing; they see everywhere only the snow and ice of Europe, without considering that the human species, just as all the others, was born in the warm countries and that on two-thirds of the globe winter is hardly known. When one wishes to study men, one has to look close by; but in order to study man, one has to learn to cast one's eyes far off; first one has to observe the differences in order to discover the properties.

Mankind, born in the warm countries, spreads from there to the cold countries; it is in these that it multiplies and later flows back into the warm countries. From this action and reaction come the earth's revolutions and the continual agitation of its inhabitants. Let us try to follow the very order of nature in our investigations. I am entering upon a long digression on a subject so hackneyed that it is trivial, but to which one still has to return in order to discover the origin of human institutions.

CHAPTER IX[70]

FORMATION OF THE SOUTHERN LANGUAGES

In the first times,* men, scattered over the face of the earth, had no society other than that of the family, no laws other than those of nature, no language other than that of gesture and some inarticulate sounds.†[71] They were not bound by any idea of common fraternity, and having no other arbiter than force, they believed themselves to be one another's enemies.[72] It was their weakness and their ignorance that gave them that opinion. Knowing nothing, they feared everything; they attacked in order to defend themselves. A man abandoned alone on the face of the earth at the

---

* I call the first times those of men's dispersion, at whatever age of mankind one might wish to fix the epoch.[73]

† Genuine languages do not at all have a domestic origin; it is only a more general and more lasting convention that may establish them. The Savages of America almost never speak except outside of their homes; each keeps silent in his cabin, he spoke to his family by signs, and these signs are infrequent because a Savage is less restless, less impatient than a European, because he does not have so many needs and takes care to provide for them himself.[74]

mercy of mankind must have been a ferocious animal. He was ready to do unto others all the evil he feared from them. Fear and weakness are the sources of cruelty.

Social affections develop in us only with our enlightenment. Pity, although natural to the heart of man, would remain eternally inactive without the imagination that puts it into play. How do we let ourselves be moved to pity? By transporting ourselves outside of ourselves; by identifying ourselves with the suffering being. We suffer only as much as we judge he suffers; it is not in ourselves, it is in him that we suffer. Consider how much this transport presupposes acquired knowledge! How could I imagine evils of which I have no idea? How would I suffer in seeing someone else suffer if I do not even know that he is suffering, if I do not know what he and I have in common? He who has never reflected cannot be clement, or just, or pitying—no more than he can be wicked and vindictive. He who imagines nothing feels only himself; he is alone in the midst of mankind.[75]

Reflection is born of compared ideas, and it is the multiplicity of ideas that leads to their comparison. He who sees only a single object has no comparison to make. He who sees from his childhood only a small number and always the same ones still does not compare them, because the habit of seeing them deprives him of the attention needed to examine them; but as a new object strikes us, we want to know it, we look for relations between it and those we do know; it is in this way that we learn to consider what is before our eyes, and how what is foreign to us leads us to examine what touches us.[76]

Apply these ideas to the first men, and you will see the reason for their barbarousness. Never having seen anything but what was around them, they did not know even that; they did not know themselves. They had the idea of a Father, of a son, of a brother, and not of a man. Their cabin held all their fellows; a stranger, a beast, a monster were the same thing for them: outside of themselves and their family, the entire universe was nothing for them.

From whence the apparent contradictions seen in the fathers of nations. So much naturalness and so much inhumanity, such ferocious morals and such tender hearts, so much love for their family and aversion for their species. All their feelings, concentrated on those nearest, had more energy. Everything they knew was dear to them. Enemies of the rest of the world, which they did not see and did not know, they hated only what they could not know.

These barbarous times were the golden age; not because men were united, but because they were separated. Each, it is said, esteemed himself the master of everything; that might be so, but no one knew or desired anything other than what was at hand: his needs, far from bringing him together with his fellows took him away from them. Men, if you like, attacked one another upon meeting, but they rarely met. Everywhere reigned the state of war, and the whole earth was at peace.[77]

The first men were hunters or shepherds, and not plowmen; the first goods were herds and not fields. Before the property of the earth was divided, no one thought to cultivate it. Agriculture is an art that requires tools; to sow in order to reap is a precaution that demands foresight.[78] Man in society seeks to expand, isolated man contracts. Beyond the range that his eye can see or his arm can reach, there is no longer either right or property for him. When the Cyclops has rolled the stone in front of the entrance to his cave, his herds and he are secure.[79] But who would look after the harvest of him whom the laws do not watch over?

I will be told that Cain was a plowman and that Noah planted a vineyard.[80] Why not? They were alone, what did they have to fear? Besides, this does not affect my point; I have said above what I mean by the first times. In becoming a fugitive, Cain was indeed forced to give up agriculture; the wandering life of Noah's descendants must have made them forget it as well; the earth had to be populated before cultivating it; the two cannot very well be done together. During the first dispersion of mankind until the family had settled down and man had a fixed abode there was no more agriculture at all. Peoples who do not settle cannot cultivate the earth; such in the past were the Nomads, such were the Arabs living in their tents, the Scythians in their wagons, such are still today the wandering Tartars, and the Savages of America.

Generally, among all the peoples whose origins are known to us, the first barbarians are found to be voracious and carnivorous rather than agricultural and granivorous. The Greeks name the first person who taught them to till the earth, and it appears that they did not learn this art until quite late. But when they add that before Triptolemus they lived on nuts alone, they are stating something improbable and which their own history belies; for they were eating flesh before Triptolemus, since he forbade them to eat it. Moreover, it does not look as though they took this prohibition very seriously.[81]

At Homeric feasts an ox was slaughtered to regale one's guests, as one might slaughter a suckling pig in our day. On reading that Abraham served a calf to three persons, that Eumaeus had two kids roasted for Ulysses' dinner, and that Rebecca roasted as many for her husband's,[82] one can judge what astonishing devourers of meat the men of those times were. In order to conceive of the meals of the ancients one has only to see still today those of Savages; I almost said those of Englishmen.[83]

The first cake that was eaten was mankind's communion. When men began to settle they cleared a bit of earth around their cabin, it was a garden rather than a field. The little grain they gathered was ground between two stones, made into some cakes, which were baked under the ashes, or over the embers, or on a hot stone, and which were eaten only at feasts. This ancient usage, which was consecrated among the Jews by Passover, is still preserved today in Persia and in the Indies. There only unleavened breads are eaten, and these breads, made up of thin sheets, are baked and consumed at every meal. Only when more was needed did anyone take it into his head to leaven it, for leavening does not work very well with a small quantity.

I know that large-scale agriculture was already found from the time of the patriarchs. The proximity of Egypt must have brought it to Palestine quite early. The book of Job, perhaps the most ancient of all the books that exist, speaks of the cultivation of the fields, counting five hundred pair of oxen among Job's riches; this word pairs shows that these oxen were yoked for work; it is explicitly said that these oxen were ploughing when the Sabeans carried them off, and one can judge what an expanse of land five hundred pairs of oxen must have ploughed.[84]

All this is true; but let us not confuse times. The patriarchal age that we know is very remote from the first age. Scripture counts ten generations from the one to the other during those centuries when men lived a long time.[85] What did they do during those ten generations? We know nothing about it. Living scattered and almost without society, they hardly spoke: how could they have written, and given the uniformity of their isolated life what events would they have passed on to us?

Adam spoke; Noah spoke; so be it. Adam had been taught by God himself. Upon separating, the children of Noah gave up agriculture, and the common language perished with the first society. This would have happened even if there had never been a tower of Babel.[86] Solitary individuals living on desert islands have been seen to forget their own language. Rarely do men who are away from their country preserve their first language after several generations, even when they work together and live in society among themselves.

Scattered in this vast desert of the world, men fell back into the stupid barbarism in which they would have found themselves if they had been born of the earth. By following these ideas, such natural ones, it is easy to reconcile the authority of Scripture with ancient records, and one is not reduced to treating as fables traditions as ancient as the people who have passed them on to us.

In that brutish state one had to live. The more active, the more robust, those who were always in front could only live off fruits and the hunt; so they became hunters, violent, bloodthirsty, and then, in time, warriors, conquerors, usurpers. History has stained its records with the crimes of these first Kings; war and conquests are merely manhunts. After having conquered them, it only remained for them to devour them. That is what their successors have learned to do.[87]

The greater number, less active and more peaceable, settled down as soon as they could, gathered livestock, tamed them, made them compliant to the voice of man, learned to look after them, propagate them, in order to feed themselves; and so began the pastoral life.

Human industry expands with the needs that give rise to it. Of the three ways of life possible for man, namely hunting, tending herds, and agriculture, the first trains the body for strength, dexterity, and speed, the soul for courage, cunning, it hardens man and makes him ferocious. The country of the hunters is not for long that of the hunt;* game has to be pursued over a long distance, hence horsemanship. The very game that flees has to be reached; hence light arms: the sling, the arrow, the javelin. The pastoral art, father of repose and of the idle passions, is the one that is most self-sufficient. It furnishes man with livelihood and clothing almost effortlessly. It even furnishes him with his dwelling; the tents of the first shepherds were made of animal skins: the roof of the ark and of Moses' tabernacle were of none other material.[88] As for agriculture, which is slower to arise, it depends on all the arts; it brings property, government, laws, and gradually misery and crimes, which for our species are inseparable from the knowledge of good and evil. Consequently, the Greeks did not regard Triptolemus merely as the inventor of a useful art, but as a founder and a wise man from whom they held their first discipline and their first laws. On the other hand, Moses seems to have issued a judgment of disapprobation upon agriculture by attributing its invention to a wicked man and having God reject his offerings; it might said that the first plowman proclaimed the bad effects of his art by his character. The author of Genesis had seen farther than Herodotus.[89]

To the preceding division there correspond the three states of man considered in relation to society. The savage is a hunter, the barbarian a herdsman, the civil man a plowman.[90]

Whether one investigates the origin of the arts or examines the first

---

*The hunter's trade is not at all conducive to population. This observation, which was made when the Islands of Santo Domingo and of Tortuga were inhabited by buccaneers, is confirmed by the state of North America. None of the fathers of any considerable nations are seen to have been hunters by station; they have all been farmers or shepherds. Hunting, therefore, must be considered here less as a resource of subsistence than as an accessory to the pastoral state.

morals, therefore, one sees that everything is related in its first principle to the means of providing for subsistence, and as for those among these means that gather men together, they are determined by the climate and by the nature of the soil. Thus, it is also by the same causes that the diversity of languages and the contrast in their characters must be explained.

Mild climates, lush and fertile lands have been the first to be populated and the last where nations have been formed, because men could more easily do without one another there, and because the needs that cause society to arise made themselves felt later there.

Assume a perpetual spring on earth;[91] assume water, livestock, pasturage everywhere; assume men leaving the hands of nature, once dispersed throughout all this: I cannot imagine how they would ever have renounced their primitive freedom and forsaken the isolated and pastoral life so suited to their natural indolence,* in order needlessly to impose on themselves the slavery, the labors, the miseries inseparable from the social state.

He who willed that man be sociable touched his finger to the axis of the globe and inclined it at an angle to the axis of the universe.[93] With this slight movement I see the face of the earth change and the vocation of mankind decided: I hear from afar the joyous cries of a senseless multitude; I see Palaces and Towns raised; I see the arts, laws, commerce born; I see peoples forming, extending, dissolving, succeeding one another like the waves of the sea: I see men gathered together at a few dwelling places in order to devour each other there, to make a frightful desert of the rest of the world; a worthy monument to social union and the usefulness of the arts.

The earth nourishes men, but when the first needs have dispersed them other needs bring them together, and it is only then that they speak and make themselves spoken of. So as not to find me in contradiction with myself, I have to be allowed time to explain myself.

If one seeks the places where the fathers of mankind were born, from whence the first colonies set out, the first emigrations came, you will not name the happy climes of Asia Minor, or of Sicily, or of Africa, or even of Egypt; you will name the sands of Chaldea, the rocks of Phoenecia. You will find the same things in all times. China has populated itself handsomely with Chinese, and it is also populated with Tartars; the Scythians in-

---

*The extent to which man is naturally lazy is inconceivable.[92] One would say that he lives only in order to sleep, to vegetate, to remain immobile; he can scarcely resolve to devote the motions necessary to prevent himself from dying of hunger. Nothing upholds the love of so many savages for their state as this delightful indolence. The passions that make man restless, provident, active, are born only in society. To do nothing is man's first and strongest passion after that of self-preservation. Were this considered carefully, it would be seen that even among us it is in order to achieve repose that each works; it is still laziness that makes us industrious.

undated Europe and Asia; the mountains of Switzerland are now pouring forth a perpetual colony into our fertile regions that promises not to run dry.

It is natural, it is said, for the inhabitants of a barren land to leave it in order to occupy a better one.[94] Very well; but why does this better land, instead of swarming with its own inhabitants, make room for others? To leave a barren land, one has to be there in the first place. Why, then, are so many men born there rather than elsewhere? One would think that barren lands must be populated only by the excess of fertile countries, and we see the opposite to be the case. Most of the Latin peoples claimed to be aboriginals,* while Magna Graecia, which is much more fertile, was populated only by foreigners. All the Greek peoples admitted that they derived their origin from various colonies, aside from the one whose soil was the worst, namely the Attic people, which called itself Autochthonous or born from itself. Finally, without piercing the night of time, modern centuries offer a decisive observation: for what climate in the world is sadder than that which has been called the factory of mankind?[95]

The associations of men are in great part the work of accidents of nature; particular floods, overflowing seas, volcanic eruptions, great earthquakes, fires kindled by lightning and which destroyed forests, everything that must have frightened and dispersed the savage inhabitants of a land must thereafter bring them together to repair in common their common losses. The traditions of the earthly calamities so current in ancient times show what instruments providence used to force human beings to come together.[96] Ever since societies have been established these great accidents have ceased and become more rare; it seems that this too must be so; the same calamities that brought together scattered men would disperse those who are united.

The revolutions of the seasons are another cause, more general and more permanent, that must have produced the same effect in the climates subject to this variety. Forced to make provision for the winter, the inhabitants there are in the position of having to help one another, there they are constrained to establish some sort of convention amongst themselves. When expeditions become impossible and the severity of the cold stops them, boredom ties them as much as need. The Lapps, buried in their ice, the Eskimos, the most savage of all peoples, come together in their caves for the winter, and in the summer no longer know one another.[97] Increase their development and their enlightenment by one degree, behold them united forever.

---

* The names *Autochthons* and *Aboriginals* mean merely that the first inhabitants of the land were savages without societies, without laws, without traditions, and that they populated it before they spoke.

Neither man's stomach nor his intestines were made to digest raw flesh; generally he cannot bear its taste.[98] With the exception perhaps of the Eskimos alone, of whom I just spoke, even savages grill their meats. To fire's use—necessary in order to cook their meats—is joined the pleasure it gives to the sight and its pleasant warmth to the body. The sight of the flame, which makes the animals flee, attracts man.* People gather together around a common hearth, have feasts, dance there; the sweet ties of habit imperceptibly bring together man and his fellows, and on this rustic hearth burns the sacred fire that carries to the depths of their hearts the first sentiment of humanity.

In warm countries, unevenly dispersed springs and rivers are additional meeting places, all the more necessary as men can do without water even less than without fire. The barbarians who live off their herds above all need common watering places, and the history of the most ancient times teaches us that it is indeed there that their treaties as well as their quarrels began.† Easy access to water can delay the society of the inhabitants in well-watered places. On the other hand, in arid places they had to cooperate in sinking wells, in drawing off canals in order to water the livestock. Associated men are seen there almost from time immemorial, for the land had to remain desert or be made habitable by human labor. But the penchant we have of relating everything to our practices makes some reflections on this necessary.

The first state of the earth differed greatly from what it is today, when it is seen adorned or disfigured by the hands of men. The chaos which the Poets feigned among the elements reigned among its productions.[101] In those remote times when revolutions were frequent, or a thousand accidents changed the nature of the soil and the look of the terrain, everything grew confusedly: trees, vegetables, shrubs, pasturage; no species had the time to lay hold of the terrain that suited it best and to choke out the others there; they would separate slowly, gradually, and then an upheaval would occur that would confound everything.

There is such a relationship between man's needs and the productions

---

* Fire gives great pleasure to animals as well as to man, once they are accustomed to its sight and have felt its gentle warmth. Often, it would even be no less useful to them than to us, at the very least to warm their young. Nevertheless, no one has ever heard of any beast, either wild or domestic, having acquired sufficient ingenuity to make fire, even after our example. These, then, are the reasoning beings who are said to form a fleeting society prior to man, whose intelligence nevertheless has never been able to raise itself to the level of striking sparks from a stone and catching them, or at least of keeping some abandoned fires going! By my word, the Philosophers make fun of us entirely openly. One clearly sees by their writings that they indeed take us for being stupid.[99]

† See the example of them both in chapter 21 of Genesis, between Abraham and Abilemech in connection with the well of the oath.[100]

of the earth that it is enough for it to be populated, and everything subsists; but before united men established a balance among its productions by their common labors, for them all to subsist nature alone had to attend to the equilibrium that the hands of men preserve today; it maintained or restored this equilibrium by means of revolutions just as men maintain or restore it by their inconstancy. War, which did not yet reign among them, seemed to reign among the elements; men did not burn towns, did not dig mines, did not fell trees; but nature ignited volcanoes, roused earthquakes, the fire of Heaven consumed forests. A bolt of lightning, a flood, an eruption did then in a few hours what a hundred thousand human arms do today in a century. Otherwise I do not see how the system could have subsisted and the equilibrium have maintained itself. In the kingdoms of organic life, the larger species would in the long run have absorbed the smaller.* The whole earth would soon have been covered with nothing but trees and ferocious beasts; in the end everything would have perished.

The waters would gradually lose the circulation that vivifies the earth. The mountains get worn down and grow smaller, the rivers sweep along, the sea fills and extends, everything imperceptibly tends toward the same level; the hands of men check this inclination and delay this progress; without them it would be more rapid, and the earth would perhaps already be under the waters. Prior to human labor, the poorly distributed springs flowed more unevenly, fertilized the earth less adequately, watered its inhabitants with more difficulty. Rivers were often inaccessible, their banks steep or marshy; as human art did not retain them in their beds, they frequently left them, overflowed on the right or left bank, changed their direction and course, forked into various branches; sometimes they were found to dry up, sometimes quicksands prevented their being approached: it was as if they did not exist, and one died of thirst in the midst of waters.

How many arid lands are habitable only by means of the ditches and canals that men have drawn off from rivers! Almost the whole of Persia continues to exist only through this artifice. China swarms with People with the help of its numerous canals: without them the Low Counties would be inundated by rivers, as they would be by the sea without their

---

* It is claimed that by a kind of natural action and reaction, the various species of the animal kingdom would of themselves maintain themselves in a perpetual balance which for them would take the place of an equilibrium.[102] Once the devouring species has increased too much at the expense of the devoured species, it is said, then the first, no longer finding its subsistence, will have to decrease and allow the second time to repopulate itself, until, furnishing anew an abundant subsistence for the first, it again decreases while the devouring species repopulates itself anew. But such an oscillation does not seem at all probable to me: for according to this system there has to be a time when the species that serves as prey increases and the one that feeds on it decreases, which seems to me against all reason.

dikes. Egypt, the most fertile land on earth, is habitable only by means of human labor. On the great plains lacking rivers and where the grade of the soil is not steep enough, there is no resource other than wells. If, then, the first peoples of which there is mention in history did not inhabit lush lands or easily accessible shores, it is not that these happy climes were deserted, but that their numerous inhabitants, able to do without one another, lived isolated in their families and without communication. But in arid places, where water can be had only through wells, people simply had to unite to sink them, or at least to agree about their use. Such must have been the origin of societies and of languages in warm countries.

There were formed the first ties between families; there the first meetings between the two sexes took place. Young girls came to fetch water for the household, young men came to water their herds. There eyes accustomed to the same objects from childhood began to see sweeter ones. The heart was moved by these new objects, an unfamiliar attraction made it less savage, it felt the pleasure of not being alone. Imperceptibly water became more necessary, the livestock were thirsty more often; they arrived in haste and parted reluctantly. In this happy age when nothing marked the hours, nothing obliged them to be counted; time did not have any measure other than amusement and boredom. Beneath aged oaks, conquerors of years, an ardent youth gradually forgot its ferocity, gradually they tamed one another; through endeavoring to make themselves understood, they learned to explain themselves. There the first festivals took place, feet leaped with joy, eager gesture no longer sufficed, the voice accompanied it with passionate accents; mingled together, pleasure and desire made themselves felt at the same time. There, finally, was the true cradle of peoples, and from the pure crystal of the fountains came the first fires of love.[103]

What then! Before that time were men born of the earth? Did the generations succeed one another without the two sexes being united and without anyone being understood? No, there were families, but there were no Nations; there were domestic languages, but there were no popular languages; there were marriages, but there was no love. Each family was self-sufficient and perpetuated itself through its own stock. Children born of the same parents grew up together and gradually found ways of expressing themselves among themselves; with age the sexes were distinguished, natural inclination sufficed to unite them, instinct took the place of passion, habit took the place of preference, they became husbands and wives without ceasing to be brothers and sisters.* Nothing in this was animated

---

*The first men simply had to marry their sisters.[104] Given the simplicity of the first morals, this practice was perpetuated without drawback as long as families remained isolated and even after the coming together of the most ancient peoples; but the law that abolished

enough to unloose the tongue, nothing that could draw forth the accents of the ardent passions frequently enough to turn them into institutions, and one could say as much about the rare and not very pressing needs that may have led some men to cooperate in their common labors: one began the basin of the fountain, and the other later completed it, often without their having had need of the slightest agreement and sometimes without even having seen one another. In a word, in mild climates, in fertile terrains, it took all the liveliness of the agreeable passions to begin to make the inhabitants speak. The first languages, daughters of pleasure and not of need, long bore the sign of their father; their seductive accent faded only with the feelings that had caused them to arise, when new needs introduced among men forced each to consider only himself and to withdraw his heart within himself.

CHAPTER X[106]

FORMATION OF THE LANGUAGES OF THE NORTH

In the long run all men become similar,[107] but the order of their progress is different. In southern climates, where nature is prodigal, needs arise from the passions, in cold countries, where nature is miserly, the passions arise from needs, and the languages, unhappy daughters of necessity, show their severe origin.

Although man becomes accustomed to inclement weather, to the cold, to discomfort, even to hunger, there is nonetheless a point at which nature succumbs. As a victim to these cruel ordeals, everything that is weak perishes; all that remains is strengthened, and there is no middle ground between vigor and death. That is why northern peoples are so robust;[108] it is not at first the climate that has made them such, rather it has suffered only those who are so to exist, and it is not surprising that children retain the good constitution of their fathers.

It is seen by now that men who are more robust must have less delicate organs, their voices must be harsher and stronger. Besides, what a difference there is between the touching inflections which come from the movements of the soul and the cries wrested by physical needs. In these dread-

---

it was no less sacred for being a human institution. Those who consider it only in terms of the tie it forms between families do not see its most important side. Given the familiarity that domestic commerce[105] necessarily establishes between the two sexes, from the moment when such a sacred law should cease to speak to the heart and impose on the senses, there would no longer be decency among men and the most frightful morals would soon cause mankind's destruction.

ful climates where everything is dead for nine months of the year, where the sun warms the air for a few weeks only to teach the inhabitants about the goods of which they are deprived and to prolong their misery, in those places where the earth yields nothing but to the force of labor and where the source of life seems to be in the arms more than in the heart, men, constantly occupied with providing for their subsistence, scarcely thought of gentler ties, everything was limited to physical impulsion, opportunity dictated choice, ease dictated preference.[109] The idleness that nourishes the passions gives way to the labor that represses them. Before thinking of living happily, they had to think of living. Mutual need united men much better than feeling would have done, society was formed only through industry, the constant danger of perishing did not allow them to limit themselves to the language of gesture, and the first word among them was not "love me," but "help me."[110]

Those two expressions, although similar enough, are pronounced in a very different tone. There was nothing one had to make felt, everything to be made understood; it was therefore a matter not of energy but of clarity. For accent, which the heart did not furnish, strong and sensible articulations were substituted, and if there was any natural imprint in the form of the language, this imprint contributed still further to its harshness.

Indeed, northern men are not without passions, but theirs are those of another type. Those of warm countries are the voluptuous passions that concern love and softness. Nature does so much for the inhabitants that there is almost nothing for them to do. Provided that an Asiatic has women and repose he is content. But in the North, where the inhabitants consume a great deal off of a barren soil, men, subject to so many needs, are easily irritated; everything that happens around them disturbs them: since they continue to exist only with difficulty, the poorer they are, the more they cling to the little they have; to approach them is to make an attempt on their lives. This accounts for their irascible temper, so quick to turn in fury against everything that offends them. Thus, their most natural voices are those of anger and threats, and those voices are always accompanied by strong articulations that make them harsh and noisy.

CHAPTER XI

REFLECTIONS ON THESE DIFFERENCES

These are, in my opinion, the most general physical causes of the characteristic difference between primitive languages. Those of the south must have been lively, sonorous, accented, eloquent, and often obscure by dint of their energy; those of the North must have been muted, crude, articulated, shrill, monotonous, clear by dint of their words rather than by a good construction. Modern languages, mingled and recast a hundred times, still retain something of these differences. French, English, and German are the private languages of men who help one another, who coolly reason with one another, or of quick-tempered people who get angry; but the ministers of the Gods proclaiming the sacred mysteries, the wise giving laws to peoples, leaders carrying along the multitude must speak Arabic or Persian.* Our languages are better written than spoken, and there is more pleasure in reading us than there is in listening to us. In contrast, when written, oriental languages lose their life and warmth. Only half of the meaning is in the words, all its force is in the accents. To judge the genius of the Orientals by their Books is like wanting to paint a man from his corpse.

In order to appraise men's actions properly, they have to be considered in all their relations, and this is what we have not at all learned to do. When we put ourselves in the place of others, we always put ourselves there such as we have been modified, not such as they must have been, and when we think we are judging them by reason, we are only comparing their prejudices with ours. Someone who can read a little Arabic smiles when leafing through the Koran, had he heard Mohammed in person proclaim it in that eloquent and rhythmic language, with that sonorous and persuasive voice which seduced the ear before the heart, and constantly animating his aphorisms with the accent of enthusiasm, he would have prostrated himself on the earth while crying out: great Prophet, Messenger of God, lead us to glory, to martyrdom; we want to conquer or to die for you. Fanaticism always appears ridiculous to us, because among us it has no voice to make itself heard.[111] Even our fanatics are not true fanatics, they are merely knaves or fools. Our languages, instead of inflections for the inspired, have only cries for those possessed by the Devil.

CHAPTER XII

ORIGIN OF MUSIC

Along with the first voices were formed the first articulations or the first sounds, depending on the kind of passion that dictated the one or the

---

*Turkish is a northern language.

other. Anger wrests menacing cries which the tongue and the palate articulate; but the voice of tenderness is gentler, it is the glottis that modifies it, and this voice becomes a sound. Only its accents are more or less frequent, its inflections more or less acute depending on the feeling that is joined to them. Thus cadence and sounds arise along with syllables, passion makes all the vocal organs speak, and adorns the voice with all their brilliance; thus verses, songs, and speech have a common origin.[112] Around the fountains of which I have spoken, the first discourses were the first songs; the periodic and measured recurrences of rhythm, the melodious inflections of accents caused poetry and music to be born along with language; or rather, all this was nothing but language itself in those happy climates and those happy times when the only pressing needs that required another's help were those to which the heart gave rise.

RELATIONSHIPS[113]

The first stories, the first harangues, and the first laws were in verse;[114] poetry was discovered before prose; this had to be so, since the passions spoke before reason. The same was so for music: at first there was no music at all other than melody, nor any other melody than the varied sound of speech, the accents formed the song, the quantities formed the meter, and one spoke as much by sounds and rhythm as by articulations and voices. In olden days to speak and to sing were the same thing, says Strabo; which shows, he adds, that poetry is the source of eloquence.* He ought to have said that they both had the same source and at first were merely the same thing. Considering the way in which the first societies were bound together, was it surprising that the first stories were set to verse and that the first laws were sung? Was it surprising that the first Grammarians subordinated their art to music and were at the same time teachers of them both?†

A language that has only articulations and voices therefore has only half its riches; it conveys ideas, it is true, but in order to convey feelings, images, it still needs a rhythm and sounds, that is, a melody; that is what the Greek language had, and what our lacks.

We are always astonished by the prodigious effects of eloquence, poetry, and music among the Greeks;[117] these effects cannot be sorted out at all in our heads because we no longer experience similar ones, and all that we can manage for ourselves, seeing them so well attested, is to pretend

---

*Geogr., Bk. 1.[115]

†*Architas atque Aristoxenes etiam subjectam grammaticen musicae putaverunt, et eosdem utriusque rei praeceptores, fuisse. . . . Tum Eupolis apud quem Prodamus et musicen et literas docet. Et Maricas, qui est Hyperbolus, nihil se ex musicis scire nisi literas confitetur.* Quint. Bk. I, chap. X.[116]

to believe them out of indulgence for our Scholars.* Burrette, having transcribed as best he could some pieces of Greek music into our musical notation, was simple enough to have these pieces performed at the Academy of Belles-Lettres, and the Academicians had the patience to listen to them.[118] I admire this experiment in a country whose music is indecipherable for every other nation. Give any foreign Musicians you please a monologue from a French opera to perform: I defy you to recognize any of it. These are nonetheless the same Frenchmen who presume to judge the melody of an Ode of Pindar set to Music two thousand years ago!

I have read that the Indians in America, seeing the astonishing effect of firearms, used to pick up the musket balls from the ground, then, throwing them with their hands while emitting a loud noise from their mouths, were quite surprised that they had not killed anyone. Our orators, our musicians, and our Scholars resemble these Indians. The wonder is not that we no longer accomplish with our music what the Greeks did with theirs, on the contrary, it would be that the same effects should be produced with such different instruments.

CHAPTER XIII

ON MELODY

Man is modified by his senses, no one doubts it; but because we fail to distinguish their modifications, we confound their causes; we attribute both too much and too little dominion to sensations; we do not see that often they affect us not only as sensations but as signs or images, and that their moral effects also have moral causes.[120] Just as the feelings that painting arouses in us are not at all due to colors, so the dominion music has over our souls is not at all the work of sounds. Beautiful colors, finely shaded, please the sight, but that pleasure is purely one of sensation. It is

---

* Doubtless allowance has to be made for Greek exaggeration in all things, but it is to concede too much to modern prejudice to carry such allowances to the point of making all differences vanish. "When the Music of the Greeks of the time of Amphion and of Orpheus," says the Abbé Terrasson,[119] "was at the level at which it is today in the towns furthest from the Capital, it was at that time that it interrupted the course of rivers, that it attracted oaks, that it made rocks move. Today, having reached a very high level of perfection, it is much beloved, its beauties have even been penetrated, but it leaves everything in place. It was the same with the verses of Homer: a Poet born in the times which still showed the effects of the childhood of the human mind, in comparison with those that followed. People were enraptured by these verses, and today they content themselves with savoring and appreciating the verses of good Poets." There is no denying that the Abbé Terrasson is sometimes philosophic, but he certainly doesn't show it in this passage.

the design, it is the imitation, that endows these colors with life and soul, it is the passions which they express that succeed in moving our own, it is the objects which they represent that succeed in affecting us. Interest and feeling do not depend on colors; the contours of a touching painting touch us in an engraving as well; remove those contours from the Painting, the colors will no longer do anything.[121]

Melody does in music precisely what design does in painting; it is melody that indicates the contours and figures, of which the accords and sounds are but the colors. But will it not be said that melody is merely a succession of sounds? Doubtless; but design is also merely an arrangement of colors. An orator makes use of ink to pen his writings; does that mean that ink is a most eloquent liquid?

Imagine a country where no one had any idea of design, but where many people who spend their lives combining, mixing, and blending colors believed themselves to excel in painting; those people would reason about our painting precisely as we reason about the music of the Greeks. Even if they were told about the emotion that beautiful paintings cause in us and about the charm of being touched by a pathetic subject, would their scholars not straightaway probe the material, compare their colors with ours, examine whether our green is more delicate or our red more brilliant; would they not try to find out which accords of colors could cause weeping, which others could arouse anger? The Burettes[122] of that country would put together a few disfigured fragments of our paintings on rags; then it would be asked with surprise what was so marvelous about such coloration.

And if, in a neighboring nation, someone began to form some sort of contour, a sketch, a still imperfect figure, it would all pass for scribbling, for a capricious and baroque painting, and, in order to preserve taste, they would hold onto this simple beauty, which in truth expresses nothing, but which makes fine shadings, large well-colored slabs, extended progressions of hues without any contour.

Finally, they might perhaps by dint of progress arrive at the experiment with the prism.[123] Straightaway, some celebrated artist would establish a beautiful system on the basis of it. Gentlemen, he would say to them, in order to philosophize properly, one has to go back to the physical causes. Here you have the decomposition of light, here you have all the primary colors, here you have their ratios, their proportions, here you have the true principles of the pleasure that painting causes for you. All this mysterious talk of design, representation, figure is a pure chicanery on the part of French painters, who think that by their imitations they produce I know not what movements in the soul, while it is known that there is nothing in it but sensations. You are told of the marvels of their paintings, but look at my hues.

French Painters, he would continue, may perhaps have observed the rainbow; they may have received from nature some taste for shading and some instinct for coloration. But I, I have shown you the great, the true principles of the art. What am I saying, of the art? Of all the arts, Gentlemen, of all the sciences. The analysis of colors, the calculation of the refractions of the prism, gives you the sole exact relationships found in nature, the rule of all relationships.[124] Now, everything in the universe is merely relationship. One therefore knows everything once one knows how to paint, one knows everything once one knows how to match colors.[125]

What would we say about a painter so lacking in feeling and taste as to reason in this way, and stupidly to limit the pleasure that painting causes in us to the physics of his art? What would we say of the musician who, filled with similar prejudices, believed he saw in harmony alone the source of the great effects of music? We would send the first off to paint woodwork, and would condemn the other to compose French opera.

As painting is, therefore, not the art of combining colors in a way pleasing to the sight, no more is music the art of combining sounds in a way pleasing to the ear.[126] If there were nothing but this in them, they would both be counted among the ranks of the natural sciences, and not the fine arts. It is imitation alone that elevates them to that rank. Now, what makes painting an imitative art? It is design. What makes music another? It is melody.

CHAPTER XIV

ON HARMONY

The beauty of sounds is from nature; their effect is purely physical, it results from the interaction of the various particles of air set in motion by the sounding body, and by all its aliquots, perhaps to infinity. All of this together produces a pleasant sensation: every man in the universe will take pleasure in listening to beautiful sounds; but unless this pleasure is animated by melodious inflections that are familiar to them, it will not be delightful, it will not pass into voluptuous pleasure. The most beautiful songs, to our taste, will always only indifferently touch an ear that is not at all accustomed to them; it is a language for which one has to have the Dictionary.

Harmony, properly so called, is in a still less favorable situation. Having only conventional beauties, it in no way appeals to ears that are not trained in it; one has to have been long habituated to it in order to feel and savor it. Rustic ears hear only noise in our consonances. When the natural proportions are distorted, it is not surprising that the natural pleasure no longer exists.

A sound carries with it all of its concomitant harmonies, in the relations of strength and interval that they must have among themselves in order to produce the most perfect harmony of this same sound. Add to this the third or fifth or some other consonance, you do not add to it, but redouble it; you leave the relation of interval unchanged, but you alter that of the strength; by reinforcing one consonance and not the others, you disrupt the proportion. Wanting to do better than nature, you do worse. Your ears and your taste are spoiled by a misunderstood art. By nature there is no other harmony than unison.

M. Rameau claims that treble parts of a comparative simplicity naturally suggest their basses, and that a man who has a true but unpracticed ear will naturally intone this bass.[127] That is a musician's prejudice, belied by all experience. Not only will a person who has never heard either a bass or harmony not find either this harmony or bass on his own, but they will even displease him if he is made to hear them, and he will like simple unison much better.

Even if one were to calculate the ratios of sounds and the laws of harmony for a thousand years, how will this art ever be made an imitative art? Where is the principle of this supposed imitation, of what is harmony the sign, and what do these chords have in common with our passions?

Were the same question put about melody, the answer would come of itself: it is in the readers' minds beforehand. Melody, by imitating the inflections of the voice, expresses complaints, cries of sadness or of joy, threats, and moans; all the vocal signs of the passions are within its scope. It imitates the accents of languages, and the turns of phrase appropriate in each idiom to certain movements of the soul; it not only imitates, it speaks, and its language, inarticulate but lively, ardent, passionate, has a hundred times more energy than speech itself. Here is from whence the strength of musical imitations arises; here is from whence the dominion of song over sensitive hearts arises. Harmony may, in certain systems, cooperate with this by linking the succession of sounds through certain laws of modulations, by making the intonations more exact, by providing the ear with reliable evidence of this exactness, by bringing together and determining imperceptible inflections into consonant and linked intervals. But by thus shackling the melody, it deprives it of energy and expression, it eliminates passionate accent in order to substitute the harmonic interval for it, it subjects to two modes alone songs which should have as many modes as they have oratorical tones, it effaces and destroys multitudes of sounds or intervals that do not enter into its system; in a word, it separates song from speech so much that these two languages combat one another, contradict one another, deprive each other of every characteristic of truth and cannot be united in a pathetic subject without being absurd. That is how it happens that the people always find it ridiculous for strong and serious passions to be expressed in song; for it knows that in our languages these passions have no musical inflections, and that the men of the north no more die singing than swans do.[128]

By itself harmony is even inadequate for the expressions that appear to depend uniquely upon it. Thunder, the murmuring of waters, winds, and storms are poorly rendered by simple chords. Whatever one may do, noise alone says nothing to the mind, objects have to speak in order to make themselves heard, in every imitation a type of discourse always has to supplement the voice of nature. The musician who wants to render noise with noise is mistaken; he knows neither the weakness nor the strength of his art; he judges it without taste, without enlightenment; teach him that he should render noise with song, that if he would make frogs croak, he has to make them sing.[129] For it is not enough for him to imitate, he has to touch and to please, otherwise his glum imitation is nothing, and, not interesting anyone, it makes no impression.

CHAPTER XV

THAT OUR LIVELIEST SENSATIONS OFTEN ACT THROUGH MORAL IMPRESSIONS[130]

As long as one wants to consider sounds only in terms of the disturbance they excite in our nerves, one will not have the true principles of music and its power over our hearts. The sounds of a melody do not act on us solely as sounds, but as signs of our affections, of our feelings; it is in this way that they excite in us the emotions they express and the image of which we recognize in them. Something of this moral effect is perceived even in animals. The barking of one dog attracts another. If my cat hears me imitate meowing, I see him immediately attentive, restless, agitated. If he perceives that it is I who is counterfeiting the voice of his fellow, he sits back and relaxes. Why this difference in impression, since there is none in the disturbance of the fibers, and since he himself was at first deceived by it?[131]

If the greatest dominion our sensations have over us is not due to moral causes, why then are we so sensitive to impressions which mean nothing to barbarians? Why is our most touching music but an empty noise to the ear of a Carib? Are his nerves of a different nature than ours, why are they not disturbed in the same way, or why do these same disturbances affect some people so much and others so little?

The cure of Tarantula bites is cited as a proof of the physical power of sounds.[132] This example proves entirely the contrary. What is required to heal everyone who has been bitten by this insect is neither absolute sounds nor the same tunes: each of them needs tunes of a melody familiar to him and lyrics he understands. Italian tunes are needed for the Italian, for the Turk, Turkish tunes would be needed. Each is affected only by accents that are familiar to him; his nerves yield to them only insofar as his mind disposes them to it: he must understand the language that is spoken to him for what is said to him to be able to move him. Bernier's cantatas have, it is said, cured the fever of a French musician; they would have given one to a musician of any other nation.[133]

The same differences can be observed in all the other senses, down to the crudest of all. Let a man whose hand is placed and whose glance is fixed on the same object alternately believe it to be alive and not alive: although the senses are struck the same way, what a change in the impression! The roundness, whiteness, firmness, gentle warmth, elastic resistance, and successive rising no longer produce anything except a soft but insipid touch for him if he does not believe he feels a heart full of life throbbing and beating underneath it all.

I know only one sense whose affections have no admixture of anything moral in them. It is taste. So gluttony is always the dominant vice only of people who feel nothing.[134]

Let whoever wishes to philosophize about the strength of sensations therefore begin by setting aside purely sensual impressions apart from the intellectual and moral impressions which we receive by way of the senses, but of which the senses are only the occasional causes; let him avoid the error of attributing to sensible objects a power that they do not have or that they derive from the affections of the soul which they represent to us. Colors and sounds are capable of a great deal as representations or signs, of little as simple objects of the senses. Series of sounds or chords will amuse me for perhaps a moment; but in order to charm me and to move me, these series have to offer me something that is neither a sound nor a chord, and that succeeds in moving me in spite of myself. Even songs that are only pleasant and say nothing are still tiresome; for it is not so much the ear that carries pleasure to the heart as the heart that carries it to the ear. I believe that by developing these ideas better, we would have been spared much stupid argumentation concerning ancient music. But in this century, when every effort is made to materialize all the operations of the soul and to deprive human feelings of all morality, I am mistaken if the new philosophy does not become as fatal to good taste as to virtue.

CHAPTER XVI

FALSE ANALOGY BETWEEN COLORS AND SOUNDS

There is no sort of absurdity to which physical observations have failed to give rise in the treatment of the fine arts. The same relationships have been found in the analysis of sound as in that of light. Straightaway this analogy was keenly seized upon without troubling about experience and reason. The systematizing spirit[135] confounded everything, and for want of knowing how to paint for the ears, they took it into their heads to sing to the eyes. I have seen that famous clavichord on which music was supposedly made with colors;[136] it was to have quite misunderstood the operations of nature not to have seen that the effect of colors is due to their permanence and that of sounds to their succession.

All the riches of coloration are spread out all at once over the face of the earth. Everything is seen by the first glance of the eye; but the more one looks, the more one is enchanted. One has only to admire and contemplate, endlessly.

This is not so for sound: nature does not analyze it and separate out its harmonics; on the contrary, it hides them under the appearance of unison; or if it occasionally separates them in the modulated song of man and in the warbling of certain birds, it is successively and one after another; it inspires songs and not chords, dictates melody and not harmony. Colors are the finery of inanimate beings; all matter is colored; but sounds proclaim movement, the voice proclaims a sensitive being; only animated bodies sing. It is not the automated flautist that plays the flute, it is the mechanic who measured the air flow and made the fingers move.[137]

Thus each sense has a field proper to it. The field of music is time, that of painting is space. To multiply the sounds heard at the same time or to develop colors one after another is to change their economy, to put the eye in the place of the ear, and the ear in the place of the eye.

You say: just as each color is determined by the angle of refraction of the ray that produces it, so too are sounds determined by the number of vibrations of the sounding body in a given time. Now, the relationships between these angles and these numbers being the same, the analogy is evident. So be it, but this analogy is one of reason, not sensation, and this is not what is at issue. In the first place, the angle of refraction is perceptible and measurable, and the number of vibrations is not. Sounding bodies, being subject to the action of the air, constantly change dimension and tone. Colors are durable, sounds vanish, and it is never certain that the sounds that reemerge were the same as those that faded. Furthermore, each color is absolute, independent, whereas each sound is for us only relative and is distinguished only by comparison. A sound does not in itself have any absolute character by which it might be recognized; it is low or high, loud or soft, in relation to another sound; in itself it is none of these. In the harmonic system, a given sound is no longer anything naturally: it is neither tonic nor dominant, neither harmonic nor fundamental; since all these properties are only relationships, and since the entire system can vary from low to high, each sound changes rank and position in the system as the system changes in degree. But the properties of colors do not at all consist in relations. Yellow is yellow independently of red and blue, it is everywhere perceptible and recognizable, and as soon as the angle of refraction that produces it is determined, one will be sure of having the same yellow at all times.

Colors are not in the colored bodies but in the light; for an object to be seen, it has to be illuminated. Sounds also need a moving body, and for them to exist, a sounding body must be struck. This is another advantage for sight: for the perpetual emanation from the stars is the natural instrument that acts upon it, whereas nature alone engenders few sounds, and, unless the harmony of the celestial spheres[138] is admitted, living beings are required for it to be produced.

It is seen from this that painting is closer to nature and that music depends more on human art. One also senses that the one holds more interest than the other precisely because it brings man together with man to a greater degree and always gives us some idea of our fellows. Painting is often dead and inanimate; it can transport you to the depths of a desert; but as soon as vocal signs strike your ear, they proclaim a being similar[139] to yourself; they are, so to speak, the organs of the soul, and if they also depict solitude for you, they tell you that you are not alone there. Birds whistle, man alone sings, and one cannot hear either a song or an instrumental piece without immediately saying to oneself: another sensitive being is present.

One of the great advantages of the musician is to be able to depict things that cannot be heard, while it is impossible for the Painter to represent those that cannot be seen, and the greatest marvel of an art that acts only through movement is to be able to form it even into the very image of rest.[140] Sleep, the calm of the night, solitude, and silence itself enter into music's portraits. It is known that noise can produce the effect of silence and silence the effect of noise, as when one falls asleep to an even and monotonous reading and wakes up the instant it stops. But music acts upon us more intimately by arousing through one sense affections similar to those that can be aroused through another, and as the relationship is perceptible only insofar as the impression is strong, painting, stripped of this power, cannot convey to music the imitations that music takes from it. Let nature as a whole be asleep, he who contemplates it sleeps not, and the musician's art consists in substituting for the imperceptible image of the object that of the movements that its presence excites in the heart of the contemplator. Not only will it agitate the sea, fan the flames of a blaze, make streams run, rain fall, and torrents swell, but it will depict the horror of a frightful desert, darken the walls of an underground dungeon, calm a tempest, make the air tranquil and clear, and spread from the orchestra a renewed freshness over the groves. It will not represent these things directly, but will awaken the same feelings in the soul that are experienced in seeing them.

CHAPTER XVII

AN ERROR OF MUSICIANS HARMFUL TO THEIR ART

See how everything continually brings us back to the moral effects of which I have spoken, and how far the musicians who consider the power of sounds only in terms of the action of air and the disturbance of fibers are from knowing wherein resides the strength of this art. The more they assimilate it to purely physical impressions, the farther they take it from its origin, and the more they also take from it its primitive energy. By giving up oral accent and adhering to harmonic institutions alone, music becomes noisier to the ear and less sweet to the heart. It has already ceased to speak; soon it will no longer sing and then, with all its chords and all its harmony, it will no longer have any effect on us.

CHAPTER XVIII

THAT THE MUSICAL SYSTEM OF THE GREEKS DID NOT HAVE ANY RELATION TO OURS

How have these changes come about? By a natural change in the character of languages. Our harmony is known to be a gothic invention. Those who claim to find the system of the Greeks in our own are making fun of us.[141] The system of the Greeks had absolutely no harmony in our sense except what was required to tune instruments on perfect consonances. All peoples who possess stringed instruments are forced to tune them by consonances, but those who do not possess them have inflections in their songs which we call false because they do not enter into our system and because we cannot notate them. This has been noted about the songs of the American savages, and it might also have been noted about the various intervals of the music of the Greeks, if this music had been studied with less bias toward our own.[142]

The Greeks divided their Diagram into tetrachords as we divide our keyboard into octaves, and the same divisions were repeated on each tetrachord among them exactly as they are repeated on each octave among us: a similarity which would not have been possible to preserve in the unity of the harmonic mode and which would not even have been imagined. But as one proceeds by smaller intervals when speaking than when singing, it was natural for them to regard the repetition of tetrachords in their oral melody as we do the repetition of octaves in our harmonic melody.

They recognized as consonances only those which we call perfect consonances; they excluded thirds and sixths from this class.[143] Why so? It is because, since the interval of the minor tone was unknown to them or at least proscribed from practice, and since their consonances were not tempered at all, all their major thirds were too strong by a comma, while their minor thirds were too weak by as much and, consequently, their major and minor sixths were reciprocally impaired in the same way. Consider now what notions of harmony one could have and what harmonic modes one could establish after banishing thirds and sixths from the class of consonances! If even the consonances they did accept had been known to them, by a true feeling for harmony, they would have at least made implicit use of them within their songs,[144] and the tacit consonance of the fundamental progressions would have lent its name to the diatonic progressions they would suggest to them. Far from having had fewer consonances than we do, they would have had more of them, and, for example, occupied with the bass *do sol*, they would have given the name consonance to the second *do re*.

But why then, it will be asked, diatonic progressions? By an instinct that leads us in an accented and tuneful language to choose the most convenient inflections: for between the overly strong modifications which must be given to the glottis in order continually to intone large intervals of consonances and the difficulty of regulating the intonation in the very complicated relations of the smaller intervals, the organ took a middle course and naturally hit on intervals smaller than consonances and simpler than commas—which did not stop the smaller intervals from also having their use in the more pathetic genera.[145]

CHAPTER XIX

HOW MUSIC HAS DEGENERATED

In proportion as language was perfected, melody imperceptibly lost its ancient energy by imposing new rules upon itself, and the calculation of intervals was substituted for the subtlety of inflections.[146] It is in this way, for example, that the practice of the enharmonic genus was gradually eliminated. Once theaters had assumed a regular form, one no longer sang in them except in the prescribed modes, and in proportion as the rules of imitation were multiplied imitative language grew weaker.

The study of philosophy and the progress of reason, having perfected grammar, deprived language of that lively and passionate tone which had at first made it so tuneful. From the time of Menalippides and Philoxenus, instrumental players—who were at first the employees of the Poets and worked only under them and, so to speak, at their dictation—became independent of them, and it is of this license that Music complains so bitterly in the Comedy by Pherecrates, a passage of which Plutarch has preserved for us.[147] Thus melody, beginning to no longer be so attached to discourse, imperceptibly assumed a separate existence, and music became more independent of the words. That was also when the wonders that it had produced when it was only the accent and the harmony of poetry gradually ceased, and when it gave to poetry that dominion over the passions which speech has since exercised only over reason. Also, ever since Greece was filled with Sophists and Philosophers neither famous poets nor musicians were seen there any longer.[148] By cultivating the art of convincing, that of moving the emotions was lost. Plato himself, jealous of Homer and Euripides, decried the one and was unable to imitate the other.[149]

Soon servitude added its influence to that of philosophy. Greece in chains lost that fire that warms only free souls, and no longer found for the praise of its tyrants the tone with which it had sung of its Heroes. The intermixture of the Romans further weakened what harmony and accent the language retained. Latin, a more muted and less musical language, wronged music in adopting it. The singing employed in the capital gradually altered that of the provinces; the theaters of Rome harmed those of Athens; when Nero was carrying off prizes, Greece had ceased to merit them, and the same melody shared by two languages suited both of them less well.[150]

Ultimately the catastrophe occurred that was to destroy the progress of the human mind without removing the vices that were its work. Europe, inundated with barbarians and enslaved by the unlearned, lost at the same time its sciences, its arts, and the universal instrument of them both, namely, perfected harmonious language. These crude men whom the north had engendered imperceptibly accustomed all ears to the coarseness of their organ; their voices, harsh and devoid of accent, were noisy without being sonorous. The Emperor Julian compared the speech of the Gauls to the croaking of frogs.[151] Since all their articulations were as harsh as their voices were nasal and muted, they could give only a sort of brightness to their singing, which was to stress the sound of the vowels in order to cover up the abundance and harshness of the consonants.

This noisy singing, joined to the inflexibility of their organs, obliged these newcomers and the subjugated peoples who imitated them to slow down all their sounds in order to make them understood. Tedious articulation and stressed sounds likewise contributed to drive away from melody every feeling for meter and rhythm; as what was hardest to pronounce was always the passage from one sound to another, there was nothing better to do than to pause at each one as long as possible, expand it, and make it burst forth as much as one could. Song was soon nothing more than a tiresome and slow series of drawn out and shouted sounds, without sweetness, without meter, and without grace; and if some scholars have said that the long and short syllables in Latin song had to be observed, it is at least certain that verse was sung like prose, and that it was no longer a question of feet, rhythms, or any species of measured song.[152]

Song, thus stripped of all melody and consisting uniquely in the strength and duration of sounds, must finally have suggested ways of making it still more sonorous with the aid of consonances. Several voices, endlessly drawing out in unison sounds of an indefinite duration, accidentally hit upon certain chords that, reinforcing the noise, made it seem more pleasant to them, and it is in this way that the practice of descant and of counterpoint began.

I know not how many centuries musicians twiddled about frivolous questions where the known effect of an unknown cause made them debate for so long. The most tireless reader would not endure the verbiage of eight or ten large chapters in Jehan des Murs in order to learn whether in the interval of the octave divided into two consonances it is the fifth or fourth that must be the lower one; and four hundred years later, one still finds in Bontempi no less tiresome enumerations of all the basses that must carry the sixth instead of the fifth.[153] In the meantime, though, harmony imperceptibly took the route that analysis prescribed to it, until finally the invention of the minor mode and of dissonances introduced into it the arbitrariness of which it is full, and which prejudice alone prevents us from perceiving.*

Melody being forgotten and the attention of the musician having been turned entirely toward harmony, everything was gradually directed toward this new object; the genera, the modes, the scale, everything took on a new appearance; it was harmonic successions that regulated the progression of the parts. Once this progression had usurped the name of melody, it was indeed impossible to mistake its mother's features in this new melody, and as our musical system gradually became purely harmonic, it is not surprising that oral accent suffered for it, and that music lost almost all its energy for us.

This is how singing gradually became an art entirely separated from the speech from which it takes its origin; how the harmonics of sounds have caused vocal inflections to be forgotten; and how, finally, limited to the purely physical effect of the combination of vibrations, music found itself deprived of the moral effects that it used to produce when it was doubly the voice of nature.

CHAPTER XX

RELATIONSHIP OF LANGUAGES TO GOVERNMENTS

This progress is neither fortuitous nor arbitrary, it depends on the vicissitudes of things. Languages are naturally formed according to men's needs; they change and decay in accordance with the changes in these same needs. In ancient times, when persuasion took the place of public force, eloquence was necessary. What use could it serve today, when public force substitutes for persuasion? Neither art nor figures of speech are needed to say, *such is my pleasure*. What discourses are then left to deliver to

---

* By relating all harmony to the very simple principle of the resonance of strings in their aliquots, M. Rameau bases the minor mode and dissonance on his supposed experimental finding that a sounding string in motion makes longer strings vibrate at its twelfth and at its major or lower seventeenth. According to him, these strings vibrate and quiver over their entire length, but do not resonate. That appears to me to be a singular physics; it is as if one were to say that the sun was shining and that one saw nothing.

These longer strings make only the sound of the highest note because they are divided, vibrate, resonate on its unison, combine their sound with its, and appear not to make any of their own. The error is to have believed to see them vibrate over their entire length, and not to have observed the knots carefully. That two sounding strings which form a given harmonic interval can make their fundamental sound heard in the bass, even without a third string, is an experimental result known and confirmed by M. Tartini;[154] but one string alone has no other fundamental sound than its own; it does not make its multiples resonate or vibrate, but only its unison and its aliquots. As sound has no other cause than the vibrations of the sounding body, and since where the cause acts freely the effect always follows, it is absurd to speak of separating the vibrations from the resonance.

the assembled people? Sermons. And what does persuading the people matter to those who deliver them, since it is not the people that confers benefices? Popular languages have become as perfectly useless to us as eloquence has. Societies have assumed their final form; nothing is changed in them any longer except by arms and cash, and as there is no longer anything to say to the people but, *give money*, it is said to them with placards at street corners or with soldiers in their homes; it is not necessary to assemble anyone for this: on the contrary, the subjects have to be kept scattered; this is the first maxim of modern politics.[155]

There are languages favorable to liberty; these are sonorous, prosodic, harmonious languages, in which discourse can be made out from a distance. Ours are made for the murmuring in sultans' Council-chambers. Our preachers torment themselves, work themselves into a sweat in churches, without anyone having known anything of what they have said. After tiring themselves out shouting for an hour, they leave the pulpit half dead. Surely this was not worth such an effort.

Among the ancients it was easy to make oneself heard by the people in the public square; one could speak there a whole day without becoming uncomfortable. Generals harangued their troops; they could make themselves heard and did not tire themselves out. Modern historians who have wanted to put such harangues in their histories have gotten themselves laughed at. Imagine a man haranguing the people of Paris in French in the Place Vendôme. Let him scream his head off: people will hear that he is screaming; not a word of it will be made out. Herodotus read his history to the peoples of Greece assembled in the open air and all rang out with applause.[156] Today the academician who reads a paper on a day of public assembly can hardly be heard in the back of the hall. If the charlatans in the public squares are less bountiful in France than in Italy, it is not that in France people listen to them any less, it is only that they cannot hear them as well. M. d'Alembert believes a French recitative could be delivered in the Italian fashion;[157] it would have to be delivered right in one's ear, otherwise none of it would be heard. Now, I say that every language with which one cannot make oneself understood by the assembled people is a servile language; it is impossible for a people to remain free and speak that language.

I shall conclude these superficial reflections, but ones which may give birth to more profound ones, with the passage that suggested them to me.

*It would be the matter of a rather philosophic study to observe in fact and show by examples how much the character, morals, and interests of a people influence its language.**

---

* *Remarks on the gen. and reason. gramm.*, by M. Duclos, page 11.[158]

Pronunciation

Let one make oneself heard distinctly while speaking lowly and producing the fewest inflections possible. Now, in order to make oneself heard distinctly in this manner only prosody and accent can substitute for the strength of the voice and the variety of inflections.

Thus, the one who will make himself heard most distinctly and at the greatest distance with the same volume and the same tone of voice without inflection and without declamation will be without contest the one who pronounces best.

The French language shows the inclinations of those who speak it, everything is fashion and style even in pronunciation.

Donne-me le. [Give it to me.]

Accent. Error in its definition.
It is true that the voice is different but the tone is absolutely the same.

I have seen fashionable young people do no more than mutter instead of speaking; they assumed that the attention one must put into listening to them excused them from any care to make themselves heard.

degoutant and *dégoutant*. Anecdote by M. de Crebillon.[1]

words whose pronunciation I have seen change
Charolois — Charolès
secret — segret
persecuter — perzecuter
registre — regître
Les hommes — le shommes
Cervus — Servus

Vice of pronunciation in the organ, or in the accent, or in the habit. *Grasseyer*, etc.

The analysis of thought is made by speech, and the analysis of speech by writing; speech represents thought by conventional signs, and writing represents speech in the same way; thus, the art of writing is only a mediated representation of thought, at least as regards vocal languages, the sole ones which are in use among us.

Is it not quite ridiculous that one is obliged to say to a man: Write for me what you are saying so that I may understand it?

I doubt that the same equivocation was found originally in Latin pronunciation. For the Latin language being above all in its beginnings spoken much more than written, it was not natural for equivocations to be left in discourse which were removed only by orthography.

Languages are made in order to be spoken, writing serves only as a substitute for speech; if there are some languages that are only written and that cannot be spoken, they belong to the sciences alone, they have no use in civil life. Such is algebra, such doubtless was the universal language which Leibniz looked for.[2] It would probably be more convenient for a Metaphysician than for an Artisan. The greatest use of language thus being in speech, the greatest concern of Grammarians should be to determine its modifications, but on the contrary they occupy themselves almost uniquely with writing. The more the art of writing is perfected, the more that of speaking is neglected. Orthography is endlessly discoursed upon and there are hardly any rules regarding pronunciation. This makes it so that by being perfected in books, language is distorted in speech. It is more clear when one writes, more mute when one speaks, syntax is purified and harmony is lost, the French language is becoming day by day more philosophical and less eloquent, soon it will no longer be good except to read, and all its value will be in libraries.

The reason for this abuse is, as I have said elsewhere,[3] in the form that governments have taken and that makes it so that there is nothing to be said to the people other than the things in the world which least touch them and with which they care about least, of listening to sermons and academic discourses. When it has not heard any of all that, the public has not lost anything great and often the orator has gained much from it. For a long time the public has no longer been spoken to except by books, and if something is still said to it in a strong voice which interests it, this is at the theater. In addition, the Players daring not alter the received usage in pronunciation are forced to sing in order to make themselves heard even though they are in an enclosed place. If some man in office was going, on the most important occasion, earnestly to take on the tone an actor takes in the theater, instead of persuading he would produce laughter. It is a tone of convention that is permitted only on the stage.

Well-written books go everywhere. In the provinces, in the villages, into foreign lands. There is no place so removed that one may not study the rules of the language in works which treat it and see the application of those rules in the writings of good authors. The same is not true for the rules of pronunciation. It is not books that convey them, it is men. Now, people who speak well are not common in any country of the world, and those who pronounce well are even less so. It is striking how much prosody and accent are lost and are disfigured to the degree one goes away from the capital. Not having any assured model to regulate one's voice, tones, and accents, one abandons oneself uniquely to the corrupt accent of one's province. Such a person, having arrived in Paris, knows his language perfectly [but] can hardly make himself understood by speaking and causes laughter as soon as he opens his mouth. Further still, the law of usage, not having the same publicity in pronunciation as in grammar, becomes arbitrary; each takes his particular usage for the good one, and having the prejudice that his accent is the sole natural one, so accuses of affectation every accent that is distant from his, so that then it is even a vice to speak well. It is thus that each province, each canton assuming a particular pronunciation, makes of the common written language its own language in speaking, so that, being spoken, Gascon French and Piccard French would be taken for two particular languages which far from being reciprocally understood are hardly understood by those who speak true French.

It is singular that in proportion as letters are cultivated, as the arts multiply, as the ties of the general society are drawn tighter, language is so much perfected by writing and so little by speech. Why are men in coming together so careful about speaking well, about the art of speaking at a distance, and so little careful about the art of speaking in a strong voice? It is that pronounced discourse is drowned amidst so many speakers and that celebrity is acquired only by books.

If there was a less necessary connection between written language and spoken language, they would imperceptibly grow apart and so separate from one another that in the end they would form two different languages, as has happened with Latin and Italian. For the pronunciation always changing and the orthography remaining the same, one would write in one manner and speak in another to the point that in the end one would have two idioms instead of one. What prevents this from happening thus commonly is that the alterations in speech are ultimately transmitted into writing. As there are more people who write as they speak than those who write according to the rules, the changes which occur in the manner of pronouncing and likewise in locutions in speaking are adopted in writing by the majority of men and thus gradually assuming power in usage ultimately cause the one that preceded it to disappear. This is how a language changes its spirit and character by degrees, and it is not surprising that these changes are more prompt and more perceptible in the French language than in any other seeing that its pronunciation, being less fixed, less subject to rules, alters more easily. If after a hundred years this alteration appears less perceptible, this does not happen solely from the excellent books of the century of Louis XIV, which have in some way become classics in this one, but also from changes which have occurred in the government, by which Paris, having a more marked ascendancy over all the Provinces, so to speak imposes on them the law of language as promptly as that of the Prince and, keeping them all dependent on its usage, sufficiently prevents them from communicating their own with one another so that they prevail within the totality.

When they speak Latin the French are understood by practically no other people.

Writing is only the representation of speech, it is bizarre that more care is given to determining the image than the object.

In certain cases it is necessary to follow the retrograde order, and pronunciation which should always regulate orthography is often reduced to consulting it.

For the Grammarians the art of speaking is practically only the art of writing and this is also seen by the use they make of accents, several of which make some distinction or remove some equivocation for the eye but not for the ear.

On Theatrical Imitation
An Essay Drawn from Plato's Dialogues[1]

Notice

This short Writing is merely a kind of extract of various places where Plato treats theatrical Imitation. I hardly had any other part in it other than that of having assembled and connected them into the form of a continuous discourse instead of that of the Dialogue which they had in the original. The occasion for this labor was the Letter to M. d'Alembert on the Theatre;[2] but not having been able to fit it into that work comfortably, I put it aside in order to use it elsewhere or to suppress it entirely. Since then, having left my hands, this writing happened to be involved—I know not how—in a transaction which did not concern me. The Manuscript has been returned to me, but the Bookseller has demanded it back as acquired by him in good faith, and I do not want to gainsay the person who gave it to him. This is how this bagatelle makes its way today into Print.[3]

On Theatrical Imitation

The more I ponder the establishment of our imaginary Republic, the more it seems to me that we have prescribed for it laws that are useful and appropriate to the nature of man. I find, above all, that it was important to set, as we have done, limits to the license of Poets and to forbid them all the parts of their art that are related to imitation. We shall even take up this subject again, if you wish, now that more important things have been examined, and, in the hope that you will not denounce me to those dangerous enemies, I will admit to you that I regard all the dramatic Authors as the corrupters of the People, or of whoever, allowing himself to be amused by their images, is not capable of considering them under their true aspect, nor of giving to these fables the corrective they need. Whatever respect I may have for Homer, their model and their first master, I do not believe that I owe more to him than to the truth; and in order to begin by assuring myself of it, I will first inquire into what imitation is.[4]

In order to imitate a thing, one must have the idea of it. This idea is abstract, absolute, unique, and independent of the number of examples of this thing which may exist in Nature. This idea is always anterior to its execution: for the Architect who builds a Palace has the idea of a Palace before beginning his own. He does not fabricate its model, he follows it, and this model is in his mind in advance.[5]

Limited by his art to that sole object, this Artist knows how to make only his Palace or other similar Palaces; but there are much more universal ones who can make everything that can be executed in the world by any Workman whatsoever, everything that Nature produces, everything that can be made visible in the heavens, on the earth, in the underworld, the Gods themselves. You well understand that these so very marvelous Artists are the Painters, and even the most ignorant of men can do as much with a mirror. You will say to me that the Painter does not make these things, but their images; the Workman who actually fabricates them does as much, since he copies a model which existed before them.

I see there three quite distinct Palaces.[6] First, the model or the original idea which exists in the understanding of the Architect, in nature, or at the very least in its Author along with all the possible ideas of which he is the source; in the second place, the Architect's Palace, which is the image of this model; and, finally, the Painter's Palace, which is the image of that of the Architect. Thus, God, the Architect, and the painter are the authors of these three Palaces. The first Palace is the original idea, existing by itself; the second is its image; the third is the image of the image, or what we properly call imitation. From whence it follows that the imitation does not, as is believed, hold the second rank in the order of beings, but the third, and that, no image being exact and perfect, the imitation is always one degree further from the truth than is thought.

The Architect can make several Palaces on the same model, the Painter several paintings of the same Palace; but as for the original type or model, it is unique; for if it should be supposed that there are two alike, they would no longer be original, they would have an original model common to them both, and it is this one alone that would be the true one. Everything that I say here of painting is applicable to theatrical imitation; but before coming to that, let us examine the Painter's imitations in more detail.

Not only does he imitate only the images of things in his pictures, namely, the perceptible productions of nature and the works of Artists; he does not even seek to render the truth of the object exactly, but the appearance; he paints it such as it appears to be, and not such as it is. He paints it from a single point of view, and choosing this point of view at his will, he renders, in accordance with what suits him, the same object to the eyes of the spectators as pleasant or deformed. Thus, they are never responsible for judging the thing imitated in itself, but they are forced to judge it based on a certain appearance and as it pleases the imitator: often they even judge it only by habit, and something arbitrary enters even into the imitation.*[7]

The Art of representing objects is very different from that of making them understood. The first pleases without instruction; the second instructs without pleasure. The Artist who draws up a plan and takes exact dimensions does nothing very pleasant for the sight; in addition, his work is sought out only by people in the art. But the one who draws a perspective flatters the people and the ignorant because he makes nothing understood by them and offers them only the appearance of what they already knew. Add to this that measurement, giving us successively one dimension and then the other, instructs us slowly about the truth of things, whereas the appearance offers us the whole at one time, and, under the presumption of a greater capacity of mind, flatters the senses by seducing amour-propre.

The representations of the Painter, deprived of all reality, produce even this appearance only with the help of some vain shadows and of some flimsy simulacra that he causes to be taken for the thing itself. If there was

---

*Experience teaches us that beautiful harmony does not at all flatter an unprepared ear, that it is habit alone that makes consonances pleasant to us and makes us distinguish the most discordant intervals. As for the simplicity of ratios on which some have wished to found the pleasure of harmony, I have shown in the *Encyclopedia* at the word *Consonance* that this principle is unsustainable, and I believe it is easy to prove that all our harmony is a barbarous and gothic invention which has become an art of imitation only by the stretch of time.[8] A studious Magistrat who, in his moments of leisure, instead of going to hear music amused himself with delving into systems, has found that the ratio of the fifth is two to three only by approximation, and that this ratio is strictly incommensurable.[9] At least no one can deny that this is so on our harpsichords by virtue of temperament, which does not prevent these fifths thus tempered from seeming pleasant to us. Now, where, in such a case, is the simplicity of ratio which should make them so for us? We still do not at all know whether our system of music is not founded on pure conventions; we do not at all know whether its principles are not completely arbitrary and whether an entirely different system, substituted for that one, would not succeed, by habit, in pleasing us equally well. This is a question discussed elsewhere.[10] By a fairly natural analogy these reflections might awaken others on the subject of painting regarding the tone of a picture, the concord of colors, certain parts of the design in which perhaps more arbitrariness enters than is thought, and in which imitation itself might have rules of convention. Why do Painters not dare undertake new imitations which have nothing against them but their novelty and otherwise seem entirely within the competence of the art? For example, it is a game for them to make a plane surface appear to be in relief. Why, then, doesn't anyone among them not attempt to give the appearance of a plane surface to a relief? If they make a ceiling seem to be a vault, why do they not make a vault appear to be a ceiling? Shadows, they will say, change appearance from different points of view, which does not happen in the same way with plane surfaces. Let us remove this difficulty and ask a Painter to paint and color a statue in such a way that it appears flat, level, and of the same color, without any design, in a single light, and from a single point of view. These new considerations would perhaps not be unworthy of being examined by the enlightened amateur who has philosophized about this art so well.[11]

any admixture of truth in his imitations, he would have had to know the objects he imitated; he would be a Naturalist, a Workman, a Physicist, before being a Painter. But, on the contrary, the compass of his art is founded only on his ignorance, and he paints everything only because he does not need to know anything. When he offers us a Philosopher in meditation, an Astronomer observing the stars, a Geometer drawing figures, a Lathe Worker in his workshop, does he thereby turn, calculate, meditate, or observe the stars? Not at all; he merely paints. Not in a position to give a rational account of any of the things that are in his picture, he takes advantage of us doubly by his imitations, either by offering us a vague and deceptive appearance, the error of which neither he nor we would know how to distinguish, or by employing false measurements in order to produce this appearance, that is, by distorting all the genuine dimensions in accordance with the laws of perspective; so that, if the senses of the spectator are not led astray and limit themselves to seeing the picture as it is, he will be mistaken about all the relations of the things that are presented to him or will find them all false. Nevertheless, the illusion will be such that simpletons and children will be taken in by it, they will believe they are seeing the objects which the Painter himself did not know and workers in arts about which he understands nothing.

Let us learn by this example to mistrust those universal people, skilled in all the arts, versed in all the sciences, who know everything, who reason about everything, and seem to unite in themselves alone the talents of every mortal. If someone tells us that he knows one of these wondrous men, let us assure him without hesitating that he is the dupe of the magic tricks of a charlatan and that all the knowledge of this great Philosopher is founded only on the ignorance of his admirers, who do not know how to distinguish error from truth, nor imitation from the thing imitated.[12]

This leads us to the examination of the tragic Authors and of Homer, their leader.* For some maintain that a tragic Poet must know everything, that he profoundly understands virtues and vices, politics and morality, divine and human laws, and that he must possess the science of all the things he treats or that he will never do anything well. Let us seek to discover, then, whether those who elevate the Poet to this degree of sublimity do not also allow themselves to be imposed upon by the imitating art of the Poets; whether their admiration for these immortal works does not prevent them from seeing how far they are from the truth, from feeling that these are colors without consistency, vain phantoms, shadows, and

---

*It was the common sentiment of the Ancients that their tragic Authors were merely the copyists and imitators of Homer. Someone said of Euripides' Tragedies: *They are the leftovers from Homer's banquets which a guest took home with him.*[13]

that, in order to draw such images, there is nothing less necessary than the knowledge of the truth; or indeed, whether there is any real utility in all this and whether the Poets actually know this multitude of things about which the vulgar find they speak so well.

Tell me, my friends, if someone could have his choice between the portrait of his mistress and the original, which do you think he would choose? If some Artist could equally make the thing imitated or its simulacrum, would he prefer the latter, in objects of any worth, and would he content himself with a house in painting when he could make himself one in actuality? If, then, the tragic Author really knew the things he claims to paint, if he had the qualities he describes, if he himself did everything he makes his characters do, would he not exercise their talents? Would he not practice their virtues? Would he not raise monuments to his glory rather than to theirs? And would he not prefer that he himself do laudable actions rather than limit himself to lauding those of someone else? Certainly his merit would be totally otherwise, and there is no reason why, being capable of more, he would limit himself to less. But what to think of the one who wants to teach us what he has not been able to learn? And who would not laugh at seeing an imbecilic group go to admire all the springs of politics and of the human heart put into play by a twenty-year-old scatterbrain to whom the least sensible person in the assembly would not want to confide the least of his affairs?

Let us leave off what concerns talents and arts. When Homer speaks so well of Machaon's knowledge,[14] we do not at all demand from him an account of his own on the same matter. We do not at all inquire about the illnesses he has cured, the students he has had in medicine, the masterpieces of engraving and of silver-smithing he has completed, the Workmen he has formed, the monuments to his industry. Let us endure him teaching us all this without knowing whether he has been instructed in them. But when he converses about war, government, laws, sciences, which demand the longest study and which matter most to men's happiness, let us dare interrupt him a moment and interrogate him in this way: O divine Homer! We admire your lessons, and in order to follow them we await only to see how you practice them yourself; if you are really what you strive to appear to be; if your imitations are not of the third rank, but the second after the truth, let us see in you the model which you paint for us in your works; show us the Captain, the Legislator, and the Wise Men whose portrait you so boldly offer us. Greece and the entire World celebrate the blessings of great men who possess these sublime arts whose precepts cost you so little. Lycurgus gave laws to Sparta, Charondas to Sicily and to Italy, Minos to the Cretans, Solon to us.[15] Is it a matter of life's duties, of the wise government of the household, of the conduct of a citizen in every state? Thales of Miletus and the Scythian Anacharsis gave the example and the precepts at the same time.[16] Is it necessary to learn these same duties from others and to instruct Philosophers and Wise Men who practice what they have been taught? This Zoroaster did for the Magis, Pythagoras for his disciples, Lycurgus for his fellow-citizens.[17] But you, Homer, if it is true that you have excelled in so many fields, if it is true that you can instruct men and make them better, if it is true that to the imitation you have joined intelligence and to speeches knowledge, let us see the works that prove your skill, the States you have instituted, the virtues that honor you, the disciples you have produced, the battles you have won, the riches you have acquired. Have you not won over crowds of friends who make you loved and honored by everyone? How can it be that you have attracted to yourself only Cleophon alone?[18] You still made only an ingrate. What! A Protagoras of Abdera, a Prodicus of Ceos, without departing from a simple and private life have gathered their contemporaries around themselves, have persuaded them to learn from them alone the art of governing their country, their family, and themselves;[19] and these very wondrous men, a Hesiod, a Homer, who knew everything, who could teach everything to the men of their time, were neglected by them to the point of going wandering, begging everywhere in the universe, and singing their verses from city to city, like vile Mountebanks! In those coarse centuries, where the weight of ignorance began to make itself felt, where the need and the avidity for knowledge concurred to make every man a little more instructed than the others useful and respectable, if they had been as learned as they seemed to be, if they had had all the qualities they made shine with such pomp, they would have passed for prodigies; they would have been sought after by everyone; each would have rushed to have them, possess them, retain them in their homes; and those who could not establish them with themselves would have followed them all over the earth rather than lose such a rare occasion of being instructed and of becoming Heroes like those they were made to admire.*

Let us agree, then, that all the Poets, beginning with Homer, represent to us in their pictures not the model of virtues, of talents, of qualities of the soul, nor the other objects of the understanding and of the senses they do not themselves have, but the images of all these objects drawn from for-

---

*Plato did not wish to say that a man competent in his interests and versed in lucrative affairs might not, by trafficking in Poetry, or by other means, attain a great fortune. But it is very different to enrich oneself and to win renown by the Poet's trade than to enrich oneself and win renown by the talents the Poet claims to teach. It is true that one could cite the example of Tyrtaeus to Plato, but he could extricate himself from the situation with distinction by considering him rather as an Orator than as a Poet.[20]

eign objects; and that they are thereby no nearer to truth in that when they offer to us the features of a Hero or of a Captain, that a Painter who, painting for us a Geometer or a Workman, is not concerned at all with the art of which he understands nothing but only with the colors and the shape. Thus, the names and the words cause an illusion for those who, sensitive to rhythm and to harmony, allow themselves to be charmed by the enchanting art of the Poet and yield to seduction by the attraction of the pleasure; so that they take the images of objects, which are not known either by themselves or by their authors, for the objects themselves, and who fear being undeceived about an error which flatters them, whether by throwing their ignorance off the track or by the pleasant sensations by which their ignorance is accompanied.

Indeed, take from the most brilliant of these pictures the charm of the verses and the foreign ornaments which embellish it, strip it of the Poet's coloration or of its style and leave it only the design, and you will have difficulty recognizing it, or, if it is recognizable, it will no longer please—like those children who, rather pretty than beautiful, adorned solely with the flower of their youth, alone lose all their graces along with it without having lost anything of their features.

Not only does the imitator or the author of the simulacrum know only the appearance of the thing imitated, but the genuine knowledge of that thing does not belong even to the one who has made it. I look into this picture of horses harnessed to Hector's chariot; these horses have harnesses, bits, reins; the Silversmith, the Blacksmith, the Saddler have made these various things: the Painter has represented them, but neither the Workman who makes them nor the Painter who draws them knows what they should be; it is for the Horseman or for the Driver who makes use of them to determine their form by their use; it is for him alone to judge whether they are well or badly made and to correct their defects. Thus, in every possible instrument there are three objects of practice to consider, namely, the use, the fabrication, and the imitation. These last two arts manifestly depend upon the first, and there is nothing imitable in nature to which one may not apply the same distinctions.

If the utility, the goodness, the beauty of an instrument, of an animal, of an action is related to the use drawn from it, if it belongs only to the one who puts them to work to give their model and to judge whether this model is faithfully executed, far from the imitator being in a position to pronounce upon the qualities of the things he imitates, this decision does not even belong to the one who has made them. The imitator follows the workman whose work he copies, the Workman follows the Artist who knows how to make use of them, and this last one alone assesses likewise the thing and its imitation, which confirms that the pictures of the Poet and of the Painter occupy merely the third place after the first model or the truth.

But the Poet, who has as judge only the ignorant People whom he seeks to please, how will he not disfigure the objects he presents to them in order to flatter them?[21] He will imitate what appears beautiful to the multitude without caring whether it is so in actuality. If he paints valor, will he have Achilles for a judge? If he paints ruse, will Ulysses take it up? Wholly the contrary: Achilles and Ulysses will be his characters, Thersites and Dolon his spectators.[22]

You will object to me that the Philosopher himself does not know all the arts about which he speaks either, and that he often extends his ideas as far as the Poet extends his images.[23] I admit it; but the Philosopher does not present himself as knowing the truth: he seeks it, he examines, he discusses, he extends our views, he even instructs us by allowing himself to be misled; he proposes his doubts as doubts, his conjectures as conjectures, and he affirms only what he knows. The Philosopher who reasons submits his reasonings to our judgment; the Poet, and the imitator puts himself forward as judge. By offering us his images, he affirms that they conform to the truth: he is therefore obliged to know it, if his art has any reality; by depicting everything, he presents himself as knowing everything. The Poet is the Painter who makes the image; the Philosopher is the Architect who draws up the plan.[24] The one does not even dare approach the object in order to paint it; the other measures before drawing.

But for fear of being misled by false analogies, let us try to see more distinctly to what part, to what faculty of our soul, the imitations of the Poet are related and let us first consider from whence the illusion of those of Painter come.[25] The same bodies seen at various distances do not seem to be the same size, nor their shapes equally perceptible, nor their colors of the same vivacity. Seen in the water, they change appearance; what was straight appears broken; the object seems to float with the waves. Through a spherical or hollow glass all these relations of the features are changed; with the help of light and shadows a plane surface is raised or recessed to the Painter's liking; his brush engraves features as deeply as the Sculptor's chisel, and in the reliefs he knows how to draw on cloth, touch—contradicted by sight—leaves in doubt which of these two should be trusted. All these errors obviously have their source in the precipitous judgments of the mind. It is this weakness of human understanding, always in a hurry to judge without knowing, which gives rise to all those magical tricks by which Optics and Mechanics mislead our senses. We reach a conclusion, based on appearance alone, from what we do know to what we do not know, and our false inductions are the source of a thousand illusions.

What resources are we offered against these errors? Those of examination and of analysis. The suspension of the mind, the art of measuring, of weighing, of counting, are the aids which man has for verifying the relations of the senses so that he does not judge what is large or small, round or square, rarefied or dense, far or near, by what they seem to be, but by what number, measure, and weight give to him as such. The comparison, the judgment of relations found by these various operations incontestably belongs to the reasoning faculty, and this judgment is often in contradiction with the one to which the appearance of things leads us. Now, we have seen beforehand that it can not be by the same faculty of the soul that it holds contrary judgments of the same things considered under the same relations.[26] From which it follows that it is not at all the most noble of our faculties, namely reason, but a different and inferior faculty which judges by appearance and yields to the charm of the imitation.[27] This is what I wanted to express beforehand in saying that Painting, and the art of imitating generally, practices its operations far from the truth of things by combining with a part of our soul deprived of prudence and reason and incapable of knowing by itself anything of reality and of truth.* Thus, the art of imitating, low by its nature and by the faculty of the soul on which it acts, can only be further so by its productions, at least as regards the material sense that makes us judge the Painter's pictures. Let us now consider the same art applied by the Poet's imitations immediately to the internal sense, that is, to the understanding.

The stage represents men acting voluntarily or by force, assessing their actions as good or bad according to the good or ill they think come to them from them, and variously affected, due to them, by pain or by sensual pleasure.[28] Now, by the reasons we have already discussed, it is impossible for the man, thus presented, ever to be in accord with himself; and as the appearance and the reality of sensible objects give him contrary opinions, likewise he assesses the objects of his actions differently, accordingly as they are far or near, conformable or opposed to his passions; and his judgments, mobile like them, constantly put his desires, his reason, his will, and all the powers of his soul into contradiction.

The stage therefore represents all men, and even those who are given to us as models, as otherwise affected than they should be to maintain them-

---

*This word *part* here must not be taken in a precise sense, as if Plato supposed the soul to be really divisible or composed. The division he assumes and which makes him use the word *part* regards only the various kinds of operations by which the soul is modified, and which are otherwise called *faculties*.

selves in the state of moderation which suits them.[29] Let a wise and courageous man lose his son, his friend, his mistress, finally, the object most dear to his heart: he will not be seen to abandon himself to an excessive and unreasonable grief; and if human weakness does not permit him to overcome his affliction completely, he will temper it by constancy; a just shame will make him close up within himself a part of his pains, and, constrained to appear to the eyes of men, he will blush to say and do in their presence some things which he does and says when alone. Not being able to be in himself such as he wishes, he at least tries to offer himself to others such as he should be. What troubles him and agitates him is grief and passion; what stops him and contains him is reason and law; and in these opposed movements his will always declares itself for the latter.

Indeed, reason desires that adversity be endured patiently, that its weight not be aggravated by useless complaints, that human things not be estimated above their worth, that, in weeping over one's ills, one not waste the forces one has to soften them, that, finally, one sometimes think that it is impossible for man to foresee the future and to know himself well enough in order to know whether what happens to him is a good or an evil for him.[30]

Thus, the judicious and temperate man will comport himself as a victim of ill fortune. He will try to turn to profit his very reverses, as a prudent gambler seeks to take advantage of a bad mark that chance brings him; and, without lamenting like a child who falls and cries over the rock that has struck him, he knows how to bear, if necessary, a hot iron that is salutary for his wound and to make it bleed in order to heal it. We shall therefore say that constancy and firmness in the face of disgrace are the work of reason, and that mourning, tears, despair, moans belong to one part of the soul opposed to the other one, weaker, more cowardly, and much inferior in dignity.

Now, it is from this sensitive and weak part that the touching and varied imitations seen on the stage are drawn.[31] The man who is firm, prudent, and always like himself is not so easy to imitate, and, even if he were, the imitation, being less varied, would not be as pleasant to the Vulgar; they would be interested with difficulty in an image which is not their own, and in which they recognized neither their morals, nor their passions: never does the human heart identify with objects that it feels are absolutely foreign to it. In addition, the skillful Poet, the Poet who knows the art of succeeding, seeking to please the People and vulgar men, is quite wary of offering them the sublime image of a heart that is master of itself, that hears only the voice of wisdom; but he charms the spectators by characters who are always in contradiction, who want and do not want, who make the Theaters ring with cries and moans, who force us to pity them, even when they do their duty, and to think virtue is a sad thing since it makes its friends so miserable. It is by this means that, with easier and more diverse imitations, the Poet moves and further flatters the spectators.

This habit of submitting the people we are made to admire to their passions so spoils and changes our judgments about laudable things that we accustom ourselves to honor the soul's weakness under the name of sensitivity, and to treat those in whom the severity of duty prevails on every occasion over natural affections as hard men without feeling. On the contrary, we esteem as good-natured men those who, vividly affected by everything, are the perpetual playthings of events; those who cry like women at the loss of what was dear to them; those who are made unjust by a deranged friendship so as to serve their friends; those who know no other rule than the blind penchant of their heart; those who—always praised by the sex that subjugates them and that they imitate—have no virtues other than their passions, nor any merit other than their weakness. Thus, equality, force, constancy, the love of justice, the empire of reason imperceptibly become detestable qualities, vices that are decried; men are honored for everything that makes them worthy of scorn, and this inversion of healthy opinions is the infallible effect of the lessons one goes to receive at the Theater.

It is therefore with reason that we blamed the Poet's imitations and we put them into the same rank as those of the Painter, whether for being equally distant from the truth, or because both of them, likewise flattering the sensitive part of the soul and neglecting the rational, invert the order of our faculties and make us subordinate the better to the worse. As the one who would occupy himself in the Republic by submitting the good to the bad, and the true leaders to the rebels, would be an enemy of the Fatherland and a traitor to the State, so the Poet imitator carries dissensions and death into the Republic of the soul by elevating and nourishing the lowest faculties at the expense of the most noble, by lavishing and using his powers on those things least worthy of occupying him, by confounding through vain simulacra true beauty with the lying attraction that pleases the multitude and apparent grandeur with genuine grandeur.

What strong souls will dare believe themselves equal to the care the Poet takes to corrupt them or to discourage them? When Homer or some tragic Author shows us a Hero overburdened with affliction, crying out, lamenting, beating his breast; an Achilles, son of a Goddess, now stretched out on the earth pouring the warm sand over his head with his two hands, now wandering like a deranged man along the shore and mixing his frightening howls with the sound of the waves; a Priam, venerable by his dignity, by his great age, by so many illustrious children, rolling in the mire, soiling his white hair, making the air ring with his curses, and shouting out at Gods and men: who among us, insensible to these plaints, does not yield to them with a sort of pleasure?[32] Who does not feel the feeling represented to us arise in himself? Who does not seriously praise the Author's art and does not regard him as a great Poet due to the expression he gives to his portraits and the affections he communicates to us? And, nevertheless, when a domestic and real affliction reaches ourselves, we glory in bearing it moderately, in not letting ourselves be overwhelmed to the point of tears; we then regard the courage we force ourselves to have as a virtue of a man and we would believe ourselves as cowardly as women to cry and to groan like these Heroes who have touched us in the scene. Are these not very useful Spectacles rather than those which we would blush to imitate, and wherein we are interested in the weaknesses from which we take such trouble to protect ourselves in our own calamities? The most noble faculty of the soul, thus losing the power and the empire over itself, grows accustomed to bend under the law of the passions; it no longer represses our tears and our cries; it delivers us over to our tenderness for objects which are foreign to us; and under the pretext of commiseration for chimerical misfortunes, far from being indignant that a virtuous man abandons himself to excessive grieving, far from preventing us from applauding his degradation, it lets us applaud ourselves for the pity which it inspires in us; it is a pleasure we believe we have gained without weakness and taste without remorse.[33]

But in allowing ourselves to be thus subjugated to the pains of another, how will we resist our own and how will we endure our own ills more courageously than those of which we perceive only a vain image? What! Will we be the only ones who do not have a hold over our sensitivity? Who is it that will not sometimes adopt those emotions to which he lends himself so willingly? Who is it that will know how to refuse his own misfortunes the tears he lavishes on those of another? I say as much of Comedy,[34] of the indecent laughter it draws from us, of the habit taken from it of turning everything to ridicule, even the most serious, the gravest objects, and of the almost inevitable effect by which it turns the most respectable Citizens into Theatrical buffoons and jokers. I say as much of love, of anger, and of all the other passions, which, becoming day by day more palpable by amusement and by play, we lose all our power to resist when they assail us in earnest. Finally, in whatever sense the Theater and its imitations are envisioned, one always sees that by animating and by fomenting in us dispositions which must be contained and repressed, it makes dominate what should obey; far from making us better and more happy, it makes us worse and still more unhappy, and we are made to pay at our own expense for the care that is taken to please us and to flatter us.

When, therefore, friend Glaucus,[35] you encounter Homer's enthusiasts, when they tell you that Homer is the institutor of Greece and the master of all the arts, that the government of States, civil discipline, the education of men, and all the ordering of human life are taught in his writings, honor their zeal, love and support them as men endowed with exquisite qualities; admire along with them the wonders of this fine genius; agree with them with pleasure that Homer is the Poet *par excellence*, the model and the leader of all the tragic Authors. But always consider that the Hymns in honor of the Gods and the praises of great men are the sole type of Poetry which should be admitted into the Republic, and that, if it once allows within it that imitative Muse which charms us and deceives us by the sweetness of its accents, men's actions will soon no longer have as their object either the law or good and beautiful things, but pain and sensual pleasure; aroused passions will dominate instead of reason; the Citizens will no longer be virtuous and just men, always subject to duty and to equity, but sensitive and weak men who will do good or evil indifferently according as they are led by their inclination. Finally, never forget that by banishing Dramas and Theatrical Pieces from our State, we are not following a barbarous obstinacy and do not at all scorn the beauties of the art, but we prefer to them the immortal beauties that result from the harmony of the soul and from the concord of its faculties.

Let us do still more. In order to protect ourselves from all partiality and to grant nothing to that ancient discord that reigns between the Philosophers and the Poets,[36] let us not take from Poetry and from imitation anything they may allege in their defense, nor from ourselves the innocent pleasures they can procure for us. Let us render that honor to the truth of respecting even its image and of allowing all who celebrate it the freedom of making themselves heard. By imposing silence on the Poets, let us accord to their friends the freedom of defending them and of showing us, if they can, that the art condemned by us as harmful is not only pleasant, but useful to the Republic and to the Citizens. Let us listen to their reasons with an impartial ear and agree whole-heartedly that we have gained much for ourselves if they prove that one can yield oneself without risk to such sweet impressions. Otherwise, my dear Glaucus, as a wise man, smitten by the charms of a mistress, seeing his virtue ready to abandon him, breaks, although with regret, such a sweet chain and sacrifices love to duty and to reason; thus, given over from our childhood to the seductive attractions of Poetry and perhaps too sensitive to its beauties, we shall nonetheless provide ourselves with force and reason against its magic tricks. If we dare grant something to the taste which attracts us, we will at least fear yielding ourselves to our first loves. We will always say to ourselves that there is nothing serious or useful in all that dramatic apparatus. In sometimes lending our ears to Poetry, we will prevent our hearts from being imposed upon by it and we will not allow it to trouble order and freedom, either in the interior Republic of the soul or in that of human society. The alternative of making oneself better or worse is no slight matter, and one cannot weigh with too much care the deliberation that conducts us. O my friends! It is, I admit, a sweet thing to yield to the charms of an enchanting talent, to acquire by means of it goods, honors, power, glory. But power, glory, riches, and pleasures are all eclipsed and disappear like a shadow before justice and virtue.

The Levite of Ephraïm

[First Draft Preface]

As for the third [piece],[1] which is merely a kind of short poem in prose, a paraphrase of the last three chapters of *Judges*,[2] I admit that it will always be precious to me and that I never reread with without an inner satisfaction, not from some stupid vanity of an author, whose ineptness on this point would be inexcusable, but from a more decent feeling and one about which I even dare boast. It is enough to make myself understood to say that this writing was done en route the tenth, the eleventh, and the twelfth of June, 1762.[3] This is what I occupied myself with during the cruelest moments of my life, overcome with miseries for which an honorable man is not even allowed to prepare himself. Plunged into a sea of misfortune, overcome with evils from my ungrateful and barbarous contemporaries, a single one from which I escape in spite of them and which remains to them for my vengeance is that of hatred.

This is with what that unfortunate defender of truth occupied himself during those instants of peril and of turmoil in which anger and indignation should have been devouring his heart. My enemies have indeed overwhelmed me with all the evils of which their rage [could] think of devising. There is one which remains to them for my vengeance and which I defy them to make me ever experience. That is the torment of hate.

from enemies whom I don't even know, to whom I have never done nor wished the least ill.
. . . and who think that one will always love
. . . hate me only due to the one who has made them

This epoch unhappily too celebrated says enough about it to excuse the mediocrity of the work and to portray [something ?] of the author. If ever some equitable man deigns to take up my defense in compensation for so many outrages and libels, I wish only these words for praise: In the cruelest moments of his life, he wrote *The Levite of Ephraïm*.

As for me, I console myself. The sole praise that I desire and that I accord myself without shame because it is due to me. In the cruelest moments of his life he wrote *The Levite of Ephraïm*.

[Second Draft Preface]

I left Paris my heart pained with distress after the Parlement's warrant.[4] It seemed to me that having asked no other favor from men than that of not doing me any evil, I would have well merited having obtained it. Even while assuming in me the most dangerous errors, weren't my intentions pure enough and clear enough to merit some indulgence. What, then, is this much-vaunted society that never recompenses good, that often dissimulates evil and always punishes it less severely than its appearance. This is what I said to myself in the bitterest suffering while rendering to myself the testimony that no man of good sense and of good faith could refuse me. These sad ideas followed me in spite of myself, and made my voyage disagreeable. I chased them away with all my power, there wasn't one with which my heart was occupied less voluntarily than that of the wrongs that could be done to me, and I was much more angry with the injustices of which I was the witness than those of which I was the victim. I thought of diverting my reverie by occupying myself with some subject; this one came to mind, and I found it suited enough to my views. It offered me a type of intermediary between the condition I was in and that into which I wished to pass, I could from time to time abandon myself to my somber mood then substitute the sweetest objects for it and as soon as my subject permitted it, I imitated it, but . . . the delightful images of M. Gessner.[5] In this fashion I almost fulfilled my goal and pleasantly completed my voyage. This bagatelle was for a long time forgotten. I took it up and touched it up on a somewhat similar occasion and with the same success. I would hope that readers take some of the pleasure in reading it that I took in imagining it. It would be hard to judge it very severely given the occasion on which it was written. But it has an aspect for which decent men will applaud it, I am sure of it, and they will feel that a man who occupied himself in this way when he was tormented is not a very dangerous enemy.

The Levite of Ephraïm

FIRST CANTO

Sacred anger of virtue, come animate my voice. I will tell of the crimes of Benjamin and the vengeance of Israel; I will speak of unprecedented infamy and of still more terrible punishments. Mortals, respect beauty, morals, hospitality. Be just without cruelty, merciful without weakness. And know how to pardon the guilty rather than punish the innocent.

O you, easy-going men, enemies of every inhumanity; you who for fear of contemplating the crimes of your brothers prefer to let them go unpunished, what picture am I going to offer to your eyes? The body of a woman cut into pieces, her torn and palpitating limbs sent to the twelve Tribes; the whole people, seized with horror, raising a unanimous protest to the Heavens, and crying out together: No, nothing like it has been done in Israel since the day our fathers left Egypt until this day. Sacred people, assemble yourself; pronounce on this horrible act and discern the price it has merited. He who averts his glance from such infamy is a coward, a deserter from justice; genuine humanity contemplates it in order to know it, to judge it, to detest it. Let us dare enter into these details and go back to the source of the civil wars which caused one of the Tribes to perish and cost the others so much blood. Benjamin, sad child of grief, who brought death to his mother,[6] it is from your bosom that came the crime that has ruined you; it is your impious race that could commit it and that had to atone for it too much.

In the days of freedom in which no one reigned over the people of the Lord, there was a time of license in which each, without recognizing either magistrate or judge, was alone his own master and did all that seemed to him good. Israel, then scattered in the fields, had few great cities, and the simplicity of its morals rendered superfluous the empire of laws. But all hearts were not equally pure, and the wicked found the impunity of vice in the security of virtue.[7]

During one of those short intervals of calm and equality that remain in oblivion because no one commands others and no evil at all is done, a Levite of the mountains of Ephraïm saw in Bethlehem a young woman who pleased him. He said to her: Young woman of Judah, you are not of my Tribe, you have no brother; you are like the daughters of Salphaad, and I cannot marry you according to the law of the Lord.* But my heart is yours; come with me, let us live together; we will be united and free; you will make my happiness, and I will make yours. The Levite was young and handsome; the young woman smiled; they were united, then he took her into his mountains.

There, passing a sweet life, so dear to tender and simple hearts, in his retreat they trusted the charms of a shared life; there, on a sistrum of gold made to sing the praises of the Almighty, he often sang of the charms of his young wife. How many times did the slopes of mount Hebal ring with his lovely songs? How many times did he lead her into the shade, into the valleys of Sichem, to cut the country roses and to taste the freshness by the shore of the streams? Sometimes he sought in the hollows of the rocks the

---

*_Numbers_, chap. XXXVI, v. 8. I know that the children of Levi could marry in all the Tribes, but not in the case supposed.[8]

combs of a golden honey from which she made her sweets; sometimes in the foliage of the olive trees he set deceptive traps for birds and he carried to her a fearful turtledove which she kissed while stroking it. Then, closing it up in her bosom she shivered with joy feeling it struggle and beat. Daughter of Bethlehem, he said to her, why do you always weep for your family and your country? Do the children of Ephraïm not also have feasts, are the daughters of smiling Sichem without grace and without gaiety, do the inhabitants of ancient Atharot lack strength and deftness? Come see their games and embellish them. Give me pleasures, O my beloved; are there for me any others than yours?

However the young woman grew bored with the Levite, perhaps because he left nothing for her to desire. She slipped away and fled to her father, to her tender mother, to her frolicsome sisters. She believed she found there the innocent pleasures of her childhood, as if she bore the same age and the same heart.

But the abandoned Levite could not forget his fickle wife. Everything in his solitude recalled for him the happy days he had passed near her, their games, their pleasures, their quarrels, their tender reconciliations. Whether the rising sun gilded the summit of the mountains of Gelboe, or a sea breeze came in the evening to refresh their burning rocks, he wandered sighing in the places the unfaithful one had loved, and at night, alone in his nuptial bed, he watered his bed with his tears.

After having drifted four months between regret and vexation, like a child who, being chased by others in play, feigns, no longer wanting to continue while burning to start again, then finally tearfully asks to get back in, the Levite, driven by his love, takes his mount and, followed by his servant with two donkeys of Epha loaded with his provisions and gifts for the relatives of the young woman, he returns to Bethlehem to be reconciled with her and to try to bring her back.

The young woman, perceiving him from far off, shivers, runs before him, and greeting him with caresses, introduces him into the house of her father; who, learning of his arrival, runs up also full of joy, embraces him, receives him—him, his servant, his baggage—and busies himself with treating him well. But the Levite, his heart wrenched with emotion, could not speak; nevertheless, moved by the good welcome of the family, he raised his eyes to his young wife and said to her, Daughter of Israel, why do you flee me? What evil have I done to you? The young woman began to cry, covering her face. Then he said to the father: Give me back my companion; give her to me for love of her; why would she live alone and abandoned? Who other than I can honor as his wife the one whom I received a virgin?

The father looked at his daughter, and the daughter's heart was touched by the return of her husband. The father therefore said to his son-in-law: My son, give me three days; let us pass these three days in joy, and on the fourth day, you and my daughter will leave in peace. The Levite therefore remained three days with his father-in-law and all his family, eating and drinking familiarly with them; and on the night of the fourth day, rising before the sun, he wanted to leave. But his father-in-law, stopping him with his hand, said to him: What! You want to leave on an empty stomach? Come fortify your stomach and then you will leave. They sat down opposite each other at table and, after eating and drinking, the father said to him: My son, I beg you to enjoy yourself further with us today. Nonetheless, the Levite, rising, wanted to leave; he believed the time he passed far from his retreat robbed him of love, was given over to others rather than to his beloved. But the father, not being able to resolve himself to be separated from her, engaged his daughter to obtain yet another day; and the daughter, caressing her husband, had him remain until the morrow.

As soon as it was morning, as he was ready to leave he was stopped yet again by his father-in-law, who forced him to seat himself at table while awaiting full daylight; and the time flowed by without them perceiving it. Then the young man got up to leave with his wife and his servant, and having prepared everything: O, my son! the father said to him: You see that the day advances and that the sun is on its decline. Do not set out so late; for pity's sake, gladden my heart further the rest of this day; tomorrow at the break of day you will leave without delay. And speaking in this way, the good old man was entirely stricken; his paternal eyes welled with tears. But the Levite did not surrender, and wished to leave at that instant.

What regrets this fatal separation cost! What touching farewells were said and resumed! What tears the sisters of the young woman shed on her face! How many times they took her again by turns in their arms! How many times did her mother, in tears, holding her once again to her breast, feel the pain of a new separation! But her father in embracing her did not cry; his mute clasps were doleful and convulsive; sharp sighs lifted his chest. Alas! He seemed to foresee the horrible fate of the unfortunate one! O! if he had known that she would never again see the dawn! If he had known that that day was the last of her days. . . . They finally leave followed by the tender benedictions of their whole family, and wishes worthy of being granted. Happy family, whose peaceful days flow in the most perfect union from the bosom of friendship, and which seems to have only one heart for all its members. O innocence of morals, sweetness of soul, antique simplicity, how lovable you are! How has the brutality of vice been able to find a place amidst you? How is it that the furies of barbarism did not respect your pleasures?

SECOND CANTO

The young Levite followed his route with his wife, his servant, and his baggage, transported with joy in bringing back his heart's friend, and, uneasy about the sun and the dust, like a mother who brings back her son from the nurse's and fears for him the air's ravages. Already the city of Jebus[9] was spied on the right hand, and its age-old walls, already centuries old, offered them a refuge for the approaching night. The servant then said to his master: You see the day ready to end; before the darkness takes us unawares let us enter the city of the Jubusites, let us seek a refuge there, and tomorrow, continuing our voyage, we can arrive at Geba.

God forbid, said the Levite, that I lodge among an infidel people and that a Canaanite give shelter to the Lord's minister.[10] No, but let us go as far as Gibeah to seek hospitality among our brothers. They thus left Jerusalem behind them, they arrived after the setting of the sun at the heights of Gibeah, which is of the Tribe of Benjamin. They turned off to pass the night there, and having entered, they went to seat themselves in the public plaza, but no one offered them a shelter, and they remained unprotected.

Men of our days, do not malign the morals of your fathers. These first times, it is true, did not abound like yours in the comforts of life; vile metals did not suffice there for everything; but man had innermost emotions, which did the rest. Hospitality was not for sale, and they did not then traffic in the virtues. The sons of Jemini[11] were not the only ones, doubtless, whose hearts of iron were hardened; but that hardness was not common. With patience brothers were found everywhere; the voyager deprived of everything did not lack anything.

After having waited a long time uselessly, the Levite was going to unfasten his baggage, in order to make the young woman a bed less hard than the naked earth, when he perceived an old man, returning late from his fields and from his rustic labors. This man was, like him, from the mountains of Ephraïm, and he had come in bygone days to establish himself in this city among the children of Benjamin.

Raising his eyes, the old man saw a man and a woman seated in the middle of the plaza, with a servant, beasts of burden, and baggage. Then drawing near he said to the Levite: Stranger, where are you from and where are you going? He answered him: We come from Bethlehem, city of Judah; we are going back to our dwelling place on the slopes of the mountain of Ephraïm, from whence we have come; and now we seek a hospice of the Lord, but no one has wanted to lodge us. We have grain for our animals, bread, wine for me, for your servant, for the young man who follows us; we have everything that is necessary for us, we lack only shelter. The old man answered him: peace be with you, my brother; you will not remain in the plaza; if you are lacking something, let the crime be mine. Then he led them into his house, had their baggage unloaded, filled the rack for their beasts, and having had the feet of his guests washed, he made for them a feast of the Patriarchs, simple and without ostentation, but abundant.

While they were at table with their host and his daughter,* promised to a young man of the country, and while amidst the gaiety of a meal offered with joy, they relaxed agreeably, the men of this city, children of Belial,[12] without restraint, unbridled, without reserve, and braving Heaven like the Cyclops of Mount Etna, came and surrounded the house, rudely knocking at the door, and crying to the old man in a menacing tone: Deliver to us that young stranger whom you received within our walls without leave, so that his beauty may pay us the price of this shelter and so that he may atone for your temerity. For they had seen the Levite in the plaza, and, by a trace of respect for the most sacred of all rights they had not wanted to lodge him in their houses so as to do him violence, but they had plotted together to come to surprise him in the middle of the night, and having learned that the old man had given him refuge, they ran without justice and without shame to tear him from the house.

Hearing these madmen the old man was disturbed, was afraid, and said to the Levite: We are lost. These wicked men are not people to be brought round by reason and they will never reconsider what they have resolved upon. Nevertheless, he went out before them to try to sway them. He prostrated himself and, raising his hands, free from plunder, to Heaven, he said to them: O my brothers! what speech have you pronounced? Ah! Do not do this evil before the Lord! Do not thus outrage nature, do not violate sacred hospitality. But seeing that they did not listen to him at all, and were ready to mistreat him, that they were going force the house, the old man, despairing, instantly made his choice and, making a sign with his hand in order to make himself heard amidst the tumult, he began again with a stronger voice: No, my living at such a price will not dishonor my guest and will not soil my house. But listen, cruel men, to the supplications of an unhappy father. I have a daughter still a virgin, promised to one among you; I am going to lead her to be sacrificed to you, but only so that

---

* In the old custom the women of the house did not sit at table with their guests when they were men, but when they were women they did sit with them.

your sacrilegious hands abstain from touching the Levite of the Lord. Then, without awaiting their response, he ran to seek his daughter to redeem his guest at the expense of his own blood.

But the Levite, whom terror had made immobile until that instant, awakening to this deplorable sight, forestalled the generous old man, threw himself before him, forced him to return with his daughter, and himself taking his beloved companion, without saying a single word to her, without raising his eyes to her, dragged her to the door and gave her up to those cursed men. Straightaway they surrounded the half-dead young woman, seized her, and fought over her without pity; in their brutal fury they were like a pack of hungry wolves returning to a watering place at the foot of the icy Alps which surprises a weak heifer, throws itself on her and tears her to pieces. O wretches, who destroy your species through the pleasures destined to reproduce it, how does her dying beauty not dampen your ferocious desires? See her eyes already closed to the light, her faded features, her dying face; the pallor of death has covered her cheeks, livid violets have chased away roses, she no longer has a voice to moan, her hands no longer have the force to repulse your outrages. Alas! She is already dead! Barbarians, unworthy of the name men, your howls resemble the cries of the horrible Hyena and like it you devour corpses.

The approach of the day which chases ferocious beasts back into their lairs having dispersed these brigands, the unfortunate woman uses the remainder of her force to drag herself back to the old man's abode; she falls before the door, her face against the earth and her hands extended on the threshold. Nonetheless, after having passed the night filling the house of his host with imprecations and tears, the Levite, ready to leave, opens the door and finds in this state the one whom he had loved so much. What a sight for his broken heart! He raises a plaintive cry toward Heaven avenger of crime: then, addressing the young woman: rise, he says to her, let us flee the curse that covers this earth. Come, O my companion! I am the cause of your ruin, I will be your consolation. May the unjust and vile man who ever reproaches you for your misery perish; you are more respectable to me than before your misfortunes. The young woman does not respond at all; he is troubled, his heart, seized with fright, begins to fear the worst evils. He calls her once again, he looks at, he touches her; she was no longer. O young woman too lovable and too much loved! Is it then for this that I have taken you from your father's house? Here, then, is the fate that my love prepared for you? He finished these words ready to follow her, and survived her only in order to avenge her.

From that instant, occupied with the sole plan with which his soul was filled, he was deaf to every other feeling; love, regret, pity, were all changed into fury in him. Even the appearance of that body, which should have made him dissolve in tears, drew from him neither complaint nor weeping. He contemplated it with a dry and somber eye; he no longer saw anything in it except an object of rage and despair. Aided by his servant, he loads it onto his mount and takes it into his house. There, without hesitating, without trembling, the barbarous man dares cut that body into twelve pieces; with a firm and sure hand he strikes without fear, he cuts the flesh and the bones, he separates the head and the limbs, and afterward had these frightful parcels sent to the Tribes, he precedes them to Mizpah, tears his clothing, covers his head with ashes, prostates himself as they arrive and calls out with great cries for the justice of the God of Israel.

THIRD CANTO

In the meantime, you would have seen the whole People of God be moved, assemble, leave their dwelling places, all the Tribes hastening to Mizpah before the Lord, as a numerous swarm of bees gathers while humming around their King. They all came, they came from every part, from all the cantons, all in agreement like a single man from Dan to Beer-sheba, and from Galead to Mizpah.

Then the Levite, having presented himself dressed in mourning, was interrogated by the Elders before the assembly about the murder of the young woman, and he spoke to them thus: I entered Gibeah the city of Benjamin with my wife to pass the night there, and the people of the country surrounded the house in which I was lodged, desiring to commit an outrage against me and make me perish. I was forced to deliver my wife to their debauchery, and she died in leaving their hands. Then I took her body, I tore it in pieces, and I sent it to you each within your boundaries. People of the Lord, I have spoken the truth; do what will seem to you just before the Almighty.

Instantly a single cry arose in all Israel, but resounding, but unanimous: Let the blood of the young woman fall back upon her murderers. Long live the Eternal One! We will not go back to our dwelling places and none of us will return beneath his roof until Gibeah is exterminated. Then the Levite cried out with a strong voice: Blessed be Israel who punishes infamy and avenges innocent blood. Daughter of Bethlehem, I carry you good news; your memory will not remain without honor. In saying these words, he fell on his face and died. His body was honored with public funerals. The limbs of the young woman were reassembled and put into the same sepulcher, and all Israel wept over them.

The preparations for the war they were going to undertake began with a solemn oath to put to death anyone who failed to be present. Then they numbered all the Hebrews carrying arms, and they chose ten out of a hundred, and a hundred out of a thousand, and a thousand out of ten thousand, the tenth part of the entire people, which made up an army of forty thousand men who had to act against Gibeah, while a like number was charged with the convoys of munitions and of victuals for the provisioning of the army. Then the People came to Silo before the ark of the Lord, saying: which Tribe will command the others against the children of Benjamin? And the Lord answered: it is the blood of Judah that cries out for vengeance; let Judah be your chief.

But before drawing the sword against their brothers, they sent Heralds to the Tribe of Benjamin, who said to the Benjaminites: Why is this horrible thing found amidst you? Give those who have committed it over to us so that they may die and that the evil may be removed from the bosom of Israel.

The fierce sons of Jemini, who had not been unaware of the assembly at Mizpah, nor of the resolution that had been taken there, having for their part been preparing, believed that their valor excused them from being just. They did not listen at all to the exhortation of their brothers, and, far from according them the satisfaction they owed them, they left in arms from all the villages of their portion, and rushed to Gibeah's defense without letting themselves be frightened by the number and resolved to combat alone the whole people united. The army of Benjamin had twenty-five thousand men bearing swords, aside from the inhabitants of Gibeah, of the number of seven hundred seasoned men, handling arms with both hands with the same dexterity and all such excellent slingers that they could throw from a horse without the stone missing on one side or the other.

The army of Israel, being assembled and having elected its chiefs, came to set up camp before Gibeah, counting on taking that place easily. But the Benjaminites, having left in good order, attacked it, broke it, pursued it with fury, terror preceded them and death followed them. The routed able-bodied of Israel were seen falling by the thousands beneath their swords, and the fields of Ramah were covered with corpses, as the sands of Elath are covered with the grasshoppers' shells that a burning wind brings and kills in one day. Twenty-two thousand men of Israel's army perished in that combat, but their brothers did not grow discouraged, and having faith in their force and in their great numbers still more than in the justice of their cause, they returned the next day and ranged themselves for battle in the same place.

Nevertheless, before risking a new combat, they went up that day before the Lord, and weeping until evening in his presence, they consulted him on the issue of that war. But he said to them: go and fight; does your duty depend on the outcome?

As they thus marched toward Gibeah, the Benjaminites made a sortie from all the doors, and, falling on them with more fury than the previous day, they defied them and pursued them with such determination that eighteen thousand more men of war perished that day in the army of Israel. Then all the people came once again to prostrate itself and weep before the Lord, and fasting until evening, they offered oblations and sacrifices. God of Abraham, they said moaning, your people, spared so many times in your just anger, will it perish for desiring to remove the evil from its bosom? Then presenting themselves before the fearsome ark, and consulting the Lord once again through the mouth of Phineas son of Eleazar, they said to him: shall we march again against our brothers, or shall we leave Benjamin in peace? The voice of the Almighty deigned to respond to them. March, and no longer have faith in your numbers, but in the Lord who gives and takes away courage as it pleases him. Tomorrow I shall deliver Benjamin into your hands.

Instantly they already felt the effect of this promise in their hearts. A cold and sure valor succeeded their brutal impetuosity, enlightening and leading them. They calmly prepared for combat and no longer presented themselves for it as wild men, but as wise and brave men who know how to vanquish without fury and die without despair. They hid their troops behind the hillside of Gibeah, and ranging themselves for battle with the remainder of their army, they drew far off from the City the Benjaminites, who, full of deceptive confidence after their first successes, left rather to kill them than to combat them; they impetuously pursued the army, which yielded and purposely drew back before them; they came before it at the place where the fields of Bethel and of Gibeah join, and cried out, rousing themselves for the carnage: they are falling before us as they did the first time. Blind men, who in the dizziness of a vain success do not see the Angel of vengeance who already flies over their ranks, armed with the exterminating sword.

Nonetheless, the body of Troops hidden behind the hillside left its ambush in good order in the number of ten thousand men, and extending around the City attacked it, forced it, and passed all its inhabitants under the edge of the sword, then raising a great column of smoke, it gave the army the agreed-upon signal while the relentless Benjaminite roused himself to pursue his victory.

But the able-bodied of Israel, having perceived the signal, went to face the enemy in Baal-tamar. The Benjaminites, surprised to see Israel's Battalions forming, developing, extending, converging on them, began to lose courage, and turning their back, they saw with fear the whirlwinds of smoke that announced to them the disaster of Gibeah. Then, struck with terror in their turn, they knew that the arm of the Lord had reached them, and fleeing in rout toward the desert, they were surrounded, pursued, killed, trampled underfoot, while various detachments that entered the cities were put to death there each in his abode.

On this day of anger and of murder, almost the whole Tribe of Benjamin in the number of twenty-six thousand men perished under Israel's sword; namely, eighteen thousand men in their first retreat from Menuhah to the east of the hillside, five thousand in the rout toward the desert, two thousand that reached Gidom and the rest in the places that were burned, and all of whose inhabitants, men and women, young and old, large and small, even down to beasts, were put to death, without mercy being given to any. In this way, this beautiful country, formerly so lively, so peopled, so fertile, and now reaped by flame and by iron, no longer offered anything but a frightful solitude covered with ashes and bones.

Six hundred men, the last remainder of that unhappy Tribe, alone escaped the sword of Israel and took refuge in the rocks of Rimmon, where they remained hidden four months, crying too late for the infamous deed of their brothers and the misery to which it had reduced them.

But the victorious Tribes seeing the blood they had shed felt the wound they had made. The people came and, assembling in the house of the mighty Lord, raised an altar on which they rendered to him his homage, offering him sacrifices and thanksgiving; then, raising their voices, they wept: they wept for their victory after having wept for their defeat. God of Abraham, they cried out in their affliction, oh, where are your promises, and how has this evil happened to your people that a Tribe was extinguished in Israel? Unhappy humans who do not know what is good for you, you have desired well to sanctify your passions; they always punish you for the excesses they make you commit, and it is by fulfilling your unjust vows that Heaven makes you atone for them.

FOURTH CANTO

After having bemoaned the evil they had done in their anger, the children of Israel sought some remedy in it that could reestablish the mutilated race of Jacob in its entirety. Moved with compassion for the six hundred men in refuge in the rocks of Rimmon, they said: what shall we do to preserve this last and precious remainder of one of our nearly extinguished Tribes? For they had sworn by the Lord, saying: may never any among us give his daughter to the son of a child of Jemini and mix his blood with the blood of Benjamin. Then, in order to elude such a cruel oath, meditating new carnage, they took the number of the army to see whether, despite the solemn engagement, any one of them had failed to comply, and none of the inhabitants of Jabesh-gilead was found. This branch of the children of Manasseh, looking less to the punishment of the crime than to the effusion of fraternal blood, had turned away from vengeance more atrocious than infamy without considering that perjury and desertion of the common cause are worse than cruelty. Alas! Death, barbarous death was the price for their unjust pity. Ten thousand men detached from the army of Israel ran up and executed this frightful order: Go, exterminate Jabesh-gilead and all its inhabitants, men, women, children, except only the virgin women, whom you shall lead back to camp so that they may be given in marriage to the children of Benjamin. Thus, to make amends for the desolation of so many murders, this fierce people committed still greater ones, similar in its fury to those flaming iron globes thrown by our machines, which, fallen to the ground, arise after their first effect with a new impetuosity and in their unexpected bounds overturn and destroy entire ranks.

During this disastrous discharge, Israel sent words of peace to the six hundred of Benjamin in refuge in the rocks of Rimmon, and they came back among their brothers. Their return was not at all a return of joy; they had a downcast countenance and their eyes lowered; shame and remorse covered their faces, and all Israel dismayed carried on their lamentations at seeing these sad remainders of one of its blessed Tribes, of which Jacob had said: "Benjamin is a devouring wolf; in the morning it will tear apart its prey, and in the evening it will share the booty."[13]

After the ten thousand men sent to Jabes had made their return, and after having numbered the young women they had led back, only four hundred of them were found, and they were given to as many Benjaminites, like prey they had just abducted for them. What weddings for the timid young virgins, whose brothers, fathers, mothers had just been slaughtered before their eyes, and who received ties of attachment and of love from hands filthy with the blood of their near ones! A sex always slave or tyrant, which man oppresses or adores, and which he can nevertheless make happy or be so himself only by leaving it equal to him.

Despite this terrible expedient, there remained two hundred men to provide for, and that people, cruel even in its pity and for whom the blood of its brothers cost so little, would perhaps have thought of making new widows for them when an old man of Lebonah speaking to the elders said to them: Israelite men, listen to the advice of one of your brethren. When will your hands weary of the murder of innocents? Behold the days of solemnity of the Eternal One in Shiloh. Say then to the children of Benjamin: Go, and set an ambush in the vines; then, when you see that the women of Shiloh leave to dance with flutes, then surround them, and each abduct his woman, return to establish yourselves along with them the country of Benjamin.

And when the fathers and the brothers of the young women come to complain to us, we shall say to them: have pity on them for love of us and of yourselves who are their brothers; since we have not been able to provide for them after this war and have not been able to give them our daughters against the oath, we shall be guilty of their loss if we leave them to perish without descendants.

The children of Benjamin then did as he told them, and when the young women left Shiloh to dance, they sprang out and surrounded them.[14] The fearful troop fled, dispersed; terror succeeded their innocent gaiety; each called out in loud cries for her companions, and ran with all her might. The vine stocks tore their veils, the earth was strewn with their finery, the race animated their color and the ardor of their abductors. Young beauties, where do you run? In fleeing the oppressor who pursues you, you fall into arms which enchain you. Each abducted his own, and trying hard to calm the fright even more by their caresses than by their violence. At the tumult that arose, at the cries they made heard long off, the whole people ran up; fathers and mothers pushed aside the crowd and wanted to extricate their daughters; the abductors, so authorized, defended their prey; at last, the elders made their voices heard, and the people, moved by compassion for the Benjaminites, took an interest in their behalf.

But the fathers, indignant at the outrage done to their daughters, did not cease their outcries. What? they cried vehemently, will the daughters of Israel be subjected and treated as slaves beneath the eyes of the Lord? Benjamin will be to us as the Moabite and the Idumean? Where is the freedom of the people of God? Torn between justice and pity, the assembly at last pronounces that the captives would recover their freedom and decide their fate for themselves. The abductors, forced to cede to the judgment, released them with regret, and tried to substitute for force with more powerful means over their young hearts. As soon as they escaped and all fled together, they followed them, held out their arms, and cried to them: daughters of Shiloh, will you be more happy with others? Are the remnants of Benjamin unworthy of swaying you? But several among them, already tied by secret affections, quivered with joy at having escaped their abductors. Axa, the tender Axa, among others, in throwing herself into the arms of her mother, whom she saw run up, furtively cast her eyes on young Elmachin to whom she had been promised and who came full of grief and of rage to free her at the price of his blood. Elmacin saw her again, extended his arms, cried out and could not speak; the race and emotion had put him out of breath. The Benjamite perceived this transport, this glance; he divined all, he moaned, and ready to withdraw, he saw Axa's father arrive.

This was the same old man, author of the counsel given to the Benjaminites. He had himself chosen Elmacin for his son-in-law, but his probity had prevented him from warning his daughter of the risk to which he exposed those of other people.

He arrives, and taking her by the hand: Axa, he said to her, you know my heart; I love Elmacin, he would have been the consolation of my aged days, but the salvation of your people and the honor of your father must win out over him. Do your duty, my daughter, and save me from opprobrium among my brothers, for I have counseled everything that has been done. Axa kisses his head and sighs without responding, but finally, raising her eyes, she encounters those of her venerable father. They said more than his mouth; she makes her choice. Her weak and trembling voice scarcely pronounces, in a weak and last farewell, the name of Elmacin, at whom she dares not look, and instantly turning round half dead, she falls into the arms of the Benjamite.

A noise arises in the assembly. But Elmacin advances and makes a sign with his hand. Then, raising his voice: hear, O Axa, he says to her, my solemn vow. Since I cannot be yours, I shall never be another's. The sole remembrance of our young years which innocence and love have embellished are enough for me. Never has the steel passed over my head, never has wine moistened my lips, my body is as pure as my heart. Priests of the living God: I dedicate myself to your service; receive the Nazarene of the Lord.

Straightaway, as by a sudden inspiration, all the young women, carried along by the example of Axa, imitate her sacrifice, and renouncing their first loves, they deliver themselves to the Benjaminites who pursued them. At this touching sight arose a cry of joy in the midst of the People. Virgins of Ephraïm, through you Benjamin is going to be reborn. Blessed be the God of our fathers! There are still virtues in Israel.

Dictionary of Music

Ut psallendi materiem discerent.
Martian. Cap.[1]

Preface

Music is, of all the fine Arts, the one whose Vocabulary is the most extensive, and for which a Dictionary is, consequently, the most useful. Thus, this one should not be classed among those ridiculous compilations multiplied each day by the fashion or rather the mania for Dictionaries. If it is bad, this is neither for the choice of subject nor for the form of the work. Thus, it would be wrong to be put off by its title. One must read it in order to judge it.

The utility of the subject does not, I admit, establish that of the Book; it justifies me solely for having undertaken it, and this is also all I can claim; for, moreover, I feel quite acutely what is wanting in its execution. Here you have less a Dictionary in form than a collection of materials for a Dictionary, which await only a better hand to be utilized. The basis of this Work was dashed off in such haste, fifteen years ago, in the *Encyclopedia*, that, when I wanted to take it up again as a work, I could not give it the solidity it might have had if I had had more time to digest its plan and to execute it.

I did not conceive of this enterprise on my own, it was proposed to me; it was added that the entire manuscript of the *Encyclopedia* had to be complete before a single line of it would be printed; I was given only three months to fulfill my task, and three years could scarcely have sufficed to read, extract, compare, and compile the Authors I required; but the zeal of friendship blinded me to the impossibility of success. Faithful to my word, I wrote quickly and badly, at the expense of my reputation, not being able to do it well in such a short time; at the end of three months my entire manuscript was written, neatly drafted, and delivered; I have not seen it since. If I had worked from volume to volume as the others did, this attempt, better digested, might have remained in the condition into which I would have put it. I do not regret having been punctual; but I do regret having been reckless, and having promised more than I could perform.

Increasingly distressed by the imperfection of my articles as the volumes of the *Encyclopedia* appeared, I resolved to recast the whole based upon my draft, and to make of it at leisure a separate work treated with more care. When I recommenced this labor, I was within reach of all the necessary help. Living in the midst of Artists and Literary People, I could consult them both. The Abbé Sallier furnished me the books and manuscripts I needed from the King's Library, and I often derived enlightenment more certain than my researches from my conversations with him.[2] I believe I owe to the memory of that decent and learned man a tribute of gratitude that all the Literary People whom he served will surely share with me.

My withdrawal to the country took all of these resources from me at the moment when I was beginning to take advantage of them. This is not the place to explain the reasons for this withdrawal:[3] it will be understood, from my fashion of thinking, that the hope of writing a good Book on Music was not one to hold me back. Far from the amusements of the City, I soon lost the tastes that related to it; deprived of the communication which might enlighten me concerning my old aim, I also lost all sight of it; and whether the Art or its theory have made progress since that time, because I was not within reach of finding out anything about this, I was no longer in a position to follow it. Convinced, nevertheless, of the utility of the labor I had undertaken, I applied myself to it from time to time, but always with less success, and always feeling that the difficulties of a Book of this type require, to conquer them, enlightenment which I was no longer in a position to acquire, and a warmth of interest which I had ceased to put into it. Finally, despairing of ever being within reach of doing better, and wanting to take leave forever of ideas from which my mind grew more and more distant, I occupied myself, in these Mountains, with gathering together what I had done in Paris and at Montmorency;[4] and, from this undigested mass has resulted a Dictionary of the sort seen here.

This review seemed necessary to me to explain how circumstances have forced me to bring out a Book in such poor condition that I might have done better with the assistance I was deprived of. For I have always believed that the respect one owes to the Public is not to tell it insipid things, but to tell it only what is true and useful, or at least what one judges to be such; not to present anything to it without having given to it all the care one is capable of, and to believe that in doing one's best, one never does well enough for it.

I did not believe, nonetheless, that the imperfect condition in which I was forced to leave this work ought to prevent me from publishing it; since a Book of this type is useful to the Art, it is infinitely easier to write a good one based on the one I am presenting than it is to begin by creating everything. The knowledge requisite for this is perhaps not extremely great, but it is extremely varied, and is rarely found united in the same brain. Thus, my compilations may spare those who are in a position to put them in the necessary order a great deal of labor; and by noting my errors, someone who is able to write an excellent Book might never do as well without mine.

I therefore warn those who want to permit only well-written Books not to undertake the reading of this one; they would soon be put off: but those whom the bad does not turn away from the good; those who are not so preoccupied by faults that they count as nothing what redeems them; those, finally, who will wish to seek here something to compensate for my own, they will perhaps find in it enough good articles to tolerate the bad ones, and, even in the bad ones, enough new and true observations to make worthwhile the trouble of sifting through and choosing among the rest. Musicians read little, and I nevertheless know few Arts where reading and reflection are more necessary. I thought that a Work in the form of this one would be precisely what would suit them, and that, in order also to make it as profitable as possible to them, it was necessary less to tell them what they knew than what they might need to learn.

If Unskilled Laborers and Note-Scrapers often set aright errors here, I hope that true Artists and men of genius will find in it useful views which they will know how to take advantage of. The best Books are those which the Vulgar decry, and from which talented people profit without speaking about them.

After having set forth the reasons for the mediocrity of the Work and those for the utility I deem can be drawn from it, I might now enter into the detail of the Work itself, give a precis of the plan I have traced out for myself and of the manner in which I have tried to follow it. But in proportion as the ideas related to it have been effaced from my mind, so the plan according to which I arranged them has likewise been effaced from my memory. My initial plan was to treat my articles in close connection with one another, to link the results so closely together by cross-references, that, along with the convenience of a Dictionary, the whole would have the advantage of a coherent Treatise; but in order to execute this plan, it would have been necessary to have kept all the parts of the Art present to my mind, and not to have treated any of them without remembering the others—which the lack of resources and my tepid taste soon made impossible for me, and which I might even have had trouble doing amidst my first guides and full of my initial fervor. Abandoned to myself alone, no longer having either Scholars or Books to consult, consequently forced to treat each article in itself and without regard to those related to it, I would have had to make numerous repetitions so as to avoid gaps. But I believed that in a Book of this type it was still a lesser evil to commit faults than to make omissions.

I therefore adhered above all to completing the Vocabulary fully, and not only to not omitting any technical term, but sometimes to passing beyond the limits of the Art rather than not always reaching them. And this made it necessary for me frequently to sprinkle this Dictionary with Italian words and Greek words: the first so consecrated by usage that it is necessary to understand them even in practice; the second, adopted in the same way by many Scholars, and for which, given the desuetude of what they express, synonyms could not be given in French. I have tried, nevertheless, to confine myself to my rule, and to avoid the excess of Brossard,[5] who, while producing a French Dictionary, makes its Vocabulary wholly Italian, and swells it with words absolutely foreign to the Art he treats. For, who would ever imagine that *Virgin*, *Apostles*, *Mass*, *Dead* were Musical terms since there are types of Music relative to what they express, that these other words, *Page*, *Leaflet*, *Four*, *Five*, *Throat*, *Reason*, *Already*, were also technical terms since they are sometimes used when speaking of the Art?

As for the parts that relate to the Art without being essential to it, and which are not absolutely necessary to the understanding of the rest, I have avoided entering into them as much as I could. Such is that of Musical Instruments, a vast part and one that would alone fill a Dictionary, especially in relation to the Instruments of the Ancients. M. Diderot was charged with this part in the *Encyclopedia*, and as it did not enter into my initial plan, I was careful not to add it in the succeeding one, after having felt so keenly the difficulty of executing this plan as it was.

I have treated the Harmonic part in accordance with the system of the Fundamental Bass, even though, imperfect and defective in so many regards, it is not at all, in my opinion, that of Nature and of truth, and even though a muffled and confused padding results from it rather than a good Harmony. But, in the end, it is a system; it is the first, and it was the only one until M. Tartini's,[6] in which those multitudes of isolated rules that might seem to be arbitrary were tied together, by principles, and which made of the Harmonic Art a study of memory rather than of reasoning. Since M. Tartini's system, although better in my view, is still not as widely known, and does not have the same authority as M. Rameau's, at least in France, it should not have been substituted for it in a Book destined principally for the French Nation. I have therefore contented myself with presenting the principles of this system as best as I can in an article in my Dictionary;[7] and furthermore, I believed I owed this deference to the Nation for which I wrote, to prefer its sentiment to my own concerning the basis of the Harmonic doctrine. I nevertheless ought not to have refrained, upon the proper occasion, from objections necessary for the understanding of the articles I had to treat; it would have been to sacrifice the utility of the book to the prejudices of the Readers; it would have been to flatter without instructing, and to transform deference into fawning.

I exhort Artists and Enthusiasts to read this Book without mistrust, and to judge it with as much impartiality as I put into writing it.[8] I beg them to consider that as I was not preaching, I had no other interest here than that of the Art, and if I had, I should naturally lean in favor of French Music, in which I might attain a place, against the Italian, in which I can be nothing. But sincerely seeking the progress of an Art I loved passionately, my pleasure silenced my vanity. My first habits have long attached me to French Music, and I was openly its enthusiast. Attentive and impartial comparisons carried me toward Italian Music, and I have abandoned myself to it with the same good faith. If I have sometimes joked, it was in order to respond to others in their same tone; but I have not, like them, delivered witty sayings as my entire proof, and I have joked only after having reasoned. Now that misfortunes and evils have finally detached me from a taste that had only too much dominion over me, I persist, by the love of the truth alone, in my judgments, which the love of the Art alone have induced me to make. But, in a Work such as this one, dedicated to Music in general, I know only one that, not being of any country, is that of all; and I have never entered into the quarrel over the two Musics except when it was a matter of clarifying some important point for common progress. I have committed numerous faults, doubtless; but I am certain that partiality has not made me commit a single one. If this is wrongly imputed to me by the Readers, what can I do about it? It is then they who do not want my book to be good for them.

If one sees some unimportant articles in other Works that are also in this one, those who might be able to note this will want to recall that, since the year 1750, the manuscript has left my hands without my knowing what has become of it since that time. I accuse no one of having taken my articles; but it is not just for others to accuse me of having taken theirs.[9]

Môtiers-Travers, 20 December 1764.

ACCENT [*Accent*]. Thus is called, according to the most general acceptation, every modification of the speaking voice with regard to its duration, or to the tone of the syllables and of the words of which the discourse is composed—which shows a very exact relationship between the two uses of *Accents* and the two parts of Melody, namely Rhythm and Intonation. *Accentus*, says the Grammarian Sergius in his commentary on Donatus, *quasi ad cantus*.[10] There are as many different *Accents* as there are manners of thus modifying the voice; and there are as many genres of *Accents* as there are general causes of these modifications.

Three of these genres are distinguished in simple discourse, namely: grammatical *Accent*, which encompasses the rule for *Accents* properly speaking, by which the Sound of syllables is low or high, and that of the quantity by which each syllable is short or long; logical or rational Accent, which some inappropriately confuse with the preceding one, this second sort of *Accent*, indicating the relationship, the greater or lesser connection which propositions and ideas have with one another, is marked in part by punctuation; finally, pathetic or oratorical *Accent*, which, by various inflections of the voice, by a more or less elevated tone, by a more lively or slower speech, expresses the feelings by which the one who is speaking is agitated and which he communicates to those who listen to him. The study of the various *Accents* and of their effects in language should be the great business of the Musician, and Dionysius of Helicarnassus reasonably regards *Accent* in general as the germ of every Music.[11] In addition, we should admit as an incontestable maxim that more or less *Accent* is the true cause that makes languages more or less musical: for what would the relationship of Music to discourse be if the tones of the singing voice did not imitate the *Accents* of speech? From which it follows that the less a language has such *Accents*, the more its Melody must be monotonous, slack, and insipid, at least if it doesn't seek in noise and the force of sounds the charm it cannot find in their variety.

With regard to pathetic and oratorical *Accent*, which is the most immediate object of the imitative Music of the theater, it should not be said in opposition to the maxim I have just established that since all men are subject to the same passions they must likewise possess their language: for the universal *Accent* of Nature which draws from every man inarticulate cries is one thing, and the *Accent* of the Language which engenders the Melody peculiar to a Nation is another. The sole difference of more or less imagination and sensitivity which is observed from one people to another must introduce an infinity of differences into the accented idiom, if I dare speak in this way. The German, for example, raises his voice equally and strongly in anger; he always cries out in the same tone. The Italian, who is rapidly and successively agitated in the same case by a thousand different emotions, modifies his voice in a thousand ways. The same basis of passion reigns in his soul; but what a variety of expressions in his *Accents* and in his language! Now, it is to this variety alone, when the Musician causes it to be imitated, that he owes the energy and the grace of his song.

Unfortunately, all these various *Accents*, which agree perfectly in the Orator's mouth, are not so easy to reconcile under the Musician's pen, already so hampered by the peculiar rules of his Art. It cannot be doubted that the most perfect, or at least the most expressive, Music would be that in which all the *Accents* were observed most precisely; but what makes this combination difficult is that too many rules in this Art are liable to contradicting one another, and to contradicting one another all the more in proportion as the language is less musical; for none of them is perfectly so: otherwise those who make use of them would sing instead of speaking.

This extreme difficulty in following the rules of all the *Accents* at the same time therefore often obliges the Composer to give preference to one or another of them, according to the various genres of Music with which he is dealing. Thus, Dance tunes in particular require a rhythmic and Cadenced *Accent*, whose character in each Nation is determined by the language. The grammatical *Accent* should be the first consulted in Recitative so as to make the articulation of the words—subject to being lost by the quickness of the flow—more perceptible in the harmonic resonance. But the passionate *Accent*, in its turn, holds sway in dramatic Arias. And both are subordinated, especially in Instrumental Pieces, to a Third sort of *Accent* which could be called musical and which is in some manner determined by the type of Melody which the Musician wants to adopt to the words.

In actuality, the first and the principal object of all Music is to please the ear; thus, every Aria should have a pleasant song. This is the first law, which it is never permitted to break. One should therefore consult primarily the Melody and the musical *Accent* in the design of any Aria whatsoever. Then, if it is a question of a dramatic and imitative song, one must seek the pathetic *Accent*, which gives its expression to the feeling, and the rational *Accent*, by which the Musician renders the ideas of the Poet with exactness. For in order to inspire others with the warmth with which we are animated when speaking to them, they must be made to hear what we are saying. The grammatical *Accent* is necessary for the same reason; and this rule is no less indispensable than the two preceding ones for being the last in order here, since the meaning of propositions and of phrases absolutely depends on that of the words. But the Musician who writes his own language rarely has need of thinking of this *Accent*; he cannot sing his Aria without perceiving whether he speaks correctly or incorrectly, and it suffices for him to know that he should always speak correctly. How fortunate, nonetheless, when a flexible and flowing Melody never ceases to lend itself to what the language requires! French Musicians in particular have aids that render their errors on this point unpardonable, and especially the treatise on French Prosody by M. the Abbé d'Olivet, which they should all consult.[12] Those who are in a position to ascend higher can study the Port-Royal Grammar and the learned notes of the Philosopher who has commented upon it.[13] Then, by resting usage on rules and rules on principles, they will always be sure of what they should do in using grammatical *Accent* of every type.

As for the two other types of *Accents*, they are less subject to being reduced to rules, and their use demands less study and more talent. One does not find the language of the passions by keeping one's head, and it is a hackneyed truth that one must oneself be moved in order to move others. In the search for the pathetic *Accent*, therefore, nothing can take the place of that genius which awakens all the feelings at will, and there is no other Art in this part than that of kindling in one's own heart the fire which one wants to carry into that of others. (See GENIUS* [*Génie*].) Is it a question of the rational *Accent*? Art has altogether little hold to grasp it for same the reason that the deaf cannot be taught to hear. It must also be admitted that this *Accent*, less so than the others, falls within the competence of Music because it is much more the language of the senses than that of the mind. Therefore give the Musician many images or feelings and a few simple ideas to render: for it is only the passions that sing; the understanding does nothing but speak.

AIR or TUNE [*Air*].[14] A Song adapted to the words of a Chanson, or to a short Piece of Poetry appropriate for being sung, and, by extension, the Chanson itself is called an *Air*.

In Operas the name *Airs* is given to all measured Songs in order to distinguish them from the Recitative, and one generally calls an *Air* any complete portion of vocal or instrumental Music forming a Song, whether that portion alone makes up an entire Piece or it can be detached from the whole of which it makes up a part and be performed separately.

* * *

The *Airs* of our Operas are, so to speak, the canvas or the basis on which the pictures of imitative Music are painted; Melody is the design, Harmony is the coloration; all the picturesque objects of beautiful nature,[15] all the pondered feelings of the human heart are the models which the Artist imitates; attention, interest, the charm of the ear, and the emotion of the heart, are the aim of these imitations. (See IMITATION* [*Imitation*].) A learned and pleasant *Air*, an *Air* found by Genius and composed by Taste, is the masterpiece of Music; it is there that a beautiful voice develops, that a beautiful Instrumental piece shines; it is there that passion imperceptibly succeeds in moving the soul by the senses. After a beautiful *Air*, one is satisfied, the ear desires nothing more; it remains in the imagination, one carries it with oneself, one repeats it at will; without being able to render a single Note of it, one performs it in one's head such as it was heard at the Theater; one sees the Scene, the Actor, the Theater; one hears the accompaniment, the applause. The genuine Enthusiast never loses the beautiful *Airs* he hears throughout his life; he makes the Opera begin anew when he wishes.

The words of *Airs* do not always form a continuous meaning, are not recited like those of the Recitative; although usually quite short, they are broken up, repeated, transposed at the Composer's pleasure. They do not make up a narration that moves along; they depict either a picture that must be seen from various points of view, or a feeling in which the heart takes pleasure, from which it cannot, so to speak, detach itself, and the various phrases of an *Air* are only so many ways of envisioning the same image. This is why the subject should be a unity. It is by those quite extensive repetitions, it is by those redoubled blows that an expression which cannot move you initially finally sways you, agitates you, transports you outside of yourself, and it is also by the same principle that Roulades, which seem so misplaced in pathetic *Airs*, are nevertheless not always so: the heart, pressed by a very lively feeling, often expresses it more vividly by inarticulate Sounds than by words. (See NEUMA [*Neume*].)

* * *

SONG or SINGING [*Chant*], *n. masc.* A sort of modification of the human voice, by which one forms varied and discernible Sounds. Let us observe that in order to give this definition all the universality it should have, one must understand by *discernible Sounds* not only those that one can assign by the Notes of our Music, and produce by the keys of our Keyboard, but all those whose Unison can be found or felt and whose Intervals can be calculated in any way whatsoever.

It is very difficult to determine in what manner the voice that forms speech differs from the voice that forms *Song*. This difference is perceptible, but what it consists in is not very clearly seen, and when it is sought, it is not found. M. Dodart has made anatomical observations thanks to which he truly believes to find the cause of these two sorts of voices in the various conformations of the Larynx.[16] But I do not know whether these observations, or the conclusions he draws from them, are very certain. (See Voice* [*Voix*].) It seems that the Sounds that form speech lack only permanence to form a genuine *Song*; it also appears that the various inflections given to the voice when speaking form Intervals that are not at all harmonic, that do not make up part of our systems of Music, and that, consequently, since they cannot be expressed in Notation, are not properly speaking *Song* for us.

Song does not seem to be natural to man. Although the Savages of America sing, because they speak, the true Savage never sang. Mutes do not sing at all; they form only voices without permanence, muted howls which need wrests from them. I would doubt that Master Pereira,[17] with all his talent, could ever draw any musical *Song* from them. Children scream, cry, and do not at all sing. The first expressions of nature have nothing melodious and sonorous about them, and they learn to Sing as they do to speak, after our example. Melodious and discernible *Song* is only a calm and artificial imitation of the accents of the speaking or passionate Voice; one cries and one complains without singing, but one imitates cries and complaints by singing, and as, of all imitations, the most interesting is that of the human passions, of all the manners of imitating the most pleasant is *Song*.

Song, applied more particularly to our Music, is its melodious part, that which results from the duration and the succession of Sounds, that on which all the expression depends, and to which the rest is subordinated. (See Music* [*Musique*], Melody* [*Mélodie*].) Pleasant *Songs* are initially striking, they are easily engraved into the memory; but they are often the stumbling block of Composers, because only learning is needed to heap up Chords, and because talent is needed to imagine graceful *Songs*. In each nation there are trivial and well-worn phrases of *Song* into which bad Musicians constantly fall; there are baroque ones that are never used, because the Public always rebuffs them. To invent new *Songs* belongs to the man of genius; to find beautiful *Songs* belongs to the man of taste.

Finally, in its most restricted sense, *Song* is said solely of vocal Music, and when combined with Instrumental Parts those which are destined for Voices are called *Singing* Parts.

Composer [*Compositeur*], *n. masc.* Someone who composes Music or who knows the rules of Composition. See an explanation of the knowledge necessary to know how to compose at the word Composition* [*Composition*]. This is still not enough to form a true *Composer*. All the learning possible does not at all suffice without the genius that puts it to work. Whatever effort one might make, whatever experience one might have, it is necessary to be born for this Art; otherwise one will never write anything but what is mediocre. It is the same for the *Composer* as for the Poet: if Nature does not form him such at birth:

> *If he has not received from Heaven the secret influence,*
> *For him Phoebus is deaf and Pegasus restive.*[18]

What I mean by genius is not at all that bizarre and capricious taste that everywhere sows the baroque and the difficult, that knows how to ornament the Harmony by dint of Dissonances, contrasts, and noise. It is that interior fire that burns, that torments the *Composer* despite himself, that constantly inspires him with new and always pleasant Songs, with expressions that are lively, natural, and that always penetrate to the heart, with a pure, touching, majestic Harmony that strengthens and adorns the Song without stifling it. It is this divine guide that led Corelli, Vinci, Perez, Rinaldo, Jomelli, Durante, more learned than them all, into the sanctuary of Harmony; Leo, Pergolesi, Hasse, Terradeglias, Galuppi into that of good taste and of expression.[19]

COMPOSITION [*Composition*], *n. fem.* This is the Art of inventing and of writing Songs, of accompanying them with a suitable Harmony, in a word, of producing a complete Piece of Music with all its Parts.

The knowledge of Harmony and of its rules is the foundation of *Composition*. Doubtless it is necessary to learn to fill out Chords, to prepare, to resolve Dissonances, to find Fundamental Basses, and to possess all the other paltry elementary knowledge; but with the rules of Harmony alone one is no closer to knowing *Composition* than one is to being an Orator with those of Grammar. I will not at all say that it is necessary, besides this, to be quite familiar with the range and the character of Voices and of Instruments, with Songs that are easy or difficult to perform, with what produces an effect and what does not, to feel the character of the different Meters, that of the different Modulations in order always to apply them both properly, to know all the specific rules established by convention, by taste, by caprice or by pedantry, as Fugues, Imitations, constrained subjects, *etc*. All these things are still merely preparations for *Composition*; but one must find in oneself the source of beautiful Songs, of grand Harmony, of Portraits, of expression; finally, to be capable of seizing upon or forming the ordering of the whole work, of following conventions of every type, and of filling oneself with the spirit of the Poet without amusing oneself by running after the words. It is with reason that our Musicians have given the name "words" to the Poems they put into Song. One sees clearly, by the way in which they render them, that for them they really are merely words. It seems, especially for the last several years, that the rules for Chords have made them forget or neglect all the others, and that Harmony has acquired facility only at the expense of the Art in general. All our Artists know filling out, we have hardly any of them who know *Composition*.

* * *

In a *Composition*, the Author has for his subject Sound physically considered, and for his object the pleasure of the ear alone, or rather he elevates himself to imitative Music and seeks to move his Listeners by moral effects. In the first regard, it is enough for him to seek beautiful Sounds and pleasant Chords; but in the second he should consider Music by its relations to the accents of the human voice, and by the possible conformities between harmonically combined Sounds and imitable objects. One will find in the article OPERA* [*Opéra*] some ideas about the means of elevating and ennobling the Art, by making of Music a language more eloquent than discourse itself.

CONSONANCE [*Consonnance*], *n. fem.* Is, according to the etymology of the word, the effect of two or more Sounds heard at the same time; but the meaning of this term is usually restricted to the Intervals formed by two Sounds whose Accord[20] pleases the ear, and it is in this sense that I shall speak of it in this article.

Among that infinity of Intervals that can divide Sounds, there are only a very small number of them that make *Consonances*; all the others shock the ear and are for this reason called *Dissonances*. It is not that a number of these are not employed in Harmony, but they are so only with precautions of which *Consonances*, always pleasant by themselves, do not have an equal need.

The Greeks accepted only five *Consonances*; namely, the Octave, the Fifth, the Twelfth—which is the replica of the Fifth, the Fourth, and the Eleventh—which is the replica of the Fourth. We add to this major and Minor Thirds and Sixths, doubled and tripled Octaves, and, in a word, the various replicas of all these without exception, in accordance with the entire extent of the system.

Consonances are distinguished into perfect or just, whose Interval does not vary at all, and into imperfect ones, which can be major or minor. Perfect *Consonances* are the Octave, the Fifth, and the Fourth; Imperfect ones are Thirds and Sixths.

Consonances are further divided into simple and complex. The only simple *Consonances* are the Third and the Fourth: for the Fifth, for example, is made up of two Thirds; the Sixth is made up of a Third and a Fourth, etc.

The physical character of *Consonances* is derived from their production in a single Sound; or, if one likes, from the vibration of strings. Of two strings in close accord, forming between them an Interval of an Octave or of a Twelfth, which is the Octave of the Fifth, or of the Seventeenth, which is the double Octave of the Major Third, if the lower one is made to be sounded, the other vibrates and resonates. With regard to the major and Minor Sixth, the Minor Third, the simple Major Fifth and Third, which are all combinations and inversions of the preceding *Consonances*, they are not found directly, but among the various strings that vibrate to the same Sound.

If I play the string *Do*, the strings raised to its Octave *do*, to the Fifth *sol* of this Octave, to the Third *mi* of the double Octave, even to the Octaves of all these, all vibrate and resonate simultaneously; and if the first string were alone sounded, one would still distinguish all these Sounds in its resonance. Here, then, are the direct Octave, Major Third, and Fifth. The other *Consonances* are also found by combinations; namely, the Minor Third from the *mi* to the *sol*; the Minor Sixth from the same *mi* to the *do* above it; the Fourth from *sol* to this same *do*; and the Major Sixth from the same *sol* to the *mi* above it.

Such is the generation of all the *Consonances*. It would be a matter of accounting for the Phenomena.

First, the vibration of strings is explained by the action of the air and the concurrence of the vibrations. (See UNISON [*Unisson*].) 2nd. That the sound of a string is always accompanied by its Harmonics (See this word), seems a property of Sound which depends upon its nature, which is inseparable from it, and which can be explained only with hypotheses that are not without their difficulties. The most ingenious that has been imagined until the present concerning this matter is, unquestionably, M. de Mairan's, which M. Rameau says he has used to his advantage.[21]

3rd. With regard to the pleasure that *Consonances* cause for the ear to the exclusion of every other Interval, the source is clearly seen in their generation. *Consonances* all arise from the Perfect Chord, produced by a unique Sound, and the Perfect Chord is reciprocally formed by the assemblage of *Consonances*. It is therefore natural that the Harmony of this Chord is communicated to its Parts; that each of them participate in it, and that every other Interval that does not make up part of this Chord does not participate in it. Now, Nature, which has endowed the objects of each sense with qualities proper for flattering it, has wanted every Sound whatsoever to be accompanied by other pleasant Sounds, as it has wanted a ray of light always to be formed of the most beautiful colors. If one presses the question, and one asks further from whence arises the pleasure that the Perfect Chord causes for the ear, whereas it is shocked by the concurrence of every other Sound, what can be responded to this, except to ask in one's own turn why green rather than gray delights the sight, and why the perfume of a rose enchants whereas the odor of the poppy displeases?

Haven't Physicists explained all this—and what do they not explain? But how conjectural all these explanations are, and how little solidity is found in them when they are closely examined! The Reader will pass judgment on this through an explanation of the principles, which I shall try to do in a few words.

They say, then, that since the sensation of the Sound is produced by the vibrations of the sounding body propagated to the tympanum by those the air receives from that same body, when two Sounds are heard together the ear is simultaneously affected by their different vibrations. If these vibrations are isochronic, that is, if they accord simultaneously at the beginning and end, this concurrence forms the Unison, and the ear, which grasps the Accord of these equal and very concordant recurrences, is pleasantly affected by it. If the vibrations of one of these two Sounds are twice the duration of those of the other, during each vibration of the lower one, the higher will make precisely two of them, and on the third they will start off together. Thus, every second one, every odd vibration of the higher will concur with every vibration of the lower, and this frequent concordance which constitutes the Octave, which according to them is less sweet than Unison, will be more so than any other *Consonance*. After this comes the Fifth, wherein one of the Sounds makes two vibrations whereas the other makes three of them, in such a way that they are in accord only at every third vibration of the higher one; then the double Octave, wherein one of the Sounds makes four vibrations while the other makes only one of them, being in accord only at every fourth vibration of the higher one; as for the Fourth, its vibrations correspond every fourth for the higher and every third for the lower; those of the Major Third are as 4 and 5, of the Major Sixth as 3 and 5, of the Minor Third as 3 and 6, and of the Minor Sixth as 5 and 8. Beyond these numbers it is only their multiples that produce *Consonances*, that is, Octaves of these; all the rest are dissonant.

Others, finding the Octave more pleasant than Unison, and the Fifth more pleasant than the Octave, give as a reason for this that the equal returns of the vibrations in the Unison and their too frequent concurrence in the Octave confound, identify the Sounds and prevent the ear from discerning their diversity. As much as one may, with pleasure, compare Sounds, it is quite necessary, they say, for the vibrations to accord by Intervals, but not for them to be confounded too often, otherwise, instead of two Sounds, one would believe that one hears only one of them, and the ear would lose the pleasure of the comparison. It is in this way that, from the same principle, one deduces the for and the against at one's pleasure, as one judges the experience requires it.

But first, one sees, this whole explanation is founded only on the pleasure it is claimed the soul receives by the organ of hearing from the concurrence of vibrations—which, at bottom, is only pure supposition. Furthermore, in order to justify this system it must further be assumed that the first vibration of each of the two sounding bodies begins exactly with that of the other; for however little the one precede it, they would no longer ever concur in the determined ratio, perhaps they never would concur, and consequently the perceptible Interval must change; the *Consonance* would no longer exist or would no longer be the same. Finally, it must be assumed that the different vibrations of the two Sounds of one *Consonance* strike the organ without confusion, and transmit to the brain the sensation of the Chord without mutually interfering with one another: a difficult thing to conceive of and which I shall have occasion to speak of elsewhere.

But without disputing about so many assumptions, let us see what must follow from this system. The vibrations or the Sounds of the last *Consonance*, which is the Minor Third, are as 5 and 6, and their Accord is extremely pleasant. What must naturally result from two other Sounds whose vibrations would be to one another as 6 and 7? A *Consonance* a little less harmonious, it is true, but still pleasant enough, due to the smallness of the difference of the ratios; for they differ only by a thirty-sixth. But tell me how it can be that two Sounds, of which the first makes five vibrations whereas the other makes six of them, produces a pleasant *Consonance*, and that two Sounds, of which the first makes six vibrations while the other makes seven of them, produces a Dissonance that is as harsh. What! In the first of these ratios the vibrations are in accord every sixth, and my ear is charmed, in the other they are in accord every seventh and my ear is flayed? I ask further how it happens that after this first Dissonance the harshness of the others does not increase by reason of the complexity of the ratios? Why, for example, is the Dissonance which results from the ratio of 89 to 90 not much more shocking than that which results from the ratio of 12 to 13? If the more or less frequent recurrence of the concurrence of the vibrations were the cause of the degree of pleasure or of pain which the Chords produce in me, the effect would be proportioned to this cause, and I do not find any such proportion. Thus, this pleasure and this pain do not at all come from this.

It still remains to attend to the alterations of which a *Consonance* is susceptible without ceasing to be pleasant to the ear, even though these alterations wholly disrupt the periodic concurrence of the vibrations, and even though this concurrence even becomes rarer in proportion as the alteration is smaller. It remains to consider why the Accord of the Organ or of the Harpsichord should offer to the ear only a cacophony that is all the more horrible in proportion as these Instruments are more carefully tuned, since, excepting the Octave, no *Consonance* is found in its exact ratio.

Will it be said that a ratio that is approached is assumed to be as entirely exact, that it is received as such by the ear, and that it supplies by instinct what it is lacking in the exactness of the Accord? I then ask why this unevenness of judgment and of discernment, by which it accepts ratios that are more or less approached, and rejects others in accordance with the different nature of the *Consonances*? In Unison, for example, the ear does not supply anything; it is just or false, nothing in between. It is also likewise for the Octave: if the Interval is not exact, the ear is shocked; it does not admit of any approximation. Why does it allow more in the Fifth and less in the Major Third? A vague explanation, without proof, and, contrary to the principle one wants to establish, does not account for these differences at all.

The Philosopher who gave us the principles of Acoustics, leaving aside all these concurrence of the vibrations, and renewing Descartes' system in this regard, accounts for the pleasure that *Consonances* cause for the ear by the simplicity of the ratios between the Sounds that form them.[22] According to this Author, and according to Descartes,[23] the pleasure diminishes in proportion as these ratios become more complex, and when the mind no longer grasps them, they are genuine Dissonances; thus, it is an operation of the mind which they take for the principle of the feeling for Harmony. Moreover, although this hypothesis agrees with the result of the first harmonic divisions, and although it even extends to other phenomena noted in the fine Arts, as it is subject to the same objections as the preceding one, it is not possible for reason to be contented with it.

Of all these, that which appears most satisfying has for its Author M. Estève, of the Royal Society of Montpellier.[24] Here below is how he reasons.

The feeling for the Sound is inseparable from that of its Harmonics, and since every Sound carries with it its Harmonics or rather its Accompaniment, this same Accompaniment is in the ordering of our organs. In the simplest Sound there is a gradation of sounds which are both weaker and higher, which soften the principal Sound by nuances, and make it lose the highest Sounds due to its great speed. This is what a Sound is; the Accompaniment is essential to it, by producing its softness and melody. Thus, every time this softening, this Accompaniment, its set of harmonics is strengthened and better developed, the Sounds will be more melodious, the nuances better supported. This is a perfection, and the soul must be sensitive to it.

Now, *Consonances* have this property, that when the Harmonics of each of the two Sounds concur with the Harmonics of the other, these Harmonics mutually support one another, become more appreciable, last longer, and thus make the Accord of the two Sounds that produce them more pleasant.

In order to make the application of this principle clearer, M. Estève has set up two Tables, the first of *Consonances*, the other of Dissonances according to the ordering of the Scale; and these Tables are so arranged that one sees in each the concurrence or the opposition of the Harmonics of the two Sounds that form each Interval.

By the Table of the *Consonances* one sees that the Chord of the Octave preserves almost all its Harmonics, and this is the reason for the identity that is conceived in the practice of Harmony between the two Sounds of the Octave; one sees that the Fifth Chord preserves only three Harmonics, that the Fourth preserves only two of them, that, finally, imperfect *Consonances* preserve only one of them, except the Major Sixth, which carries two of them.

By the Table of the Dissonances one sees that they do not preserve any Harmonic sound for themselves, except the minor Seventh alone, which preserves its fourth Harmonic, namely, the Major Third of the third Octave of the high Sound.

From these observations, the Author concludes that the more concurrent Harmonics there are between two Sounds, the more their Accord will be pleasant, and these are the perfect *Consonances*. The more the Harmonics are destroyed, the less the soul will be satisfied by these Chords; these are the imperfect *Consonances*. Finally, if it so happens that no Harmonic is preserved, the Sounds will be deprived of their softness and their melody; they will be sharp and as if emaciated, the soul will not lend itself to them, and instead of the softness it experiences in *Consonances*, finding everywhere only a sustained coarseness, it will experience a feeling of restlessness, unpleasantness, which is the effect of the Dissonance.

This hypothesis is, without question, the simplest, the most natural, and the most felicitous of all; but it nevertheless leaves something to be desired for the mind's contentment, since the causes it assigns are not always proportional to the differences in the effects; since, for example, it confounds in the same category the Minor Third and the minor Seventh as being equally reducible to a single Harmonic, although the first is *Consonant*, the other Dissonant, and their effect is very different for the ear.

With regard to the principle of Harmony imagined by M. Sauveur, and which he made consist in the Beats,[25] as it is in no way sustainable, and as it has not been adopted by anyone, I shall stop here, and it will be enough to refer the Reader to what I have said about it at the word BEATS [*Battemens*].

COPYIST [*Copiste*], *n. masc.* Someone who makes a profession of copying Music.

Whatever progress the Typographic Art has made, it has never been possible to apply it to Music with as much success as to writing, whether because, the tastes of the mind being more constant than those of the ear, one grows tired less quickly with the same books than with the same songs; or by the specific difficulties that the combination of Notes and of Lines adds to the printing of Music: for if one first prints the Staffs and then the Notes, it is impossible to give the necessary exactness to their relative positions; and if the character of each Note depends on a portion of the Staff, as in our printed Music, the lines are arranged so poorly with respect to one another, such a prodigious number of characters are needed, the whole makes for such a nasty effect on the eye, that this manner has reasonably been abandoned to be replaced with engraving. But aside from the fact that engraving itself is not exempt from inconveniences, it always has that of multiplying the copies or the Parts too much or too little; of putting into the Score what some would like in the separate Parts, or in separate Parts what others would like in the Score, and of offering to the curious almost nothing but Music that is already old and has passed through everyone's hands. Finally, it is certain that in Italy, the country on earth where the most Music is composed, printed Notation has been proscribed for a long time without the use of engraving having been able to be established there; from which I conclude that in the judgment of the Experts simple *Copying* is the most convenient.

It is more important for Music to be clearly and correctly copied than for simple writing: because someone who reads and meditates in his study perceives, easily corrects the mistakes in his book, and because nothing prevents him from suspending his reading or from beginning it anew. But in a Concert where each sees only his own Part, and where the speed and the continuity of the playing does not leave the time to come back to any mistake, they are all irreparable; often a sublime piece is maimed, the playing is interrupted or even stopped, everything goes awry, togetherness and effectiveness are everywhere lacking, the Listener is put off and the Author dishonored by the fault of the *Copyist* alone.

Furthermore, the understanding of a difficult piece of Music depends a great deal on the manner in which it is copied; for aside from the clarity of the Notation, there are various means of presenting more clearly to the Reader the ideas that one wishes to depict for him and which he should produce. The copying of one man is often found to be more readable than that of another who nevertheless notates more agreeably; it is that the one wishes only to please the eyes, and the other is more attentive to useful concerns. The most skillful *Copyist* is the one whose Music is played with the greatest ease, without the Musician himself guessing why. All this has persuaded me that to explain the duty and the cares of a good *Copyist* in some detail was not to write a useless Article; everything that tends toward making playing easier is not at all indifferent for the perfection of an Art for which it is always the greatest pitfall. I perceive how much I am going to harm myself if my work is compared to my rules; but I am not ignorant of the fact that he who seeks public utility should have forgotten his own. Literary Man: I have said about my position all the ill I think of it; I have written only French Music, and I love only Italian; I have shown all the miseries of Society when I was happy by means of it; a bad *Copyist*, I here explain what good ones do. O truth! My interest was never anything before you; may it in no way sully the worship I have vowed to you.

* * *

I stop so as not to extend the length of this article: I have said too much about it for every well-instructed *Copyist* who has a good hand and the taste for his trade; I would never say enough about it for the others. I will only add a word in conclusion. There are many intermediaries between what the Composer imagines and what the Listeners hear. It is for the *Copyist* to bring these two end points as close together as possible, to indicate clearly everything that should be done so that the performed Music renders to the Composer's ear exactly what he depicted in his head when composing it.

DISSONANCE [*Dissonnance*], *n. fem.*[26] Every Sound that forms with another one a Chord disagreeable to the ear, or, better, every Interval that is not consonant. Now, as there are no Consonances other than those which form the Sounds of the Perfect Chord among themselves and with the fundamental, it follows that every other Interval is a genuine *Dissonance*. Even the Ancients counted as such Thirds and Sixths, which they omitted from the consonant Chords.

The term *Dissonance* comes from two words, the one Greek, the other

Latin, which mean *to sound doubly*. In fact, what makes the *Dissonance* disagreeable is that the sounds which form it, far from being joined with each other to the ear, reject each other, so to speak, and are heard by it as two distinct Sounds, even though struck at the same time.

The name *Dissonance* is sometimes given to the Interval and sometimes to each of the two Sounds which form it. But although two Sounds are dissonant to one another, the name *Dissonance* is given more specifically to that of the two which is foreign to the Chord.

There are an infinity of possible *Dissonances*; but as in Music all the Intervals that the received System does not furnish are excluded, they are reduced to a small number; further, for practice one should choose among these only those that suit the Genre and the Mode, and, finally, even exclude from these latter ones those which cannot be employed in accordance with the prescribed rules. What are these rules? Do they have any natural foundation, or are they purely arbitrary? This is what I propose to examine in this Article.

The physical principle of Harmony is derived from the production of the perfect Chord by the resonance of any Sound whatsoever; all the Consonances arise from it, and it is Nature itself that furnishes them. This therefore does not apply to the *Dissonance*, at least such as we practice it. We do indeed find, if you like, its generation in the progressions of consonant Intervals and in their differences, but we do not perceive the physical reason that authorizes us to introduce it into the very body of the Harmony. Father Mersenne contents himself with showing the generation by calculation and the various ratios of *Dissonances*, those that are rejected as well as those that are accepted, but he does not say anything about the right to employ them.[27] M. Rameau specifically says that the *Dissonance* is not natural to Harmony, and that it can be used only by the assistance of Art. Nonetheless, in another Work he tries to find its principle in the ratios of numbers and in harmonic and arithmetic proportions, as if there were any identity between the properties of abstract quantity and the sensations of hearing. But after having quite exhausted the analogies, after many metamorphoses of those various proportions, the ones in the others, after many operations and useless calculations, he ends by establishing, on weak conformities, the *Dissonance* he has given himself such trouble to find. Thus, because the arithmetic proportion in the order of the harmonic Sounds gives him, by the lengths of the Strings, a Minor Third in the bass (notice that he gives it to the treble by the calculation of the vibrations), he adds a new Minor Third to the bass of the Subdominant. The harmonic proportion gives him a Minor Third on the treble (he would give it to the bass by the vibrations), and he adds a new Minor Third to the treble of the

Dominant. These Thirds, added in this way, do not, it is true, form any proportion with the preceding ratios; the ratios they themselves should have are found to be altered. But this doesn't matter: M. Rameau turns everything to best account; the proportion serves him to introduce the *Dissonance*, and the lack of proportion to make it felt.[28]

Since the illustrious Geometer who dared to interpret M. Rameau's System for the Public has done away with all these vain calculations, I shall follow his example, or rather I shall transcribe what he says about *Dissonance*, and M. Rameau will owe me thanks for having taken this explanation from the *Elements of Music* rather than from his own writings.[29]

Assuming one knows the essential pitches of the Key according to M. Rameau's System—namely, in the Key of *do*, the Tonic *do*, the Dominant *sol*, and the Subdominant *fa*—one must also know that this same Key of *do* has two Pitches, *do* and *sol*, in common with the Key of *sol*, and the two pitches *do* and *fa* in common with the Key of *fa*. Consequently, this progression of the Bass *do sol* can belong to the Key of *do* or to the Key of *sol*, just as the progression of Bass *fa do* or *do fa* can belong to the Key of *do* or to the Key of *fa*. Therefore, when one passes from *do* to *fa* or to *sol* in a Fundamental Bass, one still does not know at that point what Key one is in. It would, however, be advantageous to know this and to be able, by some means, to distinguish the generator from its Fifths.

This advantage will be obtained by joining the Sounds *sol* and *fa* together in a single Harmony, that is, by joining to the Harmony *sol si re* of the Fifth *sol* the other Fifth *fa*, in this manner: *sol si re fa*, this additional *fa*, being the Seventh of *sol*, making a *Dissonance*. It is for this reason that the Chord *sol si re fa* is called a dissonant Chord or a Seventh Chord. It serves to distinguish the Fifth *sol* from the generator *do*, which always contains the Perfect Chord *do mi sol do*, given by Nature itself, without mixture and without alteration. (See CHORD* [*Accord*], CONSONANCE* [*Consonnance*], HARMONY* [*Harmonie*].) It is seen by this that when one passes from *do* to *sol*, one passes at the same time from *do* to *fa*, because the *fa* is contained in the Chord of *sol*, and the Key of *do* is, by this means, completely determined because there is only this Key to which the Sounds *fa* and *sol* simultaneously belong.

Let us see now, continues M. d'Alembert, what we shall add to the Harmony *fa la do* of the Fifth *fa* below the generator in order to distinguish this Harmony from that of this same generator. It seems at first that one should add to it the other Fifth *sol* so that, passing to *fa*, the generator *do* passes at the same time to *sol*, and so that the Key would in this way be determined, but this introduction of *sol* into the Chord *fa la do*, would produce two Seconds in a row, *fa sol*, *sol la*, that is, two *Dissonances* whose union would be too unpleasant to the ear: an inconvenience which must be avoided, for if we alter the Harmony of this Fifth *fa* in order to distinguish the Key, it must only be altered as little as possible.

This is why, instead of *sol*, we shall take its Fifth *re*, which is the Sound that comes closest to it, and we shall have for the Subdominant *fa* the Chord *fa la do re*, which is called a Great Sixth Chord or the Added Sixth [Chord].

One can note here the analogy observed between the Chord of the Dominant *sol* and that of the Subdominant *fa*.

The Dominant *sol*, by ascending above the generator, has a Chord composed entirely of Thirds in ascending from *sol*: *sol si re fa*. Now, the Subdominant *fa* being below the generator *do*, by descending from *do* toward *fa* by Thirds one will find *do la fa re*, which contains the same Sounds as the Chord *fa la do re* gives to the Subdominant *fa*.

It is further seen that the alteration of the Harmony of the two Fifths consists solely in the Minor Third *re fa* or *fa re*, added on each side to the Harmony of these two Fifths.

This explanation is all the more ingenious as it simultaneously shows the origin, the use, the progression of the *Dissonance*, its intimate relationship with the Key, and the means for reciprocally determining the one by the other. The defect that I find in it, but an essential defect which makes the whole collapse, is the use of a pitch foreign to the Key as an essential Pitch of the Key, and that by a false analogy which, serving as the base of M. Rameau's System, destroys it in disappearing.

I am speaking of that Fifth below the Tonic, of that subdominant between which and the Tonic one does not perceive the slightest connection that might justify the use of that Subdominant, not only as an essential pitch of the Key, but even in any quality whatsoever. What is there really in common between the resonance, the vibration of the Unisons of *do*, and the Sound of its Fifth below? It is not at all because the entire String is a *fa* that its aliquots resonate to the Sound of *do*, but because it is a multiple of the string *do*; and there no multiple of this same *do* that does not produce a similar phenomenon. Take the septuple: it will vibrate and resonate in its Parts just as the triple does. Is this to say that the Sound of this septuple or its Octaves would be essential pitches of the Key? Enough said, since it does not form even a commensurable ratio of Notes with the Tonic.

I know that M. Rameau has claimed that with the sounding of any string whatsoever another string at its twelfth below would vibrate without resonating; but aside from the fact that a sounding string which vibrates and does not resonate is a strange phenomenon in acoustics, it is now recognized that this pretended experiment is in error, that the lower string vibrates because it is divided, and that it appears not to resonate because it renders in its parts only the unison of the higher, which is not easily distinguished.

Let M. Rameau then tell us that he takes the Fifth below because he finds the Fifth above, and that this play of Fifths appears to him convenient to establish his System: he will be congratulated for an ingenious invention; but let him not justify it by a chimerical experiment, let him not torment himself to discover the foundations of Harmony in the inversions of harmonic and arithmetic proportions, nor take the properties of numbers for those of Sounds.

Note further that if the counter-generation which he assumes could take place, the Chord of the Subdominant *fa* should not contain a Major Third, but a minor one, because the *la*-Flat is the genuine Harmonic which is assigned to it by this inversion 1 1/3 1/5: *do fa la*. So that according to this account, the Scale of the minor Mode would naturally have the Minor Sixth, but it has a major one, as a fourth Fifth, or as Fifth of the second Note; here, then, is a further contradiction.

Finally, note that the fourth Note given by the series of aliquots, from which the true natural Diatonic arises, is not at all the Octave of the pretended Subdominant in the ratio of 4 to 3, but another fourth Note, entirely different, in the ratio of 11 to 8, so that every Theorist should perceive it at the first glance.

I now call upon the experience and on the ears of Musicians. Let them hear how harsh and savage the Imperfect Cadence from the Subdominant to the Tonic is in comparison to this same Cadence in its natural place, which is from the Tonic to the Dominant. In the first case, can one say that the ear no longer desires anything after the Chord of the Tonic? Does one not expect, despite the fact one has just had it, a continuation or a conclusion? Now, what is a Tonic after which the ear desires something? Can one regard it as a genuine Tonic, and is one not really then in the Key of *fa*, whereas one thought one was in that of *do*? Let it be observed how foreign to the Mode, and even hard for the Voice, the diatonic and successive Intonation of the fourth Note and of the Leading Tone, in ascending as well as descending, seems. If long habit accustoms the ear and the Voice of the Musician to it, the difficulty of Beginners in intoning this Note should show him quite clearly how little natural it is. This difficulty is attributed to three consecutive *Keys*. Shouldn't it be seen that these three consecutive *Keys*, just as the Note that introduces them, produces a barbarous Modulation that has no foundation in Nature? It assuredly guided the Greeks better when it made them stop their Tetrachord precisely at the *mi* of our Scale, that is, at the Note which precedes this fourth one; they preferred to take this fourth one below and they thus discovered with their ear alone what all our harmonic theory has still not made us perceive.

If the testimony of the ear and that of reason unite, at least in the received System, to reject the pretended Subdominant not only from among the essential Pitches of the Key, but from among the Sounds which can enter into the Scale of the Mode, what becomes of all this theory of *Dissonances*? What becomes of the explanation of the minor Mode? What becomes of M. Rameau's whole System?

Perceiving the genuine generation of the *Dissonance* neither in Physics nor in calculation, therefore, I sought a purely mechanical origin for it, and it is in the following way that I tried to explain it in the *Encyclopedia*, without departing from M. Rameau's practical System.

I assume the necessity of the *Dissonance* to be recognized. (See HARMONY* [*Harmonie*] and CADENCE [*Cadence*].) It is a matter of seeing where one should take this *dissonance* and how it must be employed.

If all the Sounds of the Diatonic Scale are successively compared with the fundamental Sound in each of the two Modes, one will find for every *Dissonance* only the Second and the Seventh, which is merely an inverted Second and which actually makes a Second with the Octave. That the Seventh is inverted from the Second, and not the Second from the Seventh, is evident from the expression of the ratios, for that of the Second, 8: 9, being simpler than that of the Seventh, 9: 16, the Interval it represents is not, consequently, the engendered one, but the generator. I well know that other altered Intervals can become dissonant; but if the Second is not found expressed or implied in it, these are only accidents of Modulation which Harmony does not take into consideration, and these *Dissonances* are then not at all treated as such. Thus, it is certain that where there is no Second there is no *Dissonance* either; and the Second is strictly speaking the only *Dissonance* that may be employed.

To reduce all the Consonances to their least extent, let us not leave the limits of the Octave, they are all contained in the Perfect Chord. Let us then take this Perfect Chord, *sol si re sol*, and see where in this Chord, which I do not yet suppose to be in any Key, we could place a *Dissonance*, that is a Second, in order to make it as little shocking to the ear as possible. On the *la* between the *sol* and the *si* it would make a Second with them both and, consequently, it would be doubly dissonant. It would be the same between the *si* and the *re*, as between every Interval of a Third; there remains the Interval of the Fourth between the *re* and the *sol*. Here a Sound could be introduced in two ways: 1st, one could add the Note *fa*, which would make a Second with the *sol* and a Third with the *re*; 2nd, or the Note *mi*, which will make a Second with the *re* and a Third with the *sol*. It is obvious that the least harsh *Dissonance* one could find will be had in each of these two ways, for it will be dissonant with a single Sound, and it will engender a new Third, which, as with the two preceding ones, will contribute to sweetness of the total Chord. On the one hand we will have the Seventh Chord, and on the other the Added Sixth, the sole two dissonant Chords accepted in the System of the Fundamental Bass.

It is not enough to make the *Dissonance* heard; it must be resolved. You initially shock the ear only then to flatter it more agreeably. Here are two adjoining Sounds: on the one side the Fifth and the Sixth, on the other the Seventh and the Octave: as long as they thus produce the Second, they will remain dissonant; but let the Parts which make them heard move away from one another by a Degree, let the one ascend or the other descend diatonically, and your Second, on one side and the other, will become a Third, that is, one of the most pleasant Consonances. Thus after *sol fa* you will have *sol mi* or *fa la*; and after *re mi*, *mi do* or *re fa*: this is what is called resolving the *Dissonance*.

It remains to determine which of the two adjoining Sounds should ascend or descend, and which should remain in place: but the grounds for determining it leap to the eyes. Let the Fifth or the Octave remain as principal pitches, let the Sixth ascend and the Seventh descend, as accessory Sounds, as *Dissonances*. Furthermore, if, of the two adjoining Sounds, it is preferable for the one that has less distance to cover to do so, the *fa* will further descend on the *mi*, after the Seventh, and the *mi* of the Added Sixth Chord will ascend on the *fa*, for there is no other shorter route for resolving the *Dissonance*.

Let us now see what progression the fundamental Sound should make relative to the movement assigned to the *Dissonance*. Since one of the two adjoining Sounds remains in place, a connection should be made with the following Chord. The Interval that the Fundamental Bass should form in leaving the Chord should therefore be determined in accordance with these two conditions: 1st, so that the Octave of its preceding fundamental Sound may remain in place after the Seventh Chord, the Fifth after the Chord of the Added Sixth; 2nd, so that the Sound on which the *Dissonance* is resolved be one of the Harmonics of the one to which the Fundamental Bass passes. Now, the best movement of the Bass being by intervals of a Fifth, if it descends a Fifth in the first case, or ascends a Fifth in the second, all the conditions will be perfectly fulfilled, as is evident solely by inspection (Plate A, Figure 9 [below]).

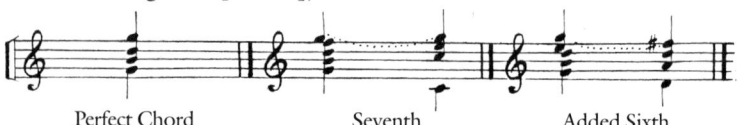

Perfect Chord   Seventh   Added Sixth

From thence is derived a means of knowing which pitch of the Key each of these two Chords best suits. What are the two most essential pitches in each Key? They are the Tonic and the Dominant. How can the Bass progress when descending a Fifth on the two essential pitches of the Key? It is by passing from the Dominant to the Tonic; thus, the Dominant is the pitch which the Seventh Chord best suits. How can the Bass progress when ascending a Fifth on the two essential pitches of the Key? It is by passing from the Tonic to the Dominant; thus, the Tonic is the Pitch which the Added Sixth Chord best suits. This is why, in the example, I have given a Sharp to the *fa* of the Chord that follows it, for the *re* being Dominant-Tonic should contain the Major Third. The Bass can have other progressions, but these are the most perfect, and the two principal Cadences. (See CADENCE [*Cadence*].)

If these two *Dissonances* are compared with the fundamental Sound, one finds the one that descends is a minor Seventh, and the one that ascends a Major Sixth, from which is derived this new rule, that major *Dissonances* should ascend and minor ones descend; for, in general, a major Interval has less distance to cover in ascending, and a minor Interval in descending; and, also in general, in Diatonic progressions the smallest Intervals are preferable.

When the Seventh Chord contains a Major Third, this Third makes another *Dissonance* with the Seventh, which is the False Fifth, or, by inversion, the Tritone. This Third vis-à-vis the Seventh is also called a major *Dissonance*, and it is prescribed for it to ascend, but this is in its quality as Leading Tone, and without the Second this pretended *dissonance* would not exist at all or would not at all be treated as such.

One observation that must not be forgotten is that the only two Notes of the Scale that are not found in the Harmonics of the two principal pitches *do* and *sol* are precisely those that happen to be introduced by the *Dissonance* and complete, by this means, the Diatonic Scale, which, without this, would be incomplete. This explains how *fa* and *la*, although foreign to the Mode, are found in its Scale, and why their Intonation, always crude in spite of habit, makes the idea of the principal Key more remote.

It must also be noted that these two *Dissonances*, namely the Major Sixth and the minor Seventh, differ only by a Semitone, and would differ still less if the Intervals were quite exact. With the aid of this observation one can derive from the principle of the resonance a very closely related origin for both of them, as I am going to demonstrate.

The Harmonics that accompany any Sound whatsoever are not limited to those that make up the perfect Chord. There are an infinity of others, less appreciable to the extent that they become higher and their ratios more complex, and these ratios are expressed by the natural series of aliquots, 1/2, 1/3, 1/4, 1/5, 1/6, 1/7, etc. The first six terms of this series give the Sounds that make up the perfect Chord and its Replicas, the Seventh being excluded from it; nevertheless, this seventh term enters like them into the total resonance of the generator Sound, although less appreciably; but it does not enter as a Consonance; it therefore enters as a *Dissonance*, and this *Dissonance* is given by Nature. It remains to see its connection with those about which I have just been speaking.

Now, this ratio is intermediate between the one and the other, and very near to them both, for the ratio of the Major Sixth is 3/5, and that of the minor Seventh 9/16. Reduced to the same terms, these two ratios are 48/80 and 45/80.

The ratio of the aliquot 1/7 reduced to simplicity by its Octaves is 4/7, and, reducing this ratio to the same terms with the preceding ones, is found intermediary between the two in this manner, 326/560, 320/560, 315/560, where it is seen that this mean ratio differs from the Major Sixth by only 1/35, or by about two Commas, and from the minor Seventh by only 1/112, which is much less than a Comma. In order to employ the same Sounds in the Diatonic genre and in various Modes, it has been necessary to alter them, but this alteration is not so great as to make us lose the trace of their origin.

I have shown, at the word CADENCE [*Cadence*], how the introduction of these two principal *Dissonances*, the Seventh and the Added Sixth, gives the means for connecting a succession of Harmony by making it ascend or descend at one's liking by the interlacing of *Dissonances*.

I do not speak here at all of the preparation of the *Dissonance*, less because it has too many exceptions to make a general rule of it than because here is not the place to do so. (See To PREPARE* [*Préparer*].) With regard to *Dissonances* by supposition or by suspension, see also these two words. Finally, I do not say anything about the Diminished Seventh either, a singular Chord of which I shall have occasion to speak at the word ENHARMONIC* [*Enharmonique*].

Although this manner of conceiving *Dissonance* gives a clear enough idea of it, as this idea is not at all drawn from the basis of Harmony, but from certain conformities between its parts, I am quite far from making more of it than it merits, and I have never given it far more than what it deserves; but until now *Dissonance* has been so badly reasoned about that I do not believe I have done worse in this than the others. M. Tartini is the first, and until now the only one, who has deduced a Theory of *Dissonances* from the true principles of Harmony.[30] In order to avoid useless repetitions, I postpone it below to the word SYSTEM [*Système*], where I explain his. I shall abstain from judging whether or not he has found that of Nature; but I should at least remark that this Author's principles would seem to have in their consequences that universality and that connection which is hardly found except in those which lead to the truth.

A further observation before finishing this Article. Every commensurable Interval is in reality consonant: only those whose ratios are irrational are truly dissonant, for it is only these to which no common fundamental Sound can be assigned. But past the point where the natural Harmonics are still appreciable, this consonance of commensurable Intervals is no longer accepted except by induction. Then these Intervals make up a great part of the Harmonic System, since they are in the ordering of its natural generation and are related to its common fundamental Sound; but they cannot be accepted as Consonances by the ear since it does not at all perceive them in the natural Harmony of the sounding body. Besides, the more complex the Interval is, the more it climbs to the high end of the fundamental Sound, which is proved by the reciprocal generation of the fundamental Sound and of the superior Intervals. (*See M. Tartini's System.*) Now, since when the distance from the fundamental Sound to the highest of the generating or engendered Interval exceeds the range of the Musical or appreciable System, everything that is beyond this range should be considered as nothing, such an Interval has no perceptible foundation at all and should be rejected from practice, or only accepted as Dissonant. This is not M. Rameau's System, nor M. Tartini's, nor mine, but the text of Nature, which, moreover, I do not undertake to explain.

EFFECT [*Effet*], *n. masc.* A pleasant and strong impression that produces excellent Music for the ear and the mind of the listeners; thus, the word *Effect* alone means in Music a great and fine *Effect*. And it will not only be said of a work that it has an *Effect*, but one will distinguish from this, under the name of *things of Effect*, all those in which the sensation produced appears superior to the means employed to arouse it.

A long practice can teach one to recognize things of *Effect* on paper; but it is only the Genius who can find them. It is the defect of bad Composers and of all Beginners to heap up Parts upon Parts, Instruments upon Instruments, in order to discover the *Effect* which flees them, and to open, as an Ancient said, a large mouth in order to blow into a small Flute. To see their Scores—so overloaded, so bristling, you would say that they are going to surprise you by prodigious *Effects*, and if you are surprised in hearing all that, it is to hear a smallish Music, scrawny, sickly, confused, without *Effect*, and more appropriate for deafening ears than for filling them. On the contrary, the eye seeks in the Scores of the great Masters those sublime and ravishing *Effects* that their Music produces when per-

GENRES OF ANCIENT MUSIC

NO. A ACCORDING TO ARIXTOXENUS

The Tetrachord being supposed to be divided into 60 equal parts

DIATONIC	CHROMATIC	ENHARMONIC
Tender or soft 12 + 18 + 30 = 60	Soft 8 + 8 + 44 = 60	6 + 6 + 48 = 60
Syntonic or hard 12 + 24 + 24 = 60	Hemiolian 9 + 9 + 42 = 60	
	Tonic 2 + 12 + 36 = 60	

NO. B ACCORDING TO PTOLEMY

The Tetrachord being represented by the ratio of its two terms

DIATONIC	CHROMATIC	ENHARMONIC
Diatonic $\frac{256}{243} \times \frac{9}{8} \times \frac{9}{8} = \frac{4}{3}$	Soft $\frac{28}{27} \times \frac{15}{14} \times \frac{6}{5} = \frac{4}{3}$	$\frac{46}{45} \times \frac{24}{23} \times \frac{5}{4} = \frac{4}{3}$
	Tight or Syntonic $\frac{22}{21} \times \frac{12}{11} \times \frac{7}{6} = \frac{4}{3}$	

Plate M, Figure 5

formed. It is because those minute details are ignored or disdained by the true genius, because he does not at all amuse you by throngs of little and puerile objects, but he moves you by grand *Effects*, and because strength and simplicity always form their character when united.

ENHARMONIC [*Enharmonique*], *adj. taken subst.*[31] One of the three Genres of the Music of the Greeks, also very frequently called *Harmony* by Aristoxenus and his sectarians.[32]

This Genre resulted from a particular division of the Tetrachord according to which the Interval which is found between the Lichanos, or the third Pitch, and since the Mese, or the fourth, was one Ditonon, or Major Third, there remained only a Semitone to divide into two Intervals in order to complete the Tetrachord on the lower end, namely, from the Hypate to the Parhypate, and from the Parhypate to the Lichanos. We shall explain at the word GENRE [*Genre*] how this division was made.

The *Enharmonic* Genre was the sweetest of the three, according to Aristide Quintilianus' report.[33] It passed as very ancient, and the majority of Authors attributed its invention to Olympus, the Phrygian. But his Tetrachord, or rather his Diatessaron of this Genre, contained only three pitches, which among them formed two uncomposed Intervals: the first of a Semitone and the other of a Major Third; and from these two Intervals alone, repeated from Tetrachord to Tetrachord, the whole *Enharmonic* Genre then resulted. It was only after Olympus that they thought of inserting, in imitation of the other genres, a fourth Pitch between the first two in order to make the division of which I was just speaking. Their ratios will be found in accordance with the systems of Ptolemy and Aristoxenus (Plate M, Figure 5).

This Genre, so marvelous, so admired by the Ancients, and, according to some, the first of the three to be found, did not long retain its vigor. Its extreme difficulty soon caused it to be abandoned, in proportion as the Art gained combinations while losing its energy and as the delicacy of the ear was supplemented by the agility of the fingers. In addition, Plutarch sharply reprimanded the Musicians of his time for having lost the most beautiful of the three Genera, and for having dared to say that its Intervals are not appreciable—as if everything that escaped their coarse senses, this Philosopher adds, must be beyond nature.[34]

Today we have a type of *Enharmonic* Genre entirely different from that of the Greeks. It consists, like the other two, in one particular Harmonic progression, which engenders *Enharmonic* Intervals in the progression of the Parts by simultaneously or successively employing, between two Notes that are one Tone apart, the Flat from the superior and the Sharp from the inferior. But although, according to the strictness of the ratios, this Sharp and this Flat should between them form an Interval (see SCALE [*Échelle*] and QUARTER-TONE [*Quart-de-ton*]), this Interval happens to be null by means of Temperament, which in the established System makes the same Sound serve two uses, which does not prevent such a transition from producing, by the force of the Modulation and of the Harmony, part of the effect that is sought in *Enharmonic* Transitions.

As this Genre is rather poorly known, and as our Authors have contented themselves with giving too succinct notions of it, I believe I should explain it here at a bit more length.

It is necessary to note first that the Diminished Seventh Chord is the only one on which truly *Enharmonic* transitions may be practiced, and that in virtue of that singular property it has of dividing the entire Octave into four equal intervals. Take from among the four Sounds which make up this Chord that which one wants as fundamental; one will always likewise find that the three other Sounds form a Diminished Seventh Chord on this sound. Now, the fundamental sound of the Diminished Seventh Chord is always a Leading Tone, so that, without changing anything in this Chord, one can, by means of double or of quadruple employment, make it serve successively on four different fundamentals, that is, on four different Leading Tones.

It follows from this that this same Chord, without changing anything either of the Accompaniment or of the Bass, can carry four different names, and consequently be figured in four different ways, namely: with a 7♭ under the name of the Diminished Seventh; with a $^6_\sharp{}^\times$ under the name of the Major Sixth and False Fifth; with a $^\times_\flat 4$ under the name of the Minor Third and Tritone; and, finally, with a × 2 under the name of the Augmented Second. It being well understood that the Clef must be differently armed in accordance with the Keys in which one is assumed to be.

These, then, are four ways of leaving a Diminished Seventh Chord, by assuming oneself to be successively in four different [Keys]: for the fundamental and natural progression of the Sound which carries a Diminished Seventh Chord is for it to be resolved on the Tonic of the minor Mode, whose Leading Tone it is.

Let us now imagine the Diminished Seventh Chord on a *do*-Sharp Leading Tone. If I take the Third *mi* as fundamental, it will become Leading Tone in its turn, and will consequently introduce the minor Mode of *fa*; now, this *do*-Sharp still remains Leading Tone in the Chord of *mi*, but it is in its capacity as *re*-Flat, that is, of the sixth Note of the Key, and of the Diminished Seventh of the Leading Tone; thus, this *do*-Sharp, which as Leading Tone was obliged to ascend in the Key of *re*, having become *re*-Flat in the Key of *fa*, is obliged to descend as a Diminished Seventh: this is an *Enharmonic* transition. If instead of the Third one takes, in the same Chord of *do*-Sharp, the Augmented Fifth *sol* as a new Leading Tone, the *do*-Sharp will then become *re*-Flat in its capacity as the fourth Note: another *Enharmonic* transition. Finally, if one takes as Leading Tone the Diminished Seventh itself, instead of *si*-Flat it must necessarily be considered as *la*-Sharp; which constitutes a third *Enharmonic* passage on the same Chord.

Thanks to these four different manners of successively considering the same Chord, one passes from one Key to another one that seems quite remote; one gives to the Parts progressions different from the one that they ought to have had in the first place, and these transitions, when properly handled, are capable not only of surprising but of delighting the Listener when they are well done.

Another source of variety in the same Genre is derived from the different ways in which one can resolve the Chord that introduces it; for although the most natural Modulation would be to pass from the Diminished Seventh Chord on the Leading Tone to that of the Tonic in the minor Mode, by substituting the Major Third for the minor one can make the Mode major, and even add to it the Seventh in order to change this Tonic into a Dominant, and to pass in this way into another Key. Thanks to these various combinations taken together, one can leave the Chord in twelve ways. But, of these twelve, there are only nine which, producing the conversion of the Sharp into a Flat or reciprocally, are genuinely *Enharmonic*, since the Leading Tone is not at all changed in the other three; furthermore, in these nine different Modulations there are only three different Leading Tones, each of which is resolved by three different transitions, so that, to grasp the thing correctly, there are on each Leading Tone only three true *Enharmonic* passages possible, all the others not being really *Enharmonic* or being related to one of the three first. (See Plate L, Figure 4, for an example of each of these transitions.)

In imitation of the Modulations of the Diatonic Genre, writing entire pieces in the *Enharmonic* Genre has several times been attempted, and, in order to give a sort of rule for the fundamental progressions of this Genre, it has been divided into *Diatonic-Enharmonic*, which proceeds by a series of major Semitones, and *Chromatic-Enharmonic*, which proceeds by a series of minor Semitones.

The Song of the first type is *Diatonic* because its Semitones are major; it is *Enharmonic* because two consecutive major Semitones form too large of a *Tone* of *Enharmonic* Interval. In order to form this type of Song, one

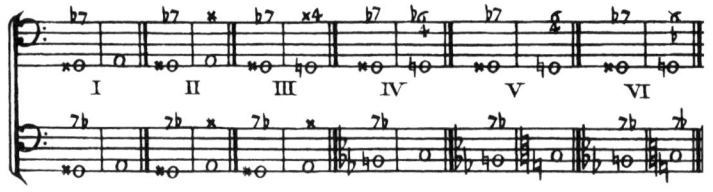

Plate L, Figure 4

must write a Bass that alternately descends a Fourth and ascends a Major Third. A part of the *Trio of the Furies* of the Opera *Hippolyte* is in this Genre, but it has never been possible to perform it at the Paris Opera, although M. Rameau assures that it has been so elsewhere by Musicians of good will, and that its effect was surprising.[35]

The Song of the second type is *Chromatic* because it proceeds by minor Semitones; it is *Enharmonic* because the two consecutive minor Semitones form too small of a *Tone* of *Enharmonic* Interval. In order to form this type of Song, one must write a Fundamental Bass that alternately descends a Minor Third and ascends a Major Third. M. Rameau informs us that he has composed an earthquake in the Opera *Indes galantes* in this Genre of Music, but that he was so badly served that he was obliged to change it into ordinary music.[36] (See M. d'Alembert's *Elements of Music*, pages 91, 92, 95, and 166.)[37]

Despite the examples cited and despite M. Rameau's authority, I believe I must warn young Artists that the *Enharmonic-Diatonic* and the *Enharmonic-Chromatic* both seem to me to be rejected as Genera, and I cannot believe that a Music modulated in this way, even with the most perfect execution, can ever be at all good. My reasons are that the brusque transitions from one idea to another, extremely remote idea are so frequent in it that it is not possible for the mind to follow these transitions with as much quickness as the Music presents them; that the ear does not have the time to perceive the very secret and very complex relationship of the Modulations, nor to infer the assumed Intervals; that one no longer finds in such successions a shadow of the Key or of the Mode; that it is equally impossible to retain that of the one being left or to foresee that of the one being entered; and that in the midst of all this one no longer knows at all where one is. The *Enharmonic* is merely an unexpected transition in which the astonishing impression is strongly formed and lasts a long time, a transition which consequently should not be repeated too brusquely or too often for fear lest the idea of the Modulation become confused and be entirely lost: for as soon as one hears only isolated Chords which no longer have a perceptible relation and common foundation, the Harmony no longer has enough unity or apparent coherence, and the effect that results from it is merely a vain noise without connection and without charm. If M. Rameau, less occupied with useless calculations, had better studied the Metaphysic of his Art, it is to be believed that the natural fire of this learned Artist would have produced prodigies whose seed was in his genius but which his prejudices have always stifled.

I do not even believe that simple *Enharmonic* Transitions can ever succeed well, either in Choruses or in Arias, because each of these pieces forms a whole in which unity should reign and whose Parts should have among themselves a more perceptible connection than this Genre can stamp them with.

What then is the true place of the *Enharmonic*? In my opinion, it is in the obligatory Recitative.[38] It is in a sublime and pathetic scene where the Voice should multiply and varying Musical inflections in imitation of the grammatical, oratorical, and often imperceptible accent; it is, I say, in such a scene that *Enharmonic* Transitions are well-placed, when one knows how to handle them for grand expressions and to firm them up, so to speak, by means of instrumental features which suspend speech and strengthen the expression. The Italians, who make admirable use of this Genre, employ it only in this manner. One can see in the first Recitative of Pergolesi's *Orfeo*[39] a striking and simple example of the effects that this great Musician knew how to draw from the *Enharmonic*, and how, far from making a modulation harsh, these transitions, having become natural and easy to sound, give an energetic sweetness to the whole declamation.

I have already said that our *Enharmonic* Genre is entirely different from that of the Ancients. I shall add that, although we do not have *Enharmonic* Intervals to sound, as they did, this does not prevent the modern *Enharmonic* from being more difficult to execute than theirs. Among the Greeks, *Enharmonic* Intervals, purely Melodious, demanded no change of ideas either in the Singer or in the listener, but only a great delicacy of the organ, whereas in our Music one must further add to that delicacy an exact knowledge of and refined feeling for the most brusque and least natural Harmonic metamorphoses: for if their phrasing is not heard, one cannot give the words the Tone that suits them, or sing in tune in a Harmonic system, if one does not feel the Harmony.

EXPRESSION [*Expression*], *n. fem.* A quality by which the Musician keenly feels and energetically renders every idea he should render and every feeling he should express. There is an *Expression* in Composition and one in performance, and it is from their concurrence that the most powerful and most pleasant musical effect results.

In order to give *Expression* to his works, the Composer should grasp and compare all the relations that can be found among the features of his object and the productions of his Art; he should know or feel the effect of every character so as to convey precisely the one that he chooses in the degree that suits it: for, as a good Painter does not give the same light to all his objects, neither will the skillful Musician give the same energy to all his feelings, nor the same strength to all his portraits, and will place each Part in the place that suits it, less to make it alone shine than to give a greater effect to the whole.

After having seen clearly what he should say, he seeks how he will say it, and here begins the application of the precepts of the Art, which is like the particular language in which the Musician wishes to make himself understood.

Melody, Harmony, Movement, the Choice of Instruments and of Voices are the elements of Musical language, and Melody, by its immediate relationship with the grammatical and oratorical Accent, is the one that gives character to all the others. Thus, it is always the Song from which the principal *Expression* should be drawn, in Instrumental Music as much as in Vocal.

What one therefore seeks to render by the Melody is the Tone, in which the feelings one wants to represent are expressed, and one should be wary of imitating therein theatrical declamation, which is itself only an imitation, but rather seek to imitate the voice of Nature speaking without affectation and without artfulness. Thus, the Musician will first seek a Genre of Melody that furnishes him with the Musical inflections most suitable to the meaning of the words, while always subordinating the *Expression* of the words to that of the thought, and the latter even to the condition of the soul of the Interlocutor: for, when one is strongly affected, the whole discourse being held takes on, so to speak, the complexion of the general feeling that dominates in us, and one does not quarrel with the person one loves in the Tone in which one quarrels with someone indifferent.

Speech is differently accented according to the various passions that inspire it, now sharp and vehement, now calm and careless, now varied and impetuous, now steady and tranquil in its inflections. From thence the Musician derives the differences in the Modes of Singing he uses and the various places where he maintains the Voice, making it proceed in the bass by small Intervals in order to express the languor of sadness and of despondency, drawing from it the sharp Sounds of rage and of pain in the treble and driving it rapidly, by all the Intervals of its Diapason, into the agitation of despair or the disorder of contrasting passions. It is above all necessary to observe that the charm of Music does not consist only in the imitation, but in a pleasant imitation, and that the declamation itself should be subordinated to the melody so as to produce such a great effect; so that the feeling cannot be portrayed without giving it that secret charm which is inseparable from it, nor touch the heart if one does not please the ear. And this is still quite conformable to nature, which gives to the tone of sensitive persons a certain indefinable touching and delightful inflections which people who feel nothing never have. Do not therefore go and take the baroque for what is expressive, nor harshness for energy; nor produce a hideous depiction of the passions you wish to render, nor act, in a word, as in the French Opera, where the passionate tone resembles cries of colic much more than the transports of love.

The physical pleasure which results from the Harmony in its turn increases the moral pleasure of the imitation by joining the pleasant sensations of Chords to the *Expression* of the Melody by means of the same principle about which I have just been speaking. But Harmony does still more: it strengthens the *Expression* itself by giving more exactness and precision to the melodious Intervals; it animates their character, and, exactly marking their place in the order of the modulation, it recalls what precedes, announces what must follow, and thus links the phrases in the Song as ideas are linked in discourse. Harmony, envisioned in this way, furnishes the Composer with great means of *Expression* which elude him when he seeks the *Expression* only in Harmony alone; for then, instead of animating the Accent, he stifles it by his Chords, and all the Intervals, muddled in a continual filling out, offer the ear only a series of fundamental Sounds that have nothing touching or pleasant about them and whose effect stops at the brain.

What will the Harmonist do, therefore, to work towards the *Expression* of the Melody and to give it more effect? He will carefully avoid covering the principal Sound under the combination of Chords; he will subordinate all his Accompaniments to the melodic Part; he will sharpen its energy with the assistance of other Parts; he will strengthen the effect of certain passages by perceptible Chords; he will shield others by supposition or by suspension by counting them as nothing on the Bass; he will make strong *Expression* come from major Dissonances; he will reserve minor ones for gentler feelings. Sometimes he will link together all the Parts by continuous and flowing Sounds; sometimes he will make them contrast in the Song by staccato Notes. Sometimes he will strike the ear with full Chords; sometimes he will strengthen the Accent by the choice of a single Interval. Everywhere he will make the linking of the Modulations present and perceptible and will make the Bass and its Harmony serve to determine the place of each passage in the Mode so that one never hears one Interval or one feature of the Song without sensing at the same time its relation with the whole.

With regard to Rhythm, in days gone by so powerful for giving strength, variety, and pleasure to Poetic Harmony, if our Languages, less accented and less prosodic, have lost the charm that resulted from it, our Music has substituted for it another, more independent of the discourse in the evenness of its Meter, and in the various combinations of its beats, whether at the same time in the whole or separately in each Part. The quantities of the Language are almost lost under those of the Notes, and the Music, instead of speaking with the speech, borrows, after a fashion, a language apart from the Meter. The strength of the *Expression* consists, in this part, in bringing together these two languages as much as is possible and in making it so that, if the Meter and the Rhythm do not speak the same way, they at least say the same things.

The gaiety that gives liveliness to all our movements should likewise give it to the Meter; sadness confines the heart, slows the movements; and the same languor is felt in the Songs it inspires. But when suffering is lively or if great combats take place in the soul, speech is uneven: it proceeds alternately with the slowness of the Spondee and with the speed of the Pyrrhic, and often ceases all of a sudden as in the obligatory Recitative. It is for this reason that the most expressive Music, or at least the most passionate, is commonly the one wherein the Beats, although equal among themselves, are the most unevenly divided, whereas the image of sleep, of rest, and of the peace of the soul are readily portrayed with equal Notes, which do not go in such a lively way or so slowly.

An observation which the Composer should not neglect is that the more studied the Harmony is, the less lively the movement should be, so that the mind has time to seize the progression of the Dissonances and the rapid linking of the Modulations. It is only the utmost fury of the passions that allows the speed of the Meter and the harshness of the Chords to be allied. Then, when he has lost his head and, due to his agitation, the Actor seems no longer to know what he is saying, this energetic and terrible disorder can be conveyed all the way to the soul of the Spectator and likewise put him outside of himself. But if you are not fiery and sublime you will be only baroque and cold; throw your Listeners into delirium, or guard against falling into it yourself, for he who loses his reason is always merely insane in the eyes of those who preserve it, and madmen are no longer interesting.

Although the greatest strength of *Expression* is drawn from the combination of Sounds, the quality of their timbre is not indifferent for the same effect. There are strong and sonorous Voices that make an impression by their mettle; others light and flexible, good for difficult performances; others sensitive and delicate that go to the heart by soft and pathetic Songs. In general, Sopranos and all high voices are more appropriate for expressing tenderness and sweetness, Basses and Baritones for rage and anger. But the Italians have banished Basses from their Tragedies as a Part whose Singing is too coarse for the heroic genre, and have substituted for it the Taille, or Tenor, whose Singing has the same character with a more pleasant effect. They employ these same Basses more suitably in Comedy for harlequins and generally for all supporting characters.

Instruments also have very different *Expressions* according to whether their Sound is strong or weak, whether their timbre is sharp or sweet, whether the Diapason is low or high, and whether Sounds can be drawn from them in greater or smaller numbers. The Flute is tender, the Oboe gay, the Trumpet warlike, the Horn sonorous, majestic, appropriate for grand *Expressions*. But there is no Instrument from which a more varied and more universal *Expression* can be drawn than from the Violin. This admirable Instrument serves as the basis for all Orchestras and suffices for the great Composer to draw out all the effects that bad Musicians uselessly seek in a hotchpotch of a multitude of different Instruments. The Composer should know the handling of the Violin to Finger his Tunes, to arrange his Arpeggios, to know the effect of open Strings, and to employ and choose his Keys according to the various characters they have on this Instrument.

In vain does the Composer know how to animate his Work if the warmth that should reign in it does not pass to those who perform it. The Singer who sees only Notes in his part is not at all in a position to grasp the Composer's *Expression*, nor give one to what he sings if he has not well grasped its meaning. He must understand what he reads in order to make it understood by others, and it is not enough to be sensitive in general if one is not so in particular to the energy of the Language that one is speaking. Begin therefore by clearly understanding the character of the Song you have to render, its relationship to the meaning of the words, the distinction of its phrases, the Accent it has of itself, what it supposes in the voice of the Performer, the energy the Composer has given to the Poet, and that which you can give in your turn to the Composer. Then you will abandon your organs to all the warmth these considerations will have inspired in you; do what you would do if you were at once the Poet, the Composer, the Actor, and the Singer, and you will have all the *Expression* that is possible for you to give to the Work you must render. In this way, it naturally happens that you will put delicacy and ornamentation in Songs that are merely elegant and graceful, piquancy and fire in those that are animated and gay, groaning and moaning in those that are tender and pathetic, and all the agitation of the *Forte-piano* in the rage of the violent passions. Wherever the musical Accent is brought together strongly with the oratorical Accent, wherever the Meter is vividly felt and serves as a guide for the Accents of the Song, wherever the Accompaniment and the Voice know how to accord and unite their effects in such a way that only one Melody results and that the deceived Listener attributes to the Voice the passages with which the Orchestra embellishes it, finally, wherever ornamentation, properly handled, bears witness to the ability of the Singer without covering and disfiguring the Song, the *Expression* will be sweet, pleasant, and strong, the ear will be charmed and the heart moved, the physical and the moral will work simultaneously toward the listeners' pleasure, and there will reign such an Accord between the speech and the Song that the whole will appear to be nothing but a delightful language that knows how to say everything and always pleases.

FUGUE [*Fugue*], *n. fem.* A piece or passage of Music in which one treats, according to certain rules of Harmony and of Modulation, a Song called the *subject* by making it pass successively and alternately from one Part to another.

Here are the principal rules for the *Fugue*, some of which belong to it and others it has in common with Imitation.

I. The subject proceeds from the Tonic to the Dominant, or from the Dominant to the Tonic, by ascending or descending.

II. Every *Fugue* has its response in the part that immediately follows the one that has begun.

III. This response should produce the subject on the Fourth or the Fifth, and by a like movement, as exactly as possible; proceeding from the Dominant to the Tonic when the subject is announced from the Tonic to the Dominant, and *vice versa*. A Part can also reprise the same subject on the Octave or on the Unison of the preceding, but then it is a repetition rather than a genuine response.

IV. As the Octave is divided into two unequal parts, of which the first contains four Degrees in ascending from the Tonic to the Dominant, and the other only three in continuing to ascend from the Dominant to the Tonic, one is obliged to consider this difference in the expression of the subject, and to make some change in the response in order not to leave the essential Pitches of the Mode. It is another thing when changing the key is proposed; then, the very precision of the response, taken on another Pitch, produces the alterations appropriate for this change.

V. The *Fugue* must be designed in such a way so that the response can enter before the end of the first Song, so that one simultaneously hears them both in part, so that by this anticipation the subject is connected, so to speak, to itself, and so that the art of the Composer is shown in this concurrence. It is foolery to present as a *Fugue* a Song that is made only to stroll from one Part to another without any other difficulty than then accompanying it as one likes. This merits at the very most the name *Imitation*. (See IMITATION [*Imitation*].)

Besides these rules, which are fundamental, in order to succeed in this genre of Composition there are others which, though being only stylistic, are no less essential. In general, *Fugues* produce a Music that is more noisy than pleasant; this is why they are more suitable in Choruses than anywhere else. Now, as their principal merit is always to fix the ear on the principal Song or subject, which is then made to pass constantly from Part to Part, and from Modulation to Modulation, the Composer should take every care always to make this Song quite distinct, or to prevent it from being stifled by or confounded among the other parts. There are two means for this. The first is in the movement, which must be constantly contrasted; so that, if the progression of the *Fugue* is precipitous the other Parts proceed deliberately by long Notes; and, on the contrary, if the *Fugue* progresses gravely, let the Accompaniments labor even more. The second means is to separate the Harmony for fear lest the other Parts, approaching too closely to the one that Sings the subject, become confounded with it and prevent it from being heard clearly enough, in such a way that what would be a vice everywhere else becomes a beauty here.

Unity of Melody: this is the great common rule that must often be practiced by different means. The Chords, the Intervals, must be chosen so that a certain Sound, and not another, produces the principal effect: *unity of Melody*. Sometimes it is necessary to bring Instruments or Voices of a different type into play so that the Part that should dominate is more easily distinguished: *unity of Melody*. Another no less necessary matter for attention in the various linkings of Modulations which direct the progression and course of the *Fugue* is to make all these Modulations correspond at the same time in all the Parts, to link the whole in its course by an exact conformity of Key, for fear lest, one Part being in one Key and another in another, the entire Harmony will not be in any, and will no longer present a simple effect to the ear, nor a simple idea to the mind: *unity of Melody*. In a word, in every *Fugue*, the confusion of the Melody or of the Modulation is what is at the same time most to be feared and most difficult to avoid; and since the pleasure this genre of Music produces is always mediocre, it can be said that a beautiful *Fugue* is the thankless masterpiece of a good Harmonist.

There are yet several other styles of *Fugues*, as *perpetual Fugues*, called *Canons*, *double Fugues*, *Counterfugues*, or *inverted Fugues*, that can each be seen at its word, and which serve more to extend the art of Composers than to flatter the ears of Listeners.

Fugue, from the Latin *Fuga, flight*, because the Parts, setting out in the same way successively, seem to flee and pursue one another.

GENIUS [*Génie*], *n. masc.*[40] Seek not, young Artist, what is *Genius*. If you have any, you feel it in yourself. If you do not, you will never know it. The *Genius* of the Musician submits the entire Universe to his Art. He paints every portrait by Sounds; he makes silence itself speak; he renders ideas by feelings, feelings by accents; and the passions he expresses, he arouses them in the bottom of hearts. Through him, sensual delight takes on new charms; the grief he causes to moan wrests cries; he burns constantly and is never consumed. He expresses wintry weather and ice with warmth; even when painting the horrors of death he carries into the soul that feeling of life which does not abandon it, and which he communicates to hearts made to feel it. But, alas! He does not know how to say anything to those in whom its seed is not present, and his wonders are little felt by anyone who cannot imitate them. Do you then want to learn whether this spark of devouring fire animates you? Run, fly to Naples to listen to the masterpieces of *Leo*, of *Durante*, of *Jomelli*, of *Pergolesi*.[41] If your eyes fill with tears, if you feel your heart beating, if you are seized with trembling, if you are suffocated by oppression amidst your transports, take Metastasio[42] and set to work: his *Genius* will warm yours, you will create after his example. This is what *Genius* does, and other eyes will soon render you the tears the Masters have made you shed. But if the charms of this great Art leave you calm, if you are neither delirious nor enraptured, if you feel what enraptures you is merely beautiful, dare you ask what is *Genius*? Vulgar man: do not profane that sublime word. What would it matter to you to know it? You would not know how to feel it: compose French Music.

TASTE [*Gout*], *n. masc.* Of all natural gifts, *Taste* is that which is best felt and least explicable; it would not be what it is if it could be defined: for it judges objects on which judgment no longer has any hold, and serves, if I dare speak this way, as the spectacles of reason.

In Melody, there are some Songs more pleasant than others, although equally well Modulated; in harmony, there are things with effect and things without effect, all of them equally regular; there is in the intermixing of parts an exquisite art that makes some shine by means of the others that depends on something finer than the law of contrasts. There are likewise in the performance of a small piece different manners of rendering it, without ever departing from its character; of these manners, some please more than others, and far from being able to submit them to rules, one can not even determine them. Reader, account for these differences, and I will tell you what *Taste* is.

Each man has a particular *Taste* by which he gives to the things he calls beautiful and good an ordering that belongs only to him. One is most touched by pathetic pieces, another prefers gay Tunes. A soft and flexible Voice loads its Songs with pleasant ornaments, a clear and strong Voice loves its own passionate accents. One will look for simplicity in the Melody; the other will attach great importance to mannered features; and they both will call what they prefer elegant *Taste*. This difference sometimes comes from the different dispositions of the organs, which *Taste* teaches one how to take advantage of; sometimes from the particular character of each man, which disposes him to be more sensitive to one pleasure or one fault rather than another; sometimes from the diversity of age or of sex, which turns the desires toward different objects. In all these cases, each having only his *Taste* to oppose to that of another, it is obvious that it must not be disputed about at all.

But there is also a general *Taste* upon which all well-constituted people are in agreement; and it is to this one alone to which one can give the name of *Taste* absolutely. Have a Concert heard by ears sufficiently trained and men sufficiently instructed: the greater number will ordinarily agree concerning the judgment of the pieces and concerning the ordering of preference that belongs to them. Ask each the reason for his judgment, there are things concerning which they will render an almost universal opinion: these things are those which are found submitted to rules; and this common judgment is then that of the Artist or of the Connoisseur. But of those things which they agree to find good or bad, there are some concerning which they will not be able to justify their judgment by any solid reason common to all; and this last judgment belongs to the man of *Taste*. If perfect unanimity is not found in this, it is because all are not equally well constituted, because all are not people of *Taste*, and because the prejudices of habit or of education often change the order of natural beauties by arbitrary conventions. As for that *Taste*, it can be disputed, since there is not one of them that is true; but I scarcely see any other means of ending the discussion than that of counting voices, when one does not even agree with that of Nature. This, then, is what should decide the preference between French and Italian Music.

Furthermore, Genius creates, but *Taste* chooses; and oftentimes a too abundant Genius needs a severe Censor who prevents it from abusing its riches. Without *Taste* one can make great things; but it is it that makes them interesting. It is *Taste* that makes the Composer grasp the ideas of the Poet; it is *Taste* that furnishes them both with everything that can ornament and makes their subject shine; and it is *Taste* that gives to the Listener the feeling for all its affinities. Nevertheless, Taste is not at all sensitivity. One can have a great deal of *Taste* with a cold soul, and such a man transported by truly passionate things is little touched by graceful ones. It sees that *Taste* fastens more willingly upon small expressions, and sensitivity on grand ones.

HARMONY [*Harmonie*], *n. fem.* The meaning the Greeks gave to this word in their Music is all the less easy to determine as, originally being a proper noun, it does not have any roots by which one may break it up in order to derive its etymology. In the ancient treatises that remain to us, *Harmony* seems to be the Part that has for its object the suitable succession of Sounds insofar as they are high or low, as opposed to the two other Parts called *Rhythmica* and *Metrica*, which relate to the Time and to the Meter, which leaves a vague and indeterminate idea for this suitability which can be fixed only by an express study of all the rules of the Art. And still, after this, *Harmony* will be very difficult to distinguish from Melody, at least unless one adds to this latter one the ideas of Rhythm and Meter, without which, in fact, no Melody can have a determinate character, whereas *Harmony* has its own by itself, independently of every other quantity. (See MELODY* [*Mélodie*].)

It is seen, by a passage from Nicomachus,[43] and by others, that they also sometimes gave the name *Harmony* to the Consonance of the Octave and to the Concerts of Voices and Instruments that were performed at the Octave, and which were more commonly called *Antiphons*.

HARMONY, according to the Moderns, is a succession of Chords according to the laws of Modulation. For a long time this *Harmony* had no other principles than rules that were almost arbitrary or founded uniquely on the approbation of a trained ear which judged the good or bad succession of Consonances and whose decisions were afterward calculated. But since Father Mersenne and M. Sauveur found that every Sound, although simple in appearance, was always accompanied by other, less appreciable Sounds which along with it formed the Perfect Major Chord, M. Rameau began from this experiment and made it the basis of his Harmonic system, with which he has filled many books, and which M. d'Alembert has finally taken the trouble to explain to the Public.[44]

M. Tartini, beginning from another experiment—newer, more delicate, and no less certain, has reached rather similar conclusions by a completely contrary path.[45] M. Rameau has the Upper partials generated by the Bass, M. Tartini the Bass by the Upper partials; the latter derives *Harmony* from Melody, and the former does entirely the opposite. In order to decide from which of these two Schools the best works must come, it is necessary only to know which should be made for the other: the Song or the Accompaniment. A short explanation of M. Tartini's will be found at the word SYSTEM [*Système*]. I continue to speak here of M. Rameau's, which I have followed in this whole work, as being the sole one accepted in the country in which I am writing.

I should nevertheless declare that this System, ingenious as it may be, is anything but founded on Nature, as he repeats incessantly; that it is established merely on analogies and conformities that an inventive man could overturn tomorrow by others more natural; that, finally, of the experiments from which he deduces it, one is acknowledged as false and the other does not at all supply the conclusions he draws from it. In fact, when this Author wanted to decorate the reasonings on which he established his theory with the title of a *Demonstration*, everyone ridiculed him; the Academy loudly disapproved of this obstreperous qualification; and M. Estève, of the Royal Society of Montpellier, made him see that, to begin with this proposition, that in the law of Nature the Octaves of the Sounds represent them and can be taken for them, there was nothing at all about it that was demonstrated nor even solidly established in his pretended Demonstration.[46] I return to his System.

The physical principle of the resonance offers us isolated and solitary Chords; it does not establish their succession. A regular succession is nevertheless necessary. A Dictionary of selected words is not a harangue, nor a collection of good Chords a Piece of Music: a sense is needed, connection is needed in Music as well as in language; something of what precedes must be transmitted to what follows so that the whole may make up an ensemble and be capable of genuinely being called a unity.

Now, the complex sensation which results from a Perfect Chord is resolved into the absolute sensation of each of the Sounds that make it up, and in the comparative sensation of each of the Intervals these same Sounds form among themselves. There is nothing perceptible in this Chord beyond this, from which it follows that it is only by the relation of Sounds and by the analogy of Intervals that the connection in question can be established; that is the true and unique principle from which all the laws of *Harmony* and of Modulation flow. If, therefore, the entire *Harmony* was formed solely by a succession of Perfect Major Chords, it would suffice to proceed in it by Intervals similar to those that make up such a Chord, for since some Sound of the preceding Chord is then necessarily prolonged in the following one, all the Chords would be sufficiently connected and the *Harmony* would be a unity, at least in this sense.

But, aside from the fact that such successions would exclude all Melody by excluding the Diatonic Genre, which forms its basis, they would not be directed toward the true goal of the Art, since Music, being a discourse, should like it have its periods, its phrases, its suspensions, its pauses, its punctuation of every type, and since the uniformity of Harmonic progressions would offer nothing of all this. Diatonic progressions required that major and minor Chords be intermixed, and the need for Dissonances to mark the phrases and pauses was felt. Now, the linked succession of Perfect Major Chords produces neither the Perfect Minor Chord nor the Dissonance, nor any type of phrasing, and punctuation is found to be totally lacking in it.

M. Rameau, wanting positively to derive all our *Harmony* from Nature in his System, has had recourse, for this result, to another experiment of his invention of which I have spoken above and which is the inversion of the first. He claimed that any Sound whatsoever furnished in its multiples a Perfect Minor Chord in the bass, of which it was the Dominant or the Fifth, just as it furnished a major in its aliquots, of which it was the Tonic or the Fundamental. He has put forward as an assured fact that one sounding String causes two other, lower Strings to vibrate in their totality without, nevertheless, causing them to resonate, one on its major Twelfth and the other on its Seventeenth; and from this fact, joined to the preceding, he has quite ingeniously deduced not only the introduction of the minor Mode and of the dissonance into *Harmony*, but the rules of harmonic phrasing and of all Modulation, such as they are found at the words CHORD [*Accord*], ACCOMPANIMENT [*Accompagnement*], FUNDAMENTAL BASS [*Bass-Fondamentale*], CADENCE [*Cadence*], DISSONANCE* [*Dissonnance*], MODULATION* [*Modulation*].

But first of all, the experiment is false. It is acknowledged that the Strings tuned below the fundamental Sound do not at all vibrate in their entirety to this fundamental Sound, but that they are divided in order to render only its unison, which, consequently, has no Harmonics below. It is furthermore acknowledged that the property that the Strings have of being divided is not at all peculiar to those which are tuned to the Twelfth and the Seventeenth below the fundamental Sound, but that it is common to all its multiples. From which it follows that since the Intervals of the Twelfth and the Seventeenth below are not unique in their way, nothing can be concluded in favor of the Perfect Minor Chord they represent.

Even were the truth of this experiment assumed, this would not come close to overcoming the difficulties. If, as M. Rameau claims, all *Harmony* is derived from the resonance of the sounding body, then it does not at all derive from it the vibrations of the sounding body, which does not resonate alone. In actuality, it is a strange theory to derive the principles of *Harmony* from something that does not resonate; and it is strange physics to make the sounding body vibrate and not resonate, as if Sound itself were anything other than air agitated by these vibrations. Besides, the sounding body does not only produce, aside from the principal Sound, the Sounds that along with it make up the Perfect Chord, but an infinity of other Sounds, formed by all the aliquots of the sounding body, which do not at all enter into that Perfect Chord. Why are the first consonant, and why are the others not, since they are all equally given by Nature?

Every Sound produces a truly Perfect Chord since it is formed from all its Harmonics and since it is by them that it is a Sound. Nevertheless, these Harmonics are not heard, and only a simple Sound is distinguished, unless it is extremely loud; from which it follows that the only good *Harmony* is Unison, and that as soon as Consonances are distinguished, the *Harmony* has lost its purity since the natural proportions are altered.

This alteration is then made in two ways. First, by having certain Harmonics sounded, and not others, one changes the relation of force that should reign between them all in order to produce the sensation of a unique Sound, and the unity of Nature is destroyed. By doubling these Harmonics, one produces an effect similar to that which would be produced by stifling all the others; for then it must not be doubted that one might hear, along with its generator Sound, those of the Harmonics that would have been left, whereas by leaving them all, they destroy one another and concur together to produce and to strengthen the unique sensation of the principal Sound. This is the same effect which the full playing of the Organ produces when, successively removing the Registers, one leaves the *Doublette* and the *Quinte* with the Principal, for then that Fifth and that Third, which remain confused, are separately and disagreeably distinguished.

Furthermore, the Harmonics that are made to be sounded themselves have other Harmonics which do not come from the fundamental Sound. It is through these added Harmonics that the one which produces them is still more harshly distinguished; and these same Harmonics which make the Chord thus felt do not at all enter into its *Harmony*. This is why the most perfect Consonances naturally displease ears little disposed to hear them; and I do not doubt that the Octave itself would be displeasing, like the others, if the mixture of the voices of men and of women did not habituate one to it from infancy.

It is still worse with the Dissonance, since not only the Harmonics of the Sound that produce it but this Sound itself does not at all enter into the harmonious system of the fundamental Sound, which makes it so that the Dissonance is always distinguished in a shocking way amongst all the other Sounds.

Every Organ key, in *plein jeu*, produces a Perfect Major Third Chord which is not distinguished from the fundamental Sound, unless extreme attention is paid and unless one draws out the playing successively; but these Harmonic Sounds are confounded with the principal one only due to the great noise and to an arrangement of registers by which the pipes that cause the fundamental Sound to resonate cover those that produce its Harmonics by their power. Now, this continual proportion is not observed and cannot be observed in a Concert since, given the inversion of the *Harmony*, it would be necessary for this greater power to pass at every instant from one Part to the another, which is not practicable and would disfigure the whole Melody.

When the organ is played, every key in the Bass causes a Perfect Major Chord to be sounded; but because this Bass is not always fundamental, and because one often modulates by a Perfect Minor Chord, this Perfect Major Chord is rarely the one which the right hand strikes; so that the Minor Third is heard with the major one, the Fifth with the Tritone, the Augmented Seventh with the Octave, and a thousand other cacophonies by which our ears are little shocked, since habit renders them accommodating; but it is not at all to be presumed that this would be so for a naturally just ear, and which, for the first time, would put this *Harmony* to the test.

M. Rameau claims that the Upper partials by some simple means naturally suggest their Bass, and that a man having a just and untrained ear will naturally intone that Bass. This is a prejudice of a Musician refuted by all experience. Not only will someone who has never heard either Bass or *Harmony* not discover either this *Harmony* or this Bass by himself, but they will displease him if he is made to hear them, and he will much prefer simple Unison.

When one considers that of all the peoples of the earth, who all have a

Music and a Singing, the Europeans are the only ones who have a *Harmony*, Chords, and who find this mixture pleasant; when one considers that the world lasted so many centuries without any of all the nations that have cultivated the Fine Arts having known about this *Harmony*; that no animal, no bird, no being in Nature produces any Chord other than Unison, nor any Music other than Melody; that the Oriental languages, so sonorous, so Musical, that Greek ears, so delicate, so sensitive, trained with such Art, never guided these voluptuous and passionate people toward our *Harmony*; that without it their Music had such prodigious effects; that with it ours has such weak ones; that, finally, it was reserved to the Peoples of the North—whose harsh and coarse organs are more touched by the shouting and noise of Voices than by the sweetness of accents and the Melody of inflections—to make this great discovery and to give it as the basis for all the rules of the Art; when, I say, one pays attention to all this, it is quite difficult not to suspect that all our *Harmony* is but a Gothic and barbarous invention which we never would have conceived of if we had been more sensitive to the genuine beauties of the Art and to truly natural Music.[47]

M. Rameau nonetheless claims that *Harmony* is the source of Music's greatest beauties; but this sentiment is contradicted by facts and by reason. By the facts: because all of Music's great effects have ceased and since it has lost its energy and its strength ever since the invention of Counterpoint—to which I add that purely harmonic beauties are learned beauties which transport only people versed in the Art, whereas Music's true beauties, being from Nature, are and should be equally perceptible to all men, learned and ignorant.

By reason, since *Harmony* does not furnish any principle of imitation by which Music, forming images or expressing feelings, may be elevated to the Dramatic or imitative genre, which is the most noble part of the Art, and the only energetic one, all that regards merely the physics of Sounds being quite limited in the pleasure they give us and having but very little power over the human heart. (See MELODY* [*Mélodie*].)

IMITATION [*Imitation*], *n. fem*. Dramatic or theatrical Music work together toward *Imitation* just like Poetry and Painting: it is this common principle to which all the Fine Arts are related, as M. le Batteux has shown.[48] But this *Imitation* does not have the same scope for all of them. Everything the imagination can represent falls within the competence of Poetry. Painting, which does not offer its portraits to the imagination, but to the sense and to a single sense, depicts only objects subject to sight. Music would seem to have the same limits with respect to hearing; nevertheless, it portrays everything, even objects which are only visible: by an almost inconceivable magic trick it seems to put the eye in the ear, and the greatest marvel of an Art that acts only by motion is to be able to form even the image of rest. Night, sleep, solitude, and silence are counted among Music's great portraits. It is known that noise can produce the effect of silence and silence the effect of noise, as when one falls asleep at an unvarying and monotonous reading and wakes up the instant it ceases. But Music acts more intimately on us by arousing by one sense affections similar to those that can be aroused by another, and, as the relationship can be perceptible only when the impression is strong, Painting, lacking this power, can give to Music only the *Imitations* that the latter draws from it. Let all of nature be asleep, he who contemplates it sleeps not, and the Musician's Art consists in substituting for the imperceptible image of the object that of the movements its presence arouses in the heart of the Contemplator. Not only will it agitate the sea, animate the flame of a blaze, make rivers flow, rain fall, and torrents swell, but it will paint the horror of a frightful desert, darken the walls of a subterranean prison, calm the tempest, make the air tranquil and serene, and spread from the orchestra a new freshness over the groves. It will not represent these things directly, but will arouse the same movements in the soul that are experienced in seeing them.[49]

I have said at the word HARMONY* [*Harmonie*] that no principle is derived from it that leads to musical *Imitation* since there is no relationship between Chords and the objects one would like to portray or the passions one would like to express. I will show at the word MELODY* [*Mélodie*] what this principle is that Harmony does not furnish and what features given by Nature are used by Music in order to represent these objects and these passions.

INTERVAL [*Intervalle*], *n. masc.* The Difference from one Sound to another from low to high; it is the entire space that one of the two [sounds] would have to cover before arriving at the Unison of the other. The difference between *Interval* and *Range* is that the *Interval* is considered as undivided and the Range as divided. In the *Interval*, only the two limits are considered; in the Range, intermediary ones are assumed between them. The Range forms a system, but an *Interval* can be detached.

Taking this word in its most general sense, it is obvious that there are an infinity of *Intervals*; but as the number of Sounds is limited in Music to those that make up a certain system, the number of *Intervals* is thereby also limited to those which these Sounds can form among themselves. So that by combining all the Sounds of any system whatsoever two by two, one will have all the possible *Intervals* in this same system; concerning which it will remain to reduce all those which are found to be equal to the same type.

The Ancients divided the *Intervals* of their Music into simple or uncompounded *Intervals*, which they called *Diastemas*, and into compounded *Intervals*, which they called *Systemas* (See these words.) *Intervals*, says Aristoxenus,[50] differ from one another in five ways. 1st. In extent; a large *Interval* differs in this way from a smaller one. 2nd. In resonance or in Accord; it is in this way that a consonant *Interval* differs from a dissonant one. 3rd. In quantity; as a simple *Interval* differs from a compounded *Interval*. 4th. In Genre; it is thus that Diatonic, Chromatic, and Enharmonic *Intervals* differ from one another. 5th. In the nature of the ratio; as the *Interval* whose ratio can be expressed in numbers differs from an irrational *Interval*. Let us say some words about these differences.

I. The smallest of all the *Intervals*, according to Baccheius and Gaudentius,[51] is the Enharmonic Diesis. The largest, taking it at the extreme low end of the Hypodorian Mode to the extreme high end of the Hypomixolydian, would be three complete Octaves; but as there is a Fifth to omit, or even a Sixth, according to a passage from Adrastus cited by Meibomius,[52] beyond the Dis-Diapason, that is, an Eighteenth, the Fourth remains as the largest *Interval* of the Diagram of the Greeks.

II. The Greeks divided *Intervals* into Consonant and Dissonant, as we do; but their divisions were not the same as ours. (See CONSONANCE* [*Consonnance*].) They further subdivided consonant *Intervals* into two types, without including in them the Unison, which they called *Homophonia*, or a parity of Sounds, and whose *Interval* is null. The first type was *Antiphonia*, or an opposition of Sounds, which is done at the Octave or at the double Octave, and which was strictly speaking only a Replica of the same Sound; but nevertheless with an opposition of low to high. The second type was the *Paraphonia*, or a distinction of Sounds, under which they comprehended every Consonance other than the Octave and its Replicas; all *Intervals*, says Theon of Smyrna,[53] which are neither Dissonants nor Unison.

III. When the Greeks speak of their Diastemas or simple *Intervals*, this term must not be taken in all strictness; for the Diesis itself is not, according to them, exempt from complexity; but it must always be related to the Genre to which the *Interval* applies. For example, the Semitone is a simple *Interval* in the Chromatic Genre and in the Diatonic, compounded in the Enharmonic. The *Tone* is compounded in the Chromatic, and simple in the Diatonic; and the Ditonon itself, or the Major Third, which is a compounded *Interval* in the Diatonic, is uncompounded in the Enharmonic.

Thus, what is a systema in one Genre can be a Diastema in another, and reciprocally.

IV. Concerning the Genres, successively divide the same Tetrachord according to the Diatonic Genre, according to the Chromatic Genre, and according to the Enharmonic, and you will have three different accords, which, when compared to one another, instead of three *Intervals*, will give you nine of them, aside from the combinations and compositions which can be made of them, and the differences of all those *Intervals*, which will produce many others. If you compare, for example, the first *Interval* of each Tetrachord in the Enharmonic and in Aristoxenus' soft Chromatic, you will have on the one side a fourth, or 3/12 of a Tone, on the other a third, or 4/12, and the two high Strings will between them produce an *Interval* that will be the difference of two preceding ones, or the twelfth part of a Tone.

V. Passing now to the ratios, this Point leads me to a small digression.

The Aristoxenians claimed to have quite simplified Music by their equal divisions of the *Intervals*, and made a great deal of fun of Pythagoras' calculations. It nevertheless seems to me that this pretended simplicity hardly existed except in the words, and that if the Pythagoreans had understood their Master and Music a little better, they would have soon shut their adversaries' mouths.

Pythagoras had not thought up the ratio of the Sounds he first calculated. Guided by experience, he only took note of his observations. Aristoxenus, inconvenienced by all these calculations, built an entirely different system in his head; and as if he might change Nature at his pleasure for having simplified the words, he believed he had simplified the things, whereas he had actually done the contrary.

As the ratios of Consonances were simple and easy to express, these two Philosophers were in agreement about these; it was likewise for the first Dissonances, for they likewise both agreed that the *Tone* was the difference between the Fourth and the Fifth; but yet how to determine this difference otherwise than by calculation? Aristoxenus nevertheless departed from that because he did not want to calculate, and he built his whole musical doctrine upon this *Tone*, whose ratio he prided himself on not knowing. What was easier to do than to show him the falsity of his procedures and the precision of those of Pythagoras? But, he would have said, I always take the doubles, or the halves, or the thirds; that is simpler and sooner done than your Commas, your Limmas, your Apotomes. I admit it, Pythagoras might have answered; but, tell me, please, how you take them, those doubles, those halves, those thirds? The other might have replied that he sounded them naturally, or that he took them on his

Monocord.⁵⁴ Well! Pythagoras might have said, sound for me exactly one quarter of a Tone. If the other were enough of a charlatan to do so, Pythagoras would have added: but is your Monocord correctly divided? Show me, please, what method have you used to take a quarter or a third of a Tone? I cannot see, in such a case, what Aristoxenus could have answered. For, to say that the Instrument had been tuned to the Voice, aside from falling into a circular reasoning, could not suit the Aristoxenians, since they wholly agree with their Leader that the Voice must be long trained on an Instrument of the utmost precision in order to attain to the point of intoning correctly the *Intervals* of the soft Chromatic and of the Enharmonic Genre.

Now, since one needs not only complex calculations and even more difficult geometrical operations in order to measure Aristoxenus' thirds and fourths of a Tone than to assign Pythagoras' ratios, it is with reason that Nicomachus, Boethius, and several other Theorists preferred the exact and harmonic ratios of their Master to the divisions of the Aristoxenian system, which were not simpler, and which did not give any *Interval* in the exactitude of its generation.

It must be noted that those reasonings that suited the Music of the Greeks would not equally suit our own, because all the Sounds of our system are put into accord by Consonances, which could not be done in theirs except for the Diatonic Genre alone.

It follows from all this that Aristoxenus reasonably distinguished *Intervals* into rational and irrational; since, although they may all be rational in Pythagoras' system, the majority of Dissonances were irrational in his own.

In modern Music *Intervals* are also considered in several manners; namely, either generally as some space or distance between two given Sounds, or as only those distances that can be notated, or, finally, as those which are marked at different Degrees. According to the first sense, every numerical ratio, as is the Comma, or muted one, as is Aristoxenus' Diesis, can express an *Interval*. The second sense applies only to the *Intervals* received in the system of our Music, the least of which is the minor Semitone expressed in the same Degree by a Sharp or by a Flat. (See SEMITONE [*Semi-ton*].) The third acceptation assumes some difference in position: that is, one or more Degrees between the two Sounds that form the *Interval*. It is in this last acceptation that the word is established in practice: so that two equal *Intervals*, such as the False Fifth and the Tritone are, nevertheless carry two different names, if the one has more Degrees than the other.

We divide, as the Ancients did, *Intervals* into Consonant and Dissonant. Consonances are perfect or imperfect (See Consonance* [*Consonnance*].) Dissonances are such by their nature, or become so by accidentals. There are only two dissonant *Intervals* by their nature, namely, the second and the seventh, including therein their Octaves or Replicas; these two can be further reduced to a single one; but all Consonances can become dissonant by accidentals. (See Dissonance* [*Dissonnance*].)

Furthermore, every *Interval* is simple or doubled. The simple *Interval* is that which is contained within the limits of the Octave. Every *Interval* that exceeds this range is doubled, that is, compounded of one of more Octaves and of the simple *Interval* of which it is the Replica.

Simple *Intervals* are further divided into direct and inverted. Take for a direct one any simple *Interval* whatsoever: its complement at the Octave is always inverted from this one, and reciprocally so.

There are only six types of simple *Intervals*, of which three are complements of the three others at the Octave, and consequently also their inversions. If you first take the smallest *Intervals*, you will have, for the direct ones, the Second, the Third, and the Fourth; for inverted ones, the Seventh, the Sixth, and the Fifth. Let the latter be direct, the others will be inverted: everything is reciprocal.

In order to find the name of any *Interval* whatsoever, one need only add one unit to the number of the Degrees it contains. Thus, the *Interval* of one Degree will give the Second; of two, the Third; of three, the Fourth; of seven, the Octave; of nine, the Tenth; etc. But this is not enough to determine an *Interval* completely: for under the same name it can be major or minor, just or false, diminished or augmented.

Imperfect Consonances and the two natural Dissonances can be major or minor, which, without changing the Degree, produces the difference of a Semitone in the *Interval*. If one reduces a minor *Interval* by a further Semitone, this *Interval* becomes diminished. If one augments a major *Interval* by a Semitone, it becomes augmented.

Perfect Consonances are invariable by their nature. When their *Interval* is what it should be, they are called *Just*. If one alters this *Interval* by a Semitone, the Consonance is called *False* and becomes a Dissonance; *augmented* if augmented by a Semitone; *diminished* if it is reduced. The name of False Fifth is given inappropriately to the Diminished Fifth; this is to take the Genre for the species: the Augmented Fifth is as wholly false as the diminished, and it is even more so in every regard.

A Table will be found (Plate C, Figure 2) of all the simple *Intervals* practicable in Music, with their names, their Degrees, their values, and their ratios.

Concerning this Table it must be noted that the *Interval* called the *Aug-*

TABLE
OF ALL THE SIMPLE INTERVALS PRACTICABLE IN MUSIC

INTERVAL expressed in Notes	NAME of the interval	DEGREES it contains	VALUE in Tones and Semitones	RATIO in Numbers
Do♯—re♭	Diminished Second	1	0	375–384
Si —do	Minor Second	1	1 Semitone	15– 16
Do —re	Major Second	1	1 Tone	8– 9
Do —re♯	Augmented Second	1	1½ Tone	64– 75
Si —re♭	Diminished Third	2	1 Tone	125–144
Mi —sol	Minor Third	2	1½ Tone	5– 6
Do —mi	Major Third	2	2 Tones	4– 5
Fa —la♯	Augmented Third	2	2½ Tones	96–125
Do♯—fa	Diminished Fourth	3	2 Tones	75– 96
Do —fa	Just Fourth	3	2½ Tones	3– 4
Do —fa♯	Augmented Fourth, called a Tritone	3	3 Tones	32– 45
Fa♯—do	Diminished Fifth, called a False Fifth	4	3 Tones	45– 64
Do —sol	Just Fifth	4	3½ Tones	2– 3
Do —sol♯	Augmented Fifth	4	4 Tones	16– 25
La♯—fa	Diminished Sixth	5	3½ Tones	125–192
Mi —do	Minor Sixth	5	4 Tones	5– 8
Sol —mi	Major Sixth	5	4½ Tones	3– 5
Re♭—si	Augmented Sixth	5	5 Tones	72–125
Re♯—do	Diminished Seventh	6	4½ Tones	75–128
Mi —re	Minor Seventh	6	5 Tones	5– 9
Do —si	Major Seventh	6	5½ Tones	8– 15
Sol♭—fa♯	Augmented Seventh	6	6 Tones	81–160
Do —do	Octave	7	6 Tones	1– 2

Plate C, Figure 2

mented Seventh by Harmonists is merely a Major Seventh with a particular Accompaniment—the genuine Augmented Seventh, such as it is marked in the Table, not having any place in Harmony, or having a place in it only successively, as an Enharmonic transition, never strictly speaking in the same Chord.

It will also be observed that the majority of these ratios can be determined in several ways; I have preferred the simplest, and that which gives the smallest numbers.

In order to compound or double one of these simple *Intervals*, it suffices to add the Octave to it as many times as one likes, and to have the name of this new *Interval*, one must add seven to the name of the simple *Interval* as many times as it contains Octaves. Reciprocally, to know the simple of a doubled *Interval* whose name one has, one must subtract seven from it as many times as one can; the remainder will give the name of the simple *Interval* that produced it. Do you want a doubled Fifth, that is, the Octave of the Fifth, or the Fifth of the Octave? To 5 add 7, you will have 12. The doubled Fifth is thus a Twelfth. In order to find the simple of a Twelfth, subtract 7 from the number 12 as many times as you can, the remainder 5 gives you a Fifth. With regard to the ratio, one need only double the second term, or take the half of the first term of the simple ratio as many times as Octaves are added, and one will have the ratio of the doubled *Interval*. Thus, 2, 3, being the ratio of the Fifth, 1, 3, or 2, 6, will be that of the Twelfth, etc. Concerning which it will be observed that in Musical terms, to compound or double an *Interval*, is not to add it to itself, it is to add to it an Octave; to triple it is to add two, etc.

I should warn here that all the *Intervals* expressed in this Dictionary by the names of Notes should always be counted from low to high, so that this *Interval*, *do si*, is not a Second, but a Seventh; and *si do*, is not a Seventh, but a Second.

LICENCE [*License*], *n. fem.* A liberty which the Composer takes and which seems contrary to the rules, even though it might lie in the principle of the rules; for this is what distinguishes *Licenses* from mistakes. For example, it is a rule in composition not to ascend from the Minor Third or from the Minor Sixth to the Octave. This rule derives from the law of harmonic connection and from that of Preparation. When, therefore, one ascends from the Minor Third or from the Minor Sixth to the Octave in such a way that there is nonetheless a connection between the two Chords, or so that the Dissonance is prepared by it, one takes a *License*; but if there is neither connection nor preparation, one makes a mistake. Likewise, it is a rule not to compose two just Fifths in succession between the same Parts, especially by a similar movement; the principle of this rule is in the law of the unity of the Mode. Every time, then, that one can compose these two Fifths without making two Modes felt at the same time, there is a *License*, but there is no mistake. This explanation was necessary because Musicians have no very clear idea of this word *License*.

As the majority of the rules of Harmony are founded on arbitrary principles and change by custom and the taste of Composers, it thereby happens that these rules vary, are subject to Fashion, and that what is a *License* at one Time is not such in another. Two or three centuries ago it was not permitted to produce two Thirds in succession, especially of the same type. Now entire pieces are written that are made up entirely of Thirds. Our ancients did not permit three consecutive Tones to be sounded diatonically. Today we sound them without scruple and without difficulty as much as the Modulation permits. It is the same with false Relations, with syncopated Harmony, and with a thousand other accidents of composition which at first were mistakes, then *Licenses*, and today have nothing irregular about them.

MELODY [*Mélodie*], *n. fem.* A succession of Sounds so ordered according to the laws of Rhythm and of Modulation that they constitute a pleasant meaning[55] for the ear. Vocal *Melody* is called Song, and Instrumental, Symphony.

The idea of Rhythm necessarily enters into that of *Melody*; a Song is a Song only inasmuch as it is measured; the same succession of Sounds can receive as many characters, as many different *Melodies* as it can be differently scanned, and the sole change of the value of the Notes can alone disfigure this same succession to the point of rendering it unrecognizable. Thus, *Melody* is nothing by itself; it is the measure which determines it, and there is no Song without a Beat. *Melody* should therefore not be compared with Harmony, an abstraction made from the Measure in them both, for it is essential to the one and not to the other.

Melody is related to two different principles, according to the manner in which it is considered. Taken by the relationships of Sounds and by the rules of the Mode, it has its principle in Harmony, since it is a harmonic analysis that produces the Degrees of the Scale, the Pitches of the Mode, and the laws of the Modulation—the unique elements of Song. According to this principle, the whole force of the *Melody* is limited to flattering the ear by pleasant Sounds, as one can flatter sight by the pleasant accords of colors; but taken as an art of imitation by which one can affect the mind by various images, move the heart by various feelings, arouse and calm the passions, work, in a word, moral effects which pass beyond the immediate empire of the senses, another principle must be sought for it: for no hold is seen by which Harmony alone, and all that comes from it can affect us in this way.

What is this second principle? It is in Nature as well as the first; but in order to discover it a more subtle, although simpler, observation and more sensitivity in the observer are needed. This principle is the same one that makes the Tone of the Voice vary when one speaks according to the things one says and the movements one experiences while saying them. It is the accent of Languages that determines the *Melody* of each Nation; it is the accent that makes one speak while singing, and speak with more or less energy according to whether the Language has more or less Accent. The one in which the Accent is more marked should produce a more lively and more passionate *Melody*; the one in which there is but little Accent or none at all can have merely a languishing and cold *Melody*, without character and without expression. These are the true principles: as long as a person departs from them and wants to speak of the power of Music over the human heart he will speak without understanding, he will not know what he is saying.

If Music depicts only by means of *Melody* and draws all its force from it, it follows that all Music that does not sing, however harmonious it may be, is not at all an imitative Music, and, not being able either to touch or to depict with its beautiful Chords, it soon wearies the ears and always leaves the heart cold. It further follows that, in spite of the diversity of the Parts which Harmony has introduced, and which are so abused today, as soon as two *Melodies* are made to be heard at the same time, they obliterate one another and remain without any effect, however beautiful they may each be separately—from which it can be judged with what taste French Composers have introduced into their Opera the custom of making an Aria serve as an Accompaniment to a Chorus or to another Aria, which is as if one took it into one's head to recite two speeches at the same time in order to give more force to their eloquence. (See UNITY OF MELODY* [*Unité de mélodie*].)

MODE [*Mode*], *n. masc.* The regular disposition of the Song and of the Accompaniment relative to certain principal Sounds based on which a Piece of Music is constituted and which are called the essential Pitches of the *Mode*.

The *Mode* differs from the Key in that the latter indicates only the Pitch, or the place in the system which should serve as a the basis for the Song, and the *Mode* determines the Third and modifies the entire Scale on this fundamental Sound.

Our *Modes* are not founded on any characteristic feeling like those of the Ancients, but uniquely on our harmonic system. The Pitches essential to the *Mode* are three in number, and together form a perfect Chord. 1st. The Tonic, which is the fundamental Pitch of the Key and of the *Mode*. (See KEY [*Ton*] and TONIC [*Tonique*].) 2nd. The Dominant on the Fifth of the Tonic. (See DOMINANT [*Dominante*].) 3rd. Finally, the Mediant, which specifically constitutes the *Mode* and which is on the Third of this same Tonic. (See MEDIANT [*Médiante*].) As this Third can be of two types, there are therefore two different *Modes*. When the mediant makes a Major Third with the Tonic, the *Mode* is major; it is minor when the Third is minor.

The Major *Mode* is immediately engendered by the resonance of the sounding body, which produces the Major Third of the fundamental Sound; but the Minor *Mode* is not at all given by Nature: it is found only by analogy and inversion. This is true in M. Tartini's system as well as in M. Rameau's.

This latter Author has explained this origin of the Minor *Mode* in different ways in his various works, one after another, none of which has contented his Interpreter, M. d'Alembert. This is why M. d'Alembert founds this same origin on another principle, which I cannot better explain than by transcribing it in this great Geometer's own terms.

"In the Song *do mi sol*, which constitutes the Major *Mode*, the Sounds *mi* and *sol* are such that the principal sound *do* causes these two to resonate, but the second Sound *mi* does not at all cause *sol*, which is only its Minor Third, to resonate.

"Now, let us imagine that instead of this Sound *mi* another Sound were placed between the Sounds *do* and *sol* that had, just like the Sound *do*, the property of causing *sol* to resonate, and which was nevertheless different from *do*; this Sound that is sought should be such that it has for its Major Seventeenth the Sound *sol* or one of the octaves of *sol*; consequently, the Sound sought should be on the Major Seventeenth below *sol*, or, what amounts to the same thing, on the Major Third below this same Sound *sol*. Now, the Sound *mi* being on the Minor Third below *sol*, and the Major Third being a Semitone larger than the Minor Third, it follows that the Sound that is sought will be a Semitone lower than the *mi*, and will consequently be *mi*-Flat.

"This new arrangement *do*, *mi*-Flat, *sol*, in which the Sounds *do* and *mi*-Flat both cause *sol* to resonate without *do* causing *mi*-Flat to resonate, is not, in truth, as perfect as the first arrangement *do*, *mi*, *sol*, because in the latter the two Sounds *mi* and *sol* are both engendered by the principal Sound *do*, whereas in the former the Sound *mi*-flat is not engendered by the Sound *do*; but this arrangement *do*, *mi* flat, *sol*, is also dictated by Nature, although less immediately than the first; and in fact experience proves that the ear accommodates itself to it nearly as well.

"In the Song *do*, *mi*-flat, *sol*, *do*, it is obvious that the Third of *do* on *mi*-Flat is minor, and such is the origin of the genre or *Mode* called *Minor*." *Elements of Music*, p. 22.[56]

The *Mode* once determined, all the Sounds of the Scale take a name relative to the fundamental and belonging to the place they occupy in that *Mode*. These are the names of all the Notes relative to their *Mode*, taking the Octave *do* as an example for the Major *Mode* and that of *la* as an example of the Minor *Mode*.

Major	Do	Re	Mi	Fa	Sol	La	Si	Do
Minor	La	Si	Do	Re	Mi	Fa	Sol	La
	Tonic	Second Note	Mediant	Fourth Note or Subdominant	Dominant	Sixth Note or Superdominant	Seventh Note	Octave

It must be noted that when the seventh Note is only a Semitone from the Octave, that is when it constitutes the Major Third of the Dominant, as *si*-natural in major or *sol*-Sharp in minor, then this seventh Note is called the Leading Tone, because it announces the Tonic and causes the Key to be perceived.[57]

Not only does each Degree take the name that suits it, but each interval is determined relative to the *Mode*. These are the established rules for this.

1st. The second Note should form a Major Second on the Tonic; the fourth one and the Dominant a just Fourth and Fifth, and that likewise in the two *Modes*.

2nd. In the major *Mode* the Mediant or Third, the Sixth and the Seventh of the Tonic should always be major—it is the character of the *Mode*. By the same reason, these three Intervals should be minor in the minor *Mode*; nevertheless, as the Leading Tone must also be perceived in it, which cannot be done without a false relation while the sixth Note remains minor, this produces exceptions to which one must pay attention in the Course of the Harmony and of the Song, but the Clef with its transpositions must always produce all the Intervals determined in relation to the Tonic according to the type of *Mode*. A general rule for this will be found at the word CLEF [*Clef*].

As all the natural Pitches of the Octave of *do* give, relative to this Tonic, all the Intervals prescribed for the Major *Mode*, and as it is likewise for the Octave *la* for the Minor *Mode*, the preceding example, which I have put forward only for the names of the Notes, should also serve as a formula for the rule of Intervals in each *Mode*.

This rule is not at all established on purely arbitrary Principles, as might be believed: it has its foundation in the harmonic generation, at least up to a certain point. If you produce the Perfect Major Chord on the Tonic, on the Dominant, and on the Subdominant, you will have all the Sounds of the Diatonic Scale for the Major *Mode*; in order to have that for the Minor *Mode*, always leaving the Major Third to the Dominant, you produce the Minor Third on the two other Chords. Such is the analogy of the *Mode*.

As this mixture of major and minor Chords introduces a false relation between the sixth Note and the Leading Tone into the Minor *Mode*, in order to avoid this false relation sometimes the Major Third is produced on the fourth Note when ascending or the Minor Third on the Dominant when descending, especially by inversion, but these are then exceptions.

There are strictly speaking only two *Modes*, as has just been seen; but, as there are twelve fundamental Sounds which give as many Keys in the system, and as each of these Keys is susceptible of the Major *Mode* and of the Minor *Mode*, one can compose in twenty-four *Modes* or manners—*Maneries*, our old Authors said in their Latin. There are even thirty-four of them possible in the manner of Notating them, but ten of them are excluded in practice, which are at bottom merely the repetitions of ten others, under much more difficult relations, in which all the Pitches would change names and in which it would be difficult to recognize them. Such are the Major *Modes* on sharp Notes and the Minor *Modes* on Flat ones. Thus, instead of composing a Major Third in *sol*-Sharp, you will compose in *la*-Flat, which gives the same keys on the keyboard, and instead of composing in *re*-Flat minor, you will take *do*-Sharp for the same reason, namely, so as to avoid in the one case an F double-Sharp, which would become a G natural, and in the other a B double-Flat, which would become an A natural.

One does not always remain in the same Key or in the same *Mode* in which one began a Tune; but, whether for expression or for variety, the Key and the *Mode* are changed according to harmonic analogy, always returning nonetheless to the one that was first heard, which is called *Modulating*.

From thence arises a new distinction of the *Mode* into *principal* and *relative*. The principal is that in which the Piece begins and ends; the relatives are those which are intermixed with the principal one in the course of the Modulation. (See MODULATION* [*Modulation*].)

In 1751, Mr. Blainville, a learned Musician from Paris, proposed to attempt a Third *Mode* which he called a *Mixed Mode* because it participates in the Modulation of the two others, or, rather, because it is comprised of them—a mixture the Author does not at all regard as an inconvenience, but rather as an advantage and a source of variety and of liberty in the Songs and in the Harmony.[58]

This new *Mode*, not at all being produced by the analysis of three Chords like the other two, is not determined like them by the Harmonics essential to the *Mode*, but by an entire Scale which belongs to it, in ascending as well as in descending; so that, in our two *Modes* the Scale is produced by the Chords, and in the mixed *Mode* the Chords are produced by the Scale.

The formulation of this Scale is in the ascending and descending series of the following Notes:

Mi   Fa   Sol   La   Si   Do   Re   Mi

whose essential difference is, as regards the Melody, in the position of the two Semitones, of which the first is found between the Tonic and the second Note and the other between the fifth and the sixth ones; and, as regards Harmony, in that it carries on its Tonic the Minor Third when beginning and the major when ending, as one can see (Plate L, Figure 5) in the Accompaniment of this Scale, in ascending as well as descending, such as it was given by the Author and performed at the *Concert Spirituel*, 30 May 1751.

It is objected to Mr. Blainville that his *Mode* has no essential Chord or Pitch or Cadence that belongs to it, and that sufficiently distinguishes it from the major or minor *Modes*. He responds to this that the difference of his *Mode* is less in the Harmony than in the Melody, and less in the *Mode* itself than in the Modulation; that it is distinguished in its beginning from the major *Mode*, by its Minor Third, and in its ending in the minor *Mode* by its plagal Cadence. To which it is replied that a Modulation that is not exclusive does not suffice to establish a *Mode*, that his is inevitably in the other two *Modes*, especially in the minor; and as for its plagal Cadence, that it necessarily has a place in the same minor *Mode* every time one passes from the Chord of the Tonic to that of the Dominant, as this was formerly practiced, even in finales, in the Plagal *Modes* and in the Quarter Tone.

Plate L, Figure 5

From which it is concluded that his mixed *Mode* is less a particular type than a new denomination for ways of intermixing and combining the major and minor *Modes*, as ancient as Harmony, practiced in all times; and this appears so true that, even in beginning his Scale, the Author does not dare to give either the Fifth or the Sixth to his Tonic for fear of determining a Tonic in the minor *Mode* by the first or a Mediant in the major *Mode* by the second. He leaves the equivocation by not filling out his Chord.

But, whatever objection may be made against the mixed *Mode*, whose name rather than its practice is rejected, this will not prevent the manner in which the Author establishes it and treats it from making him known as a man of intelligence and a Musician well versed in the principles of his Art.

The Ancients disagree prodigiously among themselves over the definitions, the divisions, and the names of their Keys or *Modes*. Obscure in all the parts of their Music, they are almost unintelligible in this one. All agree, it is true, that a *Mode* is a certain system or a constitution of Sounds, and it appears that this constitution is nothing in itself but a certain Octave filled by all the intermediary Sounds, according to the Genre. Euclid and Ptolemy[59] seem to make it consist in the various positions of the two Semitones of the Octave relative to the principal Pitch of the *Mode*, as is still seen today in the eight Tones of Plain-Song; but the greater number appear to place this difference uniquely in the place the Diapason of the *Mode* occupies in the general system, that is, in that the Bass or principal Pitch of the *Mode* is higher or lower, being taken in various places of the system, with all the Pitches of the Series always maintaining the same relationship with the fundamental, and consequently changing Chord at each *Mode* so as to preserve the analogy of this relation. This is the difference of the Keys in our Music.

According to the first meaning, there would be only seven possible *Modes* in the Diatonic system, and, in fact, Ptolemy did not accept any more than this: for, there are only seven ways of varying the position of two Semitones relative to the fundamental Sound while always keeping the prescribed Interval between these two Semitones. According to the second meaning, there would be as many *possible Modes* as there are Sounds, that is, an infinite number; but if one likewise restricts oneself to the Diatonic system, no more than seven will be found, at least if one does not want to take as new *Modes* those which would be established on the Octave of the first ones.

By combining these two approaches, one still has need of only seven *Modes*; for if one takes these *Modes* in the various places of the system, one finds at the same time the fundamental Sounds distinguished from low to high, and the two Semitones differently situated relative to the principal Sound.

But besides these *Modes,* several others can be formed by taking different Sounds for the essential Pitches of the *Mode* in the same Series and on the same fundamental Sound. For example, when the Fifth of the principal Sound is taken as Dominant, the *Mode* is Authentic; it is Plagal if the Fourth is chosen; and these are strictly speaking two different *Modes* on the same fundamental. Now, as in order to constitute a pleasant *Mode,* it is necessary, say the Greeks, for the Fourth and the Fifth to be just, or at least one of the two, it is evident that there are only five fundamental Sounds in the range of the Octave on each of which an Authentic and a Plagal *Mode* may be established. Aside from these ten *Modes,* two more are found: one Authentic, which cannot furnish a Plagal because its Fourth produces the Tritone; another Plagal, which cannot furnish an Authentic because its Fifth is false. It is perhaps in this way that a passage in Plutarch must be understood in which Music complains that Phrynis has corrupted it by wanting to derive twelve different Harmonies from five Pitches, or rather seven.[60]

These, then, are the twelve *Modes* possible in the range of one Octave or of two non-adjoining Tetrachords: if one is going to join the two Tetrachords, that is, to give a Flat to the Seventh while omitting the Octave, or if one divides the whole *Tones* by Chromatic Intervals in order to introduce into them new, intermediary *Modes,* or if, paying attention only to the differences from low to high, other *Modes* are placed at the Octave of the preceding ones, all this will furnish various means of multiplying the number of *Modes* well beyond twelve. And these are the only ways of explaining the various number of *Modes* accepted or rejected by the Ancients at various times.

Ancient Music, having at first been confined within the strict limits of the Tetrachord, the Pentachord, the Hexachord, the Heptachord, and the Octachord, at first only three *Modes* were accepted whose fundamentals were one *Tone* distant from one another. The lowest of the three was called the *Dorian*; the *Phrygian* held the middle place; the highest was the *Lydian*. By dividing each of these *Tones* into two Intervals, room was made for two other *Modes,* the Ionian and the Aeolian, the first of which was inserted between the Dorian and the Phrygian and the second between the Phrygian and the Lydian.

Later on, the system being extended on the high and the low ends, Musicians established, on each side, new *Modes* which derived their denomination from the first five by joining to them the preposition *Hyper, super,* for those on the high end and the preposition *Hypo, sub* for the two on the low end. Thus, the Lydian *Mode* was followed by the Hyperdorian, the Hyperionian, the Hyperphrygian, the Hyperaeolian, and the Hyperlydian in ascending; and after the Dorian *Mode* came the Hypolydian, the Hypoaeolian, the Hypophrygian, the Hypoionian, and the Hypodorian in descending. The enumeration of these fifteen *Modes* is found in Alypius, a Greek Author.[61] (See Plate E for their order and their Intervals expressed by the names of the Notes of our Music.) But it must be noted that the Hypodorian was the sole Mode that was performed in its entire range: in proportion as the others rose, Sounds on the high end were omitted in order not to exceed the range of the Voice. This observation serves to make intelligible other passages from the Ancients by which they seem to say that the lowest *Modes* had a higher Song: which was true in that these Songs were further raised above the Tonic. For not having understood this, *Doni* has been awfully perplexed about these apparent contradictions.[62]

Of all these *Modes* Plato rejected several as capable of corrupting morals.[63] According to Euclid, Aristoxenus permitted only thirteen of them, suppressing the two most elevated ones, namely the Hyperaeolian and the Hyperlydian, but in the work of Aristoxenus that remains to us he names only six, about which he reports the various sentiments which already reigned in his time.[64]

Finally, Ptolemy reduced the number of these *Modes* to seven, saying that the *Modes* were not introduced with the intention of varying the Songs according to low and high, for it is obvious that they might have been multiplied well beyond fifteen, but rather in order to facilitate the transition from one *Mode* to another by consonant and easily sounded Intervals.[65]

He therefore confined all the *Modes* within the space of one Octave, in which the Dorian *Mode* acted as the center, so that the Mixolydian was a Fourth above and the Hypodorian a Fourth below, the Phrygian a Fifth above the Hypodorian, the Hypophrygian a Fourth below the Phrygian, and the Lydian a Fifth above the Hypophrygian; from which it appears that, counting from the Hypodorian, which is the lowest *Mode*, to the Hypophrygian, there was an Interval of one *Tonos*; from the Hypophrygian to the Hypolydian another *Tonos*, from the Hypolydian to the Dorian one semi-*Tonos*, from this to the Phrygian one *Tonos*, from the Phrygian to the Lydian one more *Tonos*; from the Phrygian to the Mixolydian one semi-*Tonos*, which makes up the range of a Seventh, in this order:

1	2	3	4	5	6	7
Fa	*Mi*	*Re*	*Do*	*Si*	*La*	*Sol*
Mixolydian	Lydian	Phrygian	Dorian	Hypolydian	Hypophrygian	Hypodorian

GENERAL TABLE
OF ALL THE MODES OF ANCIENT MUSIC

N.B. As Authors have given various names to the majority of these Modes, the least used names have been placed in smaller characters.

	#	Note	Mode
HIGH	15	Si	Hyperlydian
	14	Si-flat	Hyperaeolian
	13	La	Hyperphrygian / Hypermixolydian*
	12	La-flat	Hyperionian / Hyperiastian / High Mixolydian
	11	Sol	Hyperdorian / Mixolydian
MEDIUM	10	Fa-sharp ...	Lydian
	9	Fa	Aeolian / Low Lydian
	8	Mi	Phrygian
	7	Mi-flat	Ionian / Iastian / Low Phrygian
	6	Re	Dorian / Hypomixolydian
LOW	5	Do-sharp	Hypolydian
	4	Do	Hypoaeolian / Low Hypolydian
	3	Si	Hypophrygian
	2	Si-flat	Hypoionian / Hypoiastian / Low Hypophrygian
	1	La	Hypodorian / Common / Locrian

*I place the Hypermixolydian Mode here, finding it noted this way in my notebooks under the citation of Euclid. But the true place of this Mode should, it seems to me, be a semitone above the Hyperlydian; thus, I think that Euclid is mistaken or that I have transcribed him incorrectly.

Ptolemy eliminated all the other *Modes*, claiming that a greater number of them cannot be placed in the diatonic system of one octave, all the Pitches which composed it being found to be employed. It is these seven *Modes* of Ptolomy which, by joining to them the Hypomixolydian — added, it is said, by Aretino[66] — today make up the eight Tones of Plain-Song. (See TONES OF THE CHURCH [*Tons de l'Église*].)

Such is the clearest notion that can be drawn from the Keys or *Modes* of ancient Music, so long as they were regarded as differing from one another only from low to high; but they also had other differences which characterized them more particularly, regarding expression. They were derived from the genre of Poetry which was put into Music, from the type of Instrument which should accompany it, from the Rhythm or the Cadence which was observed in it, from the use certain Songs had among certain Peoples and from which the names of the principal *Modes* originally came: the Dorian, the Phrygian, the Lydian, the Ionian, the Aeolian.

There were also other sorts of *Modes* that might be better called *Styles* or *genres* of composition: such were the tragic *Mode* destined for the theater, the Nomic *Mode* consecrated to Apollo, the Dithyrambic to Bacchus, etc. (See STYLE [*Style*] and MELOPOEIA [*Mélopée*].)

In our ancient Musics, certain ways of establishing the relative value of all the Notes in relation to the *Mensura* or the *Tempus* by a general sign were also called *Modes*. The *Mode* was then nearly what the Meter is today; it was marked in the same way according to the Clef, at first by circles or semicircles, dotted or without dots, followed by the numerals 2 or 3 variously combined, to which various perpendicular lines differing in number or in length were afterward added or substituted, according to the *Mode*; and it is from this antique usage that the use of C and C barred has been left to us. (See PROLATION [*Prolation*].)

There were in this sense two sorts of *Modes*: the major, which was related to the Maxima Note, and the minor, which was for the Longa. Both were divided into perfect and imperfect.

The Perfect Major *Mode* was marked with three lines or staffs that each filled three spaces of the Staff, and three others that filled only two; under this *Mode* the Maxima was worth three Longae. (See Plate B, Figure 2.)

The Imperfect Major *Mode* was marked by two lines that each spanned three spaces, and two others that spanned only two; and then the Maxima was worth only two Longae. (Figure 3.)

The Perfect Minor *Mode* was marked by a single line that spanned three spaces, and the Longa was worth three Brevae. (Figure 4.)

The Imperfect Minor *Mode* was marked by a single line that spanned only two spaces, and its Longa was worth only two Brevae. (Figure 5.)

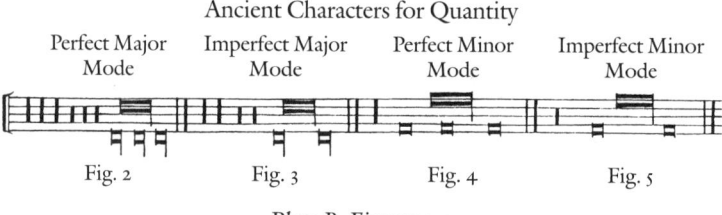

Plate B, Figures 2–5

The Abbé Brossard[67] inappropriately mixed Circles and semi-Circles with the shapes for these *Modes*. These signs brought together have never had a place in the simple *Modes*, but only when the Mensura were double or conjunct.

All this has not been in use for a long time, but these signs must necessarily be understood in order to know how to decipher ancient Musical pieces; about which the most learned Musicians are often quite perplexed.

MODULATION [*Modulation*], *n. fem.* Is properly speaking the manner of establishing and treating the Mode, but this word is taken more commonly today for the art of directing the Harmony and the Song successively in several Modes in a manner pleasant to the ear and conformable to the rules.

If the Mode is produced by the Harmony, it is also from it that the laws of *Modulation* arise. These laws are simple to understand, but difficult to observe correctly. Here is what they consist in.

In order to modulate correctly in the same Key, it is necessary: 1st. To run through all its Sounds in a beautifully Singing manner, by striking the essential Pitches more often and stressing them still more, that is, the leading Chord and the Chord of the Tonic should be struck frequently, but under different aspects and by different routes in order to prevent monotony. 2nd. To establish Cadences, or closes, only on these two Chords, or at the very most on that of the Subdominant. 3rd. Finally, never to alter any of the Sounds of the Mode, for one cannot, without leaving it, make heard a Sharp or a Flat that does not belong to it, or to omit from it one which does belong to it.

But in order to pass from one Key to another, their analogy must be consulted, attention must be paid to the relationship of the Tonics and to the number of Pitches common to the two Keys.

Let us first begin from the major Mode. Whether the Fifth of the Tonic is considered as having the simplest of all the relations with it after that of the Octave or whether it is considered as the first of the Sounds which enters into the resonance of this same Tonic, it will always be found that this Fifth, which is the Dominant of the Key, is the Pitch on which the *Modulation* most analogous to that of the principal Key can be established.

This Dominant, which made up a part of the perfect Chord of this first Tonic, also makes up part of its own, of which it is the fundamental Sound. There is therefore a connection between these two Chords. Furthermore, since this same Dominant like the Tonic contains a Perfect Major Chord by the principle of resonance, these two Chords differ from one another only by the Dissonance, which, from the Tonic passing to the Dominant, is the Added Sixth, and, from the Dominant passing again to the Tonic, is the Seventh. Now, these two Chords—distinguished in this way by the Dissonance which suits them both—form, by the Sounds that make them up them, ranked in order, precisely the Octave, or the Diatonic Scale which we call a Scale, which determines the Key.[68]

This same Scale of the Tonic, altered solely by a Sharp, forms the Scale of the key of the Dominant; which shows the great analogy of these two Keys and makes it easy to pass from the one to the other by means of a single alteration. The Key of the Dominant is therefore the first that presents itself after that of the Tonic in the order of *Modulations*.

The same simplicity of relationship we find between a Tonic and its Dominant is also found between the same Tonic and its Subdominant, for the Fifth which the Dominant produces with this Tonic on the treble, the Subdominant produces on the bass; but this Subdominant is Fifth of the Tonic only by inversion—it is directly a Fourth when placing this Tonic below, as it should be, which establishes the gradation of the ratios: for in this sense the Fourth, whose ratio is 3 to 4, immediately follows the Fifth, whose ratio is 2 to 3. If this Subdominant does not enter into the Chord in the same way as the Tonic, the Tonic on the contrary enters into its own. For let *do mi sol* be the Chord of the Tonic, that of the Subdominant will be *fa la do*; thus it is *do* that here makes the connection, and the two other Sounds of this new Chord are precisely the two Dissonances of the preceding ones. Moreover, it is not necessary to alter any more Sounds for this new Key than for that of the Dominant; all the same Pitches of the principal Key, or nearly so, are in both of them. Give a Flat to the Leading Tone *si*, and all the Notes of the Key of *do* will serve that of *fa*. The Key of the Subdominant is thus hardly less analogous to the principal Key than to that of the Dominant.

It should be further noted that after having made use of the first *Modulation* in order to pass from a principal Key *do* to that of its Dominant *sol*, one is obliged to employ the Second in order to return to the principal Key: for if *sol* is Dominant of the Key of *do*, *do* is Subdominant of the Key of *sol*; thus, one of these *Modulations* is no less necessary than the other.

The third Sound that enters into the Chord of the Tonic is that of its Third, or Mediant, and this is also the simplest of the ratios after the two preceding ones: 2/3, 3/4, 4/5. This, then, is a new *Modulation* that presents itself, and all the more analogous as two of the Sounds of the principal Tonic also enter into the minor Chord of its Mediant; for the first Chord being *do mi sol*, this one will be *mi sol si*, where it is seen that *mi* and *sol* are common.

But what makes this *Modulation* a bit remote is the number of Sounds that must be altered in it, even for the minor Mode, which best suits this *mi*. I gave the formula for the Scale for the two Modes above: now, applying this formula to *mi* in minor Mode, one finds in truth only the fourth Sound *fa* altered by a Sharp in descending, but, in ascending, one also finds two others, namely, the principal Tonic *do* and its second Note *re*, which here becomes the Leading Tone. It is certain that the alteration of so many Sounds, and above all of the Tonic, makes the Mode remote and weakens the analogy.

If the Third is inverted as the Fifth was inverted, and this third is taken beneath the Tonic on the sixth Note *la*, which should also be called Submediant, or Mediant beneath, one will form a *Modulation* more analogous to the principal Key on this *la* than that of *mi*; for the Perfect Chord of this Submediant being *la do mi*, one will again find in it, as in that of the Mediant, two Sounds that enter into the Chord of the Tonic, namely *do* and *mi*; and furthermore, the Scale of the new Key being made up, at least in descending, of the same Sounds as that of the principal Key, and having only two Sounds altered in ascending, that is, one less than the Scale of the Mediant, it follows that the *Modulation* of the sixth Note is preferable to that of this Mediant, all the more so as the principal Tonic makes up one of the essential Pitches of the Mode, which is more appropriate for establishing the idea of the *Modulation*. The *mi* can come later.

Here then are four Pitches—*mi fa sol la*—on each of which one can modulate by starting from the major Key of *do*. There remain *re* and *si*, the two Harmonics of the Dominant. The latter one, as Leading Tone, cannot become Tonic by any good *Modulation*, at least immediately: this would be brusquely to apply ideas that are too opposed to the same Sound and to give it a Harmony that is too remote from the principal one. As for the second Note *re*, thanks to a consonant progression of the Fundamental Bass, one can also modulate in it by a Minor Third, provided that one remains on it but an instant so that there is no time to forget the *Modulation* of the *do*, which is itself altered; otherwise, instead of returning immediately in *do*, it would be necessary to pass through other intermediary Keys, where there would be danger of going astray.

By following the same analogies, one will modulate in the following order in order to begin from a minor Key: the Mediant first, then the Dominant, the Subdominant, and the Submediant, or sixth Note. The Mode of each of these accessory Keys is determined by its Mediant taken in the scale of the principal Key. For example, starting from a major Key *do* in order to modulate in its Mediant, one makes the Mode of this Mediant minor, since the Dominant *sol* of the principal Key produces a Minor Third on this Mediant *mi*. On the contrary, starting from a minor Key *la*, one modulates on its Mediant *do* in the major Mode, since the Dominant *mi* of the Key from which one starts produces a Major Third on the Tonic of that into which one enters, etc.

These rules, contained in a general formula, make it so that the Modes of the Dominant and of the Subdominant are similar to that of the Tonic, and that the Mediant and the sixth Note contain the opposed Mode. It must nevertheless be noted that in virtue of the right one has of passing from the major to the minor, and reciprocally, in the same Key, one can also change the order of the Mode from one Key to another; but in thus moving away from the natural *Modulation*, it is necessary to consider the return: for it is a general rule that every piece of Music should finish in the Key by which it began.

I have gathered together all the Keys into which one can immediately pass into two very short examples: the first, by beginning from the major Mode, and the other, by beginning from the minor Mode. Each Note indicates one *Modulation*, and the value of the Notes in each example also indicates the relative duration suitable to each of these modes according to its relationship with the principal Key. (See Plate B, Figures 6 and 7.)

These immediate *Modulations* furnish the means for passing into the most remote Keys by the same rules, and of returning afterward to the principal Key, which must never be lost from sight. But it is not enough to know the routes one must follow; one must also know how to enter into them. Here is the summary of the precepts which can be given on this Subject.

In the Melody it is necessary, in order to announce the *Modulation* one

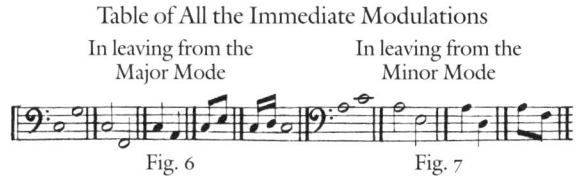

Plate B, Figures 6 and 7

Plate B, Figure 8

has chosen, to make heard the alterations it produces in the Sounds of the Key from which one starts in order to make them suitable to the Key into which one is entering. Is one in *do* major? It is only necessary to sound a *fa*-Sharp in order to announce the Key of the Dominant, or a *si*-Flat in order to announce the Key of the Subdominant. Then run through the essential Pitches of the Key into which you are entering; if it is well chosen, your *Modulation* will always be good and regular.

In the Harmony there is a little more difficulty, for as the change in Key must be done at the same time in all the Parts, one should be careful about the Harmony and the Song in order to avoid following two different *Modulations* at the same time. Huygens has remarked quite correctly that the proscription of two consecutive Fifths has this rule for its basis;[69] in fact, one can hardly form several just Fifths in a row between two Parts without modulating in two different Keys.

In order to announce a Key, some claim that it suffices to form the Perfect Chord of its Tonic, and that this is indispensable in order to give the Mode; but it is certain that the Key can be well determined only by the Leading or Dominant Chord; it is therefore necessary to make this Chord heard when beginning the new *Modulation*. The good rule would be for the Seventh or minor Dissonance always be prepared by it, at least the first time one makes it heard; but this rule is not practicable in all the permissible *Modulations*, and provided that the Fundamental Bass progresses by consonant Intervals, that harmonic connection and the analogy of the Mode are observed, and that false Relations are avoided, the *Modulation* is always good. Composers give as another rule that of changing Key only after a Perfect Cadence; but this rule is useless, and no one submits himself to it.

All the possible ways of passing from one Key into another are reduced to five for the major mode and to four for the minor mode, which will be found set forth by a Fundamental Bass for each *Modulation* in Plate B, Figure 8. If there is another *Modulation* that is not reducible to one of these nine, unless this *Modulation* is not Enharmonic, it is infallibly bad. (See ENHARMONIC* [*Enharmonique*].)

MORALS [*Moeurs*], *n. fem*. A considerable Part of the Music of the Greeks, called by them *Hermosmenos*, which consisted in knowing and choosing what is befitting in each Genre, and did not allow them to give to every feeling, to every object, to every character each form of which it was susceptible, but obliged them to limit themselves to what was suitable to the subject, to the occasion, to the persons, to the circumstances. *Morals* further consisted in so according and proportioning all the Parts of the Music, the Mode, the Tempo, the Rhythm, the Melody, and even the changes, in a Piece so that one might feel in the whole a certain conformity which did not leave any disparate element and which made it perfectly one. This sole Part, the idea of which is not even known in our Music, shows to what point of perfection an Art should be carried in which one has even reduced to rules what is decent, suitable, and befitting.

MUSICIAN [*Musicien*], *n. masc*. This name is equally given to the person who composes Music and to the person who performs it. The first is also called a COMPOSER* [*Compositeur*]. See that word.

Ancient Musicians were Poets, Philosophers, Orators of the first order. Such were Orpheus, Terpander, Stesichorus, *etc*.[70] In addition, Boethius does not want to honor with the name of *Musician* the person who only practices Music by the servile ministration of the fingers and the voice, but the person who possesses this knowledge through reasoning and speculation.[71] And it seems, furthermore, that in order to raise oneself to the grand expressions of oratorical and imitative Music, one must have made a special study of the human passions and of the language of Nature. Nevertheless, the *Musicians* of our days—limited, for the most part, to the practice of Notes and of some phrasings of Song—will hardly be offended, I think, if they are not taken for great Philosophers.

MUSIC [*Musique*], *n. fem*. The Art of combining Sounds in a manner pleasant to the ear. This Art becomes a science, and even a very profound one, when one seeks to discover the principle of these combinations and the reasons for the affections they cause in us. Aristides Quintilianus defined *Music* as the Art of beauty and of propriety in Voices and in Motions.[72] It is not astonishing that, with definitions so vague and so general, the Ancients gave a prodigious scope to the Art they defined in this way.

It is commonly supposed that the word *Music* comes from *Musa*, since it is believed that the Muses invented this Art; but Kircher, following Diodorus,[73] has this noun come from an Egyptian word, claiming that it is in Egypt that Music began to be reestablished after the flood and that the first idea of it was taken from the Sound that the reeds which grow on the banks of the Nile produced when the wind blew through their pipes. Whatever the etymology of the noun may be, the origin of the Art is certainly nearer to man, and if speech did not begin by Song, it is at least sure that there is singing everywhere there is speaking.[74]

Music is naturally divided into *theoretical* or *speculative Music* and *practical Music*.

Speculative *Music* is, if one can speak in this way, the knowledge of musical matter, that is, of the different relations—from low to high, from fast to slow, from sharp to sweet, from loud to soft—to which Sounds are susceptible, relations which, taking all the possible combinations of Music and of Sounds, seem thus to comprehend all the causes of the impressions their succession can make on the ear and on the soul.

Practical Music is the Art of applying and making use of the principles of the speculative part, that is, of directing and disposing the Sounds in relation to consonance, duration, succession, in such a way that the whole produces the proposed effect on the ear; it is this Art which is called Composition* [*Composition*]. (See this word.) As regards the actual production of Sound by Voices or by Instruments, which is called *Performance*, this is the purely mechanical and operative part, which, assuming only the faculty of justly intoning the Intervals, of correctly marking the durations, of giving to the Sounds the degree prescribed in the Key and the value prescribed in the Beats, strictly speaking demands no other knowledge than that of the characteristics of *Music* and the habit of expressing them.

Speculative *Music* is divided into two parts: namely, the knowledge of the relation of Sounds or of their Intervals and that of their relative durations, that is, of the Meter and of the Beats.

The first is properly speaking what the Ancients called *harmonic Music*. It teaches what the nature of Song consists in and indicates what is consonant, dissonant, pleasant, or unpleasant in the Modulation. In a word, it makes known the various manners in which Sounds affect the ear by their timbre, by their volume, by their Intervals, which applies equally to their Accord and to their succession.

The second was called *Rhythmic* since it treats Sounds with regard to Beats and quantity. It contains the explanation of the *Rhythmos*, of the *Metron*, of long and short, lively and slow Meters, of Beats, and of the various parts into which they are divided in order to apply the succession of Sounds to them.

Practical Music is also divided into two Parts that correspond to the two preceding ones.

That which corresponds to *harmonic Music*, and which the Ancients called *Melopoeia*, contains the rules for combining and varying consonant and dissonant Intervals in a pleasant and harmonious manner. (See Melopoeia [*Melopée*].)

The second, which corresponds to *Rhythmic Music*, and which they called *Rhythmopoeia*, contains the rules for the application of Beats, of Feet, of Meters, in a word, for the practice of Rhythm. (See Rhythm [*Rhythme*].)

Porphyry gives[75] another division of *Music*, inasmuch as *Music* has for its object mute or sonorous Motion, and, without distinguishing it into speculative and practical, he finds in it the six following parts: *Rhythmikê*, for the movements of Dance; *Metrikê*, for the Cadence and number of Verses; *Organikê*, for the practice of the Instruments; *Poêtikê*, for the Tones and the Accent of the Poetry; *Hypocritikê*, for the poses of the Pantomimes; and *Harmonikê*, for the Song.

Music is today divided more simply into *Melody* and *Harmony*, for Rhythmikê is no longer anything to us, and Metrikê is of very little importance, seeing that, in Song, our Verses take their Meter almost uniquely from the *Music* and lose the little they have by themselves.

By the melody one directs the succession of the Sounds in a manner to produce pleasant Songs. (See Melody* [*Mélodie*], Song* [*Chant*], Modulation* [*Modulation*].)

The Harmony consists in uniting to each of the Sounds of a regular succession two or more other Sounds which, simultaneously striking, the ear gratify it by their concurrence. (See Harmony* [*Harmonie*].)

One might and perhaps should further divide *Music* into *natural* and *imitative*. The first, limited to the physics of Sounds alone and acting only on the sense, does not at all convey its impressions to the heart, and can produce only more or less pleasant sensations. Such is the Music of Chansons, of Hymns, of Canticles, of all the Songs that are merely combinations of Melodious Sounds, and in general all Music that is merely Harmonious.

The second, by lively, accented, and, so to speak, speaking inflections, expresses every passion, paints every portrait, renders every object, submits all Nature to its learned imitations, and thus conveys to the heart of man the feelings appropriate for affecting it. This truly lyrical and theatrical Music was that of ancient Poems, and is in our days that which they endeavor to apply to Dramas which are performed in Song in our Theaters. It is only in this *Music*, and not in the Harmonic or natural one, that one must seek the reason for the prodigious effects that it produced in the past. As long as one seeks moral effects in the physics of Sounds alone, they will not be found and one will reason without understanding.

The ancient Writers differ greatly with one another over the nature, object, extent, and parts of *Music*. In general, they gave to this word a much more extensive meaning than that which remains to it today. Not only did they comprehend Dance, Gesture, Poetry under the noun *Music*, as has just been seen, but even the collection of all the sciences. Hermes defined *Music* as the knowledge of the order of all things.[76] This was also the doctrine of Pythagoras' school and that of Plato, which taught that everything in the universe was *Music*. According to Hesychius, the Athenians gave to all their Arts the name *Music*[77]; and all this is no longer astonishing since a modern Musician has found the principle of all relations and the foundation of all the sciences in Music.[78]

From thence all the sublime *Musics* of which the Philosophers tell us: divine *Music*, the *Music* of men, celestial *Music*, terrestrial *Music*, active *Music*, contemplative *Music*, enunciative, intellective, oratorical *Music*, etc.

It is under these vast ideas that several passages of the ancients on *Music*, which are unintelligible in the sense which we give to the word today, must be understood.

It seems that *Music* was one of the first Arts: it is found mixed among the most ancient records of the Human Race. It is also quite likely that Vocal *Music* was discovered before Instrumental, if indeed there was ever among the Ancients a truly Instrumental *Music*, that is, composed uniquely for Instruments. Not only must men, before having discovered any Instrument, have made observations on the different Tones of their Voices, but they must have learned quite early to modify their voices and their windpipes in a pleasant and melodious manner from the natural concert of birds. After that, wind Instruments must have been the first to have been invented. Diodorus and other Authors attribute their invention to the observation of the whistling of the winds in reeds and other plant stalks.[79] This is also Lucretius' sentiment:

> *At liquidas avium voces imitarier ore*
> *Ante fuit multò, quam levia carmina cantu*
> *Concelebrare homines possint, aureisque juvare;*
> *Et Zephyri cava per calamorum sibila primùm*
> *Agrestis docuêre cavas inflare cicutas.*[80]

Regarding other sorts of Instruments, sounding Strings are so common that men must have early observed their different Tones, which gave birth to Stringed Instruments. (See STRING [*Corde*].)

Instruments that are beaten in order to draw a Sound from them, as Drums and Timpani, owe their origin to the muted noise that hollow bodies produce when they are struck.

It is difficult to depart from these generalities in order to certify any fact about the invention of *Music* reduced to an Art. Without going back before the flood, several Ancients attribute this invention to Mercury, as well as that of the Lyre. Others want the Greeks to be indebted for it to Cadmus, who, running away from the Court of the King of Phoenicia, brought into Greece the Musician Hermione, or Harmony, from which it would follow that this Art was known in Phoenicia before Cadmus. In one place in the Dialogue by Plutarch on *Music*, Lysias says that it is Amphion who invented it; in another, Soterichus says that it is Apollo; in still another he seems to give the honor to Olympus: there is hardly any agreement on all this, and this does not matter very much either. To these first inventors succeeded Chiron, Demodocus, Hermes, Orpheus, who, according to some, invented the lyre. After these came Phemius, then Terpander, a contemporary of Lycurgus who gave rules to *Music*. Some people attribute to him the invention of the first Modes. Finally Thaletas and Thamyris are added, who it is said was the inventor of instrumental *Music*.[81]

Most of these great Musicians lived before Homer. Others more modern are Lasus of Hermione, Melanippides, Philoxenus, Timotheus, Phrynnis, Epigonus, Lysander, Simicus, and Diodorus, who all considerably perfected *Music*.[82]

Lasus is, as is claimed, the first who wrote on this Art in the time of Darius Hystaspes. Epigonus invented the Instrument with forty Strings that bore his name. Simicus also invented an Instrument of thirty-five Strings, called a *Simicion*.[83]

Diodorus perfected the Flute and added new holes to it, and Timotheus the lyre, to which he added a new String, which caused him to be fined by the Lacedaemonians.[84]

As the ancient Authors speak quite obscurely about the inventors of *Musical* Instruments, they are also quite obscure about the Instruments themselves. We hardly know anything about them except their names. (See INSTRUMENT [*Instrument*].)

Music was held in the greatest esteem among the various Peoples of Antiquity, and principally among the Greeks, and this esteem was proportioned to the power and the surprising effects they attributed to this Art. Their Authors did not think they were giving too grand an idea of it by telling us that it was in use in Heaven and that it was the principal amusement of the Gods and of the souls of the Blessed. Plato had no fear of saying that no change could be made in *Music* that was not a change in the constitution of the State, and he claims that one can assign sounds that are capable of giving rise to the soul's servility, insolence, and the contrary virtues.[85] Aristotle, who seems to have written his politics only in order to oppose his sentiments to those of Plato, is nevertheless in accord with him regarding the power of *Music* on morals.[86] The judicious Polybius tells us that *Music* was necessary to soften the morals of the Arcadians, who inhabited a country in which the air is dreary and cold; that those of Cynaetha, who, neglecting *Music*, surpassed all the Greeks in cruelty and that there was no City in which there were so many crimes.[87] Athenaeus assures us that in the past all the divine and human laws, the exhortations to virtue, the knowledge of what concerned the Gods and Heroes, the lives and actions of illustrious men were written in verse and sung publicly by Choruses to the sound of Instruments; and we see by our sacred Books that such were, from the first times, the customs of the Israelites.[88] No more efficacious means has been found to carve the principles of Morality and the love of virtue into the minds of men; or, rather, all this was not the effect of a premeditated means, but of the grandeur of the sentiments and of the elevation of ideas which sought, by proportionate accents, to make a language worthy of them.

Music made up part of the study of the ancient Pythagoreans. They made use of it to rouse the heart to laudable actions and to take fire with love of virtue. According to these Philosophers, our soul was so to speak formed solely of Harmony, and by means of sensual Harmony they thought to reestablish the intellectual and primitive Harmony of the faculties of the soul, that is, that which according to them existed in it before it animated our bodies and when it inhabited the Heavens.

Music has today fallen from this degree of power and majesty to the point that we are made to doubt the truth of the marvels it once produced, although attested by the most judicious Historians and by the gravest Philosophers of Antiquity. Nevertheless, one finds in modern History some similar facts. If Timotheus aroused Alexander's fury by the Phrygian Mode and calmed it by the Lydian Mode, a more modern *Music* went still further by rousing, it is said, in Eric, King of Denmark, such a fury that he killed his best domestics.[89] These unfortunates were doubtless less sensitive to *Music* than their Prince, otherwise half the danger might have been his. D'Aubigné reports another story entirely similar to that of Timotheus. He says that, under Henri III, the Musician Claudin, playing at the wedding of the Duke of Joyeuse in the Phrygian Mode, animated, not the King, but a Courtier who forgot himself so far as to take up arms in the presence of his Sovereign; but the Musician hastened to calm him by taking the Hypophrygian Mode. This is said with as much assurance as if the Musician Claudin could have known in what exactly the Phrygian Mode and the Hypophrygian Mode consisted.

If our *Music* has little power over the affections of the soul, it is on the contrary capable of acting physically on the body. Witness the story of the Tarantula, too well known to speak of it here.[90] Witness that Gascon

Knight of whom Boyle speaks,[91] who could not retain his urine at the sound of Bagpipes, to which it must be added what this same Author recounts concerning those women who dissolved in tears when they heard a certain Tone by which the rest of the Listeners were not at all affected, and I know a woman of station in Paris who cannot listen to any *Music* without being seized with involuntary and convulsive laughter. One also reads in the History of the Academy of Sciences of Paris that a Musician was cured from a violent fever by a Concert played in his bedroom.

Sounds act even on inanimate bodies, as is seen by the trembling and resonance of one sounding body at the sound of another with which it is attuned in a certain ratio. Morhoff makes mention of a certain Petter, a Dutchman, who broke a glass at the sound of his voice.[92] Kircher speaks of a large rock which trembled at the sound of a certain Organ pipe.[93] Father Mersenne also speaks of a sort of tile which the Playing of an Organ broke as an earthquake might have done.[94] Boyle adds that stalls often tremble at the sound of Organs, that he has felt them tremble beneath his hand at the sound of the Organ or of the voice, and that he has been assured that those which were well made all tremble at some determinate Tone.[95] Everyone has heard of the famous pillar of a Church in Reims which rattled perceptibly at the sound of a certain bell whereas the other pillars remained immobile; but what robs the sound of the honor of being a marvel is that this same pillar rattled equally when the clapper of the bell was removed.

All these examples, the majority of which concern sound more than *Music*, and of which Physics can give some explanation, do not make any more intelligible or more believable the marvelous and almost divine effects which the Ancients attribute to *Music*. Several Authors have troubled themselves over trying to account for them. Wallis attributes them in part to the novelty of the Art and rejects them in part as the exaggeration of the Authors.[96] Others grant this honor only to Poetry. Others suppose that the Greeks, more sensitive than us by the constitution of their climate or by their manner of living, could have been moved by things that would not touch us at all. M. Burette, even while accepting all these facts, claims that they cannot at all prove the perfection of the *Music* which produced them; he sees nothing more to them than what miserable Village gut-scrapers might have produced, in his opinion, entirely as well as the foremost Musicians of the world.[97]

The majority of these sentiments are founded on the persuasion we have of the excellence of our *Music* and on the scorn we have for that of the Ancients. But is this scorn itself as well founded as we claim? This is what has been examined many times and which, given the obscurity of the matter and the insufficiency of the judges, is in great need of being better so.

444 *Dictionary of Music*

Of all those who have gotten involved in this examination, Vossius, in his Treatise *De Viribus cantus et rhythmi*,[98] seems to be the one who has best discussed the question and most closely approached the truth. I have put forth some ideas on this point in another writing not yet public in which my opinions will be better placed than in this work, which is not made in order to stop the Reader to discuss them.[99]

There has been great desire to see some fragments of ancient *Music*. Father Kircher and M. Burette have worked on this to satisfy the Public's curiosity. In order to put their labors more within reach, in Plate C I have transcribed two pieces of Greek *Music* transcribed in modern Notation by these Authors.[100] But who will dare judge ancient *Music* based on such samples? I assume them to be faithful. I even want those who would like to judge them to be acquainted sufficiently with the genius and the accent of the Greek language to let them reflect that an Italian is an incompetent judge of a French Tune, that a Frenchman understands nothing at all about Italian Melody: then let him compare times and places and let him pronounce if he so dare.

In order to put the Reader in a position to judge the various musical Accents of Peoples, in Plate N, I have also transcribed a Chinese Tune taken from Father du Halde, a Persian Tune taken from the Chevalier Chardin,

Plate C, Figure 1

and two Chansons of the American Savages taken from Father Mersenne.[101] A conformity of Modulation with our *Music* will be found in all these pieces which will possibly make some admire the goodness and universality of our rules, and for others will perhaps render suspect the intelligence or the fidelity of those who have transmitted these Tunes to us.

In the same Plate I have added the celebrated *Rans-des-vaches*, that Tune so cherished by the Swiss that they have forbidden it from being played in their Troops on pain of death, since it would cause those who heard it to dissolve in tears, desert, or die, so much would it arouse in them the ardent desire to see their country again. One would seek in vain in this Tune the energetic accents capable of producing such astonishing effects. These effects, which do not take place on foreigners, come solely from habit, from memories, from a thousand circumstances which, recounted by this Tune to those who hear it and recalling for them their country, their old pleasures, their youth, and all their ways of living, arouse in them a bitter pain for having lost all that. The *Music* therefore does not precisely act as *Music*, but as a memorative sign. This Tune, although always the same, today no longer produces the same effects it formerly produced on the Swiss, because, having lost the taste for their first simplicity, they no longer regret it when it is recalled for them. So true it is that it is not in their physical action that the greatest effects of Sounds on the human heart must be sought!

The manner in which the Ancients notated their *Music* was established on a very simple basis, which was the relationship of numerals, that is, by the letters of their Alphabet; but, instead of confining themselves in this idea to a small number of easily retained characters, they lost themselves among the multitudes of different signs with which they gratuitously muddled their *Music*, so that they had as many manners of notating as they did Genres and Modes. Boethius took those characters in the Latin alphabet corresponding to those of the Greeks.[102] Pope Gregory perfected his method.[103] In 1024, Guido of Arezzo, a Benedictine, introduced the use of Staffs (see STAFF [*Portée*]), on the lines of which he marked the Notes in the form of Points (see NOTES [*Notes*]), designating by their position the elevation or lowering of the voice.[104] Kircher claims,[105] however, that this invention is anterior to Guido, and, in fact, I have not seen in this Monk's writings that he claims it for himself, but he did invent the Scale and applied to the Notes of his Hexachord the names derived from the Hymn of John the Baptist which are still preserved today. Finally, this man born for *Music* invented different instruments called *Polyplectra*, such as the Clavichord, the Spinette, the Vielle, *etc*. (See SCALE [*Gamme*].)

According to the common opinion, the characters of *Music* received

Chinese Tune

Chanson of Canadian Savages

Ca ni de jou ve, Ca ni da jouve He he he he he heu - - - - - - - - - - ra heura on cé bé.

Canadian Dance

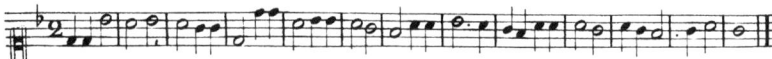

Swiss Tune called the Rans des Vaches

Persian Chanson

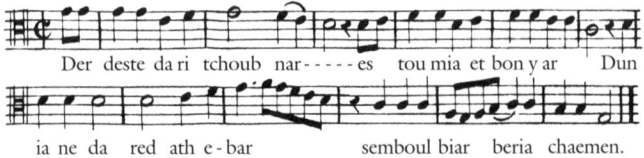

Der deste da ri tchoub nar - - - - - es tou mia et bon y ar   Dun
ia ne da   red ath e-bar   semboul biar   beria chaemen.

TRANSLATION OF THE PERSIAN WORDS

Your complexion is vermilion like the flower of Granada,
Your speech a perfume whose inseparable friend I am;
There is nothing stable in the world, everything passes in it.
Refrain: Bring these scented flowers to revive the heart of my King.

Plate N

their last considerable increase in 1330, the time at which, it is said, Jehan des Murs—improperly called by some *Jean de Meurs* or *de Muriâ*, a Doctor of Paris, although Gessner would make him English—invented the different forms of the Notes that designate their duration or quantity, and which we call today Whole Notes, Half Notes, Quarter Notes, etc. But this sentiment, although very common, appears to me poorly founded, judging from his Treatise of *Music*, entitled *Speculum Musicae*, which I had the courage to read almost in its entirety in order to confirm the invention attributed to this Author. Besides, like the King of the Poets, this great Musician had the honor of being claimed by various Peoples, for the Italians also claim he is of their Nation, apparently deceived by a fraud or an error by Bontempi, who says *Perugino* instead of *Parigino*.[106]

Lasus is, or appears to be, the first who wrote on *Music*, as was said above, but his work is lost, as are several other books of the Greeks and Romans on the same matter. Aristoxenus, a disciple of Aristotle and head of the sect in *Music*, is the most ancient Author who remains to us on this science. After him came Euclid of Alexandria. Aristides Quintilianus wrote after Cicero. Alypius came afterward, then Gaudentius, Nicomachus, and Baccheius.[107]

Marcus Meibomius has given us a fine edition of these seven Greek Authors with Latin translation and Notes.[108]

Plutarch wrote a Dialogue on *Music*. Ptolomy, the celebrated Mathematician, wrote the principles of Harmony, in Greek, around the time of the Emperor Antoninus. This Author occupies a middle position between the Pythagoreans and the Aristoxenians. Long afterward, Manuel Bryennius also wrote on the same subject.[109]

Among the Latins, Boethius wrote in the time of Theodoric, and not far from the same time as Martianus, Cassiodorus, and Saint Augustine.[110]

The Moderns are many in number. The best known are Zarlino, Salinas, Valgulio, Galileo, Mei, Doni, Kircher, Mersenne, Parran, Perrault, Wallis, Descartes, Holder, Mengoli, Malcolm, Burette, Vallotti, and finally M. Tartini, whose book is full of profundity, of genius, of overlong passages, and of obscurities, and M. Rameau, whose books have something singular about them in that they have made a great fortune without having been read by anyone. This reading has become superfluous anyway ever since M. d'Alembert took the trouble to explain to the Public the system of the Fundamental Bass, the only useful and intelligible thing found in the writings of this Musician.[111]

OPERA [*Opéra*], *n. masc.* A Dramatic and lyric Spectacle in which one endeavors to bring together all the charms of the fine Arts in the representation of a passionate action in order to arouse interest and illusion with the help of pleasant sensations.

The constituent parts of an *Opera* are: the Poem, the Music, and the Decoration. Through the Poetry one speaks to the mind, through the Music to the ear, through the Painting to the eyes, and the whole should bring them together in order to move the heart and convey to it the same impression simultaneously by the various organs. Of these three parts, my subject does not permit me to consider the first and the last except as they may relate to the second; thus, I pass immediately to that one.

The Art of combining Sounds pleasantly can be envisioned in two very different aspects. Considered as an institution of Nature, Music limits its effect to sensation and to the physical pleasure which results from the Melody, from the Harmony, and from the Rhythm. Such ordinarily is Church Music; such are dancing Tunes and those of Chansons. But taken as an essential part of the lyric Scene, whose principal object is imitation, Music becomes one of the fine Arts, capable of painting every Portrait, of arousing every feeling, of struggling with the Poetry, of giving it a new force, of embellishing it with new charms, and of triumphing over it by crowning it.

The Sounds of the speaking voice, being neither sustained nor Harmonic, are inappreciable and consequently cannot be allied in a pleasing way with those of the singing voice and of Instruments, at least in our Languages, too remote from any musical character. For the passages of the Greeks on their manner of doing recitation can be understood only by supposing their Language so accentuated that the inflections of the discourse in sustained declamation formed among themselves appreciable musical Intervals; thus, it can be said that their Theatrical Pieces were species of *Opera*, and it is for this same reason that there could have been among them no *Opera*, strictly speaking.

It is easy to perceive by the difficulty of uniting Song with discourse in our Languages that the intervention of the Music as an essential part must give to the lyric Poem a character different from that of Tragedy and of Comedy, and make of it a third type of Drama which has its specific rules; but these differences cannot be determined without an exact knowledge of the added part, of the means of uniting it to speech, and of its natural relations with the human heart—details which belong less to the Artist than to the Philosopher and which must be left to a pen made for illuminating all the Arts in order to show to those who profess them the principles of their rules and to men of taste the sources of their pleasures.

Limiting myself, then, to some observations on this subject that are more historical than reasoned, I shall first note that the Greeks did not have a lyric genre in their Theater as we do, and that what they called by this name did not at all resemble ours. As they had a great deal of accent in their Language and little din in their Concerts, all their Poetry was musical and all their music declamatory, so that their Singing was almost merely a sustained discourse and so that they actually sang their verses, as they so announce at the head of their Poems, which, through imitation, gave to the Latins and then to us the ridiculous custom of saying *I sing* when one does not at all sing. As for what they called the lyric genre in particular, it was a heroic Poetry whose style was stately and ornamented, which was accompanied by the Lyre or Cithara in preference to any other Instrument. It is certain that Greek Tragedies were recited in a manner quite similar to Song, that they were accompanied by Instruments, and that Choruses had a part in them.

But if one holds for this reason that they were *Operas* similar to ours, it is therefore necessary to imagine *Operas* without Arias, for it seems to me to be proved that Greek Music, without excepting even the Instrumental, was merely a genuine Recitative. It is true that this Recitative, which brought together the charm of Musical Sounds with all the Harmony of Poetry and all the strength of declamation, must have had much more energy than modern Recitative, which can hardly manage one of these advantages except at the expense of the others. In our living Languages, which are for the most part affected by the severity of the climate in which they originated, the application of Music to speech is much less natural. An uncertain prosody accords poorly with regularity of the Meter; silent and indistinct syllables, harsh articulations, dull and less varied Sounds lend themselves with difficulty to Melody, and a Poetry cadenced uniquely by the number of syllables takes a Harmony that is little perceived in the musical Rhythm and is constantly opposed to the diversity of the values and of movements. These are the difficulties which had to be vanquished or eluded in the invention of lyric Poetry. They therefore tried to make an appropriate Language by the choice of words, of turns of phrase, of verses, and this Language, which was called lyric, was rich or poor in proportion to the sweetness or severity of the one from which it was derived.

Having in a way prepared speech for Music, it was then a question of applying the Music to the speech and of making it so appropriate for the lyric Scene that the whole could be taken for a single and identical idiom, which led to the necessity of always singing in order always to appear to be speaking—a necessity which increases due to a Language being little musical, for the less sweetness and accent a Language has, the more harsh and shocking the alternating transition from speech to Song and from Song to speech becomes for the ear. From whence the need to substitute a discourse in Song for the discourse in recitation, which might imitate it so closely that it was only the justness of the Chords that distinguished it from speech. (See RECITATIVE [*Récitatif*].)

This manner of uniting Music to Poetry in the Theater which, among the Greeks, sufficed for interest and illusion because it was natural, by the contrary reason could not suffice among us for the same end. When listening to a hypothetical and constrained language, we have difficulty conceiving what is trying to be said to us; with a great deal of noise little emotion is produced in us: from this arises the necessity of bringing physical pleasure to the aid of the moral, and of making up for the energy of the expression with the attraction of the Harmony. Thus, the less one knows how to touch the heart, the more one must know how to flatter the ear, and we are forced to seek in sensation the pleasure which feeling denies us. This is the origin of Arias, of Choruses, of Instrumental parts, and of that enchantress Melody with which modern Music is often embellished at the expense of the Poetry, but which the man of taste rebuffs at the Theater when it flatters him without moving him.

At the birth of *Opera,* its inventors, wanting to avoid what was scarcely natural in the unison of Music with discourse in the imitation of human life,[112] took it into their heads to transport the Scene into the Heavens and into Hell, and, for want of knowing how to make men speak, they preferred to make Gods and Devils sing rather than Heroes and Shepherds. Soon magic and the marvelous became the foundations of the Lyric Theater, and, content with enriching themselves with a new genre, they did not even dream of inquiring whether that was the one they should have chosen. In order to sustain such a strong illusion they had to lavish everything human art could imagine that was more seductive amidst a People whose taste for pleasure and for the fine Arts reigned while vying with one another. That celebrated Nation which retained of its ancient grandeur only that of some ideas in the fine Arts, lavished its taste, its enlightenment in order to give to this Spectacle all the splendor it needed. Theaters in all of Italy were seen rising equal in size to the Palaces of Kings and in elegance to the monuments of Antiquity with which it was filled. The Arts of Perspective and Decoration were invented to ornament them. Artists of every sort vied with each other to make their talents shine. The most ingenious machines, the most daring flights, tempests, thunderbolts, lightning, and all the magic tricks of the wand were employed to fascinate the eyes while multitudes of Instruments and voices astonished the ears.

With all this the action always remained cold and every situation lacked interest. As there was no intrigue that wasn't easily resolved with the aid of some God, the Spectator, who was acquainted with the Poet's full powers, calmly left to him the care of delivering his Heroes from the greatest dangers. Thus, the apparatus was immense and produced little effect, because the imitation was always imperfect and crude, because the action, taken beyond Nature, was without interest for us, and because the senses lend themselves poorly to illusion when the heart does not become involved in it, so that all in all it would have been difficult to bore an assembly at a greater price.

This Spectacle, as imperfect as it was, long filled its contemporaries—who knew no better one—with admiration. They even congratulated themselves on discovering such a beautiful genre. Here, they said, is a new principle joined to those of Aristotle; here admiration is joined to terror and to pity.[113] They did not see that this apparent richness was at bottom only a sign of sterility, like the flowers that cover the fields before the harvest. It was for want of knowing how to touch that they desired to surprise, and this pretended admiration was in effect only a puerile astonishment at which they should have blushed. A false air of magnificence, of extravagance, and of enchantment impressed them to the point that they spoke only with enthusiasm and with respect of a Theater which merited only boos. They had, with the best faith in the world, as much veneration for the scene itself as for the chimerical objects they tried to represent in it—as if there were more merit in making the King of the Gods speak as insipidly as the lowest of mortals, and as if Molière's Valets were not preferable to Pradon's Heroes![114]

Although the Authors of these first *Operas* had hardly any other aim than that of dazzling eyes and dazing ears, it was difficult for the Musician never to be tempted to try to draw from his Art the expression of the feelings scattered through the Poem. The Songs of Nymphs, the Hymns of Preachers, the cries of Warriors, infernal howls did not so fill these crude Dramas that some moment of interest and situation was not found in which the Spectator asked only to be moved. Soon it began to be felt that, independently of the Musical declamation, the Language was oftentimes inappropriate, that the choice of the Movement, of the Harmony, and of the Songs was not indifferent to the things that were to be said, and that, consequently, the effect of the Music alone, limited until then to the sense, could be conveyed all the way to the heart. Melody, which at first was separated from Poetry only by necessity, took advantage of its independence to produce beauties that were absolutely and purely musical. Harmony, having been discovered or perfected, opened up for it new routes to please and to move. And Meter, emancipated from the constraint of poetic Rhythm, also acquired a sort of Cadence apart which it possessed of itself alone.

Music, having thus become a third Art of imitation, soon had its language, it expression, its portraits completely independent of the Poetry. The Instrumental part itself learned to speak without the help of words, and often feelings came from the Orchestra that were no less lively than those from the mouths of the Actors. It was then that, beginning to be disgusted by all the flashiness of the extravaganza, of the puerile din of the machines, and of the fantastic image of things which had never been seen, more interesting and truer portraits were sought in the imitation of Nature. Until then *Opera* had been constituted as it could be; for what better use could be made in the Theater of a Music that didn't know how to portray anything than to employ it for the representation of things that could not exist and of which no one was in a position to compare the image to the object? It is impossible to know whether one is affected by the portrayal of *merveilleux*[115] as one would be by their presence, whereas every man can judge for himself whether the Artist has learned well how to make the passions speak their language and whether the objects of Nature are well imitated. Also, as soon as Music had learned to portray and to speak, the charms of feeling soon caused those of the wand to be neglected, the Theater was purged of the jargon of Mythology, interest was substituted for *merveilleux*, the machines of the Poets and of the Carpenters were destroyed and lyric Drama took a more noble and less gigantic form. All that could move the heart was employed in it with success, there was no longer need to impress upon it with beings of reason or rather of folly, and the Gods were chased from the Stage when they learned how to represent men. This wiser and more regular form was further found to be the most suitable for illusion; it was felt that the Masterpiece of Music was to make itself forgotten, that by plunging the Spectator's soul into disorder and turmoil, it prevented the tender and pathetic Singing of a moaning Heroine from being distinguished from the true accents of distress, and that Achilles in fury could make our blood run cold with the same language that would be shocking to us from his mouth at any other time.

These observations gave rise to a second reform no less important than the first. It was felt that nothing cold and reasoned was needed for *Opera*, nothing which the Spectator could listen to tranquilly enough to reflect on the absurdity of what he was hearing, and it is above all in this that the essential distinction of lyrical Drama from simple Tragedy consists. All political deliberations, all conspiratorial plans, expositions, narrations, sententious maxims, in a word everything that speaks to reason alone was banished from the language of the heart, with witty phrases, Madrigals, and everything that was merely thoughts. The very tone of simple gallantry, which tallies poorly with the grand passions, was hardly admitted into the padding of tragic situations, in which it almost always spoils the effect; for it is never more strongly felt that the Actor sings than when he speaks a Song.

The energy of every feeling, the violence of every passion are thus the principal object of lyric Drama, and the illusion that produces charm is always destroyed as soon as the Author and the Actor leave the Spectator to himself for an instant. Such are the principles on which modern *Opera* is established. Apostolo Zeno, the Corneille of Italy, his affectionate student, who is their Racine, opened up and perfected this new course.[116] They dared to put the Heroes of History into a Theater which seemed suited only to the phantoms of Fable. Cyrus, Caesar, Cato himself have appeared on the Stage with success, and the Spectators most repulsed at hearing such men sing soon forgot that they sang, subjugated and delighted by the brilliance of a Music as full of nobility and dignity as of enthusiasm and fire. One readily supposes that feelings so different from our own should also be expressed in another tone.

These new Poems, which genius had created, and which it alone could sustain, effortlessly pushed aside the bad Musicians who possessed only the mechanics of their Art and, deprived of the fire of invention and of the gift of imitation, made *Operas* as they would have made clogs. Scarcely were the cries of Bacchants, conjurations of Sorcerers, and every Song which was merely vain noise banished from the Theater, scarcely were they tempted to substitute the accents of anger, of suffering, of menaces, of tenderness, of tears, of moaning, and all the movements of an agitated soul for this barbarous din than, forced to give feelings to Heroes and a language to the human heart, a Vinci, a Leo, a Pergolesi disdained the servile imitation of their predecessors and opened up a new course, went beyond it on the wing of Genius, and found themselves at their goal almost from their first steps.[117] But one cannot long walk in the path of good taste without rising or falling, and perfection is a point at which it is difficult to maintain oneself. After having tested and felt its forces, Music, in a position to walk alone, began to disdain the Poetry it should accompany and believed it would be better off drawing from itself the beauties it shared with its companion. It still proposed, it is true, to render the ideas and the feelings of the Poet, but it took on another language, after a fashion, and although the object was the same, the Poet and the Musician, too separated in their work, offered at the same time two similar, but distinct images which worked against one another. The mind, forced to divide itself, chose and remained fixed on one image rather than the other. Then the Musician, if he was more artful than the Poet, eclipsed him and caused him to be forgotten. The Actor, seeing that the Spectator sacrificed the words to the Music, in his turn sacrificed gesture and theatrical action to the Song and to the brilliance of the voice, which caused the Piece to be completely forgotten and changed the Spectacle into a veritable Concert. If, on the contrary, the advantage is found on the side of the Poet, the Music in its turn becomes almost indifferent, and the Spectator, deceived by the noise, is thrown off the scent to the point of attributing the merit of an excellent Poet to a bad Musician, and of believing he is admiring masterpieces of Harmony while admiring well-composed Poems.

Such are the defects which the absolute perfection of Music and its faulty application to Language can introduce into *Opera* in proportion to the concurrence of these two causes. Concerning this it should be noted that the Languages most suited to yield to the laws of the Meter and of the Melody are those in which the doubleness of which I have just been speaking is least apparent, because, since Music lends itself solely to the ideas of the Poetry whereas the latter lends itself in its turn to the inflections of the Melody, and because when the Music ceases to observe the Rhythm, the Accent, and the Harmony of the verse, the verse bends and yields to the cadence of the Meter and to the musical accent. But when the Language has neither sweetness nor flexibility, the harshness of the Poetry prevents it from submitting to the Song, the very sweetness of the Melody prevents it from lending itself to the good recitation of the verse, and a perpetual constraint felt in the forced union of these two Arts shocks the ear and destroys at the same time the appeal of the Melody and the effect of the Declamation. This defect is without remedy, and to want to apply the Music with all one's force to a Language that is not musical is to give it more severity than it would otherwise have.

By what I have said up to this point, it can be seen that there is a closer relationship between the apparatus for the eyes, or the decoration, and the Music, or the apparatus for the ears, than there appeared to be between two senses that seem to have nothing in common, and that in certain regards *Opera*, constituted as it is, is not as monstrous a whole as it appears to be. We have seen that, wanting to offer to view the interest and the movements which the Music lacked, crude tricks of machines and flights were devised, and that until they learned how to move us they contented themselves with surprising us. It is therefore quite natural that music, having become passionate and pathetic, would have sent back those poor supplements which it no longer needed in its own to the Theaters of the Fairs.[118] Then *Opera*, purged of all that miraculousness which had debased it, became a Spectacle equally touching and majestic, worthy of pleasing people of taste and of interesting sensitive hearts.

It is certain that one might be able to omit the pomp of the Spectacle to the same extent as one added to the interest of the action; for the more one is occupied with the characters the less one is occupied with the objects which surround them. But it is nonetheless necessary for the place of the Scene be suitable for the Actors who are made to speak in it, and the imitation of Nature, often more difficult and always more pleasant than that of imaginary beings, only becomes more interesting by becoming more plausible. A beautiful Palace, delightful Gardens, clever ruins please the eye still more than the fantastic image of Tartarus, of Olympus, of the Chariot of the Sun—an image all the more inferior to that which everyone can trace for himself, as with chimerical objects it costs the mind nothing to go beyond the possible and to make up models beyond any imitation. From this it follows that *merveilleux*, although out of place in Tragedy, are not so in the epic Poem, in which the imagination, always industrious and spendthrift, sees to the execution and draws from it a completely different component than the talent of the best Machinist and the munificence of the most powerful King could produce in our Theaters.

Although Music taken as an Art of imitation has an even closer relationship to Poetry than to Painting, the latter, in the manner in which it is employed in the Theater, is not, like Poetry, as subject to making a double representation of the same object with the Music, because the first renders the feelings of men and the other only the image of the place where they are found, an image which strengthens the illusion and transports the Spectator everywhere the Actor is assumed to be. But this transportation from one place to another must have rules and limits; in this regard it is permissible to take advantage of the agility of the imagination only while consulting the law of plausibility, and, although the Spectator seeks only to lend himself to the fictions from which he derives all his pleasure, his credulity must not be abused to the point of making him ashamed of it. In a word, one should consider that one is speaking to sensitive hearts without forgetting that one is speaking to reasonable people. It is not that I want to carry into the *Opera* that strict unity of place that is required in Tragedy and to which one can hardly subject oneself except at the expense of the action, so that one is accurate in some respect only in order to be absurd in a thousand others. Besides, this would be to deprive oneself of the advantage of changes of Scene, which mutually enhance one another: this would be to expose oneself, by a misguided uniformity, to ill-conceived oppositions between the Scene, which always remains, and situations that change; this the effect of the Music and that of the decoration would be mutually spoiled, like making voluptuous Instrumental pieces heard amongst rocks or gay tunes in the Palaces of Kings.

It is thus with reason that changes of Scene from Act to Act have been allowed to remain, and in order for them to be regular and admissible it is enough that one could naturally be taken from the place from which one departed to the place to which one passes in the Interval of time which passes or which the action assumes between the two Acts, so that, as the unity of time should be contained within about twenty-four hours' duration, the unity of place should be contained within about the space of a day's journey. With regard to the changes of Scene sometimes practiced in a single Act, they seem to me likewise contrary to illusion and to reason, and should be absolutely proscribed from the Theater.

    This is how the combination of Acoustics and Perspective can perfect the illusion, flatter the senses by diverse, but analogous impressions, and convey to the soul a single interest with a double pleasure. Thus, it would be a great error to think that the ordinance of the Theater has nothing in common with that of the Music, unless it is the general agreement they derive from the Poem. It is for the imagination of the two Artists to determine between themselves what that of the Poet leaves to their disposal, and to agree so well in this that the Spectator always feels the perfect accord of what he sees and what he hears. But it must be admitted that the Musician's task is the greater one. The imitation of painting is always cold, since it lacks that succession of ideas and of impressions which warms the soul by degrees, and since everything is said at the first glance. The imitative power of this Art, with so many apparent objects, is in fact limited to very weak representations. It is one of the great advantages of the Musician to be able to depict things that cannot be heard, while it is impossible for the Painter to depict those that cannot be seen, and the greatest marvel of an Art that acts only through movement is to be able to form it even into the image of rest. Sleep, the calm of the night, solitude, and silence itself enter into Music's portraits. Sometimes noise produces the effect of silence, and silence the effect of noise, as when a man falls asleep at an even and monotonous reading and wakes up the instant it stops, and it is the same for the other effects. But Art possesses more fertile and much finer substitutions than these; it knows how to arouse through one sense affections similar to those that can be aroused by another; and, as the relation is perceptible only insofar the impression is strong, painting, stripped of this power, gives to Music with difficulty the imitations that the latter draws from it. Let all of Nature be asleep, he who contemplates it sleeps not, and the Musician's art consists in substituting for the imperceptible image of the object that of the movements its presence arouses in the mind of the Spectator; it does not represent the thing directly, but awakens in our soul the same feeling experienced in seeing it.

    Thus, although the Painter has nothing to draw from the Musician's

Score, the skillful Musician will not at all leave the Painter's studio without fruit. Not only will he agitate the sea as he likes, fan the flames of a blaze, make streams flow, rain fall, and torrents swell, but he will increase the horror of a frightful desert, darken the walls of an underground dungeon, calm a tempest, make the air tranquil, the Sky clear, and spread from the Orchestra a new freshness over the groves.[119]

We have just seen how the union of the three Arts which constitute the lyric Scene form amongst themselves a very well-connected whole. The attempt has been made to introduce a fourth one therein of which it remains for me to speak.

All the movements of the body organized according to certain laws in order to affect one's sight by some action take in general the name of gestures. Gesture is divided into two types, of which the first serves as an accompaniment to speech and the second as its supplement. The first, natural to every man who speaks, is differently modified according to men, Languages, and characters. The second is the Art of speaking to the eyes without the aid of writing through movements of the body which have become conventional signs. As this gesture is more difficult, less natural for us than the use of speech, and as it renders it useless, excludes it, and even assumes its deprivation, this is what called the Art of Pantomimes. Add to this Art a choice of agreeable poses and cadenced movements, and you will have what we call Dance, which hardly merits the name of Art when it says nothing to the mind.

This established, it is a matter of knowing whether Dance, being a language and consequently capable of being an Art of imitation, can enter with the other three into the course of the lyric action, or, indeed, whether it can interrupt and suspend this action without spoiling the effect and the unity of the Piece.

Now, I do not see how this last case could even raise any question. For everyone senses that the whole interest of a coherent action depends upon the continual and redoubled impression its representation makes on us, that all objects which suspend or divide attention are so many counter-attractions which destroy that of the interest, that by breaking up the Spectacle by other Spectacles foreign to it the principal subject is divided into independent parts which have nothing in common among them other than the general relation of the material which makes them up, and, finally, that the more pleasant the inserted Spectacles are the more deformed would be the mutilation of the whole. So that, by assuming an *Opera* broken up by whatever Divertimenti one can imagine, if they allow the principal subject to be forgotten, the Spectator will find himself at the end of each Festivity as little moved as at the outset of the Piece, and to move him anew and to reanimate interest would be always to begin anew. This is why the Italians finally banished from the Entr'actes of their *Operas* those comic Intermezzi which were inserted into them—a sort of pleasant Spectacle, titillating and well-drawn from Nature, but so misplaced in the midst of a tragic action that the two Pieces mutually spoil one another and that one of the two could never be interesting except at the expense of the other.[120]

It therefore remains to see whether Dance, being unable to enter into the composition of the lyric genre as a foreign ornament, would be able to enter into it as a constituent part, and to make this Art cooperate with an action which it must not suspend. But how simultaneously to admit two languages which mutually exclude one another and to join the Art of Pantomime to the speech that renders it superfluous? The language of gesture, being the resource of mutes or of people who cannot make themselves heard, becomes ridiculous amongst those who speak. One does not at all respond to words with gamboling, nor to gesture with discourses, otherwise I do not at all see why someone who understands someone else's language does not respond to him in the same tone. Therefore suppress speech if you want to employ Dance: as soon as you introduce Pantomime into *Opera,* you should banish Poetry from it; because of all the unities, the most necessary is that of the language, and it is absurd and ridiculous to say the same thing at the time to the same person both orally and through writing.

The two reasons I have just put forward combine in all their force to banish from lyric Drama the Festivals and Divertimenti which not only suspend its action, but either say nothing or abruptly substitute for the language that is adopted another, opposed language whose contrast destroys plausibility, weakens interest, and, whether in the same continuous action or in an inserted episode, likewise offends reason. It would be much worse if these Festivals offered to the Spectator merely leaps without connection and Dances without object, a gothic and barbarous tissue in a sort of work in which everything should be painting and imitation.

It must nonetheless be admitted that Dance is so advantageously placed in the Theater that to remove it entirely would be to deprive it of one of its greatest pleasures. In addition, although one should not at all debase a tragic action by leaps and capers, the Spectacle is very pleasantly concluded when a Ballet is given after the *Opera,* as with a short piece after the Tragedy. In this new Spectacle, which does not depend at all upon the preceding one, the choice of another Language can also be made; it is another Nation which appears on the Stage. The Art of Pantomime or Dance then becoming the Language of convention, speech should in its turn be banished from it, and the Music, remaining the means of connection, is applied to the Dance in the short Piece as it was applied in the large one to the Poetry. But before employing this new Language, it must be created. To begin by giving Ballets in action without having first established the convention of the gestures is to speak a Language to people who do not have its Dictionary and who, consequently, will not at all understand it.

PREPARE [*Préparer*], *v. act. To Prepare* the Dissonance is to treat it in the Harmony in such a way that, thanks to what precedes it, it is less harsh to the ear than it would be without this precaution: according to this definition every Dissonance wants to be prepared. But when, in order *To Prepare* a Dissonance, one makes it a requirement for the Sound which forms it to have previously formed a consonance, then there is fundamentally only a single Dissonance which is *Prepared*, namely, the Seventh. Furthermore, this Preparation is not at all necessary in the Leading Chord, because then, since the Dissonance is characteristic both in the Chord and in the Mode, it is sufficiently announced, because the ear hears it, recognizes it, and is deceived neither about the Chord nor its natural progression. But when the Seventh is made to be heard on a fundamental Sound which is not essential to the Mode, it should be *Prepared* in order to prevent any equivocation, in order to prevent the ear of the listener from going astray, and, as this Seventh Chord is inverted and combined in several ways, there also arise various apparent ways of *Preparing* which, at bottom, nonetheless always come down to the same thing.

Three things must be considered in the use of Dissonances: namely, the Chord that precedes the Dissonance, the one in which it is found, and the one that follows it. The Preparation regards only the first two; as for the Third, see RESOLVING [*Sauver*].

When one wants *To Prepare* a Dissonance regularly, one must, in order to reach its Chord, choose such a progression of the Fundamental Bass that the Sound which forms the Dissonance is a prolongation of the strong Beat of a Consonance struck on the weak Beat in the preceding Chord: this is what is called *Syncopating*. (See SYNCOPATION [*Sincope*].)

Two advantages result from this Preparation; namely: 1. That there is necessarily a harmonic connection between the two Chords since the Dissonance itself forms this connection; and, 2. That this Dissonance, being merely the prolongation of a consonant Sound, becomes much less harsh to the ear than it would be on a newly struck Sound. Now, this is all that is sought in Preparation. (See CADENCE [*Cadence*], DISSONANCE* [*Dissonnance*], HARMONY* [*Harmonie*].)

It is seen by what I have just said that there is no Part specifically destined *To Prepare* the Dissonance other than the very one that makes it heard, so that if the Treble sounds the Dissonance, it is for it to syncopate; but if the Dissonance is in the Bass, the Bass must syncopate. Although there is nothing in this that isn't very simple, the Masters of Composition have tremendously muddled all this.

There are Dissonances which are never *prepared*, such as the Added Sixth; others which are rarely *prepared*, such as the Diminished Seventh.

RECITATIVE [*Récitatif*], *n. masc.* Discourse recited in a musical and harmonious tone. It is a manner of Singing which very closely approaches speech, a declamation in Music in which the Musician should imitate, as far as possible, the inflections of the voice of the Declaimer. This Singing is called *Recitative* because it is applied to Narration, to recitation, and because it is used in dramatic Dialogue. It has been said in the Dictionary of the Academy that *Recitative* should be uttered distinctly;[121] there are *Recitatives* which should be uttered, others which should be sustained.

The perfection of *Recitative* very much depends on the character of the Language. The more accented and melodious the Language is, the more natural the *Recitative* is and the more it approaches true discourse; it is merely notated accent in a truly musical Language. But in a heavy, indistinct, and accentless Language, the *Recitative* is merely song, cries, Psalmody: speech is no longer recognized in it. Thus, the best *Recitative* is that in which one sings the least. This, it seems to me, is the sole true principle drawn from the nature of the thing, on which one should base oneself in order to judge *Recitative* and to compare that of one Language to that of another.

Among the Greeks all Poetry was in *Recitative* because, since the Language was melodious, it sufficed to add to it the Cadence of the Meter and sustained Recitation in order to make this Recitation altogether Musical. From thence it happens that those who versified it called it *singing*. This usage, having passed ridiculously into other Languages, still makes the Poets say, *I sing*, when they do not produce any sort of song. The Greeks could sing while speaking; but among us it is necessary to speak or to sing —both cannot be done at the same time. It is this very distinction that makes it so that we need *Recitative*. Music dominates too much in our Arias, Poetry is almost forgotten in them. Our Lyric Dramas are too much sung always to be so. An Opera that was simply a series of Arias would be almost as tiresome as a single Aria of the same extent. The Songs must be divided and separated by speech; but this speech must be modified by the Music. The ideas should change, but the Language should remain the same. Once given, to change this Language during the course of a Piece would to be to want to speak part French, part German. The transition from discourse to Song, and reciprocally, is too disparate: it simultaneously offends both the ear and plausibility. Two interlocutors should speak or sing; they cannot do them both alternately. Now, the *Recitative* is the means of union between Song and speech: it is what separates and distinguishes the Arias; what rests the ear astonished by what preceded and disposes it to enjoy what follows; finally, it is by the aid of the *Recitative* that what is only dialogue, recital, narration in the Drama can be rendered without leaving the given Language and without displacing the eloquence of the Arias.

Recitative is not at all put into meter when singing. This Meter, which characterizes the Arias, would ruin recitative declamation. It is the Accent, whether grammatical or oratorical, that should alone direct the slowness or quickness of the Sounds, as well as their raising or their lowering. By notating the *Recitative* in some specific Meter, the Composer has in view only determining the correspondence of the Thoroughbass and of the Song, and indicating more or less how one should mark the quantity of the syllables, of cadencing and scanning the verses. The Italians never make use of anything but Meter in quadruple Time for their *Recitative*; but the French intermingle all sorts of Meters in theirs.

These latter also arm the Clef with all sorts of Transpositions, as much for the *Recitative* as for the Aria: this the Italians do not do, but they always notate the *Recitative* in natural. The quantity of modulations with which they burden it and the quickness of the Transitions, making it so that the Transposition suited to one Key is no longer suited to those into which one passes, would multiply the Accidentals on the same Notes too much and would make the *Recitative* almost impossible to follow and very difficult to notate.

In fact, it is in the *Recitative* that one should make use of the most studied harmonic Transitions and the most learned Modulations. The Arias, offering only one feeling, only one image, ultimately restricted to some unity of expression, barely allow the Composer to move away from the principal Key, and, if he wanted to modulate a great deal in such a short space, he would offer merely strangled, heaped up Phrases which would have neither connection, nor taste, nor Song. A very common defect in French Music, and even in German.

But in the *Recitative*, where expressions, feelings, ideas vary at every instant, equally varied Modulations should be employed which may represent by their contextures the successions expressed by the discourse of the Recitant. The inflections of the speaking Voice are not limited to musical Intervals; they are infinite and impossible to determine. Not being able to fix them with a certain precision, therefore, the Musician, in order follow speech, should at least imitate them as much as possible, and, in order to convey to the mind of the Listeners the idea of the Intervals and of the Accents he cannot express in Notes, he has recourse to Transitions which assume them. If, for example, he needs the Interval from the major Semitone to the minor, he will not notate it—he would not know how to; but he will give you its idea with the help of an Enharmonic transition. A progression of the Bass often suffices to change all the ideas and to give the Accent and the inflection which the Actor cannot perform to the *Recitative*.

Moreover, since it is important for the Listener to be attentive to the *Recitative* and not to the Bass, which should produce its effect without being heard, it follows from this that the Bass should remain on the same Note as much as possible; for it is at the moment it changes Note and strikes another Pitch that it makes itself heard. These moments, being rare and well-chosen, do not at all use up great effects; they distract the Spectator less frequently and leave him more easily in the conviction that he hears only speaking, even though the Harmony acts continually on his ear. Nothing marks a poor *Recitative* more than those perpetually leaping Basses which run from Eighth Note to Eighth Note after the harmonic succession, and produce another sort of very flat and very tiresome Melody underneath the Melody of the Voice. The Composer should know how to prolong and vary his Chords on the same Bass Note, and to change it only at the moment when the inflection of the *Recitative*, becoming more lively, receives greater effect by this change of Bass and prevents the Listener from noticing it.

The *Recitative* should be used only to tie the contexture of the Drama, to separate and set off the Arias, to prevent the stupor which the continuation of the great noise would produce; but, as eloquent as the Dialogue may be, as energetic and learned as the *Recitative* may be, it should last only as long as is necessary for its object, because it is not at all through the *Recitative* that the Music's charm acts, and because it was however only in order to display this charm that the Opera was instituted. Now, it is in this that the error of the Italians lies, they who, by the extreme length of their scenes, make poor use of the *Recitative*. However beautiful it may be in itself, it grows tiresome because it lasts too long and because it is not in order to hear the *Recitative* that one goes to the Opera. Demosthenes speaking all day would grow tiresome in the end, but it does not thereby follow that Demosthenes was a tiresome Orator. Those who say that the Italians themselves find their *Recitative* poor speak quite gratuitously since, on the contrary, there is no other part of Music of which the Connoisseurs make so much and concerning which they are also difficult to please. It even suffices to excel in this part alone, being mediocre in all the others, to raise oneself to the rank of the most illustrious Artists, and the celebrated *Porpora*[122] was immortalized solely on this account.

I add that although the same energy of expression is not commonly sought in the *Recitative* as in the Arias, it is nonetheless sometimes found there, and when it is found there it produces a greater effect than in the Arias themselves. There are few good Operas in which some principal piece of *Recitative* arouses the admiration of Connoisseurs and their interest in the whole Spectacle; the effect of these pieces sufficiently shows that the defect imputed to the genre is solely in the manner of treating it.

M. Tartini relates having heard in 1714 at the Opera at Ancona a piece of *Recitative* of a single line, and without any Accompaniment other than the Bass, produce a prodigious effect, not only on the Professors of the Art, but on all the Spectators. "It was," he says, "at the beginning of the third Act. At each presentation a profound silence in the whole Theater announced the approach of this astounding piece. Faces were seen to grow pale; one felt oneself trembling, and everyone looked at one another with a sort of fright: for there weren't either tears or plaints; it was a certain feeling of bitter and contemptuous severity which troubled the soul, gripped the heart, and chilled the blood." The original passage must be transcribed; these effects are so little known in our Theaters that our Language is little practiced in expressing them.

L'anno quatordecimo del secolo presente nel Dramma che si rapresentava in Ancona, v'era su'l principio dell' Atto terzo una riga di Recitativo non accompagnato da altri stromenti che dal Basso; per cui, tanto in noi professori, quanto negli ascoltanti, si destava una tal e tanta commozione di animo, che tutti si guardavano in faccia l'un l'altro, per la evidente mutazione di colore che si faceva la ciascheduno di noi. L'effetto non era di pianto (mi ricordo benissimo che le parole erano di sdegno) ma di un certo rigore e freddo nel sangue, che di fatto turbava l'animo. Tredeci volte si recitò il Dramma, e sempre seguì l'effetto stesso universalmente; di che era segno palpabile il sommo previo silenzio, con cui l'Uditorio tutto si apparecchiava à goderne l'effetto.[123]

SOUND [*Son*], *n. masc.* When the agitation communicated to the air by the collision of one body struck by another reaches the auditory organ, it produces a sensation there called *Noise*. (See NOISE [*Bruit*].) But there is a resonant and discernible Noise called *Sound*. Research concerning absolute *Sound* belongs to the Physicist. The Musician examines only relative *Sound*; he examines it only by its perceptible modifications; and it is only according to this last idea that we are viewing it in this Article.

There are three principal objects to consider in *Sound*: the Tone, the strength, and the timbre. Under each of these relationships, *Sound* is considered as modifiable: 1st, from low to high; 2nd, from loud to soft; 3rd, from sharp to mild, or from muted to striking, and reciprocally.

I first assume that, whatever the nature of *Sound* might be, its vehicle is nothing other than the air itself; first, because the air is the only intermediary body whose existence one is perfectly assured of between the sounding body and the auditory organ; because beings must not be multiplied unnecessarily; because the air suffices to explain the formation of *Sound*; and, furthermore, because experimentation teaches us that a sounding body does not render *Sound* in a place totally deprived of air. If one wants to imagine another fluid, one can easily apply to it everything that I say about air in this Article.

The resonance of *Sound*, or, to speak more precisely, its permanence and its prolongation, can arise only from the duration of the agitation of the air. As long as this agitation lasts, the air struck comes constantly to strike the auditory organ and thus prolongs the sensation of the *Sound*. But there is no simpler way at all to conceive of this duration than to assume vibrations in the air which succeed one another, and which thus renew the impression at each instant. Furthermore, this agitation of the air, of whatever type it may be, can be produced only by a similar agitation in the parts of the sounding body; now, it is a certain fact that the parts of the sounding body experience such vibrations. If one touches the body of a Cello while a *Sound* is being drawn from it, one feels it vibrate under one's hand and one sees quite perceptibly the vibrations of the String last until the *Sound* is extinguished. It is likewise with a bell that has been sounded by striking its clapper; one feels it, one even sees it vibrate, and one sees grains of sand thrown on its surface jump about. If the String is slackened, or if the Bell is cracked, the more vibration, the more *Sound*. If, then, this bell or this String can communicate to the air only the motions it itself has, it cannot be doubted that the *Sound* produced by the vibrations of the sounding body is propagated by vibrations similar to those this body communicates to the air.

All this assumed, let us first examine what constitutes the relationship of *Sounds* from low to high.

I. Theon of Smyrna says that Lasus of Hermione, as well as the Pythagorean Hipassus of Metapontum, made use of two similar vases which resonated in Unison in order to calculate the ratio of Consonances; that, leaving one of the two empty, and filling the other to a quarter full, striking them both caused the Consonance of the Fourth to be heard; that, further filling the second to a third full, then to half full, striking them both produced the Consonance of the Fifth, then of the Octave.[124]

Pythagoras, according to Nicomachus' and Censorin's report,[125] took another route for calculating the same ratios. He suspended different weights from the same sounding Strings, they say, and determined the ratios of the various *Sounds* by those he found between the hanging weights; but Pythagoras' calculations are too exact to have been made in this way, since everyone today knows, from Vincenzo Galilei's experiments,[126] that *Sounds* are to one another not as the hanging weights, but by the double inverse ratio of these same weights.

Finally, the Monocord was invented, called by the Ancients a *Canon harmonicus*, because it gave the ordering of the harmonic divisions. Its principle must be explained.

Two Strings of the same metal, equal and equally hung, form a Unison that is perfect in every sense: if the lengths are unequal, the shorter one will give a higher *Sound*, and therefore have more vibrations in a given time; from which it is concluded that the difference of *Sounds* from low to high proceeds only from that of the vibrations made in a certain space of time by the Strings or sounding bodies which cause them to be heard. Thus, the ratios of the *Sounds* are expressed by the number of vibrations they produce.

It is further known, by experiments no less certain, that, everything else being equal, the vibrations of Strings are always reciprocal to their lengths. Thus, a String double the length of another will have only half the number of vibrations in the same time as this one, and the ratio of the *Sounds* they cause to be heard is called an *Octave*. If the Strings are as 3 and 2, the vibrations will be as 2 and 3, and the ratio of the *Sounds* will be called a *Fifth*; etc. (See INTERVAL* [*Intervalle*].)

It is seen by this that with moveable Bridges it is easy to form on a single string divisions which produce *Sounds* in all the possible ratios, whether between themselves or with the entire String. This is the Monocord of which I was just speaking. (See MONOCORD [*Monocorde*].)

Sounds can be made high or low by other means. Two Strings of equal lengths do not always form a Unison; for if one is thicker or less taut than the other, it will make fewer vibrations in an equal time, and consequently will produce a lower *Sound*. (See STRING [*Corde*].)

By means of these principles it is easy to explain the construction of Stringed Instruments, such as the Harpsichord, the Dulcimer, and the playing of Violins and Basses, which, by different shortenings of the Strings under the fingers or mobile bridges, produce the diversity of *Sounds* which are drawn from these Instruments. One must reason in the same way for wind Instruments: the longer ones form lower *Sounds*, if the wind is the equal. The holes, as on Flutes and Oboes, serve to shorten them in order to produce higher *Sounds*. By producing more wind one makes them go to the octave, and the *Sounds* become still higher. The column of air then forms a sounding body, and the various Tones of the Trumpet and of the Hunting Horn have the same principles as the harmonic *Sounds* of the Cello and of the Violin, etc. (See SOUNDS, HARMONIC [*Sons, Harmonique*].)

If one of the large Strings of a Violin or of a Cello is made to resonate with a certain amount of force by passing the bow a bit closer to the bridge than ordinarily, as little trained and attentive one's ear may be, aside from the *Sound* of the entire String, one will distinctly hear at least that of its Octave, that of the Octave of its Fifth, and that of the double-Octave of its Third: one will likewise see vibrate and will hear resonate all the Strings raised to the Unison of these *Sounds*. These accessory *Sounds* always accompany any principal *Sound* whatsoever, but when this principal *Sound* is high, the others are less perceptible. These are called the Harmonics of the principal *Sound*: it is by these, according to M. Rameau,[127] that every *Sound* is discernible, and it is in them that he and M. Tartini have sought the principle of all Harmony, but by completely opposite routes. (See HARMONY* [*Harmonie*], SYSTEM [*Système*].)

One difficulty which remains to be explained in the theory of *Sound* is that of knowing how two or more *Sounds* can be made to be heard at the same time. For example, when one hears the two *Sounds* of the Fifth, of which the first makes two vibrations while the other makes three of them, it is not very easily understood how the same mass of air can simultaneously furnish these different numbers of vibrations, which are distinct from one another, and still less so when more than two *Sounds* are produced together and when they are all dissonant with one another. Mengoli and others deal with it by comparisons.[128] It is, they say, as with two rocks one throws into the water at the same time, and whose different circles cross one another without becoming confounded. M. de Mairan gives a more philosophic explanation.[129] According to him, the air is divided into particles of various sizes, each of which is capable of one particular Tone and is not susceptible of any other, so that to each *Sound* formed, the particles of air analogous to it are alone struck, they and their Harmonics, while all the others remain tranquil until they are moved in their turn by the *Sounds* that correspond to them; so that one hears two *Sounds* at the same time as one sees two colors at the same time, because, being produced by different parts, they affect the organ at different points.

This system is ingenious, but the imagination lends itself with difficulty to the infinity of particles of air different in size and in motion which must be spread through each point of space in order always to be ready, as needed, to everywhere render the infinity of all possible *Sounds*. When they have once reached the tympanum of the ear, it is still less conceivable how, several of them striking it together, they can produce in it a vibration capable of transmitting to the brain the sensation of each in particular. It seems that the difficulty has been put further off rather than resolved. The example of light, whose rays cross one another at a single point without confounding the objects, is alleged in vain: for, aside from the fact that one difficulty is not resolved by another, the parity is not exact, since the object is seen without exciting in the air a movement similar to that which the sounding body must excite in order to be heard. Mengoli seemed to want to anticipate this objection by saying that the masses of the air charged, so to speak, with different *Sounds* strike the tympanum only successively, alternately, and each in its turn, without considering too carefully what would occupy those which are obliged to wait for the first ones to have achieved their task, or without explaining how the ear, struck with so many successive blows, can distinguish those which belong to each *Sound*.

With regard to the Harmonics which accompany any *Sound* whatsoever, they offer less a new difficulty than a new case of the preceding one; for as soon as one should explain how several *Sounds* can be heard at the same time, one will easily explain the phenomenon of Harmonics. Indeed, let us assume a *Sound* putting into motion the particles of air susceptible of the same *Sound*, and the particles susceptible of the higher *Sounds* all the way to infinity; of these various particles, there will be some, whose vibrations beginning and ending precisely with those of the sounding body, will be constantly aided and renewed by it; these particles will be those which will produce the unison. Then comes the Octave, whose two vibrations are in accord with one of the principal *Sound*'s, are aided and reinforced by it only every other one; consequently the octave will be perceptible, but less than the Unison. Then comes the Twelfth or the Octave of the Fifth, which makes precisely three vibrations while the fundamental *Sound* makes one of them; thus, receiving a new blow only at every third vibration, the Twelfth will be less perceptible than the Octave, which receives this new blow as soon as the second one. By following this same gradation, one finds the concurrence of the vibrations later, the blows less often renewed, and consequently the Harmonics always less perceptible, until the ratios are made complex to the point that the idea of the too rare concurrence is effaced, and the vibrations, having the time to be extinguished before being renewed, the Harmonic is no longer heard at all. Finally, when the ratio ceases to be rational, the vibrations never concur; those of the highest *Sounds*, always contrary, are soon stifled by those of the String, and this high *Sound* is absolutely dissonant and null. Such is the reason why the first Harmonics are heard and why all the other *Sounds* are not heard. But this is already too much concerning the first quality of *Sound*; let us pass on to the other two.

II. The strength of the *Sound* depends upon that of the vibrations of the sounding body: the larger and stronger the vibrations are, the stronger and more vigorous the *Sound* is and the better it is heard from afar. When the String is taut enough, and when the voice or the Instrument is not forced too much, the vibrations always remain isochronic, and, consequently, the Tone remains the same, whether one increases or weakens the *Sound*; but by bowing too strongly, by slackening the String too much, by blowing out or shouting too much, one can make the vibrations lose the isochronism necessary for the identity of the Tone; and this is one of the reasons why in French Music, in which the first merit is to shout well, one is more subject to singing falsely than in Italian, where the Voice is moderated with more mildness.

The speed of the *Sound*, which would seem to depend upon its strength, does not at all depend upon it. This speed is always equal and constant if it is not accelerated or retarded by the wind: that is, the *Sound*, loud or soft, always extends uniformly, and it always covers twice the distance in two seconds that it did in one. According to Halley's and Flamstead's report, in England *Sound* covers 1070 French feet in one second, and 174 toise in Peru, according to M. de La Condamine. Father Mersenne and Gassendi have maintained that favorable or contrary wind would neither accelerate nor retard the *Sound*; this has passed for an error ever since the experiments Derham and the Academy of Sciences have made concerning this subject.[130]

Without slowing its progress, *Sound* grows weaker as it extends, and this weakening—if the propagation is free, if it is not impeded by any obstacle or slowed by the wind—usually proceeds at the ratio of the square of the distances.

III. As for the further difference found between *Sounds* by the quality of their Timbre, it is obvious that it depends neither upon the degree of elevation, nor even upon that of loudness. An Oboe can well be put into Unison with a Flute, it can well soften its *Sound* to the same degree; the *Sound* of the Flute will always have an indefinable mellowness and sweetness; that of the Oboe will have an indefinable coarseness and sharpness which will prevent the ear from confusing them, without speaking of the variety of the Timbre of Voices (See VOICE* [*Voix*]). There is no Instrument that does not have its own particular one, which is not at all that of another, and the Organ alone has twenty stops all of a different Timbre. Nevertheless, no one I know of has examined *Sound* in this aspect, which, just as the others, is perhaps found to have its difficulties: for the quality of the Timbre can depend upon neither the number of vibrations, which produces the degree from low to high, nor the size or the strength of these same vibrations, which produces the degree of loud and soft. One will therefore have to find a third cause in the sounding body different from these two in order to explain this third quality of *Sound* and its differences—which, perhaps, is not too easy to do.

The three principal qualities of which I have just been speaking all enter into the object of Music, although in different degrees, which is *Sound* in general.

In actuality, the Composer does not only consider whether the *Sounds* he employs should be treble or bass, low or high, but whether they should be loud or soft, sharp or mild, muted or striking, and he distributes them to the different Instruments, to the different Voices, in Recitation or in Choruses, to the extremities or in the *Middle* of the Instruments or of the Voices, with *Pianos* or *Fortes*, according to the conventions for all these.

But it is true that it is uniquely in the comparison of *Sounds* from low to high that the whole Harmonic science consists: so that, as the number of *Sounds* is infinite, one can say in the same sense that this science is infinite in its object. The limits of the extent of *Sounds* from low to high is not known at all, and as small as the Interval between two *Sounds* may be, it will always be conceived as divisible by a third *Sound*; but nature and art have limited this infinity in the practice of Music. One soon finds the limits of practicable *Sounds* in the Instruments, on the low as well as the high end. Elongate or shorten a sounding String to a certain point and it will no longer have a *Sound*. Nor can one increase or diminish at will either the capacity of a Flute or of an Organ pipe, or its length; there are limits past which neither one will resonate any longer. The blowing also has its measure and its laws. Too weak, it no longer produces a *Sound*; too strong, it produces only a piercing shout that is impossible to discern. Finally, it is confirmed by a thousand experiments that every perceptible *Sound* is contained in a certain latitude, past which—either too low or too high—it is no longer discernible or becomes indiscernible to the ear. M. Euler has even fixed its limits after a fashion, and according to his observations, reported by M. Diderot in his "Principles of Acoustics," every perceptible *Sound* is contained between the numbers 30 and 7552: that is, according to this great Geometer, the lowest *Sound* discernible to our ear makes thirty vibrations per second, and the highest 7552 vibrations in the same time—an Interval which contains about eight Octaves.[131]

From another point of view, it is seen by the harmonic generation of *Sounds* that in their potential infinity there is only a very small number of them that can be accepted into the harmonic system. For all those which do not form Consonances with fundamental *Sounds*, or which do not arise mediately or immediately from the differences of these Consonances, should be proscribed from the system. This is why, as perfect as our own is assumed to be today, it is nonetheless limited to but twelve *Sounds* in the range of one Octave, all the other Octaves containing merely replicas of these twelve. If one wants to count all these replicas for as many different *Sounds*, multiplying them by the number of Octaves to which the range of perceptible *Sounds* is limited, one will find ninety-six in all for the largest number of *Sounds* practicable in our Music on a single fundamental *Sound*.

The number of *Sounds* practicable in ancient Music could not be estimated with the same precision. For the Greeks formed, so to speak, as many systems of Music as they had different ways of tuning their Tetrachords. It appears from reading their Musical treatises that the number of these ways was large and perhaps indeterminate. Now, each particular Chord changed the *Sounds* of half the system, that is, the two mobile Pitches of each Tetrachord. Thus, one sees quite clearly what *Sounds* they had in a single manner of Tuning; but one can not calculate precisely how much in all this number multiplied the changes of Genre and of Mode which introduced new *Sounds*.

With regard to their Tetrachords, they divided *Sounds* into two general classes: namely, stable and fixed *Sounds* whose Accord never changed, and mobile *Sounds* whose Accord changed with the type of Genre. The first were eight in all, namely, the two extremes of each Tetrachord and the Proslambanomenos String; the second were also at the very least eight in number, sometimes nine or ten, since the two neighboring *Sounds* were sometimes merged into one and sometimes separated.

In tight Genres, they further divided stable *Sounds* into two types, the first of which contained three *Sounds* called *Apycnoi*, or *non-tight*, since they formed neither Semitones nor small Intervals on the bass; the three *Apycnoi Sounds* were the Proslambanomenos, the Nete Synemenon, and the Nete Hyperbolaeon. The other type carried the name of *Barypycnoi Sounds*, or *sub-tight*, since they formed the low end of the small Intervals; *Barypycnoi Sounds* were five in number: namely, the Hypate Hypaton, the Hypate Mese, the Mese, the Parameson, and the Nete Diezeugmenon.

Mobile *Sounds* were similarly subdivided into *Mesopycnoi Sounds*, or middling in tightness, which were also five in number, namely, the second in ascending from each Tetrachord; and by five other *Sounds* called *Oxpycnoi*, or extremely-high, which were the third in ascending from each Tetrachord. (See TETRACHORD [*Tétracorde*].)

With regard to the twelve *Sounds* of the modern system, their Accord never changes and they are all immobile. Brossard claims[132] that they are all mobile, based on the fact that they can be altered by a Sharp or by a Flat; but it is one thing to change Pitch and another thing to change the Tuning of a String.

SUBJECT [*Sujet*], *n. masc.* A term of composition: it is the principal part of the Design, the idea which serves as the foundation for the others. (See DESIGN [*Dessein*].) All the other parts require only art and labor; this one alone depends upon genius, and it is in it that invention consists. The principal *Subject* in Music produce Rondos, Imitations, Fugues, etc. See these words. A sterile and cold Composer, after having with difficulty found some meager *Subject*, merely makes it return, and parades it from Modulation to Modulation; but the Artist who has warmth and imagination knows, without letting his *Subject* be forgotten, to give it a new aspect[133] every time he represents it.

TEMPERAMENT [*Tempérament*], An operation by which, through a slight alteration in the Intervals, making the difference between two neighboring Sounds vanish, they are combined into one, which, without shocking the ear, forms Intervals with respect to the others. By this operation, the Scale is simplified by diminishing the number of Sounds necessary. Without *Temperament*, instead of the twelve Sounds alone which the Octave contains, more than sixteen of them would be necessary in order to modulate in all the Keys.

On the Organ, on the Harpsichord, on every other Keyboard Instrument, there is not, and one can scarcely have, any Interval in perfect Accord other than the Octave alone. The reason for this is that since three Major Thirds or four Minor Thirds come to make up a just Octave, the latter surpass it and the former do not reach it. For $5/4 \times 5/4 \times 5/4 = 125/64 < 128/64 = 2/1$; and $6/5 \times 6/5 \times 6/5 \times 6/5 = 1296/625 < 1296/628 = 2/1$. Thus, one is constrained to widen the Major Thirds and to shorten the minor ones so that the Octaves and all the other Intervals correspond exactly, and so that the same keys on the keyboard may be employed under their various relationships. In a moment I shall say how this is done.

This necessity did not make itself felt all of a sudden; it was recognized only while perfecting the musical system. Pythagoras, who was the first to discover the ratios of harmonic Intervals, claimed that these ratios were observed in all mathematical strictness, without according anything to the tolerance of the ear. This severity might have been good for his time, when the whole range of the system was still limited to a very small number of Strings.[134] But as the majority of the Ancients' Instruments were made up of Strings that were played unaltered, and which consequently had one

String for each Sound, they saw that, in proportion as the system expanded, by multiplying the Strings too much, Pythagoras' rule prevented the appropriate uses from being drawn from them.

Aristoxenus, Aristotle's disciple, seeing how much the precision of calculations harmed the progress of Music and the ease of performance, suddenly took the opposite extreme; almost entirely abandoning calculation, he gave himself over to the judgment of the ear alone, and rejected as useless everything Pythagoras had established.

This formed two sects in Music that divided the Greeks for a long time, the one of the Aristoxenians, who were practicing Musicians, the other of the Pythagoreans, who were Philosophers. (See ARISTOXENIANS [*Aristoxénniens*] and PYTHAGOREANS [*Pythagoriciens*].)

Later on, Ptolemy and Didymus,[135] finding with reason that Pythagoras and Aristoxenus had gone into two equally vicious extremes, and simultaneously consulting the senses and reason, each worked in his own way to reform the ancient diatonic system. But as they did not depart from the established principles for the division of the Tetrachord, and as they finally recognized the difference between the major *Tonos* and the minor *Tonos*, they did not dare touch the latter in order to apportion it, like the other, into two reputedly equal Parts by a chromatic Pitch; the system remained still long afterward in a state of imperfection which did not allow the true principle of *Temperament* to be perceived.

Finally came Guido of Arezzo,[136] who in a certain way recast Music and who, it is said, invented the Clavier. Now, it is certain that this Instrument, or the Organ, could have existed only at the same time that *temperament* was discovered, without which it is impossible to tune them, and it is at least impossible for the first invention to have long preceded the second; this is almost everything we know about it.

But although the necessity of *Temperament* was long known, the same is not the case for the best rule to follow in order to determine it. The last century, which was the century of discoveries of every kind, is the first which gave us very clear knowledge concerning this matter. Father Mersenne and M. Loulié made calculations; M. Sauveur found the divisions that furnish every possible *Temperament*; finally, M. Rameau, after all the others, believed he was the first to develop the genuine theory of *Temperament*, and himself claimed, by this theory, to establish as new a very ancient practice of which I shall speak in a moment.[137]

I have said that in order to temper the Sounds of the Harpsichord it was a matter of widening the Major Thirds and of shortening the minor ones, and of distributing these alterations in such a way as to make them as little perceptible as possible. For this, it is necessary to allocate the Tuning of the Instrument, and this Tuning is ordinarily done by means of Fifths; it is therefore by its effect on these Fifths that we have to consider *Temperament*.

If four consecutive Fifths, such as *do sol re la mi*, are tuned quite justly, one will find that this fourth Fifth *mi* will make a Major Third with the *do* from which it has started that is discordant and much too wide; and in fact this *mi*, produced as the Fifth of *la*, is not the same Sound which the Major Third of *do* should make. Here is the proof.

The ratio of the Fifth is 2/3 or 1/3, due to the Octaves 1 and 2 taken indifferently for one another. Thus, the series of Fifths forming a triple progression, will give *do* 1, *sol* 3, *re* 9, *la* 27, *mi* 81.

Let us at present consider this *mi* as the Major Third of *do*; its ratio is 4/5 or 1/5, 4 being merely the double Octave of 1. If from Octave to Octave we draw near this *mi* of the preceding one, we will find *mi* 5, *mi* 10, *mi* 20, *mi* 40, and *mi* 80. Thus, the Fifth of *la* being *mi* 81, and the Major Third of *do* being *mi* 80, these two *mis* are not the same, and their ratio is 80/81, which makes precisely the major Comma.

If we pursue the progression of the Fifths to the twelfth power, which arrives at *si*-Sharp, we will find that this *si* exceeds the *do* with which it should make a unison, and which is with it in the ratio of 531441 to 524288, a ratio that gives Pythagoras' Comma. So that, by the preceding calculation, the *si*-Sharp should exceed the *do* by three major Commas, and by this it exceeds it only by Pythagoras' Comma.

But this same Sound *mi*, which makes the Fifth of *la*, must also serve to make the Major Third of *do*; the same *si*-Sharp, which forms the twelfth Fifth of this same *do*, must also make its Octave, and, finally, these different Chords must concur in constituting the general system without multiplying the Pitches. This is what is done by means of *Temperament*.

For this: 1st. One begins by the *do* in the middle of the Keyboard, and one shortens the first four Fifths in ascending until the fourth *mi* makes the Major Third quite justly with the first Sound *do*; this is what is called the first test. 2nd. By continuing to tune by Fifths, as soon as one has arrived at the Sharps, one widens the Fifths a little, although the Thirds suffer for it, and when one has arrived at *sol*-Sharp, one stops. This *sol*-Sharp should make a just or at least bearable Major Third with the *mi*; this is the second test. 3rd. One takes up the *do* again and tunes the Fifths on the low end; namely, *fa*, *si*-Flat, etc., at first weakly, then, widening them by Degrees, that is, shortening the Sounds until one reaches *re*-Flat, which, taken as *do*-Sharp, should be found to be in tune with and make a Fifth with the *sol*-Sharp, at which one had formerly stopped; this is the third test. The last Fifths will be found to be a little too wide, as with the Major

Thirds; this is what makes the major Keys of *si*-Flat and of *mi*-Flat somber and even a bit harsh. But this harshness will be bearable if the Score is well composed, and, moreover, these Thirds, by their position, are less used than the first ones, and should be so only by choice.

Organists and Organ Builders regard this *Temperament* as the most perfect that may be used. In actuality, by this method the natural Keys enjoy all the purity of the Harmony, and the transposed Keys, which form less frequent modulations, offer great resources to the Musician when he needs more marked expressions: for it is good to observe, says M. Rameau,[138] that we receive different impressions of the Intervals in proportion to their different alterations. For example, the Major Third, which naturally arouses joy in us, impresses upon us even ideas of fury when it is too strong; and the Minor Third, which leads us to tenderness and to softness, saddens us when it is too weak.

Skillful Musicians, continues this same Author, know how to profit opportunely from these different effects of the Intervals, and exploit, by the expression they draw from them, the alteration that might be condemned in them.

But, in his *Harmonic Generation*, this same M. Rameau takes an entirely different tone.[139] He reproaches himself for his condescension toward present usage, and destroying everything he had formerly established, he gives a formula for eleven proportional means between the two limits of the Octave, by which formula he wants the entire series of the chromatic system to be regulated; so that as this system results in twelve perfectly equal Semitones, it is necessary for all the like Intervals which are formed from them also to be perfectly equal to one another.

For practice, he says, take whatever key of the Keyboard you like; first tune to it the just Fifth, then diminish it a tiny bit: proceed in this way from one Fifth to another, always by ascending, that is from low to high, until the last one whose high Sound is the low part of the first one; you can be certain that the Keyboard will be in good accord.

This method M. Rameau proposes to us today was already proposed and abandoned by the famous Couperin. It is also found throughout Father Mersenne, who made its Author a certain Gallé, and who even took the trouble to calculate the eleven proportional means for which M. Rameau gives us the algebraic formula.[140]

In spite of the scientific air of this formula, it does not appear that the practice which results from it has until now been sampled by Musicians or Organ Builders. The first cannot resolve to deprive themselves of the energetic variety they find in the various affections of the Tones the established *Temperament* causes. M. Rameau tells them in vain that they are mistaken, that the variety is found in the intermixings of Modes or in the various Degrees of the Tonics, and not at all in the alteration of the Intervals; the Musician answers that the one does not exclude the other, that he confines himself to convincing by means of an assertion, and that the various affections of the Tones are not at all proportional to the Degrees of their finales. For, they say, although there is only a Semitone in distance between the finale of *re* and that of *mi*-Flat, as between the finale of *la* and of *si*-Flat, nevertheless, the same Music will affect us quite differently in A *la mi re* than in B *fa*, and in D *sol re* than in E *la fa*; and the attentive ear of the Musician will never be mistaken, even when the general Key is raised or lowered by a Semitone and more—an obvious proof that the variety come from elsewhere than the simple different elevation of the Tonic.

With regard to the Organ Builders, they find that a Keyboard tuned in this manner is not at all as well tuned as M. Rameau maintains. The Major Thirds appear to them harsh and shocking, and when they are told that they only have to alter the Thirds as they had previously done to the Fifths, they reply that they do not understand how the Organ will be able to suppress the beats[141] that are heard by this manner of tuning, or how the ear will cease to be offended by them. Since by the nature of Consonances the Fifth can be more altered than the Third without shocking the ear and without producing beats, is it not proper to throw the alteration toward the side where it is least shocking, and preferably to leave the Intervals that cannot be altered without rendering them discordant more just?

Father Mersenne maintained[142] that it was said in his time that the first people who utilized Semitones on the Keyboard, which he calls *feintes*, first tuned all the Fifths in just about the same way as the equal Tuning proposed by M. Rameau; but since their ear could not bear the discord of the Major Thirds being necessarily strong, they tempered the Chord by weakening the first Fifths in order to lower the Major Thirds. It therefore appears that to accustom oneself to this manner of Tuning is not, for a trained and sensitive ear, a habit that is easy to acquire.

Besides, I cannot prevent myself from recalling here what I said at the word CONSONANCE* [*Consonnance*] about the reason for the pleasure that Consonances produce for the ear derived from the simplicity of the ratios. The ratio of a tempered Fifth according to M. Rameau's method is this: $\frac{\sqrt[3]{80}^4 \times \sqrt[4]{81}}{120}$. This ratio nonetheless pleases the ear. I ask: Is this by its simplicity?

TRIO [*Trio*]. In Italian *Terzetto*. Music in three principal or reciting Parts. This type of Composition passes for the most excellent and should also be the most regular of all. Aside from the general rules of Counterpoint, there are more rigorous ones for the *Trio*, the perfect observation of which tends to produce the most pleasant of all Harmonies. These rules all follow from this principle, that since the Perfect Chord is made up of three different Sounds, one must distribute these three Sounds in each Chord, as much as possible, to the three Parts of the *Trio* in order to fill out the Harmony. With regard to Dissonances, as they should never be doubled and as their Chord is made up of more than three Sounds, it is a still greater need to diversify them, and to properly choose, apart from the Dissonance, the Sounds which should preferably accompany it.

From whence these various rules: of not passing through any Chord without making its Third or Sixth heard; consequently, of avoiding striking the Fifth and the Octave simultaneously, or the Fourth and the Fifth; of using the Octave only with great precaution and of never sounding two in a row, even among different Parts; of avoiding the Fourth as much as is possible: for all the Parts of a *Trio*, taken two by two, should form perfect Duos. From whence, in a word, all those little detailed rules which are observed even without having been learned when their Principle is known well.

As all these rules are incompatible with the unity of Melody, and as a regular and harmonious *Trio* is never heard to have a determined and perceptible Song in performance, it follows that the *Trio* strictly speaking is a poor genre of Music. Furthermore, these rules, so severe, have been long abolished in Italy, where a Music that did not sing was never recognized as good, however harmonious it may otherwise be and whatever trouble it may have cost to compose.

It should be recalled here what I have said at the word Duo [*Duo*]. These terms *Duo* and *Trio* are understood only of the principal and obligatory Parts, and include neither Accompaniments nor filling out. In this way, a Music in four or five Parts can nevertheless be merely a *Trio*.

The French, who very much like to multiply the Parts, seeing that they discover Chords more easily than Songs, not content with the difficulties of the ordinary *Trio*, have also devised what they call a *Double Trio*, in which the Parts are doubled and all obligatory. They have a *Double Trio* by Mr. Duché[143] which passes for a Masterpiece of Harmony.

UNITY OF MELODY [*Unité de mélodie*]. All the fine Arts have some *Unity* of object, a source of pleasure they give to the mind: for the attention divided settles nowhere, and when two objects occupy us, it is a proof that neither of them satisfies us. In Music, there is a successive *Unity* that relates to the subject, and by which all the parts, when well linked, compose a single whole whose ensemble and all of whose relationships are perceived.

But there is another *Unity* of object, finer, more simultaneous, and from which—without it being thought of—the Music's energy and the strength of its expressions arises.

When I hear our Psalms in four Parts sung, I always begin by being gripped, delighted by that full and nervous Harmony; and the first pitches, when they are intoned quite justly, move me to the point of trembling. But hardly have I heard what follows for a few minutes than my attention relaxes, the noise gradually dazes me. Soon it wearies me and I am finally bored by hearing nothing but Chords.

This effect does not occur at all when I hear good modern Music, even though its Harmony may be less vigorous; and I recall that at the Opera in Venice, far from a beautiful Aria ever boring me, as long as it lasted I gave it an always renewed attention and heard it with more interest at the end than at the beginning.

This difference comes from that of the character of the two Musics, of which the first is merely a succession of Chords and the second is a succession of Song. Now, the pleasure of Harmony is merely a pleasure of pure sensation, and the enjoyment of the senses is always short—satiety and boredom follow close behind; but the pleasure of Melody and of Song is a pleasure of interest and of feeling which speaks to the heart, and which the Artist can always sustain and renew by dint of genius.

Music should therefore necessarily sing in order to touch, to please, to sustain interest and attention. But how in our Systems of Chords and Harmony will Music set about singing? If each Part has its own Song, all these Songs, heard at the same time, will mutually destroy one another and will no longer produce Singing; if all the parts produce the same Song, there will no longer be Harmony, and the Concert will be entirely in Unison.

The way in which a Musical instinct, a certain feeling deaf to genius, has removed this difficulty without seeing it, and has even derived an advantage from it, is quite remarkable. The Harmony, which should have stifled the Melody, animates it, strengthens it, determines it; the various Parts, without being confounded, work toward the same effect, and, even though each of them seems to have its own Song, from all these Parts brought together one hears emitted only one and the same Song. This is what I call *Unity of Melody*.

This is how Harmony itself works toward this *Unity*, far from harming it. It is our Modes that characterize our Songs, and our Modes are founded on our Harmony. Every time, then, that the Harmony strengthens or determines the feeling of the Mode and of the Modulation, it adds to the Song's expressiveness, provided that it does not cover it up.

Relative to the *Unity of Melody*, the Art of the Composer is therefore: 1st. When the Mode is not sufficiently determined by the Song, to determine it better by means of the Harmony. 2nd. To choose and work its Chords so that the most salient Sound is always that which sings, and so that the one that makes it proceed best might be in the Bass. 3rd. To add to the energy of each transition by harsh Chords if the expression is harsh, and sweet ones if the expression is sweet. 4th. To pay attention in the phrasing of the Accompaniment to the *Forte-piano*[144] of the Melody. 5th. Finally, to compose in such a way that the Song of the other Parts, far from contradicting that of the principal Part, sustains it, seconds it, and gives to it a more lively accent.

In order to prove that the energy of Music comes wholly from the Harmony, M. Rameau gives the example of a single Interval, which he calls a single Song, that takes on entirely different characters according to the various ways of accompanying it. M. Rameau has not seen that he proved wholly the contrary of what he wanted to prove: for in all the examples he gives, the Accompaniment of the Bass serves merely to determine the Song. A simple Interval is not at all a Song, it becomes a Song only when it has its place assigned in the Mode; and the Bass, by determining the Mode and the place this Interval has in the Mode, thereby determines this Interval to be this or that Song; so that, if the place it has in its Modulation is well determined by what precedes the Interval in the same Part, I maintain that it will have its effect without any Bass: thus, on this occasion the Harmony acts merely by determining the Melody to be this or that sort, and it is purely as Melody that the Interval has different expressions according to the place of the Mode where it is employed.

The *Unity of Melody* requires that two Melodies never be heard at the same time, but not that the Melody never pass from one Part to another; on the contrary, it is often elegant and tasteful to handle this transition properly, even from the Song to the Accompaniment, provided that the speech always be understood. There are even learned and properly handled Harmonies in which the Melody, without being in any Part, results solely from the effect of the whole. One will find (Plate M, Figure 7) an example, which, although crude, suffices in order to make what I want to say understood.

A Treatise would be needed in order to show in detail the application of this principle to *Duos*, *Trios*, *Quartets*, to Choruses, to Instrumental Pieces.

Song Derived from the Harmony

Plate M, Figure 7

Men of genius will sufficiently discover its extent and use, and their works will instruct others. I therefore conclude, and I say, that from the principle I have just established it follows: firstly, that every Music that does not sing is tiresome, whatever Harmony it may have; secondly, that every Music in which several simultaneous Songs are distinguished is bad, and that the same effect results as from two or more discourses pronounced at the same time in the same Tone. By this verdict, which admits of no exception, it is seen what should be thought of those marvelous pieces of Music in which an Aria serves as the Accompaniment to another Aria.

It is this principle of the *Unity* of Melody which the Italians have felt and have followed without knowing it, but which the French have neither known nor followed. It is, I say, in this great principle that the essential difference between these two Musics consists; and it is, I believe, what every impartial judge will say who should give the same attention to them both, if however the thing is possible.

When I had discovered this principle, I wanted to try applying it on my own before proposing it. This attempt produced the *Devin du Village*; after this success, I spoke of it in my *Letter on French Music*.[145] It is for the Masters of the Art to judge whether the principle is good, and whether I have indeed followed the rules which flow from it.

VOICE [*Voix*], *n. fem.* The sum of all the Sounds that a man can—by speaking, singing, or shouting—draw from his organ forms what is called his *Voice*, and the qualities of this *Voice* also depend upon those of the Sounds that form it. Thus, one should first of all apply to the *Voice* everything I have said about Sounds in general. (See SOUND* [*Son*].)

Physicists distinguish different sorts of *Voice* in man, or, if one likes, they consider the same *Voice* under different aspects.

1. As a simple Sound, such as the cry of children.
2. As an articulated Sound, such as it is in speech.
3. In Song, which adds Modulation and variety of Tones to speech.
4. In declamation, which appears to depend upon a new modification in Sound and in the very substance of the *Voice*—a modification different from that of Song and that of speech, since it can be united to either of them, or omitted from them.

From whence these divisions are drawn can be seen from the explanation M. Duclos gives of these different sorts of *Voices* in the *Encyclopedia* at the article *Declamation of the Ancients*.[146] I shall content myself with transcribing here what he says about the singing or musical *Voice*, the sole one that relates to my subject.

"Following Aristoxenus, Ancient Musicians established: 1st. That the Singing *Voice* passes from one degree of raising or of lowering to another degree, that is, from one Tone to another, by leaping, without moving through the Interval that separates them; whereas that of discourse is raised and lowered by a continuous movement. 2nd. That the Singing *Voice* is sustained on the same Tone, considered as an indivisible point, which does not happen in simple pronunciation.

"This progression by leaps and with pauses is in fact that of the Singing *Voice*; but is there nothing more in Singing? There is a tragic Declamation which allows the transition by leaping from one Tone to another, and pausing on a Tone. The same thing is noted in certain Orators. Nevertheless, this Declamation is still different from the Singing *Voice*.

"M. Dodart, who joins to an intelligence in discussion and research the greatest knowledge of Physics, of Anatomy, and of the working of the parts of the human body, has applied his especial attention to the organs of the *Voice*.[147] He observes, 1st, that a man whose speaking *Voice* is displeasing sometimes has a very pleasant Singing, and, on the contrary, 2nd, that if we have not heard someone sing, whatever knowledge we have of his speaking *Voice*, we will not recognize his Singing *Voice*.

"By continuing his researches, M. Dodart discovered that there is more movement of the larynx in the Singing *Voice* than in the speaking [*Voice*], that is, of the tracheal artery which forms a new canal that ends at the glottis, which envelops and supports its muscles. The difference between the two *Voices* therefore comes from the difference between the taut larynx being stable and at rest on its cords, in speech, and this same larynx suspended on its cords in action and moved by a swaying back and forth from high to low and from low to high. This swaying can be compared to the movement of birds who hover, or of fish who remain in the same place against the flow of the water. Although the wings of the ones and the fins of the others appear immobile to the eye, they make continual vibrations, but so short and so quick that they are imperceptible.

"In the Singing *Voice*, the moving back and forth of the larynx produces a type of undulation which is not found in simple speech. The undulation, sustained and moderated in beautiful *Voices*, makes itself perceived too much in quivering or weak *Voices*. This undulation should not be confused with the Cadenzas or the Roulades that are made by very quick and very delicate motions of the opening of the glottis, and which are made up of the Interval of a Tone or of a Semitone.

"The *Voice*, whether of Singing or of speech, comes entirely from the glottis for the Sound and for the Tone; but the undulation comes entirely from the moving back and forth of the whole larynx; it does not at all make up part of the *Voice*, but it affects its totality.

"It results from what has just been explained that the Singing *Voice* consists in the progression by leaps from one Tone to another, in it remaining on the Tones, and in this undulation of the larynx which affects the totality and the very substance of the Sound."

Although this explanation is quite clear and quite philosophic, in my view it leaves something to be desired, and this characteristic of undulation, given by the moving back and forth of the larynx to the Singing *Voice*, appears to me to be no more essential to it than the progression by leaps and the resting on Tones which, in M. Duclos's view, are not specific characteristics of this *Voice*.

For, first of all, this undulation can be given to or taken away from the *Voice* at will when singing, and one does not any less sing when one draws out a purely unified Sound without any type of undulation. Secondly, the Sounds of Instruments do not differ in any way from those of the Singing *Voice* as to the nature of their musical Sounds, and themselves have nothing of this undulation. Thirdly, this undulation is formed in the Tone and not in the Timbre; the proof of this is that this undulation is imitated on the Violin and on other Instruments, not by any moving back and forth like the motion assumed in the larynx, but by moving the finger back and forth on the String, which, thus alternately and almost imperceptibly shortened and lengthened again, renders two alternating Sounds in proportion as the finger moves back or advances. Thus, the undulation, whatever M. Dodart says about it, does not consist in a very slight moving back and forth of the same Sound, but in the more or less frequent alternation of two very close Sounds, and when the Sounds are too far removed, and if the alternating jolts are too abrupt, then the undulation becomes shaky.

I would think that the true distinctive characteristic of the Singing *Voice* is that of forming discernible Sounds whose Unison can be taken or perceived, and of passing from one to another by harmonic and commensurable Intervals, whereas, in the speaking *Voice*, either the Sounds are not sufficiently sustained, and, so to speak, sufficiently unified to be capable of being discerned, or the Intervals which separate them are not sufficiently harmonic, or their relationships sufficiently simple.

The observations M. Dodart made concerning the difference of the speaking *Voice* and the Singing *Voice* in the same man, far from contradicting this explanation, confirm it; for, as there are more or less harmonious Languages, whose accents are more or less Musical, it is also noted that in these languages the speaking and Singing *Voices* draw near or grow distant from one another in the same proportion. Thus, as the Italian Language is more Musical than the French, its speech is less distant from Singing; and it is easier to recognize the man one has heard speaking when he is Singing. In a Language which was totally harmonious, such as the Greek Language was in its beginnings, the difference between the speaking *Voice* and the Singing *Voice* would be null; one would have only one and the same *Voice* for speaking and for singing; perhaps this is still the case today for the Chinese.

This is perhaps too much concerning the different genera of *Voices*; I return to the Singing *Voice*, and I will confine myself to it for the remainder of this article.

Each Individual has his particular *Voice* which distinguishes him from every other *Voice* by some difference that belongs to it, as one face is distinguished from another; but there are also those differences which are common to several people, and which, forming so many types of *Voices*, each requires a specific denomination.

The most general characteristic that distinguishes *Voices* is not that which is derived from their Timbre or from their Volume, but from the Degree this Volume occupies in the general System of Sounds.

Voices are therefore generally distinguished into two classes; namely, high *Voices* and low *Voices*. The common difference from one to the other is just about an Octave; which makes high *Voices* actually sing at the Octave of the low *Voices*, when they seem to be singing in Unison.

Low *Voices* are usually those of grown men; high *Voices* are those of women. Eunuchs and children also have about the same Diapason of *Voice* as women; all men can even approach it by singing Falsetto. But of all the high *Voices*, it must be agreed that, despite the predilection of the Italians for Castrati, there is no type comparable to that of women, either for the range or for the beauty of the Timbre. The *Voices* of children have little consistency and no lower register at all; that of Eunuchs, on the contrary, has brilliance only in the high register; and as for the Falsetto, it is the most disagreeable of all the Timbres of the human *Voice*: to be convinced of this, it is enough to hear the Choruses at the *Concert Spirituel* in Paris, and to compare the Sopranos there with those at the Opera.[148]

All these different Diapasons, united and put into order, form a general range of about three Octaves, which has been divided into four parts, three of which, called the High Tenor, the Tenor, and the Bass, belong to the low *Voices*, and the fourth alone, which is called the Soprano, is assigned to high *Voices*. Concerning which here are some remarks which present themselves.

I. According to the compass of ordinary *Voices*, which can be fixed at about a major Tenth, by placing two Interval Degrees between each type of *Voice* and that which follows it, which is the whole degree of difference that can be given to them, the general System of human *Voices* in the two sexes is made to exceed three Octaves, and should contain only two Octaves and two Tones. It was in fact to this range that the four Parts of Music were confined, long after the invention of Counterpoint, as is seen in the Compositions of the Fourteenth century, where the same Clef, placed from Line to Line at four consecutive positions, served for the Bass, which they called *Tenor*, for the Tenor, which they called *Contratenor*, for the High Tenor, which they called *Mottetus*, and for the Soprano, which they called *Triplum*. This distribution must in truth have made Composition very difficult; but at the same time Harmony was more restricted and more pleasant.

II. To push the vocal System to the range of three Octaves with the gradation of which I was just speaking, six Parts were needed instead of four; and nothing would be more natural than this division, not in relation to the Harmony, which did not include so many different Sounds, but in relation to the *Voices*, which are now fairly poorly distributed. Indeed, why are there three Parts in men's *Voices* and only one in women's *Voices* if the totality of the latter contains as great a range as the former? Let one measure from the Interval of the highest Sounds of the highest feminine *Voices* to the lowest Sounds of the lowest feminine *Voices*, let one do the same thing for men's *Voices*, and not only will one not find a sufficient difference to establish three Parts on the one hand and only one on the other, but this very difference, if there is any, will be reducible to a very small degree. In order to judge this soundly, one must not limit oneself to examining things such as they are, but one must further see what they could be and consider that custom contributes a great deal to forming *Voices* according to the character one wants to give them. In France, where Basses and Countertenors are wanted, and where no importance at all is attached to Contraltos, men's *Voices* take on different characters and women's *Voices* hold to only a single one; but in Italy, where as much importance is attached to beautiful Altos as to the highest *Voice*, are found very beautiful low *Voices* among the women which they call *Contr'alti*, and very beautiful high *Voices* which they call *Soprani*; on the contrary, they have for recitation only *Tenori* for the men's *Voices*, so that while there is only one character for women's *Voices* in our Operas, in theirs they have only one character for men's *Voices*.

With regard to Choruses, if their Parts are generally distributed in Italy as they are in France, it is a universal, but arbitrary custom which has no natural foundation at all. Besides, are not very beautiful pieces of Music for grand Chorus, performed solely by young women, admired in several places, and singularly so in Venice?[149]

III. The distance which is too great between *Voices* and makes them all exceed their range often obliges one to subdivide several of them. It is in this way that Basses are divided into Countrabasses and Bass Tenors, Tenors into High Tenors and Concordants, Sopranos into firsts and seconds; but nothing determinate is perceived in any of this, nothing regulated according to any principle. The general spirit of French Composers is always to force *Voices* in order to make them shout rather than sing: it is for this reason that they today appear to confine themselves to Basses and High Tenors, which are in the two extremes. With regard to the Tenor, a Part so natural to man that it is called the *human Voice par excellence*, it is already banished from our Operas, where nothing natural is desired; and by the same reason, it will not take long for it to be so from all French Music.

Voices are further distinguished by many other differences than those of low and high. There are loud *Voices* whose Sounds are loud and striking, soft *Voices* whose Sounds are soft and flute-like, big *Voices* which have a large range, beautiful *Voices* whose sounds are full, just, and harmonious, and there are also those contrary to all these. There are harsh and heavy *Voices*; there are flexible and light *Voices*; there are some whose beautiful Sounds are unequally distributed, some of them in the high range, others in the *Middle*, others in the low range; there are also equal *Voices*, which make the same Timbre heard through their whole range. It is for the Composer to take advantage of each *Voice* so that its character is most advantageous. In Italy, where each time an Opera is put on again in the Theater it is always a new Music, the Composers always take great care to apportion all the roles to the *Voices* that should sing them. But in France, where the same Music endures for centuries, each role must always serve for all the *Voices* of the same type, and this is perhaps one of the reasons why French Singing, far from acquiring any degree of perfection, becomes every day more drawn out and ponderous.

The most extensive, the most flexible, the sweetest, the most harmonious *Voice* that has perhaps ever existed appears to have been that of the Chevalier Baldassare Ferri, a Perugian, from the last century.[150] A unique and prodigious Singer, whom all the Sovereigns of Europe took turns in fighting over, who was heaped with goods and with honors during his lifetime, and whose talents and glory after his death all of Italy's Muses vie with one another in celebrating. All the works written to praise this famous Musician breath with rapture, enthusiasm, and the agreement of all his contemporaries shows that a talent so perfect and so rare was even above envy. Nothing, they say, can express the brilliance of his *Voice*, nor the gracefulness of his Singing; he had, in the highest degree, all the characteristics of perfection in all the genera; he was gay, haughty, grave, tender at his will, and hearts melted at his pathos. Among the infinity of *tours de force* he made with his *Voice*, I will cite only a single one. He ascended and redescended two full Octaves in a single breath by a continual Trill marked on all the chromatic Degrees with such justness, although without Accompaniment, that if this Accompaniment was struck quickly under the note on which he was, whether Flat or Sharp, the Accord was instantly perceived with a justness that surprised all the Listeners.

The vocal and reciting parts for which a Piece of Music is composed are also called *Voices*; thus, one speaks of a Motet in a single *Voice* instead of saying a Motet in recitative, a Cantata in two *Voices* instead of saying a Cantata in Duo or in two Parts, etc. (See Duo [*Duo*], Trio* [*Trio*].)

Letter to Mr. Burney and Fragments of Observations on Gluck's "Alceste"

Letter from J. J. Rousseau to Doctor Burney, Author of the General History of Music[1]

You have given me several precious gifts of your writings in succession, Sir, each of which well deserved express thanks. The almost absolute impossibility of writing has until now prevented me from fulfilling this duty; but, by reanimating in me a remnant of zeal for an Art upon which your own zeal has made you spend so much work, time, travel, and expense, the first volume of your *General History of Music* rouses me to show you my gratitude by conversing with you for awhile on the favorite subject of your researches, which should immortalize your name among the true enthusiasts of this fine art.

If I had had the fortune of conferring with you about it at some leisure while some ideas remained to me that were still fresh, I would have been able to derive from your own many lessons from which the Public could profit, but which will be lost on me, from now on deprived of memory and beyond being in a position to read anything. But I can at least here cursorily record some of the points on which I would have liked to consult you, so that artists might not be deprived of clarifications on your part which may be worthwhile to them; and, letting those who, without knowing anything about it do not fail to astonish the Public with their learned speculations, chatter about Music in fine phrases, I shall limit myself to what relates most immediately to practice, which does not lend itself so easily to the oracles of witty minds, but for which study alone is useful to the genuine progress of the art.

1st. You have taken too much of an interest in it, Sir, not to have often remarked how confused, muddled, and often equivocal our manner of writing music is, which is one of the reasons that makes its study so long and so difficult. Struck by these inconveniences, forty years ago I devised a manner of writing it by numerals that is less voluminous, simpler, and, in my opinion, much clearer. I read the plan for it to the Academy of Sciences in 1742, I proposed it the following year to the Public in a brochure which I have the honor of sending you.[2] If you take the trouble of glancing over it, you will see therein to what point I reduced the number and simplified the expression of signs. As there are only seven diatonic notes in the scale, I have no more than seven characters in order to express them. All the others, which are only their replicas, appear therein by their degree, but always in the form of their original sign; the major, minor, augmented, and diminished intervals never become confused with regard to their position, as in ordinary music, but each has its inherent and proper character which, without regard to position or to the clef, appear at the first glance. I proscribe the natural as useless; I never have either a flat or a sharp on the clef; finally, chords, harmony, and the sequence of modulations appear in a score with a clarity that allows nothing to escape the eye, so that its succession is as clear to the sight of the reader as in the mind of the composer himself.

But the newest and most useful part of this system, and that which has nonetheless been least remarked about it, is that which relates to the values of the notes and to the expression of the duration and the quantities in the beat. It is the great simplicity of this part that prevented it from creating a sensation. I have no specific figures at all for the whole notes, half notes, quarter notes, eighth notes, sixteenth notes, etc.; all this, related by position alone back to equal aliquots, presents the divisions of the measures and of the beats to the eye, almost without having need of their own signs for this. The zero alone suffices to express any rest whatsoever; the dot, after a note or a zero, indicates all the possible prolongations of a rest or of a sound. It can represent all sorts of values; thus, whole rests, half rests, quarter rests, eighth rests, sixteenth rests, etc., are proscribed just as are the various shapes for notes. I have taken precisely the opposite route of the ordinary notation in everything: it represents the values by figures, and the intervals by positions; me, I express the values by position alone and intervals by the numerals, etc.

This manner of notating has not been adopted at all—how could it have been? It was new and I was the one who was proposing it. But its defects, which I was the first to observe, do not prevent it from having great advantages over the other, especially for training in composition, for teaching music to those who do not know it, for easily notating tunes one hears and which one wants to remember in a small volume. I have therefore preserved it for my use, I have perfected it by practicing it, and I employ it above all to notate the bass under any song whatsoever, because this bass, written this way by a line of numerals, saves me a staff, doubles my space, and makes it so that I am obliged to turn the page half as often.[3]

2nd. By perfecting this manner of notating, I have found another with which I have combined it, and of which I have now to give you an account.

In the examples you have given of the song of the Jews,[4] you have notated them, reasonably, from right to left. This direction of lines is the most ancient, and it is retained in Oriental writing. The Greeks themselves made use of it at first; then they thought of writing lines in furrows, that is, alternately from right to left and from left to right. Ultimately, the difficulty of reading and of writing in the two directions made them completely abandon the ancient direction, and they wrote as we do today, uniquely from left to right, always going back to the left hand side to recommence each line.[5]

This procedure has as an inconvenience in the leap the eye is forced to make from the end of each line to the beginning of the following one, and from the bottom of each page to the top of that which follows. This inconvenience, which habit makes imperceptible to us in reading, makes itself more strongly felt in reading music, where, the lines being longer, the eye has a greater leap to make, and where the quickness of this leap is fatiguing in the long run, especially in quick movements,[6] so that it sometimes happens in a Concerto that the Instrumentalist is mistaken about his staff, and the performance is stopped.

I thought that this inconvenience might be remedied and make Music easier, and less tiring to read, by renewing for it the method of writing by furrows practiced by the ancient Greeks, and this all the more felicitously so as this method does not have the same difficulty for Music as for writing, for the notation is equally easy to read in both directions, and there is no more difficulty, for example, in reading the plain-song of the Jews as you have notated it than if it were notated from left to right, like our own. It is a fact of experience, which everyone can verify on the spot, that he who sight-sings from left to right will sight-sing in the same way from right to left without having been coached in any way. Thus, no inconvenience for practice.

In order to assure myself of this method by experience so as to foresee every objection and to remove every difficulty, I have written a great deal of Music in this manner, vocal as well as instrumental, in separated parts as well as in a score, always adhering to that constant rule of so arranging the series of the lines and of the pages that the eye never has a leap to make either from right to left or from left to right or from bottom to top, but so that it always recommences the following line or page, even when turning the page at the very place where the preceding one ends, which makes half of my pages proceed alternately from bottom to top, as half of my lines do from left to right.[7]

I shall not speak at all of the advantages of this manner of writing music; it suffices to perform a sonata notated in this fashion in order to perceive them. As for the objections, I have been able to discover only a single one, and only for vocal Music, which is the difficulty of reading written words backwards, a difficulty that recurs every other line, and I admit that I see no other means of overcoming it than by practicing reading and writing in this fashion for some time, as printers do, a habit which is acquired very promptly. But even if one did not wish to overcome this slight obstacle for the singing parts, the advantages would still remain in their entirety without any inconvenience for the instrumental parts and for every type of instrumental music, and, certainly, in the performance of a sonata or of a Concerto, these advantages would save a great deal of fatigue for the accompanyists and especially for the principal instrument.

3rd. The two fashions of notating of which I have just spoken each having its advantages, I thought of bringing them together in a notation combining them both, especially in order to save space and to have to turn the page less often. For this, I notate the singing and accompanying parts in the ordinary Music, but in the Greek manner, that is by furrows; and as for the Bass, which ordinarily proceeds by simpler and less ornamented notes, I likewise notate it in furrows, but by numerals between the lines which separate the staffs. In this way, each accolade has a staff less, which is that of the bass, and as this bass is written in the place where the words are ordinarily placed, I write these words above the song, instead of putting them below, which is indifferent in itself and prevents the numerals of the bass from being confused with the writing. When there are only two parts, this manner of notating saves half the space.[8]

4th. If I had been in a condition to confer with you before the publication of your first Volume, in which you present the history of ancient music, I would have offered, Sir, to discuss some points with you regarding the Music of the Greeks, the clarification of which it appears to me, should throw great light on the nature of that Music—so often judged and so little understood—points which nevertheless have never given rise to questioning among our erudite people because they have not even taken it into their heads to think of them.

Among these questions, I am not at all renewing the one concerning our harmony, asking whether it was known and practiced by the Greeks, because this question seems to me not capable of being such for anyone who has any notion of the art and of what remains to us on this matter in the Greek authors. One must leave that point to the erudite to squabble over and content oneself with laughing. You have put a very fine bass under the ancient tune to an Ode by Pindar.[9] But I am quite certain that there was not a Greek ear that this Bass would not have flayed to the point of not being able to endure it.

But I would dare ask: 1st. Whether Greek poetry was susceptible of being sung in several manners, whether it was possible to compose several different tunes on the same words, and if there is any example of this having been practiced. 2nd. What was the characteristic distinction between lyric or accompanied poetry as opposed to purely oratorical poetry? Did this distinction consist only in the meter and the Style, or did it also consist in the tone of the recitation? Was there nothing song-like about poetry that was not lyric, and was there any case where, as among us, cadenced rhythm without any melody was practiced? What exactly was the instrumental Music of the Greeks? Did they have Instrumental pieces, properly speaking, composed without any words? They played Tunes which were not sung, that I know; but did they not originally have words on all these tunes, and were there any which had not been sung or meant to be so? You sense that this question would be quite ridiculous if the one who put it believed that they had accompaniments similar to our own, which were made up of parts different from the vocal one; for, in such a case, our accompaniments would have been made up of purely instrumental Music. It is true that their notation was different for instruments and for voices, but, in my opinion, that does not prevent the tune notated in the two fashions from having been the same one.

I do not know whether these questions are superficial; but I do know that they are not idle. They all pertain in some manner or other to other interesting questions, such as knowing whether there is only one Music, as our learned people majestically pronounce, or if, perhaps, as I and some other vulgar minds have dared to think, there is essentially and necessarily a music that belongs to each language, except for languages which, not having any accent at all and not being able to have music of their own, make use as they are able of that of another, claiming, for this reason, that those foreign musics, which they usurp to the prejudice of our ears, belong to no one or to everyone; in addition, such as clarifying that great principle of *the unity of Melody*: followed too precisely by Pergolesi and by Leo not to have been known by them; also followed very often, but by instinct and without knowing it, by modern Italian composers; followed very rarely by chance by some German composers, but not known to any French composer, nor ever followed in any French Music other than the *Devin du Village* alone, and proposed by the author of the *Letter on French Music* and of the *Dictionary of Music*, without having been either understood, or followed, or perhaps read by anyone—a Principle from which modern Music moves away more and more every day, to the point that it may finally degenerate into such a hullabaloo that, ears no longer being able to bear it, Authors may be forcibly led back to that much-disdained principle and to the march of nature.[10]

This, Sir, would lead me to discuss technicalities which would bore you, perhaps by their lack of utility and infallibly so by their length. Nevertheless, as it might be possible by chance to find some good ideas in my old musical reveries, I had proposed to myself to cast a few into some remarks M. Gluck asked me to make on his Italian Opera *Alceste*, and I had begun this job when he took his Opera back from me without asking me for my remarks, which were only begun, and the indecipherable draft of which was not in a condition to be sent to him.[11] I thought of transcribing this fragment here on this occasion and of sending it to you so that, if you have the whim to glance over it, my unformed ideas on lyric music may suggest to you better ones from which the public will profit in your history of modern Music.

I can neither complete this extract nor give the necessary coherence to its scattered pieces because I no longer have the Opera about which they were written. Thus, I limit myself to transcribing here what is done. As the Opera *Alceste* has been printed in Vienna,[12] I suppose that it might easily come before your eyes, and if worst comes to worst, there can be found here and there in this fragment some general idea which can be understood without an example and without much application. What gives me some confidence in the judgments I previously made in this extract is that they have almost all been confirmed afterward by the Public with regard to the French *Alceste* which M. Gluck presented for us this year at the Opera, and in which he used, with good reason, as much as possible the same Music as in his Italian *Alceste*.[13]

Fragments of Observations on M. le Chevalier Gluck's Italian "Alceste"[14]

The examination of M. Gluck's Opera *Alceste* is too far beyond my powers—especially in the state of wasting away in which my ideas, my memory, and all my faculties have been for several years—for me to have presumed for my part to take up the difficult enterprise, which, besides, cannot be good for anything; but M. Gluck so strongly pressed me that I could not refuse him this kindness, although as fatiguing for me as it is useless for him. I am no longer capable of giving the necessary attention to such a polished work. All my observations may be false and badly founded; and, far from presenting them to him as rules, I submit them to his judgment, without wanting in any way to defend them; but even though I were mistaken in all of them, what will always remain real and true is the testimony that they render to M. Gluck of my deference to his wishes and of my esteem for his works.

In first considering the total development of this piece, I find in it a sort of general misconception in that the first act is the strongest in terms of the music and the last the weakest, which is directly contrary to the good gradation of a Drama, in which the interest should always proceed by becoming stronger. I admit that the great pathos of the first act would be out of place in the following ones, but the powers of Music are not exclusively in the pathetic, but in the energy of every feeling and in the vivacity of every portrait. Everywhere that the interest is liveliest, the music should be more animated, and its resources are no less in brilliant and lively expressions than in groans and tears.

I agree that this is more the fault of the Poet than of the Musician;[15] but I do not believe that the latter is thereby entirely excused. This requires some explanation.

I do not know of any Opera in which the passions were less varied than in *Alceste*: practically everything in it turns on two feelings alone, affliction and fear, and these two feelings, always prolonged, must have cost the Musician unbelievable pains so as not to fall into the most lamentable monotony. In general, the more warmth there is in situations and in expressions, the more promptly and rapidly they should pass, otherwise the force of the emotion relents in the Listeners, and when this limit has been exceeded, while the Actor might well continue to thrash about, the spectator grows lukewarm, grows cold, and ends by becoming impatient.

From this defect it results that the interest, instead of growing warmer by degrees during the development of the piece, on the contrary grows lukewarm up to the denouement, which, with all due respect to Euripides himself,[16] is cold, insipid, and almost laughable by dint of its simplicity.

If the Author of the Drama believed he had resolved this defect by the little celebration he has placed in the second act, he is mistaken. This celebration, badly placed and ridiculously introduced, must shock in performance because it is contrary to all probability and all propriety, as much due to the quickness with which it is prepared and executed as to the absence of the Queen, about which no one is troubled, until the King finally takes it into his head to think of her.*[17]

I will dare to say that this Author, too full of his Euripides, has not drawn from his subject what it could have furnished him to sustain the interest, vary the scene, and give to the Musician the material for new Musical characters. He should have had Alceste die in the second act and employed the whole of the third one in order to prepare, by a new interest, her resurrection, which could have led to a theatrical stroke as admirable

---

*I presented an idea of how to frame this celebration better and to make it touching and rending by its very gaiety from which M. Gluck has profited in his French *Alceste*.[18]

and striking as this cold return is insipid. But, without pausing over what the Author of the Drama should have done, I return here to the Music.

Its Author therefore had to conquer the boredom from that uniformity of passion and to prevent the depression which must be its effect. What was the first, the greatest means which presented itself for this? It was to make up for what the Author of the Drama did not do by so increasing its development that the Music always increased in warmth while moving forward and finally became so vehement as to transport the Listener; and he might have so managed this development that this agitation ended or changed its object before throwing the ear and the heart into exhaustion.

This is what M. Gluck seems to me not to have done, since his first act, as strong in its Music as the second, is much more so than the third, so that the vehemence therefore does not at all proceed by increasing; and since the Author lavished all the powers of his Art ever since the first two scenes of the second act, he can do no more in the continuation than weakly sustain emotions of the same genre, which he brought too soon to the highest peak.

The objection presents itself here of itself. It was for the Author of the words to strengthen the warmth and the interest by a gradually increased development. That of the Music could render the affections of his characters only in the same order and to the same degree as the Drama presented them to him. He would have produced contradictions if he had given to his expressions nuances other than those required by those of the words he had to render. This is the objection; here is my response. M. Gluck will soon perceive that among all the Musicians in Europe, it is made for him alone.

Three things concur to produce the great effects of Dramatic Music: namely, accent, harmony, and rhythm. The accent is determined by the Poet, and the Music can hardly stray in this, either by choice or by force, from the exact expression of the words without producing contradictions. But as for the two other parts, which do not so inhere in the language, one can, up to a certain point, combine them at one's liking in order gradually to modify and increase the interest as it suits the development prescribed for it.[19]

I will even dare say that the pleasure of the ear should sometimes prevail over the truthfulness of the expression; for Music can go to the heart only through the charm of the melody, and if it were only a question of rendering the accent of the passion, the art of declamation would alone suffice, and Music, having become useless, would be intrusive rather than agreeable. This is one of the pitfalls which the Composer, too full of his expression, should carefully avoid. In all good Operas, and especially in those by M. Gluck, there are a thousand pieces which make tears flow by the Music, and which would produce only a moderate emotion or none at all if deprived of its help, however well declaimed they may be.

It follows from this that, without spoiling the truthfulness of the expression, the Musician who modulates for a long time in the same keys and only changes them rarely is master of varying their nuances by the combination of the two accessory parts that must be made to concur with it, namely, the harmony and the rhythm. Let us first speak of the former. I distinguish three types of it. Diatonic harmony, the simplest of the three and perhaps the sole natural one. Chromatic harmony, which consists of continual changes of key by fundamental successions of fifths. And, finally, the harmony that I call pathetic, which consists of interlacings of augmented and diminished chords by means of which keys that have little analogy among themselves are covered.[20] The ear is affected by rending intervals and the soul by rapid and lively ideas, capable of troubling it.

Diatonic harmony is nowhere out of place; it suits every character. With the help of the rhythm and of the melody, it can admit of every expression. It is necessary for the two other harmonies, and every Music into which it does not enter at all can never be anything but a detestable Music.

Chromatic harmony likewise enters into the pathetic harmony, but it can do very well without it and render the most pathetic expressions, although without it perhaps more weakly. Thus, by the well-handled succession of these three harmonies, the Musician can gradually increase and strengthen the feelings of the same genre which the Poet has sustained too long in the same degree of energy.

There is a second resource for this in the melody, and especially in its cadence as variously scanned by the rhythm. Extreme movements of fast and slow, contrasted meters, unequal values, mixtures of slowness and quickness, all this can likewise be graduated in order to sustain and reanimate interest and attention. Finally, there is more and less noise and brilliance, a more or less full harmony, the silences of the Orchestra, whose perpetual roar would be overwhelming for the ear, however beautiful its effects may be.

As for the rhythm, in which the greatest strength of Music consists, it requires great artfulness for it to be felicitously handled in the vocal part. I have said, and I believe it, that Greek Tragedies were true Operas. The Greek language, truly harmonious and musical, had of itself a melodious accent; it needed only to have rhythm joined to it in order to produce musical declamation; thus, not only tragedies, but all poetry was necessarily sung; Poets said *I sing* at the beginning of their poems with reason—a formula which our own have very ridiculously preserved.[21] But as for our modern languages, a production of barbarous peoples, being not at all naturally musical, not even Italian, when one wants to apply Music to them one must take great precautions in order to make this union bearable and to make it natural enough in imitative Music so as to create illusion in the theater, and in whatever manner one sets about it, one will never succeed in persuading the listener that the song he is listening to is anything but speech; and if one were to succeed, this would never be but by fortifying one of the great powers of Music, which is musical rhythm, quite different for us from poetic rhythm, and which can even be associated with it only very rarely and very imperfectly.

Determining to what point one can make language sing and Music speak is a great and fine problem to resolve. The whole theory of Dramatic Music depends upon a good solution to this problem. On this point, instinct alone has led the Italians as well as was possible in practice, and the enormous defects of their Operas do not come from a bad genre of music, but from a bad application of a good genre.

The oral accent by itself doubtless has great power, but this is only in the declamation, this power is independent of all Music; and, with this accent alone, one can make a good tragedy heard, but not a good Opera. As soon as Music is mixed in, it must be armed with all its charms to subjugate the heart through the ear; if all its beauties are not deployed, it will be intrusive, as if one had an Orator be accompanied by instruments; but as for mixing in its riches, this must be done with great discretion in order to prevent the exhaustion into which our organs would soon be cast by a prolonged action entirely in Music.

From these principles it follows that in a drama one must vary the application of the Music, sometimes by allowing the accent of the language and the poetic rhythm to dominate it, and sometimes by making the Music dominate in its turn, and by lavishing all the riches of melody, harmony, and musical rhythm in order to strike the ear and touch the heart by charms which it cannot resist. These are the reasons for the division of an Opera into simple recitative, obligatory recitative,[22] and arias.

When the discourse, rapid in its progress, must simply be recited, this is an instance of giving oneself over uniquely to the accent of the declamation, and when the language has an accent, it is merely a matter of making this accent perceptible by notating it by musical intervals, by faithfully adhering to the prosody, to the poetic rhythm, and to the passionate inflections which the meaning of the discourse requires. This is the simple recitative, and this recitative should be as near to simple speech as possible; it should adhere to the Music only because Music is the language of the Opera, and because speaking and singing alternately, as is done here in comic Operas, is to express oneself alternately in two different languages, which always makes the transition from the one to the other shocking and ridiculous, which is supremely absurd at the moment when, gripped by passion, one changes voice in order to speak a chanson.

The accompaniment of the Bass is necessary in the simple recitative, not only to sustain and guide the actor, but also to determine the type of intervals and to mark with precision the interlacings of modulation which produce such an effect in a beautiful recitative; but far from it being necessary to make this accompaniment striking, I would like on the contrary for it to be not at all remarkable and for it to produce its effect without any attention being paid to it. Thus, I believe that the other instruments ought not meddle in it at all, even if this were only to allow the ears of the listeners as well as the Orchestra to rest—something which should be completely forgotten, and whose well-handled reentries thereby produce a great effect, whereas, when the instrumental part reigns the whole length of the piece, beginning by pleasing, it ends by overwhelming. The recitative bores in the theaters of Italy not only because it is too long, but because it is badly sung and more badly placed. Lively, interesting scenes, as there should always be in an Opera, done with warmth, with truthfulness, and sustained by a natural and lively playing cannot fail to move and to please thanks to illusion; but coldly and dully recited by castrati, like school-boys' lessons, they will without doubt bore and especially when they are too long; but this will not be the fault of the recitative.

In the moments when the recitative, less like a recitation and more passionate, takes on a more touching character, one can successfully place a simple accompaniment of held notes there, which, by the aid of this harmony, give more sweetness to the expression. It is the simple accompanied recitative which, returning by rare and well-chosen intervals, contrasts with the dryness of the naked recitative and produces a very good effect.

Finally, when the violence of passion causes speech to be broken into by half-begun and interrupted words, due as much to the strength of feelings which do not find terms sufficient to express themselves as to their impetuosity, which makes them succeed one another tumultuously with a quickness without coherence and without order, I believe that only the alternate mixture of speech and of instrumental music can express such a situation. The actor, wholly yielding to his passion, should find only its accent. Melody, too little suited to the accent of the language, and musical rhythm, which does not lend itself to it at all, would weaken, would enervate all the expressiveness by being mixed with it; nevertheless, this rhythm and this melody have a great charm for the ear and through it a great power over the heart. What, then, is to be done to employ all these types of forces at the same time? Do exactly what is done in the obligatory recitative: give to speech all the accent possible and suitable to what it expresses, and throw into the instrumental ritonelli all the melody, all the cadence and rhythm that can come to its aid. The silence of the actor then says more than his words; and these reticences, well placed and well handled and filled on the one side by the voice of the Orchestra and on the other with the mute acting of an actor who feels both what he says and what he cannot say, these reticences, I say, produce an effect superior even to that of declamation, and they cannot be removed from it without removing from it the greatest part of it power. There is no good Actor who does not make long pauses in these violent moments, and these pauses, filled with an analogous expression by a [melodious and well-handled][23] ritornello, ought they not become even more interesting than when an absolute silence reigned in them? I desire for proof of this only the astonishing effect which every well-placed and well-treated obligatory recitative never fails to produce.

Persuaded that the French language, destitute of all accent, is not at all appropriate for Music, and principally for recitative, I have devised a genre of Drama[24] *in which the words and the Music, instead of proceeding together, are made to be heard in succession, and in which the spoken phrase is in a way announced and prepared by the musical phrase. The scene "Pygmalion" is an example of this genre of composition, and it has not had imitators.*[25] *By perfecting this method, one would bring together the double advantage of relieving the Actor through frequent rests and of offering to the French Spectator the type of melodrama most suited to his language. This union of the declamatory art with the musical art will produce all the effects of the true recitative only imperfectly, and delicate ears will always notice with displeasure the contrast that reigns between the language of the Actor and that of the Orchestra which accompanies him; but a sensitive and intelligent Actor, by bringing together the tone of his voice and the accent of his declamation with what the musical line expresses, mixes these foreign colors with such artfulness that the spectator cannot discern its nuances. Thus, this type of work might constitute a mean genre between simple declamation and genuine melodrama, whose beauty it will never attain. Furthermore, some difficulties which the language presents are not insurmountable; the Author of the* Dictionary of Music *has invited French Composers to make new attempts, and to introduce into their Operas the obligatory recitative, which, when it is employed properly, produce the greatest effects.*[26]

What produces the charm and energy of the obligatory recitative? Could the oratorical and pathetic accent of the Actor alone produce such an effect? No, doubtless. But the alternating lines of the instrumental part, reawakening and sustaining the feeling for the meter, which the recitative by itself would allow to be extinguished, join to the purely declamatory expression all that of the musical rhythm, which strengthens it. I distinguish rhythm and meter here because they are actually two very different things: meter is only the periodic return of equal beats; rhythm is the combination of values or quantities which fill the same beat, suited to the expressions one wants to render and the passions one wants to arouse. There can be meter without rhythm, but there is no rhythm at all without meter.

. . . It is by plumbing this part of his art that the Composer gives flight to his genius; all the science of chords cannot suffice for his needs.

It is important to remark here, contrary to the prejudice of all Musicians, that harmony by itself, being able to speak to the ear alone and imitating nothing, can have only very weak effects. When it enters successfully into imitative Music, this is always only in determining and strengthening the melodious accents, which by themselves are not always sufficiently determinate without the assistance of the accompaniment. Absolute intervals have no character by themselves; an augmented second and a minor third, a minor seventh and an augmented sixth, a false fifth and a tritone are the same intervals, and take on affections which make them determinate only by their place in a modulation, and it is for the accompaniment to determine this place for them, which would often remain equivocal by the song alone. This is the use and the effect of harmony in imitative and theatrical music. It is by the accents of the melody, it is by the cadence of the rhythm, that music, imitating the inflections which the passions give to the human voice, can penetrate to the heart and move it by feelings, whereas harmony alone, not imitating anything, can produce only a pleasure of sensation. Simple chords can flatter the ear, as beautiful colors flatter the eyes; but neither of them will ever convey the least emotion to the heart because neither of them imitate anything, unless design comes to animate the colors and unless the melody comes to animate the chords. But, on the contrary, the design by itself can, without coloration, represent touching objects to us, and imitative melody can likewise move us on its own without the assistance of chords.

This is what makes all French Music so languid and insipid, because, full of their stupid prejudices and their cold science—a science which is, at bottom, simply veritable ignorance since they do not know what the greatest beauties of their Art consist in—French composers seek in the chords alone the great effects whose energy is only in the rhythm. M. Gluck knows better than I that rhythm without harmony acts much more powerfully on the soul than harmony without rhythm; he who, with a harmony that is somewhat monotonous, in my view, does not fail to produce such great emotions since he feels and he employs all the magic tricks of meter and quantity with a profound artfulness. But I exhort him not to be too biased in favor of declamation, and always to keep in mind that one of the defects of purely declamatory Music is to lose one part of the resources of rhythm, whose greatest power is in the arias.

I have fulfilled the least difficult part of the task I imposed upon myself; a general observation on the development of the Opera Alceste *has led me to treat this truly interesting question: what license should one grant to the Musician who works on a Poem of which he is not the Author? I have distinguished three parts of imitative Music and, while admitting that the accent is determined by the Poet, I have made it seen that the harmony, and especially the rhythm, offer to the Musician resources from which he should profit.*

[The details must be entered into.][27] It is a great strain for me to follow scores which are somewhat laden; that of *Alceste* is very much so, and moreover quite intricate, full of false clefs, of false notes, of confusedly heaped up parts.

In examining the Drama of *Alceste* and the manner in which M. Gluck believes himself to be obliged to treat it, one can hardly understand how he was able to make it bearable in presentation. Not that this Drama, written on the plan of Greek Tragedies, does not shine with substantial beauties, not that its Music is not admirable, but from the difficulties he had to overcome in such a great uniformity of characters and of expression in order to prevent exhaustion and boredom and to sustain interest and attention until the end.

The overture, of a single piece of a beautiful and simple ordering, is well and regularly laid out; by means of it, the Author intended to prepare the spectators for the sadness into which he was going to plunge them from the beginning of the first act and throughout the entire Piece, and for this he modulated his overture almost entirely in the minor mode, and even with affectation, since in this entire piece, which is quite long, only the first brace on page 4, and the first related brace on page 9, are in the major mode. He moreover allocated augmented and diminished dissonances and sustained and forced sounds to the treble in order to express trembling and plaints; all this is good and well conceived in itself, since the overture should be employed only to dispose the heart of the spectator to the sort of interest by which he is going to be moved; but three inconveniences result from it. The first, the use of a kind of harmony that is not sonorous enough for an overture destined to awaken the spectator by filling his ear and preparing it for attention. The second, of anticipating this same kind of harmony, which one will be forced to employ for such a long time, and which consequently must be handled very carefully in order to prevent satiety; and the third, of also anticipating the sequence of time, by expressing for us in advance a distress which is not yet in the scene and which the announcement of the public Herald alone is going to arouse, and I do not believe that one should indicate in a retrograde order what is going to come as having already passed. In order to remedy all this, I would have thought of composing the overture in two pieces of different characters, but both of them treated in a sonorous and consonant harmony. The first, conveying into hearts the feeling of a gentle and tender gaiety, would have represented the happiness of the reign of Admetus and the charms of the conjugal union; the second, in a more complex meter and by more lively movements and a more interrupted phrasing would have expressed the People's uneasiness concerning Admetus' illness, and would have served as a very natural introduction to the start of the piece and to prepare the Herald.

Page 12. After the two notes that follow the word *Udite*,[28] I would have had the accompaniment cease until the end of the recitative. This would have better expressed the silence of the people listening to the town crier, and the spectators, curious to hear this announcement clearly, do not need this accompaniment; the Bass suffices all by itself, and the entrance of the chorus which follows would have produced still more of an effect. This alternative chorus with the short solos by Evander and Ismene seem to me a beautiful start and of a good character. The ritornello of four measures which is taken up again several times is sad without being somber and of an exquisite simplicity. This whole chorus would be of a very good tone if expressions that are too pathetic were not mixed in too often, and from the second measure. Nor do I scarcely like any better the clap of thunder on page 14;[29] it has the look of a play on words and one which seems misplaced to me; but I very much like the manner in which the same chorus, reprised on page 34, then comes to life at the idea of the unhappiness ready to strike it down.

E vuoi morire o misera.[30] This gloomy psalmody is of a sublime simplicity and should produce a great effect. But the same held note, repeated in the same manner on these other words, *Altro non puoi raccogliere*,[31] seems cold and almost insipid to me. It is natural for the voice to rise a little when it speaks several times in succession to the same person; if this same psalmody had therefore been made to ascend the second time alone by a semitone on *dis*, that is, on *mi*-flat, this might have sufficed to make it more natural and even more energetic; but I believe that it must be varied a little in some way. Furthermore, in both the eighth and in the tenth measure there is a tritone, neither of which can be resolved, even though it might appear to be so the second time by the second violin; this produces a series of chords that does not have a good foundation and that is against the rules. I know that one can do anything on a held note, especially in such a case, and this is not what I disapprove of in the passage, although I note its irregularity.[32]

This should not be a flight of precipitation, as before the enemy, but a flight of consternation which, so to speak, should be shameful and clandestine rather than striking and rapid. If the author had wanted to compose an exhortation to joy at the end of this chorus, he couldn't have succeeded better. [From whence the] double melody (the last measure on p. 60 and the three following measures.)][33]

After the chorus *fuggiamo*,[34] I would have had the entire Orchestra be quiet and would have declaimed the recitative *ove son* with a simple bass. But, immediately after these words, *V'è chi t'ami à tal segno*, I would have begun a recitative accompanied by a noble, brilliant, sublime instrumental part which would announce with dignity the decision Alceste is going to make, which would dispose the listener to feel all the energy of these words, *Ah! vi son io*, too little prepared by the two measures that precede it. This instrumental part would have offered the image of these two verses, *già tutta alla mia mente luminosa, si mostra la grande idea* would have been sustained with the same brilliance through all the ritornelli of this recitative. I would have treated the aria which follows, *ombre larve*,[35] in two contrasting movements, namely a somber and fearsome *allegro* until these words, *non voglio pietà*, and an *adagio* or *largo* full of sadness and of gentleness on these, *se vi tolgo l'amato consorte*. M. Gluck, who does not like rondos, will allow me to tell him that here would be an instance to employ one quite felicitously by making the second part of the aria of the remainder of this monologue and taking up again only the *allegro* in order to finish.

The aria *io non chiedo eterni Dei*[36] seems very beautiful to me; I would have only desired that the expressions in it did not have to be varied by different meters. Two, when they are necessary, can form agreeable contrasts; but three, this is too many, and this breaks the unity. Oppositions are much more beautiful and produce a greater effect when they are done without changing meter and through combinations of value and of quantity alone. The reason why it is better to make a contrast in the same movement than to change it is that artfulness must be hidden as much as possible in order to produce illusion and interest, and that as soon as one changes movement, the artfulness is detected and makes itself perceived. For the same reason, in the same aria I would have liked for the key to have been changed as little as possible, for the cadences to have been restricted as much as possible to two alone, principal and dominant, and for effects to have been sought in beautiful phrasing and in melodious combinations rather than in a mannered harmony and changes of key.

The aria *io non chiedo eterni Dei* p. 27[37] is, especially at its beginning, an exquisite song, as are almost all those by the same Author. But where in this aria is the unity of design, of portraiture, of character? This is not at all, it seems to me, an aria, but a succession of several arias. The children mix their song into their mother's; this is not what I disapprove of. But the meter is often changed in it, not in order to contrast and alternate the two parts by a single motive, but in order to pass successively through absolutely different songs. No common design can be shown in this piece that connects it and makes it a unified whole. Nevertheless, this is what seems to me necessary in order genuinely to constitute an aria. The Author, after having modulated in several keys, nonetheless believes he is obliged to finish in *E la fa*,[38] as he began. He himself therefore clearly perceives that the whole should be treated on a single design and form a unity. Nevertheless, I cannot see it in the different parts of this aria, unless one would like to find it in the modified repetition of the *allegro, non comprende i mali miei*,[39] with which this piece ends, which does not seem to me sufficient to make a connection among all the parts of which it is composed. I admit that the first change of meter admirably renders the meaning and the punctuation of the words. But it is no less true that this could also be attained without changing it, that, in general, these changes of meter in a single aria must produce a contrast and also change the movement, and that, finally, this one brings about a cadence on the same dominant two times in a row, a sort of monotony which should be avoided as much as possible. I will take the further liberty of saying that the last measure on page 27 seems to me to be a very weak expression for the accent of the word it should render. This fifth which the song makes on the Bass, and the minor third that is joined to it, produce a chord that is a bit languid to my ear. I would have preferred to make the song a bit more lively, and to substitute the sixth for the fifth, in something like the following way, which I do not have the impertinence to present as a correction, but which I propose solely in order better to explain my idea.[40]

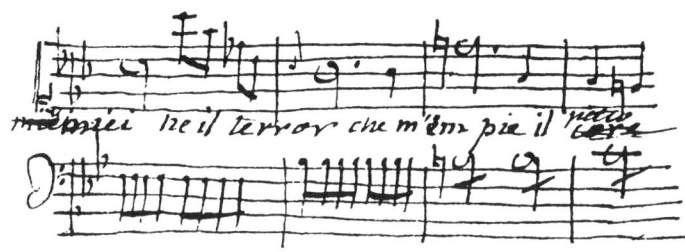

The sole reproach I might make to this recitative[41] is that it is too beautiful. But, given the place it occupies, this is indeed a reproach. If the Author begins from this point to be lavish with the enharmonic, what will he then do in the rending situations that must follow? This recitative should be touching and pathetic, I know it well, but not, it seems to me, to such a high degree, because to the extent one advances, forceful blows must be used in order to reawaken the listener when he begins to weary of beautiful things. This gradation seems to me absolutely necessary in an Opera.

The High Priest's recitative, page 55, is a fine example of the effect of the obligatory recitative. The oracle and the majesty of the person who is going to deliver it cannot be better prepared. The sole thing that I would desire in it would be a declaration that was more brilliant than terrifying, for it seems to me that Apollo should neither appear nor speak like Jupiter. For the same reason, I would not like to give to this God, who is represented to us in the figure of a handsome young blond man, the voice of a countertenor.

> Page 39 Dilegua il nero turbine
> Me freme al trono intorno,
> O faretrato Apolline
> Col chiaro tuo splendor[42]

This whole Chorus[43] in rondo could be better; these four verses should be sung first by the High Priest, then repeated in their entirety by the Chorus, without excepting the last two, which the Author has spoken only by the High Priest. On the contrary, the High Priest should speak only the following verses:

> Sai che ramingo, esule,
> T'accolse Admetto un di
> Che del anfriso al margine
> Tu fosti il suo pastor.[44]

And the Chorus, instead of these verses, which it no more than the High Priest should repeat, should take up the first four again. I also find that the response in the first two measures, a kind of imitation, does not have enough gravity. I would prefer that the whole Chorus were syllabic.[45]

Furthermore, I have noted, with great pleasure, the equally pleasant, simple, and learned manner in which the author passes from the key of the mediant to that of the seventh note of the key in the three last measures of page 39. And, after having stayed there quite long enough, he returns by a progression analogous to its principal key, by passing once again through the mediant in the 2nd, 3rd, and 4th measure of page 43; but what I don't find nearly so simple is the recitative *nume eterno*, page 52.[46]

I will not talk about the dance tune on page 17,[47] nor about any of those in this work. I have said, in my article *Opera*[48] what I thought of ballets breaking up pieces and suspending the development of the interest. I have not changed my mind since then on this point, but it is quite possible that I am mistaken.

I would not at all want any accompaniment to Evander's recitative, pp. 20, 21, and 22,[49] other than the Bass.

I also find the Chorus, page 22, much too pathetic, despite the dolorous expression with which it is filled, but the alternations from the right to the left, and the responses by various instruments, must, it seems to me, make this Music very interesting in the theater.[50]

Popoli di Tessaglia, page 24.[51] I will cite this recitative by Alceste as an example of a touching and tender modulation, without becoming entirely pathetic, even if it becomes so in the end. It is by inversions of a fairly simple harmony that M. Gluck produces these beautiful effects. He might have been the master of sticking to the same route for a long time without becoming languid and cold. But one sees by the accompanied recitative *nume eterno*, on page 52,[52] that he does not take long to seize the opportunity.

Has given too much emphatic and declamatory expression and not enough tuneful and melodious expression.[53]

This final fall is a misconception, and instead of falling on the tonic G, should have remained on the dominant D so as to indicate the question.[54]

The majority of these interlaced chords are merely different facets of a single one; which casts monotony into the harmony.

The more M. Gluck rushes toward declamatory expression, the more he loses the charm of the melody.

And he carries even into the melodious singing of his arias an austerity of system that is not part of his genius . . . only these three arias, all three of them delectable, but all three of the same character,

The art so little known but so necessary in music and above all in opera of graduating the strength and the expression so as to strike with redoubled blows that grow ever stronger. The beginning of his first act is as laden with harmony as the rest of his work.

Because hearts are warmed only by degrees. Because in order to produce great effects it is not enough to strike with great blows, it is necessary to strike with redoubled blows that grow ever stronger.

. . . this piece of music is very beautiful, but too graduated and too studied.

Extract from a Response by the Underlaborer to His Frontman Concerning a Piece from Gluck's "Orfeo" [1]

As for the enharmonic passage in Gluck's *Orfeo* which you tell me you have so much difficulty sounding out and even listening to, I know very well the reason for this: it is that you can do nothing without me and that, when deprived of my assistance you will never be anything but an ignoramus in any genre whatsoever. At least you sense the beauty of this passage, and that is already something; but you are ignorant of what produces it; I am going to teach you.

It is that this great Musician has known how to derive from the same passage, and, what is more, from the same chord, the two most contrary effects in all their force: the ravishing sweetness of Orpheus's song and the rending *stridor*[2] of the cry of the Furies. What means has he chosen for this? A very simple means, as those which produce great effects always are. If you had mediated more carefully upon the article *enharmonic*, which I once dictated to you, you would have understood that this remarkable cause must be sought not simply in the nature of intervals and in the succession of chords, but in the ideas which they arouse, and whose greater or lesser relations, so little known to Musicians, are nevertheless, without their suspecting it, the source of all the expressions that they find solely by instinct.[3]

The piece in question is in *mi*-flat major, and something worthy of being noted is that this admirable piece is, as far as I can recall it, entirely in the same key, or at least so little modulated that the idea of the principal key is not effaced for a moment. Furthermore, no longer having this piece before my eyes and recalling it only imperfectly, I can speak of it only with uncertainty.

To begin with, this *nò* by the furies, struck and reiterated each time as their entire response, is one of the most sublime inventions in this genre that I know of, and if it is perhaps owing to the Poet,[4] it must be admitted that the Musician has seized upon the manner of appropriating it. I have heard it said that at the performance of this Opera no one could stop shaking each time this terrifying *nò* was repeated, even though it was sung only in unison or at the octave, and without departing in its harmony from the perfect chord until the passage in question. But, at the moment when one least expects it, this dominant, made sharp, forms a frightful screeching which the ear and the heart cannot bear, while at the same instant Orpheus's song redoubles in sweetness and in charm; and what is most astonishing is that in ending this short passage, one finds oneself in the same key by which one just entered it, almost without being able to comprehend how we have been able to be transported so far and brought back so close with so much power and speed.

You will have difficulty believing that all this magic is worked by a tacit passage from the major mode to the minor, and by the sudden return to the major. You will easily convince yourself of this on the Harpsichord. At the moment when the Bass, which sounds the dominant with its chord, is to play *do*-flat, you change not the key but the mode and pass into a *mi*-flat minor third: for not only does this *do*, which is the sixth note of the key, take the flat that belongs to the minor Mode, but the preceding chord, which keeps close to the fundamental, becomes for it that of the diminished seventh on *re*-natural, and the diminished seventh on the *re* naturally calls for the perfect minor chord of *mi*-flat. Orpheus's song, *furie, larve*, belonging equally to the major and to the minor, remains the same in them both; but on the words *ombre sdegnose* it suddenly establishes the minor Mode. It is probably due to not having soon enough grasped the idea of the Mode that you have had difficulty justly sounding out this passage from its beginning; but it returns by concluding in the major; the great effect of this passage comes from this new transition at the end of the word *sdegnose*; and you will realize that the whole difficulty of singing it vanishes precisely when, in leaving this *la*-flat, one instantly grasps the idea of the major Mode in order to sound *sol*-natural, which is its mediant.

This augmented second or diminished seventh is suspended by passing alternately and rapidly from the major to the minor—and *vice versa*—by the alternation of the Bass between the dominant *si*-flat and the sixth note *do*-flat, then it is finally completely resolved on the tonic whose Bass sounds the mediant *sol*, after having passed by the subdominant *la*-flat while carrying with it a minor third and a tritone, which always produces the same chord of the diminished seventh on the leading tone *re*.

Let us now move on to the screeching *nò* of the Furies on *si*-natural. Why this *si*-natural and not *do*-flat, as in the Bass? Because this new sound, although entering into the preceding chord by virtue of the enharmonic, is not however in the same key at all and announces a completely different one. What is this key announced by this *si*-natural? It is the key of *do* minor, of which it becomes the leading tone. Thus, the sharp discordance of the cry of the Furies comes from this duplicity of key which it makes felt, yet keeping, which is admirable, a strict analogy between the two keys; for *do* minor, as you must at least know, is the analog corresponding to *mi*-flat major, which is the principal key here.

You will make an objection to me. All this beauty, you will tell me, is only a beauty of convention and exists only on paper since this *si*-natural is really only the octave of the *do*-flat of the Bass: for, as it is not at all resolved as the leading tone, but disappears or reascends on the *si*-flat dominant of the key, when one would notate it by *do*-flat, as in the Bass, the passage and its effect would be absolutely the same in the judgment of the ear. Thus, this whole marvelous enharmonic is only such for the eyes.

This objection, my dear Frontman, would be solid if the tempered division of the Organ and of the Harpsichord were the genuine harmonic division and if the intervals were modified in the intonation of the voice in accordance with the relationships whose idea is given by the modulation, and not in accordance with the alterations of the temperament. Although it might be true that on the Harpsichord the *si*-natural is the octave of the *do*-flat, it is not true that by sounding each of these two sounds, relative to the mode that produces them, you will sound exactly either the unison or the octave. The *si*-natural, as leading tone, will move still further away from the *si*-flat dominant and will approach it by as much by the excess of the tonic *do*, which calls for this natural; and the *do*-flat, as the sixth note in the minor mode, will move away less from the dominant which it recalls and on which it will descend again. Thus, the semitone which the Bass makes by ascending from *si*-flat to *do*-flat is much smaller than that which the furies make by ascending from *si*-flat to its natural. The augmented seventh which seems to produce these two sounds exceeds even the octave, and this excess causes the discordance of the cry of the Furies; for the idea of the leading tone joined to the natural naturally carries the voice higher than the octave of the *do*-flat, and this is so true that this cry no longer produces its effect on the Harpsichord as with the voice because the sound of the instrument is not modified in the same way.

This, I well know, is directly contrary to established calculations and to common opinion, which gives the name of a minor semitone to the transition from one note to its sharp or to its flat, and of major semitone to the transition from one note to the superior flat or to the inferior sharp. But more regard is paid in these denominations to the difference of the degree than to the true relationship of the interval, as every man who has an ear and good faith will soon be convinced of. And regarding calculation, some day I will develop for you, but for you alone, a more natural theory, which will make you see how misconceived is that on which the intervals have been calculated.⁵

I shall conclude these observations with a remark that must not be omitted; it is that the whole effect of the passage I have just examined comes from the fact that the portion in which it is found happens to be in the major mode: for had it been in minor, Orpheus' song, remaining the same, would have been without power and without effect, the intonation of the Furies by the natural would have been impossible and absurd, and there would have been nothing of the enharmonic in this passage. I would wager everything in the world that a Frenchman, having had this piece to compose, would have treated it in the minor Mode. He would have been able to put other beauties into it, doubtless, but none which would have been as simple and which would have been as worthy as this one.

This is what my memory has been able to suggest to me concerning this passage and its explanation. These great effects are found by genius, which is rare, and are felt by a sensitive organ, of which so many people are deprived; but they are explained only by a well-considered study of the art. You would not have need of my analyses now if you had meditated somewhat upon the reflections we once made when I dictated our *Dictionary* to you. But, along with a very lively nature, you have a mind of an inconceivable slowness. You do not seize any idea except long after it has been presented to you, and you see today only what you looked at yesterday.⁶ Believe me, my dear Frontman, let us never quarrel with one another;⁷ for without me you are nothing. I am indulgent, as you know; I never refuse any task you desire when you take the trouble to call me and the time to wait for me; but never attempt anything without me in any genre, never meddle extemporaneously in anything whatsoever if you do not wish to ruin in an instant by your ineptness what you have done up until now so as to give yourself the air of a thinking man.

Appendix
"Enfin, il est en ma puissance," from Lully's *Armide*

Notes

Barker	*Greek Musical Writings.* 2 vols. Edited by Andrew Barker. Cambridge: Cambridge University Press, 1989.
Bloom	Jean-Jacques Rousseau. *Emile.* Edited by Allan Bloom. New York: Basic Books, 1979.
Collected Writings, I	Jean-Jacques Rousseau. *Rousseau, Judge of Jean-Jacques: Dialogues. Collected Writings of Rousseau*, Vol. I. Edited by Roger D. Masters and Christopher Kelly. Hanover, N.H.: University Press of New England, 1991.
Collected Writings, II	Jean-Jacques Rousseau. *First Discourse and Polemics. Collected Writings of Rousseau*, Vol. II. Edited by Roger D. Masters and Christopher Kelly. Hanover, N.H.: University Press of New England, 1992.
Collected Writings, III	Jean-Jacques Rousseau. *Discourse on the Origins of Inequality (Second Discourse), Polemics, and Political Economy. Collected Writings of Rousseau*, Vol. III. Edited by Roger D. Masters and Christopher Kelly. Hanover, N.H.: University Press of New England, 1992.
Collected Writings, IV	Jean-Jacques Rousseau. *Social Contract, Discourse on the Virtue Most Necessary for a Hero, Political Fragments, and Geneva Manuscript. Collected Writings of Rousseau*, Vol. IV. Edited by Roger D. Masters and Christopher Kelly. Hanover, N.H.: University Press of New England, 1994.
Collected Writings, V	Jean-Jacques Rousseau. *The Confessions and Correspondence, Including the Letters to Malesherbes. Collected Writings of Rousseau*, Vol. V. Edited by Roger D. Masters, Christopher Kelly, and Peter G. Stillman. Hanover, N.H.: University Press of New England, 1995.
Encyclopedia	*Encyclopédie, ou Dictionnaire raisonné des sciences, des arts, et des mètiers*, facsimile edition published by Friedrich Frommann Verlag. Stuttgart; Bad-Cannstatt: Friedrich Frommann Verlag, 1966.
Gossett	Jean-Philippe Rameau, *Treatise on Harmony.* Translated and edited by Philip Gossett. (Reprint.) New York: Dover, 1971.
Jacobi	Jean-Philippe Rameau. *Complete Theoretical Writings of Rameau.* 5 vols. Edited by Erwin R. Jacobi. 6 vols. New York: American Institute of Musicology, 1967–1971.
Launay	Denise Launay, ed., *La querelle des bouffons.* 3 vols. Genève: Minkoff Reprint, 1973.

Leigh   Jean-Jacques Rousseau. *Correspondance complète*. 50 vols. Edited by R. A. Leigh. Geneva: Institute et Musée Voltaire, 1965 ff.

Pléiade   Jean-Jacques Rousseau. *Oeuvres complètes*. 5 vols. Paris: NRF-Éditions de la Pléiade, 1959–1995.

NOTES TO THE INTRODUCTION

1. The fullest treatments of Rousseau's musical writings in relation to his thought in general are: Robert Wokler, *Rousseau on Society, Politics, Music and Language: An Historical Interpretation of His Early Writings* (London: Garland, 1987); Michael O'Dea, *Jean-Jacques Rousseau: Music, Illusion and Desire* (New York: St. Martin's Press, 1995); Downing A. Thomas, *Music and the Origins of Language: Theories from the French Enlightenment* (Cambridge: Cambridge University Press, 1995); and John T. Scott, "The Harmony Between Rousseau's Musical Theory and His Philosophy," *Journal of the History of Ideas* 59 (1998), 287–308, upon which this introduction draws.

2. Rousseau, *Dialogues*, Dialogue I (*Collected Writings*, I, 22–23). For Rousseau's own statements about his "system" as the unifying principle of all his works, see also *Lettre à Beaumont* (Pléiade, IV, 935–936). See also Arthur M. Melzer, *The Natural Goodness of Man: On the System of Rousseau's Thought* (Chicago: University of Chicago Press, 1990), esp. 9–12.

3. Rousseau, *Dialogues*, Second Dialogue (*Collected Writings*, I, 164).

4. Rousseau, *Confessions*, I (*Collected Writings*, V, 10); II (*Collected Writings*, V, 60). See also Maurice Cranston, *Jean-Jacques: The Early Life and Work of Jean-Jacques Rousseau, 1712–1754* (New York: Norton, 1982), 55–56.

5. Rousseau, *Confessions*, III (*Collected Writings*, V, 98–103), V (*Collected Writings*, V, 174–176). See also Cranston, *Jean-Jacques*, 82–83.

6. Rousseau, *Confessions*, IV (*Collected Writings*, V, 123–126).

7. See Rousseau, *Dialogues*, First Dialogue (*Collected Writings*, I, 16–22); Second Dialogue (*Collected Writings*, I, 160–165).

8. Rousseau, *Confessions*, V (*Collected Writings*, V, 152).

9. See Julien Tiersot, *Jean-Jacques Rousseau*, "Les Maîtres de la Musique," 2nd rev. ed. (Paris: Libraire Félix Alcan, 1920), 59.

10. Rousseau, *Confessions*, VII (*Collected Writings*, V, 247). For the libretti to the operas, see Pléiade, II, 797–842.

11. Rousseau, *Confessions*, V (*Collected Writings*, V, 155). Rousseau's "outline" of Rameau's treatise can be found at the Bibliothèque de Genève. See Tiersot, *Rousseau*, 58.

12. Rousseau, *Confessions*, IV (*Collected Writings*, V, 143). Rousseau was, in fact, a highly skilled copyist who wrote about the demands of the work at length in the article COPYIST [*Copiste*] in his *Dictionary of Music* (translated in part herein). On Rousseau's account of his trade, see *Dialogues*, Second Dialogue (*Collected Writings*, I, 136–145, 160–165).

13. See Rousseau, *Confessions*, VI (*Collected Writings*, V, 227–228); VII (ibid., 235).

14. See Rousseau, *Confessions*, VII (*Collected Writings*, V, 241).

15. Rousseau, *Confessions*, VII (*Collected Writings*, V, 241). For the Academy's judgment of Rousseau's *Plan*, see Leigh, I, 317–322.

16. For a discussion of Rousseau's notation system and its novelty and influence, see Sydney Kleinman's helpful introduction to the Pléiade edition of the *Plan* and the "Dissertation" (Pléiade, V, xlvii–lxxiii). The translator had just read Kleinman's introduction when he picked up his daughter's small electronic keyboard, made in Singapore, and discovered that the keys on it were marked using Rousseau's notation!

17. Rousseau, "Dissertation on Modern Music," pp. 64–65 below.

18. See Rousseau, "Letter on Italian and French Opera," translated herein. See also the remarks on the dating of this letter in the editorial introduction to the writing.

19. Rousseau, *Confessions*, VII (*Collected Writings*, V, 263–264).

20. See Tiersot, *Rousseau*, 68, 79–80.

21. Rousseau, *Confessions*, VII (*Collected Writings*, V, 279–281). See also Leigh, I, 83–86. Rameau made the incident public a decade later in his *Errors on Music in the Encyclopedia*, translated herein.

22. Rousseau, "Avertissement" to *Les Muses galantes*, Pléiade, II, 1052.

23. Rousseau, *Confessions*, VII (*Collected Writings*, V, 279–281, 286)

24. See Rousseau, *Confessions*, VII (*Collected Writings*, V, 281–284). Rousseau reprints his correspondence with Voltaire concerning the opera within the *Confessions*.

25. See Rousseau, *Examination of Two Principles Advanced by M. Rameau*, pp. 271–272 below; *Dictionary of Music*, Preface, pp. 366–367 below. For a listing of Rousseau's articles in the *Encyclopedia*, see Alfred Richard Oliver, *The Encyclopedists as Critics of Music* (New York: Columbia University Press, 1947), Appendix A.

26. Rousseau to Mme de Warens, 27 January 1749 (Leigh, II, 132–133).

27. See Rousseau to d'Alembert, 26 June 1751 (Leigh, II, 159–162).

28. Jean Le Rond d'Alembert, *Preliminary Discourse to the Encyclopedia of Diderot*, trans. Richard N. Schwab (Indianapolis: Bobbs-Merrill, 1963), 100–101.

29. See Thomas Christensen, *Rameau and Musical Thought in the Enlightenment* (Cambridge: Cambridge University Press, 1993), 7–11.

30. Rousseau, ACCOMPANIMENT [*Accompagnement*], (*Encyclopedia* version), p. 202 below.

31. O'Dea, the only close student of the *Encyclopedia* articles, characterizes the article on accompaniment as "a covert attack on French music generally and on Rameau in particular as the leading exponent of the French style," and concludes that Rousseau's *Encyclopedia* articles reveal some of the essential elements of his mature musical thought (*Music, Illusion and Desire*, 10, 16).

32. D'Alembert, *Preliminary Discourse to the Encyclopedia of Diderot*, 103–104, 133.

33. Rousseau, *Confessions*, VIII (*Collected Writings*, V, 294). Rousseau compares the lively remembrance of the impression of the event and his inability to recall the details to his capacity for music: "Before I learned it, I knew multitudes of songs by heart: since I have known how to sing tunes that were noted down, I have been unable to retain any of them, and today I doubt that I can repeat one of those I have loved most fully" (ibid., 294–295).

34. Rousseau, *First Discourse* (*Collected Writings*, II, 15).

35. Lecat, *Refutation of the Observations of Jean-Jacques Rousseau of Geneva* (*Collected Writings*, II, 68). See also Lecat's remarks about the corrupt taste for intricate Italian music in his *Refutation of the Discourse which Won the Prize of the Academy of Dijon in the Year 1750, by an Academician of Dijon Who Denied It His Vote* (ibid., 161–162). For Rousseau's reply, see *Letter by Jean-Jacques Rousseau of Geneva About a New Refutation of His Discourse by a Member of the Academy of Dijon* (*Letter to Lecat*) (ibid., 178), and the "Preface" to *Narcisse* (ibid., 188).

36. For accounts of the "Quarrel of the Bouffons," see Louisette Reichenberg, *Contribution à l'histoire de la "Querelle des Bouffons"* (Philadelphia: University of Pennsylvania Press, 1937; publ. Ph.D. Diss); Oliver, *Encyclopedists as Critics of Music*, chap. VII.

37. See Cuthbert Girdlestone, *Jean-Philippe Rameau: His Life and Work* (New York: Dover, 1969; reprint), 481–483.

38. Cranston, *Jean-Jacques*, 280.

39. While Grimm's *Letter* is often seen as having opened the "Quarrel of the Bouffons," it is more accurate to think of it as the final shot of the dispute between the Lullistes and Ramistes. See Paul-Maurice Masson, "La 'Lettre sur Omphale,'" *Revue de musicologie* 27 (1945), 1–19. Compare Cranston, *Jean-Jacques*, 275–276.

40. The attribution of the letter to Raynal is generally accepted but not certain.

41. Rousseau, *Letter to Grimm*, pp. 129 and 130 below.

42. On his engraving of Pergolesi's opera, see Rousseau to Toussaint-Pierre Lenieps, 22 October 1752 (Leigh, II, 198–200); see also Reichenburg, *Contribution à l'histoire de la "Querelle des Bouffons,"* 30–31. For Rousseau's statement of Pergolesi's influence on his own work, see *Confessions*, VIII (*Collected Writings*, V, 314–315). In his article COPYIST [*Copiste*] in the *Dictionary of Music* (translated herein), Rousseau laments that he was only ever able to write French music.

43. Rousseau, *Confessions*, VIII (*Collected Writings*, V, 314–320). See also Cranston, *Jean-Jacques*, 263–267.

44. Cynthia Verba, *Music and the French Enlightenment: Reconstruction of a Dialogue, 1750–1764* (Cambridge: Cambridge University Press, 1993), 11 n; James Miller, *Rousseau: Dreamer of Democracy* (New Haven: Yale University Press, 1984), 138. Berlioz's estimation of Rousseau and account of the last performance of the *Devin du village*, in which he denies his complicity, is found in his *Mémoires* (chap. 15):

Poor Rousseau, who attached as much importance to his score of the "Devin du village" as to the masterpieces of eloquence which have immortalized his name, he who firmly believed himself to have entirely crushed Rameau, to have vanquished [Rameau's] "Trio of the Furies" with the little songs, the little flons-flons, the little rondeaux, the little solos, the little bergeries, the little drôleries of every sort that make up his little intermezzo.... Poor Rousseau! Could he have foreseen that his dear opera, which aroused so much applause, would one day fall, no longer to be raised up again, beneath the blow of an enormous white powdered wig thrown at the feet of Colette by an insolent scoffer? (quoted by Eve Kisch, "Rameau and Rousseau," *Music and Letters* 22 [1941], 97–114; 104).

45. Rousseau, *Dialogues*, First Dialogue (*Collected Writings*, I, 19–20); Second Dialogue (160–163).

46. See Wokler, "Rousseau on Rameau and Revolution," 256, 259–260.
47. Rousseau, *Letter on French Music*, p. 144 below.
48. Rousseau, *Letter on French Music*, p. 174 below.
49. Rousseau, *Letter on French Music*, p. 148 below.
50. See Cranston, *Jean-Jacques*, 284; Leigh, II, 234.
51. Rousseau, *Confessions*, VIII (*Collected Writings*, 322–323).
52. Cranston, *Jean-Jacques*, 283–384. See also Charles B. Paul, "Music and Ideology: Rameau, Rousseau, and 1789," *Journal of the History of Ideas* 32 (1971), 395–410; Robert Wokler, "Rousseau on Rameau and Revolution," *Studies in the Eighteenth Century* 4 (1978), 251–283; Verba, *Music and the French Enlightenment*, 13–15. Rousseau explains that the realm was divided between the aristocratic party defending French music and the more popular party extolling Italian music (*Confessions*, VIII, *Collected Writings*, V, 322). For an argument concerning the democratic spirit or implications in Rousseau's *Letter on French Music*, see Colm Kiernan, "Rousseau and Music in the French Enlightenment," *French Studies* 26 (1972), 156–165.
53. The main brochures from the "Quarrel," including the responses to Rousseau's *Letter on French Music*, are reprinted in Launay.
54. In his *Réponse de M. Rameau à MM. les Editeurs de l'Encyclopédie sur leur dernier Avertissement* (1757; Jacobi, V, 347), Rameau asks: "What does this *Letter on French Music* mean? Was it French Music that is intended, or the French Musician?"
55. Rousseau, *Letter on French Music*, p. 168 below.
56. For an extended examination of Rousseau's and Rameau's treatment of Lully's recitative, see Verba, *Music and the French Enlightenment*, 21–30; "The Development of Rameau's Thoughts on Modulation and Chromatics," *Journal of the American Musicological Society* 26 (1973), 72–91.
57. Rameau, *Observations on Our Instinct for Music*, Preface, p. 175 below.
58. Cranston, *Jean-Jacques*, 279.
59. Verba, *Music and the French Enlightenment*, 8.
60. Cranston, *Jean-Jacques*, 288.
61. Rameau, *Errors on Music in the Encyclopedia*, p. 226 below.
62. As Verba suggests, Rameau's *Errors* should be viewed as much as a response to Rousseau's *Letter on French Music* as an attack on specific articles in the *Encyclopedia* (*Music and the French Enlightenment*, 4). See also Wokler, "Rousseau on Rameau and Revolution," 261–262.
63. Rameau, *Errors on Music in the Encyclopedia*, p. 231 below.
64. Rameau, *Génération harmonique* (Jacobi, III, 6).
65. For a discussion of Rameau's and Rousseau's differing views of nature as the basis of their different understandings of music, see Kintzler, "Rameau et Rousseau: Le choc de deux esthétiques," Preface to Rousseau, *Écrits sur la Musique* (Stockholm: Stock, 1979), xiii–xxiv; and Kiernan, "Rousseau and Music in the French Enlightenment," 156–165. For an extensive treatment of the scientific sources of Rameau's musical theory, see Christensen, *Rameau and Musical Thought in the Enlightenment*.
66. Earlier critics of Rameau had questioned his arguments for the primacy of harmony, but they did not base their argument on a theory of nature and human nature similar to Rousseau's. For example, Johann Mattheson early on criticized

Rameau's theory in his *Der vollkommene Capellmeister* (1739). Part of this treatise is reprinted in *Musical Aesthetics: A Historical Reader*, ed. Edward A. Lippman (New York: Pendragon, 1986), 123–162. See also Erwin R. Jacobi's introduction to *Complete Theoretical Writings of Rameau*, II, xiii–xiv; III, xiv–xv, xxxi–xxviii; Oliver, *Encyclopedists as Critics of Music*, 111.

67. Rousseau, *Examination of Two Principles Advanced by M. Rameau*, pp. 272–273 below.

68. Rameau, *Errors on Music in the Encyclopedia*, p. 232 below.

69. Rousseau, *Examination of Two Principles Advanced by M. Rameau*, p. 279 below.

70. Rousseau, *Examination of Two Principles Advanced by M. Rameau*, p. 276 below.

71. The digression in the original draft of the *Examination of Two Principles*, entitled *On the Principle of Melody, or Response to the "Errors on Music,"* is translated below as "The Origin of Melody."

72. See Rousseau, *Essay on the Origin of Languages*, Draft Preface, p. 289 below.

73. Two scholars simultaneously and independently published the digression on the origin of melody from Rousseau's draft of *The Principle of Melody*: Marie-Élisabeth Duchez, "*Principe de la Mélodie* et *Origine des langues*: Un brouillon inédit de Jean-Jacques Rousseau sur l'origine de la mélodie," *Revue de musicologie*, 60 (1974), 33–86; and Robert Wokler, "Rameau, Rousseau, and the *Essai sur l'origine des langues*," *Studies on Voltaire and the Eighteenth Century*, 117 (1974), 179–238. See also Wokler's *Social Thought of J. J. Rousseau* (New York: Garland, 1987), chap. IV and Appendix.

74. Duchez, "Principe de la mélodie," 48. See also Cranston, *Jean-Jacques*, 289; Michèle Duchet and Michel Launay, "Synchronie et diachronie: l'*Essai sur l'origine des langues* et le deuxième *Discours*," *Revue internationale de philosophie* 82 (1967); Glyn P. Norton, "Retrospective Time and the Musical Experience in Rousseau," *Modern Language Quarterly* 34 (1973), 131–145; 135.

75. Rousseau, *Emile*, IV (Pléiade, IV, 672; Bloom, 340). In the original edition of the work (1762) Rousseau refers his reader to "an essay on the *Principles of Melody*," but in 1764 he corrected the citation in his copy of the work to refer to an essay on "the origin of languages." See Duchez, "*Principe de la Mélodie* et *Origine des langues*," 49.

76. Jacques Derrida, *Of Grammatology*, trans. Gayatri Chakravorty Spivak (Baltimore: Johns Hopkins University Press, 1974); original edition, *De la grammatologie* (Paris: Les éditions de minuit, 1967); see also his "The Linguistic Circle of Geneva," in *Margins of Philosophy*, trans. Allan Bass (Chicago: University of Chicago Press, 1982), 137–153; *Memoires for Paul de Man*, trans. Cecile Lindsay, Jonathan Culler, Eduardo Cadava, and Peggy Kamuf, rev. ed. (New York: Columbia University Press, 1989). See Jean Starobinski, "Rousseau and the Origin of Languages," in *Jean-Jacques Rousseau: Transparency and Obstruction*, trans. Arthur Goldhammer (Chicago: University of Chicago Press, 1988); Paul de Man, "The Rhetoric of Blindness: Jacques Derrida's Reading of Rousseau," chap. VII of *Blindness and Insight: Essays in the Rhetoric of Contemporary Criticism* (New York: Oxford University Press, 1971); see also his *Allegories of Reading: Figural Language in Rous-*

seau, Nietzsche, Rilke, and Proust* (New Haven: Yale University Press, 1979). For discussions of Derrida's reading of Rousseau, see Newton Garver, "Derrida on Rousseau on Writing," *Journal of Philosophy* 74 (1977): 663–673; Irene Harvey, "Doubling the Space of Existence," in *Deconstruction and Philosophy*, ed. John Sallis (Chicago: University of Chicago Press, 1987), 60–70.

77. For accounts of the various positions on the dating of the *Essay* and its relationship to his work as a whole, see Wokler, *Rousseau on Society, Politics, Music and Language*, 301–324; Charles Porset, "L'inquiétante étrangeté' de l'*Essai sur l'origine des langues*: Rousseau et ses exégètes," *Studies on Voltaire and the Eighteenth Century* 154 (1976), 1715–1754.

78. Rousseau, *Essay on the Origin of Languages*, chap. I, pp. 289 and 293 below.

79. Rousseau, *Second Discourse* (*Collected Writings*, III, 26).

80. For an extended treatment of the relationship between Rousseau's theory of linguistic and musical variation and his understanding of the basis of a culturally distinct community, including the legitimate community, see John T. Scott, "Rousseau and the Melodious Language of Freedom," *Journal of Politics* 59 (1997), 803–829.

81. Rousseau, *Essay on the Origin of Languages*, chap. II, p. 294 below.

82. Rousseau, *Essay on the Origin of Languages*, chap. III, pp. 294–295 below.

83. Rousseau, *Essay on the Origin of Languages*, chap. I, pp. 289–290 below.

84. Rousseau, *Second Discourse* (*Collected Writings*, III, 44).

85. Rousseau, *Essay on the Origin of Languages*, chap. IX, p. 306 below.

86. For an alternative explanation of Rousseau's ambiguous account of pity, see Derrida, *Of Grammatology*, 165–194.

87. See Rousseau, *Second Discourse* (*Collected Writings*, 14–15, 36–37 [emphasis supplied]). For Rousseau's discussion of pity, see Roger D. Masters, *The Political Philosophy of Rousseau* (Princeton: Princeton University Press, 1968), 71–72.

88. Rousseau, *Essay on the Origin of Languages*, chap. IX, p. 306 below.

89. Rousseau, *Essay on the Origin of Languages*, chap. IX, p. 314 below.

90. Rousseau, *Essay on the Origin of Languages*, chap. IX, p. 314 below.

91. Rousseau, *Second Discourse* (*Collected Writings*, III, 47).

92. For a more extensive discussion of the relationship between the "physical" and the "moral" modes of human existence in Rousseau's thought, see John T. Scott, "The Theodicy of the *Second Discourse*: The 'Pure State of Nature' and Rousseau's Political Thought," *American Political Science Review* 86 (1992), 696–711.

93. Rousseau, *Second Discourse* (*Collected Writings*, III, 46). Just before his discussion of languages in the First Part of the work, Rousseau suggests the line of argument he will take in the *Essay* when he conjectures that development of the mind and the passions is proportioned to the needs that "peoples" experience and notes in particular the differences between the peoples of the north and south (ibid., 116).

94. However, in the *Essay* he explains that Italian "by itself is no more a musical language than is French. The difference is merely that the one lends itself to music and the other does not" (chap. VII, p. 303 below).

95. Rousseau, *Essay on the Origin of Languages*, chap. XII, p. 318 below.

96. Rousseau, *Essay on the Origin of Languages*, chap. XII, below.

97. Rousseau, *The Principle of Melody*, p. 262 below.

98. See Scott, "Rousseau and the Melodious Language of Freedom."

99. Rousseau, *Essay on the Origin of Languages*, chap. XII, p. 318 below.

100. Rousseau, *On the Principle of Melody*, pp. 269–270 below.

101. Rousseau, *Essay on the Origin of Languages*, chap. XIII, p. 319 below.

102. Rousseau, *Confessions*, IX (*Collected Writings*, V, 343–344): "From how many errors would reason be saved, how many vices would be kept from being born if one knew how to force the animal economy to favor the moral order it so often troubles! Climates, seasons, sounds, colors, darkness, light, the elements, food, noise, silence, motion, rest, all act on our machine and consequently on our soul; all offer us a thousand almost guaranteed holds for governing in their origin the feelings by which we let ourselves be dominated. Such was the fundamental outline for which I already had on paper.... Nonetheless, I worked very little on this work whose title was *sensitive morality, or the Wise Man's materialism*." See also XII (ibid., 509).

103. Rousseau, *Essay on the Origin of Languages*, chap. XV, p. 323 below.

104. Rousseau, *Essay on the Origin of Languages*, chap. XV, pp. 324–325 below.

105. Rousseau, *Essay on the Origin of Languages*, chap. XIX, pp. 329–330 below.

106. Rousseau, *Essay on the Origin of Languages*, chap. XX, p. 332 below. For the classical background to Rousseau's discussion of rhetoric and freedom, see Jean Starobinski, "Eloquence and Liberty," *Journal of the History of Ideas* 38 (1977), 195–210; esp. 204–207.

107. There have been two studies devoted to Rousseau's *On Theatrical Imitation*: Lawrence Sorenson, "Rousseau's Socratism: The Political Bearing of 'On Theatrical Imitation,'" *Interpretation* 20 (1992–1993), 135–156; and Pamela K. Jensen, "The Quarrel Between Philosophy and Poetry Reconsidered: Rousseau's *On Theatrical Imitation*," in *Rousseau and Criticism* (*Pensée libre* 5; Ottawa: North American Society for the Study of Jean-Jacques Rousseau, 1995), 183–194. Both studies are suggestive, but since they did not consult the edition used by Rousseau (Ficino's Latin translation) their results must be viewed as provisional.

108. See Rousseau, *Confessions*, XI (*Collected Writings*, V, 485–491).

109. For an interpretation of Rousseau's *Levite* and a discussion of the additions he made to the original story, see Thomas M. Kavanagh, *Writing the Truth: Authority and Desire in Rousseau* (Berkeley: University of California Press, 1987), chap. 5.

110. See Rousseau, *Essay on the Origin of Languages*, chap. I, p. 291 below. See also chap. XI, p. 317 below.

111. See, e.g., Kisch, 109. Kisch's assumption of the essential identity of the *Encyclopedia* articles and the *Dictionary* leads her to claim mistakenly that Rousseau's contributions to the *Encyclopedia* (which she does not appear to have examined) are "extremely personal articles" attacking Rameau, thus explaining Rameau's hostile reaction in his *Errors*. As noted above, Rousseau's articles are not overtly hostile to Rameau.

112. Cynthia Verba, "Jean-Jacques Rousseau: Radical and Traditional Views in his *Dictionnaire de musique*," 320. Verba draws on Thomas Webb Hunt, "The *Dictionnaire de musique* of Jean-Jacques Rousseau" (Ph.D. Diss, North Texas State University, 1967), esp. Appendix VII. Out of the 904 articles in the *Dictionary*, 524

were totally new. Of those carried over from the *Encyclopedia*, only 166 are identical to the original. Wokler dates the articles by Rousseau that appeared in the later *Supplement* to the *Encyclopedia*, such as HARMONY and OPERA, as having been written around 1756 ("Rameau, Rousseau, and the *Essai sur l'origine des langues*," *Studies on Voltaire and the Eighteenth Century* 117 (1974), 179–238; 200 n50).

113. See d'Alembert, "Notice" to Volume VI of the *Encyclopedia*, translated herein (note 63 to Rameau, *Errors on Music in the Encyclopedia*).

114. See Rousseau, *Examination of Two Principles Advanced by M. Rameau*, Preface, p. 271 below.

115. I here follow the editor of the Pléiade edition of the *Dictionary of Music*, Jean-Jacques Eigeldinger. See Eigeldinger's "Introduction" to the *Dictionnaire de la musique* (Pléiade, V, cclxx–cclxxxiii).

116. Rousseau, *Confessions*, IX (*Collected Writings*, V, 344).

117. See Rousseau, *Confessions*, XII (*Collected Writings*, V, 521).

118. Hunt, "The *Dictionnaire de musique* of Jean-Jacques Rousseau," 358–359.

119. John F. Strauss, "Jean Jacques Rousseau: Musician," *Musical Quarterly* 64 (1978), 474–482; 475.

120. Rousseau reveals d'Alembert's influence on his theory of imitation in a letter to him of 26 June 1751 (Leigh, II, 159–162): "For my part, I find your idea concerning musical imitation quite correct and quite new. In fact . . . the art of the musician does not at all consist in immediately depicting objects, but in putting the soul in a disposition similar to that in which their presence would put it." Rousseau's emphasis on music and language as expressions of the passions distinguishes his theory of imitation from that of d'Alembert. See O'Dea, *Jean-Jacques Rousseau*, 47–61.

121. While Dubos is often seen as the father of modern aesthetics because of his emphasis on "sentiment," several scholars of musical aesthetics have concluded that his theory is essentially classical and that Rousseau is the true father of romantic aesthetics. See Kintzler, *Poétique de l'opéra française de Corneille à Rousseau* (Paris: Minerve, 1991), 492–514; and Verba, *Music and the French Enlightenment*, 36–38. Compare Georges Snyders, *Le Goût musical en France aux XVIIe et XVIIIe siècles* (Paris: Vrin, 1968), 121–134; Béatrice Didier, *La Musique des lumières* (Paris: PUF, 1985), Part I, chap. 1.

122. Rousseau, *Dictionary of Music*, s.v. ACCENT [*Accent*], p. 371 below.

123. Rousseau, *Dictionary of Music*, s.v. MUSIC [*Musique*], p. 445 below. Judith Shklar discusses the effect of the Swiss tune in her *Men and Citizens: A Study of Rousseau's Social Theory* (Cambridge: Cambridge University Press, 1969), 141.

124. Claude Lévi-Strauss, "Jean-Jacques Rousseau: fondateur des sciences de l'homme," in *Jean-Jacques Rousseau*, ed. Marc Eigeldinger (Neuchâtel: La Baconnière, 1962), esp. 240. For discussions of Rousseau's influence on ethnomusicology, see Nettl, *Theory and Method in Ethnomusicology* (London: Free Press, 1964), 13; Didier, *La Musique des lumières*, Part I, chap. 3.

125. Rousseau, *Dictionary of Music*, s.v. UNITY OF MELODY [*Unité de la mélodie*], pp. 477 and 479 below. See also HARMONY [*Harmonie*] and MELODY [*Mélodie*], both translated below.

126. See Rousseau, *Dictionary of Music*, s.v. FUGUE [*Fugue*], OPERA [*Opéra*],

TRIO [*Trio*], UNITY OF MELODY [*Unité de la mélodie*], all translated below. See also BALLET and OUVERTURE, which are not translated herein.

127. See Rousseau, *Dictionary of Music*, s.v. COMPOSITION [*Composition*], translated below.

128. See Rousseau, *Dictionary of Music*, s.v. GENIUS [*Génie*], p. 406 below. See also COMPOSER [*Compositeur*] and TASTE [*Gout*], both translated below.

129. See Immanuel Kant, *Critique of Judgment*, §§46–50. For a discussion of the possible influence of Rousseau's musical theory on Kant, see Marian Hobson, "Kant, Rousseau et la musique," in *Reappraisals of Rousseau*, ed. Simon Harvey, Marian Hobson, and David Kelly (Manchester: Manchester University Press, 1980), 290–307. For an excellent discussion of Rousseau's influence on Kant more generally, see Richard L. Velkley, *Freedom and the End of Reason: On the Moral Foundations of Kant's Critical Philosophy* (Chicago: University of Chicago Press, 1989).

130. See Bernard Gagnebin, "Les écrits sur la musique, la langue et le théâtre" (Pléiade, V, xxviii).

131. Van der Veen, *Le Mélodrame musical de Rousseau au romantisme* (The Hague, 1955), cited by Strauss, "Jean-Jacques Rousseau: Musician," 480–481.

132. Du Roullet, letter to Dauvergne, *Mercure de France* (October 1772), quoted and translated by Ernest Newman, *Gluck and the Opera: A Study in Musical History* (reprint; Westport, Conn.: Greenwood, 1976).

133. Gluck, *Letter to the Editor of the "Mercure de France"* (February 1, 1773), quoted and translated by Alfred Einstein, *Gluck*, trans. Eric Blom (New York: McGraw-Hill, 1972), 136–137.

134. See Rousseau, *Dialogues*, First Dialogue (*Collected Writings*, I, 16–17).

135. See Einstein, *Gluck*, 137–138; Olivier Pot, "Introduction" to *Lettre à Burney* (Pléiade, V, ccxi–ccxii).

136. Quoted by Oliver, *The Encyclopedists as Critics of Music*, 121.

137. See Pléiade, I, 1626 (n. 1 to 679).

138. Cited by Pot, "Introduction" (Pléiade, V, ccvii–ccviii). For Burney's account of his meeting with Rousseau, see his *The Present State of Music in France and Italy*, 2 vols., 2nd ed. (Oxford: Oxford University Press, 1959), I, 313–315.

139. For strong claims concerning Rousseau's influence on Gluck, see Samuel Baud-Bovy, "Jean-Jacques Rousseau et la musique," *Annales de la société Jean-Jacques Rousseau*, 38 (1969–71), 258–263; 159–169; 163; Tiersot, *Jean-Jacques Rousseau*, 189; Jensen, *Rousseau als Musiker*, 400–401; and, less strongly, Oliver, *The Encyclopedists and Critics of Music*, 119. For accounts that stress Gluck's motives in courting Rousseau, see Einstein, *Gluck*; Newman, *Gluck and the Opera*.

140. The case is argued most vigorously by Catherine Kintzler in several of her writings: "Rameau et Rousseau: Le choc de deux esthétiques"; *Jean-Philippe Rameau: Splendeur et naufrage de l'esthétique du plaisir à l'âge classique* (Paris: Le Sycomore, 1983); *Poétique de l'opéra française de Corneille à Rousseau*. Edward Lowinsky makes a broader argument in his "Taste, Style, and Ideology in Eighteenth-Century Music," in *Aspects of the Eighteenth Century*, ed. Earl R. Wassman (Baltimore: Johns Hopkins University Press, 1965), 163–205. Cranston makes a similar case for Rousseau as the apostle of the Romantic movement, in music and otherwise, in his *Jean-Jacques*, 288–289, as well as in his *The Romantic Movement*

(London: Blackwell, 1994). See also Irving Babbitt, *Rousseau and Romanticism* (Boston: Houghton Mifflin, 1919). For dissents, see Eric Taylor, "Rousseau's Conception of Music," *Music and Letters* 30 (1949), 231–242; and Strauss, "Jean Jacques Rousseau: Musician."

EDITOR'S NOTES TO
Plan Regarding New Signs for Music

This translation is based on the text in Pléiade, V, 127–154. The Pléiade edition is based on the manuscript deposited in the archives of the Académie des sciences in Paris. Previous editions of the *Plan* were based on a revised version of the writing.

1. For Rousseau's account of his experiment, see *Confessions*, VII (*Collected Writings*, V, 241).
2. "Movement" translates "*mouvement*." "*Mouvement*" can mean tempo or meter, and sometimes both, so the cognate "movement" has been used consistently to render the term.
3. See p. 12 below.
4. Michel Pignolet de Montéclair (1666–1737) was a French composer and music theorist, and author of a book of music lessons.
5. I.e., a three or a four with a dot above it would be higher ("worth more") than a six or seven without any dot above it.
6. Rousseau refers to the Academy of Sciences in Paris, to which he presented his plan August 22, 1742. For his account of his plan and its reception at the Academy, see *Confessions*, VI and VII (*Collected Writings*, V, 227–228, 237–240). After the tepid reception of the *Plan* by the Academy, Rousseau published an extended version, the "Dissertation on Modern Music," translated below.

EDITOR'S NOTES TO
Letter to the Mercure *on a New System of Musical Notation*

This translation is based on the text found in Leigh, I, 169–176. The Letter first appeared in the February 1743 edition of the *Mercure de France*, pp. 321–323.

1. The addressee "Mr. D" is not identified and is probably fictitious, but has been tentatively identified as Jean-Baptiste-Louis Vuillet de la Saunière, Comte d'Amézin (or Damesin), to whom Rousseau refers in his *Confessions* as a "Savoyard Gentleman" (VII; *Collected Writings*, V, 238). The count later married Rousseau's former pupil Mlle de Menthon.
2. Jehan des Murs (c. 1300–c. 1350) was a widely influential musical theorist of the later Middle Ages best known for his treatment of musical proportions and mensural notation. The major work attributed to him, the *Speculum musicae*, was actually written by Jacques de Liège (c. 1260–c. 1330). Guido of Arezzo (991–c. 1033) was one of the most influential musical theorists of the Middle Ages. He developed a system of precise pitch notation by lines and spaces and developed a method of sight-singing relying on the syllables *ut, re, mi, fa, sol, la, si*, which he de-

rived from a hymn to St. John and which is known as the Aretinian system. Like Rousseau, Guido introduced his new system by complaining of the awkwardness of the existing one.

3. *C sol do* is equivalent to the key of C major.

4. The tune mentioned never appeared in print.

EDITOR'S NOTES TO
Dissertation on Modern Music

This translation is based on the text found in Pléiade, V, 167–245. The Pléiade edition is based on the original edition (Paris, G. F. Quillau père, 1743).

1. Lucretius, *De rerum natura*, V.1415: "the mind is changed from its pristine condition." Rousseau later realized that he had mistakenly written "*animus*" (mind) instead of Lucretius' "*sensus*" (sense, taste). The citation comes from Lucretius' account of the development of humans from a rude to a civilized condition. Rousseau would later draw on Book V of Lucretius' poem for his own account of human history in the *Second Discourse*.

2. Jean-Baptiste Lully (1632–1687) was an Italian-born court composer to Louis XIV of France and director of the Royal Academy of Music, later known as the Grand Opera. Lully was best known for his operas, including *Armide* (1686), which Rousseau criticizes at length in his *Letter on French Music*, translated below.

3. Michel-Richard de Lalande (1657–1726) was a French composer and superintendent of the royal chapel. Arcangelo Corelli (1653–1713) was an Italian composer whose works were important in the development of the baroque sonata form. Nicolas Bernier (1665–1734) was a French composer and theorist of composition whose cantatas Rousseau relates learning by heart (*Confessions*, V; *Collected Writings*, V, 155).

4. Rousseau refers to Jean-Philippe Rameau (1683–1764), composer of keyboard music, dramatic music, and opera and influential musical theorist, and his quarrel with the defenders of Lully during the dispute between the "lullistes" and "ramistes."

5. In the solmization of the Middle Ages founded on the hexachord there were only six syllables (*do, re, mi, fa, sol*) to sing the twelve notes of the chromatic scale, while the seven letters from A to G were used to name them. The seventh syllable *si* was introduced toward the end of the sixteenth century, although the system of using six syllables remained in use long after, especially in Italy.

6. For Rousseau's account of his own use of his notational system in teaching, see *Confessions*, VII (*Collected Writings*, V, 241).

7. The Academy of Sciences noted that systems of numerical notation similar to Rousseau's had already been proposed, naming in particular that proposed by Father Jean-Jacques Souhaitti in 1677, and cited Rousseau's lack of novelty as one of the reasons for not further supporting his plan. Rousseau here protests the essential novelty of his system.

8. Rousseau refers to his *Plan Regarding New Signs for Music*, translated above.

9. No such continuation of the "Dissertation" exists, although some of Rousseau's ideas on the subjects he mentions can be gleaned from the articles ACCOM-

paniment [*Accompagnement*] and Fundamental Bass [*Bass-Fondamentale*] from the *Encyclopedia* and *Dictionary of Music*, the first of which (in the *Encyclopedia* version) is translated herein.

10. Joseph Sauveur (1653–1716) was a theorist of acoustics (a term he coined) and inventor of a system of musical notation who tried to extend the idea of frequency to standardize an absolute pitch.

11. Guido of Arezzo (c. 991–c. 1033) was one of the most influential musical theorists of the Middle Ages. He developed a system of precise pitch notation by lines and spaces and developed a method of sight-singing relying on the syllables *ut*, *re*, *mi*, *fa*, *sol*, *la*, *si*, which he derived from a hymn to St. John and which is known as the Aretinian system. Like Rousseau, Guido introduced his new system by first complaining of the awkwardness of the existing one. Jehan des Murs (c. 1300–c. 1350), a widely influential musical theorist of the later Middle Ages, was best known for his treatment of musical proportions and mensural notation. The major work attributed to him, the *Speculum musicae*, was actually written by Jacques de Liège (c. 1260–c. 1330).

12. Rousseau refers here to the notation proposed by Demotz de la Salle, whose proposal was published in 1727, and who was mentioned in the report on his *Plan* by the Academy of Sciences.

13. Rousseau refers to Sauveur's system of notation. For Sauveur, see note 10 above.

14. See note 9 above.

15. Jean-Jacques Dortous de Mairan (1678–1771) was a physicist and mathematician who also published on music, and one of the three people named by the Academy of Sciences to study Rousseau's *Plan Regarding New Signs for Music*.

16. The pitch on which instruments were tuned was different at the Paris Opera and in the Royal Chapel, and also varied from country to country.

17. For Sauveur and his attempt to establish a system of absolute pitch, see note 10 above.

18. *C sol do* is equivalent to the key of C major.

19. "Root" translates "*fondement*," which is closely related to "*fondementale*," which is translated "fundamental," as in "fundamental sound." Following Rameau in particular, Rousseau speaks of the "fundamental sound" as generating its harmonics, and therefore as their basis or, in modern terminology, their "root."

20. Rameau, *Nouveau Système de musique théoretique* (1726), 21 (Jacobi, II, 31); and *Treatise on Harmony* (1712), 12–13 (Gossett, 15–17). Both passages show Rameau's attempts to find a natural origin (that is, a generation from the vibrating string) for the minor mode, in particular for the minor third.

21. What are traditionally the black and white keys on the harpsichord are reversed on the modern piano. The black keys on the harpsichord are also called the "natural" keys, and playing on them alone is called playing "naturally."

22. All of the examples cited in this text will be found at the end of this work.

23. A single word in French (*touche*) is used to mean both a fingerboard on a string instrument and a key on a keyboard instrument. Because of the possible confusion between the key (*touche*) of an instrument and the key (*ton*) in which one plays, "*touche*" has been translated as "key of the keyboard."

24. *A mi la* is equivalent to the key of A major, and *F do fa* is equivalent to the key of F major.

25. *G re sol* is equivalent to the key of G major.

26. *C sol do* minor is equivalent to the key of C major, and *D la re* is equivalent to the key of D dorian.

27. *F do fa* minor is equivalent to the key of F major.

28. For Sauveur, see note 10 above. Sauveur divided the octave logorithmically into forty-three "proportional means" called "meridians," and then similarly divided the meridians, arriving at 3010 units which he called "decameridians."

29. The select committee appointed by the Academy of Sciences to report on Rousseau's system concluded that it worked well for vocal music, but not for instrumental music.

30. For Souhaitti, see note 7 above.

31. The roundness of the figure gives the French name for the whole note (*ronde*). In the following passage further uses of *ronde* are translated as "whole note," the "term of comparison" of which Rousseau speaks.

32. For Sauveur, see note 10 above. Sauveur's "Echometer" was an acoustical machine capable of producing sounds of a given number of vibrations per second.

33. Michel Pignolet de Montéclair (1666–1737) was a French composer and music theorist, and author of a book of music lessons.

34. *B fa si* is equivalent to the key of B-flat major, and *C sol do* is equivalent to the key of C major.

35. In his *Confessions*, VII (*Collected Writings*, V, 241), Rousseau reports the progress of one of his students: "in three months she was capable of deciphering any music whatsoever by means of my notation, and even of singing at sight better than myself anything that was not burdened with difficulties. The success was striking, but unknown."

36. See note 9 above.

37. Although he did not publish such an example of the manner of notation by lines discussed in this work, Rousseau did include an example of such notation in the plates to his *Dictionary of Music*, where he speaks of his notational system at the article NOTATION [*Notation*].

38. *Dardanus* (1739) is a lyric-tragedy by Rameau on a libretto by Le Clerc de La Bruère.

Volez, plaisirs, volez,
Amour prête leur tes charmes,
répare les alarmes qui nous ont troublés.
Que ton empire est doux, vien, vien,
nous voulons tous sentir les coups, enchaîne nous;
mais ne te sers que de ces chaînes dont les peines sont des bienfaits.
[Fly, pleasures, fly,
  Love, lend them your charms,
  make amends for the alarms that have troubled us,
  May your empire be soft, come, come,
  we all want to feel your blows, enchain us;
  but I only serve those chains whose penalties are kindnesses.]

39. The Carillon (a song after a carillon, or set of bells) is from an unidentified source:

Campana che sona da lutto e da festa.
Fa romper la testa,
Din di ra din di ra din di, . . .
[The bell that rings for mourning and feast,
It makes one's head burst,
Ding dong ding dong ding. . . .

The line translated "makes one's head burst" contains a pun suggesting that the bells also "make you wonder."

40. *Les talens lyriques*, also known as *Les Fêtes d'Hébé* (1739), is an opera-ballet by Rameau.

L'objet qui regne dans mon âme,
Des mortels et des dieux doit être le vainqueur;
Chaque instant il m'enflamme
D'une nouvelle ardeur.
Je m'abandonne à mon amour extrême,
Et je fixe à jamais mes plaisirs en ces lieux:
C'est où l'on aime que sont les cieux.
The object that reigns in my soul,
Must be the conqueror of mortals and gods;
It enflames me every instant
With a new ardor.
I abandon myself to my extreme love,
And I never fix my pleasures in these places:
It is where one loves what is heavenly.

EDITOR'S NOTES TO
Letter on Italian and French Opera

This translation is based on text found in Pléiade, V, 247–257. The title is given to the manuscript letter by the editors of the Pléiade edition. The letter was first printed by Albert Jansen (*Jean-Jacques Rousseau als Musiker* [Berlin, 1884], 455–463). Jansen conjectured that it was addressed to Rousseau's then friend Grimm and dated it as having been written about 1750. Based upon internal evidence, the editors of the Pléiade edition date it between December 1744 and September 1745, or shortly after Rousseau's return from Italy. The dating of the letter is an important issue because Rousseau's estimations of French and Italian music and opera in this letter largely contradict his mature opinion as intimated in his *Letter to Grimm on "Omphale"* (April 1752) and fully revealed in his *Letter on French Music* (November 1753). If Jansen were right to date this letter from 1750, that would mean that Rousseau's opinion soon afterward underwent a sudden and dramatic reversal. The earlier date suggests that his view changed over a longer period of time.

1. The editors of the Pléiade edition suggest that if there is an actual addressee of Rousseau's letter, it is likely Touissant Rémond de Saint-Mard (1682–1757), a French poet and critic whose *Réflexions sur l'opéra* was published in 1741.

2. "Spectacle" translates "*spectacles*." The term might have been translated "theater," as is usually done for Rousseau's *Letter to d'Alembert on the Theater*, but since Rousseau contrasts the operatic "*spectacle*" to the dramatic "*théatre*," the term has been left as "spectacle."

3. Aristotle treats tragedy and comedy in his *Poetics*, although only the part concerning tragedy survives, and Horace concentrates on epic and dramatic poetry in his *Ars poetica*, where he generally follows Aristotle's theory. By "our modern Greeks and Latins," Rousseau refers to the partisans of the Ancients, including Nicholas Boileau, who condemned departures in opera and theater from the Aristotelian unities of time, place, and action against the partisans of the Moderns, who championed these innovations. The partisans of the Ancients included Boileau, La Bruyère, Bossuet, La Fontaine, Racine, and many other leading literary figures of the time. Among the partisans of the Moderns were Perrault and Molière. Rousseau refers to Boileau, *L'Art poétique* (1674), Satire X.

4. Jean de La Bruyère speaks of "getting bored" at the Opera in his *Les Caractères ou les moeurs de la siècle* (1688). Rousseau agrees with him in his *Julie, ou la Nouvelle Héloïse*, II, xxiii (Pléiade, II, 280–289; trans. Philip Stewart and Jean Vaché [Hanover, N.H.: University Press of New England, 1997], 229–236). As for Dacier, Rousseau refers to his *Commentaires sur la Poétique d'Aristote* (1692).

5. Jean-Baptiste Lully or Lulli (1632–1687) was an Italian-born composer to King Louis XIV who often collaborated with Philippe Quinault (1635–1684), the dramatist and librettist. Lully and Quinault established the classic form of French opera. Rousseau alludes to Lully's epigones, whom he satirically compares to Amphion, the mythological lyre player who was said to have moved stones with his playing.

6. Charles Grandval (1710–1784) was a celebrated actor whose roles included Cinna in Corneille's play by that name. Claude Sarrazin (b. 1689) was a well-known actor at the Comédie-Française.

7. *Isis* (1677), *Phaeton* (1683), and *Persée* (1682) are all lyric-tragedies by Lully on libretti by Quinault. *Iphigénie en Tauride* (1704) is a lyric-tragedy by Desmarets (one of the epigones of Lully alluded to by Rousseau above) and Campra on a libretto by Duché de Vancy and Danchet. Operas were written about the historical figures Rousseau mentions, many of them in the early eighteenth century.

8. Generic tunes were often added to works and given different words to suit the occasion.

9. For Quinault, see note 5 above. Pietro Metastasio (1698–1782) was an Italian poet and very popular librettist.

10. "*Merveilleux*" is a term often used in discussing classical French opera, and refers to the supernatural or magical element so often used in such opera and employed by means of elaborate stage machinery.

11. Dardanus is the title character in Rameau's lyric-tragedy *Dardanus* (1739). Perseus is the title character in Lully's and Quinault's lyric-tragedy *Persée* (1682). The "Father" refers to Jupiter (which Rousseau originally wrote in the manuscript and then crossed out), and Rousseau could be referring to any number of operas.

12. *Thésée* (1675) and *Atys* (1676) are lyric-tragedies by Lully and Quinault. *Thétis et Pélée* (1689) is a lyric-tragedy by Fontenelle and Colasse.

13. Rousseau refers especially to a dispute over the relative merits of French and

Italian music that took place in the beginning of the eighteenth century. Rousseau would become involved in a similar dispute during the "Quarrel of the Bouffons."

14. The Theater of Paris refers to the Theater of the Palais-Royal, or the Royal Academy of Music, better known as the Paris Opera.

15. Rousseau refers to Lully's lyric-tragedy *Atys* (1676), Act II, Scene VI: "*Vous me perdez, Atys, et vous êtes aimé*." *Pyrame et Thisbé* (1726) is a lyric-tragedy with music by Rebel and Francoeur on a libretto by La Serre. *Iphigénie en Tauride* (1704) is a lyric-tragedy with music by Desmarets on a libretto by Duché de Vancy and Danchet. *Dardanus* (1739) is a lyric-tragedy by Rameau on a libretto by Le Clerc de La Bruère.

16. The *Indes galantes* (1735) is an opera-ballet by Rameau on a libretto by Fuzelier.

17. *Jephté* (1732) is a lyric-tragedy by Montéclair on a libretto by Pellegrin. For *Les Indes galantes*, see the previous note. For *Pyrame et Thisbé*, see note 15 above. *Hippolyte et Aricie* (1733) is a lyric-tragedy by Rameau on a libretto by Pellegrin.

18. The manuscript breaks off suddenly.

EDITOR'S NOTES TO
Letter on "Omphale"

This translation is based on the text of the original edition (March 1752) as reproduced in Launay, I, 3–54. Frederic Melchior Grimm (1723–1807) was born and educated in Germany and came to Paris in 1748 or 1749, where he became the editor of the *Correspondance littéraire* and a leading member of the circle of *philosophes* associated with the *Encyclopedia*, including Rousseau, who addressed Grimm in one of his defenses of the *First Discourse*, the *Letter to Grimm* (*Collected Writings*, II, 84–92).

1. *Omphale* (1701) is a lyric-tragedy by André-Cardinal Destouches (1672–1749), a French composer of operas and other music and later director of the Paris Opera, based on a libretto by Antoine Houdar Lamotte (or La Motte) (1672–1731), a French dramatist and librettist. *Omphale* was reprised in 1721, 1733, 1735, and then in 1752, by the Royal Academy of Music, better known as the Paris Opera, where it was first performed January 14, 1752.

2. Horace, *Satires*, I.4, 43–44: "If he has inspired genius, a divine mind, and a grand style, he may be honored with the title [of a poet]."

3. The addressee of Grimm's *Letter* is almost certainly fictitious.

4. Jean-Philippe Rameau (1683–1764) was a composer of keyboard music, dramatic music, and opera; author of influential theoretical writings on music. *Platée* (1745) is Rameau's successful comic opera-ballet on a libretto by Autreau. Grimm will shortly complain of Rameau's *Pygmalion* (1748), the most successful of his one-act ballets.

5. Marie Fel (1713–1794) was one of the most famous singers of the Paris Opera. Rousseau wrote his *Salve regina* (1752) for her and she played Colette in the production of his *Devin du village* (1752) at Fontainebleau. Rousseau also relates in his *Confessions* that Grimm claimed to be hopelessly in love with her, but failed to become her lover (Book VIII; *Collected Writings*, V, 310–311, 315–316).

6. *Médée et Jason* (1713) is a lyric-tragedy by Joseph-François Salomon on a libretto by Simon-Joseph Pellegrin.

7. For De la Motte, or La Motte, see note 1 above. La Motte wrote the libretti for the works by Destouches mentioned in the text: *L'Europe galante* (1697), an opera-ballet, and *Issé* (1697), a heroic pastoral. As noted above, the lyric-tragedy *Omphale* was composed by Destouches on a libretto by Lamotte.

8. For Destouches, see note 1 above.

9. Ludovico Ariosto (1474–1533) was an Italian poet best known for his *Orlando furioso*, which served as a popular setting for madrigals for long afterward. Torquato Tasso (1544–1595) was an Italian poet best known for his *Jerusalem Delivered*, which also served as a popular setting for madrigals, ultimately eclipsing Ariosto's popularity. Tasso was one of Rousseau's favorite poets, and he translated part of his famous epic poem into French. Giovanni Battista Pergolesi (1710–1736) was a composer of operas and other vocal pieces, including the opera buffa *La serva padrona*. Buranello, or "Il Buranello," is the nickname of Baldasare Galuppi (1706–1785; born at Burano, hence "Il Buranello"), Italian composer crucial to the development of the *opera buffa* style. Andrea Adolfati (1711–1760) was a Venetian composer, principally of sacred music.

10. Rousseau was, of course, the author of the *Discourse on the Sciences and Arts* (*First Discourse*), which won the prize of the Academy of Dijon in 1750. He was commissioned by Diderot to write most of the articles on music for the *Encyclopedia*. Rousseau's *Les Muses galantes* (1745) is an opera-ballet.

11. Rameau's opera-ballet *Les Indes galantes* (1735) was a failure when it was first produced.

12. *Armide* (1686), *Atys* (1676), and *Thésée* (1675) are all lyric-tragedies by Lully on libretti by Quinault. French tragedies often contained Italian ariettas during the first half of the eighteenth century.

13. In the portion omitted, Grimm examines several selections from *Omphale*, concluding that French recitative is below the dignity of the tragic genre. Grimm praises Rameau for having succeeded despite the limitations of the language.

14. *Atys* (1676) and *Armide* (1686) are lyric-tragedies by Lully on libretti by Quinault. *Hippolyte et Aricie* (1733) is a lyric-tragedy by Rameau on a libretto by Pellegrin. *L'Europe galante* (1697) is an opera-ballet by Destouches on a libretto by Lamotte. *Les Fêtes d l'Hymen et de l'Amour* is from Rameau's opera-ballet *Les Indes galantes* (1735) on a libretto by Fuzelier. *Issé* (1697) is a heroic pastoral by Destouches on a libretto by Lamotte. *Platée* (1745) is Rameau's comic opera-ballet on a libretto by Autreau.

15. Jean le Rond d'Alembert (1717–1783) was co-editor of the *Encyclopedia* along with Diderot and author of the *Preliminary Discourse* (1751) to the collection. D'Alembert also wrote a popularized version of Rameau's musical theory, the *Eléments de musique théoretique et pratique* (1st ed. 1752).

16. Pierre de Jelyotte (1711–1782) was a celebrated singer who performed in Rousseau's *Les Muses galantes* and his *Le Devin du village*.

17. French operas were frequently criticized for the tendency to overuse melismas on words which have a facile potential for word-painting.

18. In the remainder of the note, omitted here, Grimm gives examples of Italian arias.

19. *G re sol* is equivalent to the key of G major, and *E si mi* major is equivalent to the key of E major.

20. The lyric-tragedy *Zoroastre* (1749) and comic opera-ballet *Platée* (1745) are both by Rameau. The "divertimento of the Rose" refers to the third entrée in Rameau's opera-ballet *Les Indes galantes* (1735), where Tacmas sings "L'éclat des roses," which is followed by a divertimento.

21. Grimm refers to d'Alembert, who writes of Voltaire: "No one has known the rare art of presenting each idea effortlessly in the phrase which is proper to it, of embellishing everything without mistaking the proper shading for each thing, and finally, of never being either above or below his subject—a quality that characterizes great writers more than we would imagine" (*Preliminary Discourse to the Encyclopedia of Diderot*, trans. Richard N. Schwab [Indianapolis: Bobbs-Merrill, 1963], 98).

22. Mlle Puvignée was a celebrated dancer who danced the title role of Pygmalion in Rameau's lyric-ballet and who also danced in the 1756 revival of Rameau's lyric-ballet *Les Fêtes d'Hébé*.

23. The editor has not been able to identify Maurice.

24. The "Conqueror of Silesia" is Frederick II the Great (1712–1786), King of Prussia, who conquered that territory during the War of the Austrian Succession (1740–1748). Frederick was known first for his patronage of the arts and sciences, as well as his playing of the flute, and later for his autocratic rule. The "Bard of Henri IV" is Voltaire (François Marie Arouet) (1694–1778), writer, historian, and leading figure of the Enlightenment. Among Voltaire's numerous works are the *Henriade* (1723), an epic poem on King Henry IV of France, and a *History of Charles XII of Sweden* (1731). Voltaire stayed in Berlin from 1750 to 1753 under the protection of Frederick the Great and in his service.

25. The "Orpheus of France" presumably refers to Rameau (see note 4 above). For Pergolesi, see note 9 above.

26. Louis Dupré (1697–1774) was a celebrated French dancer and creator of Rameau's ballets after 1733.

27. Jean-Joseph Cassanéa de Mondonville (1711–1772) was a violinist and composer who wrote sacred and secular music.

28. For Pergolesi, see note 9 above.

29. For Fel, see note 5 above.

30. The editor has not been able to identify Astroa any further, although he appears from the information Grimm gives to be an Italian castrato who worked largely in Berlin. Felice Salimbeni was a well-known castrato singer of the mid-eighteenth century who worked mostly in Germany, including Dresden after 1751.

31. For Jelyotte, see note 16 above.

32. Edme de Bouchardon (1698–1762) and Jean-Baptiste Pigale (1714–1785) were popular sculptors of the time. Grimm compares them to Praxiteles, the great Athenian sculptor of the Periclean age. Rousseau makes the same comparison of Pigale to Praxiteles, but unfavorably, in his *First Discourse* (*Collected Writings*, II, 15–16).

33. Charles-André Vanloo or Van Loo (1705–1765), known as "Carle," was a famous painter of the time. Compare Rousseau, *First Discourse* (*Collected Writings*, II, 15–16).

34. Jean-Baptiste-Marie Pierre (1713–1789) was a popular painter of the time. Compare Rousseau, *First Discourse* (*Collected Writings*, II, 15–16).

35. Maurice Quentin de La Tour (1704–1788) was the most famous portrait painter of the day. His well-known pastel portrait of Marie Fel now hangs in the Louvre. La Tour did the portraits of many well-known people of that era, including Rousseau.

36. Marie Françoise Marchand (1711–1803), called Mademoiselle Dumesnil, was a well-known actress. Dumesnil apparently played Merope, the wife of Sisyphus in Greek mythology, in a drama.

37. Henri-Louis Caïn (1728–1778), called Lekain, was a well-known tragic actor of the time. Orosmane is a character in Voltaire's drama *Zaïre*.

38. Claude Sarrazin (b. 1689) was a well-known actor at the Comédie-Française. Luzignan is a character in Voltaire's *Zaïre*.

39. The editor has not been able to identify *Andrienne*, but it appears to be a French comedy, and probably included the stock character of an old man. See note 42 below.

40. Jeanne Gaussem (1711–1767), called Mademoiselle Gaussin, was a well-known actress of the time. The editor has not been able to identify Zeneide.

41. Charles Grandval (1710–1784) and his wife were celebrated actors. For Sarrazin see note 38 above.

42. Armand was the stage name of a famous French actor of the early- and mid-eighteenth century known in particular for his roles as a conniving valet. Dangeville was the stage name for Marie-Anne Botot (1714–1796), a famous French actress. Momus is the God of irony, sometimes depicted as a satyr-like old man. Thalie is the muse of comedy.

43. Grimm refers to Charles de Secondat, Baron de Montesquieu (1689–1755), author of *The Spirit of the Laws* and other philosophical and literary works.

44. André-Noël Pagin (1721–1785) was a French violinist and composer.

EDITOR'S NOTES TO
Remarks on the Subject of the Letter by M. Grimm on "Omphale"

This translation is based on the text of the original edition as reproduced in Launay, I, 55–81. The work was originally published anonymously in March 1752, a few weeks after the appearance of Grimm's *Letter on "Omphale."* The work is signed "D," and is generally attributed to Grimm's friend, Guillaume-Thomas-François Raynal (1713–1796), a member of the circle associated with the *Encyclopedia* and Grimm's successor in 1753 as the editor of the *Correspondance littéraire*. Raynal was among the first to reply to Rousseau's *First Discourse*, in his *Observations on the Discourse*, to which Rousseau replied with his *Letter to M. the Abbé Raynal* (*Collected Writings*, II, 23–27).

1. Raynal refers to the March 1752 edition of the *Mercure de France*.
2. See Grimm, *Letter on "Omphale,"* p. 108 above.
3. See Grimm, *Letter on "Omphale,"* p. 107 above.
4. *Platée* (1745) is Rameau's comic opera-ballet on a libretto by Autreau.

5. "Take thirty, twenty, fifty, sixty bitter snails and a rare radish brewed in Burgundy." The editor has not been able to identify the source of this quotation, which is evidently intended to be comic, since it is a bowdlerized combination of (bad) Latin and Italian.

6. See Grimm, *Letter on "Omphale,"* p. 108n† above.
7. See Grimm, *Letter on "Omphale,"* p. 108n† above.
8. See Grimm, *Letter on "Omphale,"* p. 108n† above.
9. Soldiers were stationed at French opera houses to maintain order.
10. See Grimm, *Letter on "Omphale,"* p. 108n† above.
11. Johann Adolf Hasse (1699–1783) was the most widely admired composer of *opera seria* in Italy and Germany at that time. Hasse was in the employ of the Elector of Saxony, who became King of Poland. Rousseau called Hasse's orchestra at Dresden "the most perfect ensemble in Europe" (*Dictionary of Music*, s.v. ORCHESTRE; Pléiade, V, 963–964).
12. See Grimm, *Letter on "Omphale,"* p. 114 above.
13. See Grimm, *Letter on "Omphale,"* p. 110 above.
14. See Grimm, *Letter on "Omphale,"* pp. 113–114 above.
15. Georg Friederich Händel, or George Frederick Handel (1685–1759) was one of the greatest composers of the Baroque era in both vocal and instrumental music. Handel was born in Saxony but later became a naturalized British subject.
16. French operas were frequently criticized for the tendency to overuse melismas on words which have a facile potential for word-painting.
17. See Grimm, *Letter on "Omphale,"* p. 111n* above.
18. Antonio Maria Bernacchi (1685–1756) was a celebrated Italian alto castrato known for his lengthy cadenzas.
19. François Mainard (1582–1646) was a French poet. Jean Maigret (1604–1686) was a French dramatist whose *Sophonisbe* (1634) is known for being the first French lyric tragedy to observe the Aristotelean three unities. Gian Giorgio Trissino (1478–1550) was an Italian poet and dramatist who rigorously followed the Aristotelian theory of the three unities, and whose own *Sofonisba* (1524) is his most famous work. The idea that a dramatic work should have a unity in time, place, and action is derived from Aristotle's *Poetics* (see chaps. 6–8; 1449b21–1451a36). The controversy over whether the three unities should be observed in modern tragedy was a leading question of the so-called "Quarrel of the Ancients and Moderns," which raged in France and elsewhere at the end of the seventeenth and beginning of the eighteenth centuries.
20. Pietro Metastasio (1698–1782) was an Italian poet and very popular librettist.
21. Nicola Porpora (1686–1768) was a Neopolitan composer of vocal music and opera. Giovanni Buononcini or Bononcini (1670–1745) was an Italian composer known for his graceful arias
22. See Grimm, *Letter on "Omphale,"* p. 110 above.
23. The editor has not been able to locate this passage from Voltaire.
24. Leonardo Leo (1694–1744) was a leading Neopolitan composer whose *Il Viaggiatori* was performed in Paris in 1754. Leonardo Vinci (c. 1690–1730) was a leading Neopolitan composer of *opera seria*. Domenico Terradellas or Terradeglias (1713–1751) was a Spanish-born composer of opera and other vocal music. Pietro

Pulli (c. 1710–c. 1759) was a Neopolitan composer of less renown. For Hasse see note 11 above. Niccolò Jomelli (1714–1774) was a prolific Italian composer of opera and sacred music.

25. King Louis XIV of France established at least five academies during his reign.

26. The "Academy of painting" refers to the *Académie royale de peinture et de sculpture* referred to in the previous note. Le Normant de Tourenhem was General Director for Buildings in France at this time.

27. See Grimm, *Letter on "Omphale,"* p. 110 above.

28. See Grimm, *Letter on "Omphale,"* p. 110 above.

29. See Grimm, *Letter on "Omphale,"* p. 111 above.

30. In a portion of Grimm's *Letter* omitted above, he wishes that the celebrated singer Marie Fel would apply the same boldness to French recitative.

31. Raynal refers to the end of Grimm's *Letter* where, having unfavorably compared Destouches' *Omphale* to Rameau's *Pygmalion* (only the conclusion of which passage is translated above), he speaks of the "temple" to taste in which he would place Rameau and a whole host of others. See pp. 113–114 above.

32. See Grimm, *Letter on "Omphale,"* pp. 113–114 above.

33. Raynal refers to André-Noël Pagin (1721–1785), French violinist and composer whose successful career in Paris as a violin virtuoso was mysteriously cut short, in around 1751, reportedly for daring to play in the Italian style. Pagin's teacher was Giuseppe Tartini (1692–1770), Italian composer, violinist, teacher, and musical theorist much admired by Rousseau.

34. Pagin left Paris and settled at the court of the Duc de Clérmont.

EDITOR'S NOTES TO
Letter to M. Grimm On the Subject of the Remarks Added to His Letter on "Omphale"

This translation is based on the text found in Pléiade, V, 259–274. The Pléiade edition is based on the original edition of the work, which appeared in April 1752. Rousseau's authorship of the anonymous writing was effectively acknowledged when it was reprinted in the 1764 Neuchâtel edition of his works published by Duchesne.

1. Persius, *Satires*, Prologue, 9: "Who teaches magpies to copy our speech?" Rousseau alters the original verse slightly to make an independent clause of what was a dependent clause.

2. Nicholas Boileau (1693–1711) was a French poet and literary theorist best known for his *Art poétique* (1674). Boileau's commentator was Claude Brossette (1671–1743), a literary figure of minor importance.

3. See Raynal, *Remarks*, p. 116 above.

4. See Raynal, *Remarks*, p. 117 above. Giovanni Battista Pergolesi (1710–1736) was a composer of operas and other vocal pieces, including the opera buffa *La serva padrona*. Buranello, or "Il Buranello," is the nickname of Baldasare Galuppi (1706–1785; born at Burano, hence "Il Buranello"), an Italian composer crucial to the development of the *opera buffa* style. Andrea Adolfati (1711–1760) was a Venetian composer, principally of sacred music.

5. See Raynal, *Remarks*, p. 118n* above. Antonio Maria Bernacchi (1685–1756) was a celebrated Italian alto castrato known for his lengthy cadenzas.

6. See Raynal, *Remarks*, p. 119 above.

7. See Raynal, *Remarks*, p. 119 above.

8. See Raynal, *Remarks*, p. 116 above.

9. See Raynal, *Remarks*, p. 118 and n† above.

10. "Metanasius" is painted as the very type of the pedant in Thémiseul de Saint-Hyacinthe's *Le Chef-d'oeuvre d'un inconnu* (1714) and is cited as such during this time and in the same way as Rousseau by both Raynal and Grimm. François Mainard (1582–1646) was a French poet. Gian Giorgio Trissino (1478–1550) was an Italian poet and dramatist who rigorously followed the Aristotelian theory of the three unities, and whose own *Sofonisba* (1524) is his most famous work. Jean Mairet (Rousseau, following Raynal, mistakenly writes Maigret) (1604–1686) was a French dramatist who spoke of the Aristotelian "three unities" in the preface to his tragicomedy *La Silvanire* (1630).

11. French operas were frequently criticized for the tendency to overuse melismas on words which have a facile potential for word-painting.

12. See Raynal, *Remarks*, p. 117 above.

13. Rousseau makes the same joke in a similar context in his *Julie, ou La Nouvelle Héloïse* (II, xxiii; Pléiade, II, 286).

14. See Raynal, *Remarks*, p. 115 above. *Platée* (1745) is Rameau's successful comic opera-ballet on a libretto by Autreau.

15. *Tartuffe* (1664) is a comedy by Molière (Jean-Baptiste Poquelin; 1622–1673), produced with music by Lully. The original line (I, ii, 171) reads: "*Marchons, gaupe, marchons*" ("Be off, slut, be off").

16. Ibid., V, i, 1604.

17. *La serva padrona*, Pergolesi's most popular *opera buffa*, was performed in Paris in 1752. For Pergolesi, see note 4 above.

18. See Raynal, *Remarks*, p. 117 above. For Adolfati, Pergolesi, and "Burnello" (Galuppi), see note 4 above.

19. A colloquial expression (used by Molière, for example) meaning to be skillfully defrauded of something. Rousseau alludes to the surprising lack of success of Adolfati's *In exitu* at the November 1748 Concert spirituel (an annual concert given at the Tuileries in Paris).

20. Johann Adolf Hasse (1699–1783) was the most widely admired composer of *opera seria* in Italy and Germany at that time. See p. 117 above.

21. Georges de Scudéry (1601–1667) was a French author of plays and poetry, protected by Richelieu and enemy of Boileau. In 1643 Scudéry was named by Richelieu Governor of Notre-Dame de la Garde, the basilica dominating Marseille, largely for his role in attacking Corneille's *Le Cid* for not observing the "three unities" (of time, place, and action) thought to be required for the classical form. The controversy over Corneille's work was the focus in the "Quarrel of the Ancients and Moderns." For Boileau, see note 2 above. Boileau, de Scudéry, and others took the side of the ancients by demanding that the Aristotelian "three unities" be observed.

22. See Raynal, *Remarks*, p. 119 above. Domenico Terradellas or Terradeglias (1713–1751) was a Spanish-born composer of opera and other vocal music.

23. Ludovico Ariosto (1474–1533) was an Italian poet best known for his *Orlando furioso*, which served as a popular setting for madrigals for long afterward. Grimm refers to Ariosto in his *Letter on "Omphale,"* p. 108n† above.

24. See Raynal, *Remarks*, p. 120 above. André-Noël Pagin (1721–1785) was a French violinist and composer. Pagin's teacher was Giuseppe Tartini (1692–1770), Italian composer, violinist, teacher, and musical theorist much admired by Rousseau. Pagin's successful career in Paris as a violin virtuoso was mysteriously cut short, in around 1751, reportedly for daring to play in the Italian style.

25. See Raynal, *Remarks*, p. 118 above.

26. Pierre Corneille (1616–1684) and Jean Racine (1639–1699) were the two great French dramatists of their time. Philippe Quinault (1635–1684) was a playwright and librettist who collaborated with Molière and Lully.

27. See Raynal, *Remarks*, pp. 118 and 116 above.

28. See Raynal, *Remarks*, p. 116 above.

29. See Raynal, *Remarks*, p. 119 above.

30. An indirect criticism of Rameau, who is called a "philosophical musician" by d'Alembert in the *Preliminary Discourse* to the *Encyclopedia* (1751), and who was also lionized as "the Newton of music."

31. Philip of Macedon criticized his son, the future Alexander the Great. Alexander's teacher was Aristotle. Rousseau refers to Quintus Curtius Rufus, *Historiarum Alexandri Magni Macedonis*, Book I.

32. A reference to Frederick the Great of Prussia, who played and composed for the flute. See Raynal, *Remarks*, p. 120 above.

33. Louis Dupré (1697–1774) was a celebrated French dancer and creator of Rameau's ballets after 1733. Pierre de Jelyotte (1711–1782) was a celebrated French singer who frequently appeared in Rameau's works and also in Rousseau's *Le Devin du village* (1752).

34. The 1764 version of this work published by Duchesne begins with this paragraph. Rousseau refers to the controversy between the *"lullistes"* and the *"ramistes"* from the 1730s onward over Rameau's supposed departure from the operatic model of Lully. In the following text, Rousseau will allude to several of the charges brought against Rameau's music.

35. Rousseau refers to d'Alembert's *Eléments de Musique Théoretique et Pratique suivant les Principes de M. Rameau*, published in 1752, shortly before Rousseau's *Letter to M. Grimm* appeared.

36. Rousseau discusses Rameau's theory of harmony in several articles he wrote for the *Encyclopedia*, including ACCOMPANIMENT [*Accompagnement*], FUNDAMENTAL BASS [*Basse fondamentale*], and several other articles which appeared around the same time as his *Letter to M. Grimm*.

37. Rousseau refers to the musical and theatrical entertainments at the annual fair along the Seine in Paris, for which Rameau wrote music early in his career.

38. *Roland* (1685) is a lyric-tragedy by Lully. *Dardanus* (1739) is a lyric-tragedy by Rameau.

39. Rousseau literally says "a troupe of Quinze-Vingts." The Hôpital des Quinze-Vingts was a hospital for the blind.

40. By insisting upon a unity of "design," Rousseau here anticipates the con-

cept of the "unity of melody" he develops in his *Letter on French Music* and his later musical writings. He discusses "design" in the article DESIGN [*Dessein*] in his *Dictionary of Music* (Pléiade, V, 752–753): "It is the invention and the direction of the subject, the disposition of every Part, and the general ordering of the whole. It is not enough to write beautiful Songs and a good Harmony; it is necessary to tie all this together by a principal subject, to which all the parts of the work are related, and by which it is a *one*."

41. Rousseau refers to the monasteries and churches, where medieval polyphony could still be heard.

42. Horace, *Ars poetica*, 32–35: speaking of a bronze-smith, "He depicts nails and imitates waving hair in metal. Yet he fails in that work because he cannot represent the whole."

43. The 1764 version of this work published by Duchesne ends here.

44. Plato, *Ion*, 531e–535e. The actor is Ion and the poet who takes him outside of himself is Homer.

45. Voltaire (François Marie Arouet) (1694–1778) was a writer, historian, and leading figure of the Enlightenment, among whose numerous works is the epic poem the *Henriade* (1723).

EDITOR'S NOTES TO
"Notice" to Rinaldo da Capua's La Zingara

This translation is based on the text found in Pléiade, V, 1428 (ed. n. 7 to p. 264). Rousseau's edition of Rinaldo da Capua's *La Zingara* appeared in the summer of 1753. A draft of the "Notice" was found among his papers after his death and was first reprinted by Albert Jansen in *Jean-Jacques Rousseau als Musiker* (Berlin, 1884), pp. 464–465.

1. Rinaldo da Capua (c. 1705–c. 1780) was a Neopolitan composer of sacred music and opera. The first performance of *La Zingara* was June 19, 1753, in Paris. The opera enjoyed considerable success and was translated and adapted by Favart as *La Bohémienne*. Rinaldo's *La Donna superba* was performed in December 1752 with great success.

2. Pourceaugnac is a comic character from Molière's *Monsieur de Pourceaugnac* (1669), an intermède with music by Lully.

3. Rousseau refers to the Royal Academy of Music, better known as the Paris Opera.

EDITOR'S NOTES TO
Letter from a Symphonist

This translation is based on the text found in Pléiade, V, 275–285. The Pléiade edition is based on the original edition of the work, which appeared anonymously in late September 1753. It was reprinted in the 1781 Geneva edition of Rousseau's works. The original edition is reproduced in Launay, I, 358–374.

1. The Royal Academy of Music is the official name for the Paris Opera. The symphonists commonly addressed one another as *"camarades."* *"Symphoniste,"* here translated by the cognate "symphonist," might have been rendered as "instrumentalist" except that Rousseau also uses the term *"instrumentaliste."* The connection between "symphonists" and the "instrumental pieces" (*symphonies*) they play should be kept in mind.

2. The order for the dismissal of Bambini's troupe of *opera buffa* performers, the "Bouffonists," was issued sometime after late February 1753, but they did not depart until March 1754.

3. The "Queen's corner" was the term used for the proponents of Italian music, who gathered around the queen, including the Encyclopedists. The "King's corner" denoted the proponents of French music. See *Confessions*, VIII (*Collected Writings*, V, 322).

4. The players at the Opera had been accused of intentionally misplaying the Italian works, for example in a pamphlet by Holbach early in the "Quarrel."

5. Troops were stationed at the Opera to control the often rowdy crowds.

6. The members of the Chambre des Comptes, the accounting and finance office in Paris, enjoyed their perquisites according to the length of time of their membership. Rousseau alludes here to the split among social classes during the "Quarrel of the Bouffons," with the upper classes—such as those residing in the fashionable district of St. Denis—taking the side of French music and the lower classes—who would sit in the Parterre of the theater—that of Italian music. In his *Confessions* he explains: "The more powerful, more numerous" side, "composed of Nobles, the rich, and the women, supported French music" (VIII; *Collected Writings*, V, 322).

7. *Isée* (1697) is a heroic pastoral by Destouches on a libretto by Lamotte. *Alcyone* (1706) is a lyric-tragedy by Marin Marais on a libretto by Lamotte. *Roland* (1685) is a lyric tragedy by Lully on a libretto by Quinault; Logistille is a wise and powerful fairy in the opera.

8. *La serva padrona* is by Giovanni Battista Pergolesi (1710–1736), composer of operas and other vocal pieces. Pergolesi's popular *opera buffa* was performed in Paris in 1752. Rousseau was the first in France to engrave and publish the work.

9. The "scandalous epigram" was attributed by Grimm to Diderot and reported by him in the February 1753 issue of the *Corréspondance littéraire*. The satyr Marsyas invented or played a sort of flute and challenged Apollo, who played the lyre, to a musical contest. Apollo defeated him and then flayed him alive. See Plato, *Republic*, III.399e.

10. In his *Arrêt rendu à l'Amphithéâtre de l'Opéra* (1753), Diderot names as the culprit Francoeur, one of the members of the "Queen's Corner" during the "Quarrel of the Bouffons."

11. Eustachio Bambini (1697–1770) was an Italian musician who at that time was impresario of the ducal theater of Milan, director of the Strasbourg theater, and leader of the troupe of "Bouffonists."

12. The Comédie-Française, like the "Theater" of the Paris Opera, or Royal Academy of Music, was patronized by the King.

13. *La Bohémienne* was the translation of Rinaldo da Capua's *La Zingara* by

Favart. The opera announced was *Bertoldo in Corte,* with music by Goldoni, Ciampi, and Leo.

14. Niccolò Jomelli (1714–1774) was a Venetian composer of opera and sacred music. Jommelli's *Il Paratajo*, also known as *L'Oiseleuse Angloise*, was first produced, in Paris, in early September 1753. The poor reception of Jomelli's piece led to the reaction against the Bouffonists and their departure.

15. Joseph-Barnabé de Saint-Sévin (1727–c. 1790), known as "L'Abbé" or "L'Abbé fils," was a well-known violinist. As for Caraffe, Rousseau could be referring to several members of the Caraffe dynasty of violinists at the Paris Opera.

16. Anna Tonelli was *prima donna* of Bambini's troupe of Bouffonists.

17. Durant was a copyist. The "parts of the fifths" refers to the cello parts, or in earlier times the viola part, which sometimes second the violin part or other higher parts on the octave below.

18. "Taking the octave" means applying more pressure to a string (or wind in a wind instrument) to force the tone an octave higher. Violin parts were commonly "doubled," that is, their "simple" part was ornamented by the player.

19. Marie-Jeanne Fesch, known as Mlle Chevalier (1722–1789), was a celebrated singer frequently cast in compositions by Rameau.

20. Dances used in the intermèdes in French opera, notably by Rameau.

EDITOR'S NOTES TO
Letter on French Music

This translation is based on the text found in Pléiade, V, 287–328. However, whereas the Pléiade edition is based on the first edition of the work, which appeared at the end of November 1753, this translation is based on the second edition, which appeared several months after the first, and also includes Rousseau's additions to his personal copy of the 1764 edition published by Duchesne. Major variations and additions to the different editions are noted.

1. "They are words and [vocal] sounds, and nothing else." The epigraph is derived from Horace, *Epistles*, I.1 (to Maecenas), 34. Horace explains why he has laid aside poetry to devote himself to the truth, especially through reading Stoic moral philosophy, saying: "They are words and speeches that can soothe pain and put down the disease in part." The first clause, *Sunt verba et voces* ("They are words and [vocal] sounds"), is found in Horace; the second clause, *praetereaque nihil* ("and nothing else"), was either added by Rousseau himself or taken by him so altered from another, unknown source.

2. The order for the dismissal of Bambini's troupe of *opera buffa* performers, the "Bouffonists," was issued sometime after late February 1753, but they did not actually leave Paris until March 1754.

3. The "Notice" to the first edition of the *Letter on French Music* ended here, and the remaining text of the "Notice" comes from the second edition. Rousseau's draft of the "Notice" contains the following two paragraphs, which were suppressed from the first edition during the printing process and were not included in subsequent editions:

> This Letter, in just about these words, was written over a year ago, and I issue it in order to remove from my Portfolio and my eyes all that belongs to the subject it treats, and which I confess to have loved too passionately.
>
> Arbiters of Music and of Opera, fashionable men and women: I take leave of you forever, and I shall be happy all the days of my life for having overcome the temptation to bore you a second time with my amusements. It is time to renounce Verses and Music for good and to employ the leisure that remains to me in more useful and more satisfying occupations, if not for the Public at least for myself.

By speaking of his "amusements," Rousseau refers with false modesty to the successful performances of his opera *Le Devin du village* in 1752 and 1753. The tone of these suppressed paragraphs, which is that of Rousseau the author of the *First* and *Second Discourses*, should be compared to the contemporary "Preface" to *Narcisse* (*Collected Writings*, II, 186–198).

4. This note was added by Rousseau in his copy of the 1764 edition of the *Letter*.

5. The author of the *Letter on the Deaf and the Dumb, For the Benefit of those who Hear and Speak*, is Denis Diderot (1713–1784), director of the *Encyclopedia* and at that time a close friend of Rousseau. Diderot's *Letter* appeared in 1751 and was reissued with "Additions" a few weeks later. In the *Letter*, Diderot writes: "The French language is made to teach, to enlighten, and to convince; Greek, Latin, Italian, and English, to persuade, to move, and to deceive. Speak Greek, Latin, and Italian to the masses; but to the wise, speak French" (*Selected Writings*, ed. Lester G. Crocker, trans. Derek Collman [New York: Macmillan, 1966], 35–36). Rousseau elaborates on the persuasive and convincing characters of different languages in his *Essay on the Origin of Languages*, chap. IV, translated below.

6. Bernard le Bovier de Fontenelle, *Histoire des oracles* (1686), 1st dissertation, chap. IV.

7. This sentence and the note to it were added by Rousseau to his copy of the 1764 edition of the *Letter*.

8. Plato, *Laws* (known as *De Legibus* in Latin), II.658e–659a: "For my part I go along with the many to this extent, at least, that music must be judged by pleasure, but the most beautiful Muse is she who pleases the best and best educated men." Rousseau uses Ficino's Latin translation, and omits, after "*voluptate musicam judicandam. . .*", "*. . .non tamen quorumvis hominum voluptate; sed iliam. . . .*" ("but not by the pleasure of any chance listeners"). In the context of the *Laws* from which Rousseau quotes, the Athenian Stranger asks his interlocutors to imagine what sort of presentation the people would approve, and then argues that it is not the people but the "educated" individual who is the true judge. The quotation from Plato and the note which identifies it were added by Rousseau to his copy of the 1764 edition of the *Letter*.

9. The "Queen's Corner" refers to the partisans of the Italian opera under the favor of the Queen in opposition to the partisans of the French opera under the favor of Louis XV, or what came to be called the "King's Corner." Rousseau refers to an "ancient partisan of the Queen's Corner" since the long Latin quotation that follows was taken by him, indirectly, from a writing dating from the quarrel over French and Italian music that took place earlier in the century. See the following note.

10. Rousseau identifies the source of this citation and provides a translation in the article PLAIN-SONG [*Plein-Chant*] in his *Dictionary of Music*. The source identified is *Annalium et historiae Francorum ad anno DCCVIII ad annum DCCCCXC scriptores coaetanei*, Francofurti [Frankfurt am Main], 1594, under the life of Charlemagne. However, this passage is not contained in that work and appears to have been taken by Rousseau from J. Bonnet's *Histoire de la musique* (Paris, 1715), 425, while Bonnet took it from the relation contained in a 1713 issue of the *Mercure de France* of the "antipathy of Italian Musicians against French Musicians, which has subsisted since the Emperor Charlemagne." The following translation is based on Rousseau's own translation of the passage, which is quite accurate, in the above-mentioned article in the *Dictionary of Music*.

The most pious King Charles, having returned from celebrating Easter in Rome with the Apostolic Lord, was disturbed during the festivities by a quarrel between the Roman singers and the French singers. The French claimed to sing better and more agreeably than the Romans; the Romans, claiming to be the most knowledgeable about ecclesiastical song, which they had learned from Pope Saint Gregory, accused the French of corrupting, flaying, and disfiguring true singing. The dispute having been taken before the lord King, the French, who quite relied on his support, insulted the Roman singers; the Romans, haughty from their great knowledge, and comparing the doctrine of Saint Gregory to the rusticity of the others, treated them as ignoramuses, rustics, and stupid and gross beasts: since this altercation did not end, the most pious King Charles said to his singers: Tell us what is the purest and best water, that which is taken from the live spring of a fountain, or that from the rivulets which flow from but far off. They all said that the water from the spring was the purest, and that of the rivulets is altered and dirty to the degree of the distance it came. Go back, then, replied the lord King Charles, to the fountain of Saint Gregory, whose song you have evidently corrupted. Then the lord King asked Pope Adrien for singers to correct French song, and the pope gave him Theodore and Benoist, two very knowledgeable singers and instructed by Saint Gregory; he also gave him Saint Gregory's antiphons, which he had noted himself in Roman notes. Of these two singers, the lord King Charles, on returning to France, sent one to Metz and the other to Soissons, ordering all the singing masters of the cities of France to give them their antiphons to correct, and to learn to sing from them. Thus were corrected the French antiphons, which each altered by additions and subtractions according to his mode, and all the singers of France learned Roman song, which they now called French song; but as for the trembling, flattering, beaten, shortened sounds of the song, the French never could make them well, producing quavering rather than rolling because of the natural rudeness and barbarousness of their throats. Besides, the principal singing school always remained in Metz; and to the degree that the Roman song surpassed that of Metz, the song of Metz surpassed that of the other French schools. The Roman singers learned how to accompany with instruments in the same way as the French; and the lord King Charles, having once again brought back with him masters of grammar and calculating, ordered that there be everywhere established the study of letters, for before the aforementioned lord king there was in France no knowledge of the liberal arts.

Pope Gregory the Great (c. 540–604) is credited with developing the plainchant, or "Gregorian chant," and collecting antiphons, that is, psalms or verses sung responsively. Charlemagne introduced a more homogeneous plainchant under the direction of Alcuin (735–804), who also supervised the introduction of the liberal arts into Charlemagne's realm. The hybrid Franco-Roman plainchant was widely used in France for centuries afterward.

11. Rousseau refers to Plato. See note 8 above.

12. "Movement" translates "*mouvement*." "*Mouvement*" can mean tempo or meter, and sometimes both, so the cognate "movement" has been used consistently to render the term.

13. Eighteenth-century aesthetic theory generally included the overcoming of difficulties as one of the signs of good taste and genius. Rousseau speaks disparagingly of all this "learning" instead of true "genius" at the end of this work.

14. "[Vocal] sounds, and nothing else." This is part of the epigraph to this work. See note 1 above.

15. Literally: play the softs (*doux*) loud (*fort*) and the louds (*forts*) soft (*doux*).

16. In the article SOFT [*Doux*] in his *Dictionary of Music* (Pléiade, V, 789), Rousseau explains: "The Italians write *Dolce* and more commonly *Piano* in the same sense; but their Musical Purists maintain that these two words are not synonyms, and that it is by misuse that many Authors use them as such. They say that *Piano* means simply a moderation of sound, a diminution of noise; but that *Dolce* indicates, besides this, a way of playing *più soave*, more sweetly, more flowingly, and answering more or less to the word *Louré* of the French."

17. In both the note, which was added by Rousseau to the second edition of the *Letter*, and the passage to which it is attached, Rousseau alludes to his *Letter from a Symphonist*, translated herein. "*Symphoniste*" was translated as "symphonist" in the *Letter from a Symphonist*, but is translated as "instrumental player" here and elsewhere. See note 1 to *Letter from a Symphonist*, translated above.

18. Tasso, *Jerusalem Delivered*, XVI.25, speaking of Armida:
Tender scorning, and placid and tranquil
Refusals, and precious sporting, and joyous truces,
Smiling endearments, and teardrops sweet,
Broken sighs, and kisses soft
She blended all these together and then united,
And in the fire tempered with a slow flame;
And of them shaped that girdle so marvelous
With which she kept her fair waist belted.

19. Tasso, *Jerusalem Delivered*, IV.3:
The screeching sound of the Tartarean trumpet
Calls up the inhabitants of the eternal shades:
The gloomy spacious caverns tremble,
and the blinded air resounds to that sound;
Nor ever so strident from the supernal
Regions of Heaven the thunderbolt plummets,

Nor ever so shaken does the earth tremble
When she closes up fumes in her pregnant womb.

20. Tasso's *Jerusalem Delivered* served as the basis for a number of libretti in French, including that by Quinault set to music by Lully as *Armide*. Rousseau will criticize *Armide* at length below. Rousseau's point is that the Italian cannot be adequately translated into French.

21. Rousseau paraphrases Anthony Ashley Cooper, Third Earl of Shaftesbury (1671–1713), *Characteristics* (London, 1732), III, 398–399:

> I can my-self remember the Time, when, in respect of MUSICK, our reigning Taste was in many degrees inferior to the *French*. The long Reign of Luxury and Pleasure under King CHARLES the Second, and the foreign Helps and study'd Advantages given to *Musick* in a following Reign, cou'd not raise our Genius the least in this respect. But when the Spirit of the Nation was grown more *free*, tho engag'd at that time in the fiercest War, and with the most doubtful Success, we no sooner began to turn our-selves towards *Musick*, and enquire what ITALY in particular produc'd, than in an instant we outstrip'd our Neighbours the FRENCH, enter'd into a Genius far beyond theirs, and rais'd our-selves an *Ear*, and *Judgment*, not inferior to the best now in the World.

Rousseau appears to draw on the translation sent to him in 1745 by Diderot, who translated and popularized Shaftesbury in France.

22. This note was added by Rousseau to the second edition of the *Letter*.

23. The first example is from *Hippolyte et Aricie* (1733), a lyric-tragedy by Rameau on a libretto by Simon Joseph Pelegrin. The second example, said to be by Baldasare Galuppi (1706–1785), an Italian composer crucial to the development of the *opera buffa* style, cannot be identified.

24. Marie Fel (1713–1794) was a celebrated singer who played Colette in Rousseau's *Devin du village* (1752). Pierre de Jelyotte (1711–1782) was a celebrated singer who frequently played in Rameau's works and in Rousseau's *Les Muses galantes* (1743) and then his *Le Devin du village*. The example of Jelyotte was added by Rousseau to the second edition of the *Letter*.

25. Pietro Metastasio (1698–1782) was an Italian poet and very popular librettist. Nicola Porpora (1686–1768) was a Neapolitan composer of vocal music and opera. For Galuppi, see note 23 above. Gioacchino Cocci (1715–1804) was a Neapolitan composer of tragic and comic opera whose *La scaltra governatrice* was the first full-length opera performed by the Bouffonists in Paris. Niccolò Jomelli (1714–1774) was a prolific Neapolitan composer of opera and sacred music. David Perez (1711–1779) was a Neapolitan opera composer of Spanish descent. Domenico Terradellas or Terradeglias (1713–1751) was a Spanish-born composer of opera and other vocal music in the Neapolitan style.

26. "*Quando sciolto avrò il contratto*" is from *Il Maestro di musica* with music by Pergolesi and Pietro Auletta (September 1752); "*Io ò un vespajo*" is from *La Finta cameriera* by Gaetano Latilla (November 1752); "*O questo o quello t'ai a risolvere*" is from an unknown source; "*A un gusto da stordire*" is from *Il Maestro di musica* with music by Pergolesi and Pietro Auletta (September 1752); "*Stizzoso mio, stizzoso*" is from *La Serva padrona* by Pergolesi (August 1752); "*Io sono una Donzella*" is from *Il Cinese rimpatriato* or *Le Chinois de retour* by Joseph Selletti (June 1753); "*Quanti

maestri, quanti dottori" and "*Gli Sbirri già lo aspettano*" are from *La Gouvernante rusée* by Cocchi (December 1752); "*Ma dunque il testamento*" is from an unknown source; "*Senti me, se brami stare, O che risa! che piacere!*" is from an unknown source (the second half of the verse, "*O che risa! che piacere!*" was added by Rousseau to the second edition of the *Letter*).

27. Rousseau gives the French title, *La Fausse Suivante*, for *La Finta cameriera*, by Gaetano Latilla (1711–1788), originally produced in 1738 and played by the Bouffonists in Paris in November 1752. Certain omissions were made from the Sunday performances of the piece.

28. Rousseau discusses "design" in the article DESIGN [*Dessein*] in his *Dictionary of Music* (Pléiade, V, 752–753): "It is the invention and the direction of the subject, the disposition of every Part, and the general ordering of the whole. It is not enough to write beautiful Songs and a good Harmony; it is necessary to tie all this together by a principal subject, to which all the parts of the work are related, and by which it is a *one*." Rousseau first makes this point about "design" in his *Letter to M. Grimm*, anticipating his discussion of the unity of melody in the *Letter on French Music*. See p. 130 above.

29. Rousseau develops his conception of the "unity of melody" in later writings and insists upon its importance. See the article UNITY OF MELODY [*Unité de mélodie*] in his *Dictionary of Music*, translated below.

30. All of these pieces were performed by the Bouffonists during their stay in Paris. Rousseau gives the French titles for the works: *Le Maître de Musique* is *Il Maestro di musica*, with music by Pergolesi and Pietro Auletta (September 1752). *La Femme orgueilleuse* is *La Donna superba* by Rinaldo da Capua (December 1752). *Tracollo* is *Tracollo, medioco ignorante*, attributed to Pergolesi but principally or wholly by Mariani (May 1753). *La Bohèmienne* is *La Zingara* by Rinaldo da Capua (June 1753).

31. Diderot, *Letter on the Deaf and the Dumb* (1751).

32. The article DIMINUTION [*Diminution*], which was written by Rousseau, appeared in 1754: "An old word which means the division of a long Note, such as a whole note or a half note, into several other Notes of lesser value. By this word were also understood all the Grace notes and other passages which have since been called *Roulemens* or *Roulades*" (*Dictionary of Music* version, Pléiade, V, 762–763).

33. See note 13 above.

34. For Terradeglias, see note 25 above. Rousseau may have met the composer during his 1743–1744 stay in Venice.

35. Arcangelo Corelli (1653–1713) was an Italian composer whose works were important in the development of the baroque sonata form; Lully was court composer to Louis XIV of France. Rousseau repeats a rumor about Lully and Corelli which apparently has no foundation.

36. Rousseau refers to the practice in France of using *notes inégales*, that is, writing music with different values than it has when performed.

37. Abbé Jean-Baptiste Du Bos, *Réflexions critiques sur la poésie, la peinture, et la musique* (1719), sec. XLVII. Roland de Lassus (1532–1594) and Claude Goudimel (c. 1520–1572) were important French musicians of the time. Giovanni Buononcini or Bononcini (1670–1745) was an Italian composer known for his graceful arias.

Leonardo Vinci (c. 1690–1730) was a leading Neapolitan composer of *opera seria*. Giovanni Battista Pergolesi (1710–1736) was a composer of operas and other vocal pieces, including the opera buffa *La serva padrona*, of which Rousseau speaks below. In his copy of the 1764 edition of the *Letter*, Rousseau omitted the phrase "Lully added a little rhythm."

38. See note 28 above.

39. *L'Impromptu de Campagne* (1673) is a comedy by Philippe Poisson, and *Le Baron de la Crasse* (1662) is a comedy by Raymond Poisson. The former comedy was reprised by the Comédie-Française in July 1752.

40. Grimm, *Letter on "Omphale."* In a passage not translated above, Grimm writes: "Duos also generally have the inconvenience of being beyond nature. It is not natural for two persons to speak going round and round about the same words for half an hour." Rousseau refers to Grimm's *Letter on "Omphale"* on this subject in his article Duo [*Duo*] in the *Dictionary of Music* (Pléiade, V, 790–791).

41. The duo between Mandane and Arbace is from the lyric-tragedy *Artaserse* (1744), with music by Terradeglias on a libretto by Metastasio. Rousseau could have heard this opera while in Venice. The duo between Lybia and Epaphus is from *Phaéton* (1683), a lyric-tragedy by Lully on a libretto by Quinault.

42. *La Serva padrona* is Pergolesi's best-known comic opera. See note 37 above.

43. The editor has not been able to identify this passage attributed to Cicero.

44. Rousseau refers to Felice Bambini (1742–1810), son of the director of the troupe of Bouffonists. He later composed and wrote a treatise on keyboard playing.

45. Charles Noblet (1715–1769) was an accompanist at the Paris Opera until 1762 and composer of sacred and instrumental music.

46. Literally, "*quintes*," which refers to the part for the cello or, in older times, for the viola.

47. "An art which does everything thereby reveals nothing" (reading *scoprire* for *scuopre*). From Tasso, *Jerusalem Delivered*, XVI.9.

48. Compare Rousseau, *Second Discourse* (*Collected Writings*, III, 49): "all subsequent progress has been in appearance so many steps toward the perfection of the individual, and in fact toward the decrepitude of the species."

49. Although "*air*" has been generally translated as "aria," since what is in question here is the difference between a French "*air*" and an Italian "*aria*," "*air*" has been translated by "air" and "*aria*" by "aria." There is a similar problem with "*ariette*" in the following passages. The term can mean a small *air*, but it came to refer to an Italian *aria* and especially a small *aria*, or *arietta*, which were often included in French operas during the first half of the eighteenth century.

50. The first of the three examples suggests the aria "*Veggo un'ombra che orribile severa*" from *Tito Manlio* (1742) by Gennaro Manna (1715–1779) on a libretto by Metastasio. The second, *La Clemenza di Tito* (1734) is frequently attributed to Cocchi but is actually by Antonio Caldara (c. 1670–1736) on a libretto by Metastasio (the same libretto was later set to music by Mozart). The third, *Sara*, is not listed among Metastasio's works, and Rousseau may instead mean his drama *Siroe, re di Persia* (1733).

51. *Iphigénie en Tauride* (1704) is a lyric-tragedy by Campra and Desmarets on a libretto by Duché de Vancy and Danchet based on a play by Racine.

52. Gaetano Majorano (1710–1783), called Caffarelli, was a celebrated Italian mezzo-soprano castrato who was in Paris during the 1753–1754 season, when he sang at the Concert Spirituel (an annual concert given at the Tuileries) on November 5, 1753.

53. Rousseau refers to the pamphlet *Au petit prophète de Boehmischborda et au grand prophète Monet*, by Diderot, which appeared anonymously in February 1753. Diderot's pamphlet replied to two other pamphlets: *Le petit prophète de Boehmischborda*, by Grimm, which appeared anonymously in January 1753, and *Les prophéties du grand prophète Monet*, by Pidansat de Mairobert, which responded to Grimm's pamphlet and appeared soon after it. In his reply to these two writings, Diderot compared Lully's *Armide* (1686), on a libretto by Quinault, to Terradeglias' *Nitocris* (1739), on a libretto by Metastasio. In doing so, Diderot takes up a suggestion by Pidansat.

54. In his copy of Duchesne's 1764 edition of the *Letter*, Rousseau adds here: "This monologue is found engraved with its Thoroughbass and the fundamental Bass in d'Alembert's *Elements of Music*, 1766, in 8°." See the Appendix to this volume for the text and music of the monologue.

55. Rameau analyzed this same monologue in his *Nouveau système de musique théoretique* (1726).

56. *E si mi* is equivalent to the key of E minor.

57. "*Cadence*" in French can refer either to a "cadence" (a harmonic or melodic formula that occurs at the end of a composition, a section, or a phrase) or a "trill," which is how the term has normally been translated.

58. In his personal copy of the first edition of the *Letter*, Rousseau crossed out "the prodigious change taking place in Armide's soul and in her speech" and added "the tumult of which Armide complains and the uncertainty that has upset her resolve."

59. Marie Françoise Marchand (1711–1803), called Mlle Dumesnil, was a well-known actress.

60. See note 53 above.

61. Rousseau appears to refer to *Les Troqueurs*, a comic opera by Joseph Vadé, after La Fontaine, with music by Dauvergne, produced July 30, 1753.

EDITOR'S NOTES TO
Observations on Our Instinct for Music

This translation is based on the text of the original edition found in Jacobi, III, 257–329. Rameau's footnotes are included only where necessary.

1. Rameau argued from his earliest theoretical writings that melody is derived from harmony. See *Treatise on Harmony*, II, chap. 19 (Gossett, 152–154).

2. "Movement" translates "*mouvement*." "*Mouvement*" can mean tempo or meter, and sometimes both, so the cognate "movement" has been used consistently to render the term. The word translated "motions" in the previous sentence renders "*mouvement*," a usage which underscores the relationship between musical movement, in terms of both rhythm and tempo, and physical movement, as in dance.

3. *Les Troqueurs* is a comic opera after La Fontaine by Joseph Vadé with music

by Dauvergne, and was produced July 30, 1753. *La Coquette Trompée* was a comic opera by Dauvergne on a libretto by Favart. Rameau's own comic opera-ballet, *Platée* (1745), was successfully reprised in 1753.

4. The "sounding body" (*corps sonore*) refers to a body that produces sounds upon vibrating and which causes other bodies tuned to the same frequency or a harmonic thereof to resonate. Rameau's entire musical theory is based upon the harmonics produced by a sounding body.

5. Charles-Étienne Briseux, *Traité du beau essentiel dans les Arts* (1752).

6. Rameau, *Nouveau Système de musique théoretique* (1726), chap. 10 (Jacobi, II, 64–65).

7. When he alludes to having himself contributed to the erroneous belief that the ancients did not practice harmony, Rameau refers to his earlier and more extreme view that the ancients did not practice harmony properly speaking. In the portion omitted here, Rameau discusses the nature of the tetrachord and the generation of sounds from the sounding body.

8. In the portion omitted here, Rameau discusses the generation of the notes of the major and minor modes in terms of harmonic and arithmetical proportions. He then analyzes a scene from Lully's *Armide* to show that the expressiveness of the scene derives from Lully's having followed a natural instinct in music.

9. Rameau uses the term "mode" (*mode*) here as essentially equivalent to the term "key" (*ton*). In the short portion omitted here, Rameau returns to the example from Lully's *Armide* in order to illustrate his point.

10. *Dardanus* (1739) is a lyric-tragedy by Rameau on a libretto by Le Clerc de La Bruère.

11. *Castor and Pollux* (1737) is a lyric-tragedy by Rameau.

12. Rameau now turns to an analysis of Rousseau's *Letter on French Music*, accusing him of contradicting what he had said in the articles he wrote for the *Encyclopedia* (written in 1749).

13. See Rousseau, *Letter on French Music*, p. 169 above.

14. "Trill" translates "*tril*" and "cadenza" translates "*cadence*," which has otherwise been translated "trill." Rameau criticizes Rousseau's use of the term "*cadence*" because of its association with a "cadence" (a harmonic or melodic formula that occurs at the end of a composition, a section, or a phrase). "Cadenza" has been used here to translate "*cadence*" even though true cadenzas are stylized ornaments used in singing very much as trills are stylized ornaments in music generally.

15. Example B presents a simplified and annotated score of "*Enfin il est en ma puissance, Ce fatal ennemi, Ce superbe vainqueur*," from Lully's *Armide*. See Appendix.

16. See Rousseau's article CADENCE [*Cadence*] from the *Encyclopedia*, p. 211 below. "Close" translates "*repos*" and "cadence" translates "*cadence*." A "*repos*" is a type of melodic or harmonic "close," and is often used synonymously for "cadence" (*cadence*), as Rameau suggests. Rameau generally prefers the term "*repos*," while Rousseau uses the term "*cadence*."

17. See Rousseau's article CADENCE [*Cadence*] from the *Encyclopedia*, p. 209 below.

18. See Rousseau's article CADENCE [*Cadence*] from the *Encyclopedia*, pp. 208–209 below.

19. Example B presents a simplified and annotated score of "*Enfin il est en ma puissance, Ce fatal ennemi, Ce superbe vainqueur*," from Lully's *Armide*. See Appendix.

20. See Rousseau, *Letter on French Music*, p. 169 above.

21. See Rousseau, *Letter on French Music*, pp. 160–161 above.

22. Example C presents a simplified and annotated score of "*Ce superbe vainqueur, Je vais percer son invincible coeur*" from Lully's *Armide*. See Appendix.

23. See Rousseau, *Letter on French Music*, p. 170 above.

24. See Rousseau, *Letter on French Music*, p. 170 above.

25. See Rousseau, *Letter on French Music*, p. 170 above.

26. Example D presents a simplified and annotated score of "*Le charme du sommeil le livre à ma vengeance*," from Lully's *Armide*. See Appendix.

27. See Rousseau, *Letter on French Music*, p. 170 above.

28. See Rousseau, *Letter on French Music*, p. 170 above.

29. See pp. 184–185n† above.

30. See Rousseau's article CADENCE [*Cadence*] from the *Encyclopedia*, p. 209 below.

31. See Rousseau's article CADENCE [*Cadence*] from the *Encyclopedia*, pp. 210–211 below.

32. See Rousseau, *Letter on French Music*, p. 170 above.

33. Example F presents a simplified and annotated score of "*-cible coeur. Par lui mes Captifs sont sortis d'esclavage. Qu'il éprouve toute ma rage*," from Lully's *Armide*. See Appendix.

34. See Rousseau's article CADENCE [*Cadence*] from the *Encyclopedia*, p. 209 below.

35. See Rousseau, *Letter on French Music*, p. 171 above.

36. See Rousseau, *Letter on French Music*, p. 171 above.

37. Example G presents a simplified and annotated score of "*peut m'arrêter, Achevons . . . je frémis! vengeons-nous . . . je soupire!*" from Lully's *Armide*. See Appendix.

38. See Rousseau, *Letter on French Music*, p. 161 above.

39. See above pp. 182 and 186.

40. See Rousseau, *Letter on French Music*, p. 172 above.

41. See Rousseau, *Letter on French Music*, p. 172 above.

42. See Rousseau, *Letter on French Music*, p. 172 above.

43. See Rousseau, *Letter on French Music*, pp. 172–173 above.

44. See Rousseau, *Letter on French Music*, p. 170 above.

45. See Rousseau, *Letter on French Music*, p. 172 above.

46. See Rousseau, *Letter on French Music*, p. 172 above.

47. See Rousseau, *Letter on French Music*, p. 169 above.

48. See Rousseau, *Letter on French Music*, p. 170 above.

49. See Rousseau, *Letter on French Music*, p. 170 above.

50. See Rousseau, *Letter on French Music*, p. 172 above.

51. See Rousseau's article CHORUS [*Choeur*] from the *Encyclopedia*, p. 213 below.

52. See Rousseau, *Letter on French Music*, p. 157 above.

53. Volume 3 of the *Encyclopedia* (1753) contains articles beginning with "C," including Rousseau's article CHORUS [*Choeur*].

EDITOR'S NOTES TO
Articles from the Encyclopedia

This translation is based on the original text of the *Encyclopédie, ou Dictionnaire raisonné des sciences, des arts, et des mètiers* as found in the facsimile edition published by Friedrich Frommann Verlag (Stuttgart; Bad-Cannstatt: Friedrich Frommann Verlag, 1966). Only those articles by Rousseau that Rameau directly examines are included here. The articles translated here are from the following volumes of the *Encyclopedia*: ACCOMPANIMENT [*Accompagnement*], vol. 1 (1751), 75–77; CHORD [*Accord*], vol. 1 (1751), 78–79; CADENCE [*Cadence*], vol. 2 (1751), 513–515; CHORUS [*Choeur*], vol. 3 (1753), 362; CHROMATIC [*Chromatique*], vol. 3 (1753), 387; DISSONANCE [*Dissonance*], vol. 4 (1754), 1049–1050; ENHARMONIC [*Enharmonique*], vol. 5 (1755), 688–689.

Rousseau's articles for the *Encyclopedia* are signed "S." D'Alembert, the editor responsible for the articles on music, added materials to Rousseau's articles for clarification or amplification. His additions, which are signed "O," are included here in brackets. Finally, the additions to the article CHORUS [*Choeur*] signed "B," and also included here in brackets, are by Cahusac.

Major variations and additions to these articles in versions in the *Dictionary of Music* are noted in the footnotes, except for the articles DISSONANCE [*Dissonnance*] and ENHARMONIC [*Enharmonique*], the *Dictionary of Music* versions of which are translated below in their entirety.

1. The conception of what constitutes a "complete" or "perfect" harmony, which will be at issue between Rousseau and Rameau, goes back to at least to Zarlino's discussion of a *harmonia perfetta*, which he defined as the triad of the final, dominant, and mediant. Several French musical theorists of the mid-sixteenth century who directly influenced Rameau translated Zarlino's term as *harmonie parfaite*, or "perfect harmony." See Thomas Christensen, *Rameau and Musical Thought in the Enlightenment* (Cambridge: Cambridge University Press, 1993), 45, 180.

2. Rameau, *Dissertation sur les méthodes différents d'accompagnement* (1732). In that work, Rameau proposes a set of seven figures to indicate the accompaniment. Rousseau generally follows Rameau's proposals to simplify the figures used to indicate the accompaniment and its fingering.

3. François Campion (c. 1686–c. 1748) was a guitarist and composer who published a treatise on accompaniment, the *Traité d'accompagnement et de composition selon la règle des octaves de musique* (1716).

4. In the version of this article in the *Dictionary of Music*, Rousseau added the following paragraph, in response to Rameau's criticism:

> If it is asked how this omission of Sounds accords with the definition of the *Accompaniment* by a complete Harmony, I answer that these omissions are, in truth, merely hypothetical and only within M. Rameau's System; that, according to Nature, these Chords, in appearance so mutilated, are no less complete

than the others, since the Sounds here supposed omitted would make them shocking and often unbearable; that, indeed, dissonant Chords are not at all filled out in M. Tartini's system as they are in M. Rameau's; that, consequently, defective Chords in the latter are complete in the former; that, finally, since good taste in performance often requires one to depart from the general rule and since the most regular *Accompaniment* is not always the most pleasant one, the definition ought to dictate the rule and custom apprise one when one should depart from it.

5. In the version of this article in the *Dictionary of Music*, Rousseau added the following sentence: "In Italian Recitative, whatever duration a Note in the Bass may have, it can never be struck except once and then strongly with its whole Chord; the Chord is restruck only when it changes on the same Note: but when an *Accompaniment* of Violins rules over the Recitative, then the Bass must be sustained and the Chord arpeggiated."

6. In the version of this article in the *Dictionary of Music*, instead of this paragraph Rousseau wrote: "When one accompanies vocal Music, one should, by means of the *Accompaniment,* sustain the Voice, guide it, give it the Pitch on all its reentrances, and put it back onto it when it is off pitch: the Accompanist, always having the Song before his eyes and the Harmony present to his mind, is particularly charged with preventing the Voice from going astray. (See ACCOMPANIST [*Accompagnateur*].)"

7. "Trills" translates "*cadences*," which refers to stylistic ornaments or grace notes used in playing.

8. Rameau, *Treatise on Harmony* (Gossett, 89).

9. Rameau, *Génération harmonique* (1737), 186 (Jacobi, III, 107).

10. In the version of this article in the *Dictionary of Music*, instead of this paragraph Rousseau wrote:

M. Rameau, who spoke about this *Cadence* first, and who allows several inversions of it, prohibits us, in his *Treatise on Harmony*, page 117, from allowing the one in which the added Sound is in the bass bearing a Chord of the Seventh, and that by a hardly solid reason about which I have spoken at the word CHORD [*Accord*]. He has taken this Chord of the Seventh as fundamental, so that he has a Seventh resolved by another Seventh, a Dissonance by a like Dissonance, by a similar movement on the fundamental Bass. If such a manner of Treating Dissonances could be tolerated, it would be necessary to put one's fingers in one's ears and throw the rules in the fire. But the Harmony, under which this Author has placed such a strange fundamental Bass, is manifestly the inversion of an *Imperfect Cadence* avoided by an augmented Seventh on the second Note. And this is so true that the Thoroughbass which strikes the Dissonance is necessarily obliged to ascend diatonically in order to resolve it, without which the transition would be useless. I admit that in the same work, page 272, M. Rameau gives a similar example with the true fundamental Bass, but since he disapproves, in very definite terms, of the inversion which results from this Bass, such a passage serves only to show an additional contradiction in his Book. And although in a later work (*Harmon. Gener.* page 186), the same Author seems to recognize the true foundation of this transition, he speaks of it so obscurely, and still says so clearly that the Seventh is resolved by another, that it is very clearly seen that he only glimpses it here and that at bottom he does not change his opinion, so that one has a right to cast on him the reproach that he makes to Masson of having not been able to see the *Imperfect Cadence* in one of his Inversions.

Rousseau's reference here is to Charles Masson, *Nouveau Traité des règles de la composition de la musique* (1699), p. 99. Masson was one of the most important works on counterpoint of his time. Rameau criticizes Masson's discussion of inversions and the irregular cadence in Book I, chap. 7, of his *Treatise on Harmony* (Gossett, 73–78). For Rousseau's citations of Rameau, see the previous two notes.

11. In the version of this article in the *Dictionary of Music*, before quoting the above three paragraphs, written by d'Alembert and signed "O," Rousseau writes: "After having expounded of the Rules for and constitution of various *Cadences*, let us pass to the reasons M. d'Alembert gives, following M. Rameau, for their denominations."

Then, after quoting d'Alembert, he comments:

> These explanations are ingenious and show what use can be made of Double Employment in passages that seem to be the least related. Nevertheless, M. d'Alembert's intention is surely not for one actually to use these in practice, but only for understanding Inversion. For example, the Double Employment of the *Interrupted Cadence* would resolve the Dissonance *fa* by the Dissonance *mi*, which is contrary to the rules, to the spirit of the rules, and above all to the ear's judgment; for in the sensation of the second Chord *sol si re mi*, after the first, *sol si re fa*, the ear is obstinate rather in rejecting the *re* from being the among the class of Consonances than in admitting the *mi* as a Dissonant. In general, Beginners should know that Double Employment can be admitted in a Seventh Chord after a consonant Chord, but that as soon as a Seventh Chord is followed by a similar one, Double Employment cannot take place. It is good for them also to know that one Tone should not be changed for any dissonant Chord other than the leading one; from which it follows that in the *Deceptive Cadence* no change of Tone can be supposed.

12. Instead of this paragraph, in the version of this article in the *Dictionary of Music*, Rousseau wrote: "No Author that I know of, until M. Rameau, has spoken of that harmonic ascent: he himself only causes it to be glimpsed, and it is true that one would not be able either to practice a long series of like *Cadences* because of the major Sixths that would prolong the Modulation, or even fill out, without precautions, the whole Harmony."

13. See note 9 above.

14. "Cadenza" translates "*cadence*," which is otherwise translated as "trill" when used in this sense (see note 7 above). True cadenzas are stylized ornaments used in singing, very much as trills are stylized ornaments in music generally. It was necessary to use "cadenza" here in order to convey the connection Rousseau establishes here between a "cadence" and a "trill."

15. *Jephté* (1732) is a Biblical opera based on a libretto by the Abbé Pellegrin (1663–1745), Rameau's first librettist, then set to music by Michel Pinolet de Montéclair (1667–1737).

16. *Trancrède* (1702) is an opera-ballet by André Campra (1660–1744). *Phaéton* (1683) is a lyric-tragedy by Lully.

17. *Les Indes galantes* (1735) is an opera-ballet by Rameau.

18. Boethius, *De institutione musica*, I.1. Timotheus of Meletus was a dithyrambic poet and innovator in the "new music" of the late fifth-century B.C. Athenaeus, *Deipnosophistai*, XIV.637f-638a. Epigones (c. sixth century B.C.) is said to have been the first tragic poet.

19. Aristoxenus, *Elementa Harmonica*, I.24–26, II.50–52 (Barker, II, 142–144, 164–166).

20. Ptolemy (Claudius Ptolemaeus), *Harmonica*, II.xiii (Barker, II, 342–345).

21. In the version of this article in the *Dictionary of Music*, Rousseau added the following paragraph: "The consecutive Semitones practiced in the *Chromatic* are not all of the same Genre, but almost alternately Minor and Major, that is, *Chromatic* and *Diatonic*; for the interval of a Minor *Tone* contains a Minor Semitone or *Chromatic* and a Major Semitone or Diatonic—a Measure which temperament makes common to all the Tones, so that one cannot proceed by two adjoining and consecutive minor Semitones without entering into the Enharmonic; but two major Semitones follow each other twice in the *Chromatic* order of the Scale."

22. The version of this article from Rousseau's *Dictionary of Music* will be found below among the selected articles from that work, so variants will not be noted here.

23. Marin Mersenne, *Harmonie universelle contenant la théorie et la pratique de la musique* (1636), Book II, "Des dissonances," 113 ff.

24. Rameau, *Nouveau système de musique théoretique* (1726), chap. 11 (Jacobi, II, 65 ff.). The second work in question is his *Génération harmonique*, chap. 9 (Jacobi, III, 68 ff.)

25. D'Alembert refers to his *Éléments de la musique théoretique et pratique* (1st ed.; 1752).

26. The version of this article from Rousseau's *Dictionary of Music* will be found below among the selected articles from that work, so variants will not be noted here.

27. Aristoxenus (fl. fourth century B.C.) was a student of Aristotle and the most important musical theorist of his time. His "sectarians" opposed the Pythagorean school.

28. Aristide Quintilianus, *De musica*, I.9 (Barker, II, 417–419).

29. Pseudo-Plutarch, *De musica*, 1134f–1135a; 1145a (Barker, I, 215–216, 244–245).

30. The "Trio of the Furies" is the second trio of the Furies in Rameau's lyric-tragedy *Hippolyte et Aricie* (1733). The trio was successfully performed by the private orchestra of Rameau's patron, La Pouplinière, but the singers at the Paris Opera were unable to sing it and it had to be omitted. Rameau recounts the episode and claims that it was elsewhere performed in his *Génération harmonique* (1737), chap. XIV (Jacobi, III, 89 ff.) and his *Démonstration du principe de l'harmonie* (1750), 95–96 (Jacobi, III, 213–214). See d'Alembert's discussion of the example in his addition to this article, just below.

31. D'Alembert refers to his *Éléments de la musique théoretique et pratique* (1st ed.; 1752), p. 87.

32. Rameau, *Génération harmonique* (1737), 149 ff. (Jacobi, III, 89 ff.); *Nouveau système de musique théoretique* (1726), 42 (Jacobi, II, 52). See also his *Observations on Our Instinct for Music*, p. 178 above.

33. See note 30 above.

34. Rameau describes the bad performance and poor reception of this part of his heroic opera-ballet *Les indes galantes* (1735) in his *Démonstration du principe de l'harmonie* (1750), 95 (Jacobi, III, 213–214). See also note 30 above.

35. D'Alembert, *Éléments de la musique théoretique et pratique* (1st ed.; 1752), Book 1, chaps. 20 and 22, Book 2, chap. 14. In the last chapter cited here, d'Alembert refers to several works by Rameau where the enharmonic is employed, including the example of the earthquake in his opera-ballet *Les Indes galantes*.

EDITOR'S NOTES TO
Errors on Music in the Encyclopedia

This translation is based on the text of the original edition as photostatically reproduced in Jacobi, V, 197–261. Rameau's work first appeared anonymously in 1755, and while he never acknowledged his authorship, it was almost universally known to be his work.

1. Rameau usually refers to page numbers, then to paragraphs (with a simple numeral), and then sometimes to the line number. I have added the symbol for a paragraph (¶) where he refers to one in order to avoid confusion.

2. See Rousseau, ACCOMPANIMENT [*Accompagnement*], p. 198 above.

3. See Rousseau, ACCOMPANIMENT [*Accompagnement*], p. 198 above.

4. Rameau refers to Rousseau, who grew up in Geneva, where music was restricted and theater prohibited.

5. See Rousseau, ACCOMPANIMENT [*Accompagnement*], pp. 200–201 above.

6. Rameau, *Dissertation sur les méthodes différents d'accompagnement* (1732) (Jacobi, V, 28).

7. See Rousseau, ACCOMPANIMENT [*Accompagnement*], p. 202 above.

8. See Rousseau, ACCOMPANIMENT [*Accompagnement*], p. 203 above.

9. See Rousseau, *Letter on French Music*, pp. 150–151 above.

10. "Rhythm" translates "*Mesure*," which is usually translated "meter" or "measure."

11. "Movement" translates "*mouvement*." "*Mouvement*" can mean tempo or meter, and sometimes both, so the cognate "movement" has been used consistently to render the term.

12. See Rousseau, *Letter on French Music*, pp. 151–152 above; and the article ACCOMPANIMENT [*Accompagnement*] from the *Encyclopedia* (or the *Dictionary* or *Encyclopedic Dictionary*, as Rameau sometimes calls it), p. 202 above.

13. *Pygmalion* (1748) is an opera-ballet by Rameau.

14. See Rousseau, *Letter on French Music*, p. 159 above.

15. *Jephté* (1732) is a Biblical opera by Montéclair based on a libretto by the Abbé Pelegrin, Rameau's future librettist.

16. *Hippolyte et Aricie* (1733), *Castor et Pollux* (1737), and *Dardanus* (1730) are

lyric-tragedies by Rameau. *Les Talens Lyriques*, otherwise known as *Les Fêtes d'Hébé* (1739) is an opera-ballet by Rameau.

17. Rameau refers to Rousseau's opera-ballet *Les muses galantes*, first performed in 1745 at the home of Rameau's patron, Alexandre-Jean-Joseph Le Riche de La Pouplinière, a wealthy tax farmer and patron of the arts. Rousseau claims that his opera was accepted by the Paris Opera, but that he withdrew it. For Rousseau's account of the event, see *Confessions*, VII (*Collected Writings*, V, 280–281). See also the Introduction, p. xvii above.

18. I.e., meteors fall from high to low.

19. Father Louis-Bertrand Castel (1688–1757) was a Jesuit priest, long-time contributor to the *Journal de Trévoux*, and scientist known among other things for his theory of the analogy between music and colors and the "ocular clavichord" he built based on these theories. Castel was an early proponent of Rameau's theory of harmony, but later one of his most dogged critics. Rousseau also knew Castel and ridicules his theory and his ocular clavichord in his *Essay on the Origin of Languages*, chap. XVI, translated herein.

20. Gioseffo Zarlino (1517–1590) was an Italian composer and important musical theorist best known for his exposition and defense of a "modern" system of music. Athanasius Kircher (1601–1680) was a German music theorist whose *Musiciqua universalis* was one of the most influential musical treatises of the time.

21. Rameau, *Nouveau Système* (1726), chap. 8 (Jacobi, II, 53–58).

22. See note 13 above.

23. See note 16 above.

24. The "Trio of the Furies" is the second trio of the Furies in Rameau's lyric-tragedy *Hippolyte et Aricie* (1733). The trio was successfully performed by the private orchestra of Rameau's patron, La Pouplinière, but the singers at the Paris Opera were unable to sing it and it had to be omitted. Rameau recounts the episode and claims that it was elsewhere performed in his *Génération harmonique* (1737), chap. XIV (Jacobi, III, 89 ff.) and his *Démonstration du principe de l'harmonie* (1750), 95–96 (Jacobi, III, 213–214).

25. Rameau, *Démonstration du principe de l'harmonie* (1750), 40 (Jacobi, III, 186). The word translated "close" is "*repos*," which is often used synonymously with "*cadence*," here translated "cadence."

26. See Rameau, *Dissertation sur les méthodes différents d'accompagnemnt* (1732).

27. See Rousseau, ACCOMPANIMENT [*Accompagnement*], p. 202 above.

28. See Rousseau, ACCOMPANIMENT [*Accompagnement*], p. 202 above. Rameau refers to Rousseau's article FIGURING [*Chiffrer*] in the *Encyclopedia*, where he writes (vol. 3, pp. 334–337, quoting pp. 336–337): "In his *Dissertation on the various methods of accompaniment*, M. Rameau has found a great number of defects in the established figures. He has made it seen that they are far too numerous, and nevertheless insufficient, obscure, and equivocal, that they uselessly multiply the number of chords, and that they show no sort of connection.... After having made very good observations on the mechanics of the fingers in the practice of accompaniment, M. Rameau proposes other figures, much simpler, that make this accompaniment totally independent of the thoroughbass, so that, without regard to this bass and even without seeing it, one would accompany with these figures alone with more

precision than can be done by the established method with the aid of the bass and the figures."

29. Rameau is still quoting Rousseau's article FIGURING [*Chiffrer*] in the *Encyclopedia* (see previous note) where he writes of Rameau's method (p. 337): "As simple as this method may be, as favorable as it may seem for practice, it nevertheless does not seem to be totally exempt of inconveniences. For, although it simplifies the signs, and although it diminishes the apparent number of chords, the genuine fundamental harmony is still not at all expressed by it."

30. That is, in Rameau's discussion of Rousseau's article CADENCE [*Cadence*], below.

31. See Rousseau, ACCOMPANIMENT [*Accompagnement*], p. 202 above.

32. See Rousseau, DISSONANCE [*Dissonnance*], p. 216 above.

33. See Rousseau, CHORD [*Accord*], p. 207 above.

34. Psalm 115: 5–6: "They have eyes and do not see, they have ears and do not hear."

35. See Rousseau, CHORD [*Accord*], pp. 206–207 above.

36. For Rameau's theory of notes or chords "by supposition," see Thomas Christensen, *Rameau and the Musical Enlightenment*, pp. 63–66, 99–100.

37. See Rousseau, DISSONANCE [*Dissonnance*], p. 217 above.

38. See Rousseau, CADENCE [*Cadence*], p. 209 above.

39. See Rousseau, CADENCE [*Cadence*], p. 209 above. See Rameau, *Observations on Our Instinct for Music*, p. 184–185n§ above.

40. See Rousseau, CADENCE [*Cadence*], p. 209 above.

41. See Rousseau, CADENCE [*Cadence*], p. 211 above.

42. See Rousseau, ACCOMPANIMENT [*Accompagnement*], p. 201 above. Rameau refers to his *Dissertation sur les différentes méthodes d'accompagnement* (1732), 22–24 (Jacobi, IV, 28–30).

43. See Rousseau, ACCOMPANIMENT [*Accompagnement*], p. 201 above.

44. See Rameau, *Treatise on Harmony*, Supplement (Jacobi, I, 468). Rameau describes the effect of the dissonance as arising from the closeness of the two sounds of the second chord and compares it to the friction resulting from two bodies rubbing together.

45. See Rousseau, *Letter on French Music*, p. 157 above, and Rameau, *Observations on Our Instinct for Music*, p. 197 above.

46. See Rousseau, CHROMATIC [*Chromatique*], p. 214 above.

47. See Rousseau, DISSONANCE [*Dissonnance*], p. 215 above. Rameau's version of the latter passage is quite different from Rousseau's original.

48. Rameau, *Generation Harmonique* (1737), chap. 9 (Jacobi, III, 68–74):

> The necessity of the Dissonance is recognized in the uniformity of the Harmony which produces the three fundamental Notes of the Mode, so that by this uniformity each of them can attain the same empire over the Ear.
>
> In fact, if the first two fundamental Notes which succeed one another did not have anything which distinguished them in their Harmony, the third would always be arbitrary, whereby the principal Note, and consequently the Mode, would never be entirely determined.

49. For d'Alembert's addition to Rousseau's article DISSONANCE [*Dissonnance*], which is signed "O," see p. 218 above.

50. See Rousseau, DISSONANCE [*Dissonnance*], p. 215 above.
51. See Rousseau, CHORD [*Accord*], pp. 204–205 above.
52. Rameau, *Extrait d'une réponse de M. Rameau à M. Euler sur l'identité des octaves* (1753), 5 ff. (Jacobi, V, 170 ff.).
53. See Rousseau, CHORD [*Accord*], pp. 204–205 above.
54. Rameau, *Démonstration du principe de l'harmonie* (1750). The first selection he cites (pp. 19–20 [Jacobi, III, 176]) begins:

> All this established, I enter into the matter, and as I have the honor of speaking to Mathematicians, I will borrow their language as much as my little knowledge shall permit me, so that they may not call anything into doubt.
>
> The sounding body, which I call, with just title, the *fundamental sound*, this unique principle, generator and orderer of all Music, this immediate cause of all its effects, the sounding body, I say, does not resonate while it at the same time engenders all the continual proportions from which arise the harmony, the Melody, the Modes, the Genres, down to the very last rules necessary for practice.

The second passage referred to concerns the generation of the minor mode.
55. See Rousseau, DISSONANCE [*Dissonnance*], p. 216 above.
56. See Rousseau, DISSONANCE [*Dissonnance*], p. 216 above.
57. Rameau, *Treatise on Harmony*, Supplement (Jacobi, I, 465–469), the text of which is a revision of Book II, chap. 7 of the *Treatise* on the irregular cadence; *Nouveau système de musique théoretique* (1726), chaps. 11–14 (Jacobi, II, 65–76).
58. See Rousseau, DISSONANCE [*Dissonnance*], p. 216 above.
59. See Rousseau, DISSONANCE [*Dissonnance*], p. 216 above.
60. "Relationships" can also be translated as "ratios." Rameau's point is that the relationships among sounds can be conceived as mathematical ratios.
61. Rameau, *Démonstration du principe de l'harmonie* (1750) (Jacobi, III, 176–177, 179, 181–182, 211). Rameau, *Nouveau système de musique théoretique* (1726) (Jacobi, II, 34).
62. Rameau appears to refer to his *Démonstration du principe de l'harmonie* (1750) (Jacobi, III, 183, 191).
63. The editors of the *Encyclopedia*, Diderot and d'Alembert, responded to Rameau's criticism in the "Notice" to the next volume of their work to appear (Vol. VI; 1756):

> It appeared to us that our Readers strongly approved of the resolution we took to no longer respond to anything at all that might be written against us. We shall continue to keep our word. But we believe that we should again repeat that in this Dictionary each Author is the guarantor of his articles, that we do mean to answer only for our own, that the Encyclopedia is in this regard precisely in the same position as our Academy's collections. . . . But we also have some right to demand that our just regard for our colleagues not be made a crime for us; well- or ill-founded complaints of which we may be the object should not at all fall on us.
>
> This notice, although already given numerous times, seems to have garnered scant attention on the part of an anonymous person who has just attacked some articles on Music by M. Rousseau.* "I believe," he says, "I should

put the Editors of the Encyclopedia onto the path of the truths which they *are ignorant of, neglect, or dissimulate in order to substitute for them errors, criticisms without solution, EVEN opinions.*" The declaration we have just made should shield us from such a rash accusation. Moreover, the Author should not at all regard this declaration as a tacit or indirect avowal of the justice of his remarks. M. Rousseau, who joins to considerable knowledge and taste in Music the talent of thinking and of expressing himself with clarity, which Musicians do not always have, is too much in a position to defend himself on his own for us to undertake here to uphold his suit. He could, in the Dictionary of Music he is preparing, repulse the darts that have been hurled against him if he judges what we dare not maintain, that the brochure by the anonymous person merits it. As for us, without otherwise taking any part in a dispute which would turn us from our goal, we cannot persuade ourselves that the celebrated artist to whom this production is attributed is in reality the author. Everything prevents us from believing it: the little sensation which the criticism seems to us to have produced among the Public; the imputations, as misplaced as unreasonable, which this artist incapable of charging two men of Letters who have on every occasion rendered him a distinguished justice and whom he has deigned sometimes to consult concerning his own works; immoderate manner in which he treats M. Rousseau in this brochure, who has often named with praise the musician of whom we are speaking† and for whom he has never lacked regard, even in the small number of places where he thought of combatting him; finally, the more than singular opinions which are maintained in this work, and which do not augur in his favor, among others, that Geometry is founded on Music, that one should compare to harmony any science one takes, that an ocular clavichord in which one would be limited to representing the analogy of harmony to colors would merit general approbation, and so the remainder.‡ If these are the truths which we are accused of being ignorant of, of neglecting, or of dissimulating, this is a reproach which we have unfortunately merited for a long time.

Rameau wrote a response to the "Notice": his *Réponse de M. Rameau à MM. Les Editeurs de l'Encyclopédie sur leur dernier Avertissement* (1757). An exchange ensued that included Rameau's *Lettre à M. d'Alembert sur ses opinions en musique insérées dans les articles "Fondamental" et "Gamme" de l'Encyclopédie* (1760).

  * See the Brochure which has for its title, *Errors on Music in the Encyclopedia*.
  † See the words ACCOMPANIMENT [*Accompagnement*], *page 75, col. 2, toward the end*; BASS [*Basse*], *page 119, col. 2*; and especially the end of the word FIGURE [*Chiffrer*].
  ‡ See the brochure cited, page 46, 64, and especially from page 110 to the end.

EDITOR'S NOTES TO
Continuation of the Errors on Music in the Encyclopedia

This translation is based on the text of the original edition as photostatically reproduced in Jacobi, V, 313–330. Like the *Errors on Music in the Encyclopedia*, Rameau's continuation of his criticism of Rousseau's articles first appeared anonymously in 1756. As with the earlier work, Rameau never acknowledged authorship of his *Continuation of the Errors on Music in the Encyclopedia*, even though it was widely known.

1. See Rameau, *Errors on Music in the Encyclopedia*, p. 231 above.
2. Gioseffo Zarlino (1517–1590) was an Italian composer and important musical theorist best known for his exposition and defense of a "modern" system of music.
3. See Rameau, *Observations on Our Instinct for Music*, p. 180 above.
4. Rameau, *Nouveau système de musique théoretique* (1726) (Jacobi, II, 34); *Génération harmonique* (1737) (Jacobi III, 67–68); *Démonstration du principe de l'harmonie* (1750) (Jacobi, III, 247).
5. See Rameau, *Errors on Music in the Encyclopedia*, p. 234 above.
6. See Rousseau, ACCOMPANIMENT [*Accompagnement*], p. 201 above. Rameau cites the passage he has in mind in its entirety in the next paragraph.
7. Zarlino, *Le istitutioni harmoniche* (1558), Part IV, chap. 5. Ptolemy, *Harmonica*, III.7 (Barker, II, 378–379).
8. See Rousseau, CHROMATIC [*Chromatique*], p. 214 above.
9. See Rousseau, DISSONANCE [*Dissonance*], p. 217 above.
10. See Rameau, *Errors on Music in the Encyclopedia*, p. 242 above.
11. See Rousseau, ACCOMPANIMENT [*Accompagnement*], p. 201 above.
12. See Rousseau, CADENCE [*Cadence*], p. 212 above.
13. See Rousseau, CADENCE [*Cadence*], p. 212 above.
14. See Rameau, *Errors on Music in the Encyclopedia*, p. 242 above.
15. See Rousseau, ENHARMONIC [*Enharmonique*], p. 219 above.
16. Rameau, *Génération harmonique* (1737), chap. 14, article II, p. 149 (Jacobi, III, 89). The four modes of which Rameau speaks in this chapter are the Diatonic, Chromatic, Enharmonic, and Enharmonic Diatonic.
17. See Rameau, *Errors on Music in the Encyclopedia*, p. 234 above.
18. Zarlino, *Le istitutioni harmoniche* (1558), Part II, chap. 16.
19. See Rameau, *Errors on Music in the Encyclopedia*, p. 250 above.
20. In his *Réponse de M. Rameau à MM. les Editeurs de l'Encyclopédie sur leur dernier Avertissement* (1757) (Jacobi, V, 346–347), Rameau identifies d'Alembert as the one who learned musical theory from him. Rameau claimed that he offered to review the articles on music for the *Encyclopedia*, which were written principally by Rousseau.

EDITOR'S NOTES TO
On the Principle of Melody

This translation is based on the text found in Pléiade, V, 329–343. The Pléiade text is based on Rousseau's manuscript (Neuchâtel MS R 60, ff 8–17r). The Pléiade edition is edited by Marie-Elisabeth Duchez and is based on her earlier edition of the writing published as "*Principe de la Mélodie* et *Origine des Langues*: Un brouillon inédit de Jean-Jacques Rousseau sur l'origine de la mélodie," *Revue de Musicologie* 60 (1974), 33–86. Duchez's edition appeared at the same time as a slightly different one published by Robert Wokler: "Rameau, Rousseau, and the *Essai sur l'origine des langues*," *Studies on Voltaire and the Eighteenth Century* 117 (1974), 179–238. Wokler's edition has also been consulted for the present translation. For details on the manuscript, see the discussion in Duchez's and Wokler's articles.

Only the portion of Rousseau's manuscript included in the Pléiade edition is translated here. The manuscript as a whole is entitled *On the Principle of Melody, or Response to the "Errors on Music"* and is a first draft of what would later become his *Examination of Two Principles Advanced by M. Rameau*. The manuscript contains: first, a fairly complete and final version (excluding the Notice) of the beginning of the *Examination*, then a discussion of the origin of melody (translated here), and then a much sketchier version of the remainder of what would become the *Examination*. The portion of the manuscript presented in the Pléiade edition and translated here is given the title "The Origin of Melody" by the editor. Italicized words or phrases contained in the Pléiade edition and indicating Rousseau's interlinear and marginal additions to his manuscript have been omitted in the present translation. The bracketed portions, indicating passages crossed out by Rousseau and incorporated by him into his *Examination*, have been retained in the present edition. The text of "The Origin of Melody" is only barely punctuated, so some punctuation has been added to the translation for purposes of clarity.

1. Rousseau refers to Rameau's *Errors on Music in the Encyclopedia*, translated above.

2. Compare Rousseau, *Second Discourse* (*Collected Writings*, III, 31): "Man's first language, the most universal, most energetic, and only language he needed before it was necessary to persuade assembled men, is the cry of Nature."

3. Lucretius, *De rerum natura*, V, 1028 ff. Diodorus Siculus as cited by Athanasius Kircher, *Prodromus Coptus sive Aegyptiacus* (1636), 131, 139; Rousseau also cites this story in the article MUSIC [*Musique*] in his *Dictionary of Music*, translated below.

4. See Rameau, *Démonstration du principe de l'harmonie* (1750), 12–13 (Jacobi, III, 172–173): "every cause that produces on my ear a single and simple impression makes me hear *noise*; every cause that produces on my ear an impression composed of several others makes me hear *sound*"; *Génération harmonique* (1737), chap. 1, p. 28 (Jacobi, III, 28): "Let us henceforth recognize, then, Harmony as a natural effect which results from the resonance of every sounding Body in particular; it is from there that it derives its origin: the appreciable sound is not unique in its nature, it is Harmonious. . . ."

5. See Rousseau, *Essay on the Origin of Languages*, chap. V, translated below.

6. The same Greek word, "*nomos*," can be used for both "law" and "song," as Rousseau notes in the article CHANSON [*Chanson*] in his *Dictionary of Music* (Pléiade, V, 690): "The use of *Chansons* seems to be a natural continuation of that of speech, and it is actually no less general, for everywhere there is speaking, there is singing. To imagine them, they had only to engage their organs, give an agreeable turn to the ideas to which they wanted to attend, and fortify by the expression of which the Voice is capable the feeling they wished to render of the image they wished to portray. Also, the ancients did not yet possess the art of writing when they already had *Chansons*. Their laws and their stories, the praises of gods and of

heroes were sung before being written. And from this it happens, according to Aristotle, that the same Greek noun was given to laws and to *Chansons*." See Aristotle, *Problems*, XIX.28.919b37–920a2; Plato, *Laws*, III.700b. See also Rousseau, *Essay on the Origin of Languages*, chap. XII, translated below.

7. Paragraphs in brackets were crossed out by Rousseau in the original manuscript. These paragraphs were used by him in his *Examination of Two Principles Advanced by M. Rameau*, although not all of them made it into the final version of that work. See *Examination of Two Principles*, p. 275 below. This paragraph also became, with slight alterations, the third paragraph of chap. XVIII of the *Essay on the Origin of Languages*, translated below.

8. The portion of the paragraph in brackets became with slight alterations the last paragraph of chap. XVIII of the *Essay on the Origin of Languages*, translated below.

9. Aristoxenus distinguished between melody and rhythm in his *Elementa Harmonica* I.1, II.1 (Barker, II, 126, 148), as did Aristides Quintilianus, *De musica*, I.13 (Barker, II, 434–435). For Aristotle, see *Poetics*, IV, 1449b28.

10. See Rameau, *Errors on Music in the Encyclopedia*, p. 228 above. This and the next two paragraphs in brackets became with slight alterations two paragraphs of his *Examination of Two Principles*, pp. 277–278 below.

11. This paragraph became with slight alterations the first paragraph of chap. XIX of the *Essay on the Origin of Languages*, translated below.

12. This paragraph became with slight alterations part of the second paragraph of chap. XIX of the *Essay on the Origin of Languages*, translated below.

13. See Rousseau, *First Discourse* (*Collected Writings*, II, 7–8).

14. See Plato, *Republic*, X.599c–e; Diogenes Laertius, *Lives of the Philosophers*, "Plato."

15. This paragraph became with slight alterations the third paragraph of chap. XIX of the *Essay on the Origin of Languages*, translated below.

16. This paragraph became with slight alterations the fourth paragraph of chap. XIX of the *Essay on the Origin of Languages*, translated below.

17. Flavius Claudius Julianus ("Julian the Apostate"), *Misopogon*, 337c. Julian actually compares the Gaul's speech to the cawing of hoarse birds.

18. This paragraph became with slight alterations the fifth paragraph of chap. XIX of the *Essay on the Origin of Languages*, translated below.

19. This paragraph became with slight alterations the sixth paragraph of chap. XIX of the *Essay on the Origin of Languages*, translated below.

20. This paragraph became with slight alterations the seventh paragraph of chap. XIX of the *Essay on the Origin of Languages*, translated below.

21. Jehan des Murs (c. 1300–c. 1350) was a widely influential musical theorist of the later Middle Ages best known for his treatment of musical proportions and mensural notation. The major work attributed to him, the *Speculum musicae*, was actually written by Jacques de Liège (c. 1260-c. 1330). Bontempi, or Giovanni-Andrea Angelini-Bontempi (c. 1630–c.1704), published his *Istoria musica* in 1695. Rousseau read the work attentively while living at Charmettes, and credits it with sparking his interest in musical theory (see *Confessions*, VII; *Collected Writings*, V, 206).

22. This paragraph became with slight alterations the eighth paragraph of chap. XIX of the *Essay on the Origin of Languages*, translated below.

23. This paragraph became with slight alterations the ninth, and final, paragraph of chap. XIX of the *Essay on the Origin of Languages*, translated below.

24. For Ulysses and Ajax, see Homer, *Iliad*, XXIII.740–797; for Priam, see ibid., XXIV.470–676; for Hector, see ibid., VI.369–502, and see also Rousseau, *Emile*, Book I (Pléiade, IV, 283; Bloom, 63). Rousseau develops the analogy between music and painting at greater length in chap. XIII of the *Essay on the Origin of Languages*, translated below.

25. In a manuscript, cited by Duchez (Neuchâtel MS R 72, frag. 46 v°; Pléiade, V, ed. n. 3 to p. 342), Rousseau writes of the "pathetic accent": "it is, so to speak, only the amplification of the cry of nature modified in every language by the inflections which are proper to it." See also note 2 above.

26. Rousseau defines "Piano-Forte" or "Forte-Piano" in his *Dictionary of Music* (Pléiade, V, 830): "A complex Italian noun and one which musicians should frenchify, as painters have frenchified that of *chiaro-scuro*. *Forte-Piano* is the art of softening and strengthening sounds in the imitative melody as is done in the speech which one should imitate. When one speaks with warmth one does not always express oneself with the same degree of force. Music, by imitating the variety of accents and of tones, should therefore imitate also the intense and remiss degrees of speech, and should speak sometimes softly, sometimes loudly, sometimes in a whisper." See note 15 in the following chapter for a definition of "remiss."

EDITOR'S NOTES TO
Examination of Two Principles Advanced by M. Rameau

This translation is based on the text found in Pléiade, V, 345–370. The Pléiade edition is based on the fine copy (Neuchâtel MS R 59), which was the basis of the first edition of the work as published by du Peyrou and Moultou in their 1781 *Collection complète des oeuvres de Jean-Jacques Rousseau* (*Oeuvres posthumes de Rousseau*, vol. 3: *Treatises on Music*). The editors of the Pléiade edition also provide variants from Rousseau's original draft of the work, entitled the *On the Principle of Melody, or Response to the "Errors on music"* (MS R 60). Major variants have been provided here in the editorial notes.

1. Rousseau refers to his defenses of his *Discourse on the Sciences and the Arts* (*First Discourse*), and to his declaration in the *Final Reply* that he would no longer respond to his critics (see *Collected Writings*, II, 129).

2. Rousseau's notice indicates that he prepared the final form of the *Examination of Two Principles* to serve as a preface to his *Dictionary of Music*, which was published in 1768.

3. See Rameau, *Errors on Music in the Encyclopedia*, p. 239 above.

4. Rousseau was asked by Diderot to write the articles on music for the *Encyclopedia* in June 1748 and completed them in three months. See *Confessions*, VII (*Collected Writings*, V, 292).

5. Rousseau refers to Rameau's hostility to him after the production of his *Muses*

galantes, which Rameau accused him of having plagiarized. See *Confessions*, VII (*Collected Writings*, V, 280–281). See also Rameau's version of the story in his *Errors on Music in the Encyclopedia*, p. 230 above, and the Introduction to this volume.

6. See Rameau, *Errors on Music in the Encyclopedia*, p. 228 above.

7. In the first draft of the *Examination*, entitled *The Principle of Melody*, this paragraph concludes: "relative to what is more esteemed than the song itself. Such a song indeed has the type of beauty that art gives it, but without having that from nature, it is not at all a genuine melody, it is always without warmth and without expression, and the cold approbation it arouses comes only from the habit of hearing basically similar ones."

8. The editor has not been able to identify this quotation from Rameau.

9. Rameau alludes to the experiment in his *Observations on Our Instinct for Music*, p. 178 above, and relates it in his *Démonstration du principe de l'harmonie* (1750), 11–12 (Jacobi, III, 172): "I then placed myself as well as I could into the state of a man who had neither sung nor heard singing, promising myself even to resort to extraneous experiments whenever I suspected that habit . . . might influence me despite myself. . . . My search was not long. The first sound which struck my ear was like a flash of light. I perceived right away that it was not one [sound], rather the impression it made upon me was composite. . . ." (trans. Thomas Christensen, *Rameau and the Musical Enlightenment* [Cambridge: Cambridge University Press, 1993], 217–218). See also Rameau's "Reflexions sur la manière de former la voix," *Mercure de France* (October 1752, p. 91; Jacobi, VI, 299): "What made me note for the first time that harmony was natural to us, was a man of more than seventy years old, who, in the Parterre of the Lyon Opera, set to singing very loudly and strongly, the fundamental bass of a song whose words had struck him."

10. Guinguettes were popular dance halls.

11. D'Alembert, *Preliminary Discourse* to the *Encyclopedia*: "After having created an art of learning music, one ought also create an art of listening to it" (trans. Richard N. Schwab [Indianapolis: Bobbs-Merrill, 1963], 39). D'Alembert discusses the origin of music from its possible origin as the imitation of noise to its role in the expression of the passions, and concludes that any music that does not portray anything is merely noise.

12. It is at this point in the first draft of the *Examination*, entitled *On the Principle of Melody*, that Rousseau turns to a discussion of the origin of melody, translated above. The first draft also contains the following paragraph: "It therefore seems that Melody or song, a pure work of nature, does not owe, either among the learned or among the ignorant, its origin to harmony, a work and production of art, which serves as proof and not as source for beautiful song and whose most noble function is that of setting it off to advantage."

Rousseau gives a similar explanation in reply to LeRoy's objections to his *Second Discourse*: "The reasons one opposed to me are always drawn from places like Paris, London, or some other little corner of the world. I try to draw mine only from the world itself" (*Collected Writings*, III, 133).

13. See Rameau, *Errors on Music in the Encyclopedia*, p. 231 above.

14. See Rameau, *Errors on Music in the Encyclopedia*, p. 229 above.

15. Rousseau defines "slack" [*remiss*] sounds in the article REMISSE in his *Dictio-*

nary of Music (Pléiade, V, 1016–1017): "*Slack* sounds are those which have little force, those which being very high can be produced only by extremely slack cords nor heard except quite closely. *Slack* is opposed to intense...."

16. In the first draft of the *Examination*, entitled *The Principle of Melody*, Rousseau continues: "It seems that as speech is the art of transmitting ideas, melody would be that of transmitting feelings, and nevertheless M. Rameau wants to strip it of all that serves it as a language and that cannot be given to the harmony."

17. See Rameau, *Errors on Music in the Encyclopedia*, p. 232 above.

18. Compare Diderot's more materialist account in his *Letter on the Deaf and Dumb* (1751): "In music, the pleasure of sensation depends upon a particular disposition not only of the ear, but of the whole system of nerves."

19. See Rameau, *Errors on Music in the Encyclopedia*, p. 235 above.

20. In the first draft of the *Examination*, entitled *The Principle of Melody*, Rousseau adds the following paragraph: "Consult all the nations in the world, all men not forewarned by habit, all those in whom interest or amour-propre will not at all cause them to speak, you will have a unanimous opinion and this opinion will be the voice of nature. I admit that I am strangely surprised to see this word fall from M. Rameau's pen. It seems to me that he should likewise prevent his readers and his Listeners from thinking of it."

21. Rousseau alludes to Tartini's *Trattato di musica* (1754), on which he took extensive notes while working on his reply to Rameau and while reworking his articles in the *Encyclopedia* for his *Dictionary of Music*.

22. Jean-Adam Serre (1704–1788), Genevan physicist, chemist, painter, and musical theorist who published criticisms of Rameau's theory of harmony, including his *Essais sur les principes de l'harmonie* (1753), to which Rousseau refers.

23. See Rameau, *Errors on Music in the Encyclopedia*, p. 224 above.

24. See Rameau, *Nouveau système de musique théoretique* (1726), chap. 23 (Jacobi, III, 104–116). Arcangelo Corelli (1653–1713) was an Italian violinist and influential composer.

25. Joseph Sauveur (1653–1716) was a theorist of acoustics (a term he coined) and inventor of a system of musical notation who tried to extend the idea of frequency to standardize an absolute pitch. Sauveur demonstrated at the Academy of Sciences how the vibration of one string could make vibrate the parts of another string divided into portions in a certain ratio to the first string (the points of division being called "knots").

26. D'Alembert lists music as the lowest of the arts in his "Preliminary Discourse" to the *Encyclopedia*. For Rameau's "proceedings" with regard to Rousseau, see note 5 above.

27. Rousseau refers to Rameau's accusation of plagiarism regarding his *Les Muses galantes*. See note 17 to Rameau's *Errors on Music in the Encyclopedia*, translated above.

28. Rousseau reworked this passage for the article SONG [*Chant*] in the *Dictionary of Music*, translated below.

29. Rousseau includes this sentence in the article COMPOSER [*Compositeur*] in his *Dictionary of Music*, translated below.

30. See Rameau, *Errors on Music in the Encyclopedia*, p. 244 above. As the editor

responsible for the articles on music in the *Encyclopedia*, d'Alembert added remarks in his own name to Rousseau's articles.

EDITOR'S NOTES TO
Essay on the Origin of Languages

This translation is based on the text found in Pléiade, V, 371–429. The Pléiade edition is based on the original manuscript found in the Bibliothèque publique et universitaire de la ville de Neuchâtel, Neuchâtel, Switzerland (MS R no. 11). The original manuscript was also consulted for the present translation and was provided thanks to M. René Marti of the Bibliothèque de Neuchâtel.

1. In the manuscript, Rousseau originally added "Citizen of Geneva," but crossed it out in the final copy. Rousseau was born in Geneva, but lost his citizenship when he converted to Catholicism after running away from Geneva at the age of sixteen, in 1728. His citizenship was officially restored in 1754 (see *Confessions*, VIII; *Collected Writings*, V, 329). In his *Nouvelle Héloïse*, which does not bear the designation "Citizen of Geneva," Rousseau explains that he only added "Citizen of Geneva" to the title pages of those works he believed would do honor to his native city (Seconde Préface; Pléiade, II, 27). Rousseau's reasons for removing "Citizen of Geneva" from the title page of the *Essay* are unclear.

2. Rousseau planned on publishing the *Essay* as the second text in a volume composed of *On Theatrical Imitation* and the *Levite of Ephraïm*, both translated below. This draft for a preface appears to have been written about June 1763 in the circumstances related by Rousseau there.

3. Despite Rousseau's statement about the connection of the *Essay* with the *Second Discourse*, the relationship between the two works is a matter of some dispute. See the Introduction to this volume.

4. Rousseau refers to Rameau's *Errors on Music in the Encyclopedia*, published anonymously in 1755, and translated above. The first draft of Rousseau's reply was entitled by him *On the Principle of Melody, or Response to the "Errors on Music."* A revised version of this response became the *Examination of Two Principles Advanced by M. Rameau*, translated above, and part of the response omitted from the final version, translated above as *On the Principle of Melody*, were later incorporated by Rousseau into the *Essay on the Origin of Languages*. For these passages, see the editorial notes to the *Principle of Melody*.

5. The magistrate was Chrétien-Guillaume de Lamoignon de Malesherbes (1721–1794), then head of censorship in France. Rousseau showed the *Essay* to Malesherbes in late 1761, and he counseled Rousseau to edit it as a separate work, explaining: "I believe that you would do great harm to the public by depriving them of it or by waiting for the collected edition of your works to present it" (Leigh, IX, 131, 205, 251). In his *Confessions*, Rousseau mentions that he had Malesherbes read the *Essay* and had subsequently put it into the hands of Du Peyrou, the editor of his collected works (XI; *Collected Writings*, V, 469).

6. In the draft manuscript of the *Essay* the chapter divisions are in the margin, and appear to have been added to the text by Rousseau at a later date than the ini-

tial composition of the work. The Pléiade edition uses ordinal numbers for the chapters, for example "First Chapter," but this translation follows the manuscript, which uses cardinal numbers, for example "Chapter I."

7. On the word *moeurs*, translated here as "morals," see *Collected Writings*, II, 203–204 n7.

8. "Similar" translates "*semblable*," which is elsewhere translated "fellow" or "fellowmen." Rousseau describes a man's initial recognition of a similarity between himself and his fellows in the *Second Discourse*: "Although his fellows were not for him what they are for us, and although he scarcely had more intercourse with them than with other animals, they were not forgotten in his observations. The conformities that time could make him perceive among them, his female, and himself led him to judge of those which he did not perceive" (*Collected Writings*, III, 44).

9. Rousseau alludes to the legend of Dibutade's daughter as related by Pliny the Elder, *Natural Histories*, XXXV.xliii.1: "enamored of a young man who was leaving for a faraway country, she enclosed in lines the shadow of his face as projected on a wall by the light of a lamp."

10. Rousseau incorporated this paragraph and the following one with some changes into his *Emile*, IV (Pléiade, IV, 647; Bloom, 322).

11. For Thrasybulus, see Herodotus, *Histories*, V.92. In Aristotle's version, it is Periander who advises Thrasybulus in this manner (*Politics*, III.13.1284a26–33 and V.10.1311a20–22). For the same story about Tarquin, see Livy, *History of Rome*, I.54. For Alexander, see Plutarch, *Life of Alexander*, 39. For Diogenes, see Diogenes Laertius, *Lives of the Eminent Philosophers*, "Diogenes," VI.39. For Darius, see Herodotus, *Histories*, IV.131–133. These examples are all cited by William Warburton, Bishop of Gloucester (1698–1779), in his *Divine Legation of Moses* (1737–1741), translated in French as *Essai sur les hiéroglyphes des Egyptiens* (1744). Rousseau refers to Warburton's work in his *Social Contract* (II, 7 and IV, 8).

12. See *Judges* 19–21. Rousseau wrote a prose poem based on this poem, the *Levite of Ephraïm*, which he intended to publish together with the *Essay* and his *On Theatrical Imitation*, both of which are translated below. See note 2 above.

13. See 1 *Samuel* 11: 5–10.

14. See Athenaeus, *Deipnosophists*, XIII.590e. Phryne opened her robes and corrupted her judges with her dazzling beauty.

15. Horace, *On the Art of Poetry*, V.180–182: "What enters only by the ear makes less impression on the heart than what is put before the eyes, and about which the spectator assures himself by those faithful witnesses."

16. In his *Letter to d'Alembert on the Theatre*:

> I hear it said that tragedy leads to pity through fear. So it does; but what is this pity? A fleeting and vain emotion which lasts no longer than the illusion which produced it; a vestige of natural sentiment soon stifled by the passions; a sterile pity which feeds on a few tears and which has never produced the slightest act of humanity. Thus, the sanguinary Sulla cried at the account of evils he had not himself committed. Thus the tyrant of Phera hid himself at the theatre for fear of being seen groaning with Andromache and Priam, while he heard without emotion the cries of so many unfortunate victims slain daily by his orders. Tacitus reports that Valerius Asiaticus, calumniously accused by

the order to Messalina, who wanted him to perish, defended himself before the emperor in a way that touched this prince very deeply and drew tears from Messalina herself. She went into the next room in order to regain her composure after having, in the midst of her tears, whispered a warning to Vitellius not to let the accused escape. I never see one of these weeping ladies in the boxes at the theatre, so proud of their tears, without thinking of the tears of Messalina for the poor Valerius Asiasticus. (Pléiade, V, 23, and var. a; ed. and trans. Allan Bloom in *Politics and the Arts* [Ithaca: Cornell University Press, 1968], 24–25).
See also *Second Discourse* (*Collected Writings*, III, 36).

17. Giacobbo Rodrigo Pereira or Pereire (1715–1780) presented his method for teaching the deaf to the Academy of Sciences in Paris in 1749.

18. Jean Chardin, *Voyages en Perse*, 4 vols. (Amsterdam, 1735), III, 122.

19. In his *Second Discourse*, Rousseau locates the distinctive difference between man and the animals in "the faculty of self-perfection" or "perfectibility," and relates that faculty to speech (*Collected Writings*, III, 27, and 83 n*8).

20. See esp. Julien Offray de la Mettrie, *Man: A Machine* (1748), ed. A. Vartanian (Princeton: Princeton University Press, 1960), chap. 2, esp. 160–161. More generally, Rousseau refers to a debate concerning speech and the difference between man and the other animals that was begun in the seventeenth century by Descartes (see *Discourse on the Method*, 5, end), and that included La Mettrie, Buffon, Condillac, and others.

21. Rousseau distinguishes needs from passions in the *Second Discourse* (*Collected Writings*, III, 27). "Voices" translates "*voix*" here and throughout this translation, except on two occasions indicated in the notes. Rousseau's use of the word has several different but related meanings. In general, "voice" refers to any uttered sound, but Rousseau means by "voice" especially the spontaneous accented and melodic utterance of the passions, and especially the moral passions. The opposition he draws between "voice" as the spontaneous utterance of the passions and "articulation" as the conventional sounds that require practice in order to be articulated leads him in chap. V to use the term "*voix*" to mean "vowel" as opposed to (articulated) consonants. See also *Emile*: "Man has three kinds of voice—the speaking or articulate voice, the singing or melodic voice, and the passionate or accentuated voice, which serves as language to the passions and which animates song and word" (II; Pléiade, IV, 404; Bloom, 148).

22. In this sentence "language" translates "*langage*," while "languages" translates "*langues*." The two words are related in origin and meaning, and there are no sufficiently distinct yet related equivalents for them in English. "*Langue*" is closer to the root sense of "tongue," and refers foremost to a language spoken among a people or a linguistic community, while "*langage*" is derivative and has a more specialized connotation of language as a linguistic system; in turn, "*parole*," which is translated as "speech" in the title to this chapter, refers to the act of using a language ("*langue*").

By objecting to the comparison between primitive languages and geometry Rousseau is probably alluding to Maupertuis' *Réflexions philosophiques sur l'origine des langues et la signification des mots* (1748), as well as Condillac's *Essai sur l'origine des connaissances humaines*, II, i, 15, §153, where Condillac also opposes poets to geometers with regard to language. More generally, he is objecting to the notion that philosophic language could be reduced to geometric form, and to the related tradition of "original" or "Adamic" language. This theory holds that the initial word for an object, as spoken by Adam, directly exhibits the object's nature and truth, and was held in various forms by Leibniz and others in the Berlin Academy, including Maupertuis, and in England by Thomas Sprat and others in a tradition opposed by Locke. For a discussion of the theories of language origin held by the Lockean tradition in comparison with the rival tradition of Adamic language, see Hans Aarsleff, *From Locke to Saussure: Essays on the Study of Language and Intellectual History* (Minneapolis: University of Minnesota Press, 1982).

23. See Rousseau, *Confessions*, I (*Collected Writings*, V, 7): "I felt before thinking; this is the common fate of humanity."

24. For example, by Diderot in the article "*Encyclopédie*" in the *Encyclopedia*, and by Condillac in his *Essai sur l'origine des connaissances humaines*, II, i, 1, §1 and 10, §103.

25. See Rousseau, *Second Discourse* (*Collected Writings*, III, 41, 75–76).

26. See chap. X below.

27. Rousseau draws on Bernard Lamy's discussion of tropes and figurative language in his *La Rhétorique, ou l'Art de parler* (4th ed.; 1701), II, 3: "Tropes are names that are transferred from the thing of which they are the proper name, to apply them to things which they signify only indirectly: thus, all tropes are metaphors, for the word, which is Greek, means translation." Lamy discusses how the passions may enlarge a perceived object, as in the example of supposed giants used by Rousseau just below.

28. There are stories of giants in Scripture (e.g., Genesis 6:4) and numerous classical writings. See Rousseau's discussion of such legends in his *Second Discourse*, note *8 (*Collected Writings*, III, 80).

29. Lamy, *La Rhétorique, ou l'Art de parler* (4th ed.; 1701), Preface and III, 1. In his *Second Discourse*, Rousseau exclaims that he is "convinced of the almost demonstrated impossibility that languages could have arisen and been established by purely human means" (*Collected Writings*, III, 33). However, just as he shows in the *Second Discourse* how agriculture and metallurgy might have arisen despite a similar quandary, so too in the present work he explains the origin of languages in purely natural terms, especially in chap. IX below.

30. The distinction between "persuasion" and "conviction" explained here is central to Rousseau's discussion of the Legislator in his *Social Contract* (II, 7): "Since the legislator is therefore unable to use either force or reasoning" to establish a people," he must necessarily have recourse to another order of authority, which can win over without violence and persuade without convincing." Rousseau returns to the persuasive character of the languages used by political and religious founders in chap. XI of the *Essay*. Rousseau revalues the characteristic difference between "persuasion" and "conviction" held by many of his predecessors, for example Diderot, who writes in his *Letter on the Deaf and Dumb* (1751): "The French language is made to teach, to enlighten, and to convince; Greek, Latin, Italian, and English, to persuade, to move, and to deceive. Speak Greek, Latin, and Italian to

the masses; but to the wise, speak French" (*Selected Writings*, ed. Lester G. Crocker, trans. Derek Collman [New York: Macmillan, 1966], 35–36).

31. In Plato's *Cratylus* Socrates claims that the meaning of names can be derived from the etymological origins in such a way that words are imitations of the realities named.

32. See Chardin, *Voyages en Perse*, 4 vols. (Amsterdam, 1735), III, 143.

33. The title, "*De l'Écriture*," could also mean "On Scripture." Rousseau's discussion of the relationship between written and spoken language in this chapter and the following ones includes an implicit critique of claims of scriptural religions. See the second part of the "Profession of Faith of the Savoyard Vicar" in Book IV of the *Emile* for a further consideration of the issue (Pléiade, IV, 609–635; Bloom, 296–313).

34. The "double convention" of which Rousseau speaks is also discussed by Diderot in the article "*Encyclopédie*" for the *Encyclopedia*, and is derived from the double conformity thesis put forward most importantly by Locke (*An Essay Concerning Human Understanding*, esp. II, 32, §8; III, 2, §1, 4). Locke's thesis is opposed to the univocal thesis championed by the adherents of "original" or "Adamic" language, in which the word is presumed to be a univocal representation of the object.

35. Rousseau mentions the same classification into savage, barbarous, and civilized peoples in his *Second Discourse* (*Collected Writings*, III, 49–50), and employs it in the *Social Contract* (III, 8). The classification is derived from Montesquieu, *On the Spirit of the Laws*, XVIII, 11–17; see also I, 3, and XXI, 1–4.

36. Tchelminar, or Chihil–Minar, is the ancient name of Persepolis, near the modern city of Shiraz in southern Iran. An "ectype" is a wax impression or other sort of tracing of an original object such as a coin, medal, or inscription. For example, building on his theory of the mind as a tabula rasa or wax tablet, Locke writes: "The complex Ideas of Substances are Ectypes, Copies too; but not perfect ones, not adequate" (*An Essay Concerning Human Understanding*, II, 31, §13).

37. Chardin, *Voyages en Perse*, 4 vols. (Amsterdam, 1735), II, 167–168.

38. Ibid. Rousseau's abridgments of the passage are indicated by the ellipses in brackets. The discovery of the famous Rosetta stone, in 1799, allowed this writing to be deciphered.

39. For the story that Cadmus introduced the alphabet to the Greeks, which was widely discussed in Rousseau's time, see Herodotus, *Histories*, V.58, and Pliny the Elder, *Natural Histories*, VII.192.

40. "Commerce" translates "*commerce*," which can mean both social intercourse and trading and has been translated as "intercourse" elsewhere in the *Collected Writings*. See *Second Discourse*: "It is easy to understand that such intercourse [*commerce*] did not require a language much more refined than that of Crows or Monkeys, who group together in approximately the same way"; and: "they continued to enjoy among themselves the sweetness of independent intercourse [*commerce*]" (*Collected Writings*, III, 45, 49).

41. Pausanias, *Arcadia*, V.xvii.6. The proposed etymology of "*versus*" is not found in Marius' *Ars grammatica*, but it is found in Isidore of Seville, *Origins*, VI.xiv.7. Rousseau proposed to reintroduce this manner of writing in music; see his *Letter to Burney*, pp. 486–489 below.

42. The number of letters in the Greek alphabet is discussed in Pliny the Elder, *Natural Histories*, VII.56; Tacitus, *Annals*, XI.14; Marius Victorinus, *Ars grammatica*, IV.95–97; Isidore of Seville, *Origins*, I.3–4.

43. The lustra were the five-year periods separating the purification of the Roman people after each census. See Livy, *History of Rome*, I.44.

44. "Vowels" translates "*voix*," which has otherwise been translated as "voices." Rousseau elsewhere uses "*voyelles*" to mean "vowels." See note 21 above.

45. The "Gentlemen of Port Royal" refers to Antoine Arnauld and Nicholas Lancelot, who wrote the *Grammaire générale et raisonnéee*, commonly known as the *Port-Royal Grammar*. See Pt. 1, chap. 1.

46. Charles Pinot Duclos, Rousseau's friend, wrote a commentary on the *Port-Royal Grammar* (see previous note), the *Remarques sur la Grammaire générale et raisonnée* (1754), I, 1.

47. "The vowels were of the number seven in Greek, Romulus counted six, but later usage mentioned only five, once they came to reject Υ as Greek," Martianus Capella (fl. fifth century A.D.), *De Nuptiis Mercurii et Philologiae*, Bk. III.

48. "Words" translates "*voix*," which has otherwise been translated as "voices" (see note 21 above), whereas "word" generally translates "*mot*."

49. That is, the question "*venez-vous*," "are you coming?" is readily distinguished from the statement "*vous venez*," "you are coming."

50. The manuscript of this chapter from this point on was substantially reworked by Rousseau, who altered and expanded the text in numerous places to an extent unusual for the manuscript of the work in general. Following the Pléiade edition, this translation follows the fair copy of the manuscript, apparently by Du Peyrou's secretary, Jeannin, which is added at the end of the folio containing the manuscript of the work.

51. The Story of Bellerophon is found in Homer, *Iliad*, VI.167–170: "He [Proitos] shrank from killing him [Bellerophon], since his heart was awed by such action, / but sent him away to Lykia, and handed him murderous symbols [*sêmata*], / which he inscribed in a folding tablet, enough to destroy life, / and told him to show it to his wife's father, that he might perish" (trans. Richard Lattimore [Chicago: University of Chicago Press, 1951]). The authenticity of this story was a common point of discussion in Rousseau's time. Homer's works were said to have been compiled by the Athenian tyrant Peisistratos in the second half of the sixth century B.C. Father Jean Hardouin (1646–1729) denied the authenticity of most of the works of antiquity and claimed that they were written in the middle ages, and also maintained that the New Testament had originally been written in Latin. Considering the critique of Scripture undertaken by Hobbes, Spinoza, and others, including the question of the authorship and date of the various books of the Bible, Rousseau's discussion in this chapter of Homer would apply equally well to the Bible.

52. Rousseau greatly admired the poetry of Torquato Tasso (1544–1595), and translated part of his *Jeruselum Delivered* into French. For his description of the singing of the gondoliers in Venice, see *Confessions*, VII (*Collected Writings*, V, 263–264).

53. See Plato, *Laws*, II.669e–670a, on poetry separated from song and as a written work.

54. The original title of the chapter, "On Modern French Prosody," shows the connection of the present work with Rousseau's *Letter on French Music* (1753), translated above.

55. See note 48 above.

56. "Accent" and "accent marks," i.e. written accents, both translate "*accent*." As Rousseau notes in the entry ACCENT [*Accent*] in his *Dictionary of Music*, translated below, the term "prosody" translates the Greek word for accent, and involves the study of the rhythm and accent of a language.

57. Rousseau refers above all to the article "*Accent*" by Du Marsais in the *Encyclopedia* (1751).

58. Cicero, *De oratore*, III.xliv.173–174:

> After attention to this matter comes also the consideration of the rhythm and shape of the words, a point which I am afraid Catullus here may consider childish; for the old Greek masters held the view that in this prose style it is proper for us to use something almost amounting to versification, that is, certain definite rhythms. For they thought that in speeches the close of the period ought to come not when we are tired out but where we may take breath, and to be marked not by the punctuation of the copying clerks but by the arrangement of the words and of the thought; and it is said that Isocrates first introduced the practice of tightening up the irregular style of oratory which belonged to the early days, so his pupil Naucrates writes, by means of an element of rhythm, designed to give pleasure to the ear. For two contrivances to give pleasure were devised by the musicians, who in the old days were also the poets, verse and melody, with the intention of overcoming satiety in the hearer by delighting the ear with the rhythm of the words and the mode of the notes. These two things, therefore, I mean the modulation of the voice and the arrangement of words in periods, they thought proper to transfer from poetry to rhetoric, so far as was compatible with the severe character of oratory." (Trans. H. Rackham [Cambridge: Harvard University Press, Loeb Classical Library, 1958])

59. Isidore of Seville, *Origins*, XXI.1: "In addition, there are certain signs found in the most celebrated writers, which the ancients introduced into verse and prose for distinctions in writing. The sign is a specific mark, placed in the manner of a letter to indicate the phrase pattern on each word. The number of signs introduced in verse is 26, which are named below. . . ."

60. Following the Pléiade edition, the translation here follows Rousseau's manuscript, which is almost illegible at this point, against the copyist, Jeannin. See note 50 above.

61. That is, *où*, "where," is distinguished from *ou*, "or"; *à*, "to," is distinguished from *a*, "has."

62. Duclos, *Remarques sur la Grammaire générale et raisonnée*, I, 4. Dionysius of Halicarnassus says (*Synthesis*, 15) that all the variations of the spoken voice take place within the space of a fifth. For Rousseau's remarks on Dionysius of Halincarnassus' understanding of accent and music, see the entry ACCENT [*Accent*] in the *Dictionary of Music*, p. 371 below.

63. That is, *è*, "is," is distinguished from *e*, "and." Benedetto Buonmmattei or

Buonmattei (1581–1647) was an Italian grammarian whose *Della lingua toscana* (1643) was influential in forming what is now modern Italian. See *Della lingua toscana* (1714), VI, 9.

64. Rousseau suggests a similar experiment in his *Letter on French Music*, p. 150 above.

65. See the fragment by Rousseau entitled "Pronunciation," translated below. Also consider Rousseau's discussion of the relationship between languages and government in chap. XX of the *Essay* in connection with his ironic praise in the *First Discourse* of princes' support for the arts and sciences and the establishment of academies (*Collected Writings*, II, 5, and n. 19).

66. Duclos, *Remarques sur la Grammaire générale et raisonnée*, I, 4.

67. "Points" ("*points*") and "accents" were only later added to Hebrew script. By these "*points*," Rousseau could also be referring to punctuation, which Hebrew also originally lacked. Spinoza explains in chap. 7 of his *Theologico-Political Treatise*: "Firstly, there are in Hebrew no vowels; secondly, the sentences are not separated by any marks elucidating the meaning or separating the clauses. Though the want of these two has generally been supplied by points and accents, such substitutes cannot be accepted by us, inasmuch as they were invented and designed by men of an after age whose authority should carry no weight. The ancients wrote without points (that is, without vowels and accents), as is abundantly testified; their descendants added what was lacking, according to their own ideas of Scriptural interpretation" (ed. and trans. R. H. M. Elwes [New York: Dover, 1951], 109–110).

68. Rousseau first discusses the characteristic differences between the peoples of the north and south in his *Second Discourse*, just before his long digression there on the origin of language (*Collected Writings*, III, 27). The juxtaposition of the north and south is also found foremost in Montesquieu. See *Spirit of the Laws*, XIV–XVII, esp. bk. XIV, 1–3, XVII, 1–8, XVIII, 4; see also XIX, 4, 27, XXI, 1–4.

69. See Rousseau, *Second Discourse*, note *8 (*Collected Writings*, III, 84–86); *Letter to Philopolis* (ibid., 130).

70. In Rousseau's draft this chapter was originally entitled Chapter VIII, but was later changed.

71. The account of the origin of society and languages in this chapter generally parallels the account offered by Rousseau in the Second Part of the *Second Discourse* (see *Collected Writings*, III, 46–47; also 27–34). In the *Second Discourse,* Rousseau establishes the "epoch of the first revolution" of the establishment of families as the point where true languages began to develop (ibid., 46). The "first times" spoken of in the *Essay* therefore refers not to Rousseau's description of our original condition as solitary animals, or the "pure state of nature" depicted in the First Part of the *Second Discourse*, but to the "state of nature" described in the Second Part of the work, where nascent families develop and become established.

72. See Rousseau, *Geneva Manuscript*, I, 2 (*Collected Writings*, IV, 81): "The words foreigners and enemies were long synonymous for several ancient peoples. . . . Hobbes' mistake, therefore, is not that he established the state of war among men who are independent and have become sociable, but that he supposed this state natural to the species and gave it as the cause of the vices of which it is the effect." See also *État de guerre* (Pléiade, III, 601–602).

73. Rousseau's evasive statement is clearly directed toward the possible objections of those who accept the account of human origins and language found in Scripture. Rousseau makes his intentions in this chapter clearer a few pages later, when he twice refers back to what he says here about "the first times" when speaking of the events recounted in *Genesis*. Rousseau continues to play on the Scriptural account of our origins and of the origin of language in this chapter. However, instead of locating the origin of language with the first man, Adam, or his children or immediate descendants, Rousseau finds it in the story of Isaac, Rebecca, and the encounter at the well (Gen. 24), or at the first meeting of the young of opposite sexes of dispersed families such as he describes near the end of this chapter.

74. In the *Second Discourse*, Rousseau cites approvingly the researches that Condillac made on the origin of languages, "which all fully confirm my sentiment, and which perhaps gave me the first idea of it," but objects that Condillac assumes what he himself questions, "namely, a kind of society already established among the inventors of language" (*Collected Writings*, III, 29–30). For Condillac's discussion of families and the origin of languages, with reference to the Scriptural account, see *Essai sur l'origine des connaissances humaines*, II, 1, preamble.

75. For the supposed contradiction between Rousseau's statement here about pity and his discussion in the *Second Discourse*, see Introduction, pp. xxix–xxx above.

76. See the similar account in the *Emile*, esp. Books III (Pléiade, IV, 480–488; Bloom, 202–208) and IV (Pléiade, IV, 546–548; Bloom, 251–253).

77. As in the *Second Discourse*, Rousseau is arguing against Hobbes' view that the state of nature is a condition of war: "Hobbes claims that man is naturally intrepid and seeks only to attack and fight. An illustrious Philosopher thinks, on the contrary, and Cumberland and Pufendorf also affirm, that nothing is so timid as man in the state of Nature" (*Collected Writings*, III, 20). See also the *État de guerre* (Pléiade, III, 600–603). For Hobbes, see *Leviathan*, chaps. 11, 13, and *De cive*, chap. 1.

78. Rousseau draws on Montesquieu, *Spirit of the Laws*, I, 3, for the distinction among shepherds, hunters, and plowmen. In the *Second Discourse*, Rousseau argues that the institution of agriculture and discovery of metallurgy together work to take men out of the state of nature (*Collected Writings*, III, 48–51).

79. The story of the Cyclops Polyphemos is found in Homer, *Odyssey*, IX.116–566. Augustine takes up the story with regard to property and safety in his *City of God*, XIX.12. See also Rousseau, *Social Contract*, I, 4.

80. See Genesis 4:3, 9:20.

81. Rousseau discusses the natural diet of mankind at length in the *Second Discourse* and conjectures that we may have been originally herbivores (see esp. *Collected Writings*, III, n.*4, 71). See also *Emile*, II (Pléiade, IV, 408–415; Bloom, 151–156). Pelasgos was said to have taught the Greeks to eat acorns (Pausanias, *Arcadia*, VIII.i.6), while Triptolemus was said to have taught agriculture to them and prohibited the eating of meat (ibid., VIII.iv.1; Plato, *Laws*.III.782b; Xenophon, *Hellenica*, VI.3). Rousseau mentions Triptolemus again just below and seems to assume that Herodotus includes the legend about him in his *Histories*, which is incorrect.

82. For Abraham, see Genesis 18:7; for Eumaeus, see Homer, *Odyssey*, XIV.72–80; for Rebecca, see Genesis 27:9.

83. In the *Emile*, where he is speaking of the possible unnaturalness of meat-eating, Rousseau remarks that "English barbarism is known" is this respect (IV, Pléiade IV, 411 and note).

84. Job 1:3, 14, 15.

85. Genesis 10:1, 11:10–29.

86. For Adam being taught to speak by God, see Genesis 2:19–20, 3:10, 12; for Noah, see ibid., 9:20–27; for the Tower of Babel, see ibid., 11:1–9.

87. In the *Social Contract* Rousseau writes that according to Grotius and Hobbes, who both justified conquest as a source of authority, "the human species is divided into herds of livestock, each with its leader, who tends to it in order to devour it" (I, 2; see also I, 4). See also *Second Discourse* (*Collected Writings*, III, 32–33). Compare Aristotle, *Politics*, I.8.1256b23–26.

88. Exodus 26:7–14, 36:14–19.

89. Note that Rousseau inverts the chronicle of Genesis, which is reputed to have been written by Moses. In the Scriptural account, Adam and Eve eat of the fruit of the tree of the knowledge of good and evil, then make clothes, and are then expelled from the Garden of Eden. Only with Cain, their son, does agriculture arise and are its fruits scorned by God in favor of those of the pastoral life led by Abel. After Cain kills his brother, Abel, God puts a mark on him (Gen. 3:1–4, 16). Rousseau also appeals to the Scriptural story of the origin of our knowledge of good and evil in the *Second Discourse*, where he writes that after the meeting of dispersed families and the beginnings of society, morality was introduced into human actions (*Collected Writings*, III, 48). Compare Grotius, *Droit de la Guerre et de la Paix*, II, 2, §1 (trans. Barbeyrac).

90. See note 78 above.

91. For the "perpetual spring," see Ovid, *Metamorphoses*, I.107 ff., and Pufendorf, *Droit de la nature et des gens*, II.ii.2, who cites Ovid when he speaks of the pagan poets' ignorance of the earthly paradise of the Garden of Eden.

92. On man's natural laziness, see *Second Discourse* (*Collected Writings*, III, 28). In his 1756 letter to Voltaire on providence, Rousseau explains the natural goodness of life, claiming he has proved it in his description of natural man in the *Second Discourse*: "I dare to state that there is in the upper Valais not a single Mountaineer discontented with his almost automatic life, and who would not willingly accept, even in place of Paradise, the bargain of being reborn unceasingly in order to vegetate thus in perpetuity" (*Collected Writings*, III, 111). See also *Reveries of the Solitary Walker*, Fifth Walk (Pléiade, I, 1042).

93. The inclination of the axis of the earth to the angle of that of the universe is the cause of the seasons. Rousseau uses the same image in a fragment from his projected *Political Institutions* in a treatment of the effect of climates on civilization, a discussion relevant to the present discussion: "To tilt the axis of the world with a finger or to say to man, 'Cover the earth and be sociable,' was the same thing for He who needs neither hand to act nor voice to speak" (*Collected Writings*, IV, 55).

94. See Montesquieu, *Spirit of the Laws*, XVIII, 3: "It is natural for a people to leave a bad country in search of a better and not for them to leave a good country in search of a worse one." Compare Machiavelli, *Discourses on Titus Livy*, I, 1.

95. Rousseau refers to England. See Montesquieu, *Spirit of the Laws*, XVII, 5.

96. Rousseau also speaks of these natural disasters as the cause that unites men and begins to make them speak in the *Second Discourse* (*Collected Writings*, III, 46–47). See also *Political Fragments*, X (*Collected Writings*, IV, 56). For the ancient traditions of natural disasters, aside from the flood and destruction of the Tower of Babel recounted in Genesis (7:10–8:14; 11:1–9), see, among others, Plato, *Laws*.III. 667a–682a, *Timaeus*, 22a–25d, and *Critias*, 108e–109a, *et passim*; Lucretius, *De rerum natura*, I.1027–1034, V.333–347, 380–415.

97. Compare Rousseau's similar description of the Swiss in his *Constitutional Project for Corsica* (Pléiade, III, 914).

98. See note 83 above.

99. On the use of fire among men and animals, see *Second Discourse*, note *8 (*Collected Writings*, III, 82–83). The term "fleeting society" (*société fugitive*) makes it appear that Rousseau is referring here to Helvétius, who uses the term in his *De l'Esprit* (1758; Discours premier, chap. 1). The word translated as "stupid" here also means "beasts." See Rousseau's letter to Voltaire of September 10, 1755 (*Collected Writings*, III, 105 and ed.n. 2).

100. See Genesis 21:25–33.

101. For the chaos feigned by the poets, see, e.g., Ovid, *Metamorphoses*, I.5–31; Lucretius, *De rerum natura*, II.118–122. As Gourevitch notes in his edition of the *Essay*, Descartes uses the same phrase as Rousseau (*Discourse on Method*, 5, second paragraph).

102. Rousseau appears to refer to Buffon's theory as elaborated in his *Animaux carnissiers* (1758; vol. 7), where Buffon criticizes Rousseau's theory of man's original diet as expressed in the *Second Discourse*.

103. See the parallel account in the *Second Discourse* (*Collected Writings*, III, 46). Rousseau appears in both accounts to draw on Lucretius, *De rerum natura*, V.1390–1402. For the relationship of dancing and singing in connection with the opposition of north and south, see Condillac, *Essai sur l'origine des connaissances humaines*, II, i, 8.

104. The necessary intermarriage within families in primitive times was a common subject in Rousseau's time. See, for example, Grotius, *Droit de la Guerre et de Paix*, I, 5, §12 (trans. Barbeyrac); Pufendorf, *Droit de la nature et des gens*, I, 2, §6 (trans. Barbeyrac); Montesquieu, *Persian Letters*, Letter LXVII.

105. See note 40 above.

106. In Rousseau's draft this chapter was originally entitled Chapter IX, but was later changed.

107. "Similar" translates "*semblables*," which has otherwise been translated "fellow-men."

108. See Rousseau, *Emile*, II (Pléiade, IV, 374; Bloom, 128).

109. See Montesquieu, *Spirit of the Laws*, XVIII, 4.

110. The first word among them was not "*aimez-moi*," but "*aidez-moi*." As Starobinski remarks in his edition of the *Essay*, Rousseau takes advantage here of the contrast between the hard "d" and the nasal "m" in the two phrases in order to make the opposition between them evident to the ear in French.

111. Rousseau discusses Mohammed, among others, as persuasive political and religious founders in the *Social Contract* (II, 7; see also IV, 8). As in the *Social Con-

tract, Rousseau here appears to have Voltaire's *Mahomet* (1743) in mind. See his discussion of this play in the *Letter to d'Alembert on the Theatre* (ed. Bloom, 30–32) as well as the "Profession of Faith" in the *Emile*, IV (Pléiade, IV, 632–633 and note; Bloom, 311–313).

112. The notion of a mutual origin of song and poetry was a common notion in antiquity. See also Condillac, *Essai sur l'origine des connaissances humaines*, II, i, 2, §§14–15; 5, §46; 8, §§73–79.

113. In the draft manuscript, Rousseau wrote "Relationships" in the margin in the same fashion as the chapter headings and numbers (see note 6 above), although this apparent chapter heading was not numbered.

114. The relationship between songs and laws is indicated by the Greek "*nomos*," which can mean either "law" or "song." See Aristotle, *Problems*, XIX.28; Martianus Cappela, *De Musica* (= *De Nuptiis Philologiae et Mercurii*, IX), 313g. See note 6 to Rousseau's *On the Principle of Melody*, translated above.

115. Strabo, *Geographica*, I.ii, 6.

116. Quintilian, *Institutio oratoria*, I.x.17–18: "Archytas and Aristoxenus held that the former was subordinate to the latter, while we know that the same instructors were employed for the teaching of both. . . . [The same fact is proved by] Eupolis, who makes Prodamus teach both music and literature, and whose Maricas, who was none other than Hyperbolus in disguise, asserts that he knows nothing of music but letters" (*The Institutio oratoria of Quintilian*, trans. H. E. Butler [Cambridge: Harvard University Press, Loeb Classical Library, 1920]). In his edition of the *Essay*, Gourevitch notes that Rousseau makes several errors in transcribing this passage, most notably substituting Aristoxenus where Quintilian speaks of Euenus.

117. See Rousseau's article MUSIC [*Musique*] in his *Dictionary of Music*, p. 444 below, where he refers to the *Essay*. Compare Montesquieu's discussion of ancient music in his *Spirit of the Laws*, IV, 8.

118. Pierre Jean Burette (1665–1747) was a musician and medical doctor who collaborated on the *Journal des savants* and was a member of the Académie des Inscriptions et Belles-Lettres. Burrette transcribed music set to an ode of Pindar (*Ariston men hudor*) and one by Horace. Both odes were originally reproduced by Marin Mersenne in his *Harmonie universelle* (1636). Rousseau discusses both Mersenne and Burette and at some length in the article MUSIC [*Musique*] in his *Dictionary of Music*, translated below.

119. Jean Terrasson (1670–1750), *La philosophie applicable à tous les objets de l'esprit et de la raison* (1754), published posthumously and edited by d'Alembert. In this work, Terrasson praises Rameau and attacks his adversaries, including Rousseau: "The music of Rameau is one example of the new beauties always rejected by some" (p. 30). Terrasson, professor of Greek and Latin philosophy at the Collège de France, was a partisan of the moderns in the Quarrel between the ancients and moderns. Rousseau refers to Terrasson in his *Emile* as a proponent of the superiority of the moderns (IV; Pléiade, IV, 676; Bloom, 343).

120. For a similar discussion of moral causes, physical causes, and taste, see *Emile*, IV (Pléiade, IV, 671–676; Bloom, 340–343). See also Rousseau *Dialogues*, Second Dialogue, (*Collected Writings*, I, 112–113).

121. The comparison between painting and music, with design representing the melody and coloration the harmony, was a common trope in this period. See also Plato, *Republic*, X, 600e–601b. "Contour" translates *"trait"* in this passage and in the remainder of this chapter.

122. For Burette, see note 118 above.

123. The analogy between the refraction of colors in the prism and the notes of the musical scale was made most importantly by Newton in his *Opticks* (Pt. 1, qu. 14). Newton's proposition was discussed in the article *"Coulour"* in the *Encyclopedia*, and was taken up most importantly by Castel, whose "ocular clavichord" Rousseau lampoons in chap. XVI below.

124. "Relationships" translates *"rapports,"* which can also be translated "ratios" and has been translated as such when it clearly has this sense.

125. Rousseau parodies Rameau in the previous passage. For example, in his *Nouvelles réflexions sur la démonstration du principle de l'harmonie* (1752) Rameau writes: "The beautiful edifices of the Greeks and Romans . . . were all built on the proportions drawn from music, which well justifies the idea that I have long had, that in music resides most certainly the principle of all the arts of taste" (Jacobi, V, 123–124). See also the end of Rameau's *Errors on Music in the Encyclopedia*, translated above.

126. This is the definition of music Rousseau gives at the outset of the article Music [*Musique*] in the *Dictionary of Music*, translated below.

127. Rousseau here opposes Rameau's supposed experiment as reported, among other places, in his *Treatise on Harmony*, Bk. 3, chap. 40 (Gossett, 331–341). He explains the basis of his criticism at the outset of his *Examination of Two Principles*, translated above.

128. See Plato, *Phaedo*, 84e–85a.

129. Rousseau appears to refer to Rameau's *Platée* (1745), which includes a chorus of croaking frogs.

130. In Rousseau's draft this chapter was originally entitled: "How our liveliest sensations often act through moral impressions."

131. For Rousseau's similar discussion of indications that animals as well as humans seem to show signs of natural pity, see *Second Discourse* (*Collected Writings*, III, 36). In the *Emile*, Rousseau remarks that "it is important to observe that something moral enters into everything concerned with imitation," and then writes in a note to the statement: "This is proved by an essay on the *Principle of Melody*, which will be found in the collection of my writings" (IV; Pléiade, IV, 672; Bloom, 340). In his own copy of the *Emile*, Rousseau changed the reference to the *Essay on the Origin of Languages* (Pléiade, IV, 1618).

132. Rousseau refers to the supposed cure for tarantula bites by dancing, from which comes the dance called a "Tarantella."

133. Nicolas Bernier (1664–1734) was the director of music of the Sainte-Chapelle in Paris and the chapel at Versailles. Rousseau relates the story of the musician cured by a concert in the article Music [*Musique*] in his *Dictionary of Music*, p. 443 below. In his *Confessions*, Rousseau relates learning cantatas by heart while he himself was ill (V; *Collected Writings*, V, 155).

134. See *Emile*, II (Pléiade, IV, 409–410; Bloom, 152): "Gluttony is the vice of hearts that have no substance."

135. Rousseau distinguishes the "systematizing spirit" from the "spirit of observation," upon which he says his own "system" is founded, in his *Lettres morales* (Lettre 3; Pléiade IV, 1090–1093).

136. The "ocular clavichord" was constructed by the Abbé Louis Bertrand Castel (1688–1757), whom Rousseau had met soon after arriving in Paris with his new system of musical notation (see *Confessions*, VII (*Collected Writings*, V, 238, 242–243, 274). Castel first proposed his clavichord in 1725 in the *Mercure de France* and elaborated on it in later works, most importantly his *Optique des coulours* (1740). A separate article on the "*Clavecin oculaire*" was included in the *Encyclopedia*.

137. Rousseau refers to the famous automated flautist constructed by Vaucanson (1709–1782), who published his *Mécanisme d'un flûteur automate* in 1738.

138. Rousseau refers to the ancient teaching, dating back to the Pythagorians and Plato and popular in the Middle Ages and Renaissance, that the revolution of the spheres containing the celestial bodies produced a harmonious music.

139. "Similar" translates "*semblable*," which is translated as "fellows" in the previous sentence. See note 8 above.

140. This paragraph in the *Essay* is repeated almost verbatim in the articles IMITATION [*Imitation*] and OPERA [*Opéra*] in the *Dictionary of Music*, both of which are translated below.

141. Rousseau refers foremost to Rameau, who claimed Greek music was a defective version of the harmonic theory he developed in his works. However, in his earlier works, notably the *Treatise on Harmony* (1722), Rameau claimed that the music of the Greeks was founded on melody and not harmony. In his later writings, Rameau changed his mind and insisted that Greek music was based on a defective notion of harmony. The debate between Rousseau and Rameau over the related issues of the primacy of melody and harmony and the nature of Greek music can be found in Rousseau's article ENHARMONIC [*Enharmonique*] in the *Encyclopedia* (later included in revised form in the *Dictionary of Music*) and Rameau's critical examination of that article in his *Continuation of Errors on Music in the Encyclopedia*, both translated above.

142. Rousseau elaborates on the difference among the musical systems of various peoples and includes examples of the music of the Greeks, American Indians, and others, in the article MUSIC [*Musique*] in the *Dictionary of Music*, translated below.

143. This paragraph was adapted with minor changes from the *Principle of Melody*, p. 263 above, and was also used in the *Examination of Two Principles*, p. 275 above.

144. Rousseau's formulation in the version of this sentence in the *Principle of Melody* (see p. 263 above) brings out the pun: "they would have so to speak understood them underneath [*sousentendües au dessous*] their songs."

145. See the entry PATHETIC [*Pathétique*] in the *Dictionary of Music*: "The true *pathetic* genre is in passionate accent, which is not at all determined by rules, but is what genius discovers and the heart feels, without art being able in any way to give it laws."

146. This whole chapter was adapted with changes from the *Principle of Melody*, pp. 265–268 above.

147. Plutarch, *De Musica*, XXX.1141c–1142a. The dialogue, falsely attributed to

Plutarch, contains a synopsis of Pherecrates' play *Chiron* (c. 440–420 B.C.), in which Music, dressed as a woman, complains that, instead of commanding poetry as of old, now she is stripped of her rightful place and accustomed power. Melanippides (fifth century B.C.) and Philoxenus (fourth century B.C.) were innovators in Greek music.

148. See Rousseau, *First Discourse* (*Collected Writings*, II, 7–8).

149. See Plato, *Republic*, X.599c–e; Diogenes Laertius, *Lives of the Philosophers*, "Plato."

150. Nero is the "flute player" Rousseau has Fabricius denounce in the important prosopopeia in the *First Discourse* (*Collected Writings*, II, 11).

151. Flavius Claudius Julianus ("Julian the Apostate"), *Misopogon*, 337c. Julian actually compares the Gaul's speech to the cawing of hoarse birds.

152. See Rousseau's article PLAIN-SONG [*Plain-Chant*] in his *Dictionary of Music* (Pléiade, V, 983), where he appears to allude to this discussion in the *Essay*: "The time when the Christians began to have Churches . . . was that in which Music had already lost almost all its ancient energy by a progress of which I have elsewhere set forth the causes."

153. Jehan des Murs (c.1300–c.1350), a widely influential musical theorist of the later Middle Ages best known for his treatment of musical proportions and mensural notation. Rousseau refers to the *Speculum musicae*, long attributed to Jehan des Murs, but actually written by Jacques de Liège (c.1260–c.1330). Giovanni-Andrea Angelini-Bontempi or Buontempi (c. 1630–c.1704), published his *Istoria musica* in 1695. Rousseau read the work attentively while living at Charmettes, and credits it with sparking his interest in musical theory (see *Confessions*, VII; *Collected Writings*, V, 206).

154. Giuseppe Tartini (1692–1770) was a well-known violinist, composer, and theoretician. His most influential work was the *Trattato di musica secondo al vera scienza dell'armonia* (1754). For Rousseau's discussion of Rameau's vibrating string, see *Examination of Two Principles*, end, p. 281 above.

155. In the *Emile* Rousseau writes: "I observe that in the modern age men no longer have a hold on one another except by force or by self-interest; the ancients, by contrast, acted much more by persuasion and by the affections of the soul because they did not neglect the language of signs" (IV; Pléiade, IV, 645; Bloom, 231). See also *Social Contract*, III, 15: "your indistinct languages cannot be heard outdoors" (see more generally III, 12–15). Compare Aristotle, *Politics*, VII.4.1326b5–6.

156. See Rousseau's similar description of the public reading of the poetry of Homer and the great Athenian tragedians in his *Considerations on the Government of Poland*, chap. 2 (Pléiade, III, 958).

157. D'Alembert, *De la liberté de la musique* (1758), XXIII: "If French recitative were as well composed as it could be, it ought to be able to be recited in Italian."

158. Duclos, *Remarques sur la Grammaire générale et raisonnée*, I, 1.

EDITOR'S NOTES TO
Pronunciation

This translation is based on the text found in Pléiade, II, 1248–1252. The Pléiade edition is based on Rousseau's manuscript (Neuchâtel R 19, folios 13–15), which was written in about 1761. The title "Pronunciation" was given to the manuscript by its first publisher, Streickeisen-Moultou, who took it for a fragment of the *Essay on the Origin of Languages*.

1. The editor cannot identify Rousseau's reference to Prosper Jolyot de Crebillon, commonly known as Crebillon père, French dramatist of the late seventeenth and early eighteenth century. For his analysis of Crebillon's plays, see *Letter to d'Alembert* (Pléiade, V, 25–30; ed. Bloom, 27–32).
2. The philosopher Gottfried Wilhelm von Leibniz (1646–1716) worked for much of his life on a universal philosophical language akin to algebra.
3. Rousseau appears to refer to the concluding chapter of his *Essay on the Origin of Languages*, which was not, however, published during his lifetime.

EDITOR'S NOTES TO
On Theatrical Imitation

This translation is based on the text found in Pléiade, 1195–1211. The work was first published in the 1764 Duchesne edition of Rousseau's works, and also in a separate edition in the same year by Guy, Duchesne's assistant, and in a counterfeit edition in the same year by Rousseau's former publisher, Rey.

1. The Pléiade edition of this writing does not contain the subtitle, even though the first edition of the work bears it.
2. Rousseau's *Letter to M. d'Alembert on the Theatre* was published in 1758. The *Letter* was in reaction to the article "Geneva" in the seventh volume of the *Encyclopedia*, in which d'Alembert suggested the establishment of a theater in Rousseau's fatherland, where theaters were prohibited.
3. The "transaction" in question was the separate publication of this writing by Guy, the "Bookseller" Duchesne's assistant. Rousseau sent Duchesne the writing in 1758 along with the plates to the *Nouvelle Héloïse* (see Leigh, VII, 363).
4. See Plato, *Republic*, X.595a–c.
5. Socrates uses the example of a bed maker. See Plato, *Republic*, X.596a–b.
6. See Plato, *Republic*, X.597b.
7. See Plato, *Republic*, X.598a–b.
8. See the version of the article CONSONANCE [*Consonnance*] in the *Dictionary of Music*, pp. 377–382 below. Rousseau terms modern harmony a "barbarous and gothic invention" in the article HARMONY [*Harmonie*] in the *Dictionary of Music*, p. 413 below.
9. Rousseau refers to M. de Moisgelou, (d. 1761), councilor in the Grand Council of Geneva. Rousseau speaks of Moisgelou in his article SYSTEM [*Système*] in the *Dictionary of Music*.
10. Rousseau discusses the difference among musical systems most especially in the article MUSIC [*Musique*] in the *Dictionary of Music*, translated below.
11. Rousseau may be referring to Diderot.
12. Compare the story of Emile and the "magician Socrates" in Rousseau's *Emile*, III (Pléiade, IV, 437–441; Bloom, 172–175).
13. The editor has not been able to identify the source of this quotation.

14. Machaon is the son of Asclepius, the legendary founder of the art of medicine. See Homer, *Iliad*, IV.192–218. See Plato, *Republic*, X.599b–c.

15. Lycurgus was the semimythical traditional founder of Sparta. Charondas (sixth century B.C.) was the lawgiver of Catana in Sicily. Minos was the semimythical founder and king of Crete. Solon (sixth–fifth century B.C.) was the Athenian statesman and poet who revised the Athenian legal and political system.

16. Thales of Miletus (sixth century B.C.) was a philosopher who is said to have given political advice to the Ionians. Anacharsis from Scythia (sixth century B.C.) was a sage who traveled widely in Greece.

17. Zoroaster was the mythical founder of Zoroastrianism, the Persian religion. Pythagoras (sixth century B.C.) was the founder of a philosophical cult. Lycurgus was the semimythical traditional founder of Sparta.

18. Cleophon was an Athenian politician contemporary with Socrates.

19. Protagoras of Abdera and Prodicus of Ceos were both well-known Sophists contemporary with Socrates. See Plato, *Republic*, X.600c–d. See Plato, *Apology of Socrates*, 19d–20a; *Protagoras*, 310c–317c.

20. Tyrtaeus was an elegiac poet of the seventh century B.C., probably Spartan, who was also involved in the politics of his time.

21. See Plato, *Gorgias*, 501e–502b.

22. Thersites is an ugly, foul man who rails at Agamemnon until beaten into silence by Ulysses (Odysseus) (Homer, *Iliad*, II.211–270). Dolon is an ugly, cowardly Trojan scout killed by Diomedes and Odysseus (ibid., X.313–464).

23. See Plato, *Laws*, VII.817b-d.

24. Compare Rousseau's description of the Legislator in *Social Contract*, II, 7 (*Collected Writings*, IV, 154–155).

25. See Plato, *Republic*, X.602c–603a.

26. See Plato, *Republic*, IV.436b–c, V.476d–478e.

27. See Plato, *Republic*, X.603a–b.

28. See Plato, *Republic*, X.603d–e.

29. See Plato, *Republic*, X.603e–604b.

30. See Plato, *Apology of Socrates*, 40c.

31. See Plato, *Republic*, X.605b–606b.

32. See Plato, *Republic*, III.388a–b.

33. For Rousseau's analysis of the role of pity in the theater, see *Letter to d'Alembert on the Theatre* (ed. Bloom, 24–25); *Essay on the Origin of Languages*, chap. I, p. 291 below.

34. See Plato, *Republic*, X.606c.

35. See Plato, *Republic*, 606e–607a. Rousseau writes "Glaucus" here and in the next paragraph when he appears to mean "Glaucon," Socrates' main interlocutor in the *Republic*. Glaucus is the sea-god discussed by Socrates in Book X of the *Republic* (611d) and by Rousseau in the *Second Discourse* (*Collected Writings*, III, 12).

36. See Plato, *Republic*, X.607b–c.

EDITOR'S NOTES TO
The Levite of Ephraïm

This translation is based on the text found in Pléiade, II, 1205–1223. The Pléiade edition is based on the two extant manuscripts of the work. The work (without the draft prefaces) was first published by du Peyrou and Moutou in their 1781 *Oeuvres posthumes de Rousseau*, as part of their *Collection complète des oeuvres de Jean-Jacques Rousseau*. The draft prefaces are found in separate manuscripts.

1. Rousseau intended to publish the *Levite of Ephraïm* along with *On Theatrical Imitation* and the *Essay on the Origin of Languages*, both translated above. The manuscript of this draft preface is found between two letters from February and July 1763, suggesting that Rousseau intended to publish the work at about that time.

2. See Judges 19–21.

3. Rousseau refers to his flight from France after the condemnation of his *Emile* by the Parlement of Paris and the warrant for his arrest. The order for his arrest was issued June 9, 1762. That afternoon, warned of these actions, Rousseau fled Paris for Geneva, but Rousseau's native city burned both the *Emile* and *Social Contract* and ordered his arrest. In his *Confessions*, Rousseau relates that it was on the morning after his departure from Paris that he thought of composing the *Levite of Ephraïm*, which he wrote during his voyage and completed afterward at Môtiers. Rousseau relates the circumstances of the composition of the work in his *Confessions*, XI (*Collected Writings*, V, 485–491).

4. See the previous note.

5. Rousseau explains in the *Confessions* (XI; *Collected Writings*, V, 491) that the style of his *Levite* is taken from the *Idylles et poëmes champêtres* by Salomon Gessner (1730–1788), a poet from Zurich who wrote idylls in prose that praised the simple life, as translated by Jean-Jacques Hubner, a Genevan Calvinist who converted to Catholicism. Hubner sent his translation of Gessner's *Idylles* to Rousseau at the end of 1761 (Leigh, IX, 347–348).

6. See Genesis 35:17–19. Benjamin was the son of Jacob and Rebecca.

7. This paragraph and the last one have no analog in Judges. The Scriptural version of the story begins simply: "And it came to pass in those days, when there was no king in Israel, that there was a certain Levite . . ." (Judges 19:1 [KJV]). Rousseau substantially embellishes the Scriptural account. For a treatment of Rousseau's departures from Scripture, see Thomas M. Kavanaugh, *Writing the Truth: Authority and Desire in Rousseau* (Berkeley: University of California Press, 1987), chap. 5.

8. Numbers 36:8 (KJV): "And every daughter, that possesseth an inheritance in any tribe of the children of Israel, shall be wife unto one of the family of the tribe of the father, that the children of Israel may enjoy every man the inheritance of his fathers."

9. Jebus is another name for Jerusalem.

10. Priests were drawn from the tribe of Levi.

11. Rousseau appears to have invented the term "sons of Jemini," which he uses here and below instead of the term "Benjaminites" found in the Scriptural version.

12. See Deuteronomy 13:13 (KJV): "Certain men, the children of Belial, are gone

out from among you, and have withdrawn the inhabitants of their city, saying, Let us go and serve other gods, which ye have not known."

13. Genesis 49:27 (KJV): "Benjamin shall ravin as a wolf: in the morning he shall devour the prey, and at night he shall divide the spoil."

14. The Scriptural version of the story concludes here, so the continuation is Rousseau's own embellishment.

EDITOR'S NOTES TO
Dictionary of Music

This translation is based on text found in Pléiade, V, 603–1191 (inclusive). The Pléiade edition of the work is not fully edited and awaits a new edition. The original edition of Rousseau's *Dictionary of Music* (Paris: Duchesne, 1768; reproduced by Georg Olms Verlagsbuchhandlung and Johnson Reprint Company [Hildesheim and New York, 1969]), has also been consulted.

The articles from the *Dictionary of Music* included here have been selected for their importance to understanding Rousseau's musical and aesthetic theory. Rousseau himself claims the importance of some of these articles. In his *Dialogues* (*Collected Writings*, I, 17–18) he indicates the following articles: ENHARMONIC [*Enharmonique*], EXPRESSION [*Expression*], FUGUE [*Fugue*], GENIUS [*Génie*], HARMONY [*Harmonie*], LICENSE [*Licence*], MODE [*Mode*], MODULATION [*Modulation*], PREPARATION [*Préparation*], RECITATIVE [*Récitatif*], and TRIO [*Trio*]. In a letter to Joseph-Jerôme le François de Lalande (March 4, 1768; Leigh, XXXV, 160–161), Rousseau lists the following articles as particularly important: ACCENT [*Accent*], CONSONANCE [*Consonnance*], DISSONANCE [*Dissonnance*], ENHARMONIC [*Enharmoniqe*], EXPRESSION [*Expression*], TASTE [*Gout*], HARMONY [*Harmonie*], INTERVAL [*Intervalle*], LICENSE [*Licence*], OPERA [*Opéra*], SOUND [*Son*], TEMPERAMENT [*Tempérament*], UNITY OF MELODY [*Unité de mélodie*], VOICE [*Voix*]. The other articles included here were selected by the translator because they expand on the theory of musical expression that underlies Rousseau's musical and aesthetic doctrine.

The articles included here are alphabetized by the French term. This ordering does not usually pose any difficulty for the English reader because of the similarity or identity of most of the French and English terms. Within his articles, Rousseau includes frequent cross-references to other articles. The articles included in this translation have been indicated by an asterisk added to the cross-referenced article. For example, the article HARMONY* [*Harmonie*] is included in this translation, but the article SYSTEM [*Systeme*] is not included.

1. "So as to learn about the matter of songs," Martianus Capella, *De Musica* (= *De Nuptiis Philologiae et Mercurii*, IX), 904. The passage refers to the crowd of maidens who gather to hear Harmony expound upon her art.

2. Claude Sallier (1685–1761) was a philologist and bibliographer who directed the Royal Library toward the end of his life.

3. For Rousseau's explanation for his withdrawal from Parisian society to the

Hermitage near Montmorency in April 1756, see *Confessions*, IX (*Collected Writings*, V, 337–351).

4. Rousseau was then living in Môtiers-Travers, as indicated in the dating at the end of the Preface, below. For Rousseau's account of his flight from Paris and then Geneva and his stay at Môtiers, See *Confessions*, XII (*Collected Writings*, V, 499–532).

5. Abbé Sébastien de Brossard, whose *Dictionnaire de musique, contenant une explication des termes grecs, latins, italiens, et françois* (1703) was the first musical dictionary in France, and the only one before Rousseau's.

6. Giuseppe Tartini (1692–1770) was an Italian composer, violinist, teacher, and musical theorist whose *Trattato di musica secondo la vera scienza* (1754), which tried to reconcile empirical observation with classical harmonics and the laws of physics, was admired by Rousseau.

7. In the article SYSTEM [*Système*], Rousseau explains:

Until our century, Harmony, born gradually and as by chance, had only scattered rules, established by the ear, confirmed by use, and which seemed absolutely arbitrary. M. Rameau is the first who, by the System of the Fundamental Bass, gave principles to these rules. Since his *System*, on the basis of which this Dictionary has been assembled, has been sufficiently developed in its principal Articles, it will not be explained in this one, which is already too long, and which those senseless repetitions would elongate still further to the point of excess. Moreover, the object of this work does not oblige me to explain all *Systems*, but solely to explain well what one *System* is, and to clarify that explanation as need be with examples. Those who would like to see M. Rameau's *System*—so obscure, so vague in his own writings—explained with a clarity of which one would not believe possible will be able to refer to M. d'Alembert's *Elements of Music*.

M. Serre of Geneva, having found M. Rameau's principles insufficient in quite a number of respects, has devised another *System* based on his own, in which he claims to show that every Harmony is borne on a double Fundamental Bass; and as this Author, having traveled in Italy, is not unaware of M. Tartini's experiments, he composed, by joining them with those of M. Rameau, a mixed *System*, which he had printed in Paris in 1753, under the title: *Essays on the Principles of Harmony*, etc. The ease with which this work can be consulted, and the advantage that is found in reading it in its entirety, also excuses me from having to offer an account of it to the public.

It is not the same with that of the illustrious M. Tartini, of which it remains for me to speak, which, being written in a foreign language, often profound and always vague, is only within reach of being consulted by very few people, even the majority of whom are rebuffed by the obscurity of the Work, before being able to sense its beauties. I will write, as briefly as is possible for me, an extract of this new *System*, which, if it is not that of Nature, is at least, of all those that have been published until now, that whose principle is the simplest, and from which all the laws of Harmony seem to arise least arbitrarily. (Pléiade, V, 1082–1083)

D'Alembert's *Elements of Music* (*Eléments de l'harmonie théoretique et pratique*; 1st ed., 1753; 2nd ed., 1762) provided a clear explanation of Rameau's musical system.

Jean-Adam Serre (1704–1788) was a Genevan physicist, chemist, painter, and musical theorist who published criticisms of Rameau's theory of harmony, including his *Essais sur les principes de l'harmonie* (1753), to which Rousseau refers.

8. Readers of the *Dictionary* might suspect Rousseau's animus toward French music and partiality for Italian music because of his previous writings, notably the *Letter on French Music*. Rousseau alludes just below to his role in the debate over French and Italian music.

9. For Rousseau's fears that his articles on music had been plagiarized, see *Dialogues*, First Dialogue (*Collected Writings*, I, 17–18).

10. "Accent is more or less song," Sergius, or sometimes Servius (date unknown), *Commentarius in artem donati* (ed. Heinrich Keil, *Grammatici Latini*, 8 vols. [Leipzig, 1864], IV, 482). The full text of the reference is: "Spoken accent is more or less song according to the Greeks, who call it *prosodian*." Sergius' work is a commentary on the major work of the famous grammarian Aelius Donatus.

11. Dionysius of Helicarnassus, *Synthesis*, 15.

12. Pierre-Joseph Thoulier, Abbé d'Olivet, *Traité de la prosodie française* (1736).

13. The Port-Royal Grammar is the popular name for the *Grammaire générale et raisonnée* by Antoine Arnauld and Nicholas Lancelot, first published in 1664. Charles Pinot Duclos, Rousseau's friend, wrote a commentary on that work, *Remarques sur la Grammaire générale et raisonnée* (1754).

14. "*Air*" used in this sense has usually been translated elsewhere as "aria."

15. "Beautiful nature" translates "*la belle nature*," which was a technical term of eighteenth-century aesthetics that had a wide and usually vague meaning.

16. Denis Dodart, "Supplément au Mémoire sur la voix et sur les tons" (1706), 178–184.

17. Giacobbo Rodrigo Pereira or Pereire (1715–1780) presented his method for teaching the deaf to the Academy of Sciences in Paris in 1749. Rousseau mentions Pereira in his *Essay on the Origin of Languages*, chap. I, translated above.

18. Originally in French verse, drawn from d'Alembert's article "*Compositeur*" in the *Encyclopedia* (1753; III, 769).

19. Arcangelo Corelli (1653–1713) was an Italian composer whose works were important in the development of the baroque sonata form. Leonardo Vinci (c. 1690–1730) was a leading Neapolitan composer of *opera seria*. David Perez (1711–1779) was a Neapolitan opera composer of Spanish descent. Rinaldo da Capua (c. 1705–c. 1780) was a Neapolitan composer of sacred music and opera. Niccolò Jomelli (1714–1774) was a prolific Neapolitan composer of opera and sacred music. Francesco Durante (1684–1755) was a Neapolitan composer of sacred music and influential teacher. Leonardo Leo (1694–1744) was a leading Neapolitan composer. Giovanni Battista Pergolesi (1710–1736) was a composer of operas and other vocal pieces, including the opera buffa *La serva padrona*. Johann Adolf Hasse (1699–1783) was the most widely admired composer of *opera seria* in Italy and Germany at that time. Domenico Terradellas or Terradeglias (1713–1751) was a Spanish-born composer of opera and other vocal music in the Neapolitan style. Baldasare Galuppi (1706–1785) was a Venetian composer crucial to the development of the *opera buffa* style.

20. In this article, "Accord" translates *"Accord,"* which is usually translated "Chord." The two usages are related, for a chord is the recognized accord of two or more sounds heard simultaneously.

21. Jean-Jacques Dortous de Mairan (1678–1771) was a mathematician, physicist, and philosopher whose study of accoustics, the "Discours sur la Propagation du Son dans les différents Tons qui le modifient," was published in the *Histoire de l'Académie Royale des Sciences* in 1737. Mairan was one of the three academicians commissioned in 1741 to examine further Rousseau's "Plan Concerning New Signs for Music." Rameau adopted Mairan's hypotheses in his *Génération harmonique* (1737). Mairan, and Rameau after him, drew an analogy of light and color to sound, an analogy to which Rousseau alludes just below. For a discussion of Mairan and Rameau, see Thomas Christensen, *Rousseau and Musical Thought in the Enlightenment* (Cambridge: Cambridge University Press, 1993), 139–142.

22. The "Philosopher" in question is Denis Diderot, whose "Principes généraux d'acoustique" was published in 1748 as the first of his *Mémoires sur différens sujets de mathématiques*. See 235–239, 255–258.

23. René Descartes (1596–1650), the great philosopher, also wrote a work on music, the *Compendium musicae* (1618).

24. Pierre Estève (1720–after 1758) was a French physicist, academician, and literary figure who wrote works on the fine arts, including his *L'Esprit des beaux-arts* (1753), and on music, including his *Nouvelle découverte du principle de l'harmonie, avec un examen de ce que M. Rameau a publié sous le titre de Démonstration de ce principe* (Paris, 1751). Estève later wrote a pamphlet against Rousseau's *Letter on French Music*.

25. Sauveur, *Principes d'acoustique et de musique* (1701). "Beats" are an accoustical phenomenon resulting from the interference of two sound waves of slightly different frequencies that are heard as minute but perceptible intensifications of a sound at regular intervals.

26. For the version of this article in the *Encyclopedia*, see pp. 215–218 above.

27. Marin Mersenne, *Harmonie universelle contenant la théorie et la pratique de la musique* (1636), Book II. Mersenne tries to explain the origin of the dissonance as a "supposed" fifth below the tonic.

28. The first work to which Rousseau refers is Rameau, *Nouveau système*, chap. 11: "If one does not at all hear a Dissonance in the resonance of a sounding Body, this proves that they are not natural in Harmony and, consequently, they can be introduced into it only with the aid of Art" (Jacobi, II, 65). The second work in question is his *Génération harmonique* (1737), chap. 9 (Jacobi, III, 68).

29. Rousseau presents a summary of d'Alembert's discussion of dissonance in his *Eléments de l'harmonie théoretique et pratique* (2nd ed., 1762).

30. Giuseppe Tartini (1692–1770) was an Italian composer, violinist, teacher, and musical theorist whose *Trattato di musica secondo la vera scienza* (1754), which tried to reconcile empirical observation with classical harmonics and the laws of physics, was admired by Rousseau.

31. For the version of this article in the *Encyclopedia*, see pp. 219–221 above.

32. Rousseau refers to Ptolemy's discussion of Aristoxenus, *Elementa Harmonica*, I.12 (Barker, II, 301–303).

33. Aristides Quintilianus (third or fourth century A.D.), *De musica*, I.9 (Barker, II, 417–418).

34. Pseudo-Plutarch, *De musica*, 1134f–1135b, 1145a (Barker, I, 215–218, 244–245). *De musica* was formerly attributed to Plutarch.

35. The "Trio of the Furies" is the second trio of the Furies in Rameau's lyric-tragedy *Hippolyte et Aricie* (1733). The trio was successfully performed by the private orchestra of Rameau's patron, La Pouplinière, but the singers at the Paris Opera were unable to sing it and it had to be omitted. Rameau recounts the episode and claims that it was elsewhere performed in his *Génération harmonique* (1737), chap. XIV (Jacobi, III, 89 ff.) and his *Démonstration du principe de l'harmonie* (1750), 95–96 (Jacobi, III, 213–214).

36. Rameau describes the bad performance and poor reception of this part of his heroic opera-ballet *Les Indes galantes* (1735) in his *Démonstration du principe de l'harmonie* (1750), 95–96 (Jacobi, III, 213–214)

37. D'Alembert, *Eléments de musique théoretique et pratique* (2nd ed.; 1762), Book I, chaps. 20 and 22, Book II, chap. 14. In the last chapter cited, d'Alembert refers to several works by Rameau where the enharmonic is employed, including the example of the earthquake in his *Indes galantes*.

38. Rousseau defines the obligatory recitative as a recitative intermixed with melody played by the orchestra, thereby so to speak obliging the person doing the recitative and the orchestra to be attentive to and to await one another, and cites his own *Le Devin du village* as the first use of the device in French music (OBLIGATORY RECITATIVE [*Récitatif obligé*]; Pléiade, V, 1012–1013).

39. *Orfeo* is one of the many works attributed to Pergolesi (see note 19 above) but actually by another composer, in this case Luigi Rossi (1598–1653), singer, organist, and composer whose *Orfeo* was first produced in 1647.

40. Rousseau claims in his *Dialogues* that he included this article "only as a joke" (*Collected Writings*, I, 19). As he also notes there, however, the article was much-cited, and it would also become quite influential as a sort of manifesto of a new aesthetics. Rousseau's suggestion that the article was a joke may be intended to be provocative rather than serious.

41. For Leo, Durante, Jomelli, and Pergolesi, see note 19 above.

42. Pietro Metastasio (1698–1782) was an Italian poet and extremely popular librettist.

43. Nicomachus (c. A.D. 50–100), *Enchiridion*, chap. 2 (Barker, II, 248–250).

44. Sauveur, *Principes d'acoustique et de musique* (1701). For Mersenne see note 27 above. For d'Alembert see note 7 above.

45. For Tartini, see note 6 above.

46. Rousseau refers to Rameau's *Démonstration du principe de l'Harmonie* (1750). The *Demonstration* was originally presented as a "*Mémoire*" to the Academy of Sciences, whose approbation he published with the work. D'Alembert, a member of the committee which examined and approved of Rameau's "*Mémoire*," justified his later criticisms of Rameau's theories (for example in his article FONDEMENT in the *Encyclopedia*) by complaining that Rameau abused the Academy's authority and misled the public by entitling his work a "Demonstration." Pierre Estève (b. 1720),

French physicist, academician, and literary figure who wrote works on the fine arts, including his *L'Esprit des beaux-arts* (1753) and on music, including his *Nouvelle découverte du principle de l'harmonie, avec un examen de ce que M. Rameau a publié sous le titre de Démonstration de ce principe* (1751). Estève later wrote a pamphlet against Rousseau's *Letter on French Music*.

47. Compare Rousseau, *Essay on the Origin of Languages*, chap. XVIII, translated above.

48. Charles Batteux, *Les Beaux-arts réduits à un même principe* (1746).

49. Rousseau uses almost exactly the same passage in his *Essay on the Origin of Languages*, chap. XVI, translated above. See also a letter to d'Alembert (June 26, 1751; Leigh, II, 159–160): "The art of the musician does not at all consist in immediately portraying the objects, but in putting the soul into a disposition similar to that in which their presence would put it."

50. Aristoxenus, *Elementa Harmonica*, I.15–16 (Barker, II, 136–137).

51. Baccheius Geron (third–fourth century A.D.), *Eisagoge*; Gaudentius, *Harmonica introductio*.

52. Adrastus (c. second century A.D.) was a Greek philosopher cited by Meibomius in his edition of Theon of Smyrna (Barker, II, 222). Marc Meibom (latinized as Marcus Meibomius) (1620–1711) was a Danish historian and philologist who edited an influential collection of ancient musical writings, the *Antiquae musicae auctores septem, Graece et Latine*, 2 vols. (Amsterdam, 1652). Rousseau used Meibomius' collection as his major source on ancient music.

53. Theon of Smyrna (second century A.D.), *Mathematics Useful for Reading Plato*, II.xiii (Barker, II, 213).

54. For Rousseau's explanation of the Monocord, see the article SOUND [*Son*], translated below.

55. "Meaning" translates "*sens*," which can also mean "sense" or "sensation." Rousseau's argument is that, through melody, music is a kind of language.

56. Rousseau gives a very rough paraphrase of d'Alembert, *Eléments de musique théoretique et pratique* (2nd ed.; 1762), Book I, chap. 2, pp. 22 ff.

57. That is, the "leading tone" (*note sensible*) is so called because it causes to the key to be pereived (*fait sentir*).

58. Charles-Henri de Blainville (1711–1769) was a cellist, composer, and musical theorist whose *Essai sur le troisième mode* was published in 1751 and who at the same time presented a concert as an example of his theory at the *Concert Spirituel* at the Tuileries palace. See a letter from Rousseau to Raynal on hearing the concert, May 30, 1751 (Leigh, II, 155–159). See also a letter from Blainville to Rousseau, September 1751 (Leigh, II, 164–166).

59. Pseudo-Euclid (c. 300 B.C.), *Elements of Geometry*; Ptolemy, *Harmonics*, II.10–11 (Barker, II, 336–340).

60. Pseudo-Plutarch, *De musica*, 1141c–1142a (Barker, I, 235–238). *De musica* was formerly attributed to Plutarch. The dialogue contains a synopsis of Pherecrates' (c. 440–420 B.C.) play *Chiron*, in which Music, dressed as a woman, complains that instead of commanding poetry as of old, now she is stripped of her rightful place and accustomed power.

61. Alypius (third or fourth century A.D.), *Eisagoge*.
62. Giovanni Battisti Doni (1595–1647) was an Italian classicist, philologist, and musical theorist who devoted himself to the rediscovery of Greek music.
63. "Morals" translates the French "*moeurs*," which has the broad sense of customs or mores. See Plato, *Republic*, III.398c–399e.
64. Pseudo-Euclid (c. 300 B.C.), *Elements of Geometry*. Aristoxenus, *Elementa Harmonica*, II.37–38 (Barker, II, 153–154).
65. Ptolemy, *Harmonics*, II.7–11 (Barker, II, 331–340).
66. Guido of Arezzo (991–c. 1033), sometimes called "Aretino," was one of the most influential musical theorists of the Middle Ages. He developed a system of precise pitch notation by lines and spaces and developed a method of sight-singing relying on the syllables *ut, re, mi, fa, sol, la, si*, which he derived from a hymn to St. John and which is known as the Aretinian system.
67. Abbé Sébastien de Brossard, *Dictionnaire de musique, contenant une explication des termes grecs, latins, italiens, et françois* (1703), s.v., "*Modo*," "*Tempo*," and "*Prolazione*."
68. The first word in this sentence that is translated "scale" is "*gamme*," which is the "natural" scale derived from just intonation, while the second word translated "scale" is "*échelle*," which is any scale, "natural" or tempered. The word translated as "scale" in the next paragraph is "*gamme*."
69. Christiaan Huygens (1629–1695), the physicist and astronomer, also wrote a work on music, the *Novus cyclus harmonicus* (1661).
70. Orpheus was a mythical or semimythical musician, poet, and mystic. Terpander was a Greek musician and poet of the seventh century B.C. Stesichorus was a Greek lyric poet of about the sixth or seventh century B.C.
71. Boethius (fifth century A.D.), *De Institutione Musica*.
72. Aristides Quintilianus (third or fourth century A.D.), *De Musica* I.4, where music is defined as "knowledge of what is appropriate in sounds and in the movements of bodies."
73. Athanasius Kircher, *Prodomus Coptus Aegyptiacus* (1635), 131, 138. Diodorus Siculus (c. 80–c. 21 B.C.) discusses the invention of music by Hermes in his *General History*, I.i.16.
74. For the relationship between speech and song, see *Essay on the Origin of Languages*, chaps. XII and XIV, translated above.
75. Porphyry (c. 232–c. 300 A.D.), *Commentary on the Harmonics of Ptolemy*, I.1.
76. Rousseau's reference is unclear.
77. Hesychius (fifth century A.D.), *Lexicon*.
78. The modern musician to whom Rousseau refers is Rameau, who argues in his *Observations on Our Instinct for Music*, and other works, that music is the "mother" of all the sciences and arts (see p. 177 above).
79. Diodorus Siculus (first century B.C.–first century A.D.), *General History*, I.i.16.
80. Lucretius, *De rerum natura*, V.1379–1383: "But imitating the flowing voices of birds with the mouth was long in use before men could try with tuneful song to enchant the ear; and Zephyr's whistling through hollow reeds first taught rustic men to blow through shepherd's hollow pipes."
81. Chiron the centaur was the legendary teacher of Achilles. Demodocus was a

blind epic singer mentioned in Homer's *Odyssey* (IX.44 ff.). Hermes was the Greek messenger God. Orpheus was a mythical or semimythical musician, poet, and mystic. Phemius was a renowned epic singer mentioned in Homer's *Odyssey* (XI, XVI). Terpander was a Spartan musician and poet of the seventh century B.C. (Lycurgus was the semilegendary refounder of Sparta). Thaletas was a Spartan aeolist and musician of the seventh century B.C. Thamyris was a mythical epic singer from Thrace discussed in the pseudo-Plutarchian *De Musica* (1132a–b).

82. Rousseau's general source is the pseudo-Plutarchian, *De Musica*, 1141c–1142a. Lasus (b. c. 548–545 B.C.) was born in Hermione and lived at the court of Hipparchus, tyrant of Athens, where he composed hymns and dithyrambs. Melanippides (c. 480–c. 414 B.C.) was an innovative composer of dithyrambs. Philoxenus (c. 435–380 B.C.) was an innovative composer of dithyrambs. Timotheus (c. 450–c. 360 B.C.) was an innovative composer of dithyrambs and music for the cithar. Phrynnis (b. c. 475 B.C.) was an aulist and citharist and leading innovator of the period. Epigonus (sixth century B.C.) was a musician who was said to have invented a forty-stringed instrument called an Epigoneion. Lysander (sixth century B.C.) was a musician and citharist said to have instituted solo cithar playing. Simicus is unknown except for it being assumed that the thirty-five-stringed instrument called a "simicion" was named after him. Diodorus (fifth century B.C.), known also as Pronomus, was a famous aulist who was the first to play all of the harmonia on the same aulos.

83. For Lasus, Epigonus, and Simmicus, see the previous note.

84. For Diodorus and Timotheus, see note 82 above.

85. Plato, *Republic*, IV.424c: "For never are the ways of music moved without the greatest political laws being moved" (trans. Bloom). See also III.398c–402a.

86. Aristotle, *Politics*, VIII.5–7. "Morals" in this sentence and the next one translates "*moeurs*," which has a broader sense of customs or mores.

87. Polybius, *Histories*, IV.20–21.

88. Athenaeus, *Deipnosophistae*, 626a–629c.

89. For Timotheus, see note 82 above. Rousseau's source for the example of King Eric of Denmark and the examples in this and the following several paragraphs is Chamber's *Cyclopedia* (1741–1743), the model for Diderot's *Encyclopedia*.

90. For Rousseau's discussion of the supposed cure for tarantula bites through music, see *Essay on the Origin of Languages*, chap. XV, translated above. See also the article "*Tarantule*" in the *Encyclopédie*.

91. Robert Boyle (1627–1691), the great chemist and physicist, also wrote on music and acoustics.

92. Daniel Georg Morhoff (1639–1691) was a philologist who also wrote on music.

93. Athanasius Kircher (1601–1680) was an influential musical theorist and mathematician.

94. For Mersenne, see note 27 above.

95. For Boyle, see note 91 above.

96. John Wallis (1616–1703) was a highly influential English mathematician who also wrote on music, specifically on the phenomenon of resonance and the division of the octave.

97. Pierre-Jean Burette, "Dissertation sur la Mélopée de l'ancienne musique" (1729).

98. Isaac Vossius (1618–1689) was a Dutch theologian, philosopher, and scientist whose *De poematum cantu et viribus rhythmi* was delivered as a lecture at Oxford in 1673.

99. Rousseau appears to refer to his *Essay on the Origin of Languages*, which was not published until after his death.

100. Rousseau presents two tunes published by Kircher in his *Musurgia Universalis* (1650). The first is the beginning of Pindar's first Pythian Ode, written in 470 B.C. to celebrate the chariot race victory of the tyrant Hiero of Aetna (later of Syracuse), and is now generally thought to be a forgery. The Greek text Rousseau takes from Kircher contains several errors, which have not been corrected in the figures reproduced in the text. The second is an Ode to Nemesis, now attributed to Mesomedes, a contemporary of Hadrian (second century A.D.).

Their translations follow:

Ode by Pindar

O golden lyre, jointly possessed by Apollo and
violet-tressed Muses; which the footstep hears, as it begins the festivities,
and whose orders the singers obey,
whenever you make ready with quivering strings to strike up the prelude to
   the chorus leader's overture.
You lull even the warring thunderbolt [of everlasting fire].

Hymn to Nemesis

Nemesis, winged one who tilts life's balance, dark-eyed
goddess, daughter of Justice, who checks the proud
neighing of mortals [with your adamant bit . . .]

101. See Jean-Baptiste du Halde, *Description de la Chine*, 4 vols. (1735), III, 267; Chardin, *Voyages en Perse*, 4 vols. (1735), II, 114; Mersenne, *Harmonie universelle* (1636), II, ii. Mersenne's source is Jean de Léry, *Histoire d'un voyage fait en la terre de Brésil dite Amérique* (1611), 174, 315, 322.

102. Boethius (fifth century A.D.), *De Institutione Musica*.

103. Pope Gregory the Great (c. 540–604) is credited with developing the plainchant, or "Gregorian chant," and collecting antiphons, that is, psalms or verses sung responsively.

104. For Guido de Arezzo see note 66 above.

105. Kircher, *Musurgia universalis* (1650), 44.

106. Jehan des Murs (c .1300–c. 1350) was a widely influential musical theorist of the later Middle Ages best known for his treatment of musical proportions and mensural notation. The major work attributed to him, the *Speculum musicae*, was actually written by Jacques de Liège (c. 1260–c. 1330). The editors have not been able to identify the source of the claim by the Swiss poet and painter Salomon Gessner that Jehan des Murs was English. The claim by Giovanni Andrea Bontempi that Jehan des Murs was Perugian (*Perugino*), like Bontempi himself, instead of Parisian (*Parigino*) is from his *Istoria musica* (1695), 199.

107. Lasus (c. 548–545 B.C.) lived at the court of Hipparchus, tyrant of Athens,

where he composed hymns and dithyrambs. Aristoxenus (fourth century B.C.) was the most important and influential musical theorist of ancient Greece. The major musical works once attributed to the great mathematician Euclid (fourth–third century B.C.), are no longer thought to have been written by him. Aristides Quintilianus (c. second century A.D.) was the author of an important treatise on music that follows the Pythagorian system. Alypius (third or fourth century A.D.) is the fullest source for our knowledge of Greek musical scales. Gaudentius (c. second century A.D.) was a Greek musical theorist. Nicomachus (c. 100 A.D.) was a neo-Pythagorian mathematician and musical theorist. Baccheius Geron (c. third century A.D.) was author of a dialogue on music that largely follows Aristoxenian principles.

108. For Meibom (or Meibomius) see note 54 above.

109. The dialogue *De musica* once attributed to the philosopher and historian Plutarch (first–second century A.D.), is no longer thought to have been written by him. Ptolemy (c. 108–c. 165 A.D.) wrote an important treatise on music. Manuel Bryennius (fourteenth century A.D.) was a Byzantine scholar and musical theorist.

110. Boethius (fifth century A.D.), the philosopher, also wrote on music. Martianus Capella, the author of a didactic treatise on the arts, Aurelianus Cassiodorus, historian and writer on education, and St. Augustine, the great philosopher and theologian, all lived around the fifth century A.D.

111. Gioseffo Zarlino (1517–1590) was an Italian composer and important musical theorist. Francisco de Salinas (1513–1590) was a Spanish organist and musical theorist. Valgulio has not been identified by the editor. Vincenzo Galilei (Rousseau mistakenly writes Galileo) (c. 1520–1591) was a Florentine musical theorist and composer, father of the famous scientist, who was himself also interested in music. Girolamo Mei (b. 1519) was a Florentine humanist and historian of Greek music. Giovanni Battista Doni (1595–1647) was a classicist and musical theorist. Athanasius Kircher (1601–1680) was an influential musical theorist and mathematician. Antoine Parran (1587–1650) was a French composer and musical theorist. Claude Perrault (b. 1613) was a French scientist who wrote on acoustics. John Wallis (1616–1703) was a highly influential English mathematician who also wrote on music, specifically on the phenomenon of resonance and the division of the octave. René Descartes (1596–1650), the great French philosopher, also wrote a work on music. William Holder (1616–1696) was an English mathematician and musician. Pietro Mengoli was an Italian musical theorist of the same period. Alexander Malcolm (1685–1763) was a Scottish mathematician and musical theorist whose work synthesized the work of Kircher, Mersenne, Descartes, and others. Pierre-Jean Burette (1665–1747) was a French author who wrote particularly on ancient Greek music. Francesco Antonio Vallotti (1697–1780) was an Italian composer and musical theorist. Giuseppi Tartini (1692–1770) was an Italian musician, teacher, and musical theorist much admired by Rousseau. Jean-Philippe Rameau (1683–1764) was the most influential French composer and musical theorist of that time. D'Alembert's *Eléments de musique théoretique et pratique* (1st ed.; 1752) popularized Rameau's musical theories.

112. Compare to Aristotle, *Poetics*, chaps. 1–3, 1147a9–1148b3.

113. See Aristotle, *Poetics*, chaps. 1–6, 1447a9–1450b20.

114. Rousseau discusses the valets in Molière's comedies in a letter to Georges-Louis Le Sage père (1 July, 1754; Leigh, II.1–3): "If Molière consulted his servant, it is doubtless with respect to the *Medecin malgré lui*, regarding Nicole's sallies and Sosie's and Cléantis' quarrels. But unless Molière's servant was a very extraordinary person, I would indeed wager that this great man did not consult him with regard to *Misanthrope* nor *Tartuffe*, nor concerning the beautiful scene between Alcméne and Amphitrion." For a discussion of these comedies, see Rousseau's *Letter to d'Alembert on the Theatre* (Bloom, 34–46, and on the valets in particular, 36). Pradon (c. 1632–c. 1698) was a French tragic dramatist of the late eighteenth century who was often compared critically to Corneille, his great contemporary.

115. "*Merveilleux*" is a term often used in discussing classical French opera, and refers to the supernatural or magical element so often used in such operas and employed by means of elaborate stage machinery.

116. Apostolo Zeno (1668–1750) was an Italian librettist and literary scholar who began a reform in the form and content of the libretto which separated the spheres of drama and music. His "student" was Pietro Metastasio (1698–1782), the Italian poet and very popular librettist who succeeded Zeno at the Imperial Court in Vienna.

117. For Vinci, Leo, and Pergolesi, see note 19 above.

118. The Fairs were annual fairs at which theater troupes gave plays.

119. This paragraph and the previous one are variations of passages in the article IMITATION [*Imitation*], translated above, as well as in the *Essay on the Origin of Languages*, chap. XVI, translated above.

120. "Opera buffa" originated as a two-act play inserted between the three acts of a tragic opera and was gradually performed on its own.

121. *Dictionnaire de l'Académie françoise* (4th ed.; 1762), s.v. "*Récitatif*."

122. Nicola Porpora (1686–1768) was a Neopolitan composer of vocal music and opera.

123. Tartini, *Trattato di musica secondo la vera scienza* (1754). Here is a more literal translation of the passage:

> In the fourteenth year of this century in the Drama which was performed in Ancona there was at the beginning of the third Act a line of Recitative, not accompanied by any instrument other than the Bass, by which, as much in our professors as in every other listener, was produced such and so much a commotion of the soul, which everyone looking into one another's faces could see by the evident change of color it produced in all of ours. The effect was not of plaints (I well remember that the speech was of anger [or: contempt]); but of a certain rigor and chilling in the blood which caused the soul's turmoil. Thirteen times the Drama was performed, and every time the same effect universally followed; of which a palpable sign of the advent of this high point was the silence with which every Listener awaited to to enjoy the effect.

124. Theon of Smyrna (second century A.D.), *Mathematics Useful for Reading Plato*, II.xii. Lasus of Hermione (c. 548–545 B.C.) was a pioneering poet and composer of hymns and dithyrambs; Hipassus of Metapontum was an early Pythagorean.

125. Nicomachus, *Enchiridion*, chap. 6 (Barker, II, 256); Censorinus (third century A.D.), *De die natali*, X.viii.

126. Vincenzo Galilei, *Dialogo della musica antica e moderna* (1602), 104.

127. Rameau, *Génération harmonique*, 8 ff. (Jacobi, III, 18 ff.).

128. Pietro Mengoli, *Speculazioni di musica* (1670), Speculatione quarta.

129. Jean-Jacques Dortous de Mairan, "Discours sur la Propagation du Son dans les différent Tons qui le modifient," *Histoire de l'Académie Royale des Sciences* (1737; publ. 1740).

130. Rousseau takes Halley's and Flamstead's report from Diderot, "Principes généraux d'acoustique," the first of his *Mémoires sur différens sujets de mathématiques* (1748). La Condamine's report comes from his *Relation abrégée d'un voyage fait à l'intérieur de l'Amerique méridionale* (1745). A toise is about six and one half feet. Pierre Gassendi's and Marin Mersenne's experiment is from Gassendi, *Syntagmatis Philosophici* (1658), 418. William Derham's experiments are recounted in his "Experimenta et Observationes de *Soni Motu* aliisque ad id attinentibus, *Philosophical Transactions* (1708), no. 313, art.1, and taken by Rousseau from Diderot's "Principes généraux d'acoustique" (1748; published as the first of his *Mémoires sur différens sujets de mathématiques*), 239.

131. Leonhard Euler, *Tentamen novae theoriae musicae, ex certissimis harmoniae principii dilucide expositae* (1739), as reported by Diderot, "Principes généraux d'acoustique" (1748; published as the first of his *Mémoires sur différens sujets de mathématiques*).

132. Abbé Sébastien de Brossard, *Dictionnaire de musique, contenant une explication des termes grecs, latins, italiens, et françois* (1703).

133. "Aspect" translates "*air*," which can also mean "tune."

134. "Strings" translates "*cordes*," which can also be translated "pitches." One unaltered string produces one principal pitch.

135. Ptolemy (c. 108–165 A.D.) was an astronomer, mathematician, and musical theorist. Didymus (c. 63 B.C.–10 A.D.) was a grammarian and musical theorist. both were discussed by Brossard in his *Dictionnaire de musique*, s.v. "*Temperamento*."

136. Guido of Arezzo (c. 991–c.1033), one of the most influential musical theorists of the Middle Ages, as cited by Athanasius Kircher, *Musurgia universalis* (1650), 215.

137. Mersenne, *Harmonie universelle* (1636); Étienne Loulié, *Nouveau système de musique ou nouvelle division de moncorde* (1698), cited by Brossard, *Dictionnaire de musique*, s.v. "Temperamento." Rameau discusses his theory of temperament at length in his *Génération harmonique* (1737), chap. 7 (Jacobi, III, 52–66).

138. Rameau, *Nouveau système de musique théoretique* (1726), 107 ff. (Jacobi, II, 117 ff.)

139. Rameau, *Génération harmonique* (1737), 94 ff. (Jacobi, III, 61 ff.)

140. François Couperin, "le Grand" (1668–1733), French organist and composer of music for harpsischord and of sacred music. Mersenne, *Harmonie universelle* (1646), Book I, prop. xiv. Jean Gallé was a mathematician who was contracted in 1636 to teach the Liège organ-builder André Severin how to construct a keyboard with equal temperament (see Mersenne, *Harmonie universelle*, Book III, props. i, viii).

141. "Beats" translates "*battements*." See note 25 above.

142. Mersenne, *Harmonie universelle* (1636), Book I, prop. xiv.

143. Rousseau appears to refer to Joseph-François Duché de Vancy (1668–1704), a tragic poet and composer.

144. See note 26 to *The Principle of Melody*, translated above.

145. See *Letter on French Music*, pp. 154–156 above. Rousseau's *Devin du village* was produced in 1752, and the *Letter on French Music*, which was written around the beginning of 1753, was published in November 1753.

146. Charles Duclos' article "Déclamation des anciens" is found in vol. 4 of the *Encyclopedia* (1754), 686–691. The citation is from p. 688.

147. Denis Dodart (1634–1707) was a French physician and academician who wrote on music. The reference is to his "Mémoire sur les causes de la voix humaine, et de ses différens tons," *Mémoires de l'Académie royal des sciences* (1700), 244–293.

148. The Concert Spirituel was the annual concert given at the Tuilleries palace. The Opera refers to the Paris Opera.

149. Rousseau alludes to the famous Venetian *Scuole* or *ospidale*, hospices for young women who were trained in music. Rousseau recounts a visit to one of the four *ospidale* in his *Confessions*, VII, (*Collected Writings*, V, 264–265).

150. Baldassare Ferri (1610–1680) was an Italian castrato who sang largely in Poland and Austria. He was eulogized by the great castrato, composer, and musical theorist Giovanni Andrea Bontempi, in whose works Rousseau probably read about Ferri.

EDITOR'S NOTES TO
Letter to Mr. Burney and Fragments of Observations on Gluck's "Alceste"

This translation is based on the text found in Pléiade, V, 431–457. The Pléiade edition is based on the autograph manuscript (Neuchâtel MS R. 63). The letter and the accompanying observations on Gluck's *Alceste* are in fragmentary form and appear to have been written about October 1777. It is uncertain whether Rousseau ever sent the letter to Burney. Rousseau gave the manscript of the letter to Pierre Prévost, of the Royal Academy of Sciences and Belles-Lettres of Berlin, who sent it to du Peyrou and Moultou to be published. The observations on Gluck's *Alceste* were first published by Grimm in the *Correspondance littéraire* (March–May 1778) and were then published along with the letter to Burney by du Peyrou and Moutou in their 1781 *Oeuvres posthumes de Rousseau*, as part of their *Collection complète des oeuvres de Jean-Jacques Rousseau*. A separate modern edition in Rousseau's *Correspondance complète* (Leigh, XL, 146–158) has also been consulted for the translation.

Charles Burney (1726–1814) was an English organist and historian of music who made several journeys to the continent to assemble the contents for his general history of music. His trips resulted in his *Present State of Music in France and Italy* (1771) and *The Present State of Music in Germany, the Netherlands and United Provinces* (1773). The first volume of his *General History of Music* appeared in 1776, and Rousseau received it from a friend in July 1776. Burney's whole project was completed, in four volumes, in 1789. Rousseau was among the original subscribers to Burney's *General History of Music*.

1. This is the title given at the head of Rousseau's letter by Prévost. See the introductory editorial remarks above.

2. Rousseau refers to his *Plan Regarding New Signs for Music* and his *Dissertation on Modern Music*, translated above. Since Rousseau did not possess any copies of his *Dissertation*, it appears that he intended to send Burney some version of his *Plan*.

3. The manuscript of the letter includes the following continuation, which is not contained in the original edition: "You will find among the examples, Sir, under the sign A, a sample of this manner of adapting the bass by numerals to the ordinary notation for the song." Rousseau may be referring to the examples published as part of his *Dissertation on Modern Music* (and included with the translation of that work above), but in any case the manuscript letter to Burney contains no such examples.

4. Burney, *General History of Music*, ed. F. Mercier (1935; 2nd ed., 1957), I, 342–343.

5. Rousseau also discusses the direction of writing in his *Essay on the Origin of Languages*, chap. V, translated above.

6. "Movements" translates "*mouvements*." "*Mouvement*" can mean tempo or meter, and sometimes both, so the cognate "movement" has been used consistently to render the term.

7. The manuscript of the letter includes the following continuation, which is not contained in the original edition: "All this will be better explained by the examples in notation which I am joining to this writing, under the sign B." See note 3 above.

8. The manuscript of the letter includes the following continuation, which is not contained in the original edition: "You will also find examples of this joined below under the sign C." See note 3 above.

9. Rousseau transcribes the same tune on a Pindaric ode at the end of the article MUSIC [*Musique*] in his *Dictionary of Music*, translated above.

10. Rousseau is the author of the *Devin du Village*, the *Letter on French Music*, and the *Dictionary of Music*. For his discussions of the "unity of melody," see *Letter on French Music*, p. 155 above, and the article UNITY OF MELODY [*Unité de la mélodie*] in the *Dictionary of Music*, translated above.

11. Rousseau apparently wrote his comments on Gluck's *Alceste* in the winter of 1774–1775. Gluck left Paris in March 1775, taking the score with him.

12. Gluck's Italian *Alceste* was first performed in Vienna, December 16, 1767, and was published there in 1768.

13. Gluck wrote the Italian version of *Alceste* on a libretto by Calzabigi in 1767. He later wrote a French version of the work on a libretto by Du Roullet, which was first performed at the Paris Opera, April 23, 1776. The Italian version of *Alceste* premiered in Paris on July 30, 1776.

In the Dedication to the Italian *Alceste* (1769), Gluck explains:
> When I undertook to put the Opera *Alceste* into music, I planned to avoid

all the abuses which the mistaken vanity of Singers and the excessive complaisance of Composers had introduced into Italian Opera and which have made of the most solemn and most beautiful of all spectacles the most tiresome and most ridiculous. I sought to reduce the music to its true function, that of seconding the poetry in order to fortify the expression of the feelings and of the interest of situations without interrupting the action and dampening it by superfluous ornaments. I believed that music should add to the poetry what is added to a correct and well-composed design by the vivacity of colors and the harmonious concord of light and shadows, which serve to animate the figures without altering their contours.

14. This is the title given at the head of the following fragmentary writings by the original editors of the work. See note 1 above.

15. That is, Gluck's librettist, Ranieri de Calzabigi (1713–1795), who also wrote the libretti for Gluck's *Orfeo ed Euridice* and other pieces.

16. Gluck's *Alceste* is patterned on Euripides' *Alcestis*.

17. In the Italian version of *Alceste*, Act II begins with a scene in which Alceste is in a forest consecrated to the infernal deities and attended by a pantomine of demons. The following scene represents a room in the royal palace where a joyous entertainment celebrating the return of the king is in progress.

18. Rousseau suggested that Gluck introduce Alceste's lamentation, "O Gods, sustain my courage, I can no longer hide the extent of my griefs," into the midst of the joyous entertainment in Act II, Scene 1, in order to provide a striking contrast.

19. A break in the manuscript occurs here, represented here and elsewhere below by a space. The Pléiade edition does not contain these spaces, but instead indicates manuscript breaks in editorial notes.

20. Rousseau seems to refer to the enharmonic genre. See his analysis of Gluck's *Orfeo* in his *Extract from an Answer by the Underlaborer to His Frontman*, translated below.

21. Rousseau makes the same point in the articles OPERA [*Opéra*] and RECITATIVE [*Récitatif*] in the *Dictionary of Music*, pp. 449 and 460 above.

22. Rousseau defines the obligatory recitative as a recitative intermixed with melody played by the orchestra, thereby so to speak obliging the recititant and the orchestra to be attentive to and to await one another, and cites his own *Le Devin du village* as the first use of the device in French music (OBLIGATORY RECITATIVE [*Récitatif obligé*], Pléiade, V, 1012–1013).

23. The passage in brackets is not found in Rousseau's manuscript and was apparently added by the editors of the first edition.

24. Rousseau's manuscript has a break at this point and is continued in Prévost's handwriting. Passages in Prévost's handwriting were put into italics by the original editors, who relate that Prévost told them he wrote these passages under Rousseau's direct supervision. The editors of the Pléiade edition follow the practice.

25. Rousseau's *Pygmalion*, which he calls a "lyric scene," was written about 1762 and first performed in April 1770, then at the Paris Opera in March 1772, then at the Comédie-Française in October 1772, and finally reprised, without Rousseau's con-

sent, at the Comédie-Française in October 1775. The work was published in 1771, and, contrary to Rousseau's statement, would actually become a very influential and much discussed work, especially in Germany.

26. See Rousseau, *Dictionary of Music*, OBLIGATORY RECITATIVE [*Récitatif obligé*] (Pléiade, V, 1012–1013): "Until now, French Music has not known how to make any use of the *obligatory recitative*. Some idea has tried to be given of it in a scene of the *Devin du village*; it seems that the public has found that a lively situation thus treated becomes more interesting. . . ." Rousseau is the author of the *Devin du village*, which was first produced in 1752.

27. The passage in brackets is not found in Rousseau's manuscript and was apparently added by the editors of the first edition.

28. Gluck's *Alceste* (Act I, Scene 1) opens with the Herald's announcement of the impending death of King Admetus:
Popoli che dolenti della sorte d'Admeto
in lui piangete più il padre
che il regnante, udite:
[People, who are mourning the fate of Ademtus
who weep for him more as a father
than as ruler, hear me:]

29. This occurs at the beginning of Act I, Scene 2.

30. The Infernal Deities address Alceste in a dark wood sacred to the gods of the underworld (Act II, Scene 2):
E vuoi morire, oh misera,
quando di gioventù
t'adorna il fiore?
[And you wish to die, unhappy woman,
while the flower of youth
still adorns you?]

31. Still Act II, Scene 2 (see the previous note):
Altro non puo raccogliere
[No other can receive.]

32. In the original edition of this work, the editors added at this point: "(*The end of an observation on the chorus* Fuggiamento *the beginning of which is lost*.)" "*Fuggiamento*" should read "*Fuggiamo*." There are numerous errors in the Italian in the original edition. For Rousseau's discussion of the chorus "*fuggiamo*," see just below.

33. Rousseau refers to the chorus "*fuggiamo*" (Act I, Scene 4) which he discusses just below, where the psalmody on the word "*fuggiamo*" comes to be superimposed over the principal chorus. The passage in brackets is added by the editors of the Pléiade edition.

34. Rousseau here analyzes Act I, Scene 5, where the chorus serves as a congregation and Alceste replies to its reaction to the oracle that someone must die if King Admetus is to live:
Congregation:
Che annunzio funesto
di nuovo terrore!

Fuggiamo, fuggiamo
da questo soggiorno d'orrore.
Alceste:
Ove so, che ascoltai!
Morrà lo sposo...
Misero Admeto! Prence infelice!
Ove trovar chi voglia
per prolungari i giorni,
sè stesso e i giorni suoi porre in oblio?
V'è chi t'ami a tal segno?
[Congregation:
What a gloomy pronouncement
of fresh terror!
Let us fly, let us fly
from this sojourn of horror.
Alceste:
Where am I, what did I hear?
My husband will die...
Wretched Admetus! Unhappy prince!
Where can someone be found
who, to prolong the days,
would let himself and his days fall into oblivion?
Is there anyone who loves you to such a degree?]

35. Still Act I, Scene 5 (see the previous note):
Ombre, larve, compagne di morte,
no vi chiedo, non voglio pietà....
[Shades, phantoms, companions of death,
I do note ask you, I do not wish for pity....]

36. Rousseau goes back to analyze the song Alceste sings after emerging from the palace (Act I, Scene 2):
Io non chiedo, eterni dei,
tutto il ciel per me sereno.
Ma il mio duol consoli almeno,
consoli almeno qualche raggio di pietà.
Non comprende mali miei....
[I do not ask, eternal gods,
that all heaven should be serene for me.
But at least let some ray
of pity console my grief.
No one understands my sufferings....]

37. See the previous note.

38. *E fa la* is equivalent to the key of E minor.

39. See note 36 above.

40. The editors of the Pléiade edition reproduce Rousseau's musical sketch at the end of the letter instead of here, where it is in Rousseau's manuscript.

41. Rousseau appears to refer to the second, longer recitative of the Grand Priest of Apollo in Act I, Scene 4.

42. Rousseau analyzes the High Priest's sacrifice at the Temple of Apollo (Act I, Scene 3):

Dilegua il nero turbine
che freme al trono intorno.
Oh fa ritrato, Apolline,
col chiaro tuo splendor.
[Dispel the black whirlwind
that roars about the throne.
Oh make it retreat, Apollo,
with your bright splendor.]

43. Rousseau continues to analyze the same scene as above, where the Chorus replies to the High Priest in responsorial fashion (Act I, Scene 3).

44. Rousseau continues to analyze the same scene as above (Act I, Scene 3). The first two lines are given to the chorus by Gluck with the High Priest taking up the last two:

Sai che ramingo ed esule
t'accolse Admeto un giorno,...
... che dell'Anfriso al margine
tu fosti il suo pastor.
[You know that as a wandering exile
Admetus one day received you,...
... that by the shores of the Amphrysus
you were his shepherd.]

45. The Chorus's pantomime (still Act I, Scene 3) is done in dactylic rhyme on a slow tempo.

46. Alceste's recitative (Act I, Scene 4) comes after the interchange between the High Priest and chorus Rousseau has just analyzed:

Nume, eterno, immortal,
se col tuo sguardo...
[Deity, eternal one, immortal one,
if with your glance...

47. Act I, Scene 1. Gluck's Italian *Alceste* includes numerous balletic pieces.

48. See Rousseau, *Dictionary of Music*, s.v. OPERA [*Opéra*], translated above.

49. Evander's recitative is in Act I, Scene 1.

50. The chorus (Act I, Scene 1) is structured like an antiphon, with a "right-hand chorus," associated with the oboes for Admetus, and a "left-hand chorus," associated with the flutes for Alceste.

51. Alceste's recitative (Act I, Scene I) comes immediately after the chorus just analyzed by Rousseau:

Popoli di Tessaglia,
ah mai più giusto fu il vostro pianto;...
[People of Thessaly,
never more justified were your tears;...]

52. Rousseau returns to Alceste's recitative (Act I, Scene 4), which he analyzed above.

53. This fragment and the following ones until the end of the writing were not included in the original edition of the writing.

54. Rousseau refers to the end of one of the arias in the opera. By "misconception," Rousseau means that the movement of the music contradicts the sense of the words or introduces an equivocation. In the Dedication to *Alceste* Gluck remarked: "I did not want to end the *aria* with a misconception for the sole aim of arranging it so that the singer who might want to show off could vary as he pleased a single passage in several ways."

EDITOR'S NOTES TO
Extract from a Response by the Underlaborer to His Frontman

This translation is based on the text found in Pléiade, V, 459–465. The Pléiade text is based on Rousseau's manuscript (Neuchâtel MS. R. 62). The *Extract* was first published by du Peyrou and Moutou in their 1781 *Oeuvres posthumes de Rousseau*, as part of their *Collection complète des oeuvres de Jean-Jacques Rousseau*, and in the same year as part of the *Mémoires pour servir à l'histoire de la révolution opérée dans la musique par M. le Chevalier Gluck* (Bailly, Paris, 1781). Rousseau appears to have written the *Extract* shortly before his *Letter to Burney*, perhaps after seeing the production of the French version of Gluck's *Orfeo* in 1774.

The title of this piece—"*Extrait d'une réponse du Petit Faiseur à son Prête-Nom*"—poses certain difficulties for translation. A "*petit faiseur*" is a sort of apprentice worker or assistant to an artisan or artist, and has been translated here as "underlaborer" in a deliberate evocation of Locke's ironic description of himself in the "Epistle to the Reader" from his *Essay Concerning Human Understanding*. The term "*faiseur*" can also mean "prankster," so Rousseau's allusion in the title to the joke of his piece is lost in translation. A "*prête-nom*" is someone who acts on behalf of the person principally interested, for example a broker or an agent, and in a derogative sense it can mean "frontman," "figurehead," or "straw man." "Frontman" has been chosen to reflect the fact that Rousseau is alluding in the title to charges, including those by Rameau, that he was not himself the composer of his major musical compositions or the author his writings on music, but that he either plagiarized or secretly commissioned the works or portions of them from someone else. He alludes to these charges in the "Editor's Notice" to the collection of songs he entitled *Consolations for My Life's Miseries*, in this case with reference to his lyric scene *Pygmalion*: "Truly if he did not write it, it was because he was not capable of it. My Underlaborer [*petit-Faiseur*] can only blow into pipes; he would have needed a Master Workman [*grand Faiseur*] for it. I know of only M. Gluck who is capable of understanding this work . . ." (Pléiade, V, ed. n. 2 to p. 461). Rousseau presents himself in the *Extract* as both the underlaborer and the frontman.

1. Gluck's *Orfeo ed Euridice* was written on a libretto by Ranieri de Calzabigi (1713–1795), who also wrote the libretti for Gluck's *Alceste* and other pieces. The Italian version premiered in 1762 in Vienna. A later French version, on a translated libretto by P. L. Moline, debuted April 19, 1774, in Paris. The piece in question is near the beginning of Act II, where Orpheus encounters the Furies and tries to charm them with his singing, which they resist with their repetitive "*Nò*"—"No." Patricia Howard offers a reading of the piece in chap. 4 of *G. W. von Gluck, Orfeo*,

ed. Patricia Howard, Cambridge Opera Handbooks (Cambridge: Cambridge University Press, 1981).

2. Rousseau uses the Latin "*stridor*," which means a grating, humming, or whistling noise, as the blowing of the wind, the humming of bees, or even the trumpeting of elephants. The French equivalent—"*strideur*"—was not in use at that time.

3. See Rousseau, *Dictionary of Music*, s.v. ENHARMONIC [*Enharmonique*], translated above.

4. That is, the librettist Calzabigi. See note 1 above.

5. See Rousseau, *Dictionary of Music*, s.v. TEMPERAMENT [*Tempérament*], translated above. Berlioz disagreed with Rousseau's analysis: "Gluck has established an enharmonic relationship between two parts in an *indeterminate* key. I refer to the passage about which J. J. Rousseau and others have written so many foolish things on account of the difference which they believed existed between the G flat and the F sharp" (*Grand traité d'instrumentation et d'orchestration*, quoted by Howard, in *Orfeo*, 88).

6. Rousseau's description here of the "Frontman" matches his self-description in the *Confessions* and his other autobiographical writings, above all in his *Dialogues*, where he speaks of his dual reputation as two persons: "the first—timid to the point of stupidity—scarcely dared to show his friends the works of his leisure time. The second—with an even more stupid impudence—proudly and publicly attributed to himself the works of others about the things he understood least . . ." (First Dialogue; *Collected Writings*, I, 15).

7. This phrase—"*ne nous brouillons jamais ensemble*"—also suggests that they should never be confused with one another.

Index

Aarsleff, Hans, 569n22
Academy of Sciences, xv, 21, 23, 468
Adolfati, Andrea, 108n*, 116, 121, 124, 532n9, 536n4, 537(nn18, 19)
Alembert, Jean Le Rond d', xix, xxxvi, 110n*, 276, 286, 332, 337, 386, 409, 423, 447, 517(nn27, 28, 32), 523(nn113, 120), 532n15, 533n21, 538(nn30, 35), 548n54, 551, 553n11, 554(nn25, 30, 31), 555n35, 557n49, 558n63, 560n20, 564n11, 565n26, 566n30, 567n16, 577n119, 580n157, 581n2, 582n33, 585n7, 586n18, 587n29, 588(nn37, 44), 589(nn49, 56)
Alexander the Great, 538n31
Alypius, 447, 592n107
Amphion, 441
Anacharsis, 342, 582n16
Andrastus, 415, 589n52
Ariosto, Ludivico, 124, 532n9, 538n23
Aristotle, xxxvii, 99, 441, 447, 472, 530n3, 535n19, 538n31, 554n27, 562n6, 567n11, 575n87, 577n114, 580n156, 593(nn112–113)
Aristoxenus, 219, 416, 429, 447, 472, 480, 554(nn19, 27), 562n9, 577n116, 587n32, 589n50, 590n64, 592n107
Armand, 114n**, 534n42
Armide (lyric-tragedy by Lully), 168–173, 184–196, 511–514, 526(nn2, 4), 530(nn5, 7, 11–12), 532(nn12, 14), 545n20, 548n53, 549n8, 554n16,
Arnauld, Antoine, 571n45, 586n13
Athenaeus, 214, 442, 567n14, 591n88
Augustine, Saint, 447, 574n79, 593n110
Auletta, Pietro, 545n26, 546n30

Babbitt, Irving, 525n140
Baccheius Geron, 415, 447, 589n51, 592n107
Bambini, Eustachio, xxi, 135, 136, 540(nn2, 11), 547n44
Bass, Allan, 520n76
Batteux, Charles, 413, 589n48
Baud-Bovy, Samuel, 524n139
Berlioz, Hector, 518n44, 603n5
Bernacchi, Antonio Maria, 117, 118, 118n*, 121, 123, 535n18, 537n5
Bernier, Nicholas, 28, 324, 526n3, 578n133
Blainville, Charles-Henri, 425–427, 589n58

Blom, Eric, 524n133
Boethius, 214, 439, 445, 447, 554n18, 590n71, 593n110
Boileau, Nicholas, 99, 121, 124, 530n3, 536n2, 537n21
Bontempi (Buontempi), Giovanni-Andrea Angelini, 267, 330, 562n21, 580n153
Bossuet, Jean-Bénigne, 530n3
Botot, Marie-Anne (Mlle Dangeville), 114n**, 534n42
Bouchardon, M. de, 113n‡‡, 533n22
Boyle, Robert, 443, 591(nn91, 95)
Briseux, Charles-Étienne, 177n*, 549n5
Broussard, Abbé Sebastien de, 369, 432, 470, 590n67, 595(nn132, 135, 137)
Bryennius, Manuel, 447, 593n109
Buffon, Georges Louis Leclerc, Compte de, 576n102
Buonmmattei, Benedette, 303n*, 572n63
Buononcini (Bononcini), Giovanni, 118n*, 157n*, 535n21, 546n37
Burney, Charles, xli, 524n138, 596, 597n4
Burrette, Pierre-Jean, 319, 443, 444, 447, 577n118, 578n122, 592n97, 593n111
Butler, H. E., 577n116

Cadmus, 298, 441
Caffarelli (Gaetano Majorano), 167n*, 548n52
Caïn (Lekain), Henri Louis, 113n§§§, 534n37
Caldara, Antonio, 547n50
Calzagibi, Raniero di, xl, xli
Campion, François, 199, 551n3
Campra, André, 530n7, 547n51, 554n16
Capella, Martianus, 299n†, 336, 447, 571n47, 577n114, 584n1, 593n110
Capua, Rinaldo da, 133, 376, 539n1, 540n13, 546n30, 586n19
Caraffe, 137, 541n15
Cassiodorus, 447, 593n110
Castel, Father Louis-Bertrand, 231, 556n19, 578n123, 579n136
Censorin, 464
Chardin, Jean-Baptiste-Simon, 292–298, 298n*, 444, 568n18, 570(nn32, 37), 592n101
Charondas, 341, 582n15

605

Christensen, Thomas, 517n29, 519n65, 551n1, 557n36, 564n9, 587n21
Cicero, 302n*, 447, 547n43, 572n58
Cleophon, 342, 582n18
Cocci, Gioacchino, 153, 545n25, 546n26
Condamine, M. de La. *See* La Condamine, M. de
Condillac, Étienne Bonnot, Abbé de, 574n74, 576n103, 577n112
Corelli, Arcangelo, 28, 157n*, 158, 283, 376, 526n3, 546n35, 565n24, 586n19
Corneille, Thomas, 126, 136, 530n6, 537n21, 538n26
Cranston, Maurice, xxiii, 516n4, 518(nn38–39, 43), 519(nn50, 52, 58, 60), 520n74, 524n140
Crebillon, Prosper Jolyot de, 333, 581n1
Crocker, Lester G., 570n30

Dacier, Émile, 99, 530n4
Darius, 291
Demodocus, 441, 590n81
Demotz de la Salle, Abbé, 527n12
Derham, William, 468, 595n130
Derrida, Jacques, xvii, 520n76, 521n86
Descartes, René, 381, 447, 568n20, 587n23
Destouches, André-Cardinal, 108n*, 531n1, 532(nn7–8, 14), 536n31, 540n7
Dialogues, xiii, xiv, xl
Dictionary of Music, xvi, xxvi, xxxvi–xxxix, xli, 490, 509, 559n63
Diderot, Denis, xviii, 142n*, 156, 369, 469, 517n32, 532(nn10, 15), 540(nn9–10), 542n5, 545n21, 546n31, 548n53, 558n63, 569n24, 570n34, 581n111, 587n22, 591n99, 595(nn130–131)
Didier, Béatrice, 523(nn121, 124)
Didymus, 472, 595n135
Diodorus Siculus, 260, 437, 440, 441, 561n3, 590(nn73, 79), 591(nn82, 84)
Diogenes, 291
Dionysius, 586n11
Dionysius of Halicarnassus, 302, 371, 586n11
Discourse on the Sciences and Arts, see *First Discourse*
Discourse on the Origin of Equality, see *Second Discourse*
Dissertation on Modern Music, xvi, 21, 597n3
Dodart, Denis, 374, 480–482, 586n16, 596n147
Dolon, 344, 582n22
Donatus, Aeluis, 371, 586n10
Doni, Giovanni Battisti, 447, 590n62
Du Roullet, Marie François Louis Gand Bailli, xl, 524n132, 597n13
Dubos (Du Bos), Jean-Baptiste, Abbé, xxxvii, 157n*, 523n121, 546n37

Duché de Vancy, Joseph-François, 476, 530n7, 531n15, 574n51
Duchet, Michèle, 520n24
Duchez, Marie Elizabeth, xvii, 520(nn73–75), 560, 563n25
Duclos, Charles Pinot, 299, 302, 304, 332n*, 480–481, 571n46, 572n61, 573n66, 580n158, 586n13, 596n146
Dupré, Louis, 113n*, 128, 533n26, 538n33
Durant, 138, 541n17
Durante, Francesco, 376, 406, 586n19, 588n41

Eigeldinger, Jean-Jacques, 523n115
Einstein, Alfred, 524(nn133, 139)
Enharmonic, 181, 183, 219, 251–259, 395, 506–509, 579n141, 584, 603n3
Epigones, 214, 441, 554n18, 591n82
Estève, Pierre, 381, 382, 587n24, 588n46
Euclid (Pseudo-Euclid), 427, 429, 430n*, 447, 589n59, 590n64, 593n107
Euripides, 266, 340n*, 329

Fel, Marie, 107, 113n§, 119, 153, 531n5, 533n29, 534n35, 536n30, 545n24
Ferri, Baldassare, 485, 596n150
Fesch, Marie-Jeanne (Mlle Chevalier), 139, 541n19
First Discourse, xiii, xviii, 108n*, 531, 532n10, 562n13, 573n65
Flamstead, 468, 595n130
Fontenelle, Bernard le Bovier de, 142, 542n6
Frederick the Great, 113, 533n24
French music, xvi–xviii, xxi–xxii, xxxi, 99–107, 116, 121, 126–127, 141–143, 149–153, 157–159, 166–169, 173–176, 303, 408, 498–499

Gagnebin, Bernard, 524n130
Galilei, Vincenzo, 447, 465, 593n111, 595n126
Gallé, Jean, 595n140
Galuppi, Baldasare (Il Buranello), 108n*, 116, 117, 121, 127, 152, 153, 376, 532n9, 536n4, 537n18, 545(nn23, 25), 586n19
Garver, Newton, 521n76
Gassendi, Pierre, 468, 595n130
Gaudentius, 415, 447, 589n51, 592n107
Gaussem, Jeanne (Mlle Gaussin), 114, 534n40
Gessner, Salomon, 352, 447, 583n5, 592n106
Girdlestone, Cuthbert, 518n37
Gluck, Christoph Willibald von, xiii, xxxix, xli, 491–505, 506–509, 524(nn133, 139), 596, 597(nn11–13), 598(nn15–16, 18, 20), 599n28, 602n54
Goudimel, Claude, 157n†, 546n37

Index

Gourevitch, Victor, xliv, 576n101, 577n116
Government, 331–332, 334
Grandval, Charles, 100, 114n§, 530n6, 534n41
Greek music, xxxii–xxxiii, xxxviii, 116, 146, 219, 251–259, 262, 265, 275, 299–301, 318–319, 327–329, 399, 415–417, 428–431, 448–450, 470, 489–500, 579n141, 580n147, 590n62
Gregory, St., 445, 592n103
Grimm, Friedrich Melchior, xx, xli, 158, 518(nn39, 41), 529, 531(nn3–5), 532(nn13, 18), 533(nn21, 30, 32), 534(nn43, 2–3), 535(nn6–10, 12–14, 17, 22), 536(nn27–32), 537n10, 540n9, 547n40, 548n53
Grotius, Hugo, 575(nn87, 89), 576n104
Guido of Arezzo, 22, 34n*, 34–36, 431, 445, 472, 525n2, 527n11, 590n66, 592n104

Halde, Jean-Baptiste du, 444, 592n101
Halley, Edmund, 468, 595n130
Handel, George Frederick (Georg Friederich Händel), 117, 120, 125, 535n15
Hardouin Jean, 301, 571n51
Harmony, xxii, xxxii, xxxiii–xxxvi, xxxiii–xxxiv, xxxviii, 144–145, 158, 160–162, 175, 176, 182, 191–193, 226–232, 235, 263, 265, 268–269, 273–274, 278–281, 321–323, 327–328, 331, 376, 385, 392, 400, 408–413, 436, 439, 442, 448, 450, 451, 454, 523n125, 581n8, 585n7; and melody, xxii–xxvi, 144–145, 175–176, 191–193, 226–228, 231–232, 273–274, 278–280, 322–323, 373–375, 401–402, 477–479
Harvey, Irene, 521n76
Hasse, Johann Adolf, 117, 119, 120, 124n*, 124, 125, 376, 535n11, 537n20, 586n19
Herodotus, 332, 576n111, 570n39
Hesychius, 440, 590n77
Hipassus of Metapontum, 464, 594n124
Hobbes, Thomas, 571n51, 573n72, 574n77, 575n87
Hobson, Marian, 524n129
Holbach, Paul-Henri Dietrich (Thiry), Baron d', 540n4
Holder, William, 447, 593n111
Homer, 121, 131, 266, 300, 301, 329, 340n*, 340–344, 347–348, 441, 539n44, 563n24, 571n51, 574(nn79, 82)
Horace, 99, 291, 530n3, 531n2, 539n42, 541n1, 577n118
Howard, Patricia, 603n1
Hubner, Jean-Jacques, 583n5
Hunt, Thomas Webb, 522n112, 523n118
Huygens, Christiaan, 436, 591n60
Hystaspes, Darius, 441

Imitation, xxxvi, xxxvii, 265, 287, 292, 320, 322–323, 326–327, 329, 337–350, 373, 413–414, 439, 456
Isidore of Seville, 302n*, 570n41, 571n42, 572n59
Italian music, xiv, xvi–xvii, xx–xxii, xxv, 99–108, 115, 116–118, 121–127, 135, 148–154, 157–158, 162–165, 168, 176, 203, 226–227, 230–231, 303, 408

Jansen, Albert, 529, 539
Jeannin, 572n60
Jehan des Murs, 22, 34n*, 267, 330, 447, 525n2, 527n11, 562n21, 580n158, 592n106
Jelyotte, Pierre de, 111, 113n††, 128, 153, 532n16, 533n31, 538n33, 545n24
Jensen, Pamela K., 522n107, 524n139, 529
Jomelli, Niccolo, 119, 153, 376, 406, 541n14, 545n25, 586n19
Julianus, Flavius Claudus (Julian the Apostle), 266, 330, 562n17, 580n51

Kant, Immanuel, xxxix, 524n129
Kavanagh, Thomas, M., 522n109, 583n7
Kiernan, Colm, 519(nn52, 65)
Kintzler, Catherine, 519n65, 523n121, 524n140
Kircher, Athanasius, 231, 437, 443, 444, 445, 447, 556n20, 561n3, 590n73, 591n93, 592n100, 593n111
Kisch, Eve, 522n111
Kleinman, Sydney, 517n16

La Condamine, M. de, 468, 595n130
La Tour, Maurice Quentin de, 113n†††, 534n34
La Poplinière (La Pouplinière), Alexandre-Jean-Joseph Le Riche de, xvii, 556n17
La Bruyère, Jean de, 99, 530(nn3–4)
Laertius, Diogenes, 562n14, 567n11, 580n149
Lalande, Joseph-Jerôme le François de, 584
Lalande, Michel-Richard, 28, 526n3
LaMotte (La Motte), Antoine Houdar, 107n*, 531n1, 532(nn7, 14), 540n7
Lamy, Bernard, 295, 569(nn27, 29)
Lancelot, Nicholas, 571n45, 586n13
Language, xxii, xxiv, xxxviii, 106, 141–142, 144–152, 163–164, 166–167, 260–267, 279, 289–318, 331–336, 371, 421–422, 454, 460–461, 482
Lasus of Hermione, 441, 447, 464, 591(nn82–83), 592n109, 594n124
Latilla, Gaetano, 545n26, 546n27
Launay, Michel, 520n74
Laws, xxxiii, 262, 318
Le Devin du Village, xxi, xl, xli, 479, 490,

518n44, 531n5, 542n3, 588n38, 596n145, 597n10, 599(nn22, 26)
Le Sage, Georges-Louis, 594n114
Le Maître, Jacques-Louis-Nicholas, xiv
Lecat, Claude-Nicholas, 518n35
Legislator, 291
Leibniz, Gottfried Wilhelm, 569n22, 581n2
Leo, Leonardo 119, 151, 376, 406, 453, 490, 535n24, 586n19, 588n41, 594n117
LeRoy, Charles-George, 564n12
Léry, Jean de, 592n101
Les Fêtes de Ramire, xviii
Les Muses Galantes, xvii, xxv, 108n*, 230, 532n10, 556n17
Letter to d'Alembert on the Theater, xxxv, 337, 581n2
Letter on French Music, 479, 490, 519n52, 529, 549n12, 572n56, 573n64, 586n8, 589n47, 596n145, 597n10
Lévi-Strauss, Claude, xxxviii, 523n124
Liège, Jacques de, 525n2, 527n11, 562n21, 580n153, 592n106
Lippman, Edward A., 520n66
Livy, 567n111, 571n43
Locke, John, 569n22, 570n36
Louis XIV, 119, 526n2, 536n25, 546n35
Loulié, Étienne, 472, 595n137
Lowinski, Edward, 524n140
Lucretius, 27, 260, 526n1, 561n3, 576(nn96, 101, 103), 590n80
Lully, Jean-Baptiste, xxi, 27, 28, 99, 117, 119, 121, 129, 134, 151, 157n*, 158, 163n*, 166, 183, 184, 526n2, 531n15, 537n15, 538(nn26, 34, 38), 539n2, 540n7, 546n35
Lycurgus, 341, 342, 441, 582n17
Lysander, 441, 591n82
Lysias, 441

Machaon, 341, 582n14
Machiavelli, Niccolò, 575n94
Maigret (Miaret), Jean, 117, 123, 535n19, 537n10
Mainard, 117, 123, 535n19, 537n10
Mairan, Jean-Jacques Dortous de, 40, 378, 466, 527n15, 587n21, 595n129
Malcolm, Alexander, 447, 593n111
Malesherbes, Chrétien-Guillaume de Lamoignon de, xvii, xxxv, 566n5
Man, Paul de, xvii, 520n76
Manna, Gennaro, 547n50
Marais, Marin, 540n7
Marchand, Marie Françoise (Mlle Dumesnil), 113, 172, 534n36, 548n59
Marius, Victorinus, 570n41, 571n42
Marti, René, 566
Masson, Paul-Maurice, 518n39
Masson, Charles, 553n10

Masters, Roger D., 520n87
Matheson, Johann, 519n66
Maupertuis, Pierre Louis Moreau de, 568–569n22
Mei, Girolamo, 447, 591n111
Meibomius, Marcus (Marc Meibom), 415, 447, 589n52
Melanippides, 329, 580n147, 591n82
Melody, xxii, xxxiii, xxxiv, xxxviii, 144–145, 152–157, 175, 182, 187, 191, 227–228, 231–232, 260–269, 273–279, 318–324, 329–331, 366, 371–375, 400–402, 408, 421–422, 435–436, 439, 448, 450–451, 454, 523n125
Melody, unity of, xxi–xxii, xxv, xxxviii, 154–157, 229–230, 405–406, 476–479, 490, 523n125, 524n126, 539n40, 546n29, 597n10
Melzer, Authur M., 516n2
Mengoli, Pietro, 447, 466, 591n111, 595n128
Menthon, Françoise, 525n1
Mersenne, Marin, 385, 443, 445, 447, 472, 474, 554n23, 587n27, 588n44, 591n95, 592n101, 595(nn130, 137, 140), 596n142
Mesomedes, 592n100
Metanasius, 123, 537n10
Metastasio, Pietro, 101, 118, 530n9, 535n20, 545n25, 547n50, 588n42, 594n116
Mettrie, Julien Offray de la, 568n20
Miller, James, 518n44
Minos, 341, 582n15
Mohammed, 317, 576n111
Moisgelou, 581n9
Molière, 451, 530n3, 537n15, 538n26, 539n2
Mondonville, Jean-Joseph Cassanéa de, 113n†, 533n27
Montéclair, Michel Pignolet de, 18, 80, 525n4, 528n33
Montesquieu, Charles-Louis Secondat Baron de, 534n43, 570n35, 574n77, 575(nn94–95), 576(nn104, 109), 577n117
Moral effects, needs, passions, xxix, xxxiii–xxxvi, xxxix, 279, 319, 323–325, 331, 404, 421, 437, 439, 441
Morhoff, Daniel Georg, 443, 591n92
Moultou, Paul, 563

Narcisse, xv
Nature, xxv, xxvi, 22, 175, 181–182, 191, 226, 248, 255, 260, 276, 321, 376, 410–411, 421, 439, 448, 585n7
Nettl, 523n124
Newman, Ernest, 524(nn132, 139)
Newton, Isaac, 578n123
Nicomachus, 408, 447, 464, 588n43, 593n107, 595n125
Noblet, Charles, 160, 547n45
Norton, Glyn P., 520n74

Index

Oliver, Alfred Richard, 517n29, 518n36, 520n73, 524(nn136, 139)
Olivet, Pierre-Joseph Thoulier, Abbé d', 373, 586n12
Orpheus, 437, 441, 590n70, 591n81
Ovid, 575n91, 576n101
O'Dea, Michael, 516n1, 517n31, 523n120

Pagin, André-Noël, 114n‡‡, 120, 534n44, 536(nn33–34), 538n24
Parran, Antoine, 447, 593n111
Paul, Charles B., 519n52
Pausanias, 299n*, 570n41
Peisistratos, 571n51
Pereira (Pereyre or Pereire), Giacobbo Rodrigo, 375, 568n17, 586n17
Perez, David, 153, 376, 545n25, 586n19
Perfectibility, xviii
Pergolesi, Giovanni Battista, xx, xxi, 108n*, 113n‡, 116, 117, 121, 124n*, 124, 151, 157n*, 376, 399, 406, 453, 590, 518n42, 532n9, 533(nn25, 28), 536n4, 537(nn17–18), 540n8, 545n26, 547(nn37, 42), 586n19, 588n41, 594n117
Perrault, Claude, 447, 530n3, 593n111
Persius, 536n1
Persuasion, 296, 331, 569n30
Phemius, 441, 590n81
Pherecrates, 329, 580n147
Philip of Macedon, 128, 538n31
Philolaus 263
Philosophy, philosopher, philosophize, 110, 118, 115–126, 142, 144, 180, 262, 265, 305, 320, 324, 325, 329, 349, 472
Philoxenus, 329, 441, 580n147, 591n82
Phrynnis, 441, 591n82
Physical causes, physics, xxvi, xxxi, xxxiii, 279, 316, 320–321, 401, 404, 439, 443, 448
Pidansat de Mairobert, Mathieu François, 548n53
Pierre, Jean-Baptiste-Marie, 113n***, 534n34
Pigale, Jean-Bapiste 113n‡‡, 533n32
Pindar, 319, 444, 529n100
Pity, xviii–xxix, 306
Plato, xxxv, 121, 143, 266, 296, 329, 337, 345n*, 429, 440, 441, 539n44, 540n9, 542n8, 544n11, 562(nn6, 14), 571n53, 574n81, 576n96, 578(nn121, 128), 579n138, 582(nn23, 25–32, 34–36), 590n63
Pliny the Elder, 570n39, 571n42
Plutarch (Pseudo-Plutarch), 219, 329, 395, 428, 441, 447, 554n29, 567n111, 579n147, 588n34, 589n60, 591(nn81–82), 593n109
Poisson, Philippe, 547n39
Poisson, Raymond, 547n39

Polybius, 441, 591n87
Porphyry, 439, 590n75
Porpora, Nicola, 118n*, 153, 463, 535n21, 545n25, 594n122
Porset, Charles, 521n77
Pot, Olivier, 524(nn135, 138)
Pradon, Nicolas, 451, 594n114
Prévost, Pierre, 597n1, 598n24
Prodicus, 342, 582n19
Ptolemy, 427, 429, 431, 447, 472, 554n20, 560n7, 587n32, 589n59, 595n135
Pufendorf, Samuel, 575n91, 576n104
Pulli, Pietro, 119, 536n24
Puvignée, Mlle, 112n*, 533n22
Pygmalion, xxxix, 497, 555n13, 531n4, 536n31, 598n25, 602
Pythagoras, 180–182, 252, 258, 263, 342, 416, 440, 464, 471, 472, 582(nn17, 19)

Quarrel of the Bouffons, xiii, xix–xxiv, 141, 518(nn36, 39), 519n53, 531n13, 540(nn6, 10)
Quinault, Philippe, 99, 101, 126, 530(nn5, 7, 11–12), 532(nn12, 14), 538n26, 540n7, 545n20, 547n41, 548n53
Quintilian, 219, 437, 447, 554n28, 562n9, 577n116, 590n72, 592n107

Racine, Jean, 126, 136, 530n3, 538n26
Rameau, Jean-Philippe, xii, xv, xvi, xvii, xviii, xxiii, xxiv–xxxvi, xxxvii, 44n*, 65, 107, 108, 109, 115, 117, 120, 123, 128, 160, 168, 175, 199, 200–204, 209, 210, 211, 212, 214, 215, 216, 220, 221, 260, 261, 264, 265, 268, 289, 322, 331n*, 369, 378, 385–389, 398, 409–413, 423, 447, 466, 472, 474–475, 478, 517n31, 519(nn52, 57, 61–65, 68), 520n66, 522n111, 526n4, 527(nn19–20), 528n38, 531(nn4, 16), 532(nn11, 13–15), 533(nn20, 22, 25), 536n30, 537n14, 538(nn30, 33–34, 36, 38), 541(nn19–20), 545n24, 548, 549(nn4, 6–11, 14, 16), 551(nn1–2), 552(nn8–10), 553(nn11–12), 554(nn17, 24, 30), 555(nn32, 34, 1, 4, 6, 13), 556(nn19, 21, 24–26, 28), 557(nn29–30, 44–45, 47–48, 52, 60, 63), 560(nn1, 3–6, 16–17, 19–20), 561n4, 562n10, 563(nn3, 5), 564(nn6, 8–9, 14–15, 17, 19, 22–27, 30), 566n4, 578(nn125, 129), 579n141, 580n154, 585n7, 587n28, 588n46, 590n78, 595(nn138–139), 602
Rans-des-Vaches, xxxviii, 445
Raynal, Guillaume-Thomas-François, Abbé, xx, 518n40, 534, 534n1, 536(nn31, 33, 1, 4), 537(nn5–9, 12, 14, 18, 22), 538(nn24–25, 27–29, 32)
Reichenberg, Louisette, 518(nn36, 42)

Richelieu, Duc de, xviii, 537n21
Rufus, Quintus Curtius, 538n31

Saint-Hyacinthe, Themiseul de, 537n10
Saint-Mard, Touissant Rémond de, 529nl
Saint-Sevin, Joseph-Barnabé de, 137, 541n15
Salimbeni, 113n**, 533n30
Salinas, Francisco, 447, 593n111
Sallier, Claude, 367, 584n2
Salomon, Joseph-Francois, 532n6
Sarrazin, Claude, 99, 114n*, 530n6, 534n38
Sauveur, Joseph, 34, 40, 66, 79, 284, 472, 527(nn10, 13, 17), 528n32, 528n28, 587n25, 588n44
Schwab, Richard N., 517n28, 564n11, 533n21
Scott, John T., 516n7, 521(nn92, 80), 522n98
Scudéry, Georges de, 124, 537n21
Second Discourse, xxiv, xvii, xxx, xxxii, xxxiii, 289, 521n93, 561n1, 564n12, 567n8, 568(nn16, 21), 569(nn28–29), 571n81, 573(nn68–69, 71), 574(nn74–75, 77–78), 575(nn89, 92), 576n96, 578n131, 582n35
Selletti, Joseph, 545n26
Sergius, 371, 586n10
Serre, Jean-Adam, 282, 565n22, 586n7
Shaftesbury, Anthony Ashley Cooper, Earl of, 150n*, 545n21
Shklar, Judith, 523n123
Simicus, 441, 591n83
Snyders, Georges, 523n121
Social Contract, xxxiii, xxxv, 567n11, 575n87, 576n111, 582n24
Solon, 341, 582n15
Sorenson, Lawrence, 522n107
Soterichus, 441
Souhaitti (Souhaitty), Jean-Jacques, xvi, 526n7, 528n30
Spinoza, Benedict, 571n51, 573n67
Sprat, Thomas, 569n22
Starobinski, Jean, xvii; 520n76, 522n106
Stesichorus, 437, 590n70
Strabo, 318, 577n115
Strauss, John, 523n119, 525n140

Tacitus, 571n42
Tarquin, 291
Tartini, Giuseppi, 120, 331, 369, 392–393, 409, 423, 447, 463, 466, 536n33, 538n24, 552, 565n2, 580n154, 585(nn6–7), 587n30, 588n45, 593n111, 594n123
Tasso, Torquato, 532n9, 544n18, 545n20, 547n47, 571n52
Taylor, Eric, 525n140

Terpander, 437, 441
Terradeglias (Terradellas), Domenico, 119, 124, 153, 157n*, 376, 535n24, 537n22, 545n25, 546n34, 547n41, 548n53, 586n19
Terrasson, Jean, 319n*, 577n119
Thales, 342, 582n16
Thaletas, 441, 591n81
Thamyris, 441, 591n81
Theon of Smyrna, 415, 464, 589n53, 594n124
Thersites, 344, 582n22
Thomas, Downing A., 516n1
Thoulier, Pierre-Joseph, 586n12
Thrasybulus, 291, 567n11
Tiersot, Julien, 516(nn9, 11), 517n20, 524n139
Timotheus of Meletus, 214, 441, 442, 554n18, 591(nn84, 89)
Tonelli, Anna, 138, 541n16
Tournehem, Le Normant de, 119n*, 536n26
Triptolemus, 307, 574n81
Trissino, Gian Georgio, 117, 123, 535n19, 537n10

Vadé, Joseph, 548n3
Valgulio, 447, 593n111
Vallotti, Francesco Antonio, 447, 593n111
Vanloo (Van Loo), Anne-Antoinette-Christine, 113n55, 533n33
Vaucanson, Jacques de, 579n137
Velkley, Richard L., 524n129
Verba, Cynthia, xliv, 518n44, 519(nn52, 56, 59, 62), 522n112, 523n121
Vinci, Leonardo, 119, 157n*, 376, 535n24, 547n37, 586n19
Voltaire, xviii, 112, 118, 131, 136, 517n24, 523n112, 533(nn21, 24), 534(nn37, 38), 539n45, 561, 576n99, 577n111
Vossius, Isaac, 444, 592n98

Wallis, John, 443, 447, 591n96, 593n111
Warburton, William 567n11
Warrens (Vuarens), Louise Eleonor de, xiv, xv, 517n26
Wassman, Earl R. 524n140
Wokler, Robert 516n1, 519(nn46, 52, 62), 520(nn73, 77), 523n112, 561

Xenophon, 574n81

Zarlino, Giuseppe, 231, 254n*, 258, 447, 551n1, 556n20, 560(nn2, 7, 19)
Zeno, Apostolo, 453, 594n116
Zoroaster, 342, 582n17